Cases in Strategic Marketing Management

Cases in Strategic Marketing Management

Julian W. Vincze
Rollins College, Crummer Graduate School of Business

Carol H. Anderson
Rollins College, Crummer Graduate School of Business

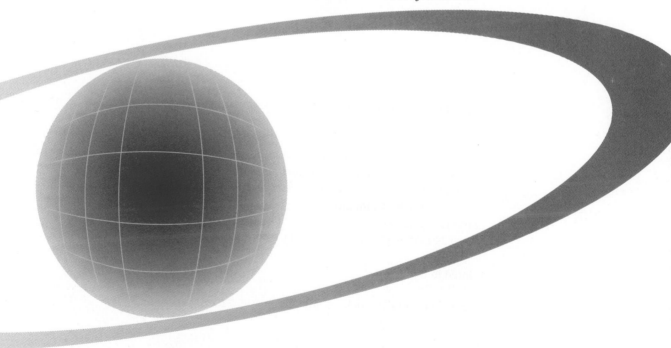

Houghton Mifflin Company   Boston   New York

Vice President and Publisher: Charles Hartford
Sponsoring Editor: George Hoffman
Associate Sponsoring Editor: Joanne Dauksewicz
Project Editor: Elizabeth Gale Napolitano
Editorial Associate: Damaris R. Curran
Editorial Assistant: Sarah Godshall
Senior Production/Design Coordinator: Sarah Ambrose
Senior Manufacturing Coordinator: Marie Barnes
Marketing Manager: Melissa Russell

Cover Design: Rebecca Fagan
Cover Image: Jim Krantz, Graphicstock

Printed in the U. S. A.

Library of Congress Catalog Card Number: 99-72025

ISBN: 0-395-87053-4

2 3 4 5 6 7 8 9-POO-03 02 01 00

This book is dedicated to the two people whose patience and understanding made this project possible: our spouses, Linda J. Vincze and Alexander T. Wood.

Julian W. Vincze and Carol H. Anderson (Wood),
Crummer Graduate School at Rollins College

Contents

Preface

We believe that the most effective learning on any subject takes place when the student is involved in the pedagogical process. Thus, we have provided a casebook that is intended to provide ample opportunity for both students and teachers to apply the concepts and principles appropriate to marketing as a discipline in a changing world. Although this casebook has been designed as a companion supplement to *Strategic Marketing Management: Meeting the Global Marketing Challenge* by Anderson and Vincze, it is also appropriate for use with any textbook that covers marketing theory, concepts, and practices.

The thirty-six cases that we have selected will appeal to students and professors alike because they are intrinsically interesting, up-to-date, and illustrate a large number of strategic marketing management issues. The cases detail decision situations that entail both consumer product and business-to-business marketing and will provide students with a broad overview of the field of marketing management. Also, because they are decision-oriented as opposed to descriptive in nature, the cases provide students the opportunity to apply what they have learned and to perform in-depth analysis of strategic issues.

The cases vary in length from short pieces describing straightforward business situations to more lengthy cases describing more complex situations. They also cover profit and nonprofit organizations as well as domestic and global marketing environments. The organizations discussed in the cases range from large, well-known companies, for which students can conduct further research, to small, entrepreneurial businesses that illustrate the uncertainty and challenge of the strategic marketing management process.

Several cases contain issues about ethical marketing and business practices and two are focused on this type of decision situation. In addition, the selection includes a number of international cases, and many of the other cases contain some element of global strategy. In short, there is enough variety in these cases and depth and breadth of coverage to satisfy the needs of most classrooms. A grid that outlines the topical coverage of each case can be found at the end of this preface (pages xiv–xvii) and in the *Instructor's Resource Manual*.

RECOGNITION OF CONTRIBUTORS

We believe that our entire case selection is unrivaled in breadth and depth. We would like to express special thanks and recognition to;

James W. Camerius, Professor of Marketing, *Northern Michigan University,* and
James W. Clinton, Professor of Management, *University of Northern Colorado*

for allowing us to use several of their cases that make an outstanding contribution to this collection.

In addition, we would like to offer special gratitude to those who contributed two cases to this collection as follows:

Brian G. Gnauck
Northern Michigan University

Bill Middlebrooke
Southwest Texas State University

Lynda L. Goulet
Univeristy of Northern Iowa

John K. Ross, III
Southwest Texas State University

Peter G. Goulet
University of Northern Iowa

Frank Shipper
Salisbury State University

Mike Keeffe
Southwest Texas State University

We have been fortunate to have a large number of excellent cases to draw on from colleagues in the field. We are grateful to all of the case authors who have contributed to this edition. A complete alphabetically ordered list of these contributors follows:

Jan Willem Bol
Miami University

Samuel P. Graci
Northern Michigan University

W. Blaker Bolling
Marshall University

Madelyn Gengelbach
University of Missouri at Kansas City

James L. Bowey
Bishop's University, Quebec

K. Matthew Gilley
James Madison University

James W. Camerius
Northern Michigan University

Troy Gleason
University of North Dakota

James W. Clinton
University of Northern Colorado

Brian G. Gnauck
Northern Michigan University

Loretta Ferguson Cochran
Clemson University

Lynda L. Goulet
University of Northern Iowa

Robert P. Crowner
Eastern Michigan University

Peter G. Goulet
University of Northern Iowa

David M. Currie
Rollins College

Walter E. Greene
The University of Texas Pan American

Timothy T. Dannels
Iowa State University

Jean M. Hanebury
Texas A & M University

Natalya V. Delcoure
Northeast Louisiana University

Craig A. Hollingshead
Marshall University

Dorothy G. Dologite
City University of New York—Baruch College

Lawrence R. Jauch
Northeast Louisiana University

Richard L. Jones
Marshall University

Marshall Foote
University of North Dakota

Michael J. Keeffe
Southwest Texas State University

Jeffrey A. Krug
University of Illinois at Urbana-Champaign

Anne T. Lawrence
San Jose State University

Aaron Martin
University of North Dakota

Charles C. Manz
University of Massachusetts, Amherst

Steven J. Maranville
University of St. Thomas

Kimberly I. McKell
Bishop's University, Quebec

Bill J. Middlebrook
Southwest Texas State University

Robert J. Mockler
St. John's University

Jaideep Mohan
Total System Services, Inc.

Brent Olson
University of North Dakota

Kay M. Palan
Iowa State University

Paul Poppler
St. John's University

Richard L. Priem
The University of Texas at Arlington

George M. Puia
Indiana State University

Madeleine E. Pullman
Southern Methodist University

Steven A. Rallis
Iowa State University

Krishnan Ramaya
University of Southern Indiana

David W. Rosenthal
Miami University

John K. Ross, III
Southwest Texas State University

Chetan Sankar
Auburn University

John L. Scott
Northeast Louisiana University

Frank Shipper
Salisbury State University

Charles B. Shrader
Iowa State University

Marilyn L. Taylor
University of Missouri at Kansas City

Joan L. Twenter
Iowa State University

Brian Wavra
University of North Dakota

Ashli White
Bowling Green, KY

Timothy E. Williams
University of Northern Iowa

Jan Zahrly
University of North Dakota

FOR THE INSTRUCTOR

Accompanying *Cases in Strategic Marketing Management* is a comprehensive *Instructor's Resource Manual* that offers very thorough teaching notes for each case in this collection. The teaching notes cover all aspects of a company's strategy and structure and provide suggestions for teaching approaches. Many of the notes also provide a series of questions that can be given to students to help them focus on the significant issues in each case. Almost all of these teaching notes have been adapted from materials supplied by the case authors and a few include a sample student case analysis report.

Julian W. Vincze
Carol Anderson (Wood)

Case	The Changing Role of Marketing	Forces of Change	Strategic Market Planning	Marketing Intelligence	Consumer Buying Behavior	Business Buying Behavior	Market Segmentation	Product Strategy	Services Marketing	Distribution Strategy	IMC Strategy	IMC Tools	Direct Marketing	Pricing Strategy	Control Marketing Performance	Marketing-Oriented Organization	Social Issues	International	Innovation	Entrepreneurial
1 MTV versus VIVA-TV (1995)	X	X	X	X	X		X		X		X									
2 W. L. Gore & Associates, Inc.: Entering 1998	X	X	X				X								X				X	
3 Perfumery on Park	X	X	X	X	X		X	X	X	X		X	X	X	X					X
4 Odwalla, Inc., and the *E. coli* Outbreak	X			X		X		X									X		X	X
5 Calgene Inc.: Marketing High-Tech Tomatoes (1995)	X	X	X	X	X	X	X	X		X				X		X	X		X	
6 Marketing Challenges Facing AUCNET USA	X	X	X	X	X	X	X		X	X			X	X		X		X	X	X
7 The Samaritan Group	X	X	X										X						X	
8 Artistic Impressions Inc.: Developing An Entrepreneurial Growth Strategy	X							X			X		X	X						X
9 Invacare Corporation (1997)	X					X		X												
10 Quality Asphalt, Inc.	X										X									
11 Circus Circus Enterprises, Inc. (1998)	X			X	X		X	X	X						X	X				

	The Changing Role of Marketing	Forces of Change	Strategic Market Planning	Marketing Intelligence	Consumer Buying Behavior	Business Buying Behavior	Market Segmentation	Product Strategy	Services Marketing	Distribution Strategy	IMC Strategy	IMC Tools	Direct Marketing	Pricing Strategy	Control Marketing Performance	Marketing-Oriented Organization	Social Issues	International	Innovation	Entrepreneurial
12 Embassy by Waterford Wedgwood PLC (1995)	X	X	X				X	X		X				X				X		
13 Black Diamond, Ltd.: Hanging on the Cutting Edge	X	X	X	X	X	X	X	X		X	X					X			X	
14 Alcoholes de Centroamerica, S.A. de C.V.	X	X	X	X	X	X		X		X	X						X	X		X
15 Frigidaire Company: Launching the Front-Loading Washing Machine		X			X			X		X				X						
16 The U.S. Internal Revenue Service: An Agency under Siege		X					X		X	X						X				
17 Outback Goes International		X				X	X	X	X	X	X			X		X			X	X
18 Dayton Hudson Corporation		X			X			X	X	X	X			X		X				
19 SAP AG (1995)	X	X	X			X	X	X		X	X	X						X		
20 Perdue Farms, Inc. (1995)	X	X	X	X	X	X	X	X		X	X	X		X		X	X			
21 Tyson Foods, Inc.	X	X	X		X	X	X	X		X	X			X						

Case	The Changing Role of Marketing	Forces of Change	Strategic Market Planning	Marketing Intelligence	Consumer Buying Behavior	Business Buying Behavior	Market Segmentation	Product Strategy	Services Marketing	Distribution Strategy	IMC Strategy	IMC Tools	Direct Marketing	Pricing Strategy	Control Marketing Performance	Marketing-Oriented Organization	Social Issues	International	Innovation	Entrepreneurial
22 AB Astra: Global Marketing Strategy (1995)			X			X	X	X		X						X		X		
23 Will Old Navy Recreate Past Successes For Gap Inc.? (1995)		X	X	X		X				X		X		X						
24 RWC, Inc.: Seeking Strategic Direction		X				X					X					X				
25 Nike, Inc. (1999)	X	X			X			X		X	X			X				X		
26 CompuSound Inc.		X			X		X	X		X	X	X		X						X
27 North Country Bank & Trust		X			X		X		X	X	X	X		X		X		X		
28 Avon Products, Inc. (1996)		X			X	X	X	X		X	X	X	X	X	X	X		X		
29 Kellogg Company	X	X						X		X	X	X		X				X		
30 Cedar Falls Utilities and the Information Superhighway (D): TCI's Response	X	X	X		X	X	X			X	X			X			X			
31 America Online (1997)	X	X	X	X	X	X	X	X	X				X	X			X	X	X	X
32 Carnival Corporation (1998)	X		X		X		X	X	X	X	X			X		X		X		

	The Changing Role of Marketing	Forces of Change	Strategic Market Planning	Marketing Intelligence	Consumer Buying Behavior	Business Buying Behavior	Market Segmentation	Product Strategy	Services Marketing	Distribution Strategy	IMC Strategy	IMC Tools	Direct Marketing	Pricing Strategy	Control Marketing Performance	Marketing-Oriented Organization	Social Issues	International	Innovation	Entrepreneurial
33 The Roche Group	X	X					X	X		X				X	X	X		X		
34 Kentucky Fried Chicken and the Global Fast-Food Industry	X	X					X	X	X	X								X		
35 Hoechst-Roussel Pharmaceuticals, Inc.: RU 486		X			X		X	X									X	X		
36 Stew Leonard's Dairy		X														X	X			

Cases in Strategic Marketing Management

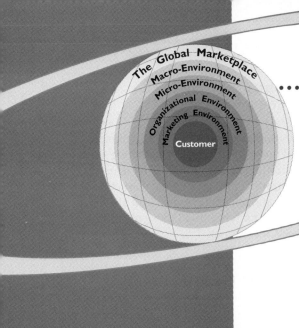

Introduction to the Case Method

We learn best by doing.

Anonymous

In view of the diverse objectives of courses on strategic marketing management, the specific contents of such courses may vary substantially. This book approaches these subjects through business cases. A case is a description of an organizational situation and frequently contains detailed information about complex issues.

The case method is a Socratic teaching method designed to help you apply theories and concepts that you have learned to actual situations. Most cases focus on some core problem or problems, but the cases can be lengthy and comprehensive. As a student, you are asked to identify those problems and to solve them.* The solution may require you to take advantage of strategic opportunities, and sometimes

you may need to propose tactical actions. At other times you will simply be asked to analyze what a firm did correctly, not what its problems were.

Cases are usually written by professors or students or by people involved in the organizational situation. Cases almost always involve real situations. Occasionally, the identity of the organization involved is disguised, but often you will know the identity of the company. Thus you will be able to obtain additional information about the organization if you wish or if your instructor asks you to. However, it is often not wise to research past the date in which the business situation occurred (unless specifically requested by the instructor). For example, if the case describes a situation that occurred in June of 1998, then gathering information that is more current may be dysfunctional. Knowing what the company actually did in the situation is extremely difficult to ignore, and students almost always assume what the company did was the correct thing to do. This knowledge of action taken may render the learning experience offered in the business situation less effective because students think they know the correct answer and fail to consider alternative actions and learn from the discussion of all the alternatives.

Cases may be accompanied by (or contain) industry notes. Your instructor may choose to utilize these industry notes or to ignore them. When used, they are supportive materials for a specific case situation, not a replacement for case materials. As you approach any case, you should obtain as much information on the company's industry as you need to understand the situation described in the case.

OBJECTIVES

The case method's objectives are

1. To add realism to the classroom and to enable students to apply what they have learned

2. To help students to integrate knowledge of the functional areas and to employ concepts of strategic marketing management

3. To improve students' decision-making ability, primarily through practice in making decisions

4. To help students see how actions are related and what they mean in a practical as well as a theoretical sense

5. To encourage students to be effective oral communicators through participation in class, through defense of their ideas, and through the need to "seize the floor" in order to participate

6. To improve students' overall communication skills

APPROACHES

Case analyses may be oral, written, or both. They may be structured or unstructured. Students may be asked to take the role of the CEO, a consultant, or some other person involved in the situation. Normally, the outside consultant's role is preferred because it forces the student to be responsible for communicating his or her basis of analysis, their reasoning that resulted in suggestions, and in addition their complete thinking relative to proposals for action and the implementation of chosen alternatives.

TYPES OF ORGANIZATIONS ENCOUNTERED

Cases cover both goods and services marketing in consumer and business-to-business marketing situations in organizations of various sizes, missions (profit and nonprofit), and geographic market penetration (local, national, multinational, and global). The problems encountered by all these organizations are similar yet distinct.

CASE PROBLEMS ENCOUNTERED

Most of the problems encountered in the cases in this book involve the formulation and control of marketing strategy or tactics. Some require lengthy analysis—which will be explained in detail by your instructor. A few cases involve social responsibility and ethical issues. All require the student analyst to work diligently to acquire an in-depth understanding of the business situation described in the case and, by doing so, to maximize his or her learning opportunity.

Group versus Individual Analysis

Students can engage in preclass and class analysis of a case in either of two ways—in a group or individually. The group method is used when the course is designed to teach people to work in teams and when it is feasible for people to meet in groups. Always be certain of the instructor's expectations relative to individual versus group case analysis. When group analysis is used, the workload should be distributed fairly, but in all groups some people do their fair share and some do not. Appropriate peer-group evaluation should be carried out. Students should resist pressures to conform and be self-reliant in group meetings. Before the group meets, each student should go individually through the steps of analysis outlined in the following section. When the individual method is used, the student prepares all work by himself or herself.

PREPARING A CASE: A SUGGESTED COURSE OF ACTION

1. Read the case; become familiar with the situation. If possible, put the case aside for awhile.

2. Reread the case.

   a. Summarize pertinent information. Use what you have learned in other courses.

   b. Identify vision, mission, goals, objectives, past marketing strategies, current strategies, key success factors, constraints, and SWOT (strengths, weaknesses, opportunities, threats).

   c. Pay special attention to information in exhibits, take notes, and perform analyses: ratios, financial statements, forecasts, pro forma financial statements.

   d. Answer any questions your instructor has provided.

3. Establish a decision framework.

   a. What are the major problems?

   b. How do you know?

   c. What are the decision constraints?

   d. What are your strategic assumptions?

4. Try to get a comprehensive view of the problem. Do you have the strategic picture in mind? Do you see the interrelationships of the key variables? If not, mull over what you do know until you obtain an overall perspective.

5. Search for and delineate alternatives. Match strengths and weaknesses against opportunities and threats. Be sure to use applicable concepts such as the various product and business matrices, the product lifecycle model, and basic strategic options, and ensure that alternatives address the problems you identify.

6. Choose the appropriate alternatives. Match your choices against vision, mission, goals, objectives, and SWOT. The evaluation process is largely rational but partly intuitive. Once you have finished your analyses, your intuition must function to help you put the complex pieces together.

7. Set priorities for your solution.

8. Be prepared to implement your recommended decisions with a plan of action. You should know how to obtain support for your choices, and you should, if your professor desires, budget for your intended actions.

CLASS PARTICIPATION

The effectiveness of the case method depends in large part on students' contributions in class. Unlike a lecture class, the case method requires the student to assume responsibility for learning, and for the learning of others. Interactions involved in sharing ideas, questioning for understanding, challenging comments, acknowledging issues, and defending positions are important parts of the classroom experience in the case method. In the classroom, you should

1. Participate often and intelligently. A portion of your classroom grade may be based on your participation. An A average on other work may become a B or a C (or worse) for the course if you do not participate appropriately.

2. Substantiate your reasoning and positions with analysis and interpretation of the facts in the business situation.

3. Do not participate just to participate. Contribute. You will soon learn that your professor and your classmates can tell the difference.

4. Respect your peers—you will learn from them. Recognize that others will have thought of issues, analyzed facts, and come to conclusions that you have not.

5. Be prepared to seize the floor. As part of the case method learning experience, you must share your efforts—to do this, you must be heard. If not, how will sharing occur—how will anyone know of your efforts? And your classroom participation grade will suffer significantly.

6. Recognize that your instructor is going to disagree with you, sometimes simply to see if you can defend your position. Furthermore, your classmates are often going to disagree with you to enhance their own situations. You must be prepared to defend your reasoning and analysis.

7. Be willing to take risks. If you make a mistake, you make a mistake, but if you don't try, you'll never get anywhere and you squander a learning opportunity.

8. Avoid use of weak words such as *maybe, I think, I feel, It appears, It tends to.* Be positive

and persuasive. Use such words as *It is* and *The analyses reveal that....*

9. Be prepared to change your mind during the discussion of the case. Others may have presented analyses that suggest you missed something. Revising your opinion will not help your written report, since presumably you already will have turned in your written report. But be flexible enough to change your mind in your oral communications if you see you were wrong, because it will help your class participation to do so, and more importantly, it will contribute to your learning experiences.

10. Try to maintain a general manager's orientation to what is going on in the classroom. Think of the way you should respond to the positions of others if you were the CEO of this organization, and react accordingly.

WRITING A CASE STUDY ANALYSIS

Often, as part of your course requirements, you will need to prepare a written case analysis. This may be an individual or a group report. Whatever the situation, there are certain guidelines to follow in writing a case analysis that will improve the evaluation your work will receive from your instructor. Before we discuss these guidelines and before you use them, make sure that they do not conflict with any directions your instructor has given you.

The structure of your written report is critical. Generally, if you follow the steps for analysis discussed in the preceding section, you *already will have a good structure for your written discussion.* All reports begin with an *introduction* to the case. This should explain briefly the organization of your report. Do this sequentially by writing, for example, "First, we discuss the business environment and organizational audit of company X.... Third, we discuss several alternatives that were considered.... Last, we provide recommendations and a detailed plan of action for turning around company X's business."

In the second part of the case write-up, the strategic analysis section (or business audit), do a thorough analysis of past marketing strategies that resulted in past successes both to understand how the organization adds value and to identify past and current key success factors. This should be fol-lowed by the SWOT analysis. Next, analyze the organization's structure and control systems, and then analyze and discuss the nature and problems of the company's business-level and corporate strategy. Make sure you use plenty of headings and subheadings to structure your analysis. For example, have separate sections on any important conceptual tool you use. Thus you might have a section on the product lifecycle concept as part of your analysis of the environment. You might offer a separate section on portfolio techniques when analyzing a company's corporate strategy. Tailor the sections and subsections to the specific issues of importance in the case.

In the third part of the case write-up, present your understanding of issues and decisions that managers face within the organization. Also try to state a specific "problem" statement that summarizes all the issues previously identified, and do not forget the time horizon as to when decisions must be made.

The fourth part of the case write-up contains the possible alternative solutions you considered. Some instructors will require that this section of your report contain a brief explanation of the alternative followed by an evaluation of the alternative. Evaluation may be as simple as a list of pros and cons. But it also may be a more detailed discussion of positive and negative aspects of each alternative considered. And some instructors also may expect a discussion of the justification of which alternative is the best given the specifics of the business situation.

The next part of the case write-up contains your solutions in the form of both a set of recommendations of what should be done and also a plan of action that details how to perform the recommended actions. Be comprehensive and as specific as possible, and make sure your proposed activities are in line with the previous analysis so that the recommendations fit together and move logically from one to the next. The recommendations section is very revealing because, as mentioned earlier, your instructor will have a good idea of how much work you put into the case from the quality of your recommendations.

Following this framework will provide a good structure for most written reports, although obviously it must be shaped to fit the individual case being considered. Some cases are about excellent companies experiencing no problems. In such instances, it is hard to write recommendations. Instead, you can focus on analyzing why the company is doing so well, using that analysis to structure the discussion. Following are some minor suggestions that can help make a good analysis even better.

1. Do not repeat in summary form large pieces of factual information from the case. The instructor has read the case and knows what is going on. Rather, use the information in the case to illustrate your statements, to defend your arguments, or to make salient points. Beyond the brief introduction to the company, you must avoid being *descriptive;* instead, you must be *analytical.*

2. Make sure the sections and subsections of your discussion flow logically and smoothly from one to the next. That is, try to build on what has gone before so that the analysis of the case study moves toward a climax. This is particularly important for group analysis, because there is a tendency for people in a group to split up the work and say, "I'll do the beginning. You take the middle. And I'll do the end." The result is a choppy, stilted analysis because the parts do not flow from one to the next, and it is obvious to the instructor that no real group work has been done.

3. Avoid grammatical and spelling errors. They make the paper sloppy.

4. Some cases dealing with well-known companies end in 1993 or 1994 because the decision was an important one and represents an unusual learning opportunity (also often no later information was available when the case was written). If expected or requested by your instructor, do a library and/or World Wide Web search for more information on what has happened to the company in subsequent years. Following are sources of information for performing this search:

   The Internet with its World Wide Web is the place to start your research. Very often you can download copies of a company's annual report from its Web site, and many companies also keep lists of press releases and articles that have been written about them. Thoroughly search the company's Web site for information such as the company's history and perfor-

mance, and download all relevant information at the beginning of your project. Yahoo is a particularly good search engine to use to discover the address of your company's Web site, although others work as well.

Compact disc sources such as Lotus One Source and InfoTrac provide an amazing amount of good information, including summaries of recent articles written on specific companies that you can then access in the library. *FINS Predicasts* provide a listing on a yearly basis of all the articles written about a particular company. Simply reading the titles gives an indication of what has been happening in the company.

Annual reports on a Form 10-K often provide an organization chart.

Companies themselves provide information if you write and ask for it.

Fortune, BusinessWeek, and *Forbes* have many articles on companies featured in the cases in this book.

Standard & Poor's industry reports provide detailed information about the competitive conditions facing the company's industry. Be sure to look at this journal.

5. Sometimes instructors hand out questions for each case to help you in your analysis. Use these as a guide for writing the case analysis. They often illuminate the important issues that have to be covered in the discussion.

If you follow the guidelines in this section, you should be able to write a thorough and effective evaluation.

ADDITIONAL PERSPECTIVES

As you engage in case analysis, the following additional issues may arise.

Degree of Difficulty

Sometimes the point of the case will be obvious. At other times it will be necessary to read, reread, and reanalyze the case in order to identify the major problem or opportunity. Many cases contain problems of technique that are not the major problems, only symptoms of a major problem.

Viewpoint

One factor to be considered is the viewpoint of the student. Should he or she envision himself or herself as a consultant or as a member of the organization? The ease with which solutions may be implemented is related to the choice of viewpoint. Be certain you understand the viewpoint your instructor expects you to use as a case analyst!

Results

Most of the time your predicted results will be attainable, but in some situations, no matter what the decision, the results may be ineffective. Many factors, especially external environmental factors, are completely beyond the control of an organization. In such situations, the best decisions may be those which allow an organization to minimize its losses.

Strength of Analyses

Most students will not uncover all the factors that eventually will be revealed in the classroom discussions. This constitutes one of the most important learning factors gained from use of the case method—the realization that there is always something the individual will overlook. This is very much like real life.

Perspective

For both the student and the instructor, the case method is a difficult process. In traditional classroom learning situations, students have been assigned the roles of listeners and nonparticipants. To be effective, the case method requires that students think, act, and participate. In order for students to receive good grades, they must achieve these more active levels of learning as opposed to being merely receptive and passive members of a lecturer's audience. The role of a strategic marketing manager, too, demands this kind of behavior.

Case Bias

One must be aware of the inherent bias in a case. The case is related as it is perceived by someone else—the case writer. The reader of a case does not have the benefit of knowing how the information was obtained or what factors the individual considered in writing the case. What is presented as fact may not be as clear-cut as it seems. How facts are presented, which facts are included, and which facts are left out are critical factors. Occasionally, facts may be distorted, especially facts related to statements about the personalities of individuals. Often, individuals' personalities are the key problems in a case, yet the reader can never be sure that the statements about these personalities are exactly accurate.

Answers

There are no right answers in a case situation. Some answers, however, are better than others. The only true test of the decision is in its implementation, and unfortunately, the case method does not allow for implementation of decisions. The right answer, then, is unknown. Only the better answer can be determined. Students whose decisions are based on insufficient analysis usually come up with worse answers and correspondingly worse grades. It is the analysis and interpretation of facts on which decisions are based that are important; several acceptable solutions may be derived from them.

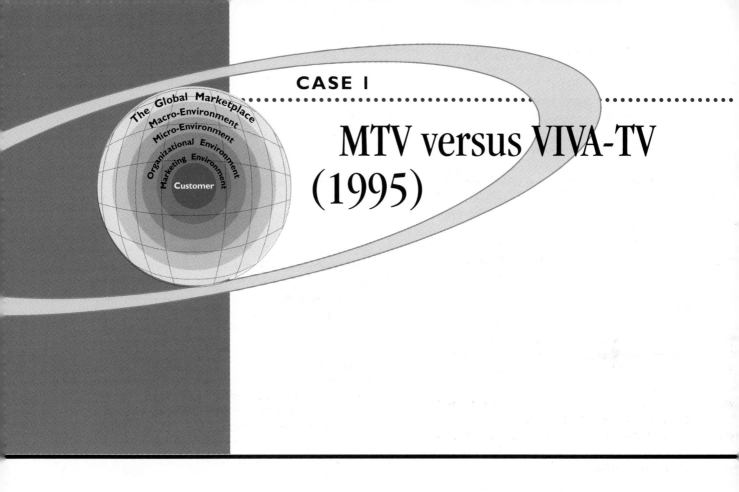

MTV versus VIVA-TV (1995)

*This case was prepared by Julian W. Vincze, Professor of Marketing,
Crummer Graduate School of Business, Rollins College.*

*The November 18, 1994 announcement by Steven
Blame, MTV's managing editor, that he was joining VIVA as its new program director was a shock
to his colleagues but especially to his boss Peter
Einstein, MTV Europe's director of network development. Blame's announcement came on the
heels of another announcement—that the European record industry's battle with MTV was esca-
lating again. Sony, Warner, Polygram, and EMI
proclaimed their intention to launch a second rival channel in Germany, VIVA 2. MTV's monopoly
in Europe had ended in 1993 when these companies had launched VIVA-TV in Germany. Now
their plans for a VIVA 2 to compete directly
against MTV's new VH1 channel for 30-
somethings indicated a greater resolve to
threaten MTV. Industry observers wondered
how MTV would react to this latest challenge.*

This case is intended to be used as a basis for class discussion
rather than as an illustration of either effective or ineffective
handling of the situation. This case was prepared by Julian W.
Vincze, Crummer Graduate School of Business, Rollins College.
Copyright © 2000 Julian W. Vincze.

HISTORY OF MTV IN EUROPE

Pop-music's MTV, a subsidiary of Viacom International Inc. of New York, was an almost immediate
success when it launched MTV Europe in 1987
with almost the same broadcasting format as in the
United States. Although MTV does not release financial figures (only consolidated financials by parent Viacom), it was estimated that MTV Europe
could be received by 60 million European households, which was slightly more than the number of
U.S. households receiving MTV in the early 1990s.
German households, at approximately one-third of
the 60 million European households, were MTV's
most important European market. In June of 1993
when VIVA was being formed, Peter Einstein, MTV
Europe's director of network development, was
quoted as saying: "We don't think our business will
suffer on the basis of a channel that plays German
music, as research has shown that viewers like
MTV how it is."[1]

MTV EUROPE PROGRAMMING

When MTV Europe first began broadcasting, it virtually replicated the pop-music programming format that had been so successful in the United States. The broadcast language was English, and the majority of video clips used were from the same sources that supplied their U.S. operations and initially were the identical video clips. With time, the number of European artists highlighted in the programming increased as MTV Europe became better able to understand the preferences of its European target viewers and also as its understanding of the European record industry matured.

HISTORY OF VIVA-TV

Cologne based VIVA-TV was owned jointly by four of the five companies that dominated the German music industry. Polygram NV, Thorn EMI Plc, Sony Corp., and Time Warner Inc.'s Warner Music jointly owned a 99 percent majority interest (24.75 percent each). Other principals were Frank Otto, owner of Hamburg's OK Radio, Hannes Rossacher and Rudi Dolezal, of the Vienna video-production company Doro Productions, and Dieter Gorny, then managing director of the Popkomm music-festival organization. These VIVA shareholders initially committed to DM100 million of total expenditures with the expectation that this amount would allow VIVA to achieve break-even operations in 4 years.

In order to begin broadcasts, VIVA had to convince regional authorities (individual German states) that they were viable. (See Exhibit A for additional information.) It was generally believed that in many states German channels would be favored over foreign channels such as MTV, but these authorities' decisions were not always predictable. Johanna Fell, a media adviser to the BLM licensing authority in Bavaria, noted that "it may well be possible that VIVA is preferred." However, Christa Michalek, director of planning and buying at the German airtime buyer, Hiemstra Media Services,[2] said that MTV's market dominance would be difficult to upset: "MTV is institutionalized, I can't imagine that it will lose its young audience. VIVA will have to promote itself a lot to succeed. It may pick up an older audience." Simon Aboud, European media manager at McCann-Erickson in London, argued that MTV is "a hard act to follow, but the new channel must represent a threat to it. The first indicator

will be if the German-only MTV advertisers switch to the tailor-made product (of VIVA)."[3]

VIVA'S MARKET VIEWPOINT

VIVA, however, was adamant that there was a market for a German music channel and aimed to fill a gap in German pop-music programming. It cited the fact that German pop music accounted for a third of total recorded music sales in the European Union. Frank Otto noted, "there are some big German artists that are liked a lot which do not get played on MTV. We will play the music German listeners want to hear." There were no Germany-only advertising spots available on MTV in 1993, but anyone wanting to reach only German-speaking markets could buy time, albeit covering all of Europe, at a cheaper rate than MTV regularly charged advertisers. These advertisers, interested in only the German-speaking audience, were mainly breweries and record companies, although this market was estimated to be worth DM40 million per year to MTV. Christophe Benning, media group manager at Media Direction, who had responsibility for buying German-language MTV ads for Clausthaler brand beer, said: "There is a market opportunity for such a program, but the main target will not be youngsters; you can catch a lot of people with national German melodic music in the 25 to 55 age group. If the channel is clever, it will do this. It will be hard for VIVA to get the young people. It should target housewives in the morning, kids in the afternoon, and yuppies in the evening."[4]

Levi Strauss & Co., which in 1993 was buying English-language pan-European airtime on MTV, refused to rule out using the new channel. Alois Burkart, Strauss's marketing services manager in Germany, said that "theoretically, VIVA could be good for us, and we will make a decision in September or October (of 1993) whether to us it is. There's no guarantee that we (will) keep using the same channels."[5] VIVA planned to pay 4.8 percent of annual advertising revenue to the German music publisher's organization, Gema, and would combine music videos, in-house magazine programming, and brought-in products. VIVA expected German rock and pop acts to account for less than half (40 percent) of the music output, with the remainder being artists from the international music scene, many of whom had strong German followings.

EXHIBIT A
··············
MTV versus VIVA: TV Media Policy for Germany

The Federal Republic of Germany (FRG) is served by two public broadcasting corporations—Arbeitsgemein-schafter der oeffentlich-rechtlichen Rundfunkanstaltern Deutschlands (ARD) and Zweites Deutsches Fernse-hen (ZDF)—and a number of private broadcasters, which all are under the indirect supervision of the states (Laender) of the FRG. Until 1984, TV broadcasting in the FRG was the exclusive domain of ARD and ZDF. There are 13 regional television corporations (which issue transmission licenses) established under state law based on an agreement among the states. ARD and ZDF compare in organization and programming to the national TV networks in the United States. Article 5 of the FRG Constitution guarantees everyone the right to free expression of opinion, "freedom of the press and freedom of reporting by radio," and forbids censor-ship. In a landmark decision based on Article 5, the FRG Federal Constitutional Court (FCC) in 1961 de-clared that all relevant social forces should be involved in controlling radio and television. In 1981, the FCC declared that private television is permissible under Article 5, thus ending ARD and ZDF's monopoly. The laying of coaxial cable in late 1983 and early 1984 permitted the rapid development of cable TV, which is the usual connection for most German households. Financial support for ARD and ZDF comes from monthly fees (split on a 70:30 ratio) paid by almost every household. In 1986, the FCC ruled that there must be ade-quate separation between a state's newly established regulatory authority for private broadcasting and the executive arm of the state (regulators must be independent of government influence). On October 3, 1986, the minister presidents of all German states agreed that public and private broadcasters have equal rights in producing and transmitting programs, and two of the four channels available from the direct-broadcasting satellite TV-SAT2 were given to private broadcasters. TV-SAT2, replacing a failed TV-SAT1, was launched Au-gust 9, 1989. However, despite the fact that private broadcasting has been introduced to all German states, the dispute over public versus private control continues.

Applicants for new broadcasting licenses must apply to the state media center established in the state where the broadcaster plans to set up headquarters. Licenses can be granted for cable, satellite, and terrestrial trans-mission. In order to receive a terrestrial license, the program must be considered a "full program" and meet certain requirements, including regional programming, cultural events, general information programs, and a minimum number of self-produced programs. Networks not able to meet "full" requirements (e.g., movie channels, music channels, etc.) may be granted satellite and/or cable licenses only. But all licenses depend on the availability of frequencies, satellite transponders, or cable channels.

The two major private telecasters, SAT 1 and RTL plus (who have terrestrial frequencies in all major cities), and the two smaller ones, TELE 5 and PRO 7, all depend solely on ad revenues, and only RTL plus has achieved profitable operations (since 1991). The market dichotomy is readily reflected in programming for private broadcasters who seek to maximize viewership and ad revenues at minimum cost by showing the cheapest obtainable popular entertainment—vintage U.S. and Italian films, U.S. serials, music videos, sports, and quiz and giveaway shows.

Deutsche Telekom provides cable transmission to all households in the FRG.

Source: 1992 National Trade Data Bank, Market Reports, "Germany—Media Policy," by Peter H. Ziemons, May 1992.

STARTUP DIFFICULTIES
•••••••••••••••••••••••••••••••
VIVA had planned its initial broadcast for Thursday, August 19, 1993, and expected it would bring VIVA into the highly competitive German market (see Exhibit B for details), which had seen half a dozen

new commercial TV stations going on the air in 1993 alone. Industry data on advertising revenue and viewer rating for the first half of 1993 showed that the biggest losers in the nightly battle for the German living room were the two state-owned net-works—ARD and ZDF—which previously had en-

EXHIBIT B

MTV versus VIVA: East German Media Scene

Prior to unification, the German Democratic Republic (GDR) was served by two state-owned broadcasters, DDR I and DDR 2. Broadcasting, which included radio and TV programming, was fully controlled by the GDR government. After opening the East German border in 1989, the two German public broadcasters (ARD and ZDF) and the two major private broadcasters (SAT I and RTL plus) began discussions with DDR I and DDR 2 to seek ways to cooperate and to use DDR I and DDR 2 frequencies for their own programs. After German reunification on October 3, 1990, the two eastern German broadcasters were renamed DFF I (Deutscher Fernsehfunk) and DFF 2 but were required to cease operation on December 31, 1991.

The new eastern German media scene is based on a state treaty (Staatsvertrag) among all German state minister presidents, passed on August 31, 1991. It includes the establishment of two public broadcasters, MDR (Mitteldeutscher Rundfunk) and ORB (Ostdeutscher Rundfunk Brandenburg). Both began operations on January 1, 1992, and are full members of the ARD (sometimes referred to as the first public broadcasting system).

Although the private broadcasters, represented through their lobbying organization, Verband Privater Rundfunk und Telekommunikation (VPRT—Association for Private Broadcasting and Telecommunications), called for a new broadcasting infrastructure in an untied Germany, particularly in terrestrial transmissions, the state treaty (Staatsvertag) gives priority to so-called basic coverage, which favors the public broadcasters in terrestrial frequency allocation. Currently, most eastern German households receive private television from satellites, in particular Astra 1A and Astra 1B.

Involvement of the European Community

On October 3, 1989, after a 3-year discussion, the EC Commission passed a directive concerning transborder television in the European Community. The EC Broadcast Directive is supposed to harmonize the EC broadcast market and includes "political goals" for commercial advertisements, sponsorship, and quotas on foreign (non-EC) programming designed to preserve national culture and its advertising limitations. The directive affected the German private broadcasters just as they were beginning to hope of achieving a stable market share. The four nationwide private broadcasters agreed that the EC directive could have strong adverse effects if the recommendation that 50 percent of programming consist of European films and serials were changed to a requirement. They felt that the current recommendation was not a legal requirement that would force them to change their policies. However, if this were to become a requirement, private broadcasters claimed that high production costs, coupled with limited coverage and low advertising revenues, would force them out of business.

German law constitutionally constrains the federal government from legislating or otherwise prescribing the content of broadcast programming, a competence that is explicitly delegated to the German states, which must establish independent supervisor boards. Although EC law would override domestic law, it is clear that stiff public opposition exists to such action.

Source: 1992 National Trade Data Bank, Market Reports, "Germany—Media Policy," by Peter H. Ziemons, May 1992.

joyed a monopoly.[6] For example, RTL plus, a private channel, had been able to achieve DM1.3 billion in ad revenue for this period of 1993, which was 39 percent of Germany's total ad spending on TV, while during the same period ZDF's ad revenue had plunged 49 percent to DM255 million and ARD's had fallen 22 percent to DM357 million. RTL had captured over a fifth of viewers aged 14 to 49, which was the audience range ad agencies considered to be the most likely to buy their goods.[7] Meanwhile, the private TV industry had continued to grow, with newcomers such as the CNN-style

N-TV, the "infotainment" channel VOX, the all-sports network Deutsche Sportfernsehen (DSF), and the movie channel RTL2 all competing for viewers and advertising.

Due to licensing and other difficulties, VIVA had been unable to begin broadcasting as planned in August of 1993. During September, managing director Michael Oplesch revealed that Frank Otto had acquired a 19.8 percent stake in VIVA by purchases from the four major founding organizations. The result was the decline of Sony, Time Warner, Thorn EMI, and Polygram stakes to 19.8 percent each.[8] Other difficulties delayed VIVA's debut until December 1, 1993, by which time managing director Dieter Gorny said: "It's a Christmas present to young Germans." VIVA's first broadcast was a 1-hour program consisting of a 10-minute promotion and 50 minutes of video clips, and it was available in only four German states.

VIVA's full broadcasting had begun December 21, 1993, by which time about 55 percent of German households had been able to receive what amounted to several hours of programming. Dieter Gorny said: "We want to enter the market step by step. It would be foolish for us to think we could come up with the whole product immediately. VIVA is intended as a channel for young people in the 14 to 29 age group, and its image will be young, trendy, and dynamic. We will be doing a lot of research to find out what our viewers want to see." However, Gorny admitted that the percentage of local acts played would be nearer 20 to 25 percent (instead of the targeted 40 percent) to begin with, but he said: "We are offering a new forum for German music. In 1 or 2 years' time I think we'll see a real boost to the German video Industry."[9]

COMPETITION INCREASES

VIVA wasted little time in its bid to shake up MTV. Within a few months of beginning programming in Germany, three of the major shareholders (Polygram, Sony, and Warner Music) had stunned the industry by announcing plans to launch a pop TV channel in the United States. In partnership with Ticketmaster, the consortium planned to go head to head with MTV in its home market. Leaked reports indicated a planned launch by autumn 1994.[10] Industry observers had felt this announcement would be a severe blow to MTV, even though

it had seen other competitors try and fail to conquer its dominant U.S. position. MTV's reliance on record companies to provide its lifeblood of pop videos made the specter of a record industry–backed rival a real threat. Margaret Wade of Warner Music said diplomatically: "It's a very big market, and there is room for a competitor." Being equally polite, MTV responded: "We think our success is based on programming and loyalty, and we welcome fair competition."

However, VIVA likely had more than a desire for healthy competition as a motive. Bruce Steinberg, head of satellite station UK Gold and a former director of MTV Europe, noted that a power struggle might be developing between TV stations and their suppliers. He said: "MTV has already taken record companies to court in Europe over the amount they charge for showing videos. MTV is also a hugely profitable company which had relatively low fixed costs and high margins, so this is a way of the record companies getting a piece of that action—whether they can command the same credibility is a different question."[11] Within a few days of this announcement, MTV was reported to have lodged a complaint against VIVA to the European Commission, alleging that it (VIVA) had an unfair competitive advantage because of easier access to music videos via its shareholders. VIVA's managing director, Dieter Gorny, responded: "VIVA was honored that MTV was already taking it seriously as a competitor," but Gorny also rejected MTV's claims.

At the same time as the complaint was being lodged, the trade press reported that VIVA was picking up a former MTV sponsor. Braun, the electrical goods manufacturer, had sponsored MTV's weekly "Europe's Top Twenty" chart program for 5 years under a contract that expired in December of 1993. Because of a cut in Braun's pan-European advertising budget, it had not renewed the MTV contract and instead negotiated a spot-advertising and sponsorship package with VIVA. Braun's advertising agency, Hiemstra Media Services, noted that VIVA would allow Braun to reach youth music channel viewers in the German market at a much lower cost than MTV. A VIVA spokesperson noted that Braun was just one of a number of advertisers that are now using VIVA or intending to do so. Also mentioned were Sega, Wrangler jeans, and Nestle foods.[12] MTV said that it recently acquired new sponsorship business for its main service from Italian jeans' manufacturer Replay and sport shoe manufacturer Fila, which would together compensate for the loss of Braun.[13]

SIZE OF AUDIENCE

VIVA believed its popularity would come from being more German oriented than MTV. VIVA, which broadcasts in the German language, said its research indicated that fully 60 percent of German MTV viewers did not understand English. VIVA also noted that since 15 percent of its music output was German-language, and since nearly one-third of the music videos it showed were both produced in Germany and featured German artists, then German audiences (the company believed) would prefer VIVA over MTV.

VIVA reached 8.8 million German cable homes when launched in December 1993 (about 66 percent of market) and expected to be available in 10 million homes by March of 1994. VIVA transmitted on the Eutelsat IIF2 satellite and had virtually no direct-to-home market. Meanwhile, MTV's German coverage was twice as big, largely because of its use of the Astra satellite for its main service. The Astra satellite gave MTV 18.2 million German homes, with an expected growth to 21 million by the end of 1994.

PRICING

In early 1994, VIVA's rate-card costs for a 30-second spot ranged from DM360 to DM2700, and it predicted that 90,000 viewers were watching at any one time. MTV, meanwhile, charged an average of about DM5900 for a 30-second spot and predicted that 180,000 Germans in the 16 to 34 age group were watching at any one time. Christophe Benning, media group manager at the Media Direction agency, who no longer used MTV, believed both were too expensive. He said: "VIVA's programming was good, but the ad rates were too expensive for the audience covered, but if he used a music channel in the future, he would probably use VIVA, but only if the audiences justified the cost."[14]

Simon Aboud, European media manager at McCann Erickson, suggested that MTV would suffer some loss of revenue to VIVA because some agencies would want to use the new channel and would do so by using some of their MTV budget rather than by increasing overall spending. But Frank Brown, sales director of MTV Europe, argued

that VIVA's arrival was a positive development for MTV because he expected VIVA's lower prices to encourage more German advertisers to use youth-targeted channels for the first time.[15]

MTV REACTS

As a result of VIVA's competitive moves, MTV reacted to secure two-thirds of its German market by persuading Deutsche Telekom to pay a fee for carrying MTV on its cable networks. This was a major breakthrough, since the German operator, which controls the bulk of the 13.5 million cable homes, had previously adamantly refused to pay any carriage fees. MTV, like other channels, paid Deutsche Telekom what was in effect a cable distribution fee. Now Deutsche Telekom had agreed to pay a fee to allow it to continue to carry MTV in the clear when MTV was encrypted (in late 1994). This fee had given Deutsche Telekom the right to decode MTV's satellite signals and to distribute MTV through its networks. Cable subscribers would not pay anything extra. Deutsche Telekom had said the fee was worthwhile because of MTV's strong brand and very high loyalty among young viewers. Thus the only way for German viewers to receive the encrypted MTV for "free" would be through the cable system.

However, in January of 1994, MTV also launched a German opt-out service on Eutelsat II F1. This MTV opt-out service offered 2 minutes an hour of advertising every evening, seen only in Germany and charged at a special low rate of DM2500 for 30 seconds.[16] This special version of MTV, which allowed for opt-outs for German advertising, was transmitted to German cable systems via the Eutelsat II-F1 satellite and also would become encrypted at the time when the main MTV service on the Astra satellite was encrypted. Encrypting MTV on Astra would allow 6.5 million German dish homes to receive MTV and also would allow MTV to join the United Kingdom's Sky Multi-Channels subscription package. MTV also was reported to be talking to Selco, the company formed by British Sky Broadcasting's Rupert Murdoch and German programmer and rights owner Leo Kirch about marketing English-language Astra pay channels to dish homes in Germany.

These activities, and especially the deal with Deutsche Telekom, were viewed as a major coup for MTV in its battle with VIVA for audiences and advertisers. It also was reported that MTV was scheduled to meet with the private cable operators of Germany to discuss a similar deal. Anga, the private cable operators' organization, said that its members might consider paying MTV.[17]

VH-I AND PAN-EUROPEAN TV MARKETS

On September 30, 1994, MTV launched a new station aimed at the United Kingdom and only the United Kingdom. The new channel, called VH-1, duplicated the channel that already existed in the United States and was targeted at the baby-boomer generation. This audience, which was the next step older than the regular MTV youth audience, was considered to favor a programming mix of "vintage and contemporary" music as opposed to MTV's usual pop-music programming. Bill Roedy, head of MTV Europe, said: "The future of the business will be to develop more national outlets." He conceded in an interview that 5 years after he began to sell the notion of a single European market to advertisers and 2 years after that market was born (December 31, 1992), it remained a difficult task. "The market was very difficult to develop early on, and it is still very difficult," he said.[18] The only people who really ever believed in the United States of Europe were the Americans," said Brian Jacobs, international media director at Leo Burnett in London. "The problem is that it remains inherently difficult to sell anything across borders. It is true in Asia. It is true in Latin America. And it is true here."[19]

Problems with pan-European advertising ranged from structural ones concerning the way advertisers organized themselves to ones of national taste and phraseology. For example, even a pan-European marketer like Kellogg, the cereal maker, which marketed from Copenhagen to Corfu, did not necessarily use the same brand name in every market. Even companies that did sell under the same name across Europe still tended to organize along national lines. Thus sales targets and crucial advertising budgets tended to be put together nationally. Mr. Roedy described the process that MTV used to sign up over 200 advertisers as very labor-intensive. "You have to sell not only their corporate headquarters but each of the national units as well," he said.[20] By all accounts, MTV had scored more successes than any other pan-European broadcaster in selling itself. But the pan-European market seemed far from approaching the sum of its national parts

and remained a tiny portion of the total market. "It is still relatively small," said Paul McGhee, director of network and business development at NBC Super Channel, who estimated the value of the pan-European advertising market for 1994 at $US150 million (roughly one-tenth of the total European ad market).[21]

THE FUTURE FOR MTV

Sometime in 1995, MTV's faith in the single European market would face a new test. By digitally compressing its signal, MTV would be able to squeeze six channels onto the satellites it used to cover Europe. Mr. Roedy was considering whether to use the new capacity for new product offerings like VH-1 or to tailor MTV for national markets. Coca-Cola, one of MTV's biggest advertisers, had started running commercials on VIVA. Hanno Hoekstra, Coke's group brand manager in Germany, said MTV "is still the most important youth channel, but it needs to maintain that position actively by getting closer to the point of sale. It needs to accompany local events and turn more into a somewhat community-based network. In shops and bars in Germany, you find more and more of VIVA."[22]

Meanwhile, it was reported that VIVA recorded advertising revenue of DM15 million by the end of September 1994 and as a result may have been able to cross the profit threshold in 1995, two years ahead of schedule. Mr. Gorny believed more and more companies were placing their TV spots with VIVA in order to round off their ad campaigns. In addition, he thought advertisers were reducing their budgets for youth magazines such as *Bravo, Maedchen,* or *Popcorn* and were placing their ads with VIVA. VIVA had expected to start broadcasting VIVA 2 by the end of 1994, and Gorny was reported to also want to enter the merchandising market via a fashion series of clothing for young people (1995) and by opening VIVA cafés and shops (1996).[23]

MTV'S CHALLENGE IN 1995

With all of VIVA's competitive activities, as well as the other changes that were taking place in the European music industry, MTV clearly faced a challenge in deciding what strategic actions to take in 1995. Peter Einstein wondered whether the decision was a relatively straightforward one of choosing between staying as a pan-European channel or was the best strategy for MTV to become a group of country-customized but integrated channels? A third alternative viewed the decision as more complicated. Perhaps what was needed was a complete re-evaluation of MTV's operating and marketing strategies?

Questions

1. What are the past operating strategies and marketing strategies that resulted in MTV's success?

2. What issues and problems are now confronting MTV?

3. What alternative actions should MTV consider to address the issues and solve the problems you identified in Question 2?

4. What competitive actions do you believe MTV should use in 1995 in both Germany and the United States?

5. What competitive reactions do you predict if MTV implements the actions you recommended in Question 4?

Endnotes

1. "Time Warner and Sony Back Music Channel," *The Financial Times,* June 10, 1993.
2. Unlike the United States, where individual advertising agencies also buy clients' TV media exposure time, in Germany (and other European Union countries), advertising media buying services are provided by separate organizations who often buy time blocks from the media (sometimes under long-term contracts) and then "sell" or "allocate" media time to match their clients' requests.
3. "Time Warner and Sony Back Music Channel," *The Financial Times,* June 10, 1993.
4. *Ibid.*
5. *Ibid.*
6. "German Answer to MTV Prepares to Hit Air Waves," *Reuter Business Report,* August 15, 1993.
7. "A German 'MTV' to Be Launched as TV War Heats Up," *Reuters Limited,* August 16, 1993.
8. "Germany: VIVA Music Channel to Broadcast from Cologne," *Sueddeutsche Zeitung,* September 2, 1993.
9. Miranda Watson, "Rock On, Germany," *The Guardian,* December 13, 1993.
10. Emily Bell, "Recording Industry Puts Heat on MTV," *The Ottawa Citizen,* February 21, 1994.
11. "Rock Giants Threaten MTV with Rival Stations," *The Observer,* February 6, 1994.
12. "VIVA Set to Pick up Former MTV Sponsor," *Satellite TV Finance,* February 17, 1994.
13. "Germany: VIVA Fernsehen Targets Net Advertising Income of DM7M," *Sueddeutsche Zeitung,* February 9, 1994.
14. *Ibid.*
15. *Ibid.*
16. *Ibid.*
17. "MTV in German Breakthrough Deal," *Satellite TV Finance,* February 17, 1994.
18. Erik Ipsen, "For MTV Europe, a New Play on Nationalism," *International Herald Tribune,* August 24, 1994.
19. *Ibid.*
20. *Ibid.*
21. *Ibid.*
22. Irene Bejenke, "In Europe, MTV is Feeling the Heat from Its Main Rival," *Wall Street Journal,* October 4, 1994.
23. "Germany: VIVA Fernsehen Expects to Cross Profit Threshold in 1995," *Reuter Textline Sueddeutsche Zeitung,* October 10, 1994.

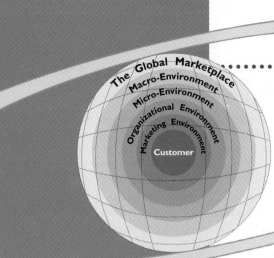

W. L. Gore & Associates, Inc.: Entering 1998

This case was prepared by Frank Shipper of the Department of Manage-ment and Marketing at Franklin P. Perdue School of Business at Salisbury State University, and Charles C. Manz, Nirenberg Professor of Business Lead-ership at the University of Massachusetts, Amherst.

"To make money and have fun."

W. L. Gore

Bursting with resolve, Jack Dougherty, a newly minted MBA from the College of William and Mary, reported to his first day at W. L. Gore & Asso-ciates on July 26, 1976. He presented himself to Bill Gore, shook hands firmly, looked him in the eye, and said he was ready for anything.

Jack was not ready, however, for what hap-pened next. Gore replied, "That's fine, Jack, fine. Why don't you look around and find something you'd like to do?" Three frustrating weeks later he found that something: trading in his dark blue suit for jeans, he loaded fabric into the mouth of a machine that laminated the company's patented Gore-Tex[1] membrane to fabric. By 1982,

Jack had become responsible for all advertising and marketing in the fabrics group. This story is part of the folklore of W. L. Gore & Associates.

Today, the process is more structured. Regard-less of the job for which they are hired, new associ-ates[2] take a journey through the business before settling into their own positions. A new sales asso-ciate in the fabrics division may spend 6 weeks ro-tating through different areas before beginning to concentrate on sales and marketing. Among other things, the newcomer learns how Gore-Tex fabric is made, what it can and cannot do, how Gore han-dles customer complaints, and how it makes its in-vestment decisions.

Anita McBride related her early experience at W. L. Gore & Associates this way:

Before I came to Gore, I had worked for a structured organization. I came here, and for the first month it was fairly structured because I was going through training, and this is what we do and this is how Gore is and all of that. I went to Flagstaff for that training. After a month, I came down to Phoenix, and my sponsor said, "Well, here's your office; it's a wonderful office" and "Here's your desk," and walked away. And I thought, "Now what do I do?" You know, I was waiting for a memo or something, or a job description. Finally, after another month I was so frustrated, I felt, "What have I gotten myself into?" And so I went to my sponsor, and I said, "What the heck do you want from me? I need something from you." And he said, "If you don't know what you're supposed to do, examine your commitment and opportunities."

COMPANY BACKGROUND

W. L. Gore & Associates was formed by the late Wilbert L. Gore and his wife in 1958. The idea for the business sprang from his personal, organizational, and technical experiences at E. I. DuPont de Nemours and particularly his discovery of a chemical compound with unique properties. The compound, now widely known as Gore-Tex, has catapulted W. L. Gore & Associates to a high ranking on the *Forbes* 1998 list of the 500 largest private companies in the United States, with estimated revenues of more than $1.1 billion. The company's avant-garde culture and people management practices resulted in W. L. Gore being ranked as the seventh best company to work for in America by *Fortune* in a January 1998 article.

Wilbert Gore was born in Meridian, Idaho, near Boise in 1912. By age 6, according to his own account, he was an avid hiker in the Wasatch Mountain Range in Utah. In those mountains, at a church camp, he met Genevieve, his future wife. In 1935, they got married—in their eyes, a partnership. He would make breakfast, and Vieve, as everyone called her, would make lunch. The partnership lasted a lifetime.

He received both a bachelor of science in chemical engineering in 1933 and a master of science in physical chemistry in 1935 from the University of Utah. He began his professional career at

American Smelting and Refining in 1936. He moved to Remington Arms Company in 1941 and then to E. I. DuPont de Nemours in 1945. He held positions as research supervisor and head of operations research. While at DuPont, he worked on a team to develop applications for polytetrafluoroethylene, referred to as PTFE in the scientific community and known as "Teflon" by DuPont's consumers. (Consumers know it under other names from other companies.) On this team, Wilbert Gore, called Bill by everyone, felt a sense of excited commitment, personal fulfillment, and self-direction. He followed the development of computers and transistors and felt that PTFE had the ideal insulating characteristics for use with such equipment.

He tried many ways to make a PTFE-coated ribbon cable without success. A breakthrough came in his home basement laboratory while he was explaining the problem to his 19-year-old son Bob. The young Gore saw some PTFE sealant tape made by 3M and asked his father, "Why don't you try this tape?" Bill then explained that everyone knew that you cannot bond PTFE to itself. Bob went on to bed.

Bill Gore remained in his basement lab and proceeded to try what everyone knew would not work. At about 4:00 A.M. he woke up his son, waving a small piece of cable around and saying excitedly, "It works, it works." The following night father and son returned to the basement lab to make ribbon cable coated with PTFE. Because the breakthrough idea came from Bob, the patent for the cable was issued in Bob's name.

For the next 4 months, Bill Gore tried to persuade DuPont to make a new product—PTFE-coated ribbon cable. By this time in his career, Bill Gore knew some of the decision makers at DuPont. After talking to a number of them, he came to realize that DuPont wanted to remain a supplier of raw materials and not a fabricator.

Bill and his wife, Vieve, began discussing the possibility of starting their own insulated wire and cable business. On January 1, 1958, their wedding anniversary, they founded W. L. Gore & Associates. The basement of their home served as their first facility. After finishing dinner that night, Vieve turned to her husband of 23 years and said, "Well, let's clear up the dishes, go downstairs, and get to work."

Bill Gore was 45 years old with five children to support when he left DuPont. He put aside a career of 17 years and a good, secure salary. To finance the first 2 years of the business, he and Vieve mortgaged their house and took $4000 from savings. All their friends told them not to do it.

The first few years were rough. In lieu of salary, some of their employees accepted room and board in the Gore home. At one point 11 associates were living and working under one roof. One afternoon, while sifting PTFE powder, Vieve received a call from the city of Denver's water department. The caller indicated that he was interested in the ribbon cable but wanted to ask some technical questions. Bill was out running some errands. The caller asked for the product manager. Vieve explained that he was out at the moment. Next, he asked for the sales manager and, finally, the president. Vieve explained that they also were out. The caller became outraged and hollered, "What kind of company is this anyway?" With a little diplomacy, the Gores were able eventually to secure an order for $100,000. This order put the company on a profitable footing, and it began to take off.

W. L. Gore & Associates continued to grow and develop new products, primarily derived from PTFE. Its best known product would become Gore-Tex fabric. In 1986, Bill Gore died while backpacking in the Wind River Mountains of Wyoming. He was then chairman of the board. His son Bob continued to occupy the position of president. Vieve remained as the only other officer, secretary-treasurer.

Company Products

In 1998, W. L. Gore & Associates has a fairly extensive line of high-tech products that are used in a variety of applications, including electronic, waterproofing, industrial filtration, industrial seals, and coatings.

Electronic and Wire Products. Gore electronic products have been found in unconventional places where conventional products will not do—in space shuttles, for example, where Gore wire and cable assemblies withstand the heat of ignition and the cold of space. In addition, they have been found in fast computers, transmitting signals at up to 93 percent of the speed of light. Gore cables have even gone underground, in oil drilling operations, and underseas, on submarines that require superior microwave signal equipment and no-fail cables that can survive high pressure. The Gore electronic products division has a history of antici-

pating future customer needs with innovative products. Gore electronic products have been well received in industry for their ability to last under adverse conditions. For example, Gore has become, according to Sally Gore, leader in human resources and communications, ". . . one of the largest manufacturers of ultrasound cable in the world, the reason being that Gore's electronic cables' signal transmission is very, very accurate and it's very thin and extremely flexible and has a very, very long flex life. That makes it ideal for things like ultrasound and many medical electronic applications."

Medical Products. The medical division began on the ski slopes of Colorado. Bill was skiing with a friend, Dr. Ben Eiseman of Denver General Hospital. As Bill Gore told the story:

> We were just to start a run when I absentmindedly pulled a small tubular section of Gore-Tex out of my pocket and looked at it. "What is that stuff?" Ben asked. So I told him about its properties. "Feels great," he said. "What do you use it for?" "Got no idea," I said. "Well give it to me," he said, "and I'll try it in a vascular graft on a pig." Two weeks later, he called me up. Ben was pretty excited. "Bill," he said, "I put it in a pig and it works. What do I do now?" I told him to get together with Pete Cooper in our Flagstaff plant and let them figure it out.

Not long after, hundreds of thousands of people throughout the world began walking around with Gore-Tex vascular grafts.

Gore-Tex–expanded PTFE proved to be an ideal replacement for human tissue in many situations. In patients suffering from cardiovascular disease, the diseased portion of arteries has been replaced by tubes of expanded PTFE—strong, biocompatible structures capable of carrying blood at arterial pressures. Gore has a strong position in this product segment. Other Gore medical products have included patches that can literally mend broken hearts by sealing holes and sutures that allow for tissue attachment and offer the surgeon silklike handling coupled with extreme strength. In 1985, W. L. Gore & Associates won Britain's Prince Philip Award for Polymers in the Service of Mankind. The award recognized especially the life-saving achievements of the Gore medical products team.

Two recently developed products by this division are a new patch material that is intended to incorporate more tissue into the graft more quickly and the Gore RideOn[3] cable system for bicycles. According to Amy LeGere of the medical division, "All the top pro riders in the world are using it. It was introduced just about a year ago, and it has become an industry standard." This product had a positive cash flow very soon after its introduction. Some associates who were also outdoor sports enthusiasts developed the product and realized that Gore could make a great bicycle cable that would have 70 percent less friction and need no lubrication. The associates maintain that the profitable development, production, and marketing of such specialized niche products are possible because of the lack of bureaucracy and associated overhead, associate commitment, and use of product champions.

Industrial Products.   The output of the industrial products division has included sealants, filter bags, cartridges, clothes, and coatings. Industrial filtration products, such as Gore-Tex filter bags, have reduced air pollution and recovered valuable solids from gases and liquids more completely than alternatives—and they have done so economically. In the future they may make coal-burning plants completely smoke-free, contributing to a cleaner environment. The specialized and critical applications of these products, along with Gore's reputation for quality, have had a strong influence on industrial purchasers.

This division has developed a unique joint sealant—a flexible cord of porous PTFE—that can be applied as a gasket to the most complex shapes, sealing them to prevent leakage of corrosive chemicals, even at extreme temperature and pressure. Steam valves packed with Gore-Tex have been sold with a lifetime guarantee, provided the valve is used properly.

In addition, this division has introduced Gore's first consumer product—Glide[4]—a dental floss. Ray Wnenchak, of the industrial products division, said:

> That was a product that people knew about for a while and they went the route of trying to persuade industry leaders to promote the product, but they didn't really pursue it very well. So out of basically default almost, Gore decided, okay, they're not doing it right. Let's go in ourselves. We had a champion, John Spencer, who took that and pushed it forward through the dentist's offices and it just skyrocketed. There

were many more people on the team, but it was basically getting that one champion who focused on that product and got it out. They told him it "Couldn't be done," "It's never going to work," and I guess that's all he needed. It was done, and it worked.

Amy LeGere added:

> The champion worked very closely with the medical people to understand the medical market, like claims and labeling, so that when the product came out on the market it would be consistent with our medical products. And that's where, when we cross divisions, we know whom to work with and with whom we combine forces so that the end result takes the strengths of all of our different teams.

As of 1998, Glide has captured a major portion of the dental floss market, and the mint flavor is the largest selling variety in the U.S. market based on dollar volume.

Fabric Products.   The Gore fabrics division has supplied laminates to manufacturers of foul-weather gear, ski wear, running suits, footwear, gloves, and hunting and fishing garments. Firefighters and U.S. Navy pilots have worn Gore-Tex fabric gear, as have some Olympic athletes. The U.S. Army adopted a total garment system built around a Gore-Tex fabric component. Employees in high-tech clean rooms also wear Gore-Tex garments.

Gore-Tex membrane has 9 billion pores randomly dotting each square inch and is feather light. Each pore is 700 times larger than a water vapor molecule, yet thousands of times smaller than a water droplet. Wind and water cannot penetrate the pores, but perspiration can escape. As a result, fabrics bonded with Gore-Tex membrane are waterproof, windproof, and breathable. The laminated fabrics bring protection from the elements to a variety of products—from survival gear to high-fashion rainwear. Other manufacturers, including 3M, Burlington Industries, Akzo Nobel Fibers, and DuPont, have brought out products to compete with Gore-Tex fabrics. Earlier, the toughest competition came from firms that violated the patents on Gore-Tex. Gore successfully challenged them in court. In 1993, the basic patent on the process for manufacturing ran out. Nevertheless, as Sally Gore explained:

EXHIBIT A
················
Gore's Family of Fabrics

Brand Name	Activity/Conditions	Breathability	Water Protection	Wind Protection
Gore-Tex	Rain, snow, cold, windy	Very breathable	Waterproof	Windproof
Immersion technology	For fishing and paddle sports	Very breathable	Waterproof	Windproof
Ocean technology	For offshore and coastal sailing	Very breathable	Waterproof	Windproof
WindStopper	Cool/cold, windy	Very breathable	No water resistance	Windproof
Gore Dryloft	Cold, windy, light precipitation	Extremely breathable	Water resistant	Windproof
Activent	Cool/cold, windy, light precipitation	Extremely breathable	Water resistant	Windproof

...what happens is you get an initial process patent and then as you begin to create things with this process you get additional patents. For instance, we have patents protecting our vascular graft, different patents for protecting Gore-Tex patches, and still other patents protecting Gore-Tex industrial sealants and filtration material. One of our patent attorneys did a talk recently, a year or so ago, when the patent expired and a lot of people were saying, "Oh golly, are we going to be in trouble!" We would be in trouble if we didn't have any patents. Our attorney had this picture with a great big umbrella, sort of a parachute, with Gore under it. Next he showed us lots of little umbrellas scattered all over the sky. So you protect certain niche markets and niche areas, but indeed competition increases as your initial patents expire.

Gore, however, has continued to have a commanding position in the active-wear market.

To meet the needs of a variety of customers, Gore introduced a new family of fabrics in the 1990s (Exhibit A). The introduction posed new challenges. According to Bob Winterling:

...we did such a great job with the brand Gore-Tex that we actually have hurt ourselves in

many ways. By that I mean it has been very difficult for us to come up with other new brands, because many people didn't even know Gore. We are the Gore-Tex company. One thing we decided to change about Gore 4 or 5 years ago was instead of being the Gore-Tex company, we wanted to become the Gore company and that underneath the Gore company we had an umbrella of products that fall out of being the great Gore company. So it was a shift in how we positioned Gore-Tex. Today, Gore-Tex is stronger than ever as it's turned out, but now we've ventured into such things as WindStopper[5] fabric that is very big in the golf market. It could be a sweater or a fleece piece or even a knit shirt with the WindStopper behind it or closer to your skin, and what it does is it stops the wind. It's not waterproof; it's water resistant. What we've tried to do is position the Gore name and beneath that all the great products of the company.

W. L. Gore & Associates' Approach to Organization and Structure
················

W. L. Gore & Associates has never had titles, hierarchy, or any of the conventional structures associ-

EXHIBIT B

·················
International Locations of W. L. Gore & Associates

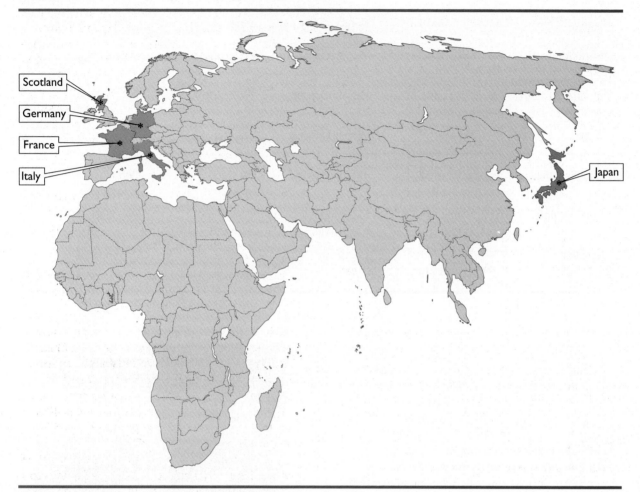

ated with enterprises of its size. The titles of president and secretary-treasurer continue to be used only because they are required by the laws of incorporation. In addition, Gore has never had a corporatewide mission or code of ethics statement, nor has Gore ever required or prohibited business units from developing such statements for themselves. Thus the associates of some business units who have felt a need for such statements have developed them on their own. When questioned about this issue, one associate stated: "The company belief is that (1) its four basic operating principles cover ethical practices required of people in business; (2) it will not tolerate illegal practices." Gore's management style has been referred to as "unmanagement." The organization has been guided by Bill's experiences on teams at DuPont and has evolved as needed.

For example, in 1965, W. L. Gore & Associates was a thriving company with a facility on Paper Mill Road in Newark, Delaware. One Monday morning in the summer, Bill Gore was taking his usual walk through the plant. All of a sudden he realized that he did not know everyone in the plant. The team had become too big. As a result, he established the practice of limiting plant size to approximately 200 associates. Thus was born the expansion policy of "get big by staying small." The purpose of maintaining small plants was to accentuate a close-knit atmosphere and encourage communication among associates in a facility.

At the beginning of 1998, W. L. Gore & Associates consisted of over 45 plants worldwide with approximately 7000 associates. In some cases, the plants are grouped together on the same site (as in Flagstaff, Arizona, with 10 plants). Overseas, Gore's

EXHIBIT C
••••••••••••
The Lattice Structure

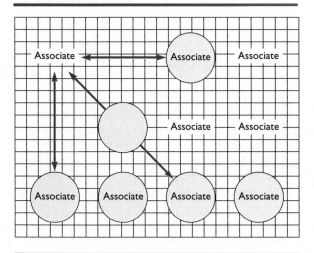

manufacturing facilities are located in Scotland, Germany, and China, and the company has two joint ventures in Japan (see Exhibit B). In addition, it has sales facilities located in 15 other countries. Gore manufactures electronic, medical, industrial, and fabric products. In addition, it has numerous sales offices worldwide, including eastern Europe and Russia.

The Lattice Organization.   W. L. Gore & Associates has been described not only as unmanaged but also as unstructured. Bill Gore referred to the structure as a "lattice organization" (see Exhibit C). The characteristics of this structure are

1. Direct lines of communication—person to person—with no intermediary

2. No fixed or assigned authority

3. Sponsors, not bosses

4. Natural leadership defined by followership

5. Objectives set by those who must "make them happen"

6. Tasks and functions organized through commitments

The structure within the lattice is complex and evolves from interpersonal interactions, self-commitment to group-known responsibilities, natural leadership, and group-imposed discipline.

Bill Gore once explained the structure this way: "Every successful organization has an underground lattice. It's where the news spreads like lightning, where people can go around the organization to get things done." An analogy might be drawn to a structure of constant cross-area teams—the equivalent of quality circles going on all the time. When a puzzled interviewer told Bill that he was having trouble understanding how planning and accountability worked, Bill replied with a grin: "So am I. You ask me how it works? Every which way."

The lattice structure has not been without its critics. As Bill Gore stated:

> I'm told from time to time that a lattice organization can't meet a crisis well because it takes too long to reach a consensus when there are no bosses. But this isn't true. Actually, a lattice by its very nature works particularly well in a crisis. A lot of useless effort is avoided because there is no rigid management hierarchy to conquer before you can attack a problem.

The lattice has been put to the test on a number of occasions. For example, in 1975, Dr. Charles Campbell of the University of Pittsburgh reported that a Gore-Tex arterial graft had developed an aneurysm. If the bubblelike protrusion continued to expand, it would explode. Obviously, this life-threatening situation had to be resolved quickly and permanently.

Within only a few days of Dr. Campbell's first report, he flew to Newark to present his findings to Bill and Bob Gore and a few other associates. The meeting lasted 2 hours. Dan Hubis, a former policeman who had joined Gore to develop new production methods, had an idea before the meeting was over. He returned to his work area to try some different production techniques. After only 3 hours and 12 tries, he had developed a permanent solution. In other words, in 3 hours a potentially damaging problem to both patients and the company was resolved. Furthermore, Hubis's redesigned graft went on to win widespread acceptance in the medical community.

Eric Reynolds, founder of Marmot Mountain Works, Ltd., of Grand Junction, Colorado, and a major Gore customer, raised another issue: "I think the lattice has its problems with the day-to-day nitty-gritty of getting things done on time and out the door. I don't think Bill realizes how the lattice system affects customers. I mean after you've established a relationship with someone about product quality, you can call up one day and suddenly find that someone new to you is handling your problem. It's frustrating to find a lack of continuity." He went on to say: "But I have to admit that I've personally seen at Gore remarkable examples of people coming out of nowhere and excelling."

When Bill Gore was asked if the lattice structure could be used by other companies, he answered: "No. For example, established companies would find it very difficult to use the lattice. Too many hierarchies would be destroyed. When you remove titles and positions and allow people to follow who they want, it may very well be someone other than the person who has been in charge. The lattice works for us, but it's always evolving. You have to expect problems." He maintained that the lattice system worked best when it was put in place in start-up companies by dynamic entrepreneurs.

Not all Gore associates function well in this unstructured work environment, especially initially. For those accustomed to a more structured work environment, there can be adjustment problems. As Bill Gore said: "All our lives most of us have been told what to do, and some people don't know how to respond when asked to do something—and have the very real option of saying no—on their job. It's the new associate's responsibility to find out what he or she can do for the good of the operation." The vast majority of the new associates, after some initial floundering, have adapted quickly.

Others, especially those who require more structured working conditions, have found that Gore's flexible workplace is not for them. According to Bill for those few, "It's an unhappy situation, both for the associate and the sponsor. If there is no contribution, there is no paycheck."

As Anita McBride, an associate in Phoenix, noted:

> It's not for everybody. People ask me do we have turnover, and yes we do have turnover. What you're seeking looks like utopia, but it also looks extreme. If you finally figure the system, it can be real exciting. If you can't handle it, you gotta go. Probably by your own choice, because you're going to be so frustrated.

Overall, the associates appear to have responded positively to the Gore system of unmanagement and unstructure. And the company's lattice organization has proven itself to be good for it from a bottom-line perspective. Bill estimated the year before he died that "the profit per associate is double" that of DuPont.

Features of W. L. Gore's Culture

Outsiders have been struck by the degree of informality and humor in the Gore organization. Meetings tend to be only as long as necessary. As Trish Hearn, an associate in Newark, Delaware, said, "No one feels a need to pontificate." Words such as *responsibilities* and *commitments* are commonly heard, whereas words such as *employees, subordinates,* and *managers* are taboo in the Gore culture. This is an organization that has always taken what it does very seriously, without its members taking themselves too seriously.

For a company of its size, Gore has always had a very short organizational pyramid. As of 1995, the pyramid consisted of Bob Gore, the late Bill Gore's son, as president and Vieve, Bill Gore's widow, as secretary-treasurer. He has been the chief executive officer for over 20 years. No second-in-command or named successor has been designated. All the other members of the Gore organization were, and continue to be, referred to as associates.

Some outsiders have had problems with the idea of no titles. Sarah Clifton, an associate at the Flagstaff facility, was being pressed by some outsiders as to what her title was. She made one up and had it printed on some business cards: Supreme Commander (see Exhibit D). When Bill Gore learned what she did, he loved it and recounted the story to others.

Leaders, Not Managers.   Within W. L. Gore & Associates, the various people who take lead roles are thought of as being leaders, not managers. Bill Gore described in an internal memo the kinds of leadership and the role of leadership as follows:

1. The associate who is recognized by a team as having a special knowledge or experience (e.g., this could be a chemist, computer expert, machine operator, salesman, engineer, lawyer). This kind of leader gives the team *guidance in a special area.*

EXHIBIT D
Sarah Clifton's card

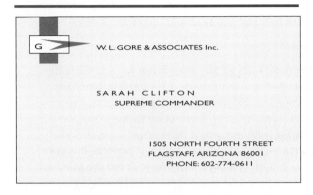

2. The associate the team looks to for coordination of individual activities in order to achieve the agreed on objectives of the team. The role of this leader is to persuade team members to *make the commitments* necessary for success (commitment seeker).

3. The associate who proposes necessary objectives and activities and seeks agreement and team *consensus on objectives.* This leader is perceived by the team members as having a good grasp of how the objectives of the team fit in with the broad objective of the enterprise. This kind of leader is often also the "commitment seeking" leader in 2 above.

4. The leader who evaluates relative contribution of team members (in consultation with other sponsors), and reports these contribution evaluations to a compensation committee. This leader also may participate in the compensation committee on relative contribution and pay and *reports changes in compensation* to individual associates. This leader is then also a compensation sponsor.

5. The leader who coordinates the research, manufacturing, and marketing of one product type within a business, interacting with team leaders and individual associates who have commitments regarding the product type. These leaders are usually called *product specialists.* They are respected for their knowledge and dedication to their products.

6. *Plant leaders* who help coordinate activities of people within a plant.

7. *Business leaders* who help coordinate activities of people in a business.

8. *Functional leaders* who help coordinate activities of people in a "functional" area.

9. *Corporate leaders* who help coordinate activities of people in different businesses and functions and who try to promote communication and cooperation among all associates.

10. *Entrepreneuring associates* who *organize new teams* for new businesses, new products, new processes, new devices, new marketing efforts, new or better methods of all kinds. These leaders invite other associates to "sign up" for their project.

It is clear that leadership is widespread in our lattice organization and that it is continually changing and evolving. The situation that leaders are frequently *also* sponsors should not confuse that these are different activities and responsibilities.

Leaders are not authoritarians, managers of people, or supervisors who tell us what to do or forbid us doing things; nor are they "parents" to whom we transfer our own self-responsibility. However, they do often advise us of the consequences of actions we have done or propose to do. Our actions result in contributions, or lack of contribution, to the success of our enterprise. Our pay depends on the magnitude of our contributions. This is the basic discipline of our lattice organization.

Egalitarian and Innovativeness. Other aspects of the Gore culture have been at promoting an egalitarian atmosphere, such as parking lots with no reserved parking spaces except for customers and disabled workers or visitors and dining areas— only one in each plant—set up as focal points for associate interaction. As Dave McCarter of Phoenix explained: "The design is no accident. The lunchroom in Flagstaff has a fireplace in the middle. We want people to like to be here." The location of a plant is also no accident. Sites have been selected on the basis of transportation access, a nearby university, beautiful surroundings,

EXHIBIT E
. . . .
Excerpts from Interviews with Associates

The first excerpt is from an associate who was formerly with IBM and has been with Gore for 2 years.

Q: What is the difference between being with IBM and Gore?

A. I spent 24 years working for IBM, and there's a big difference. I can go ten times faster here at Gore because of the simplicity of the lattice organization. Let me give you an example. If I wanted to purchase chemicals at IBM (I am an industrial chemist), the first thing I would need to do is get accounting approval, then I would need at least two levels of managers' approval, then a secretary to log in my purchase, and then the purchase order would go to Purchasing, where it would be assigned a buyer. Some time could be saved if you were willing to "walk" the paperwork through the approval process, but even after computerizing the process, it typically would take 1 month from the time you initiated the purchase requisition until the time the material actually arrived. Here they have one simple form. Usually, I get the chemicals the next day, and a copy of the purchase order will arrive a day or two after that. It happens so fast. I wasn't used to that.

Q. Do you find that a lot more pleasant?

A. Yeah, you're unshackled here. There's a lot less bureaucracy that allows you to be a lot more productive. Take lab safety, for example. In my Lab at IBM, we were cited for not having my eyewash taped properly. The first time, we were cited for not having a big enough area taped off. So we taped off a bigger area. The next week the same eyewash was cited again because the area we taped off was 3 inches too short in one direction. We retaped it, and the following week, it got cited again for having the wrong color tape. Keep in mind that the violation was viewed as serious as a pail of gasoline next to a lit Bunsen burner. Another time I had the dubious honor of being selected the functional safety representative in charge of getting the function's labs ready for a corporate safety audit. [The function was a third level in the pyramidal organization: (1) department, (2) project, and (3) function.] At the same time I was working on developing a new surface-mount package. As it turned out, I had no time to work on development, and the function spent a lot of time and money getting ready for the corporate auditors who in the end never showed. I'm not belittling the importance of safety, but you really don't need all that bureaucracy to be safe.

The second interview is with an associate who is a recent engineering graduate.

Q. How did you find the transition coming here?

A. Although I never would have expected it to be, I found my transition coming to Gore to be rather challenging. What attracted me to the company was the opportunity to "be my own boss" and determine my own commitments. I am very goal oriented and enjoy taking a project and running with it—all things that you are able to do and encouraged to do within the Gore culture. Thus I thought, a perfect fit!

However, as a new associate, I really struggled with where to focus my efforts—I was ready to make my own commitments, but to what?! I felt a strong need to be sure that I was working on something that had value, something that truly needed to be done. While I didn't expect to have the "hottest" project, I did want to make sure that I was helping the company to "make money" in some way.

At the time, though, I was working for a plant that was pretty typical of what Gore was like when it was originally founded—after my first project (which was designed to be a "quick win"—a project with meaning, but one that had a definite end point), I was told, "Go find something to work on." While I could have found something, I wanted to find something with at least a small degree of priority! Thus the whole process of finding a project was very frustrating for me—I didn't feel that I had the perspective to make such a choice and ended up in many conversations with my sponsor about what would be valuable. . . . In the end, of course, I did find that project—and it did actually turn out to be a good investment for Gore. The process to get there, though, was definitely trying for someone as inexperienced as I was—so much

EXHIBIT E
∙∙∙∙∙∙∙∙∙∙∙∙∙∙
Excerpts from Interviews with Associates (*continued*)

> ground would have been gained by suggesting a few projects to me and then letting me choose from that smaller pool.
>
> What's really neat about the whole thing, though, is that my experience has truly made a difference. Due in part to my frustrations, my plant now provides college grads with more guidance on their first several projects. (This guidance obviously becomes less and less critical as each associate grows within Gore.) Associates still are choosing their own commitments, but they're doing so with additional perspective and the knowledge that they are making a contribution to Gore—which is an important thing within our culture. As I said, though, it was definitely rewarding to see that the company was so responsive and to feel that I had helped to shape someone else's transition!

and climate appeal. Land cost has never been a primary consideration. McCarter justified the selection by stating: "Expanding is not costly in the long run. The loss of money is what you make happen by stymieing people into a box."

Bob Gore is a champion of Gore culture. As Sally Gore related:

> We have managed surprisingly to maintain our sense of freedom and our entrepreneurial spirit. I think what we've found is that we had to develop new ways to communicate with associates because you can't communicate with 6000 people the way that you can communicate with 500 people. It just can't be done. So we have developed a newsletter that we didn't have before. One of the most important communication mediums that we developed, and this was Bob Gore's idea, is a digital voice exchange which we call our Gorecom. Basically everyone has a mailbox and a password. Lots of companies have gone to e-mail, and we use e-mail, but Bob feels very strongly that we're very much an oral culture and there's a big difference between cultures that are predominantly oral and predominantly written. Oral cultures encourage direct communication, which is, of course, something that we encourage.

In rare cases an associate "is trying to be unfair," in Bill's own words. In one case the problem was chronic absenteeism, and in another, an individual was caught stealing. "When that happens, all hell breaks loose," said Bill Gore. "We can get damned authoritarian when we have to."

Over the years, Gore & Associates has faced a number of unionization drives. The company has neither tried to dissuade associates from attending an organizational meeting nor retaliated when flyers were passed out. As of 1995, none of the plants has been organized. Bill believed that no need existed for third-party representation under the lattice structure. He asked the question, "Why would associates join a union when they own the company? It seems rather absurd."

Commitment has long been considered a two-way street. W. L. Gore & Associates has tried to avoid layoffs. Instead of cutting pay, which in the Gore culture would be disastrous to morale, the company has used a system of temporary transfers within a plant or cluster of plants and voluntary layoffs.

Exhibit E contains excerpts of interviews with two Gore associates that further indicates the nature of the culture and work environment at W. L. Gore & Associates.

W. L. Gore & Associates' Sponsor Program
∙∙∙∙∙∙∙∙∙∙∙∙∙∙∙∙∙∙∙∙∙∙∙∙∙∙∙∙∙∙∙∙∙∙∙

Bill Gore knew that products alone did not a company make. He wanted to avoid smothering the company in thick layers of formal "management." He felt that hierarchy stifled individual creativity. As the company grew, he knew that he had to find a way to assist new people and to follow their progress. This was particularly important when it came to compensation. W. L. Gore & Associates developed its sponsor program to meet these needs.

When people apply to Gore, they are initially screened by personnel specialists. As many as 10 references may be contacted on each applicant. Those who meet the basic criteria are interviewed by current associates. The interviews have been described as rigorous by those who have gone through them. Before anyone is hired, an associate must agree to be his or her sponsor. The sponsor is to take a personal interest in the new associate's contributions, problems, and goals, acting as both a coach and an advocate. The sponsor tracks the new associate's progress, helping and encouraging, dealing with weaknesses, and concentrating on strengths. Sponsoring is not a short-term commitment. All associates have sponsors, and many have more than one. When individuals are hired initially, they are likely to have a sponsor in their immediate work area. If they move to another area, they may have a sponsor in that work area. As associates' commitments change or grow, they may acquire additional sponsors.

Because the hiring process looks beyond conventional views of what makes a good associate, some anomalies have occurred. Bill Gore proudly told the story of "a very young man" of 84 who walked in, applied, and spent 5 very good years with the company. The individual had 30 years of experience in the industry before joining Gore. His other associates had no problems accepting him, but the personnel computer did. It insisted that his age was 48. The individual success stories at Gore have come from diverse backgrounds.

An internal memo by Bill Gore described three roles of sponsors:

1. *Starting sponsor*—a sponsor who helps a new associate get started on a first job or a present associate get started on a new job.

2. *Advocate sponsor*—a sponsor who sees that an associate's accomplishments are recognized.

3. *Compensation sponsor*—a sponsor who sees to it that an associate is fairly paid for contributions to the success of the enterprise.

A single person can perform any one or all three kinds of sponsorship. Quite frequently, a sponsoring associate is a good friend, and it is not unknown for two associates to sponsor each other.

COMPENSATION PRACTICES

Compensation at W. L. Gore & Associates has taken three forms: salary, profit sharing, and an associates' stock ownership program (ASOP).[6] Entry-level salary has been in the middle for comparable jobs. According to Sally Gore: "We do not feel we need to be the highest paid. We never try to steal people away from other companies with salary. We want them to come here because of the opportunities for growth and the unique work environment." Associates' salaries have been reviewed at least once a year and more commonly twice a year. The reviews are conducted by a compensation team at each facility, with sponsors for the associates acting as their advocates during the review process. Prior to meeting with the compensation committee, the sponsor checks with customers or associates familiar with the person's work to find out what contribution the associate has made. The compensation team relies heavily on this input. In addition, the compensation team considers the associate's leadership ability and willingness to help others develop to their fullest.

Profit sharing follows a formula based on economic value added (EVA). Sally Gore had the following to say about the adoption of a formula:

It's become more formalized and in a way, I think that's unfortunate because it used to be a complete surprise to receive a profit share. The thinking of the people like Bob Gore and other leaders was that maybe we weren't using it in the right way and we could encourage people by helping them know more about it and how we made profit share decisions. The fun of it before was people didn't know when it was coming, and all of a sudden you could do something creative about passing out checks. It was great fun, and people would have a wonderful time with it. The disadvantage was that associates then did not focus much on, "What am I doing to create another profit share?" By using EVA as a method of evaluation for our profit share, we know at the end of every month how much EVA was created that month. When we've created a certain amount of EVA, we then get another profit share. So everybody knows and everyone says, "We'll do it in January," so it is done. Now associates feel more part of the happening to make it work. What have you done?

Go make some more sales calls, please! There are lots of things we can do to improve our EVA, and everybody has a responsibility to do that.

Every month EVA is calculated, and every associate is informed. John Mosko of electronic products commented, "... [EVA] lets us know where we are on the path to getting one [a profit share]. It's very critical—every associate knows."

Annually, Gore also buys company stock equivalent to a fixed percent of the associates' annual income, placing it in the ASOP retirement fund. Thus an associate can become a stockholder after being at Gore for a year. Gore's ASOP ensures that associates participate in the growth of the company by acquiring ownership in it. Bill Gore wanted associates to feel that they themselves are owners. One associate stated, "This is much more important than profit sharing." In fact, some long-term associates (including a 25-year veteran machinist) have become millionaires from the ASOP.

W. L. GORE & ASSOCIATES' GUIDING PRINCIPLES AND CORE VALUES

In addition to the sponsor program, Bill Gore articulated four guiding principles:

1. Try to be fair.

2. Encourage, help, and allow other associates to grow in knowledge, skill, and scope of activity and responsibility.

3. Make your own commitments, and keep them.

4. Consult with other associates before taking actions that may be "below the water line."

The four principles have been referred to as "Fairness, Freedom, Commitment, and Waterline." The waterline terminology is drawn from an analogy to ships. If someone pokes a hole in a boat above the waterline, the boat will be in relatively little real danger. If someone, however, pokes a hole below the waterline, the boat is in immediate danger of sinking. Waterline issues must be discussed across teams and plants before decisions are made.

The operating principles were put to a test in

1978. By this time, word about the qualities of Gore-Tex fabric was being spread throughout the recreational and outdoor markets. Production and shipment had begun in volume. At first a few complaints were heard. Next, some of the clothing started coming back. Finally, much of the clothing was being returned. The trouble was that the Gore-Tex fabric was leaking. Waterproofing was one of the major properties responsible for Gore-Tex fabric's success. The company's reputation and credibility were on the line.

Peter W. Gilson, who led Gore's fabrics division, recalled: "It was an incredible crisis for us at that point. We were really starting to attract attention; we were taking off—and then this." In the next few months, Gilson and a number of his associates made a number of those below-the-waterline decisions.

First, the researchers determined that oils in human sweat were responsible for clogging the pores in the Gore-Tex fabric and altering the surface tension of the membrane. Thus water could pass through. They also discovered that a good washing could restore the waterproof property. At first, this solution, known as the "Ivory Snow solution," was accepted.

A single letter from "Butch," a mountain guide in the Sierras, changed the company's position. Butch described what happened while he was leading a group: "My parka leaked, and my life was in danger." As Gilson noted, "That scared the hell out of us. Clearly, our solution was no solution at all to someone on a mountain top." All the products were recalled. Gilson remembered: "We bought back, at our own expense, a fortune in pipeline material—anything that was in the stores, at the manufacturers, or anywhere else in the pipeline."

In the meantime, Bob Gore and other associates set out to develop a permanent fix. One month later, a second-generation Gore-Tex fabric had been developed. Gilson, furthermore, told dealers that if a customer ever returned a leaky parka, they should replace it and bill the company. The replacement program alone cost Gore roughly $4 million.

The popularity of Gore-Tex outerwear took off. Many manufacturers now make numerous pieces of apparel such as parkas, gloves, boots, jogging outfits, and wind shirts from Gore-Tex laminate. Sometimes when customers are dissatisfied with a garment, they return it directly to Gore. Gore has always stood behind any product made of Gore-Tex fabric. Analysis of the returned garments found that the problem often was not the Gore-Tex fabric. The manufacturer "... had created a design flaw so that the water could get in here or get in over the zipper, and we found that when there was something negative about it, everyone knew it was Gore-Tex. So we had to make good on products that we were not manufacturing. We now license the manufacturers of all our Gore-Tex fabric products. They pay a fee to obtain a license to manufacture Gore-Tex products. In return, we oversee the manufacture, and we let them manufacture only designs that we are sure are guaranteed to keep you dry, that really will work. Then it works for them and for us—it's a win-win for them as well as for us," according to Sally Gore.

To further ensure quality, Gore & Associates has its own test facility, including a rain room for garments made from Gore-Tex. Besides a rain/storm test, all garments must pass abrasion and washing machine tests. Only the garments that pass these tests will be licensed to display the Gore-Tex label.

RESEARCH AND DEVELOPMENT

Like everything else at Gore, research and development (R&D) has always been unstructured. Even without a formal R&D department, the company has been issued many patents, although most inventions have been held as proprietary or trade secrets. For example, few associates are allowed to see Gore-Tex being made. Any associate can, however, ask for a piece of raw PTFE (known as a "silly worm") with which to experiment. Bill Gore believed that all people had it within themselves to be creative.

One of the best examples of Gore inventiveness occurred in 1969. At the time, the wire and cable division was facing increased competition. Bill Gore began to look for a way to straighten out the PTFE molecules. As he said, "I figured out that if we ever unfold those molecules, get them to stretch out straight, we'd have a tremendous new kind of material." He thought that if PTFE could be stretched, air could be introduced into its molecular structure. The result would be greater volume per pound of raw material with no effect on performance. Thus fabricating costs would be reduced, and profit margins would be increased. Going about this search in a scientific manner, Bob Gore heated rods of PTFE to various temperatures and then slowly stretched them. Regardless of the temperature or how carefully he stretched them, the rods broke.

Working alone late one night after countless failures, Bob in frustration stretched one of the rods violently. To his surprise, it did not break. He tried it again and again with the same results. The next morning Bob demonstrated his breakthrough to his father, but not without some drama. As Bill Gore recalled: "Bob wanted to surprise me, so he took a rod and stretched it slowly. Naturally, it broke. Then he pretended to get mad. He grabbed another rod and said, 'Oh, the hell with this,' and gave it a pull. It didn't break—he'd done it." The new arrangement of molecules not only changed the wire and cable division but led to the development of Gore-Tex fabric.

Bill and Vieve did the initial field-testing of Gore-Tex fabric the summer of 1970. Vieve made a hand-sewn tent out of patches of Gore-Tex fabric. They took it on their annual camping trip to the Wind River Mountains of Wyoming. The very first night in the wilderness, they encountered a hail storm. The hail tore holes in the top of the tent, and the bottom filled up like a bathtub from the rain. Undaunted, Bill Gore stated: "At least we knew from all the water that the tent was waterproof. We just needed to make it stronger, so it could withstand hail."

Gore associates have always been encouraged to think, experiment, and follow a potentially profitable idea to its conclusion. At a plant in Newark, Delaware, Fred L. Eldreth, an associate with a third-grade education, designed a machine that could wrap thousands of feet of wire a day. The design was completed over a weekend. Many other associates have contributed their ideas through both product and process breakthroughs.

Even without an R&D department, innovation and creativity continue at a rapid pace at Gore & Associates. The year before he died, Bill Gore claimed that "the creativity, the number of patent applications and innovative products [are] triple" that of DuPont.

DEVELOPMENT OF GORE ASSOCIATES

Ron Hill, an associate in Newark, noted that Gore "will work with associates who want to advance themselves." Associates have been offered many in-house training opportunities, not only in technical and engineering areas but also in leadership development. In addition, the company has established cooperative education programs with universities and other outside providers, picking up most of the costs for the Gore associates. The emphasis in associate development, as in many parts of Gore, has always been that the associate must take the initiative.

MARKETING APPROACHES AND STRATEGY

Gore's business philosophy incorporates three beliefs and principles: (1) that the company can and should offer the best-valued products in the markets and market segments where it chooses to compete, (2) that buyers in each of its markets should appreciate the caliber and performance of the items it manufactures, and (3) that Gore should become a leader with unique expertise in each of the product categories where it competes. To achieve these outcomes, the company's approach to marketing (it has no formally organized marketing department) is based on the following principles:

1. Marketing a product requires a leader, or *product champion.* According to Dave McCarter: "You marry your technology with the interests of your champions, since you've got to have champions for all these things no matter what. And that's the key element within our company. Without a product champion, you can't do much anyway, so it is individually driven. If you get people interested in a particular market or a particular product for the marketplace, then there is no stopping them." Bob Winterling of the fabrics division elaborated further on the role and importance of the product champion:

The product champion is probably the most important resource we have at Gore for the introduction of new products. You look at that bicycle cable. That could have come out of many different divisions of Gore, but it really happened because one or two individuals said, "Look, this can work. I believe in it; I'm passionate about it; and I want it to happen." And the same thing with Glide floss. I think John Spencer in this case—although there was a team that supported John, let's never forget that—John sought the experts out throughout the organization. But without John making it

happen on his own, Glide floss would never have come to fruition. He started with a little chain of drug stores here, Happy Harry's, I think, and we put a few cases in, and we just tracked the sales, and that's how it all started. Who would have ever believed that you could take what we would have considered a commodity product like that, sell it direct for $3–5 apiece. That is so un-Gore-like it's incredible. So it comes down to people, and it comes down to the product champion to make things happen.

2. *A product champion is responsible for marketing the product through commitments with sales representatives.* Again, according to Dave McCarter:

We have no quota system. Our marketing and our salespeople make their own commitments as to what their forecasts have been. There is no person sitting around telling them that is not high enough, you have to increase it by 10 percent, or whatever somebody feels is necessary. You are expected to meet your commitment, which is your forecast, but nobody is going to tell you to change it. . . . There is no order of command, no chain involved. These are groups of independent people who come together to make unified commitments to do something, and sometimes when they can't make those agreements . . . you may pass up a marketplace. . . . But that's OK, because there's much more advantage when the team decides to do something.

3. *Sales associates are on salary, not commission.* They participate in the profit-sharing and ASOP plans in which all other associates participate.

As in other areas of Gore, individual success stories have come from diverse backgrounds. Dave McCarter related another success of the company relying on a product champion as follows:

I interviewed Sam one day. I didn't even know why I was interviewing him actually. Sam was retired from AT&T. After 25 years, he took the golden parachute and went down to Sun Lakes to play golf. He played golf a few months and got tired of that. He was selling life insurance.

I sat reading the application; his technical

background interested me. . . . He had managed an engineering department with 600 people. He'd managed manufacturing plants for AT&T and had a great wealth of experience at AT&T. He said, "I'm retired. I like to play golf, but I just can't do it every day, so I want to do something else. Do you have something around here I can do?" I was thinking to myself, "This is one of these guys I would sure like to hire, but I don't know what I would do with him." The thing that triggered me was the fact that he said he sold insurance, and here is a guy with a high degree of technical background selling insurance. He had marketing experience, international marketing experience. So the bell went off in my head that we were trying to introduce a new product into the marketplace that was a hydrocarbon leak-protection cable. You can bury it in the ground, and in a matter of seconds it could detect a hydrocarbon like gasoline. I had a couple of other guys working on the product who hadn't been very successful with marketing it. We were having a hard time finding a customer. Well, I thought that kind of product would be like selling insurance. If you think about it, why should you protect your tanks? It's an insurance policy that things are not leaking into the environment. That has implications, big time monetary. So, actually, I said, "Why don't you come back Monday? I have just the thing for you." He did. We hired him; he went to work, a very energetic guy. Certainly a champion of the product, he picked right up on it, ran with it single handed. . . . Now it's a growing business. It certainly is a valuable one too for the environment.

In the implementation of its marketing strategy, Gore has relied on cooperative and word-of-mouth advertising. Cooperative advertising has been especially used to promote Gore-Tex fabric products. These high-dollar, glossy campaigns include full-color ads and dressing the salesforce in Gore-Tex garments. A recent slogan used in the ad campaigns has been, "If it doesn't Gore-Tex, it's not." Some retailers praise the marketing and advertising efforts as the best. Leigh Gallagher, managing editor of *Sporting Goods Business* magazine, describes Gore & Associates' marketing as "unbeatable."

Gore has stressed cooperative advertising because the associates believe positive experiences with any one product will carry over to purchases of other and more Gore-Tex fabric products. Apparently, this strategy has paid off. When the Grandoe Corporation introduced Gore-Tex gloves, its president, Richard Zuckerwar, noted: "Sports activists have had the benefit of Gore-Tex gloves to protect their hands from the elements. . . . With this handsome collection of gloves . . . you can have warm, dry hands without sacrificing style." Other clothing manufacturers and distributors who sell Gore-Tex garments include Apparel Technologies, Lands' End, Austin Reed, Hudson Trail Outfitters, Timberland, Woolrich, North Face, L. L. Bean, and Michelle Jaffe.

The power of these marketing techniques extends beyond consumer products. According to Dave McCarter, "In the technical end of the business, company reputation probably is most important. You have to have a good reputation with your company." He went on to say that without a good reputation, a company's products would not be considered seriously by many industrial customers. In other words, the sale is often made before the representative calls. Using its marketing strategies, Gore has been very successful in securing a market leadership position in a number of areas, ranging from waterproof outdoor clothing to vascular grafts. Its market share of waterproof, breathable fabrics is estimated to be 90 percent.

ADAPTING TO CHANGING ENVIRONMENTAL FORCES

Each of Gore's divisions has faced from time to time adverse environmental forces. For example, the fabric division was hit hard when the fad for jogging suits collapsed in the mid-1980s. The fabric division took another hit from the recession of 1989. People simply reduced their purchases of high-end athletic apparel. By 1995, the fabric division was the fastest growing division of Gore again.

The electronic division was hit hard when the main-frame computer business declined in the early 1990s. By 1995, that division was seeing a resurgence for its products partially because that division had developed some electronic products for the medical industry. As can be seen, not all the forces have been negative.

The aging population of America has increased the need for health care. As a result, Gore has invested in the development of additional medical products, and the medical division is growing.

W. L. GORE & ASSOCIATES' FINANCIAL PERFORMANCE

As a closely held private corporation, W. L. Gore has kept its financial information as closely guarded as proprietary information on products and processes. It has been estimated that associates who work at Gore own 90 percent of the stock. According to Shanti Mehta, an associate, Gore's returns on assets and sales have consistently ranked it among the top 10 percent of the Fortune 500 companies. According to another source, W. L. Gore & Associates has been doing just fine by any financial measure. For 37 straight years (from 1961 to 1997) the company has enjoyed profitability and positive return on equity. The compounded growth rate for revenues at W. L. Gore & Associates from 1969 to 1989 was more than 18 percent discounted for inflation.[7] In 1969, total sales were about $6 million; by 1989, the figure was $600 million. As should be expected with the increase in size, the percentage increase in sales has slowed over the last 7 years. The company projects sales to reach $1.4 billion in 1998. Gore financed this growth without long-term debt unless it made sense. For example, "We used to have some industrial revenue bonds where, in essence, to build facilities the government allows banks to lend you money tax-free. Up to a couple of years ago we were borrowing money through industrial revenue bonds. Other than that, we are totally debt-free. Our money is generated out of the operations of the business, and frankly we're looking for new things to invest in. I know that's a challenge for all of us today," said Bob Winterling. *Forbes* magazine estimates Gore's operating profits for 1993, 1994, 1995, 1996, and 1997 to be $120, $140, $192, $213, and $230 million, respectively. Bob Gore predicts that the company will reach $2 billion in sales by 2001.

Recently, the company purchased Optical Concepts, Inc., a laser, semiconductor technology company, of Lompoc, California. In addition, Gore & Associates is investing in test marketing a new product, guitar strings, that was developed by its associates.

When asked about cost control, Sally Gore had the following to say:

> You have to pay attention to cost or you're not an effective steward of anyone's money, your own or anyone else's. It's kind of interesting, we started manufacturing medical products in 1974 with the vascular graft, and it built from there. The Gore vascular graft is the Cadillac or BMW or the Rolls Royce of the business. There is absolutely no contest, and our medical products division became very successful. People thought this was Mecca. Nothing had ever been manufactured that was so wonderful. Our business expanded enormously, rapidly out there [Flagstaff, Arizona], and we had a lot of young, young leadership. They spent some time thinking they could do no wrong and that everything they touched was going to turn to gold. They have had some hard knocks along the way and discovered it wasn't as easy as they initially thought it was. And that's probably good learning for everyone somewhere along the way. That's not how the business works. There's a lot of truth in that old saying that you learn more from your failures than you do your successes. One failure goes a long way toward making you say, "Oh, wow!"

ACKNOWLEDGMENTS

Many sources were helpful in providing background material for this case. The most important sources of all were the W. L. Gore associates, who generously shared their time and viewpoints about the company. They provided many resources, including internal documents and added much to this case through sharing their personal experiences as well as ensuring that the case accurately reflected the Gore company and culture.

Endnotes

1. Gore-Tex is a registered trademark of W. L. Gore & Associates.
2. In this case, the word *associate* is used because in W. L. Gore & Associates' literature the word is always used instead of employees. In fact, case writers were told that Gore "never had 'employees'—always 'associates.'"
3. Gore RideOn is a registered trademark of W. L. Gore & Associates.

4. Glide is a registered trademark of W. L. Gore & Associates.

5. WindStopper is a registered trademark of W. L. Gore & Associates.

6. Similar legally to an ESOP (employee stock ownership plan). Again, Gore simply has never allowed the word *employee* in any of its documentation.

7. In comparison, only 11 of the 200 largest companies in the Fortune 500 had positive ROE each year from 1970 to 1988, and only 2 other companies missed a year. The revenue growth rate for these 13 companies was 5.4 percent, compared with 2.5 percent for the entire Fortune 500.

Bibliography

Aburdene, Patricia, and John Nasbitt, *Re-inventing the Corporation* (New York: Warner Books, 1985).

Angrist, S. W. "Classless Capitalists," *Forbes,* May 9, 1983, pp. 123-124.

Franlesca, L. "Dry and Cool," *Forbes,* August 27, 1984, p. 126.

Hoerr, J. "A Company Where Everybody Is the Boss," *Business Week,* April 15, 1985, p. 98.

Levering, Robert, *The 100 Best Companies to Work for in America* (New York: Signet, 1985), see the chapter on W. L. Gore & Associates, Inc.

McKendrick, Joseph, "The Employees as Entrepreneur," *Management World,* January 1985, pp. 12-13.

Milne, M. J. "The Gorey Details," *Management Review,* March 1985, pp. 16-17.

Price, Debbie M. "Gore-Tex Style." *Baltimore Sun,* April 20, 1997, pp. 1D & 4D.

Price, Kathy, "Firm Thrives without Boss," *AZ Republic,* February 2, 1986.

Posner, B. G. "The First Day on the Job," *Inc.,* June 1986, pp. 73-75.

Rhodes, Lucien, "The Un-manager," *Inc.,* August 1982, p. 34.

Simmons, J. "People Managing Themselves: Un-management at W. L. Gore, Inc.," *The Journal for Quality and Participation,* December 1987, pp. 14-19.

"The Future Workplace," *Management Review,* July 1986, pp. 22-23.

Trachtenberg, J. A. "Give Them Stormy Weather," *Forbes,* 137(6), March 24, 1986, pp. 172-174.

Ward, Alex. "An All-Weather Idea," *New York Times Magazine,* November 10, 1985, sec. 6.

Weber, Joseph. "No Bosses. And Even 'Leaders' Can't Give Orders," *Business Week,* December 10, 1990, pp. 196-197.

"Wilbert L. Gore," *Industry Week,* October 17, 1983, pp. 48-49.

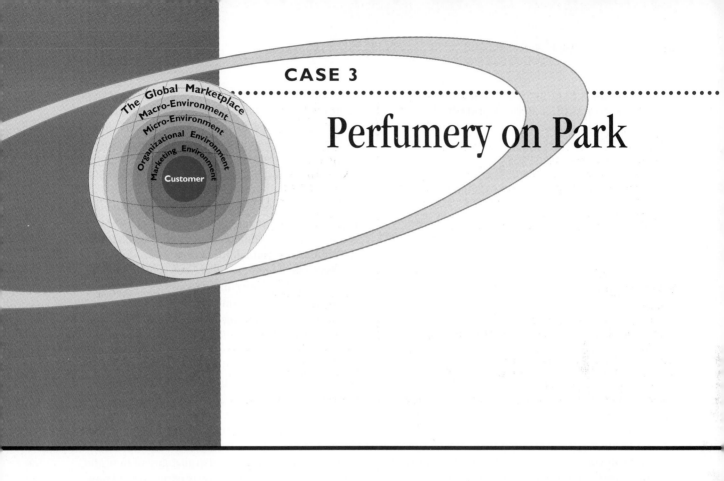

Perfumery on Park

This case was prepared by David M. Currie, Associate Professor of Economics and Finance at the Crummer Graduate School of Business, Rollins College.

In October 1998, Anna Currie wondered what she should do about Perfumery on Park, Inc. Recent development of the Internet presented an exciting opportunity for growth but would require further commitment of time and money. The opportunity occurred at a time in Anna's life when she was growing tired of the constant attention required to run a small business. Her children had grown and lived elsewhere, and vacations looked more and more attractive. The dilemma, then, was whether to put more effort into growing the business or leave the business entirely.

Whatever the option, Anna was conscious of maintaining the strengths Perfumery on Park had developed through the years—product selection, knowledge of the fragrance industry, variety of fragrances, contacts with suppliers, and quality of

service. Any strategic option would be rejected if it jeopardized or did not build on these strengths.

HISTORY

Market Niche

Anna Currie established Perfumery on Park, Inc., in Winter Park, Florida, in May 1984. After an initial period of rapid growth, revenue increases had slowed over the past few years to that of the perfume business nationally. Anna was responsible for all aspects of the boutique's operations, including ordering, personnel, finance, and marketing. Her husband, David, worked at the shop on weekends and during holidays and maintained the accounting records. The three employees in addition to Anna and David were competent both in their knowledge of the perfume business and in their ability to manage the shop during the Curries' absence.

Winter Park is an affluent community adjacent to Orlando, the tourist center of Florida. Winter Park's main street, Park Avenue, is bordered on one side by Central Park and on the other by numerous small boutiques and specialty shops. The ambience of the town is comparable with that of Carmel, California, Palm Beach, Florida, or the Hamptons of Long Island.

Perfumery on Park had carved a market niche by specializing in classic fragrances and fragrances from smaller houses or less famous designers. These fragrances appealed especially to men and women with an appreciation for fine fragrances or who had traveled to Europe and had been exposed to a broader variety of fragrances than was typically available in the United States. Personnel at department stores in the central Florida area regularly referred customers to the Perfumery. In return, the Perfumery staff referred to department stores' customers who requested fragrances from heavily advertised national launches that the Perfumery did not carry.

The Perfumery's variety of fragrances was considered unsurpassed by U.S. standards, where most fragrance marketing was through department stores. Of more than 400 fragrances on the international market in 1998, Perfumery on Park carried almost 200. Because most department stores carried perhaps 25 to 30 lines that tended to be in fashion at the time, a niche existed for a shop specializing in traditional and hard-to-find fragrances.

The success at carving a niche in the competitive fragrance market caused rapid growth in the early years of the business, but as the business matured, the rate of growth slowed. Price increases had averaged 3 percent per year recently because of lower inflation in the United States and a relatively stable value of the dollar.

Emphasis on Service

Anna's strong belief in service to customers took many aspects. An important aspect was maintenance of a fragrance once the decision was made to carry it. With an average of more than 30 fragrance launches each year in the United States, turnover of fragrances was constant as the different fragrances experienced their lifecycles. Once Anna decided to carry a fragrance, the fragrance was maintained until it was no longer manufactured. Maintaining a fragrance also meant stocking whatever stock-keeping units (SKUs) were available: perfumes, eaux de toilette, and body products such as talcum powder, lotion, and bath gel. The decision to carry a fragrance thus implied a significant investment in inventory. Over the years, the average monthly inventory had grown to about $100,000 from $70,000 in the late 1980s.

Frequently, the U.S. distribution of a fragrance changed, resulting in the product's unavailability for a period of months. Locating the new distributor required considerable effort, but meeting the needs of clients required that such information be obtained. If a fragrance line did not have an American distributor, Anna contacted the manufacturer in France about ordering the fragrances directly. As a courtesy to her customers, Anna also special-ordered other fragrances for which an established U.S. market did not exist; these fragrances then were resold at prices that barely covered the cost of importing and duties.

Great care was taken in educating the staff about all aspects of the fragrance industry—ingredients, manufacturers and couturiers, procedures for applying fragrances, and availability of new and classic fragrances. The staff was expected to know about all the fragrances carried at the Perfumery, whereas the staff at a department store typically specialized in the lines of one designer or manufacturer such as Estèe Lauder or Lancôme. The Perfumery received referrals from throughout the United States of customers trying to locate a fragrance they had worn for years but were no longer able to find in their local market.

Aspects of merchandising played a key role in satisfying customers. Gift wrapping was complementary, samples were provided as a means of testing alternative fragrances, and shopping bags were decorated with ribbons. For special occasions, customers frequently asked the staff to wrap packages from other stores because of the quality of the Perfumery's presentation. Customers who visited the shop more than once were greeted by name, although the usual joke was that the staff recognized customers by fragrance rather than by name. The staff maintained a database for the customer so the current fragrance favorite would be known to whomever was shopping for that individual.

A few years earlier Anna decided to grow the catalogue business, resulting in a mailing list that now numbered more than 8000 customers nationwide. Not only did the Perfumery receive orders from throughout the United States, it also received referrals from stores as far away as Nevada and Michigan. Because central Florida was such a popular tourist destination, visitors to Park Avenue often stopped at the shop, where they left information about fragrance preferences.

TRENDS IN THE FRAGRANCE INDUSTRY

Consolidation of Department Stores

Sales through boutiques such as Perfumery on Park account for more than 90 percent of the sales of perfumes in France. In the United States, however, the shares are reversed because the usual channel of distribution is through department stores. The department store industry in the United States had gone through a period of consolidation in the early 1990s, resulting in closure or merger of some of the famous names in the industry.

One of the major survivors nationally was Saks Fifth Avenue, which recently opened a store in the Orlando area. Although department stores generally were not competitors for the Perfumery, Saks was an exception. Not only did Saks carry new launches, it also carried a wide variety of classic perfumes, the specialty of Perfumery on Park. Customers who had comparison shopped told Anna that prices were higher at Saks. It wasn't clear how much of a threat Saks represented for the Perfumery, although the slowdown in growth roughly coincided with the opening of the Saks store in the mid-1990s.

Other department stores in the Orlando area, such as Dillard's and Burdine's, competed with the Perfumery only to a limited extent because of their different product selection. The closest full-scale mall was almost 10 miles away. Jacobson's sold fragrances at its location on Park Avenue, as did Dillard's at the Winter Park Mall (Dillard's was almost the only store remaining at the mall), but each tended to specialize in lines that were not carried at the Perfumery.

Repositioning of Fragrances

One outcome of the turmoil in department stores was a change in the positions of fragrances in the market. Manufacturers who had relied on depart-

ment stores for access to the U.S. customer found that they had lost that access. Some of the manufacturers went out of business, while others repositioned their products to become more exclusive or toward mass market. Department stores dropped lines when it became difficult to maintain contact with suppliers. Although this represented an opportunity for the Perfumery, it created confusion in the eyes of the consumer.

An example is Parfums Lanvin, a famous couturier in Paris. Lanvin's most famous fragrance was Arpège, created during the 1920s and a favorite at the Perfumery. Lanvin suffered financial difficulty in the early 1990s, partly as a result of problems in U.S. distribution. The firm was sold to new owners and stopped manufacturing all its fragrances, including Arpège. After 2 years, Arpège was re-released in France and then in the United States. Initially, distribution of Arpège was limited to a few department stores, but because Anna had maintained contact with Parfums Lanvin, the Perfumery was added to U.S. distribution. It quickly became one of the Perfumery's top-selling fragrances.

However, customers faced a rude shock when they purchased Arpège. Before leaving the market, Arpège had been manufactured in eau de cologne concentration, which did not use as many fragrant oils and therefore could be purchased for about $25. When it returned, Arpège was not available as cologne, and Lanvin decided to reposition Arpège as a more exclusive fragrance. The least concentrated form was eau de parfum, which used a higher concentration of oils; the lowest price point was $60. Women who had purchased Arpège for years first found that it was no longer available. When it became available after a 2-year hiatus, they had to pay twice as much. Customer confusion frequently was expressed as resentment toward the Perfumery for trying to gouge customers. Only through a process of patient explanation was the staff able to mollify irate customers.

Diverters

Diversion continued to be a problem in the perfume industry. Rights to sell French fragrances in the United States are purchased by a company that is authorized as the sole agent in the United States. In most cases the agent in turn sells through authorized retail outlets such as department stores or specialty shops such as the Perfumery.

Occasionally, a discount store such as TJ Maxx or Beall's obtains a fragrance that it sells at a discount from the authorized distributor's suggested retail price. Other firms specialize in wholesaling selected fragrances at prices lower than those suggested by the authorized distributor. These products sold outside the purview of the authorized distributor are called diverted (parallel imports or gray market) goods, and the source of supply for diverters is the subject of conjecture.

In most cases, diverters offer only a limited variety of products—100-ml eau de toilette sprays, for example—rather than the complete line. The product is available intermittently but may be in large quantities when it is available. The products frequently are old, resulting from distributor closeouts or repackaging.

Although authorized distributors and retailers may view these gray market goods as prohibited by the distribution contract and hence illegal, the Supreme Court of the United States upheld the right of discounters to obtain and sell diverted goods in 1988 in a suit involving K Mart, Inc.

The diversion situation created problems for Anna because some of the classic fragrances were now distributed in the United States by firms that traditionally were diverters. Her policy had always been not to deal with diverters, but she had to if she was to obtain some of the fragrances that were the Perfumery's specialty. To make the situation worse, the diverters were not reliable about shipping and availability. Orders frequently were shipped incomplete, or products on the order form were not available.

DEVELOP A PRESENCE ON THE WEB

The most exciting change in American retailing in the past few years was the development of electronic commerce. A recent article disclosed that sales via the Internet in the United States were estimated to be $30 billion in 2000, up from $2.7 billion in 1997. Internet sales accounted for less than 1 percent of retail sales in 1997 but were predicted to account for 15 percent of retail sales within 5 years. Anna considered whether she should take advantage of the opportunity by becoming one of the first perfume outlets over the Internet.

Anna wondered whether the same strengths that contributed to the success of the store—product selection, knowledgeable staff, and quality of service—would extend to success on the Internet. There were several perfume sites on the Internet, but they had characteristics similar to diverters and department stores—few product lines, limited SKUs in each line, and emphasis on fashion rather than classic fragrances. It seemed it would be possible to extend the Perfumery's market niche to the Internet. Anna also had access to some of the prestige lines in the fragrance industry—Hermès and Guerlain, for example—that were not available on-line. A recent article in *Women's Wear Daily* identified a new Internet perfumer with first-year sales of $1 million, even without many of the lines Anna carried. Anna especially liked what she read in another article that customers over the Internet tended to be loyal to the site they did business with first. Anna knew from experience that it was less expensive to retain customers than to attract new customers, so she thought that gaining an early entry would pay handsome dividends.

On the other hand, selling through a computer was much different from selling person-to-person, which had been the Perfumery's forte. Information about products must be articulated in written rather than verbal form. The shop's inventory must be computerized in a format that will allow customers to shop via the Internet. Anna must find a presentation that will encourage shoppers to return to the site repeatedly, so the pages must be updated on a regular basis. She had not yet taken the time to think of changes in management systems and increases in inventory that might be necessary to accommodate Internet customers.

Anna wasn't sure how much this effort would cost in terms of money and time. She had no experience designing Web pages, so would have to outsource the tasks associated with creating a presence on the Web. She estimated that the direct cost would range from $5000 for a low-cost effort to as much as $100,000 for a more professional presentation. *Women's Wear Daily* reported that Calvin Klein would spend as much as $10 million on its CKOne site; spending that amount of money was beyond Anna's wildest dreams. In addition to the direct monetary cost was the cost in terms of her time to develop ideas, collect information, and write text. At this point in her career, Anna wasn't sure whether she was willing to devote that much more time and money into growing the business.

FATIGUE FACTOR

The reason Anna hesitated to grow the business was that she was tired. Anna was 55 years old, had experienced two careers (in human resources and retailing), and had built a thriving business from the ground up. When she opened the shop 14 years earlier, almost everything about it was exciting. The Christmas season, when as much as 50 percent of the year's sales occurred, was especially hectic, but there had been a sense of accomplishment as the business grew.

Over the years, the sense of accomplishment became less important, and the feeling of being tied to the shop increased. The Curries' children had grown up and moved elsewhere. Traveling to visit them during Christmas was out of the question, of course, because it was the busiest shopping season of the year, and all hands were necessary at the shop. When relatives came to visit during the Christmas holidays, Anna and David saw them only in the evenings because of the need to work during the day. After one day off for Christmas, the work routine started again.

There were vacations, but they occurred during the spring and summer when business was slower. It occurred to Anna and David that they had not had Saturdays off since 1984. Although they had accepted the routine, it had begun to wear on them to the point that they wondered whether the business was worth the constant commitment of time. The shop was profitable enough that Anna and David could travel to France to maintain contacts with perfume suppliers, but on their return they had to catch up on the work that piled up during their absence. Surely there was more to life than work.

If she decided to close the business, Anna had two alternatives. The most attractive option was to sell the business as a going concern. Not only would this yield the most money, it would ensure continuation of the idea Anna had nurtured through the years. In many ways growing a business was like raising a child, with the same sense of pride, accomplishment, and love. Selling the business would hurt but would justify Anna's 15 years of hard work. A going concern was more valuable because of the intangible factors Anna had built on as the business grew—the reputation of the Perfumery, contacts with perfume suppliers, and a national customer list. In addition, she felt that the shop was well positioned for eventual presence on the Web.

The second alternative was to sell through the inventory, liquidate the assets, and sell the leasehold. Liquidating the shop was unattractive for the opposite reasons from selling the business—it was potentially less profitable and there were fewer feelings of accomplishment. However, this option was more realistic, particularly if Anna decided she needed to act quickly.

If Anna decided to leave the business, she wanted to work elsewhere. Over the past few years she had enjoyed doing volunteer work with local school children and thought she would like to continue similar efforts in a paid position. Whatever position she accepted would have to provide time during the holidays for her to visit her children.

THE DECISION

Faced with these diametrically opposed alternatives, Anna wanted to decide on an appropriate strategy. Expanding through the Web would involve additional financing beyond the cash flow generated by the shop. The Curries had invested as much of their own money as they could and looked forward to the time after the bank loan was retired so they could draw more from the boutique. Of course, expanding also offered the greatest financial reward. It was impossible to estimate the volume of sales that might be achieved through the Internet, but the number surely was quite large.

Even though there was no rush in making a decision, Anna's feeling of frustration was increasing. She and David had discussed whether they should close the shop for a few years, but inertia kept them in the business. Perhaps now was the appropriate time to decide.

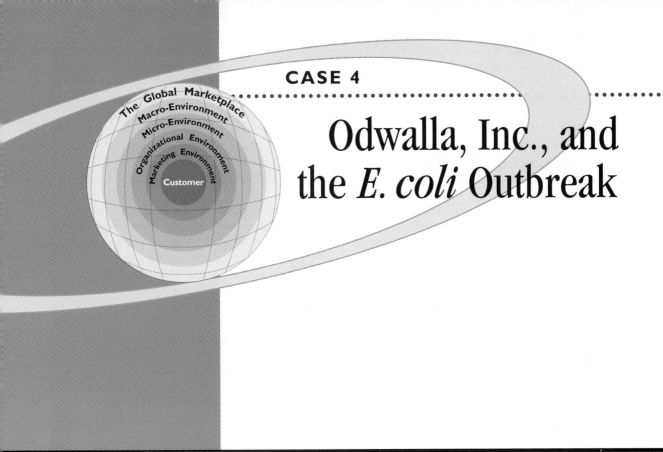

CASE 4

Odwalla, Inc., and the *E. coli* Outbreak

This case was prepared by Anne T. Lawrence, Professor of Organization and Management at San Jose State University.

October 30, 1996, was a cool, fall day in Half Moon Bay, California, a coastal town an hour's drive south of San Francisco. At the headquarters of Odwalla, Inc., a modest, two-story wooden structure just blocks from the beach, company founder and chairman Greg Steltenpohl was attending a marketing meeting. Odwalla, the largest producer of fresh fruit and vegetable–

This is an abridged version of a longer case, Anne T. Lawrence, "Odwalla, Inc., and the *E. coli* Outbreak (A), (B), and (C)" [*Case Research Journal*, 19(1), Winter 1999]. This case was written with the cooperation of management, solely for the purpose of stimulating student discussion. Sources include articles appearing in the *Natural Foods Merchandiser*, the *Nation's Business*, the *San Jose Mercury News*, the *Rocky Mountain News*, the *San Francisco Chronicle*, the *Seattle Times*, the *Fresno Bee*, the *New York Times*, the *Wall Street Journal*, and the *Squeeze* (Odwalla's in-house newsletter); press releases issued by Odwalla and by the American Fresh Juice Council; and Odwalla's annual reports and prospectus. Odwalla's Web site may be found at *http://www.odwallazone.com/*. Copyright © 1999 by Anne T. Lawrence and the North American Case Research Association. All rights reserved.

based beverages in the western United States, had just completed its best-ever fiscal year, with sales of $59 million, up 40 percent over the past 12 months.

The company's CEO, Stephen Williamson, urgently knocked on the glass door and motioned Steltenpohl into the hall. Williamson, 38, a graduate of the University of California at Berkeley and a former investment banker, had served as president of Odwalla from 1992 and 1995, when he became CEO.

It was unlike him to interrupt a meeting, and he looked worried. "I just got a call from the King County Department of Health," Williamson reported. "They've got a dozen cases of E. coli *poisoning up there in the Seattle area. A number of the families told health officials they had drunk Odwalla apple juice."* E. coli *O157:H7 was a virulent bacterium that had been responsible for several earlier outbreaks of food poisoning, including one traced to undercooked Jack-in-the-Box hamburgers in 1993.*

Steltenpohl was puzzled. "What do they know for sure?"

"Right now, not a whole lot. It's just epidemiology," Williamson replied. "They don't have any bacteriologic match-ups yet. They said it might be a while before they would know anything definitive."

"We'd better see what else we can find out."

Steltenpohl and Williamson returned to their offices, where they began placing calls to food safety experts, scientists at the Food and Drug Administration and the Centers for Disease Control, and the company's lawyers. A while later, Steltenpohl came out to speak to his next appointment, a man who had been waiting in the lobby for over an hour. "I'm awfully sorry," the chairman said apologetically. "I'm not going to be able to see you today. Something important's happening that I've got to deal with right away."

COMPANY HISTORY

Odwalla, Inc., was founded in 1980 by Steltenpohl, his wife Bonnie Bassett, and their friend Gerry Percy. Steltenpohl, then 25, was a jazz musician and Stanford graduate with a degree in environmental science. The group purchased a used hand juicer for $200 and began producing fresh-squeezed orange juice in a backyard shed in Santa Cruz, California. They delivered the juice to local restaurants in a Volkswagen van. Steltenpohl later said that he had gotten the idea from a book, *100 Businesses You Can Start for Under $100.* His motivation, he reported, was simply to make enough money to support his fledgling career as a musician and producer of educational media presentations. The company's name came from a jazz composition by the Art Ensemble of Chicago, in which Odwalla was a mythical figure who led the "people of the sun" out of the "gray haze," which the friends chose to interpret as a reference to overly processed food.

During the 1980s, Odwalla prospered, gradually extending its market reach by expanding its own distribution and production capabilities and by acquiring other juice companies. In 1983, the company moved into a larger production facility and added carrot juice to its product line. In 1985—the same year Odwalla incorporated—the company purchased a small local apple juice company, Live

Juice. With apple added to the line, the company expanded its distribution efforts, moving into San Francisco and further north into Marin County. In 1986, Odwalla purchased Dancing Bear Juice Company in Sacramento and assimilated that company's juice products and distribution network in central California.

The company financed its rapid growth in its early years through bank loans and private stock offerings in 1991, 1992, and 1993. In December 1993, the company went public, offering for sale 1 million shares of common stock at an initial price of $6.375 a share. The proceeds of the initial public offering were used in part to construct a 65,000-square-foot state-of-the-art production facility in Dinuba, in California's agricultural Central Valley.

The company also made additional acquisitions. In June 1994, the company acquired Dharma Juice Company of Bellingham, Washington, to distribute its products in the Pacific Northwest. In January 1995, Odwalla purchased J. S. Grant's, Inc., the maker of Just Squeezed Juices, which became the distributor for Odwalla products in the Colorado market. The strategy appeared to be successful. By 1996, Odwalla, which already controlled more than half the market for fresh juice in northern California, had made significant inroads in the Pacific Northwest and Colorado and was poised to extend its market dominance into New Mexico, Texas, and southern California.

PRODUCT LINE

The company considered its market niche to be "fresh, minimally processed juices and juice-based beverages." The company produced a range of products from fresh juice, some single strength and some blended. Odwalla chose fun, clever names, such as Strawberry C-Monster (a vitamin C–fortified fruit smoothie), Femme Vitale (a product formulated to meet women's special nutritional needs), and Guava Have It (a tropical fruit blend). Packaging graphics were brightly colored and whimsical. Pricing was at the premium level; a half gallon of fresh-squeezed orange juice retailed for around $5; a 16-oz blended smoothie, for $2 or more.

Odwalla was committed to making a totally fresh product. In the company's 1995 Annual Report, for example, the letter to shareholders stated:

Our juice is FRESH! We believe that fruits, vegetables, and other botanical nutrients must be treated with respect. As a result, we do not heat-treat our juice, like the heavily processed products made by most other beverage companies.

The company's products were made without preservatives or any artificial ingredients, and the juice was not pasteurized (heat treated to kill microorganisms and to extend shelf life). Unpasteurized juice, the company believed, retained more vitamins, enzymes, and what Steltenpohl referred to as the "flavor notes" of fresh fruits and vegetables.

Although Odwalla did not pasteurize its juice, it took many steps in the manufacturing process to ensure the quality and purity of its product. To avoid possible contamination, the company did not accept ground apples, only those picked from the tree. Inspectors checked field bins to see if there was any dirt, grass, or debris, and bins with evidence of ground contact were rejected. The company's manufacturing facility in Dinuba was considered the most advanced in the industry. The plant operated under a strict code of good manufacturing practices. At Dinuba, apples were thoroughly washed with a sanitizing solution of phosphoric acid and scrubbed with whirling brushes. All juice was produced under extremely strict hygienic standards.

MARKETING

Odwalla marketed its products through supermarkets, warehouse outlets, specialty stores, natural food stores, and institutions such as restaurants and colleges. Slightly over a quarter of all sales were with two accounts—Safeway, a major grocery chain, and Price/Costco, a discount warehouse.

A distinctive feature of Odwalla's strategy was the company's direct store distribution, or DSD, system. Most sites, from supermarkets to small retailers, were provided with their own stand-alone refrigerated cooler, brightly decorated with Odwalla graphics. Accounts were serviced by route salespeople (RSPs), who were responsible for stocking the coolers and removing unsold juice that had passed its "enjoy by" date. RSPs kept careful records of what products were selling well, enabling them to adjust stock to meet local tastes. As an incentive, salespeople received bonuses based on their routes' sales, in addition to their salaries.

Although the DSD system was more expensive than using independent distributors, it allowed the company to maintain tight control over product mix and quality. Moreover, because the company assumed responsibility for ordering, stocking, and merchandising its own products within the store, Odwalla in most cases did not pay "slotting" and other handling fees to the retailer.

CORPORATE CULTURE

The fresh juice company was always, as Steltenpohl put it, "values driven." In 1992, around 80 Odwalla employees participated in a 9-month process that led to the creation of the company's vision, mission, and core values statements. These focused on nourishment, ecological sustainability, innovation, and continuous learning.

Concerned that rapid growth might erode common commitment to these values, in 1995 the company initiated annual 3-day training sessions, held on site at multiple locations, known as Living Vision Conferences, for employees to talk about the application of the vision to everyday operating issues. An internal process the company called Vision Link sought to link each individual's job to the Odwalla vision. Managers were expected to model the company's values. The company called its values a "touchstone (for employees) in assessing their conduct and in making business decisions."

In addition, Odwalla instituted a "strategic dialogue" process. A group of 30 people, with some fixed seats for top executives and some rotating seats for a wide cross section of other employees, met quarterly in San Francisco for broad discussions of the company's values and strategic direction.

Social responsibility and environmental awareness were critical to Odwalla's mission. Community service efforts included aid to farm families in the Central Valley, scholarships to study nutrition, and gifts of cash and juice to many local community organizations. The company instituted a recycling program for its plastic bottles. It attempted to divert all organic waste away from landfills—for example, by selling pulp for livestock feed and citrus peel for use in teas and condiments and past-code juice for biofuels. In the mid-1990s, the company began the process of converting its vehicle fleet to alternative fuels. Odwalla's corporate responsibility extended to its employees, who received innovative benefits that included stock options, extensive "wellness" programs, and an allowance for fresh juice. The company won numerous awards for its environmental practices, and in 1993, *Inc.* magazine honored Odwalla as employer of the year.

During these years, the Odwalla brand name became widely identified with a healthful lifestyle, as well as with California's entrepreneurial business climate. In an oft-repeated story, Steve Jobs, founder of Apple Computer, was said to have ordered unlimited quantities of Odwalla juice for all employees working on the original development of the Macintosh computer.

THE *E. COLI* BACTERIUM

The virulent strain of bacteria that threatened to bring down this fast-growing company was known in scientific circles as *Escherichia coli, E. coli* for short.

The broad class of *E. coli* bacteria, microscopic rod-shaped organisms, is common in the human intestinal tract, and few pose a danger to health. In fact, most *E. coli* play a beneficial role by suppressing harmful bacteria and synthesizing vitamins. A small minority of *E. coli* strains, however, cause illness. One of the most dangerous of these is *E. coli* O157:H7. In the intestine, this strain produces a potent toxin that attacks the lining of the gut. Symptoms of infection include abdominal pain and cramps, diarrhea, fever, and bloody stools. Most cases are self-limiting, but approximately 6 percent are complicated with hemolytic-uremic syndrome, a dangerous condition that can lead to kidney and heart failure. Young children, the elderly, and those with weakened immune systems are most susceptible.

E. coli O157:H7 lives in the intestines of cows, sheep, deer, and other animals. The meat of infected animals may carry the infection. *E. coli* is also spread to humans through fecal contamination of food. For example, apples may be contaminated when they fall to the ground and come in contact with cow or deer manure. Secondary infection also may occur, for example, when food is handled by infected persons who have failed to wash their hands after using the toilet. Unfortunately, only a small amount of "157"—as few as 500 bacteria—is required to cause illness. As one epidemiologist noted, "It does not take a massive contamination or a major breakdown in the system to spread it."

E. coli O157:H7 is known as an "emergent" pathogen, meaning that its appearance in certain environments is viewed by researchers as a new phenomenon. The organism was first identified in 1982, when it was involved in several outbreaks involving undercooked meat. Since then, poisoning incidents had increased dramatically. By the mid-1990s, about 20,000 cases of *E. coli* poisoning occurred every year in the United States; about 250 people died. Most cases were believed to be caused by undercooked meat. Although a serious threat, *E. coli* is not the most common food-borne illness. In the United States, 5 million cases of food poisoning are reported annually, with 4000 of these resulting in death. Most cases are caused by mistakes in food preparation and handling, not by mistakes in food processing or packaging.

E. COLI IN FRESH JUICE

It was widely believed in the juice industry that pathogens like *E. coli* could not survive in an acidic environment such as citrus and apple juice. Odwalla apple juice had a pH (acidity) level of 4.3. (On the pH scale, 7 is neutral, and levels below 7 are increasingly acidic.) Odwalla did conduct spot testing of other, more pH-neutral products. The Food and Drug Administration (FDA), although it did not have specific guidelines for fresh juice production, indicated in its Retail Food Store Sanitation Code that foods with a pH lower than 4.6 were *not* "potentially hazardous."

In the early 1990s, however, scattered scientific evidence emerged that *E. coli* O157:H7 might have undergone a critical mutation that rendered it more acid-tolerant. In 1991, an outbreak of *E. coli* poisoning sickened 23 people in Massachusetts who had consumed fresh, unpasteurized apple cider purchased at a roadside stand. A second, similar incident occurred in Connecticut around the same time. In a study of the Massachusetts outbreak published in 1993, the *Journal of the American Medical Association* reported that *E. coli* O157:H7, apparently introduced by fecal contamination of fresh apples, had unexpectedly survived in acidic cider. The journal concluded that *E. coli* O157:H7 could survive at a pH below 4.0 at the temperature of refrigerated juice. The journal recommended strict procedures for sanitizing apples used to make fresh juice, all of which Odwalla already followed.

Although the FDA investigated both instances in New England, it did not issue any new regulations requiring pasteurization of fresh juice, nor did it issue any advisories to industry. At the time of the Odwalla outbreak, neither the FDA nor state regulators in California had rules requiring pasteurization of fresh apple juice.

CONSIDERING THE OPTIONS

In the company's second-floor conference room, later in the day of October 30, Steltenpohl and Williamson gathered the company's senior executives to review the situation. King County officials had identified about a dozen cases of *E. coli* infection associated with Odwalla apple juice products. But, as Steltenpohl later described the situation, "It was all based on interviews. They didn't yet have bacteriological proof." Washington health officials had not yet made a public announcement, nor had they ordered or even recommended a product recall.

Conversations with federal disease control and food safety specialists throughout the day had turned up troubling information. From them, Odwalla executives had learned of the two earlier outbreaks of *E. coli* illness associated with unpasteurized cider in New England. And they had been told that "157" could cause illness in very minute amounts, below levels that would reliably show up in tests. The FDA had indicated that it planned to launch an investigation of the incident but did not suggest that Odwalla had broken any rules.

Management understood that they had no *legal* obligation to order an immediate recall, although this was clearly an option. Another possibility was a nonpublic recall. In this approach, the company would quietly pull the suspect product off the shelves and conduct its own investigation. If a problem were found, the company could then choose to go public with the information.

The company carried general liability insurance

totaling $27 million. It had little debt and about $12 million in cash on hand. The cost of various options, however, was hard to pin down. No one could be sure precisely how much a full or partial product recall would cost, if they chose that option, or the extent of the company's liability exposure.

ORDERING A RECALL

At 3 P.M., Steltenpohl and Williamson, about 4 hours after they had received the first phone call, issued a public statement:

> Odwalla, Inc., the California-based fresh beverage company, issued today a national product recall of fresh apple juice and all products containing fresh apple juice as an ingredient.... Our first concern is for the health and safety of those affected. We are working in full cooperation with the FDA and the Seattle/King County Department of Public Health.

The recall involved 13 products, all containing unpasteurized apple juice. At the time, these 13 products accounted for about 70 percent of Odwalla's sales. The company did not recall its citrus juices or geothermal spring water products.

"Stephen and I never batted an eyelash," Steltenpohl later remembered. "We both have kids. What if it had turned out that something was in the juice, and we left it on the shelf an extra 2 weeks, or week, or even 2 days, and some little kid gets sick? What are we doing? Why are we in business? We have a corporate culture based on values. Our mission is nourishment. We really never considered *not* recalling the product. Looking back, I suppose the recall was the biggest decision we made. At the time, it seemed the only possible choice."

Once the decision to recall the product had been made, the company mobilized all its resources. On Thursday morning, October 31, 200 empty Odwalla delivery trucks rolled out from distribution centers in seven states and British Columbia with a single mission: to get the possibly tainted product off the shelves as quickly as possible. Organizing the recall was simplified by the facts that Odwalla operated its own fleet of delivery vehicles and that, in most cases, the product was displayed in the company's own coolers. The delivery drivers simply went directly to their own accounts and removed the recalled juices. In cases where the product was shelved with other products, Odwalla worked with retailers to find and remove it.

A group of employees in San Francisco, one of the company's major distribution centers, later recounted the first day of the recall:

> Every single person who is or was an RSP [route salesperson], express driver, or merchandiser, worked that first full day and the next.
>
> What was amazing was there were a lot of people who we didn't even have to call to come in. It might have been their day off, but they'd call to ask, "What can I do?"
>
> Right. They'd ask, "When should I come in? Where do you need me to be?" . . . It was an amazing effort. . . . We were able to make it to every single account on that first Thursday. That's a thousand accounts.

Within 48 hours, the recall was complete. Odwalla had removed the product from 4600 retail establishments in seven states and British Columbia. "This is probably as speedy as a product recall gets," a stock analyst commented. "They probably accomplished it in world-record time."

On October 31, as it was launching its recall, the company also took several additional steps:

- The company announced that it would pay all medical expenses for *E. coli* victims if it could be demonstrated that Odwalla products had caused their illness.

- The company offered to refund the purchase price of any of the company's products, even those which had not been recalled.

- The company established a crisis communications center at its headquarters and hired a PR firm, Edelman Public Relations Worldwide, to help it handle the crush of media attention. It also set up a Web site and an "800" hotline to keep the public and the media appraised of the most recent developments in the case. Twice-daily media updates were scheduled.

- The company decided to extend the recall to include three products made with carrot juice. Although these products did not contain apple juice, carrot juice was produced on the same line. Until the company had determined the cause of the outbreak, it felt it could not guarantee the safety of the carrot juice products.

On October 31, as the company's route salespeople were fanning out to retrieve the juice, Odwalla's stock price was plummeting. The company's stock lost 34 percent of its value in one day, falling from 18 3/8 to 12 1/8 on the NASDAQ exchange. Trading volume was 20 times normal, as 1.36 million shares changed hands.

TRACKING THE OUTBREAK

Over the next few days, the full extent of the outbreak became clearer. In addition to the cases in Washington, new clusters of *E. coli* poisoning were reported by health authorities in California and Colorado. As the company received reports about individual cases, Steltenpohl and Williamson attempted to telephone families personally to express their concern. They were able to reach many of them.

On November 8, a 16-month-old toddler from a town near Denver, Colorado, who had developed hemolytic-uremic syndrome, died following multiple organ failure. Tests later showed antibodies to O157:H7 in the girl's blood. It was the first, and only, death associated with the *E. coli* outbreak. Steltenpohl immediately issued a statement that read:

> On behalf of myself and the people at Odwalla, I want to say how deeply saddened and sorry we are to learn of the loss of this child. Our hearts go out to the family, and our primary concern at this moment is to see that we are doing everything we can to help them.

Steltenpohl, who had spoken with the girl's parents several times during her hospitalization, flew to Denver, with the family's permission, to attend the child's funeral. The girl's father later told the press, "We don't blame the Odwalla company at all. They had no bad intentions throughout all this, and they even offered to pay all of [our child's] hospital bills. I told them yesterday that we don't blame them, and we're not going to sue."

By the time the outbreak had run its course, 61 people, most of them children, had become ill in Colorado, California, Washington, and British Columbia. Except for the Colorado youngster, all those who had become ill, including several children who had been hospitalized in critical condition, eventually recovered.

INVESTIGATION OF THE OUTBREAK

As the outbreak itself was running its course, the investigation by both the company and federal and state health authorities proceeded. On November 4, the FDA reported that it had found *E. coli* O157:H7 in a bottle of unopened Odwalla apple juice taken from a distribution center in Washington state. As it turned out, this was the only positive identification of the pathogen in any Odwalla product. Eventually, 15 of the 61 reported cases (5 in Colorado and 10 in Washington) were linked by molecular "fingerprinting" to *E. coli* found in the Odwalla juice sample. The origin of contamination in the other 46 cases remained unknown.

Meanwhile, federal and state investigators converged on Odwalla's Dinuba manufacturing plant, inspecting it from top to bottom, in an attempt to find the source of the pathogen. On November 18, the FDA announced that it had completed its review of the Dinuba facility and had found no evidence of *E. coli* O157:H7 anywhere in the plant. The investigators then turned their attention to the growers and packers who supplied apples to the Dinuba plant, on the theory that the company might have processed a batch of juice containing some ground apples contaminated by cow or deer feces. In their interim report, the FDA noted that although no *E. coli* was found at Dinuba, "microbial monitoring of finished product and raw materials used in processing [was] inadequate." Odwalla sharply challenged this conclusion, noting that the FDA did not have any requirements for microbiologic testing.

SEARCHING FOR A SOLUTION

The recall placed enormous financial pressure on the company and challenged its executives to decide how and when to reintroduce its products to the market. As a short-term measure, Odwalla announced on November 7 that it would immediately reintroduce three of its recalled products, all juice blends, that had been reformulated without apple juice. These products would continue to be produced at Dinuba, but not on the apple processing line. In announcing the reformulation, Steltenpohl told the press, "Until we are assured of a completely safe and reliable method of producing apple juice, we will not include it in our juices."

But the reformulation of a few blended juice "smoothies" was hardly a long-term solution, since apple juice was a core ingredient in many of the company's top-selling products. Odwalla urgently needed to find a way to get apple juice safely back on the market. How to do so, however, was not obvious.

To assist it in finding a solution to the problem, Odwalla assembled a panel of experts, dubbed the Odwalla Nourishment and Food Safety Advisory Council, to recommend ways to improve product safety. In late November, with the help of these experts, Odwalla executives conducted detailed scenario planning, in which they reviewed a series of possible options. Among those they considered were the following:

- *Discontinue all apple juice products.* In this scenario, the company would eliminate all apple juice and blended juice products until it could be fully assured of their safety.

- *Improved manufacturing processes.* In this scenario, the company would take a number of steps to improve hazard control at various points in the production process, e.g., through modified product handling procedures, multiple antiseptic washes, routine sample testing, and stricter controls on suppliers.

- *Labeling.* Another option was to disclose risk to the consumer through product labeling. For example, an unpasteurized product could be sold with a disclaimer that it was not suitable for consumption by infants, the elderly, or those with compromised immune systems because of the very rare but still possible chance of bacterial contamination.

- *Standard pasteurization.* Standard pasteurization involved slowly heating the juice to a point just below boiling and holding it at that temperature for several minutes. The heat killed dangerous microorganisms and also had a side benefit of extending the shelf life of the product. Standard pasteurization, however, also destroyed many of the nutritional benefits of raw juice.

• *Modified pasteurization.* Modified pasteurization, also known as *flash pasteurization,* involved quickly heating the juice to a somewhat lower temperature, 160°F, and holding it very briefly at that temperature to kill any harmful bacteria. In tests of this procedure, Odwalla technicians found that it yielded an apple juice that had a "lighter" taste than unpasteurized juice but with a more "natural" taste than standard pasteurized apple juice. The process destroyed some nutrients, but fewer than standard pasteurization. Flash pasteurization did not, however, extend the shelf life of the product.

• *Use of alternative (non-heat-based) technologies for removing pathogens.* The company also examined a number of alternative methods of killing pathogens. These included a high-pressure process in which pressure was used to explode the cell walls of bacteria; a process in which light waves were directed at the juice to destroy pathogens; the use of electricity to disrupt bacteria; and the use of herbal antiseptic products.

A key factor in the decision, of course, was what customers wanted. The company commissioned some market research to gauge consumer sentiment and also carefully monitored public opinion as revealed in calls and letters to the company and discussions on public electronic bulletin boards, such as America Online.

The company also had to consider its financial situation. Remarkably, despite the recall, sales for the quarter ending November 30, 1996, were actually 14 percent ahead of the same period for 1995, because of excellent sales prior to the outbreak. The *E. coli* incident, however, had caused significant operating losses. By the end of November, the recall had cost the company about $5 million. Expenses had included the cost of retrieving and destroying product, legal and professional fees, and increased marketing costs. At the end of the fiscal quarter, Odwalla had a cash position of about $9 million, down from $12 million at the time of the outbreak.

On December 5, Odwalla announced that it had decided to flash pasteurize its apple juice. In a statement to the press, Williamson stated:

Odwalla's first priority is safety. After much consideration and research, we chose the flash pasteurization process as a method to produce apple juice. It is safe, yet largely preserves the great taste and nutritional value, allowing Odwalla to remain true to its vision of optimal nourishment. Importantly, we will continue to aggressively pursue the research and development of alternative methods to bring our customers safe, unpasteurized apple juice.

The following day, all apple juice and blended juice products were reintroduced to the market with flash pasteurized juice. The label had been redesigned to indicate that the product had been flash pasteurized, and Odwalla coolers prominently displayed signs so advising customers.

At the same time, the company moved forward with its expert panel to develop a comprehensive Hazard Analysis Critical Control Points (HACCP) plan (pronounced "HASSIP") for fresh juice production. HACCP was not a single step, but a comprehensive safety plan that involved pathogen control at multiple points in the juice production process, including sanitation of the fruit, testing for bacteria, and quality audits at several points in the process. The company also continued to monitor new, alternative technologies for controlling bacterial contamination.

REGULATING THE FRESH FRUIT JUICE INDUSTRY

In the wake of the *E. coli* outbreak, public concern about food safety mounted, and federal and state regulators began considering stricter regulation of the fresh fruit juice industry. On December 16, the FDA sponsored a public advisory hearing in Washington, D.C., to review current science and to consider strategies for improving the safety of fresh juice. Debate at the two-day hearings was wide-ranging.

Steltenpohl and Williamson represented Odwalla at the hearing. In their testimony, the Odwalla executives reported that they had decided to adopt flash pasteurization but argued *against* government rules requiring all juice to be heat-treated. "Mandatory pasteurization would be a premature and unnecessary step in light of the vast new technologies emerging," Steltenpohl told the hearing. He warned the panel that mandates could "lead to widespread public fears about fresh food and beverages."

Steltenpohl and Williamson called on the FDA to continue to explore different methods for producing fresh juice safely. In addition, they called for industry self-regulation aimed at adoption of voluntary standards for safe manufacturing practices and hazard control programs. The Odwalla executives reported that they viewed flash pasteurization as the "last line of defense" in a comprehensive program to eliminate pathogens.

Some other juice makers and scientists supported Odwalla's position. Several small growers vigorously opposed mandatory pasteurization, saying they could not afford the expensive equipment required. A representative of Orchid Island Juice Company of Florida asked, "What level of safety are you trying to achieve? We don't ban raw oysters and steak tartar, although the risks are much higher. Nor do we mandate that they be cooked, because it changes the flavor." A number of food safety experts testified about emerging technologies able to kill pathogens without heat treatment.

Some scientists and industry representatives, however, were on the other side. Two major firms, Cargill and Nestle, both major producers of heat-treated juice products, argued vigorously for a government mandate, saying that "other technologies just won't do the job." Dr. Patricia Griffin of the Centers for Disease Control and Prevention noted that "current production practices do not guarantee the safety of apple cider, apple juice, and or-ange juice." She called for pasteurization of apple juice and cider, as well as product labels warning customers of potential risk. A representative of the Center for Science in the Public Interest called for a label warning the elderly, infants, and persons with suppressed immune systems to avoid fresh, unpasteurized juice.

Several days after the hearing, the advisory panel recommended against mandatory pasteurization, for the moment at least, calling instead for "good hazard control" at juice manufacturing plants and in the orchards that supplied them. However, an FDA spokesman added, "We can never say that forced pasteurization is completely off the boards." The agency indicated that it would continue to study a number of alternative approaches to improving juice safety, including mandatory pasteurization.

LOOKING TO THE FUTURE

In May 1997, Steltenpohl reflected on the challenges facing Odwalla:

> Our task now is to rebuild a brand and a name. How you rebuild . . . these are important decisions. You can make what might be good short-term business decisions, but they wouldn't be the right thing. The decisions we make now become building blocks for the [company's] culture. We have to look at what's right and wrong. We need a clear moral direction.

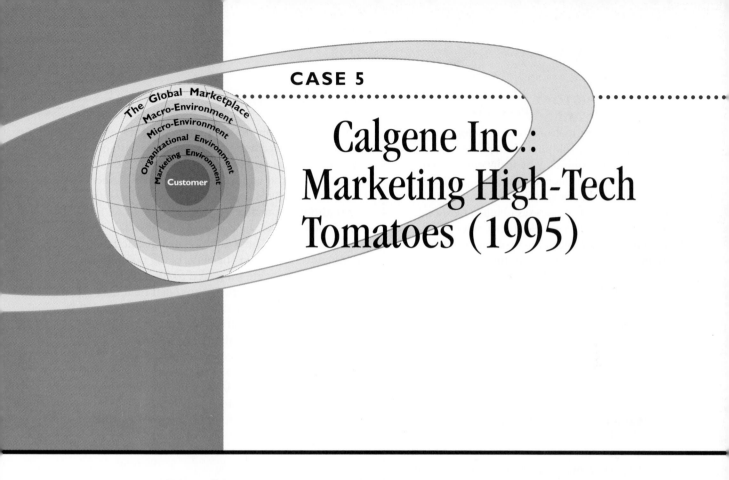

CASE 5

Calgene Inc.: Marketing High-Tech Tomatoes (1995)

This case was prepared by Julian W. Vincze, Professor of Marketing, Crummer Graduate School of Business, Rollins College.

BRUISED PRODUCT PROBLEM

By late in 1995, few customers had had the opportunity to taste the bioengineered and trademarked MacGregor's tomatoes grown from FlavrSavr tomato seeds. MacGregor's tomatoes, which were introduced with a flurry of publicity by Calgene Inc. in May of 1994, had not achieved wide distribution by 1995. Why had this occurred? The answer was that Calgene's research and development (R&D) department, after overcoming complex technological, regulatory, and environmental obstacles through years of effort and considerable expense, seemed to encounter totally unexpected tomato distribution problems. MacGregor's tomatoes were designed to have several outstanding

product features such as longer shelf life, better taste, and juicier flavor. These features were expected to differentiate MacGregor's tomatoes from ordinary fresh tomatoes. Unfortunately, during the 1994 growing season, Calgene realized that its product was not able to withstand the normal rigors of the standard picking, packing, and shipping methods used in the fresh tomato packing industry. Early shipments became bruised on their way to market, so Calgene had to undertake a costly overhaul of its packing methods (detailed later).

This damage to product, which was both unexpected and very late in the R&D cycle, had a major impact on Calgene's timetable for widespread distribution and market introduction of the MacGregor tomato. Industry analysts believed this difficulty contributed to a cash drain that in early 1995 forced Calgene to sell assets and cut its workforce by 10 percent. "This tomato has brought them to their knees," said Stan Shimoda, an analyst with BioScience Securities Inc. of Orinda, California. "The question is, can they get up again?"[1]

CALGENE'S HISTORY

Calgene Inc., an agricultural biotechnology company involved in developing, through genetic manipulation, a portfolio of genetically engineered plants and plant products for the food, seed, and oleochemical industries, focused operations in three core crop businesses (as detailed below). Headquartered in Davis, California, Calgene was formed in 1982 and became involved in the development of improved plant varieties and plant products and was the first company to introduce genetically engineered products in the fresh tomato, cottonseed, and industrial and edible plant oils (canola) markets, where it believed biotechnology could provide substantial added commercial value in consumer, industrial, and seed markets.

Fresh Market Tomato Core Crop No. I

Fresh tomatoes currently were the most visible and probably also the most important of Calgene's core crops. After 12 years of R&D efforts, Calgene's first apparent success was in May of 1994 when the U.S. Food and Drug Administration (FDA) announced its determination that the MacGregor tomato had not been significantly altered with respect to safety or nutritive value when compared with conventional tomatoes. This FDA approval allowed Calgene to begin to market MacGregor's tomatoes. However, this success was tempered by the apparent ongoing difficulties encountered in achieving widespread distribution and therefore market availability of MacGregor's tomatoes (as noted above). These difficulties caused Calgene's non-genetically engineered tomato production to be scaled back and eventually resulted in curtailment of much of Calgene's Mexican operations, although, during 1994, Calgene had made agreements with both Campbell Soup Company and Zeneca A.V.P. (the original financial backers of the R&D that produced MacGregor's tomatoes) whereby Calgene received worldwide, exclusive royalty-free rights to produce and sell fresh market tomatoes containing the FlavrSavr gene. Prior to these agreements, Calgene's commercialization rights were limited to North America and had required royalty payments to Campbell Soup Company.

Tomato Packing Methods

The traditional tomato packing method was called the *gassed-green method,* which began with either mechanical or hand field picking. The field picking occurred while the tomatoes were green and rock hard. This green picking was necessary for traditional tomatoes so that they could withstand the rigors of the remaining steps in the packing process. These additional steps included being moved by conveyor belts, being dumped into large bins, being subjected to high-pressure gas spraying, and then being boxed. If field picking was mistimed until after the tomatoes began to ripen, they would start to soften too quickly as a result of an enzyme called *polygalacturonase* (PG). If this softening occurred, the tomatoes were prone to being damaged during packing and shipping to retailers and/or by the handling that occurred within retail stores. In addition, late picking lessened the shelf life of the tomatoes at the retail store.

Customers' Reactions of Gassed-Green Tomatoes

However, the problem with the green picking and packing process was that the ultimate consumers did not want to buy green and unripened tomatoes. Therefore, the packing process included the high-pressure gas spraying step. The gas used in the spraying step was ethylene, a hormone that triggered the beginning of the reddening and ripening process. Thus almost all fresh field-grown tomatoes ripened during the packing and shipping process because the ethylene spray eventually caused the green tomatoes to turn red. However, these artificially induced ripe tomatoes did not achieve a deep red color. Instead, they turned a pale red and were somewhat mushy and to many customers were tasteless. These traditional tomato packing methods were considered by the industry to be very efficient because they minimized costs and resulted in relatively low retail prices for consumers. Unfortunately, these traditional packing methods had such a deleterious effect on the taste of tomatoes picked while still green and rock hard that many customers equated this taste with cardboard. The tomatoes certainly did not compare favorably with vine-ripened, freshly picked field tomatoes. In fact, one industry observer noted that a U.S. Department of Agriculture report gave an 84 percent dissatisfaction rate among customers of gassed-green tomatoes.[2]

Development of MacGregor's Tomato

Cognizant of this criticism of tasteless tomatoes, and anxious to capitalize on what they perceived to be a market opportunity, Calgene's geneticists bioengineered the ordinary tomato to delay softening and rotting (the maturation process) in order to enhance taste and lengthen retail shelf life. They used what was then cutting-edge technology of gene splicing. Calgene's scientists developed a procedure that prevented tomatoes from producing PG by creating an antisense, or mirror, image of the gene that carried instructions for producing the enzyme. By then inserting the antisense gene into the tomato's DNA, production of the enzyme was blocked. This began the ripening process, which in turn was responsible for breaking down the wall of tomato cells. This antisense gene also was expected to allow growers to wait until the MacGregor's tomato was turning red before harvesting.[3]

The concept seemed straightforward and rather simple: that is, the stronger the cell walls, the easier it would be to transport tomatoes without damage; the more advanced the maturation process was before picking and packing, the better the flavor and the longer the retail shelf life. However, delayed maturation, which allowed for longer time ripening on the vine, also resulted in a softer tomato when picked. With hindsight, it now seemed that Calgene had rushed to commercialize its MacGregor's Flavr-Savr tomato without considering that its tomato would not tolerate traditional packing house processes without bruising.

Cotton—Calgene's Core Crop No. 2

Calgene's second core crop and genetic engineering program focused on reducing farmers' growing costs through the development of cotton varieties that required fewer pesticides (and also the creation of cotton varieties that produced natural colors). It was estimated that U.S. cotton farmers spent over $200 million annually on herbicides and from $225 to $400 million on insecticides. Therefore, when Calgene could create herbicide resistant and insect resistant cotton varieties, the result would be not only reduced production costs for farmers but also improved crop yields and environmental benefits. Calgene believed that these product features would translate into premium pricing opportunities.

Calgene's BXN trademarked cottonseed received U.S. Department of Agriculture (USDA) deregulation in 1994. Calgene marketed conventional cottonseed varieties and their BXN cotton through its Stoneville subsidiary, which had experienced a revenue growth of 19 percent during the 1994 fiscal year. In April of 1995, Calgene introduced two new genetically engineered varieties of BXN cotton that were resistant to the herbicide bromoxynil (commonly used cotton crop herbicide) at a 45 percent price premium over Calgene's non-genetically engineered cottonseed. These two new BXN cotton varieties, like all of Calgene's BXN cotton, also were genetically engineered to contain a Bt gene for resistance to *Heliothis,* the principal cotton insect pest.

Plant Oils—Calgene's Core Crop No. 3

Calgene's third core crop was industrial and edible plant oils. This program focused on genetically engineering rapeseed oils with a broad range of food and industrial applications. Calgene's scientists had successfully genetically altered canola rapeseed varieties that produced substantial quantities of laurate, an important ingredient in detergents that was not naturally present in canola or other nontropical oil plants. In March of 1994, Calgene received a U.S. patent on the bay thioesterase gene. This gene in rapeseed plants resulted in the production of laurate, while in June of 1994, Calgene successfully purified the LPAAT enzyme. Introduction of the gene that produced this LPAAT enzyme increased laurate levels significantly beyond the 40 percent level that had been achieved previously. Thus, by July of 1995, Calgene's Laurical trademarked canola sales were reported to be 1 million pounds.

The Plant Oils Division also was conducting its eighth season of field trials with canola plants that had been genetically engineered to produce oil with increased stearate levels. Stearate had the potential to substitute for hydrogenated oils in margarine, shortening, and confectionary products. Therefore, Calgene had begun to establish strategic relationships with Procter & Gamble, Unilever, and Pfizer Food Science to explore the potential commercial opportunities for its plant oil products.

KEY STRENGTHS AND BUSINESS STRATEGY

In the president's letter to shareholders included in Calgene's 1994 Annual Report, Roderick Stacey said:

> As we look to the future, I believe the key strengths of Calgene are as follows:
>
> 1. We are the scientific and regulatory leaders in agricultural biotechnology, particularly in the science of plant oils modification. All technical hurdles are behind us in our first tomato, cotton, and oil products. We have the only FDA and USDA approvals for genetically engineered plant products.
>
> 2. Our proprietary position is strong. We resolved all of the issues regarding tomato technology with Zeneca and Campbell and have worldwide royalty-free rights to the FlavrSavr gene in fresh tomatoes. We have successfully negotiated favorable cross-licenses with Monsanto, Mogen International nv, PGS, and Agracetus to obtain freedom to operate in the most important core plant genetic engineering technologies. Seven oils gene modification patents have been issued in Europe, and U.S. counterparts (patents), starting with the Laurate gene patent, are beginning to issue. We remain confident that we will prevail in our litigation with Enzo Biochem, Inc.
>
> 3. We are in excellent position to commercialize on our scientific successes. We have a conventional operating business base which generated $35 million in product revenues in 1994. We have a seasoned senior management group and an experienced and capable field production team in each of our core crops. The supply of our MacGregor's tomatoes grown from FlavrSavr seeds will be increased in October.

> Field results of BXN cotton have exceeded expectations in 1994, and market launch is set for 1995.
>
> We are positioned to realize the promise of our 12 years' investment in plant science, regulatory innovation, and business planning.[4]

However, despite this optimism voiced by Mr. Stacey, several industry observers were skeptical of the basis for his optimism and openly wondered if Calgene could successfully market its high-tech tomatoes. However, in 10-K financial filings, Calgene noted that its business strategy was to build operating businesses in their core crop areas to facilitate the market introduction of genetically engineered proprietary products and to maximize the long-term financial return from such products. Calgene believed that implementing this strategy would provide direct access to markets where Calgene could sell fresh and processed plant products having improved quality traits or cost-of-production advantages or both. For details about Calgene's financial situation, refer to Exhibits A and B.

CALGENE REACTS TO BRUISING PROBLEM

Once aware of the bruising problem in late 1994, Calgene's first response was to approach experienced packing companies to ask them to devise gentler handling procedures; however, none could meet Calgene's requirements. Calgene then decided to build its own processing plant near Chicago for the purpose of developing gentler handling procedures. However, by the time tomatoes grown in fields in the southern states arrived at the plant, many were bruised or split or both. Finally, Calgene announced that it would spend up to $10 million in 1995 building three facilities nearer its growing areas. These facilities would be equipped with high-tech "soft touch" machines that included optical sensors to distinguish tomato size, shape, and color and which were designed originally to sort peaches.

The first location, a 90,000 square foot facility in Immokalee, Florida, was proclaimed to be on-line and operational by late March of 1995. A second location in Lake Park, Georgia, was a 65,000 square foot packing and distribution facility that was scheduled to begin operations in May 1995. The

EXHIBIT A
....
Calgene Inc. Balance Sheet (000's)[16]

	1995	1994	1993	1992	1991
Assets					
Cash	11,753	5,286	15,009	9,511	5,548
Marketable securities	10,283	15,457	24,773	31,748	30,632
Receivables	6,697	4,792	2,666	2,864	3,163
Inventories	8,148	5,068	4,774	4,461	5,529
Other current assets	1,699	2,278	6,023	7,814	7,363
Total current assets	38,580	32,881	53,245	56,636	52,235
Property, plant, and equipment	38,044	32,363	26,561	21,982	20,872
Accumulated depreciation	15,524	12,872	11,023	9,909	8,432
Net property and equipment	22,520	19,491	15,538	12,073	12,440
Investment and advances to subs	0	1,415	1,551	3,432	3,710
Intangibles	26,224	23,677	17,308	12,205	14,180
Deposits and other assets	1,907	848	759	877	571
Total assets	89,231	78,312	88,401	85,223	83,136
Liabilities					
Notes payable	7,761	8,650	7,597	9,083	7,039
Accounts payable	6,487	7,916	5,327	1,977	2,457
Current long-term debt	1,494	1,728	1,241	1,037	527
Accrued expenses	2,049	1,803	1,562	3,735	4,278
Other current liabilities	9,968	8,088	3,211	2,502	5,057
Total current liabilities	27,759	28,185	18,938	18,334	19,358
Long-term debt	14,671	4,204	3,694	4,378	5,065
Other long-term liabilities	750	1,500	N/A	N/A	N/A
Total liabilities	43,180	33,889	22,632	22,712	24,423
Minority interests	N/A	N/A	N/A	N/A	948
Preferred stock	N/A	N/A	N/A	29,506	29,627
Common stock (net)	30	27	24	18	15
Capital surplus	223,161	190,934	169,482	111,101	86,488
Retained earnings	−177,140	−146,538	−103,737	−78,114	−58,198
Other equities	N/A	N/A	N/A	N/A	−167
Total shareholder equity	46,051	44,423	65,769	62,511	57,765
Total liabilities and net worth	89,231	78,312	88,401	85,223	83,136

third location, in Irvine, California, was a modification of an existing structure that also was expected to be on-line for packing and distributing by May 1995. "We now have the facilities in place to supply demand for FlavrSavr tomatoes across the U.S.," said Danilo Lopes, CEO of Calgene Fresh, the wholly owned subsidiary of Calgene Inc. that grows, packs, distributes, and sells fresh produce.[5] In addition, Calgene noted that it would rely more heavily on manual labor in picking and packing its tomatoes grown on approximately 2000 acres in California, Florida, and Georgia. "The combination of increased acreage, new packing and distribution facilities, and an experienced management team should enable us to achieve our target expanded distribution," said Mr. Lopes.[6] Roger Salquist, Cal-

EXHIBIT B

Calgene Inc. Income Statement (000's)[17]

	1995	1994	1993	1992	1991
Net sales	55,431	38,433	27,237	21,877	26,104
Cost of goods sold	57,114	46,703	26,633	20,316	19,727
Gross profit	−1,683	−8,270	604	1,561	6,377
R&D expenditures	11,937	12,847	10,260	11,256	11,151
Selling, gen. and admin. exp.	16,081	21,279	16,494	11,318	10,161
Income before depreciation	−29,701	−42,396	−26,150	−21,013	−14,935
Nonoperating income	38	389	1,644	3,274	1,515
Interest expense	924	729	673	813	898
Income before taxes	−30,587	−42,736	−25,179	−18,555	−14,318
Provisions for income tax	15	65	44	61	61
Net income before extraord.	−30,602	−42,801	−25,223	−18,616	−14,379
Extraordinary items	N/A	N/A	−400	−1,300	−12,600
Net income	−30,602	−42,801	−25,623	−19,916	−26,979

Key Annual Financial Ratios	1994	1993	1991
Quick ratio	0.91	2.24	2.41
Current ratio	1.17	2.81	3.09
Sales/cash	1.85	0.68	0.53
Receivables turnover	8.02	10.22	7.64
Receivables days sales	44.89	35.24	47.13
Inventories turnover	7.58	5.71	4.90
Net sales/working capital	8.18	0.79	0.57
Net sales/total assets	0.49	0.31	0.26
Net sales/employees	113.707	73.021	77.578
Total liabilities/total assets	0.43	0.26	0.27
Times interest earned	−57.62	−36.41	−21.74
Total debt/equity	0.13	0.08	0.09
Net income/net sales	−1.11	−0.94	−0.91
Net income/total assets	−0.55	−0.29	−0.23

gene's CEO, said the company was on target to have its tomatoes in 2500 stores by June (1995) and added that sales of the company's tomatoes in the Midwest were "doing great."[7]

Mr. Shimoda's response to these statements was: "The technology didn't do what they thought it would do, and so they had to reinvent the wheel to deal with a soft tomato."[8] Another industry observer, Andre Garnet, analyst at A. G. Edwards, asserted that "Calgene's distribution system is all screwed up, and it costs more to produce than to sell."[9] Mr. Garnet believed that Calgene would be forced to raise additional cash before the end of 1995.

COMPETITOR TOMATO: ENDLESS SUMMER

Although there is currently only one other firm attempting to market genetically engineered fresh market tomatoes, competition is expected to intensify rapidly as existing gassed-green tomato producers react to competitive pressures by growing and marketing traditionally developed vine-ripened tomatoes. The existing direct competitor was DNA Plant Technology Corporation (DNAP) of Oakland, California, which developed a competitor to Mac-Gregor's tomato which they called the Fresh World Farms Endless Summer. FDA clearance to market Endless Summer was granted in early 1995.[10] DNAP claimed that Endless Summer tomatoes required no special handling, even though they too stay ripening longer on the vine than the so-called gassed-green tomatoes. The secret was a more-recent technology that regulated a tomato's ethylene production and slowed down the overall ripening process, including softening. This allowed Endless Summer to be picked earlier than FlavrSavr tomatoes while they were still relatively hard and therefore able to withstand traditional packing house processes. Yet because of the slowed ripening, Endless Summer tomatoes outlasted FlavrSavr on shelf life because they stayed fresh for 30 days after harvest. The relative taste factors of these two competitor high-tech tomatoes had not yet been determined by the market place. However, Carolyn Hayworth, a Calgene spokesperson, said: "It's a huge market—a $3½ billion market for fresh tomatoes in the U.S.; let's just let the consumer decide."[11]

Endless Summer, grown in Florida and California, was in test market in Rochester, New York, and national rollout was predicted for the fall of 1995. DNAP intended to apply its technology to other foods as well, starting in 1996. Potential candidate foods for its process were noted to include bananas, pineapples, peas, peppers, and strawberries.[12] Mr. Shimoda thought Endless Summer stood a better chance of success than MacGregor's tomato, and George Dahlman, an analyst with Piper Jaffray Inc. and once a Calgene advocate, seemed to agree. Mr. Dahlman said: "The future of this company [Calgene] is more controversial than ever." However, Carolyn Hayworth, a Calgene spokeswoman, noted: "We're building a business, and we believe we know what we are doing."[13] Roger Salquist, Calgene's CEO, insisted that Calgene would not have to raise more money and that the fiscal year ending in 1996 would be profitable.

CONSUMER REACTIONS UNCERTAIN

Both MacGregor's tomato and Endless Summer were the result of gene-transfer technology used to develop tomatoes that could ripen longer on the vine yet not spoil on the trip to market. The goal appeared to be a year-round tomato with flavor and juiciness. However, consumer reaction to genetically altered foods remained uncertain. When MacGregor's tomatoes were offered in Seattle's Fred Meyer stores (an upscale supermarket chain) in November and December of 1994, "We had a very positive response. The stores have been asking for more as a result of requests by shoppers," said assistant vice president Rob Boley.[14] The tomatoes carried a label noting that they were grown from genetically modified seeds and a sign that gave additional details.

However, some industry observers were critical of both Calgene and DNAP for not publicizing any marketing research studies that they may have carried out prior to or during the development of MacGregor's tomato and Endless Summer. This failure to publicize any research relative to the acceptability to customers of bioengineered fresh tomatoes was interpreted by some to indicate that little, if any, actual customer opinion surveys had been carried out by either company and that in their rush to apply the technology, the whole aspect of consumer acceptance was overlooked. If R&D scientists had pressed for quick development and upper management had not expended scarce resources on customer surveys, then, without any indication of customer acceptance of bioengineered fresh tomatoes, the probability of immediate acceptance by consumers was viewed as questionable at best and perhaps improbable in a worst-case scenario. This lack of market research therefore could represent an unexplored opportunity or potentially a tremendous oversight fraught with perils. Still other industry observers were more trusting that good management existed at both Calgene and DNAP and that such a major oversight could not have occurred. They argued that surely these two management teams had not only looked at the supply side of the market but had thoroughly analyzed the demand aspects as well. Since neither company had publicized such demand analyses, actual retail trials would have to be relied on to judge potential customer acceptance rates. And results from trial markets were not being made public by either firm.

Controversy about Genetically Engineered Food

Controversy had surrounded the idea of genetically engineered food. For example, with MacGregor's tomatoes, the use of marker genes added to the tomatoes in order to determine whether the gene for slow ripening was transferred successfully had become a public controversy. The controversial aspect of the process related to the fact that the marker genes were resistant to certain antibiotics, and critics said that such resistance might create antibiotic resistance in people who ate these altered tomatoes. Even though Food and Drug Administration (FDA) scientists had concluded that such development of resistance to antibiotics by people consuming genetically altered foods was not a possibility, the rumor still existed.

In addition, a national coalition of prominent chefs as early as mid-1992 had begun to call for a boycott of genetically engineered foods.[15] This coalition claimed support from some 1000 of their colleagues, including such nationally known figures as Wolfgang Puck of Spago in West Hollywood, Jimmy Schmidt of the Rattlesnake Club in Detroit, Jean Louis Palladin of Jean Louis in Washington, D.C., and Mark Miller of Red Sage in Washington, D.C., and was led by chef Rick Moonen of the Water Club in New York. Despite this protest, the FDA declared that genetically engineered foods were safe and special labeling was unnecessary regardless of customers who had professed to having religious or health concerns.

THE FUTURE

What does the future hold for Calgene and its MacGregor's tomato? Many investors and industry analysts are pondering this question. Stan Shimoda indicated that MacGregor's tomato had brought Calgene to its knees—his question was, Could they get up again? Others held similar views, only differing in degree of pessimism. Countering these views, however, were the optimistic statements of the management of Calgene, which implied that Calgene was on the verge of a huge success in the marketplace. Which view is the correct one? Would the MacGregor's tomato be a marketing success story? What would you predict? If you were to unexpectedly inherit $25,000 would you invest it in Calgene stock?

Questions

1. Do a traditional SWOT (strengths, weaknesses, opportunities, and threats) analysis of Calgene's situation in the spring of 1995.

2. What is your assessment of the product development procedures used by Calgene to develop the MacGregor's FlavrSavr tomato? Were they effective, or could they be improved?

3. What is your assessment of Calgene's knowledge about customer acceptance of bioengineered foods and specifically the FlavrSavr tomato? Do you think there has been an oversight, or do you agree that Calgene management has effectively considered market demand for the product?

4. Diagram the consumer purchasing process you believe is used by the average household when purchasing fresh tomatoes. List what you believe are the evaluative criteria applied when deciding which alternative fresh tomatoes to purchase?

5. Calgene seems to be planning to introduce MacGregor's FlavrSavr tomatoes to the market by traditional channels of distribution. Is this the best channel to use? What other channels might be used?

6. How much of a technological lead does Calgene enjoy over DNAP? Does the FlavrSavr tomato have a market leadership position over Endless Summer tomatoes?

7. What are the barriers to entry in the fresh tomato producing and marketing industry?

8. Assume that you have unexpectedly inherited $25,000 today. Would you invest it in Calgene?

Endnotes

1. Ralph T. King, Jr., "Low-Tech Woe Slows Calgene's Super Tomato," *Wall Street Journal*, April 11, 1995, pp. B-1, B-6.

2. Barbara DeLollis, "High-Tech Tomato Had Growing Pains; Developing the Technology Was Only Half of the Challenge," *The Fresno Bee,* April 10, 1995.

3. Del I. Hawkins, Roger J. Best, and Kenneth A. Coney, "Calgene, Inc. versus the Pure Food Campaign," *Consumer Behavior: Implications for Marketing Strategy,* 6th ed. (Homewood, IL: Irwin, 1995), p. 384.

4. *1994 Annual Report to Shareholders,* Calgene Inc., Davis, California.

5. "Calgene Tomato Packing and Distribution System Nears Completion; Senior Produce Executives Join Calgene Fresh Team," PR Newswire, March 28, 1995.

6. *Ibid.*

7. Herb Greenberg, "I Say Tomato, Some Say Tomorrow, What's Really Going On?" *San Francisco Chronicle,* January 16, 1995.

8. "Calgene Tomato Packing and Distribution System Nears Completion; Senior Produce Executives Join Calgene Fresh Team," PR Newswire, March 28, 1995.

9. Lauren Dermer, "Calgene Short Seller Stomps on Biotech-Enhanced Tomato," *Portfolio Letter,* February 6, 1995.

10. "Calgene and DNAP Vie in Tomato War," *Industries in Transition,* February 1995.

11. Judith Blake, "High-Tech Tomato May Roll onto Market Soon," *Seattle Times,* February 1, 1995.

12. "Calgene and DNAP Vie in Tomato War," *Industries in Transition,* February 1995.

13. Ralph T. King, Jr., "Low-Tech Woe Slows Calgene's Super Tomato," *Wall Street Journal,* April 11, 1995, pp. B-1, B-6.

14. Judith Blake, "High-Tech Tomato May Roll onto Market Soon," *Seattle Times,* February 1, 1995.

15. "Chefs Vow Boycott of Genetically Engineered Foods," *Nation's Restaurant News,* August 10, 1992.

16. *1995 and 1994 Annual Reports to Stockholders,* Calgene Inc., Davis, California.

17. *Ibid.*

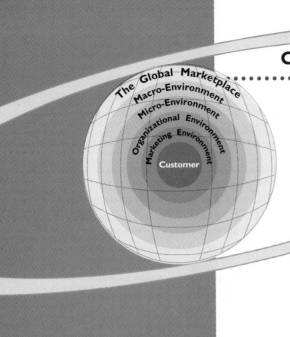

Marketing Challenges Facing AUCNET USA: A Real-Time On-Line Auto Auction Company

This case was written by Professor Chetan Sankar of Auburn University and Jaideep Mohan of Total System Services, Inc.

"The bid is $10,000. Do I hear $10,100? Ladies and gentlemen, this choice vehicle is in fine condition, has been regularly serviced, and has only 10,000 miles on the odometer. Do I hear $10,100? The gentleman from Nashville bids $10,050. Thank you, Sir. The bid is now $10,050."

Was this just another day at a used car auction? Not exactly. At this auction, the bidders were in their own offices throughout the United States, the vehicles were still on the sellers' lots, and the auctioneer was in a suburban office building of AUCNET USA in Atlanta, Georgia. With the enthusiasm of an avid sports fan, Yuko Oana, CEO of AUCNET USA, leaned forward on his chair in the Network Control Center, cheering as cars were sold using the system. Every 2 minutes a car was

put up for sale on the satellite auction system. A used car in Huntsville, Alabama, had come up for sale on the screen, and dealers in Pennsylvania, Virginia, and Georgia were bidding on the car. Mr. Oana was excited when the "sold" sign came up on the monitor—which it did many times that day. Mr. Oana wanted such momentum to not only persist but to build, and he needed his executive team to investigate the best ways to accomplish that objective.

HISTORY OF AUCNET JAPAN

In 1985, Mr. Masataka Fujisaki, an entrepreneur, saw an opportunity to transform the marketplace of wholesale auto auctions in Japan.[1] In this market, large-volume dealers sold and bought cars from other dealers; no sales were made to direct consumers. The vehicles were transported weekly to one of several established locations and sold to dealers at live auctions. This traditional method was inefficient because only about 40 percent of the inventory was sold at any auction. Mr. Fujisaki had a vision of a computerized auction system where wholesale dealers did not have to leave the workplace to buy and sell cars, and he built that business using information technologies.

The AUCNET Japan system was based on a thorough inspection system. A selling dealer called AUCNET headquarters to request inspection of the cars to be sold. The dealer filled out an inspection report form showing the results of the annual government inspection of the engine and drivetrain. An inspector was then dispatched to the dealer location to check the car, confirming the condition shown on the report form. In addition, the inspector appraised the cosmetic condition of the interior and exterior of the car. A single number between 1 and 10, with 10 being the best, summarized the inspection results. A car that did not rate at least a 4 could not be sold on AUCNET.

This auctioning system was so successful in Japan that AUCNET Japan's profits had doubled every year since 1985, and by 1995, it was the largest automobile auction house in Japan. It had more than 3200 subscribers (dealers who contracted with AUCNET to use its services) and processed 150,000 vehicles per year.[2] Mr. Fujisaki planned to transplant this technology to the U.S. market, where more than 14 million used cars were sold every year. His vision became a reality in September 1994, when AUCNET Japan created a subsidiary headquartered in Atlanta, Georgia.

AUCNET USA

In 1994, the used cars handled by U.S. auto auctions were worth $50 billion—double the value of used cars auctioned in 1989 and more than triple that of a decade ago. As a result, auto auctions, once clearinghouses for relatively old cars, had been handling growing numbers of good late-model cars.[3]

Mr. Oana was appointed the CEO of AUCNET USA in 1994. The son of a sake brewer, he had graduated from the faculty of law at Tokyo University. He envisioned AUCNET USA's core competency to be the creation of new methods of exchanging information and funds between buyers and sellers in traditional markets. He said:

> The auction business is not new. The history of the auction goes back many centuries, to when people used to get together to auction farm animals and other products. We do the same thing in trading cars electronically; the only difference is the convenience we offer. We eliminated the need for a physical auction site.

Mitsubishi dealers were the first subscribers to AUCNET USA's on-line auction system. By August 1995, AUCNET USA had 250 subscribers to their system and had sold 3500 used automobiles. By December 1995, the number of subscribers had grown to nearly 600. Of the 14,068 cars offered for sale during 1995, 52 percent were sold using the on-line system. In 1996, AUCNET offered about 35,000 used cars for sale, and about 50 percent of these were sold using the on-line system. The number of subscribers had grown to nearly 700.

In 1995, AUCNET USA had 75 employees. Yuko Oana was the president and CEO. The executive team consisted of J. D. Grogan, manager of public relations and marketing, Bruce Spengler, vice president of network systems, Dave Frazier, vice president of auction processing, and Brad Randall, manager of transportation.

Twice a week, AUCNET USA ran auctions between 9:00 A.M. and 12:00 noon from its Atlanta headquarters. Tuesday was limited to sales of cars by Mitsubishi dealers, and Friday was open to sales of cars from other dealers. Each subscriber was provided with a proprietary computer system that included a satellite dish, receiver, and a cart that housed all the computer equipment. Before the sale day, the dealers were given a preview catalog, and on the sale day, each car was listed and sold using the on-line system. After a sale had been confirmed, the transportation department at AUCNET arranged for the car to be transported from the seller's lot to the buyer's lot within a few days. AUCNET took care of the automobile title transfers. The buyers and sellers paid a fee to AUCNET for providing those services.

The Inspection Process

The vehicle inspection process was at the heart of AUCNET USA. The reliability of AUCNET's inspection process was a major reason for the acceptance of AUCNET's auction system in the United States. J. D. Grogan said:

> Reliability of the inspection process is at the core of AUCNET's auction system. The inspec-

tion process developed for the U.S. market is more detailed than the one used in Japan. This is mainly because Japan already has strict government regulations for maintenance of cars.

AUCNET USA was very methodical about its inspection process. It preferred to hire select individuals who had 10 years of automotive repair and maintenance experience. They were then given 6 weeks of training on the inspection process. For each scheduled auction, the inspectors were dispatched to appropriate dealerships, marshaling areas, and rental lots to evaluate and inspect the vehicles thoroughly.

The inspection covered 120 points on each vehicle, including the interior and exterior, and a test drive. High-resolution digital cameras were used to take pictures of the left front and right rear of the exterior and most of the interior of the vehicle. Custom-designed inspection software running on a notebook computer recorded the inspectors' performance ranking on all 120 items required for each vehicle inspection. Based on the make, model, year, vehicle condition, driveability, and history of repair, the software generated a grade for each vehicle, ranging from 5 (excellent) to 1 (poor). Exhibit A is an example of the inspection report as seen by the dealers on their monitors. Grogan commented on the inspection system:

> Given the skeptical nature of the American buyer, we had to develop this in-depth inspection process. The dealers' confidence level in our inspection had to get to a point where it was very high. They now have the confidence that if one AUCNET inspector rates a car as 4, any other of our inspectors examining the car would also rate it as a 4.

The Auction

AUCNET USA faxed a preview catalog to all its subscribers on the day before the sale day (called *preview day*). The details in this catalog (Exhibit B) included vehicle run number, mileage, vehicle locations, interior and exterior colors, options, and rating for each car.

A card was issued to every subscriber who had established a credit line with AUCNET USA. This card provided identification information that included the subscriber's credit limit, history, location, etc. With this card, a subscriber could log onto the AUCNET network control center from his or her computer. AUCNET's dedicated digital satellite transmission network ensured display of on-line real-time broadcast-quality video images and delivery of CD-quality audio at the subscribers' locations.

On the preview day, with the catalog in hand, a dealer could log onto his or her system, type in a vehicle's run number, and view inspection photographs and condition reports for that car. The dealer could look at three different views of a car, read the inspection report, and decide whether he or she might want to bid on the car the next day.

On sale day, both buyers and sellers attended an AUCNET Satellite Auto Auction from their dealerships and bid in real time on selected vehicles. The auctioneer sitting in a booth in Atlanta announced the bids for each car. Bidding by dealers was done by pushing the top button on a bid stick. Once the floor price (the price set by the seller) was reached, the SELL sign appeared on all screens, and the vehicle was sold to the highest bidder. Anytime during the bidding process, a seller could lower his or her floor price and sell the vehicle by pressing the confirmation button on the bid stick. Once the sale was confirmed, the buyer had to press the confirmation button on the bid stick to lock in the price and close the sale of that vehicle. The name of the buyer's dealership and location appeared for all to see. The vehicle was considered a "no sale" if a 2-minute time limit expired before the floor price was reached. However, the auctioneer could extend the bidding time if necessary.

Delivery

Once a buyer confirmed a bid, he or she had to pay for it and arrange for transportation of the vehicle from the seller's location. AUCNET's transportation managers were responsible for finding a transporter who would transport a buyer's car within a few days for a reasonable price. Mainly, AUCNET performed a goodwill service for the buyer by providing pertinent information about the transporters. The choice of delivery service was left to the buyer.

Financial Arrangements

Once the vehicle was sold to a buyer, AUCNET paid the seller within 24 hours, faxing a bill of sale and purchase authorization to the buyer. The buyer had 5 days to pay for the vehicle and had to

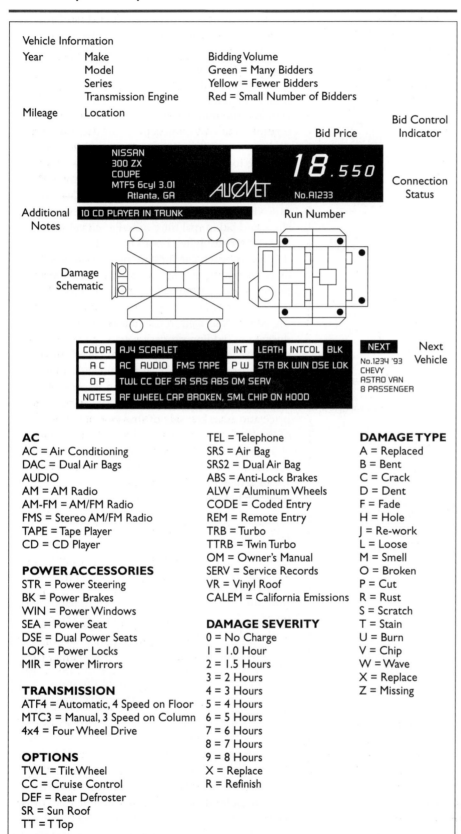

Vehicle Information

Year   Make   Bidding Volume
           Model   Green = Many Bidders
           Series   Yellow = Fewer Bidders
           Transmission Engine   Red = Small Number of Bidders

Mileage   Location

                                         Bid Control
                          Bid Price   Indicator

NISSAN
300 ZX
COUPE   ☐   **18**.550
MTF5 6cyl 3.0l   Connection
Atlanta, GA   AUCNET   No.A1233   Status

Additional   10 CD PLAYER IN TRUNK   Run Number
Notes

Damage
Schematic

COLOR	AJ4 SCARLET		INT	LEATH	INTCOL	BLK	NEXT	Next
A C	AC	AUDIO	FMS TAPE	P W	STR BK WIN DSE LOK		No.1234 '93	Vehicle
O P	TWL CC DEF SR SRS ABS OM SERV						CHEVY ASTRO VAN	
NOTES	RF WHEEL CAP BROKEN, SML CHIP ON HOOD						8 PASSENGER	

AC
AC = Air Conditioning
DAC = Dual Air Bags
AUDIO
AM = AM Radio
AM-FM = AM/FM Radio
FMS = Stereo AM/FM Radio
TAPE = Tape Player
CD = CD Player

POWER ACCESSORIES
STR = Power Steering
BK = Power Brakes
WIN = Power Windows
SEA = Power Seat
DSE = Dual Power Seats
LOK = Power Locks
MIR = Power Mirrors

TRANSMISSION
ATF4 = Automatic, 4 Speed on Floor
MTC3 = Manual, 3 Speed on Column
4x4 = Four Wheel Drive

OPTIONS
TWL = Tilt Wheel
CC = Cruise Control
DEF = Rear Defroster
SR = Sun Roof
TT = T Top

TEL = Telephone
SRS = Air Bag
SRS2 = Dual Air Bag
ABS = Anti-Lock Brakes
ALW = Aluminum Wheels
CODE = Coded Entry
REM = Remote Entry
TRB = Turbo
TTRB = Twin Turbo
OM = Owner's Manual
SERV = Service Records
VR = Vinyl Roof
CALEM = California Emissions

DAMAGE SEVERITY
0 = No Charge
1 = 1.0 Hour
2 = 1.5 Hours
3 = 2 Hours
4 = 3 Hours
5 = 4 Hours
6 = 5 Hours
7 = 6 Hours
8 = 7 Hours
9 = 8 Hours
X = Replace
R = Refinish

DAMAGE TYPE
A = Replaced
B = Bent
C = Crack
D = Dent
F = Fade
H = Hole
J = Re-work
L = Loose
M = Smell
O = Broken
P = Cut
R = Rust
S = Scratch
T = Stain
U = Burn
V = Chip
W = Wave
X = Replace
Z = Missing

send the money to AUCNET either via express mail or electronic fund transfer. Once AUCNET received the money, it mailed the car title to the buyer and arranged for the purchased vehicle to be delivered to the buyer. AUCNET handled any complications that occurred during the financial transactions.

AUCNET's revenue came from leasing equipment to the dealers and charging fees for performing different services. The fees charged by AUCNET USA during December 1995 are shown below.

Item	Fee ($US)
Vehicle inspection	25 per car
Registration (first time only)	50
Registration (prior week no sale rerun)	25
Sale fee	75
Remove vehicle from sale on preview day	25
Remove vehicle from sale on sale day	50
Buyer's fee	115
Buyer's draft fee	50
Monthly lease of system	149

Future Business Opportunities

New Clients. Mitsubishi Motor Sales of America was AUCNET USA's largest client, but in late 1994, the company was on the verge of adding more car manufacturers to its list of clients. Brad Randall, AUCNET USA's manager of transportation, commented on the new clients:

It's going to get really exciting around here. This shows that the word of mouth about our business is getting around the auto industry. People are starting to look at us seriously.

Mr. Oana commented on some future possibilities:

Our system can add another channel and provide the capability to hold two sales simultaneously. When AUCNET has a Mitsubishi program sale, it can include all Mitsubishi dealers and cut out everybody else. This can also be done on the basis of territory. For example, if a seller in Texas only wants to sell to Texas dealers, we can close everybody out and have a Texas sale. We are also beginning to advertise our services

using the Internet and have a home page at *www.aucnet.com.*

The high growth in the sale of used cars had prompted AUCNET to look into new markets. Dave Frazier, AUCNET USA's vice president, commented:

What we want to move into next is auctioning heavy earth-moving equipment. The transportation cost of moving this equipment from the seller's location to an auction site is phenomenal. With our system, we can set up the auction in a large room of a hotel with big-screen TV's. We will invite the bidders, give them a catalog, train them, and finally let them bid on the equipment.

Another possibility is to set up flower auctions in Europe, which represent a billion-dollar business—like the tulip auctions in Holland. For the flower auctions, we show the picture of the flowers in the field on the computer screen. The auction process in Europe would work in a reverse order. For instance, if the seller's price for tulips was $25,000, the bid would start at $30,000 and go down, and the first one to hit the button wins the bid. It is a one-bid process. The technical challenge for this venture involves the monetary units that will be shown on the screen. We need to develop software so that bidders can use the appropriate currency for their bids and purchases.

THE COMPETITION

No other competitors offered the full on-line services offered by AUCNET USA. A few companies provided on-line services using the Internet. For example, The Auto Shoppe in Milwaukee, Wisconsin, which advertised itself as the first Internet used car lot in Milwaukee (*www.autoshoppe.com*), offered customer services that included consignment, detailing, and locating and registering of vehicles. Another on-line competitor, the Autoboard (*www.autoboard.com*), offered a bulletin board service for advertising vehicles and charged $24.95 for a 6-week period. Sellers had to mail or fax all pictures and provide information about the cars. Buyers negotiated directly with the sellers after reviewing the information.

Grogan commented on AUCNET USA's competitors:

EXHIBIT B
Preview Catalog

All Times EST

Preview Days and Time	Wednesday 02/15/95	1:00 P.M.–6:00 P.M.
	Thursday 02/16/95	9:00 A.M.–10:00 A.M.
Sale Day	Thursday 02/16/95	
Sale Start Time	11:00 A.M.	
Training Video Start Time	10:30 A.M.	
Model Mix	Mirage Mix	8
	Mirage S	17
	Galant ES	20
	Eclipse	2
	Expo LRV	5
	Expo SP	29
	Diamante ES	8
	Diamante Wagon	11
February Calendar	Consignment Sale	February 23
	MMSA Program Sale + MMCA REPO's	February 28

Car Information (Sample)

No.	Year	Make	Series Doors	Trans	Cylinder Liter	Mile	Exterior Color	VIN	MSRP	State Plate	CAT	Location City	State	Interior Color	AC	Audio	E-Rating
A0001	94	MITSU	ES 2 doors	ATF3	4 1.5	10,114	Y96/Cairo Yellow Prl Met	JA3EA21A3 RU06400	$12,530	AL	L	Brunswick	GA	Gray	AC	FMS TP	3
A0002	94	MITSU	S 5 doors	ATF4	4 2.4	16,427	X02/Albany Black Prl Met-2	JA3ED59G8ZZ 08188	$13,840	NJ	L	Philadelphia	PA	White	AC	FMS	4
A0003	94	MITSU	Wagon 5 doors	ATF4	6 3.0	20,821	BDF/Melbourne	6MMAC49SSR T000222	$26,320	FL	L	Miami	FL	Brown	AC	FMS TP	4

There is not a competitor out there that provides services anywhere close to what we offer. Chrysler is the only company that I know of in the U.S. market that has a semi-interactive auction, but it looks more like a telethon for buying and selling used cars. Our competitors are mainly the traditional regular auction houses like Manheim auctions and independent auction houses across the country.

Art White, a used car buyer for a Mitsubishi dealership in Wexford, Pennsylvania, explained why he used AUCNET USA:

I look at the detailed schematic drawing of a car's dents and dings on the computer screen. I cannot inspect cars this thoroughly in a regular auction.

When asked about AUCNET's thorough inspection and grading process, Bob Winters of Fred Beans Mitsubishi, a used car dealer in Doylestown, Pennsylvania, commented:

I've never had any surprises when the cars are delivered. I can rely on the grades even when I don't have time to preview the cars. Also, AUCNET gives me better control over my dollar inventory. Once, I had listed two cars on the preview catalog even before I had purchased them. Due to the AUCNET system, I had buyers for those cars even before they were in my lot. AUCNET saved me a tremendous amount of time and cost.

MARKETING CHALLENGES IN THE UNITED STATES

AUCNET USA was changing the traditional marketplace for used cars—a mix of physical locations, inventory, and tangible products—to a radically different "marketspace." Marketspace transactions, in which the cars were seen on a terminal and then traded, involved new ways of thinking about making money.[4] The *content* of the transaction was different: Information about the car replaced the cars themselves. Inspection reports were a critical element in the transaction, and the customers had to trust this process. The *context* in which the transaction occurred also was different: An electronic, on-screen auction replaced a face-to-face auction. Although the auctioneer's voice and tone remained similar to those in a real auction, the infrastructure that enabled the transaction to take place was different: Buyers and sellers were not in the same place; computers and communications lines replaced used car lots.

To increase its chance of success, AUCNET had to address certain marketing challenges: overcoming dealers' reluctance to adopt the system, understanding the differences between Japanese and U.S. markets, connecting the proprietary system to other systems, including the costs of transportation in the sale price, allowing for the risks in paying sellers first, and adjusting the price structure as necessary.

Dealer Attitudes

Many U.S. dealers were not very receptive to the idea of an auto auction based on satellite services. Many felt that it didn't allow them "to kick the tires." Dianne Wyatt, sales manager at Auburn Mazda said:

I wouldn't know from whom I am buying the car. I would also worry about inspectors not doing a good job of evaluating the car.

Bobby Mattox, sales manager at Dyas Nissan, said:

I am concerned about inspectors getting bribed when evaluating the cars. Why are we going to use a satellite-based system when we can go and see the car?

Dave Frazier agreed that marketing the system was an issue, but felt that trends were in their favor:

Families own many dealerships, so especially the younger members are taking over and they are more progressive and looking to be leaner in their operations and want to save money in any way they can. Usually they are the ones that tend to be early adopters of our system.

Grogan talked about how changes in dealers' mindsets would come about:

The dealers who initially said we won't buy cars on a computer are now buying about fifteen cars a week. We can spend millions of dollars on advertising, but the grass-roots advertising that spreads through word of mouth is what's going to make the difference in this business. Although dealers sell people things, they are hesitant when others try to sell them something. When one dealer tells another dealer, "Hey! I got this system and it works and it is great," the other dealers get inquisitive and will want to find out about it.

Nobody really wanted to be first on the AUCNET system. Everybody wanted to be second or third. They wanted to wait and see the results of others. Now we have Mitsubishi, who stepped in first and has done very well with our system. Since things have moved well for Mitsubishi, we currently have five other manufacturers who are interested in joining our system.

Differences Between U.S. and Japanese Markets

There were a number of differences between the U.S. and Japanese used car markets that together created a climate in which U.S. dealers, unlike Japanese dealers, liked to physically inspect used cars before purchasing them.

- Due to the scarcity of land in Japan, auctions were held at government auction sites, and they were all scheduled for particular times. In the United States, auctions were held at private sites at various times and were not as expensive to run as they were in Japan.

- Japan had an extensive public transportation system, and fuel cost much more in Japan than in the United States. Therefore, used cars in Japan had much less mileage than used cars in the United States.

- In Japan, automobiles older than 3 years were inspected regularly to ensure they met government and environmental standards. Therefore, Japanese dealers generally felt that used automobiles would be in reasonably good condition. In contrast, there was much less government control in the United States, and regulations and inspection policies varied from state to state.

For all these reasons, U.S. buyers were hesitant to put their trust in the inspection process and the

on-line auction system. This was AUCNET USA's biggest challenge in marketing the system.

Sharing the System

The AUCNET system had been designed as a proprietary system and could not be used by the dealerships that were AUCNET clients for any other purpose. However, many dealers had leased satellite dishes that linked them to specific manufacturers' systems, such as GM's Pulsat system and Lexus's TDN, and they wanted to be able to access the AUCNET system through these systems and satellite dishes rather than only via the AUCNET satellite dishes.

AUCNET's managers were initially reluctant to connect their proprietary systems to the dealers' systems because financial data and other sensitive information were handled during the course of the auctions. In addition, AUCNET was planning to add a bulletin board to its system in the future to allow automobiles to be bought and sold all week long, and it expected its systems to be heavily used. Another advantage of the proprietary system was its simplicity; training dealers to use the control keys was relatively easy.

Despite this, AUCNET decided to enter into a few joint arrangements. In 1995, AUCNET announced that its systems were compatible with both GM's Pulsat and Lexus's TDN. This reduced the number of satellite dishes dealers had to purchase, and AUCNET expected that more dealers would now sign up for its services.

Seller-to-Buyer Transportation

Some dealers were concerned that the cost of moving a car from the seller's lot to the buyer's lot was not included in the price. Brad Randall, manager of transportation, commented:

> A transporter normally likes to carry a full load of cars to a particular destination. AUCNET deals with transporting one or more cars to different places and cannot promise a full load to a transporter. A car might be in Alabama that is sold to someone in North Carolina or Florida. Once someone has bought a car, it is his or her responsibility to transport it. As a goodwill mea-

sure, AUCNET locates a transporter who will transport the car for a reasonable price.

Collection Risks

AUCNET underwrote the risks in collecting funds from the buyer, thereby providing a valuable service to the seller. The seller was paid within 24 hours, although the buyer had up to 5 days to pay for the vehicle. This service had the potential to add significant risk to AUCNET's operations, since nonpayment by buyers could cut into profit margins. However, AUCNET did not perceive this risk to be critical at this time, since the company dealt exclusively with dealers of used cars, who were less likely to default than individual customers.

Price Structure

AUCNET needed to make sure that its pricing structure was competitive. Grogan said that AUC-NET had changed its price structure:

> We have cut down our equipment and installation fee dramatically by setting a $149 per month flat fee, down from an earlier fee of $395 per month. In reality we are not an equipment sales company, we are an auction company. Therefore, we had to cut our fee to increase the number of subscribers. Before the price change, we were adding three or four subscribers a week. This week alone, we had eight or nine subscribers sign up. The $149 per month for

dealers is a small amount in comparison to what is spent on monthly travel to on-site auctions.

AUCNET'S FUTURE

Mr. Oana wanted AUCNET's executive team to create strategies through which the company could grow in the United States. He knew that the answers to three questions could determine the future of AUCNET USA:

1. What should be done to increase the likelihood of the U.S. operation's success, given the availability of new information technologies?

2. Should AUCNET USA expand into other markets, such as auctioning heavy earth-moving equipment in the United States or auctioning flowers in Europe?

3. What other business expansion opportunities could AUCNET USA pursue?

Endnotes

1. A. Warbelow and J. Kokuryo, "AUCNET TV Auction Network System," Harvard Business Publishing 9-190-001, July 1989.

2. Smith and Associates, "AUCNET Opens New Regions, Continues Dealer Expansion," *Auto Remarketing,* January 1995, pp. 10–11.

3. G. Stern and N. Templin, "Big Used-Car Auctions Meet Critical Needs of Detroit and Dealers," *Wall Street Journal,* June 27, 1995, p. 1.

4. J. F. Rayport and J. J. Sviokla, "Managing in the Marketplace," *Harvard Business Review* 27(6), November–December 1994, pp. 141–150.

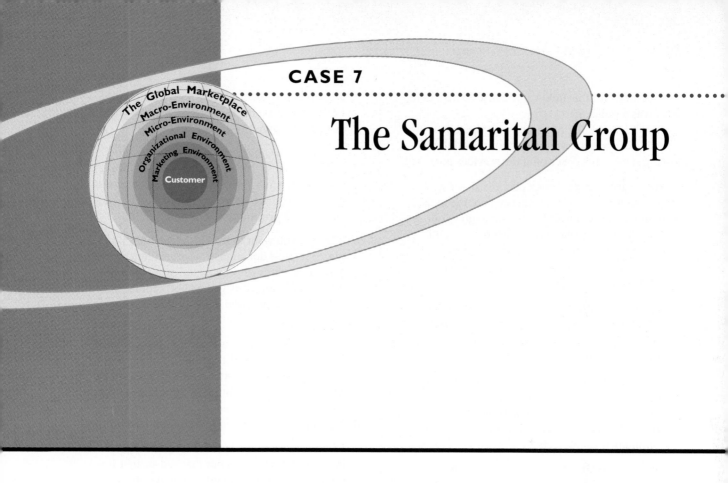

The Samaritan Group

This case was prepared by Robert P. Crowner, Professor of Management, Eastern Michigan University.

As Bill Williams contemplated developing a 3-year strategic business plan for The Samaritan Group (TSG), which he founded in 1970, he remembered how many changes had been made in the last 3 years. He had deliberately changed the basic nature of his business from a communications agency to a telemarketing company. He even changed the name to reflect the new strategy. Unfortunately, from 1990 through 9 months of 1994, the revenues had fallen 42 percent, and although profit was marginally improved, it only represented about 0.4 percent of revenue. Given his goals of expanding the company and making it profitable so that he could pass it on to his son or sell it at a good price for his retirement, he wondered if he was on the right track. Hence he began his review prior to developing his strategic plan.

COMPANY BACKGROUND

Bill Williams, the president and owner of TSG, was a graduate of the University of Dayton School of Journalism. He had various management assignments in communications, advertising, and public relations for several firms before founding his own company, The Williams Organization (TWO), in 1970. Bill is an accredited member of the Public Relations Society of America, the highest ranking available to a public relations practitioner. Accreditation is awarded only after successfully completing intensive written and oral examinations.

TWO began by offering marketing services including print design and production, publishing, and public relations/publicity to public service groups in the law enforcement and fire protection fields. TWO offered to provide brochures, newsletters, press releases, magazines, graphic design, public relations, corporate identity packages, and sales materials. In short, it was a full-service agency. Bill's initial entry into this field came through his uncle, who was a policeman.

TWO's marketing brochure with the motto "Quality, Experience & Results!" contained the following statements describing the services provided:

You've got your marketing plan. It's all set up and ready to go. Now all you need are the tools to implement it. Instead of having to go to one place for this service and another for that and possibly even a third place as your plan expands, consider The Williams Organization (TWO) for all your marketing needs.

Whatever your needs—magazines, newspapers, newsletters, brochures—TWO can customize your printed material to meet the objectives of you and your audience.

Our creative graphic arts layout, design, and production studio will achieve the professional results you are seeking. All aspects of the project are handled in-house, providing timeliness and continuity to all projects.

The Williams Organization takes a personal interest. As public relations counsel, we provide professional guidance from concept to implementation of total image-building programs, including preparation of press releases and features, arrangement of media interviews or coverage, and periodic internal and external audits to ascertain the effectiveness of the programs selected.

TELEMARKETING

TWO first became involved in telemarketing in 1976 by default when an independent contractor for TWO went bankrupt. TWO was using telemarketing as a sales tool in conjunction with other promotional techniques. For instance, Bill said that the impact of direct mail is increased from 3 to 10 percent by using telemarketing as a follow-up. The brochure noted the following about telemarketing:

More than 118 billion dollars in goods and services are sold by phone each year. In 1985, a little over 82,000 businesses used telemarketing to reach potential customers. By the year 2000, 8 million telemarketers will be employed in this country. There is a good reason for the rapid

growth in the telemarketing industry. It works! In fact, it may be the most cost-effective way to meet your marketing goals.

The Williams Organization is a proven entity when it comes to telemarketing services. We've been successfully using this (dynamic) sales tool since 1976, so we've grown and refined our services over a proven period of time.

Whether you want to host an event, sell a product, or request donations, our professional telemarketing staff will provide the manpower to get the job done. Also, you will be kept informed of the progress being generated on your account.

Over the years, the fund-raising business done in telemarketing increased, becoming a major part of TWO's business. Public-sector areas including law enforcement and firefighting became the main part of their telemarketing business. Bill began to see that telemarketing offered more potential. He noted:

I felt I wanted to get out of the area we had been in, and while it is not that bad an area, it is not highly prestigious, and I know we are very capable of doing other things. I am moving toward telemarketing in order to expand the business and shift the emphasis. The potential in telemarketing is vastly unlimited.

There is still another factor in this picture. When you do fund-raising work for law enforcement and firefighting agencies, the most success comes from male callers, which limits your labor pool. In contrast, when you do fundraising for nonprofit organizations, the most success comes from female callers. That fact allowed us to expand our labor pool enormously. It is also much easier to deal with nonprofits who are usually national charities. Negotiations are usually conducted by mail or by telephone. We have an excellent reputation. A national attorney is used to keep us apprised of what is happening nationally in the fund-raising area.

THE SAMARITAN GROUP

As a result of the evolving opportunities and advantages in telemarketing, Bill decided to shift the emphasis of his company to telemarketing for nonprofit clients. After considerable soul searching, in early 1990 he even decided to change the name of his company to more closely indicate the nature of the intended core business and coincident with the consolidation of several subsidiaries over a period of 3 years. He began to turn down business in the marketing agency area of the business and actively seek nonprofit fund-raising clients. In 1994, his business was comprised of 5 percent in publications, 10 percent in marketing, and 85 percent in telemarketing, of which the nonprofit clients were the largest group. Exhibit A shows the organization chart for TSG as of 1994.

TSG offered several kinds of telemarketing services. Included were new product introductions, product sales, lead generation, lead qualification, market research, and inactive accounts reactivation. The most important was fundraising. Seminar registration, membership campaigns, full account management, appointment setting, verification (follow-up), and in-house consultation were services that also were offered.

Currently, TSG had about 15 clients, of which 2 together accounted for about two-thirds of the revenue. Exhibit B shows a listing of clients by type of business with the sales and related expenses for each for the first 9 months of 1994. Bill believed that there was a great deal of potential for growth in nonprofit telemarketing. TSG did little formal marketing of itself, rather relying on word-of-mouth

EXHIBIT A
Organization Chart: The Samaritan Group

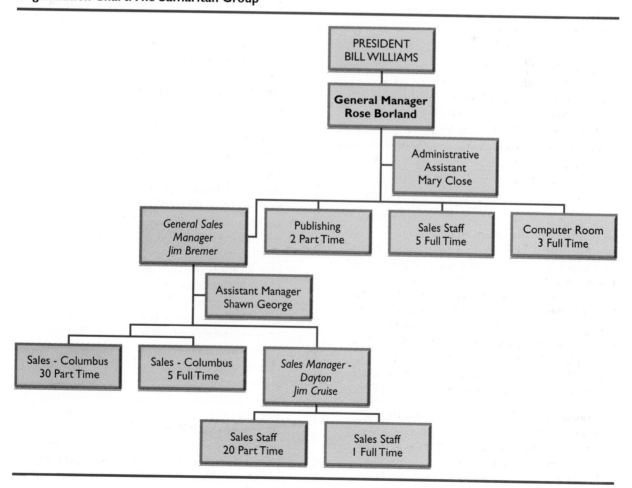

Source: Company records.

EXHIBIT B
. . . .
Schedule of Sales by Client: The Samaritan Group (In thousand dollars)

	1994 9 Months
Nonprofit	
Client A	636.0
Client D	79.1
Client E	52.0
Client G	63.0
Client H	48.7
Other	17.7
Total	896.5
Public service	
Client B	302.2
Client C	257.0
Client F	48.4
Client I	30.0
Client J	53.7
Client K	18.2
Client L	20.6
Other	34.6
Total	764.7
Credit	(0.5)
Total	1,660.7

Source: Company records.

advertising from satisfied clients. No cold calls were made, and no advertising was done. Brochures were available to mail to clients. Business was somewhat seasonal, with December and January being slow months. Bill noted that:

I can pick and choose charity clients at all times. I mean at any time I have maybe three to five requests on my desk from different charities who are interested in representation, the end result of which I can pick and choose. Oftentimes, however, there are more embryonic charities that I may choose not to represent just because getting name familiarity and recognition is an expensive process. The fee that they would pay to us is higher, but you know name recognition sometimes will outweigh the higher fee because you may have to go through a much greater process in order to gain the customer base.

In regard to fees for the services TSG performed, fees were either charged as a percent of the collected funds, which was the common way, or by the hour for the person making the call. Hourly rates varied by whether the person being called was a homeowner, $29 to $30 per hour in the evening, or business, $33 to $38 per hour depending on whether it was local or long-distance calls. Business calls required a higher caliber and more experienced caller in order to get through the screens in a business organization. The cost of the caller, including wages, overhead, and phone charges, ranged from $12 to $18.

The percentage charged as a fee ranged from 65 to 90 percent of the collected funds. Bill described the process:

Where the client may be in the range depends on whether it is an established charity, whether they have a presence in the market we are working in, and whether they have a lapsed donor or previous client base. It is a typical negotiation which takes into account many different factors. It ultimately depends on how well you negotiate.

The gross profit margin is at best 20 to 25 percent. Bill volunteered that the fees ranging up to 90 percent seemed horribly high to the public. He offered this insight:

The nonprofit fund-raising arena works like this. A new charity may go into the fund-raising business using direct mail. Using national statistics, they will lose money for the first two and a half years of continuous mailings before they break even. Then the direct mail will start to accrue profits. A one-time giver is meaningless. Half the donors are typically one-time givers. Where you gain your profits is the multiple giver. That is the initial key to all of this.

So what happens is that you have that loss curve which many charities, especially new charities, cannot afford. So they seek out telemarketing fund raisers who are willing to gamble with them and work on a percentage basis. Because I have no guarantees, I am rolling the dice, and if I guess wrong, I am the one who loses money. So let's take a really terrible position of me being the onerous businessman who has no morals or ethics who says OK new charity I will work for you and take 90 cents of every dollar I raise. What I am going to give them is a guaranteed profit of 10 cents, which is a nice beginning for them, since they can use that to help grow their charity. But what is most important is they are gaining a donor list which they can turn into direct mail. They can get the loss time down from two and a half years to maybe six months by starting to direct mail these people we have developed.

Several examples were given by Bill as to how new clients were obtained. TSG belongs to the Trade Exchange of America, located in Columbus, Ohio. There are about 4000 members. Immediately after a company joins, an article is published in their newsletter describing the product or service provided by the new member. Members can then call the exchange to secure names of firms who do what the caller is seeking.

A firm in Cincinnati who remanufactures office furniture was a client TSG obtained through the exchange. This company had been rather unsuccessful in using cold calling in its marketing effort. The company employed TSG to call its customer base to perform a quality audit. The audit turned up the fact that there was dissatisfaction with some marketing representatives who were no longer with the company. They had apparently promised things that were not accomplished, although the company did not know of the promises. The vast majority of the company's customers were pleased to hear from TSG and were very open to giving the company another chance. It was very meaningful for the company to reactivate what had been dissatisfied customers.

Another example of a potential new customer was a large second-tier public accounting firm that wished to have a public relations audit done of the principals, clients, media, former clients, prospective clients, and universities where it recruited. The CPA firm also may wish to have some professional articles ghost-written by TSG. In turn, the CPA firm may take over the accounting activities of TSG in a barter arrangement.

COMPETITION

TSG operates primarily in the Ohio and Indiana regional area. Bill said that TSG is small and has three public-service competitors, two of which are subcontractors to TSG. In the nonprofit sector, there are 12 competitors in the two-state region as well

as national firms such as Reese Brothers who handle the Mothers Against Drunk Driving (MADD) account. Unfortunately, the competition consists of privately held companies, and financial information is not available for comparative purposes.

OPERATIONS

TSG has two offices from which its calls are placed, one in Dayton and one in Columbus. Jim Williams, Bill's son, managed the Columbus office while he was working on his MBA at Ohio State University. Bill and Jim had somewhat different philosophies regarding TSG, so since finishing his degree in 1993 Jim decided to work for another company doing outside sales work. This decision does not mean that he will never wish to return to TSG.

Bill is a believer in centralized operations, having tried decentralized offices with poor results. In fact, if it were not for the high quality of the labor pool in Columbus, he would not even have an office there. In Bill's opinion, the cost of long-distance calling is more than offset by the hassle of satellite offices.

The calling operations are the heart of the business. Largely part-time college students are used in both locations to make calls. Bill expects to move toward more full-time employees as the business expands. Calls are mainly made in the evening and typically last for 1 minute. About 15 contacts, which are defined as a sale, turndown (TD), disconnect, or wrong number, are made per hour. Bill estimates that 2.3 million phone call attempts are made per year in Ohio and 300,000 in Indiana, the other major state in which TSG works.

TSG primarily uses Bresser's Cross Directory as a basis for the numbers it calls. This directory lists numbers up one side of a street and down the other by area, and thus it is easier to control geographically. Telephone directories are used in areas where Bresser's is not available.

Bill stated that TSG had a higher than normal percentage of people who pay their pledge, 70 to 80 percent versus 50 percent nationally. He attributes this high rate to the steps that are taken.

> Our callers attempt to not high pressure for a yes. We continue to talk until we receive three "no's." We call a donor back 90 percent of the time with a different caller in order to "confirm the address" and also verify the amount

pledged. Only if a pledge is verified will the two-part invoice, return envelope, and background on the client be sent to the donor. When the customer pledges, they become a "cross-off," which means they have become a repeat customer. Future calls to a repeat donor for the same or other clients will be made by a more experienced caller as though we know them.

When donors are billed, they are entered into TSG's IBM 36 computer, which currently contains 280,000 names. The custom program, which was developed over several years by a full-time employee who became part-time, cost approximately $200,000. Data for each donor include the name, address, purchase date, paid date, amount, client number, and multiple purchases if more than one client is involved.

TSG is considering the purchase of predictive dialing equipment to improve the efficiency of its operations. Each station, which costs $5000, is a PC-driven central file server. Bill estimates that eight units would be required. The equipment paces the operators by dialing ahead at a predetermined rate. Three residential shifts would be organized from 9 A.M. to 1 P.M., 1 P.M. to 5 P.M., and 5 P.M. to 9 P.M. Of these, the 5 to 9 slot is the best time to call and the 1 to 5 slot the poorest time. Predictive dialing eliminates operators handling calls that do not answer, busies, and answering machines. The computer reschedules the call and calls back later. Bill expects to move toward more full-time employees as the business expands.

In the publication area, TSG provided all the services such as creative, design, keylining and typesetting in-house. In-house work was marked up by 50 to 70 percent for billing. Printing was contracted out typically by securing three bids and marking up the printing by 10 percent. Public relations work was marked up by 66 percent.

FINANCIAL

TSG presently has a part-time accountant do its monthly financial statements, including a listing of clients. Exhibit C shows the income statements from 1988 through the first 9 months of 1994. Exhibit D shows the schedule of direct expenses, and Exhibit E shows the schedule of administrative expenses for the same time period. Exhibit F shows the balance sheets for the same time period. Exhibit G shows the income statements by each of the first three quarters for 1993 and 1994 for comparison purposes. Similarly, Exhibit H shows the

EXHIBIT C

Income Statement: The Samaritan Group (In thousand dollars)

	1988	1989	1990	1991	1992	1993	1994 9 Months
Net sales	3,403.7	3,773.2	3,846.3	3,076.9	2,786.1	2,790.9	1,660.7
Direct expenses	2,587.7	2,872.5	3,018.3	2,242.8	2,125.3	2,073.0	1,213.2
Gross profit	816.0	900.7	828.0	834.1	660.8	717.9	447.5
Gen. operating exp.	1,066.8	938.8	874.7	811.5	624.6	688.6	435.2
Other income expense							
Interest income							
Interest expense	(16.2)	(18.4)	(18.0)	(18.6)	(15.4)	(20.8)	(9.4)
Misc. income	4.2	0.7	3.2		1.5	1.9	2.1
Rental income				22.2			1.2
Total	(12.0)	(17.7)	(14.8)	3.6	(13.9)	(18.9)	(6.1)
Net income	(262.8)	(55.8)	(61.5)	26.2	22.3	10.4	6.2

Source: Company records.

EXHIBIT D
Schedule of Direct Expenses: The Samaritan Group (In thousand dollars)

	1988	1989	1990	1991	1992	1993	1994 9 Months
Sales salaries	626.8	609.9	502.2	466.6	459.0	365.6	212.4
Manager salaries	86.6	145.8	86.5	87.7	109.2	95.3	73.3
Production salaries	83.2	64.1	64.6	58.5	204.0	141.7	90.5
Total salaries	796.6	819.8	653.3	612.8	772.2	602.6	376.2
Payroll taxes	95.8	82.6	70.7	79.6	82.4	46.3	27.0
Employee insurance	27.2	8.1	8.8	(0.6)			
Production costs	125.7	109.1	130.2	32.8	6.1	1.1	0.7
Purchases	18.0	53.9	24.4	17.0			
Commissions	1,058.3	1,199.1	1,783.7	1,068.6	764.0	998.8	558.9
Postage & mailing	124.7	123.7	87.7	85.9	72.0	57.7	38.0
Telephone	239.5	281.0	200.5	238.6	256.6	171.2	100.1
Printing	58.7	60.8	42.8	88.7	79.9		
Outside labor	26.7	103.6	0.8	3.0	1.7	0.1	
Direct client expense				3.5	71.0	180.0	100.9
Sales leads	9.3	9.1	2.0	1.3	2.6	2.0	0.7
Sales incentives	4.6	16.5	4.9	5.5	6.7	6.5	5.8
Freelance labor	2.6	5.1	8.5	6.1	10.1	6.7	4.9
Total	2,587.7	2,872.4	3,018.3	2,242.8	2,125.3	2,073.0	1,213.2

Source: Company records.

schedule of direct expenses, and Exhibit I shows the schedule of administrative expenses.

TSG has used different accounting firms over the years shown on the exhibits, which accounts for some of the differences in classification of accounts. The current accountant, Kevin Straub, noted when asked why the sales were lower in 1988, "that several clients had been lost over some legal matters." He also mentioned that the commissions shown on the income statements were paid to subcontractors and represented 7 to 8 percent of the collected billings sold by the subcontractors. Subcontractors were used to cover some regional clients or clients that had specific bonding or registration requirements. He pointed out that the public-sector groups were still among the most profitable clients, even though they had been de-emphasized.

Bill sees a serious constraint in a shortage of capital. He estimates he could use $500,000 to purchase equipment and provide additional employees.

FUTURE POSSIBILITIES

Bill said he spent about 60 hours per week on TSG business. Much of it was new business development and extensive reading of local business magazines, newspapers, and telemarketing communications. He lamented that his area of expertise was in print media, which the company was phasing out. He noted, "Jim is a foot-soldier in telemarketing, while I have not even been drafted yet."

Bill did not do extensive planning or budgeting as he originally began to shift the nature of TSG's business. Rather, he began with a concept that he developed by extensive networking with competitors in the telemarketing area, many of whom were national and not current competitors. Many are quite sophisticated, and this is the direction Bill wants to move. For instance, one direct-mail company in Virginia has a lapsed-donor list of 10 mil-

EXHIBIT E
....
Schedule of Administrative Expenses: The Samaritan Group (In thousand dollars)

	1988	1989	1990	1991	1992	1993	1994 9 Months
Payroll—executive	67.2	208.8	184.4	229.0	208.4	213.3	94.2
Payroll—administrative	254.9	255.5	188.3	113.6	59.8	101.2	60.3
Payroll—clerical	18.1	15.2	66.2	89.2			6.8
Total payroll	340.2	479.5	438.9	431.8	268.2	314.5	161.3
Payroll taxes	35.2	32.5	32.8	27.4	9.2	39.4	23.8
Rent	132.4	84.8	70.3	76.1	94.4	88.3	71.1
Employee insurance	23.3	35.7	22.6	25.8	29.2	19.0	16.2
Insurance	46.0	26.1	32.5	28.6	20.6	15.4	8.4
Telephone	23.0	16.8	15.6	7.9			
Utilities	15.7	17.7	16.7	20.3	20.7	18.9	13.4
Taxes	47.3	9.2	16.4	15.4	35.5	29.8	21.1
Building maintenance	18.4	27.0	19.2	20.7	14.2	10.3	22.9
Equipment leasing	23.4	20.7	16.1	22.7	3.5		4.9
Advertising	30.7	20.2	6.4	4.8	5.5	4.8	2.3
Entertain & promotion	9.9	5.7	5.0	3.1	2.6	1.8	1.3
Travel	33.2	14.8	4.0	4.9	4.2	4.8	0.2
Depreciation	81.8	52.5	39.6	17.2	23.3	21.8	17.0
Employee leasing					3.0	22.5	13.6
Computer expense	8.5	10.9	17.2	17.3	21.7	21.6	2.3
Office expense	38.3	37.5	44.0	33.5	19.3	13.9	10.9
Professional fees	79.7	14.1	37.0	18.9	20.6	35.5	19.0
Dues & licenses	3.7	3.7	6.3	6.3	7.8	8.7	4.3
Bad debts	48.7	6.5	6.3		1.7		1.4
Contract guarantee				5.2			2.2
Auto expense	25.0	22.2	23.7	19.7	13.1	16.0	12.1
Miscellaneous	2.4	0.7	4.1	3.9	6.3	1.6	5.5
Total	1,066.8	938.8	874.7	811.5	624.6	688.6	435.2

Source: Company records.

EXHIBIT F
. . . .
Balance Sheet: The Samaritan Group (In thousand dollars)

	1988	1989	1990	1991	1992	1993	1994 9 Months
Current assets							
Cash	40.1	58.1	27.0	29.6	32.8	23.5	35.3
Accounts receivable	138.7	72.7	56.6	61.7	16.6	25.8	32.7
Officer receivable	17.7	17.7	17.7	17.7	19.3		
Total	196.5	148.5	101.3	109.0	68.7	49.3	68.0
Fixed assets							
Furniture & fixtures	177.5	172.3	172.3	184.2	179.3	202.7	202.8
Equipment	314.4	275.4	265.5	288.9	290.3	279.3	285.1
D&B master file	47.7	25.7	25.7	25.7	25.7	25.7	25.7
Leasehold imprv.	53.2	53.2	53.2	58.1	9.0	9.6	9.7
Total	592.8	526.6	516.7	556.9	504.3	517.3	523.3
Depreciation	466.9	432.7	466.8	468.2	439.4	461.2	478.2
Net fixed assets	125.9	93.9	49.9	88.7	64.9	56.1	45.1
Other assets	20.7	35.1	26.5	32.9	7.5	7.5	7.5
Total assets	343.1	277.5	177.7	230.6	141.1	112.9	120.6
Current liabilities							
Accounts payable	89.4	157.1	115.2	64.2	44.5	69.4	90.4
Accrued taxes	41.4			14.7	21.6		
Total	130.8	157.1	115.2	78.9	66.1	69.4	90.4
Long-term liabilities							
Banks	238.6	202.5	169.1	181.3	178.1	146.3	143.0
Officer	63.9	63.9	100.9	151.7	85.6	62.2	46.0
Total	302.5	266.4	270.0	333.0	263.7	208.5	189.0
Equity							
Common stock	2.0	2.0	2.0	2.0	71.0	71.0	71.0
Retained earnings	(92.2)	(148.0)	(209.5)	(209.5)	(282.0)	(246.4)	(236.0)
Current earnings				26.2	22.3	10.4	6.2
Total	(90.2)	(146.0)	(207.5)	(181.3)	(188.7)	(165.0)	(158.8)
Total liab. & equity	343.1	277.5	177.7	230.6	141.1	112.9	120.6

Notes: (1) Retained earnings at beginning of 1992 adjusted for absorption of subsidiaries. (2) Common stock at end of 1992 reflects the capitalization of part of officer loan. (3) Retained earnings at beginning of 1993 adjusted for absorption of subsidiary.

Source: Company records.

EXHIBIT G
············
Income Statement: The Samaritan Group (In thousand dollars)

	Three Months		Six Months		Nine Months	
	1993	*1994*	*1993*	*1994*	*1993*	*1994*
Net sales	654.6	584.8	1,323.7	1,131.3	1,867.4	1,660.7
Direct expenses	426.2	435.9	912.3	830.1	1,341.1	1,213.2
Gross profit	228.4	148.9	411.4	301.2	526.3	447.5
Gen. operating exp.	190.0	148.8	357.3	283.2	526.0	435.2
Other income expense						
Interest income						
Interest expense	(4.8)	(4.9)	(7.5)	(7.3)	(10.7)	(9.4)
Misc. income	0.1	1.0	0.6	1.0	0.6	2.1
Rental income	0.6	0.4	1.0	0.8	1.7	1.2
Total	(4.1)	(3.5)	(5.9)	(5.5)	(8.4)	(6.1)
Net income	34.3	(3.4)	48.2	12.5	(8.1)	6.2

Source: Company records.

EXHIBIT H
············
Schedule of Direct Expenses: The Samaritan Group (In thousand dollars)

	Three Months		Six Months		Nine Months	
	1993	*1994*	*1993*	*1994*	*1993*	*1994*
Sales salaries	91.4	76.7	193.7	144.1	281.7	212.4
Manager salaries	21.5	24.1	46.9	44.3	72.9	73.3
Production salaries	31.9	33.9	70.5	64.5	108.7	90.5
Total salaries	144.8	134.7	311.1	252.9	463.3	376.2
Payroll taxes	11.9	11.1	26.4	20.0	37.4	27.0
Employee insurance	6.7					
Production costs	0.1	0.2	0.5	0.5	0.9	0.7
Purchases						
Commissions	179.3	207.7	381.9	380.4	531.3	558.9
Postage & mailing	14.7	13.1	30.5	25.2	45.6	38.0
Telephone	31.9	34.5	88.8	67.2	132.6	100.1
Printing						
Outside labor						
Direct client expense	31.4	32.4	62.4	77.9	115.8	100.9
Sales leads	0.2	0.3	0.3	0.5	1.3	0.7
Sales incentives	1.5	1.8	3.6	3.3	5.5	5.8
Freelance labor	3.7	0.1	6.8	2.2	7.4	4.9
Total	426.2	435.9	912.3	830.1	1,341.1	1,213.2

Source: Company records.

EXHIBIT I
. . . .
Schedule of Administrative Expenses: The Samaritan Group (In thousand dollars)

	Three Months		Six Months		Nine Months	
	1993	1994	1993	1994	1993	1994
Payroll—executive	16.1	42.2	104.7	68.2	161.1	94.2
Payroll—administrative	49.0	19.4	31.7	39.5	52.2	60.3
Payroll—clerical	7.7	3.8	15.9	5.5	23.7	6.8
Total payroll	72.8	65.4	152.3	113.2	237.0	161.3
Payroll taxes	19.6	9.5	26.5	16.5	33.2	23.8
Rent	21.7	18.2	44.4	47.3	69.4	71.1
Employee insurance	6.7	5.2	10.4	10.9	14.9	16.2
Insurance	(0.6)	3.6	3.5	8.3	9.6	8.4
Telephone						
Utilities	5.6	5.6	10.5	9.5	15.3	13.4
Taxes	4.8	5.3	10.9	10.8	20.4	21.1
Building maintenance	8.2	10.0	18.6	7.8	24.3	22.9
Equipment leasing						4.9
Advertising	1.5	0.8	2.8	2.0	3.5	2.3
Entertain & promotion	0.5	0.3	0.9	0.5	1.2	1.3
Travel	0.8	0.1	2.1	0.2	3.5	0.2
Depreciation	4.1		4.1		16.3	17.0
Employee leasing	5.9	4.8	11.6	9.3	17.1	13.6
Computer expense	0.1	0.3	1.0	9.8	1.7	2.3
Office expense	5.0	3.2	8.0	6.7	9.9	10.9
Professional fees	8.7	7.4	17.9	12.0	28.6	19.0
Dues & licenses	1.4	1.7	3.7	3.4	4.7	4.3
Bad debts		1.4		1.4		1.4
Contract guarantee	17.4	2.2	17.4	1.0	3.4	2.2
Auto expense	5.6	3.6	10.0	8.7	11.3	12.1
Miscellaneous	0.2	0.2	0.7	3.9	0.7	5.5
Total	190.0	148.8	357.3	283.2	526.0	435.2

Source: Company records.

lion people for a nonprofit charity client. TSG is working with this company on a proposal to call this list, and Bill is confident that at least 10 percent can be reactivated.

Bill sees TSG's marketing niche as nonprofit telemarketing and service. An advantage enjoyed is that this business is multiyear, long-term contracts, while many large telemarketing service bureaus are project-related, which creates big swings in employment. These service bureaus did not know or understand fund-raising.

As Bill thought about creating his strategic plan, he noted:

The business is out there; I mean there is just tons of it! If there is anything else, I am in a very exciting business. I am in a wonderful growth business. It's just that right now I am just still in the gutter trying to get my nose above the edge of the curb and that is very frustrating for me. I know I will need capital to move this company forward.

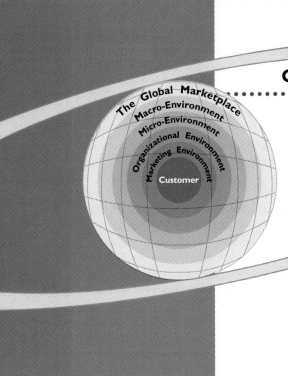

Artistic Impressions, Inc.: Developing an Entrepreneurial Growth Strategy

This case was prepared by James W. Camerius, Professor of Marketing, Northern Michigan University and James W. Clinton, Professor of Management, University of Northern Colorado.

"I think that there's plenty of opportunity out there, and I don't think that we're scratching the surface in the African-American market," suggested Bart Breighner, president and chief executive officer of Artistic Impressions, Inc. "But the reality is that African-Americans make up only 10 percent of this country's population of close to 300 million. I want the whole shot, so we're going to do things to grow the Caucasian market," he noted.

Bart Breighner was excited and optimistic about the future of the company he had created. Artistic Impressions was a rapidly growing direct seller of affordable artworks for the home and office. The firm had a plan to achieve sales of $25

million in 1998. Twice ranked in the top 500 fastest growing private companies in the United States, according to *Inc.* magazine, the company's sales had increased more than 962 percent in the past 5 years.

Artistic Impressions' corporate offices and distribution center were located in Lombard, Illinois, a western suburb of Chicago. Paintings and other artworks were sold through over 2700 salespeople in over 40 states, primarily to African-Americans via home art shows that were a form of the direct marketing party plan. The corporate strategy was based on a perceived market need and a compensation system designed to reward salespeople with substantial commissions. Breighner was certain he had positioned the firm for future growth. Breighner called a meeting of his staff to discuss repositioning the firm for the future. He asked the staff to respond to the following issues: "What do we need to do to get us where we want to go, to reach the kind of customer we want to reach, and to recruit and maintain the kind of sales force that will grow the business?"

BART BREIGHNER

Bart Breighner was a graduate of the University of Maryland. In 1962, he was making $4500 a year as a teacher of high school math. Six years later, he earned $100,000 a year as a manager for World Book Encyclopedia. He had a 30-year track record in the direct-selling field, primarily with World Book Encyclopedia. In his 21-year career with World Book, he built field sales organizations. For the last 7 years with World Book, Breighner held the position of executive vice president and director of North American sales. Reflecting on those years, he noted:

> They sent me through the Harvard University Advanced Management Program. As part of my job responsibility I traveled around the world. . . . that was an exciting career. But the company was sold twice, and I wasn't politically adept at dealing with the paternalistic environment. I wasn't comfortable, and I did move on. I decided to become an entrepreneur.

Breighner next entered the loan-consulting business on a freelance basis by starting a small but profitable financial planning company. He left after a short period of time to become a consultant to Bee Line Fashions, an $80 million company experiencing financial difficulties. Tiring again of the corporate environment, he left after 6 months, concluding

> We could not agree on how we were going to salvage [the company]. . . . it was going way down. At that point, I said, hey, who was I kidding? I'm too rambunctious to report to someone else.

After additional experience in training and recruiting programs, Breighner decided to return to direct selling. "I missed direct sales and the psychic rewards the business offers," he noted, "I looked into possibilities and capital requirements." He surveyed the field to identify an unsatisfied market need. He felt that he wanted to "control his own destiny" at that midcareer point in his life. A number of fields in direct sales are relatively crowded, such as nutrition and cosmetic and facial products,

but there are very few successful home enhancement companies. He founded Artistic Impressions, Inc., in 1985.

In 1995, Breighner authored *Face to Face Selling,* published by Park Avenue Publications, Indianapolis, Indiana. The book detailed the steps individuals needed to get started and succeed in sales, such as goal setting, mental preparation, and developing a sales presentation. It also explored what Breighner called "the art of creative confrontation" to effectively deal with others. He used many of his own experiences throughout the book, citing creative sales techniques for new and experienced salespeople.

Breighner believes that his initial motivation to enter direct selling came from a popular platform speaker whom he met early in his career. When asked why he was still working in the field at the age of 70, the speaker said, "I need the money."

Breighner started Artistic Impressions intending to be the dominant company in the industry. "Success is intentional." Breighner was finalist several times in the Entrepreneur of the Year award sponsored by Ernst & Young, an accounting and consulting firm. He also created a comprehensive videotape series for training his salesforce with an emphasis on building confidence in even the most inexperienced new consultant. He also has served on the board of directors of the Direct Selling Association, an industry organization located in Washington, D.C.

THE DIRECT-SALES ENVIRONMENT

The direct-selling industry consisted of a few well-established companies and many smaller firms that sold a broad range of products: toys, animal food, plant-care products, clothing, computer software, financial services, etc. Among the dominant companies were Avon (cosmetics), Amway Corporation (home cleaning products), Shaklee Corporation (vitamins and health foods), World Book, Encyclopedia Britannica, Tupperware (plastic dishes and food containers), Kirby (Vacuum Cleaners), and Mary Kay (cosmetics).

By the 1980s, analysts believed that the industry was in a mature stage of development, including a high concentration of firms selling nutritional products (vitamins) and facial products (cosmetics).

Spectacular sales growth, characteristic of the 1960s and 1970s, had given way to a pattern in most firms of stagnant revenues and profits. The industry found it difficult to attract new salespeople, who typically were responsible for generating much of a company's sales growth. Industry problems were blamed on the increasing number of full-time working men and women, which cut into the number of recruits and the ability to reach sales targets. Problems also were blamed on an improved economy, which encouraged some potential customers to avoid purchasing items from part-time salespersons and shop at established retail stores for more expensive products, and the increasing sophistication in the marketplace, which forced manufacturers to develop new, more upscale products and modify existing products that were outdated.

Breighner felt that Artistic Impressions offered a career in direct sales that appealed to those individuals who wanted to be independent, successful businesspeople, particularly those in other careers who feared being displaced through corporate downsizing. Breighner also believed that those individuals who had successful professional careers but were frustrated in present positions and wanted to do something they would enjoy at midcareer would find satisfaction through sale of the company's products. "Our people, who are independent contractors, see our company as a vehicle for obtaining financial independence," he suggested.

Breighner's review of the direct-selling field in 1984 led him to conclude that there were very few successful "home enhancement companies." A major competitor in the field was a firm called Home Interiors, with annual sales of about $500 million. Several smaller companies were less of a threat. Breighner indicated that while he respected their product lines and their business methods, he felt that the market would support and probably needed an art product for the home that was more upscale than what was available. He felt there was an opening for a different kind of company.

THE ORGANIZATION

Artistic Impressions was a privately held, multilevel direct-sales organization. A *multilevel organization* is one in which a hierarchical network of distribu-

tors is created to sell and distribute a product line. This approach is distinguished by the fact that each distributor in the network is not only seeking to make retail sales of goods and services to the final consumer but also is looking for distributors to join his or her distribution network. By recruiting and training new distributors, the recruiter becomes a master distributor who earns sales commissions and bonuses on the retail sales of all distributors within the network. The primary company business was selling framed art via the party plan. The party plan method of at-home retailing requires a salesperson to make sales presentations in the home of a host or hostess who has invited potential customers to a "party." Usually, the party plan includes various games and other entertainment activities in which participants receive small, inexpensive gifts. Closing the sale occurs when the salesperson takes orders from the people attending the party. The mission statement of the company stated: "Artistic Impressions exists to provide quality art at affordable prices to enhance the American home." The primary goal of the firm, or any company, was, according to Breighner, to survive. The second goal was to be consistently profitable: "Profit is not something that is left over."

Although Breighner is Caucasian, 90 percent of the company's salesforce of Artistic Impressions is African-American, as are 90 percent of the customers. According to Breighner:

> It wasn't intentional. It just went that way, because of the direction of the organization. We got some powerful management and salespeople with exceptional educational and professional backgrounds who just happened to be African-American. I would like to have a blended company, that is, a company that reflects the population as a whole. Some people call this diversity.

The primary focus of the product line was art that had an African-American appeal. "We have a very large African-American community," said Deborah Thompson-Widmer, a Caucasian, director of promotions and communications for Artistic Impressions. "It's very hard to find African-American art out there. We hit a gold mine out there [in this area], and [our products] really met a need."

Thompson-Widmer was a former associate dean of admissions at Ripon College, Wisconsin. She oversaw three departments. Field service processed new applications for sales representatives, monitored the productivity of sales representatives, and generated reports for team managers. Promotions developed ways to motivate the salesforce, such as special incentives, contests, customer specials, and hostess specials. The third department, marketing, developed promotional materials and videos.

> There's a whole trend in the economy where people are staying home more, they're doing more things at home, they're entertaining in the home, and they want to decorate the home. That has helped us. So many people don't go to galleries because they don't think they can afford gallery art. So many people want to decorate, but they don't get to the store, they don't know what to get.

The company discovered that the appeal of religious art was very strong in the African-American community. In the popular "The Last Supper," for example, by artist R. Williams, the flesh tones were darker than in other portrayals of this religious scene. A similar situation existed in "Praying Hands," by R. Williams. Artistic Impressions' version appeared as a replica of an original painting but done in darker flesh tones. The design also was available as a figurine. Other artworks depicted African-Americans in various life-experience situations. The product line also included landscapes, florals, still lifes, and abstracts that had a broader appeal and put less emphasis on ethnic background.

Another emerging market niche that the company was just beginning to explore was Hispanic art. Widmer noted:

> We have a very strong group of sellers in Puerto Rico. They're asking for more and more Hispanic art. We've started to branch into that because the marketplace is telling us that we have a segment of people saying this is what we need, and that's where we are going. We're in a really big growth spurt now. Sales for the year are up 30 percent. We're booming in the number of recruits coming in and the number of states we're in. It's a very exciting process. We really want to stay in the United States. We did Puerto Rico because it's easy to ship. If there was a direction we would go first, it probably would be Canada.

THE PROCESS

Identifying a Market Need

In the 1980s, marketing studies conducted by World Book Encyclopedia revealed that the field of home beautification was going to grow in the future. "I made a mental note at that time that the field was hot and was going to continue to be hot," suggested Bart Breighner. "I made lists of what business I could be in. Later that factor plus my more than 20 years of experience of recruiting, training, and developing direct salespeople combined to show me a way to capitalize on my assets."

In his trips to Europe, Breighner appreciated and accumulated a collection of moderately priced artworks and came to enjoy art in general. While searching for a new residence in the western suburbs of Chicago, he observed that the art that decorated people's homes was not very attractive. Often, ordinary posters served as the centerpiece of home decoration. He felt that he could provide products to the American public that would enhance their quality of life. He defined the nature of the business as "home enhancement: making homes and offices more attractive by offering beautiful, affordable pieces of artwork in the comfort of a home or office." The core of the strategy was to (1) find a need, (2) develop a product to fill it, and (3) develop a compensation system that would allow the firm to fulfill its objectives and at the same time provide above-average income for its salesforce. Entry-level participants were known as consultants. The marketing program at Artistic Impressions was based on "consultants who take pride in making homes and offices more attractive by offering beautiful, affordable art in the comfort of a home or office."

Although sales for the first year were $500,000, the company lost $120,000. The next year sales tripled to $1.5 million, doubled the next year to $3 million, were $5 million the next, and $6.5 million the next year. The company currently has recorded 91 months of consecutive increases over the previous month. Breighner anticipated doubling sales over the next 3 years.

Product

The product line featured over 375 hand-painted originals, serigraphs, lithographs, and prints with over 150 specialized framing options. The company also sold limited-edition figurines and collector plates. These items were illustrated in a 100-page company catalog.

Artistic Impressions featured art from thousands of artists around the world. It also sold a broad spectrum of art created by artists that the company contracted on an independent basis. One popular creator of Americana renderings was H. Hargrove. The company also sold ethnic and religious art, such as the works of Aaron Hicks and R. Williams, in addition to other areas of popular interest. The company felt this art appealed to a diverse audience, but the primary appeal, however, was to African-Americans and other ethnic groups.

Renee DeRosa was in charge of product development. She attended art shows around the country, and artists contacted her about their work. A product committee reviewed the art to evaluate market potential. The committee also worked with regional managers to identify regional tastes. Customer tastes and preferences filtered up from the field to the product committee, which made the marketing decision. Committee members followed trends in decorating, color schemes, and styles, noting that what was popular in California might not be in New York.

Artistic Impressions' management published new catalog supplements periodically to introduce new products. The 1998 catalog supplement showed several examples of a new process, developed by the company, called *stochastic reproduction.* It is a technique for producing tones and colors with sharper and clearer imaging. It allowed colors and images to "jump off the canvas" and provide a "lifelike appearance." The 1998 catalog supplement showed several examples of this new process.

According to Breighner:

> We were in business only two years when a Korean-American, who was in the forefront of replicating painting on canvas from original oil paintings, came to work for Artistic. We started producing paintings on canvas, what we call lithographic canvas. That was the key. It revolutionized our business. Some people call them prints on canvas, because they're reproductions from an original oil painting. We also developed a studio and hired some foreign artists—Koreans, Chinese, and Russian. We have the technol-

ogy to reproduce the same abstract painting over and over.

Promotion
• • • • • • • •

The marketing system of Artistic Impressions was made up of approximately 2700 salespeople who operated in more than 40 states. In 1997, representatives of the company conducted over 40,000 art shows. They arranged with hosts to invite friends, relatives, and acquaintances into living rooms to view 60 or more paintings, many of which were the original artwork. Guests were prescreened before each show to identify their personal art interests. This meant that from the thousands of paintings in the company's inventory, each home show was customized to the guests. Consultants can request any type of artwork. If a hostess wants burgundies and greens, contemporary works, he or she is sent 20 to 30 paintings with these color schemes.

The consultant arrived at the host's home and displayed the artwork on an easel with up to 40 framed samples. Following the show, the guests, often including both husbands and wives, had an opportunity to purchase the paintings. Five to 10 people is the typical show. The presentation is about an hour long. Future hosts were often selected from guests at the show. Hosts were eligible to purchase paintings from the company's product line at substantial discounts.

A consultant can make up to $40 to $50 an hour for a show. The hostess gets 10 percent of the show's sales, which average $1000—$100 off a piece of artwork. If two of his or her guests ask to do a show in the future, he or she get another $100 off another piece of artwork for each hostess. The typical art consultant who worked one night a week earned more than $10,000 a year. Special incentives to motivate associates included discounts on art, prizes, and trips to London, Switzerland, Hawaii, and Acapulco, Mexico. Commissions for consultants started at 22 percent and increased, depending on sales volume.

"The consultants get about $8000 in inventory they can use and trade every week through resupply to get new paintings for the shows. Our consultants do nothing more than set up shows, sell, get the commission, and recruit more people, and we take care of the other aspects of the business," noted Thompson-Widmer.

The corporate sales training program, called The System Works, was provided free to consultants by corporate management. Sales consultants were encouraged to qualify for management opportunities by recruiting others to become consultants. In this multilevel organization, consultants were eligible to initially become sales directors after recruiting three people as consultants. As sales directors, they earned commissions and bonuses on sales made by their new recruits. "The sales director gets an override, a percentage payback for training the consultants under them. The override increases with each level. We always pay four levels down," noted Thompson-Widmer. "Everything is based on current production, team building, and team sales volume." The first level of management was the sales director. At the next level was the regional manager. The regional manager supervised two sales directors. A regional manager with a team of two sales directors and 24 consultants scheduling, on average, two weekly shows each can earn in excess of $50,000 annually. Some of the senior managers supervise up to several hundred independent contractors. The next level, zone manager, included two regions with 12 people each plus 6 people under them plus the individual. The top level was the executive manager, who supervised four zones in the hierarchy: consultants, sales directors, regional managers, and zone managers. Commission and bonuses increased as one moved up the hierarchy. In 1998, the salesforce was primarily African-American. It was headed by Cedric Hill, also an African-American, who was president of the sales division. Before joining the Artistic Impressions' management team, Hill was an aerospace engineer who worked at NASA. Hill and his team generated $8 million worth of sales within 5 years of joining the company.

To motivate sales associates, the company held an annual convention at a hotel in the Chicago area. The 3-day event was designed as a business and networking environment. It featured a series of meetings of active consultants, team competition, new product introduction, entertainment, motivational sessions, and sales performance recognition. The artists who created the artwork sold by the company attended the convention, displaying their latest work and meeting personally with the company's representatives. Each year Artistic Impressions recognized top achievers at all levels in personal sales, number of shows given, recruiting of new consultants, etc. Attendees paid their own expenses to attend the convention. "We hold two regional meetings every year for our managers and keep training them," said Thompson-Widmer. "We also send our trainers from our corporate office to help train in the field as well. We pretty much run our business interacting with about 70 to 75 regional and zone managers. Although we send out mailings to all our representatives, our focus is to hit the regional managers."

The company did no national or regional advertising. Publicity was limited to feature stories on the company and its activities in magazines like *Black Enterprises.*

Distribution

Sales associates were not required to purchase inventory or deliver merchandise. The company shipped all products by United Parcel Service (UPS) from a distribution center adjacent to corporate headquarters in Lombard, Illinois, to the show host, who delivered them to customers. Approximately 7000 framed paintings per week were shipped to show hosts.

Price

Listed prices of artworks included the choice of frame from a basic line of 30 frames. The price range for the majority of artwork sold was $69 to $149. The company was concerned that the price of its product be kept within an affordable range for their customers. Additional charges were made if the customer chose the artwork of an upscale designer or specialized, higher-quality museum frame. Designer frames ranged from $10 to $30 or more, depending on the size of the frame. The museum line of frames was available in only two sizes and sold for either $60 or $80. Frame liners also were available from $10 to $30, depending on the size of artwork selected. Limited editions of figurines and plates sold exclusively by Artistic Impressions started at $29.95. Some special figurines emulating original paintings also were sold by the company. One such work was "The Last Supper," created by artist R. Williams and available for $159.

Corporate Responsibility
• • • • • • • • • • • • • • • • • • •

Artistic Impressions created a partnership with the National Foundation for Teaching Entrepreneurship (NFTE). Bart Breighner served as chairman of NFTE and maintained that it was important to "donate your talents as well as money to organizations of this type." He had raised over $500,000 in the last 5 years for NFTE. NFTE provided entrepreneurial and motivational training for inner-city youth and provided a practical plan for exiting poverty. Breighner planned to sponsor about 12 summer camps that offered a free camp to inner-city youth from up to a dozen cities throughout the country. Artistic Impressions was also honored with the Vision for Tomorrow award from the Direct Selling Association in recognition of its "contribution to support and launch the careers of disadvantaged youth."

THE CHALLENGE
• •

Bart Breighner was certain that he had positioned the firm for continued success by appealing to a wider market. Others on his executive team were not so sure. They felt that the firm already was struggling in 1998, just to get 7000 mostly African-American paintings out to current customers. Some thought that any attempt to enter new markets would distract from the highly successful niche strategy that the company had developed since its inception.

Breighner concluded:

The business we're in is selling art, framed art, and we do it primarily with a party plan, the home show method. But we're going to redo the mission because frankly, we're an opportunity-driven company.

Bibliography

Artistic Impressions, Inc., Catalog Supplement, 1998.

Artistic Impressions, Inc., "Share the Exciting World of Art," company sales brochure, 1998.

Breighner, Bart, *Face to Face Selling* (Indianapolis: Park Avenue Publications, 1995).

Breighner, Bart, Interview with Founder and President, Artistic Impressions, Inc., Lombard, Illinois, May 12, 1998.

Kuratko, Donald F., and Richard M. Hodgetts, *Entrepreneurship: A Contemporary Approach* (Fort Worth: The Dryden Press, 1998).

Pride, William M., and O. C. Ferrell, *Marketing: Concepts and Strategies* (Boston: Houghton Mifflin, 1993).

Thompson-Widmer, Deborah, Interview with Director of Promotion and Communications, Artistic Impressions, Inc., Lombard Illinois, May 12, 1998.

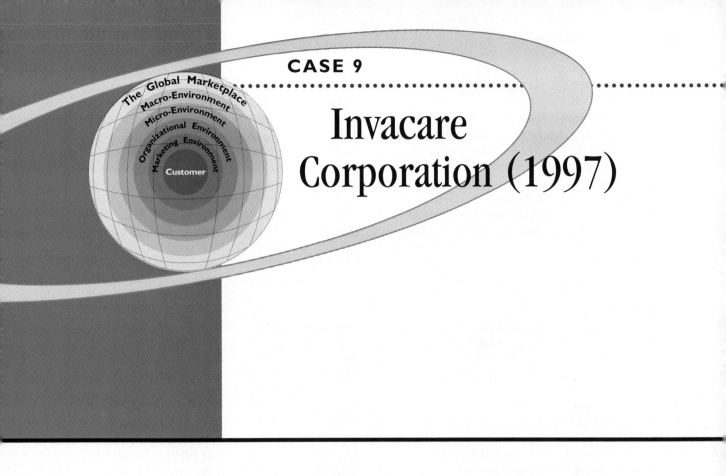

CASE 9

Invacare Corporation (1997)

This case was prepared by Walter E. Greene, Professor of Strategic Management and International Business, The University of Texas Pan American, Edinburg.

If you only had $10,000, would you try to raise $7.8 million? Malachi Mixon did just that to buy Invacare from Johnson & Johnson in 1979.

BACKGROUND

Invacare goes back a long way—112 years to be precise. The company's roots go back to the year 1885, when the Worthington Company of Elyria, Ohio, began producing "vehicles" designed for the physically handicapped.

The Worthington Company merged with a manufacturer of rubber tire wheels and casters in the early 1900s, at which time the company name changed to Colson Company. The Colson Company

became a major supplier of bicycles and placed little emphasis on the wheelchair product. When the Colson Company moved its headquarters in 1952, three of its employees purchased the wheelchair operations and renamed the company Mobilaid, Inc.

By 1960, Mobilaid, Inc., had annual sales of $150,000 and employed 15 individuals. It continued to grow modestly during the 1960s and was acquired in 1970 by Technicare Incorporated (Technicare), which renamed Mobilaid, Inc., as Invacare Corporation (Invacare) in 1971. Technicare focused most of its resources in the medical diagnostic imaging field and indeed became a leading manufacturer of such equipment. Invacare continued to grow at a modest rate, but with little direction and not much in the way of new products.

Technicare was acquired by medical giant Johnson & Johnson in 1978, and a decision was made to sell off Invacare, a relatively small and obscure part of then Technicare.

This case was originally prepared under a Department of Education Grant to the University of Tulsa International Management Center for case development. Copyright by Professor Greene.

INVACARE UNDER MIXON

Mal Mixon was then a manager at Technicare in charge of marketing computed tomographic (CT) scanners. Mixon, then 39, became very interested in acquiring Invacare; however, the asking price for it was $7.8 million. Mixon, though he had only $10,000 to invest, was not dismayed by the large asking price. Mixon knew that there was a strong growth potential for the home health care industry. Mixon convinced two real estate brokers to purchase the facility for $2 million, thereby reducing the asking price to $5.8 million. Mixon further assembled and convinced a group of Cleveland investors to purchase $1.3 million in both preferred and common shares. He was then able to secure a commitment from First Chicago Bank to lend the company $4.3 million, which note was later transferred to National City Bank. Mixon invested his $10,000, borrowed $40,000 from two personal friends, and borrowed from the company $100,000 to come up with the approximate difference of the asking price. Mixon accomplished a leveraged buyout that many would not consider feasible. However, there were some disadvantages to this leveraged buyout, namely, the high cost of the debt and equity. The bank loan was secured at a rate of 3 points over prime, which at that time in December of 1979 equated to a rate of about 20 percent.

The buyout was structured in such a way that Mixon retained a 15 percent interest in Invacare. In 1979, Invacare's sales were about $19 million, and net earnings after acquisition costs were approximately $100,000. At the time, Invacare employed about 350 individuals. In the first year of operations under Mixon, the profits of Invacare, which were about $1.4 million, were drained off by the high cost of debt. To add further to the obstacles of the company in its first year(s) were several well-established competitors, primarily Everest & Jennings, a California-based home health care company that had more than 80 percent of the wheelchair market.

Mixon's strategy was first to concentrate on the company's employees, who were demoralized and had little incentive for staying with a company that was going nowhere fast. Mixon concentrated on the sales personnel by going out himself to make sales or accompanying sales personnel on sales vis-

its. Mixon told his sales staff often that they would someday be number one in the industry. Mixon also brought in some key personnel with experience that enabled the company to begin to grow slowly.

Mixon studied Invacare's product lines and eliminated those which he considered obsolete or unprofitable. In January of 1981, Invacare entered the home care bed business with the acquisition of a small start-up company in Sanford, Florida. Also in 1981, Invacare followed a growth strategy by expanding its product line by entering the respiratory business through the acquisition of Prime Air, Inc., a manufacturer of oxygen concentrators in Hartford, Connecticut. This operation was later moved to the Cleveland Street facility in Elyria, Ohio, in 1985. (See Exhibit A for a list of acquisitions.) Sales and earnings continued to grow through the early 1980s, and by the end of 1983, Invacare had sales of $70 million and earnings of $2.8 million. (See Exhibits B and C for the latest financial data.) At that time, wheelchair sales still comprised about 50 percent of Invacare's total sales. In the first quarter of 1984, Invacare announced its first public stock offering, which was completed successfully by the end of May 1984 and raised $15 million on the issuance of 1.5 million shares.

INVACARE FOREIGN OPERATIONS

In April of 1984, Invacare obtained its first foothold in Europe through the acquisitions of Carters, Ltd., a leading United Kingdom manufacturer of wheelchairs and patient aids since 1850, and also by acquiring Gunter & Meier, a West German wheelchair manufacturer. Carters' principal products were similar to those marketed by Invacare.

As part of the 1984 transaction, Invacare also acquired substantially all the assets and business of the U.S. affiliate of Carters, Rajowalt/Carters, located in Atwood, Indiana. Rajowalt produced splints and other orthopedic equipment used in the treatment of bone fractures.

The home health care market in Europe was different in several aspects from that in the United States. In most European countries, socialized medicine was the norm; consequently, governments were the largest single customers of home health

EXHIBIT A
....
List of Acquisitions

Date Firm Acquired	Acquisitions Product	Sales (When Listed)	No. of Employees (When Listed)
1979 Technicare (Invacare)	Wheelchairs	$19.5 million	350
1981 Home Bed Care	Home beds		
1981 Prime Air, Inc.	Oxygen concentrators		
1984 Carters, Ltd.	Wheelchairs		
1984 Gunter & Meier	Wheelchairs	$.25 million	
1988 Invamex	Wheelchairs		
1991 Canadian Posture & Seating Centre, Inc.		$1.2 million	
1991 Canadian Wheelchair Manufacturing, Ltd.		$6.0 million	50
1992 Hovis Medical	Home medical equipment		60
1992 Perry Oxygen Systems	Oxygen systems		
1992 Cofipar/Poirier, S.A.	Wheelchairs	$57.3 million	
1993 Top End	Athletic wheelchairs		
1993 Dynamic Control, Ltd.	Wheelchairs	$305 million	150
1993 Geomarine Systems, Inc.	Low-air-loss therapy systems	$4–5 million	
1994 Beram, AB	Wheelchairs		
1994 Patient Solutions, Inc.	Ambulatory infusion pumps		
1994 Rehadap, S.A.	Wheelchairs		
1994 Genus Medical, Inc.	Motorized wheelchairs		
1995 Special Health Systems	Wheelchair seating		
1995 Medical Equipment Repair Service	Aftermarket oxygen Parts and repairs		
1995 Paratec, AG	Wheelchairs		
1995 Group Pharmaceutical, Ltd.	Wheelchair distributor		
1995 Thompson Rehab	Wheelchairs		
1995 Bencraft, Ltd.	Wheelchairs and seating		
1995 Patient Solutions	Ambulatory infusion pumps		
1995 PinDot Products	Custom seating systems		

Note: All 1995 acquisitions completed for approximately $31 million in cash without increasing debt-to-equity ratio, which remains 0.6 to 1.

Source: Invacare reports.

care products. The rental market in countries with socialized medicine was virtually nonexistent, with a resulting market oriented more toward price than durability. In some European countries, such as West Germany, the market was strongly geared toward quality and product features. The European market also was dominated by several companies, each of which possessed particular strengths in one or more countries.

The European market was characterized by a distribution network that relied on direct government outlets and on some independent medical

EXHIBIT B

Consolidated Balance Sheet: Invacare Corporation and Subsidiaries

	December 31				
	1995	1994	1993	1992	1991
Assets (in thousands)					
Current assets					
Cash and cash equivalents	$4,132	$7,359	$9,392	$8,181	$1,472
Marketable securities	2,437	3,044	4,155	2,533	1,723
Trade receivables, net	93,592	76,280	63,286	66,293	51,006
Investment in installment recbls., net	37,074	33,723	26,173	18,606	13,972
Inventories	54,468	49,982	44,011	47,875	42,217
Other current assets	6,831	4,088	3,590	4,357	4,648
Deferred income taxes	6,151	5,959	5,584	4,089	4,776
Total current assets	204,685	180,435	156,191	151,934	119,814
Other assets	36,581	28,840	17,341	9,059	4,897
Property and equipment, net	65,078	55,919	52,480	51,040	35,260
Goodwill, net	102,406	72,915	60,355	50,379	2,378
Total assets	$408,750	$338,109	$286,367	$262,412	$162,349
Liabilities and shareholders' equity					
Current liabilities					
Accounts payable	$33,805	$29,882	$23,267	$30,836	$15,947
Accrued expenses	45,097	34,234	32,623	39,063	22,946
Accrued income taxes	5,821	3,225	4,508	2,065	2,267
Current maturities long-term obligation	213	326	515	422	896
Total current liabilities	84,936	67,667	60,913	72,386	42,056
Long-term obligations	122,456	105,528	90,351	74,488	31,795
Deferred income taxes	39	907	141	1,538	1,788
Shareholders' equity					
Preferred shares	0	0	0	0	0
Common shares	6,148	5,573	5,192	5,004	4,522
Class B common shares	1,243	1,767	2,084	2,225	2,323
Additional paid-in capital	66,890	63,671	61,709	59,666	45,728
Retained earnings	130,100	99,086	73,242	51,132	33,393
Adjustment to shareholders' equity	993	(2,196)	(3,570)	(1,671)	(1,294)
Treasury stock	(4,055)	(3,894)	(3,695)	(2,356)	(550)
Total Shareholders' equity	201,319	164,007	134,962	114,000	86,710
Total liabilities and shareholders' equity	$408,750	$338,109	$286,367	$262,412	$162,349

Source: Invacare Annual Reports.

EXHIBIT C

Selected Financial Data: Invacare Corporation and Subsidiaries

(In thousands, except per share and ratio data)	1995	1994	1993	1992	1991	1990	1989
Earnings							
Net sales	$504,032	$411,123	$365,457	$305,171	$263,181	$229,797	$186,055
Income from operations	54,144	43,736	36,870	27,567	23,628	16,750	8,823
Net earnings	32,165	26,377	22,110	17,739	14,128	7,610	2,628
Net earnings per share	1.07	0.89	0.75	0.63	0.53	0.33	0.23
Dividends per common share	.03750	.01875	.000	.00	.00	.00	.00
Other data							
R&D expenditures	$9,002	$7,651	$6,840	$5,251	$4,518	$3,343	$3,322
Capital expenditures, net of disposals	11,027	12,217	11,961	17,301	11,396	8,600	10,828
Depreciation and amortization	14,159	12,686	12,280	10,008	8,073	6,603	4,992
Key ratios							
Return on sales	6.4%	6.4%	6.0%	5.8%	5.4%	3.3%	1.4%
Return on average assets	8.6%	8.4%	6.0%	8.4%	9.4%	5.8%	2.3%
Return on beginning shareholders equity	19.6%	19.5%	19.4%	20.5%	33.7%	23.7%	8.7%
Current ratio	2.4:1	2.7:1	2.6:1	2.2:1	2.8:1	2.4:1	3.1:1
Debt-to-equity ratio	.6:1	.6:1	.7:1	.7:1	.4:1	1.2:1	1.8:1

Source: Invacare Annual Reports.

equipment dealers. As the home health care equipment industry continued to develop, the roles of the medical equipment dealers were expected to strengthen.

Present foreign plant locations and products included Wales, patient aids and wheelchairs; Porta Germany, Gunter Meier GMB II, wheelchairs and patient aids; and Reynosa, Mexico, wheelchairs. Wheelchairs and orthopedic soft goods were manufactured in the Atwood, Indiana, facility of Rajowalt. In January 1988, Invacare began operations of its newly constructed maquiladora plant (a 78,000-square-foot manufacturing facility in Reynosa, Mexico, across the border from McAllen, Texas), named Invamex. This manufacturing plant enabled Invacare to manufacture low-cost manual wheelchairs that could compete with other foreign competitors from the Far East. In October 1991, Invacare acquired Canadian Posture & Seating Centre, Inc., a Kitchner, Ontario, maker of seating and positioning products, with annual sales of about $1.2 million. Also in October 1991, Invacare acquired Canadian Wheelchair Manufacturing, Ltd., which had annual sales of about $6 million. In August 1992, Invacare acquired Perry Oxygen Systems, a small manufacturer of liquid oxygen and oxygen delivery systems located in Port St. Lucie, Florida, whose operations were transferred to the Sanford, Florida, facility. On October 15, 1992, Invacare completed the acquisition of Poirier S.A., France's largest manufacturer and distributor of wheelchairs and other home medical products. This acquisition was made with a combination of cash and common stock for a total consideration of approximately $57.3 million. Poirier's sales for the fiscal year 1992 were $45 million, and its earnings exceeded $3 million.[1]

In August 1994, Invacare purchased all the outstanding shares of Rehadap S.A., a Spanish marketer and distributor of precision wheelchairs and other rehabilitation products for people with disabilities. In November 1994, the company purchased all the outstanding shares of Genus Medical, Inc., a manufacturer of power positioning seating systems for motorized wheelchairs and electric three- and four-wheeled scooters. In March 1993, Invacare purchased the assets of Top End, a manufacturer of specialty products for sports and recreational use for people with physical disabilities. In June 1993, Invacare acquired for cash all the shares

of Dynamic Controls Limited, a manufacturer of control systems for power-drive wheelchairs, and in July 1993 acquired Geomarine Systems, Inc., a manufacturer of low-air-loss therapy systems.

In October 1992, Invacare purchased all the outstanding shares of Gofipar/Poirier Group for approximately $57,341,000. Poirier manufactures and distributes wheelchairs and home medical products in France and other European Economic Community countries.

During 1995, Invacare completed eight acquisitions. On May 5, 1995, it acquired PinDot Products, a Northbrook, Illinois, designer, manufacturer, and distributor of contour custom seating systems under Contour U, Silhouette, and Performance brand names. On May 25, 1995, Invacare acquired Patient Solutions, of San Diego, a manufacturer of ambulatory infusion pumps, a new product category that expanded Invacare's product offering. Then, on June 6, 1995, it acquired Bencraft Limited, of Birmingham, England, a manufacturer of wheelchairs and designer and manufacturer of specialty seating systems that complemented its existing distribution in the United Kingdom.

On June 29, 1995, Invacare acquired Thompson Rehab, of Auckland, New Zealand, a manufacturer and distributor of manual and power wheelchairs. This gave Invacare a major market share position in New Zealand and a potential manufacturing base for the Australian market. On September 9, 1995, Invacare acquired Group Pharmaceutical Limited (GP Health Care), of Auckland, New Zealand, marketer and distributor of Invacare prescription wheelchairs and other rehabilitation products, giving Invacare direct control over distribution and further expansion in the Pacific Basin.

On September 13, 1995, Invacare acquired Paratec AG, of Basel, Switzerland, a manufacturer of sports active wheelchairs sold under the Juschall name, strengthening its custom lightweight wheelchair product offering throughout Europe. On September 22, 1995, it acquired Medical Equipment Repair Service (MERS), of Sarasota, Florida, an aftermarket oxygen concentrator parts and repair service and supplier of other related respiratory equipment, complementing their aftermarket part's business by expanding its respiratory presence. Finally, on November 22, 1995, Invacare acquired Special Health Systems, of Ontario, Canada, a designer and manufacturer of planar seating and positioning systems for wheelchairs. With this acquisition, Invacare had the ability to be a full-line supplier of cushions, contour seating, and planar seating systems.

INVAMEX

In 1987, Invacare began construction of Invamex. Startup was accomplished during the second half of 1988, and in the third quarter, the first wheelchairs were shipped from Invamex. This manufacturing plant enabled Invacare to manufacture low-cost manual wheelchairs that could compete with other foreign competitors from the Far East.

Invamex paid its Mexican workers $3.70 per day, slightly above the minimum wage in Mexico. Mandated benefits in Mexico were approximately 60 percent of pay. Invamex also provided retirement benefits, vacations, and health and life insurance for its Mexican workers. In addition to wages and benefits, Invamex provided other amenities for its employees, such as food stamps, uniforms, and transportation to and from work. A nurse and doctor were always available at the plant.

Invamex was highly dependent on an ample water supply. Approximately 68 thousand gallons were used daily in operations. During the severe drought over the summer of 1996, operations were threatened but not curtailed. Raw materials were shipped from Ohio. Plans called for enlargement of the plant from 78,000 square feet to twice that amount within a 3- to 5-year period.

In 1988, the border facility was producing some 150 wheelchairs per day with 136 employees. By 1990, Invamex had increased production to 180 wheelchairs per day and employed some 200 workers.

A MAJOR SETBACK

In 1984, Invacare suffered a major financial setback, posting a loss on sales of $91 million. The major reasons were nonrecurring charges against income, which included an adjustment for inventory that was carried on the books but which the company did not physically have on hand. The other major cause was a recall of a defective product that cost the company an estimated $1.5 million. On the heels of the financial setback, the U.S. government changed its Medicare reimbursement policy, which essentially required wheelchair dealers to sell more of their chairs outright rather than to lease them. This caused the dealers' income to drop because many of the motorized wheelchairs were too expensive for Medicare recipients and too costly for the dealers to finance themselves.

By the end of 1985, Invacare had restored profitability. Invacare cut costs by reorganizing its divisions and introducing new products that began to have an impact in the market. For example, in 1985 Invacare introduced the first power wheelchairs designed specifically for a child's use. Until then, the industry had offered children's seats fitted on a larger, adult-size base.

STRUCTURE

Invacare was highly centralized, with its headquarters located in Elyria, Ohio.[2] Invacare had a unique organizational structure that combined the benefits of both centralized and decentralized operations. Its internal structure consisted of four focused operating groups worldwide. Each group consisted of several dedicated business units. Externally, Invacare had one "face to the customer" because products were sold through a single domestic sales and service organization with complete account responsibility. The company's executive officers are listed in Exhibit D.

During 1995, Invacare made several important changes to strengthen its management team and realign responsibilities in a way that would provide for future growth. Domestic operations were reorganized into a business unit to further decentralize and push decision making down to lower levels and to enable more rapid market response. Invacare realigned its management organization into three operating groups reporting to its chief operating officer, Mr. Gerry Blouch. The three groups were Rehab Products, headed by Lou Tabickman, Standard Products, headed by Tom Buckley, and Respiratory Products, directed by Don Anderson.

Invacare's manufacturing plants were headed by the plant manager, and the plant's financial and cost accounting functions were headed by the local controller, who along with the plant manager was in charge of local budgeting. The distribution

EXHIBIT D
....
Invacare Executive Officers

Board of Directors	Executive Committee
1. A. Malachi Mixon, III (3) (4), Chairman of the Board of Directors, President and Chief Executive Officer	1. A. Malachi Mixon, III
2. Joseph B. Richey, II President, Invacare Technologies, Senior VP, Total Quality Management	2. Joseph B. Richey, II
3. Francis J. Callahan (2) (3), President, Crawford Fitting Co.	3. Gerald B. Blouch, Chief Operating Officer
4. Frank B. Carr (1) (4), Managing Director of Investment, General Banking, McDonald & Co. Corporate Secretary	4. Thomas R. Miklich, Chief Financial Officer, Securities Council, Treasurer and
5. Michael F. Delaney (2) (4), Associate Director of Development, Standard Products	5. Thomas J. Buckley, Group Vice President, Paralyzed Veterans of America
6. Whitney Evans (2) (4), private investor	6. Benoit Juranville, President, Invacare Europe
7. Dan T. Moore, III (1) (3), President, Dan T. Moore Co.	7. Richard A. Sayers II, VP, Human Resources
8. E. P. Nalley (1) (4), retired senior VP	8. Louis F. J. Slangen, Senior VP, Sales & Marketing
9. William M. Weber (1) (2), President, Roundwood Capita	9. M. Louis Tabickman, Gp. VP, Rehab Products

Committees: (1) audit, (2) compensation, (3) nominating, (4) investment.

Source: Invacare Annual Report.

centers also were headed by a local manager, and inventory and distribution controls were the responsibility of both the manager and the local controller, who performed similar functions as the manufacturing plant controller in terms of budgeting and financing. The company employed a just-in-time inventory method with respect to its inventory stock (however, most plants maintained a 30- to 45-day inventory). As of December 31, 1995, the company had approximately 3293 employees in 16 manufacturing locations. While Invacare had managed to work successfully with its employees and had no unions to contend with in the United States, this was not the case in the European market, where the labor forces were well organized. Up to now it has had very little

interference from the European organized labor forces primarily because of the sluggish worldwide economy. Future labor negotiations may be an important measure of how successful Invacare will perform in the European market.

Invacare issued annual audited consolidated financial statements in accordance with regulations established by the Securities and Exchange Commission. All its accounting was compiled through use of an on-line computer networking system, since such current information could be provided to its readers as soon as the transmitted information was compiled. The consolidated financial statements included the accounts of Invacare Corporation and its subsidiaries. European subsidiaries were consolidated using a November 30 fiscal year-end. All significant intercompany transactions were eliminated. Substantially all the assets and liabilities of the company's foreign subsidiaries were translated to U.S. dollars at year-end exchange rates.[3] See Exhibit E for financial data by business segments.

PRODUCTS

Invacare manufactured and distributed prescription power and manual wheelchairs, standard wheelchairs, respiratory equipment, hospital-type beds for the home, patient aids, motorized scoot-

EXHIBIT E

Selected Financial Data: Invacare Business Segments

(In thousands)	Domestic	Other North America	Total North America	Europe	Total
1995					
Net sales	$353,340	$34,154	$387,494	$116,538	$504,032
Earning before income taxes	46,930	(2,842)	44,088	7,757	51,845
Assets	227,003	56,974	283,977	124,773	408,750
Liabilities	96,129	43,718	139,847	67,584	207,431
1994					
Net sales	$293,790	27,774	321,564	89,559	411,123
Earning before income taxes	39,742	(885)	38,857	3,020	41,877
Assets	204,715	31,582	236,297	101,812	338,109
Liabilities	87,691	28,566	116,257	57,845	174,102
1993					
Net sales	$261,337	21,638	282,975	82,482	365,457
Earning before income taxes	31,681	1,057	32,738	772	33,510
Assets	172,235	25,186	198,421	87,946	286,367
Liabilities	73,880	19,604	93,484	57,921	151,405
1992					
Net sales	$224,349	61,143	19,679	80,822	305,171
Earning before income taxes	25,636	1,761	161	1,922	27,558
Assets	151,735	101,958	8,719	110,677	262,412
Liabilities	93,364	47,860	7,188	55,048	148,412

Note: The company operated in one business segment, home medical equipment. Geographic information for each of the four years ended December 31 is included here.

The operations of the company's Mexican facility are treated as Domestic for segment reporting purposes. Substantially all the products manufactured at the Mexican facility are sold to customers located in the United States.

The results of the company's Canadian and New Zealand operations were included in Other North American for segment reporting purposes. A significant portion of the New Zealand operations is components for products manufactured by the company's North American facilities.

Eliminated from above net sales for 1995, 1994, and 1993 were $11,296,000, $6,922,000, and $6,128,000, respectively, of sales by North American subsidiaries to European subsidiaries and $1,005,000, $575,000, and $761,000, respectively, of sales by European subsidiaries to North American subsidiaries. Sales between geographic areas are based on the costs to manufacture plus a reasonable profit element.

Source: Invacare Annual Reports.

ers, and other home health care and extended care equipment. By 1996, Invacare had manufacturing locations in Ohio, Florida, Texas, California, Canada, Mexico, Great Britain, Germany, and France. Its products are distributed through a worldwide network of more than 10,000 medical equipment dealers, including more than 3500 domestic dealers.

One key to the success of Invacare over the past 18 years has been its commitment to product development and technological improvements. In 1991 the company introduced more than 75 new products or enhancements of existing products in the United States. In 1992, Invacare introduced 26 new products or enhancements, a substantial decline from 1991, primarily attributed to new product delays that would be introduced in 1993. Research and development (R&D) expenditures had been running at about 2 percent of sales. In 1991 total R&D expenditures totaled approximately $4.5 million. The number two manufacturer of home health care products was Sunrise Medical, with worldwide sales of about $185 million. See Exhibit F for a list of competitors' products.

Wheelchairs represented about 61 percent of Invacare's total annual sales in 1992. The standard wheelchairs were generally purchased by older people and therefore usually reimbursed by

Medicare. They were regarded as a commodity item and therefore a price-driven type of sale. The general price range could be from about $350 to $1000. The power wheelchairs were Invacare's most attractive product line. The company lead the U.S. market with more than a 50 percent share. Power wheelchairs were purchased by people with more severe disabilities than those who purchase manual wheelchairs. Typically, users were quadriplegics who had some motor skills in at least one arm. The power wheelchair was usually controlled by a joystick, which accelerates, turns, and stops the chair. The user must have enough control in his or her arm to operate the joystick; if not, more sophisticated "sip and puff" controls are used. Invacare was the only manufacturer who designed and manufactured its own controllers (an electronic microprocessor that controls the chairs movements). Invacare had started in May of 1991 to manufacture its Action line of wheelchairs. These ultralight wheelchairs were the second-fastest growing segment of the market. Ultralight wheelchairs generally were purchased by younger, active users with permanent disabilities. These chairs allowed people with disabilities to play sports and were used in the 1996 para-Olympic games in Atlanta, Georgia. They were light by any wheelchair

EXHIBIT F

Wheelchair Competition: Major Products by Name

Invacare	E&J	Hoyer	Theradyne	Gendron
World Chair Current	Traveler	2000	Maxim "Max"	Regency Transporter 5825
1000 E	Vista	1000	Maxim "Mac"	Economy 8555
1000	Traveler	2000	Maxim "Max"	Regency Transporter 5825
1000 HEMI	Universal	N/A	Maxim "Hemi"	Lowboy Hemi
World Chair Economy	Vista	1000	Maxim "Mac"	Economy 8555
2000 Series	E-Z-Lite	(Sunrise) Quickie Breezy	Envoy	2058 QR
9000 Series	Premier 2	(Sunrise) Quickie RX	Venture	Sportlife 4000
2000 LT	Premier 2	(Sunrise) Quickie Breezy	Thunderbird	2058 QR
4000 Series	Universal	N/A	Envoy	X2 Series

standard and allowed users greater mobility. They were generally made of aluminum. However, the latest advancements in materials had enabled the production of carbon composite frames, which were lighter than the then current frames.

Invacare's home health beds accounted for about 12 percent of the company's total annual sales in 1992. They were specifically designed to aid persons with disabilities that prohibit or limit their movement. In this regard, Invacare was using the latest advancements in seating and cushions being put out by its Canadian subsidiary, Posture & Seating Centre, Inc.

Invacare's respiratory equipment accounted for about 16 percent of the company's total annual sales in 1992. Until 1992, Invacare sold only oxygen concentrators, representing a $150 million market. During 1992, the company introduced an expanded line of respiratory equipment and accessories, including nebulizers and aspirators. With the acquisition of Perry Oxygen Systems, Invacare introduced its liquid oxygen line, which will place it in a market with $450 million in annual sales. Respiratory products are heavily dependent on Medicare, since most patients are elderly.

Invacare's other products were placed under a general category of patient aids. Invacare's patient aids accounted for about 14 percent of the company's total annual sales in 1992. These products included walkers, crutches, commodes, bath rails, patient lifts, traction equipment, standard and power recliner chairs, and other home health aids. Most patient aid products were regarded as commodities.[4]

DISTRIBUTION

Early on after Invacare was acquired by the Mixon group, marketing of its products became a priority. In a competitive field that was dominated by E&J, Mixon's strategy was to become dealer-oriented. That is, in an industry that was influenced not so much by a doctor, but rather by a therapist or the dealer, Mixon began a strategy to win over the dealers, because they were for the most part the representatives of the home health medical equipment market. In the early years, contacts and product orientation were about all the company could offer the dealers because of the high costs of the leveraged buyout, so it stockpiled inventory. In 1984, when the first public stock offering was completed

successfully, Invacare had the needed capital to begin the implementation of its final strategy on dealer orientation. Invacare began an aggressive distribution strategy of offering dealers prepaid freight, 48-hour delivery, cheap financing, money for cooperative advertising, and volume discounts—a strategy of marketing saturation it had always tried to follow but had never implemented with the aggressiveness that it could now afford. Dealers became very familiar with Invacare's products because of the more available financing, volume discounts, etc. Invacare had 22 distribution centers worldwide that were serviced by 150 company salespersons, 24 telemarketing employees, and 4 independent representative organizations.[5]

During 1995, Invacare entered the retail distribution channels. Invacare kept its Invacare, Action, and PinDot brands exclusively for the HME (home medical equipment) provider channel. In early 1996, Invacare acquired Frohock-Stewart, Inc., a manufacturer of personal care products located in Northboro, Massachusetts. This acquisition permitted Invacare for the first time to offer a complete range of off-the-shelf home health care products through the retail distribution channel that will have no association with the Invacare, Action, and PinDot brands.

ONE-STOP SHOPPING PLUS

Invacare's basic product strategies were simple: make its products the most attractive products for HME dealers. Invacare was known for its one-stop shopping marketing strategy. Invacare was the only manufacturer committed to being the one source for the approximately 3500 home health care and medical equipment dealers in the United States. Invacare distributed approximately 85 percent of what dealers needed. In 1992, Invacare began its One-Stop Shopping Plus, a program that provided discounts to dealers as their percentage of sales exceeded 65 percent of Invacare products. As dealers step up through the percentage breakpoint (65 percent), the program amounts to an exclusive distribution agreement with Invacare for the dealer in that area.[6] The company had 100 dealers signed up for the program. Invacare had shown a concern for the bottom line of its dealers and had thus enjoyed a continued loyalty from many of those dealers. This strategy pushed product lines of Invacare that could be sold on the basis of value (standard wheelchairs, beds, etc.) rather than on the basis of premium price—quality (ultralight wheelchairs, highly complex motorized wheelchairs, etc.). Invacare began an advertising campaign in 1992 to create a "pull" demand from end users and clinical professionals such as therapists. The one-stop shopping concept was extended to Invacare's European operations during 1995. In addition, Invacare earned ISO 9000 certification in its manufacturing plants in France, Sweden, and the United Kingdom. Germany is anticipated to receive this certification during early 1997. Invacare's goal is to have all North American manufacturing facilities ISO 9000-certified by the end of 1997.

COMPETITION

Domestic.   The home health care industry was quickly becoming a sector of the haves and have nots. Former giants like Everest & Jennings International (E&J) continued to struggle and lose market share, while small manufacturers suffered from a lack of distribution as dealers remained cautious in dealing with companies they were not sure would survive.

A large portion of Invacare's market share success had come at the expense of E&J, which once controlled about 85 percent of the total wheelchair market. E&J continued to suffer operating losses, but its brand name retained a strong following, and its Smith & Davis bed business remained profitable. E&J had restructured its debt, but financial difficulties continued. E&J had suffered losses of about $120 million in the last 4 years (about $8 million in 1992). E&J began matching Invacare's price in 1985, and by 1989, there existed an all-out price war between Invacare and E&J, but the response by E&J to Invacare was late in coming. The price war drove Invacare's net margin to less than 1 percent in the wheelchair market in the second quarter of 1989, but E&J was pushed to the verge of bankruptcy.

The next significant challenge faced by Invacare came from the second largest manufacturer of wheelchairs—Sunrise Medical, a California-based subsidiary of Hoyer International and Japanese manufacturers of home health care products. Sun-

rise had been very successful in the manual ultralight wheelchair market. Invacare itself entered that market in May of 1991 with the introduction of its Action wheelchair line. Sunrise Medical had more than 60 percent of the ultralight wheelchair market in the United States. Sunrise also competed with Invacare in other home health care product segments such as beds. However, it concentrated primarily on the domestic market it controlled—ultralight wheelchairs—and as such was not viewed as a serious competitor in areas other than wheelchairs and patient aids. While Invacare had more than 50 percent of the U.S. home health equipment market, Sunrise did have a 30 percent domestic market share of patient aids (e.g., crutches, canes, walkers, commodes, patient lifts, etc.) as compared with Invacare's approximate 20 percent share in bed lifts.

In the area of domestic respiratory sales, Puritan-Bennett and DeVilbiss enjoyed more than 40 percent of the market. Invacare as a relative newcomer had about 8 percent of the domestic respiratory market. The acquisition of Perry Oxygen System enabled Invacare to continue to gain market share in a product line that had about $150 million in domestic sales.[7]

International.   Invacare continued to make huge inroads into the European home health care industry. With the acquisition of Poirier S.A. in 1992, Invacare was the second largest competitor in the home health care industry behind German-based giant Meyra—a privately held company. Invacare's international sales and earnings for 1992, 1993, 1994, and 1995 are summarized in Exhibit E. With the exception of Sunrise, with about $100 million in sales in 1992 in Europe, most of the European competition was focused on local markets. Invacare was establishing an infrastructure that would allow it to compete across the continent. Sunrise Medical also was solidifying its infrastructure by aggressively establishing itself in Europe—having acquired several European home health care manufacturers itself. Poirier S.A., France's largest home health care product manufacturer, sold similar products as Invacare. Poirier's sales mix was roughly 40 percent standard wheelchairs, 40 percent rehabilitation wheelchairs, and 20 percent patient aids including beds. Invacare's German subsidiary (Gunter & Meier) also was capturing market share from the giant German-based home health care product company, Meyra, as well as the second largest German home health care manufacturer, Ortopedia. Invacare capitalized on Meyra and Ortopedia's (Meyra recently acquired Ortopedia and became an even more formidable competitor) weakness of a reluctance to manufacture low-cost wheelchairs and other patient aids.

In Canada, Invacare had small competitors that competed on more of a regional basis. Its wheelchair products manufactured in Mexico were sold in both the United States and Canada primarily. With the ability to manufacture low-cost wheelchairs in Mexico, Invacare continued to dominate the standard wheelchair market with more than a 60 percent domestic market share. Exhibit F lists some of the major competitors in the home health care industry.

Mixon stated that "he isn't about to let Quickie (a subsidiary of Sunrise) do to him (Invacare) what he did to Everest & Jennings." A recent advertisement by Invacare pokes fun at its competitor by stating, "Why settle for a Quickie? Get Real Action!"[8] See Exhibit G for a comparison of Invacare's progress and sales mix.

GOVERNMENT REGULATION

While Invacare received no revenues directly from Medicare or Medicaid, a typical home medical equipment dealer generates between 40 and 50

EXHIBIT G

Invacare Sales Mix by Product Line

Then and Now: A Comparison

A group of investors including Mr. Mixon and several board members purchased Invacare from Johnson & Johnson in 1979 and have grown the company considerably since that time. This chart details the company's remarkable progress. Invacare became a public company in 1984.

	1979	*1995*
Annual sales	$19.5 million	$504.032 million
Shareholders' equity	$1.5 million	$201.319 million
Product offering line of equipment	67% standard wheelchairs, 28% patient aids and beds, 5% manual wheelchairs	World's broadest home medical equip. 36% Rehab. 22% Personal care and beds 17% Standard wheelchairs 12% Respiratory 7% Other 2% Pressure relief 2% Parts 2% Distributed products
International business	None	26.0% of sales

Invacare Sales Mix by Operating Group
Standard products 36%
Europe 23%
Rehab products 21%
Respiratory products 12%
Other 8%

Source: Invacare Annual Reports.

percent of its revenues from Medicare/Medicaid sales. Changes in Medicare/Medicaid budgets would have an effect on sales and bottom-line earnings of Invacare. One of the proposed line-item cuts in President Clinton's economic plan specified a $75 million cut in domestic home health care spending; however, the proposed cuts would focus on areas perceived as abusive, such as home infusion therapy, parental and enteral equipment, and prosthetics and orthotics, categories in which Invacare was not involved. Favorable statements were made recently by the Clinton administration in which the President's task force on national health care stated that a goal of the new long-term care program was to shift spending from nursing homes to community-based services that provided medical care and other types of assistance to people living in their own homes.

Invacare continued to be a leading home health care advocate in Washington, D.C. In addition to retaining a respected lobbyist in Washington, Invacare was an active member of all major trade associations and coalitions representing the HME industry and home health care in general.[9]

OUTLOOK

Mixon recently concluded in his annual report to the shareholders, "The long-term outlook for home health care is excellent. Recent meetings between industry representatives and the White House Task Force on Health Care Reform indicated that the Clinton administration views home care as a cost-effective alternative to institutional care. In fact, at his 1993 preinaugural economic summit, President Clinton said, 'Let's keep in-home services. . . . We can serve more people at lower cost even if we have to cut back a little on what we're doing institutionally.' Invacare will be a clear beneficiary of this policy."[10]

The company had enjoyed tremendous growth rates; in 1992, its sales rose by 16 percent over 1991 sales, while its earnings rose more than 26 percent over 1991 amounts. In 1995, Invacare had annual sales in excess of $504 million, serving an estimated $3 billion global market. Invacare had experienced a 22.5 percent compounded average sales growth rate per year since 1979. The National Association of Home Care projected that growth rates for products and related home care services will rise an average of 9 percent per year for the foreseeable 5 years commencing in 1992. During 1995, Invacare increased spending on research and development to $9 million and introduced more than 27 major new products at the Medtrade/NHHCE industry trade show. Baird Corporation estimated that revenue growth will continue in the range of 15 percent, while earnings growth will be at about 20 percent over the next few years.

Invacare Corporation had grown from a minor player in the home health care industry to the world's largest manufacturer of home health care products.

Success can be attributed to many factors, including the management of Invacare, in particular its chief executive officer, Mal Mixon, but he believed the company's success had come about because of the strategy it had always followed since 1979, which was:

1. Offer the industry's broadest product line.

2. Provide the highest levels of customer service in the industry.

3. Enhance the industry's most extensive warehouse and distribution network, and build the supporting systems to increase its efficiency.

4. Continue to build on the dealer orientation policy as well as enhance consumer demand through marketing programs.

5. Maintain the industry's most productive salesforce.

6. Be a leader in product development.

7. Maintain costs at a minimum to yield lowest cost to the consumer.

8. Above all, never lose touch with the customer.

Mixon was quoted in a recent *Forbes* article: "Everest & Jennings International had more than 80 percent of the wheelchair market, but they were arrogant and had lost touch with the customer." This is a lesson that Mixon vows never to happen to Invacare. Mixon was taking a visible role in the industry's lobbying efforts to educate the U.S. Congress about the home medical equipment industry. Despite the rhetoric, few people in Washington, D.C., have answers to health care issues, and Mixon quotes a senior policymaker in the Health Care

Financing Agency (HCFA) as saying, "You'll never convince me that taking a bath is a medical necessity."[11]

Mixon must fly to Washington, D.C., next week to give expert testimony concerning the HME industry before a congressional committee on health insurance. What, he mused, should be his next move? What issues must Invacare deal with in order to be successful in the future?

Questions

1. Evaluate the past strategy of Invacare. Will these strategies continue to work in a changing environment, especially as it pertains to domestic sales—government Medicare/Medicaid?

2. What new problems will Invacare face in the 2000s?

3. What additional factors will Invacare have to contend with in its overseas operations that it does not have in the domestic markets?

4. Evaluate Invacare's total home health care product strategy. Will some strategies in the long run eliminate all but the giant manufacturers of home health care products, or will they cause Invacare to stretch its resources (R&D) too thinly?

5. If you were an investment consultant, how would you rate the stock value prospects of Invacare over the next 4 years?

6. Can Invacare continue its lobbying efforts, and what does it need to do to win the Malcolm Baldrige National Quality Award?

Bibliography

Bendix, Jeffrey, "Invacare Rolls to #1," Enterprise Development; Weatherhead School of Management, Cleveland, Spring 1991.

Dombcik, Jerry H., "Invacare Corporation—Earnings Review and Estimate Revision," McDonald & Company Securities, Inc., Cleveland, February 22, 1993.

Emch, Peter H., "Health Care Research," Robert W. Baird & Co., Inc., Milwaukee, March 10, 1993, pp. 1–13.

Hayslett, Brenda, Telephone Interview with Human Resources, Invacare Corporation, April 12, 1993.

"Invacare Acquires Canadian Firm," *Wall Street Journal,* November 5, 1991, p. A20.

"Invacare Buys Canadian Concern," *Wall Street Journal,* October 11, 1991, p. B6.

Invacare Corporation 1991 Annual Report, Elyria, Ohio.

Invacare Corporation 1992 Annual Report, Elyria, Ohio.

Invacare Corporation 1993 Annual Report, Elyria, Ohio.

Invacare Corporation 1994 Annual Report, Elyria, Ohio.

Invacare Corporation 1995 Annual Report, Elyria, Ohio.

Invacare Corporation 1996 Annual Report, Elyria, Ohio.

Invacare Corporation 1992 Consolidated Financial Statements, Elyria, Ohio.

Invacare Corporation 1993 Consolidated Financial Statements, Elyria, Ohio.

Invacare Corporation 1994 Consolidated Financial Statements, Elyria, Ohio.

Invacare Corporation 1995 Consolidated Financial Statements, Elyria, Ohio.

"Invacare Corporation," *Wall Street Journal,* July 23, 1991, p. B9.

"Invacare Corporation—Perry Oxygen Systems," *Wall Street Journal,* August 10, 1992, p. C6.

Ledesma, Javier, Personal interview with controller of Reynosa plant, April 5, 1993.

Malkes, Lynn D., "Recommendation: Buy Progress Report," Investment Research, Roney & Co., Detroit, March 10, 1993.

Mixon, Malachi A., "The Invacare Story," Elyria, Ohio. July 1989.

Mixon, Malachi A., "A Partial Solution to the Nation's Problems with Health Care Costs," Cage University, October 23, 1992.

News from Invacare, "*Forbes* Names Invacare to 200 Best Small Companies List," Elyria, Ohio, November 4, 1992.

News from Invacare, "Invacare Adds 'Top End' to Action Wheelchair Line," Elyria, Ohio, March 4, 1993.

News from Invacare, "Invacare Completes Poirier Acquisitions," Elyria, Ohio, October 15, 1992.

News from Invacare, "Invacare Reports Record Fourth Quarter Earnings on 24 Percent Sales Gain," Elyria, Ohio, February 18, 1993.

News from Invacare, "Invacare's Support of Wheelchair Basketball Helps Slam-Dunk Outdated Perceptions," Elyria, Ohio, December 3, 1992.

Paris, Ellen, "The Perils of Being Too Successful," *Forbes,* 139(3), February 9, 1987, p. 2.

Palmeri, Christopher, "Wheel to Wheel Combat," *Forbes,* 51(4), February 15, 1993, p. 3.

Shingler, Dan, "Invacare's Record Earnings in '90 a 183% Boost from '89," *Crains Cleveland Business,* 12(9), March 4, 1991, p. 23.

Shingler, Dan, "It's the Midas Touch," *Crains Cleveland Business,* 12(42), October 21, 1991, p. 17.

Thomas, Chris, "Cities Courting Invacare to Win Headquarters," *Crains Cleveland Business,* 12(32), August 12, 1991, p. 2.

U.S. Securities and Exchange Commission, Annual Report to Section 13 or 15(D) of the Securities Exchange Act of 1934—Form 10K, Invacare Corporation for the Fiscal Year Ended December 31, 1991, Ernst & Young, Cleveland, Ohio, February 20, 1992.

U.S. Securities and Exchange Commission, Quarterly Report Under Section 13 or 15(D) of the Securities Exchange Act of 1934—Form 10Q, Invacare Corporation for the Quarter Ended September 30, 1992, Gerald B. Blouch, Vice President and General Manager Home Care Division, Cleveland, Ohio, November 3, 1992.

"Wheelchair Undergoes Streamline Makeover," *Wall Street Journal,* May 1, 1991, p. B1.

Endnotes

1. Invacare 1991 Annual Report and 1992 Consolidated Financial Statements, Invacare Corporation, Elyria, Ohio.
2. Chris Thomas, "Cities Courting Invacare to Win Headquarters," *Crains Cleveland Business,* 12(32), August 12, 1991, p. 2.
3. Invacare 1991 Annual Report, Elyria, Ohio.
4. Peter H. Emch, "Health Care Research," Robert W. Baird & Co., Inc., Milwaukee, March 10, 1993, p. 13.
5. Christopher Palmeri, "Wheel to Wheel Combat," *Forbes,* 51, February 15, 1993, pp. 62–64.
6. Emch, *op. cit.*
7. *Ibid.*
8. Palmeri, *op. cit.*
9. Malachi A. Mixon, "A Partial Solution to the Nation's Problems with Health Care Costs," speech given for Cage Western University, October 23, 1992.
10. News from Invacare, "Invacare Reports Record Fourth Quarter Earnings on 24 Percent Sales Gain," Elyria, Ohio, February 18, 1993, pp. 1–2.
11. Malachi A. Mixon, *Medical Industry Executive,* March 1993, p. 28.

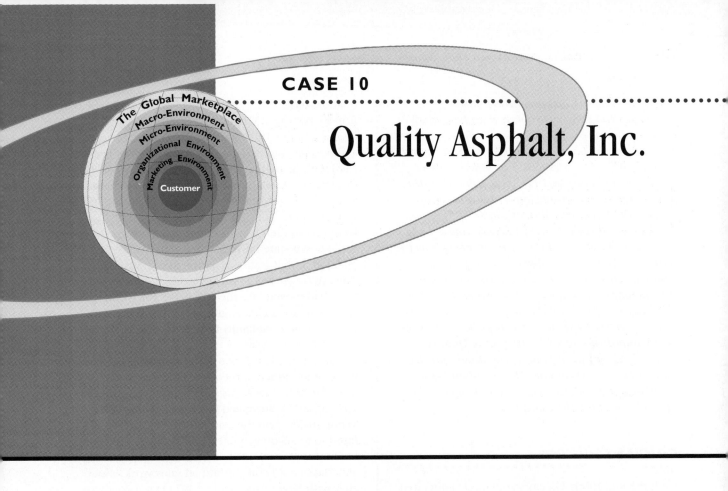

CASE 10

Quality Asphalt, Inc.

This case was prepared by Lynda L. Goulet and Peter G. Goulet of the University of Northern Iowa and Timothy E. Williams, a graduate of the MBA program at the UNI.

Greg Halvensen was alone in the office of Quality Asphalt on the day before Thanksgiving in 1995. His brother, Don, and parents, Mark and Doris, had already left. Greg was thinking about the next day because Thanksgiving was a day when the family would all be together, and traditionally, it had become the day on which the family made many major decisions. In 1971, during the Thanksgiving weekend, Mark decided to leave his position as equipment operator with the State Highway Maintenance Department and start his own asphalt paving business in Williston. He

Funding to support the development of this case was provided by the UNI John Poppajohn Entrepreneurial Center. To preserve the firm's desires for anonymity, the names of the firms and individuals and the geographic location have been disguised. The firm's financial data have been adjusted, although the actual sales growth rates, performance percentages, and key ratios have been preserved. Copyright © 1998 by Lynda L. Goulet, Peter G. Goulet, and Timothy E. Williams.

cashed in a life insurance policy and used the proceeds to purchase a small dump truck and a used asphalt paver. Seven years later, Mark and Doris decided to incorporate their business, which had been operating as a proprietorship. In 1991, both of the Halvensen children were working in the family business. Don was vice president of field operations and responsible for all the firm's construction activity. Greg was vice president of sales. That year, a record year for sales and operating profit, Mark and Doris used the Thanksgiving holiday to announce their decision to gradually retire and to give their shares of stock to their two sons.

Greg stared at the financial statements for the 1995 fiscal year, which ended September 30. Although the statements had arrived 2 weeks earlier, he hadn't had much time to examine them. A period of unusually warm weather was keeping the firm busy. He'd even seen people golfing when he was out earlier in the day delivering a quote for repaving a supermarket parking lot. Profits for that year were better than he had expected, especially since sales had declined considerably from the previous year. On the other hand, the current year's sales were not much higher than they had been in 1991, and 1995 operating profits were considerably lower than the record year of 1991. (Refer to the summary of the financial statements in Exhibit A.) It was now 4 years since their parents had announced their plans to retire, yet they still retained ownership of all the firm's 126,000 shares of stock, and as the only two members of Quality Asphalt's board of directors, they still made all the major decisions. Greg was concerned because he strongly believed that many important decisions involving Quality Asphalt's long-run future had to be made soon. He really didn't want another Thanksgiving "pow-wow" to go by without everyone sharing a common vision of the firm's future.

COMPANY HISTORY

Until the mid-1980s, Quality Asphalt (QA) operated only as an asphalt paver, purchasing its asphalt mix from Williston Asphalt Company, whose plant manager was a neighbor of Mark and Doris. The only other producer of asphalt mix in QA's immediate market area was Svenson Asphalt and Paving, the largest competitor in the area. When Williston Asphalt Company sold out to Svenson in 1985, QA's cost for its materials rose substantially, resulting in a significant loss. That Thanksgiving Mark and Doris made their decision to produce their own asphalt mix. During the winter off-season the Halvensens purchased a used asphalt plant and a one-acre tract of undeveloped land in Williston's new industrial park. By the following spring, QA had hired an asphalt plant manager and was producing its own asphalt mix. This decision subsequently led to a period of growth and profitability. During the remainder of the 1980s, net income rebounded and reached a high of $81,000 in 1989 on sales of over $2 million, about three times QA's 1985 sales level. By 1991, sales reached nearly $2.5 million, and net income was a record $166,000.

Don began working for the family business in the first year of its operation as a laborer during the summer while he was enrolled in a local liberal arts college. After graduating, he joined QA on a full-time basis and soon became supervisor of the firm's labor crew. When QA began producing its own asphalt in 1986, sales began to grow by leaps and bounds, and by 1989, QA had four labor crews, each with its own field supervisor, each managed by Don. In the fall of 1988, at his father's request, Greg quit his job and moved back to Williston, assuming full responsibility for QA's sales activities. Greg had studied construction engineering at a well-known state university and then accepted a position in that state's department of transportation (DOT). After 12 years of working for the DOT, Greg had moved into the private sector, working for 5 years for a civil engineering consulting firm before joining the family business at the start of QA's 1989 fiscal year.

During the late 1980s and early 1990s, QA hired three other nonconstruction employees. Greg hired Steve Lorens as his sales assistant shortly after arriving at QA. Steve had just graduated as a marketing major from the state university. Steve was hired to focus on acquiring jobs in the sizable market for small residential customers. That way Greg and Mark could concentrate on sales work associated with larger projects. In 1987 QA's accountant suggested to Doris that she offer an internship to a business management major at the nearby college to help her with the increasing tasks and paperwork resulting from QA's growth. After completing his internship at QA in the summer of 1987 and graduating in August, John Richards was hired as office manager at the beginning of QA's 1988 fiscal year. In 1990, working with Greg and Steve, John computerized QA's accounting and record-keeping systems. Janice Jeffries, a community college graduate, was hired in 1991 when John Richards had personal problems that necessitated his taking almost an entire year's leave of absence. After John's return in 1992 and Mark and Doris' announcement of their retirement decision, Janice agreed to continue working for QA full time for the 8-month construction season and 1 week during each of the remaining months.

In 1992, after learning about the Halvensen's decision to gradually retire, Svenson Asphalt and Paving made an offer to buy Quality Asphalt, which Mark and Doris refused. Svenson then began a price and bidding war that continued for more than a year and caused in decline in QA's profitability in both 1992 and 1993. Svenson's attack on QA ended in late 1993 when Svenson was purchased

EXHIBIT A

Quality Asphalt Financial Statements (Years Ending September 30)
($ in thousands)

	1995	1994	1993	1992	1991	1990	1989	1988	1987
Gross revenue	$2,580	$3,245	$2,433	$2,222	$2,444	$2,407	$2,180	$1,714	$1,037
Cost of construction									
Materials	$ 752	$1,026	$ 777	$ 554	$ 619	$ 766	$ 646	$ 555	$ 321
Labor	619	637	594	528	440	489	440	285	190
Subcontractors	117	501	258	312	426	388	295	275	66
Depreciation	176	113	115	117	111	91	80	68	55
Other expenses	325	401	351	308	266	276	292	212	145
Total COC	$1,989	$2,678	$2,095	$1,819	$1,862	$2,010	$1,753	$1,395	$ 777
Gross profit	$ 591	$ 567	$ 338	$ 403	$ 582	$ 397	$ 427	$ 319	$ 260
General & administrative									
Salaries	$ 86	$ 85	$ 83	$ 80	$ 62	$ 66	$ 64	$ 36	$ 17
Insurance	113	87	85	83	79	67	62	57	43
Interest	44	26	21	26	34	25	40	45	50
Other G&A expenses	183	202	135	145	139	162	148	95	66
Total G&A	$ 426	$ 400	$ 324	$ 334	$ 314	$ 320	$ 314	$ 233	$ 176
Earnings before taxes	$ 165	$ 167	$ 14	$ 69	$ 268	$ 77	$ 113	$ 86	$ 84
Income taxes	55	56	2	14	102	17	32	20	19
Net income*	$ 110	$ 111	$ 12	$ 55	$ 166	$ 60	$ 81	$ 66	$ 65
Accounts receivable	$ 620	$ 675	$ 898	$ 363	$ 902	$ 359	$ 780	$ 575	$ 282
Inventory	44	25	35	25	18	20	9	9	17
Cash + other current assets	141	25	246	166	132	286	146	132	102
Total current assets	$ 805	$ 725	$1,179	$ 554	$1,052	$ 665	$ 935	$ 716	$ 401
Net property and equipment	995	777	789	797	764	637	598	546	413
Total assets	$1,800	$1,502	$1,968	$1,351	$1,816	$1,302	$1,533	$1,262	$ 814
Current liabilities	$ 500	$ 451	$1,068	$ 421	$ 878	$ 600	$ 782	$ 553	$ 130
Long-term liabilities	339	200	160	202	265	195	304	343	384
Total liabilities	$ 839	$ 651	$1,228	$ 623	$1,143	$ 795	$1,086	$ 896	$ 514
Stockholders' equity*	961	851	740	728	673	507	447	366	300
Total liabilities + equity	$1,800	$1,502	$1,968	$1,351	$1,816	$1,302	$1,533	$1,262	$ 814

*All earnings have been retained.

by Packer Paving, the state's largest paving contractor with subsidiaries located throughout the state. Prior to its purchase of Svenson, Packer Paving had purchased controlled interest in Barnes Stone, a rock quarry in the Williston area and a major supplier to QA.

Don and Greg Halvensen were both married. Although their spouses were employed, neither of their careers were connected with construction or QA. However, Don's only son, David, was 21 and had been working at QA since he was 16. In 1995 David was one of QA's equipment operators and was likely to be promoted to field superintendent when a position opening became available. Greg's oldest child was expected to begin working at QA as a field laborer in the summer of 1996 after turning 16.

ASPHALT AND CONCRETE PAVING

Asphalt cement is a very heavy by-product of the oil refining process that is nearly solid at room temperature. The cost of asphalt cement is therefore closely related to the price of crude oil and the cost of the refining process. To produce a paving mix, asphalt cement must be heated to temperatures in excess of 300°F before it can be combined with rock aggregate that has been completely dried and heated to the same temperature. Different applications require the asphalt mix to be made from different sizes of rock and different concentrations of asphalt cement.

In order to attain the proper compaction and surface appearance, the asphalt must be laid when the mix is at a temperature exceeding 250°F. This temperature requirement limits the amount of time available to transport the asphalt from the production site to the paving site. The transit time is less than 90 minutes during favorable summer weather conditions and less than 60 minutes during the spring and fall. Projects that require additional finishing effort, such as paving irregularly shaped areas or around obstructions, further reduce the time available for transit and hence the distance from the asphalt production plant. Asphalt that cools below 250°F is considered to be waste. However, if the asphalt temperature is maintained in a heated storage facility, it can be stored for as long as 24 hours. If placed in an insulated (but not heated) storage facility, the necessary temperature can be maintained for 8 hours in hot weather and for several hours in cold weather.

The main substitute for asphalt paving is Portland cement concrete paving, although for some purposes, such as for the shoulders on some roads and for driveways in more rural areas, gravel can be used instead of paving. Concrete paving is a mixture of water, sand, rock, and a cementing agent. Portland cement is produced by superheating lime powder. Once Portland cement is mixed with water, it binds to whatever it contacts (such as sand and rock) and begins to cure (harden). The porous quality of the rock aggregate used to make concrete is a major concern. Rock that is too porous will not cure well and will not be as durable. Because highly porous rock will absorb and retain water, the expansion and contraction when water freezes and ice melts will cause the concrete paving to crack more easily than it would if less porous rock were used. Like asphalt, concrete has a limited life before it can no longer be used for paving. Evaporation during transport to the paving site and excess heat create the time limitation for concrete. Since evaporation is greatest when outdoor temperatures are high, concrete can be transported further distances in cooler weather. An "extender" also can be added to the concrete paving mix to help reduce the evaporation rate. Thus, while concrete generally can be transported further distances than asphalt can, concrete cannot be stored once the cement is mixed with water because the curing process cannot be arrested indefinitely.

The determination of whether to use asphalt or concrete pavement is made by the project developer, usually on the advice of engineers involved in the project design. The decision typically is based on several criteria, including soil conditions, expected traffic loads, past experience with paving alternatives, knowledge of the paving methods, personal preference, and cost. Roads can be paved with either concrete or asphalt, although an asphalt surface must be thicker than a concrete surface to bear the same weight. For most heavy-duty applications, such as roads, a rock underlayment is used for both asphalt and concrete paving. This rock base allows water to drain into a tiling system under the shoulders of the road. High-traffic roads paved with concrete require stress-reducing reinforcements, usually made of steel, to be laid between lanes and every 20 feet within lanes. Such "joints" in the concrete paving help to reduce the random cracking of the pavement from weather and traffic-related heaving by channeling any cracking tendency to the joints. Such reinforcement is not required for roads paved with asphalt. Concrete surfaces can be repaved with another layer of concrete or a layer of asphalt, and asphalt surfaces can be repaved with more asphalt or with a layer of concrete. Furthermore, both old concrete and asphalt roads can be "recycled" with pavement-eating machines that grind up the old surface into small pieces that can then be used as underlayment for the new pavement.

QUALITY ASPHALT'S ENVIRONMENT

National Economic Conditions

The general economy in the United States at the end of 1995 was characterized by increasing personal income, low unemployment, low inflation, relatively low interest rates, and a very strong stock market. In 1995, the national unemployment rate was 5.3 percent, down from its most recent high of 7.5 percent in 1992. Growth in consumer prices for 1995, as measured by the CPI, was 2.8 percent for all items, well below the 5.4 percent rate in 1990. Inflation in producer prices (PPI) for paving mixtures was 2.5 percent for 1995, and prices were still well below the average price from 1985. The prime interest rate charged by banks averaged 8.8 percent, up from a low of 6.0 percent in 1993 but below the 10.9 percent rate from 1989.

Construction activity in the United States was reasonably strong in 1995. Low vacancy rates encouraged the construction of additional office space. Vacancy rates for office buildings during 1995 averaged 14.3 percent, down from a high of 20.5 percent in 1992. Since 1991, the value of new construction increased in both the private and public sectors following the short recession in 1990–1991. Although consumer spending for improvements, maintenance, and repairs of residential property also increased following the recession, a slight decline occurred in 1995. Since 1993, construction employment and average hourly earnings were rising, as was the average performance of firms in the industry. (See Exhibit B for data concerning U.S. demographic information and construction activity.)

The economy was expected to remain strong, although there was some concern about inflation. Many stock market experts expected Federal Reserve Chairman Greenspan to slowly continue to raise interest rates in an effort to control inflation. Such increased interest rates would be expected to somewhat depress construction activity in both the residential and business customer segments. However, demographic trends indicated support for continued strength in construction activity for at least the next decade. The percentage of the U.S. population aged 35 to 64 was expected to continue to increase. These age groups earn more and spend more on housing than other age groups.

By 1995, construction of the Federal Interstate Highway System was essentially completed. The system, developed by President Dwight Eisenhower in the 1950s, improved our national defense system by providing a means to quickly and efficiently transport military equipment and personnel from one area of the country to another. This highway system also proved to be a large factor in the economic success of the nation. The construction and maintenance of federal and state highways had been funded in large part from fuel and road-use taxes. As of 1993, over two-thirds of the nation's highway pavement was considered to be in at least fair condition, with the major exception of interstate highways in urban areas, as shown below.

Road Pavement Condition Rating	Urban Areas		Rural Areas	
	Total	Interstate	Total	Interstate
Poor	9%	12%	6%	6%
Mediocre	15%	28%	12%	26%
Fair	38%	24%	43%	24%
Good	20%	26%	21%	33%
Very good	18%	9%	18%	11%

Source: *Statistical Abstract of the United States,* 1993.

Local Economic Conditions

Quality Asphalt, Inc., was located in Williston, which had a metropolitan area population of 178,000 in 1995. Williston was located about 60 miles from the city of Hartford with an area population of 118,000 and about 30 miles from New Brighton with an area population of 64,000. (Refer

EXHIBIT B
United States Demographic and Construction Activity Information

	1980	1985	1990	1995	2000 est.
Total population	227,726,000	238,466,000	249,913,000	263,034,000	274,634,000
Personal income per capita	$10,087	$14,421	$19,170	$23,193	NA
No. of households	80,776,000	86,789,000	93,347,000	98,990,000	103,246,000
Percent of population by age group					
24 and younger	41.4%	38.6%	36.5%	35.7%	35.3%
25–34	16.4%	17.5%	17.4%	15.6%	13.6%
35–44	11.3%	13.3%	15.1%	16.2%	16.3%
45–54	10.0%	9.4%	10.0%	11.8%	13.5%
55–64	9.6%	9.3%	8.5%	8.0%	8.7%
65 and older	11.3%	11.9%	12.5%	12.7%	12.6%

Value of New Construction ($ in millions)

Year	Total	Private	Public	Per Capita Total
1985	$ 377,358	$ 229,543	$ 77,815	$ 1,582
1986	$ 407,682	$ 323,100	$ 84,582	$ 1,694
1987	$ 419,386	$ 328,738	$ 90,648	$ 1,727
1988	$ 432,251	$ 337,516	$ 94,735	$ 1,764
1989	$ 443,651	$ 345,477	$ 98,174	$ 1,794
1990	$ 442,161	$ 334,683	$ 107,478	$ 1,769
1991	$ 403,404	$ 293,295	$ 110,109	$ 1,597
1992	$ 435,021	$ 315,696	$ 119,326	$ 1,703
1993	$ 464,501	$ 339,160	$ 125,341	$ 1,799
1994	$ 506,904	$ 376,566	$ 130,338	$ 1,945
1995	$ 526,598	$ 383,886	$ 142,711	$ 1,991

All Government Expenditures for Highways ($ in millions)

Year*	Total	Federal	State	Local	Per Capita Total
1985	$ 45,856	$ 834	$ 27,167	$ 17,854	$ 192
1990	$ 61,913	$ 856	$ 36,464	$ 24,593	$ 248
1991	$ 65,601	$ 665	$ 38,911	$ 26,025	$ 260
1992	$ 67,196	$ 813	$ 40,266	$ 26,117	$ 263
1993	$ 68,753	$ 619	$ 42,056	$ 26,078	$ 266
1994	$ 72,758	$ 691	$ 43,812	$ 28,255	$ 280

Expenditures by Residential Property Owners for Improvement, Maintenance, and Repairs and Number of New Privately Owned Housing Unit Starts
($ in millions)

Year	Residential Spending	Housing Unit Starts	Per Capita Residential Spending
1985	$ 80,267	1,742,000	$ 337
1986	$ 91,274	1,805,000	$ 379
1987	$ 94,082	1,620,000	$ 387
1988	$ 101,117	1,488,000	$ 413
1989	$ 100,891	1,376,000	$ 410
1990	$ 106,773	1,193,000	$ 427
1991	$ 97,528	1,014,000	$ 386
1992	$ 103,734	1,200,000	$ 411
1993	$ 108,305	1,288,000	$ 420
1994	$ 115,030	1,457,000	$ 441
1995	$ 111,683	1,354,000	$ 425

Construction Industry Corporations with Activity
Selected Measures of Performance for Selected Years

	1985	1990	1991	1992	1993	1994
No. of active corporations	318,000	407,000	417,000	408,000	417,000	433,000
Average assets	$ 667,000	$ 599,000	$ 582,700	$ 566,400	$ 576,500	$ 575,300
Average liabilities	$ 505,000	$ 442,300	$ 413,400	$ 390,300	$ 394,700	$ 394,700
Percent debt to assets	75.7%	73.8%	70.9%	68.9%	68.5%	68.6%
Average sales	$1,217,600	$1,313,800	$1,235,300	$1,224,000	$1,290,900	$1,369,100
Average net income	$ 13,835	$ 16,710	$ 14,630	$ 13,480	$ 17,990	$ 26,790
Percent net income to sales	1.1%	1.3%	1.2%	1.1%	1.4%	2.0%
Percent net income to assets	2.1%	2.8%	2.5%	2.4%	3.1%	4.7%

Average Hourly Earnings of Construction Workers

1985	$12.33	1985	$12.33
1990	$13.78	1993	$14.35
1991	$14.02	1994	$14.69
1992	$14.11	1995	$15.08

*Highway spending for other years not available.
Source: *U.S. Statistical Abstract,* 1995.

to Exhibit C for a map of the area and Exhibit D for demographic information and construction activity in the Williston metropolitan area.) In 1995, the average personal income level in Williston was almost identical to the U.S. average income. However, Williston's age group proportions were slightly different from the national percentages. Williston had a slightly higher percentage of its population in the 25 to 34 age group, although this percentage had been declining, but a lower percentage of its population in the 35 to 64 age groups, although the 45 to 54 age group percentage had been increasing. The Williston area's economy was a reasonably well-balanced mix of service businesses and manufacturing firms. New Brighton was primarily a service-based community, while Hartford was primarily an industrial center. The rural areas surrounding all three of these cities were almost entirely devoted to agriculture.

Although Smithtown and Mt. Pias were more than a 90-minute drive from Williston, QA had completed paving projects in the Smithtown–Mt. Pias area in the past. Smithtown, 80 miles from Williston, was a rural community with 13,000 residents. Mt. Pias, 20 miles further, had a population of 29,000. Within a 30-minute drive to the south and west of these two communities were six other towns. Including Smithtown and Mt. Pias, this area of the state had a total population of 94,000 in 1995.

The most obvious indication of the health of the local construction industry was the increase in building permits over the last decade, with very notable increases in 1987 and 1994. Although the number of building permits issued declined in 1995, the average valuation increased. The statistic causing concern for most construction contractors was the low unemployment level in Williston, 2.9 percent in 1995, which was well below both the national unemployment rate of 5.3 percent and the state unemployment rate of 3.3 percent. The unemployment rate in New Brighton, the closest city from which firms could attract labor, was 2.7 percent. At these low levels of unemployment, it is very difficult for a small company to recruit skilled employees. Paving firms face above-average difficulties in attracting and retaining a labor force because of the physical intensity of the work in the summer heat and the seasonability of the business. Weather conditions in QA's area restrict outdoor construction activities to 8 months each year (ap-

proximately 34 weeks), with the off-season from around Thanksgiving to the beginning of April. During the construction season, paving crews worked whenever the ground was dry, the temperature was above freezing, and there was no frost in the ground.

THE NATURE OF CONSTRUCTION CONTRACTING

The customers for construction paving work may be classified into three broad categories: residential owners, commercial and industrial organizations, and governments. Residential owners generally require the paving of driveways and private sidewalks. Businesses purchase parking lot and related paving work either as part of a larger building construction project or as an improvement project. Governments purchase highway and street paving, as well as parking lots and public sidewalks, often in conjunction with public building projects or sewer and other public-utility construction work.

All larger construction projects are designed by architects and/or engineers who identify the construction requirements and material specifications appropriate for the project's purpose and the preferences of the owner or governmental entity. Bids are then sought for its construction, either for the project as a whole or for major portions of the work. On publicly funded construction projects, the construction contract(s) typically must be publicly advertised and the contract(s) awarded to the lowest qualified bidder(s). When a contract is for an entire project, the construction firm that "wins" the contract is referred to as the *prime contractor.* Working directly with only one company makes the entire construction process less complicated for the owner or governmental unit. Furthermore, for privately funded projects, keeping the owner's contractual obligations simplified also makes it easier for the owner to obtain external financing.

In contrast to publicly funded construction projects, contracts for privately funded work may be either competitively bid or simply negotiated between a contractor and the owner. When bids are used, the owner is not required to select the contractor with the lowest bid but may use other considerations in awarding the contract. Negotiated contracts usually result from the owner's previous satisfactory experience with the contractor.

EXHIBIT C
....
Area Map with Distance and Population Information

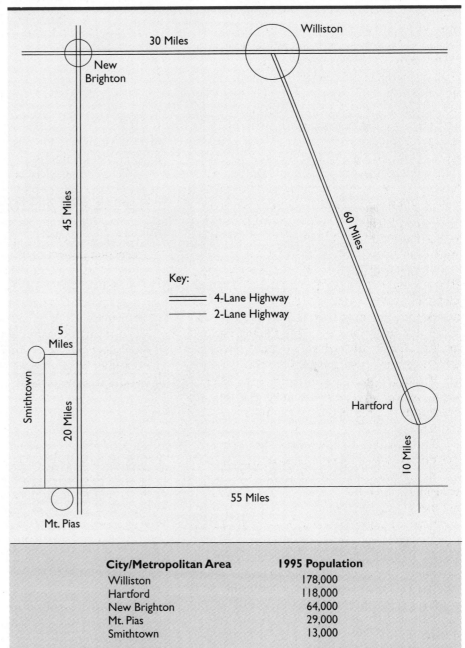

City/Metropolitan Area	1995 Population
Williston	178,000
Hartford	118,000
New Brighton	64,000
Mt. Pias	29,000
Smithtown	13,000

EXHIBIT D
Williston Metropolitan Area Demographic and Construction Activity Information

	1980	1985	1990	1995	2000 est.
Total population	170,000	165,000	170,000	178,000	186,000
Personal income per capita	$10,700	$14,200	$18,900	$23,200	$28,900
No. of households	62,000	61,000	66,000	70,000	73,000
Percent of population by age group					
24 and younger	42.6%	39.0%	36.2%	35.1%	
25–34	17.6%	17.9%	17.2%	15.1%	
35–44	11.6%	13.7%	15.5%	16.6%	
45–54	9.6%	9.4%	10.6%	12.4%	
55–64	8.5%	8.8%	8.4%	8.1%	
65 and older	10.1%	11.2%	12.1%	12.7%	

Year	No. of Building Permits*	Total Valuation	Average Valuation	No. of Residential Permits†
1985	2,946	$ 37,383,448	$ 12,690	134
1986	3,091	$ 37,462,635	$ 12,120	217
1987	4,405	$ 54,012,288	$ 12,260	351
1988	4,898	$ 68,970,036	$ 14,080	381
1989	5,058	$ 90,823,066	$ 17,955	442
1990	5,144	$ 74,080,889	$ 14,400	395
1991	5,511	$ 88,819,016	$ 16,115	404
1992	6,123	$ 94,063,486	$ 15,360	566
1993	6,387	$ 86,385,723	$ 13,525	577
1994	8,347	$126,915,514	$ 15,205	631
1995	7,338	$157,333,043	$ 21,440	525

*Includes industrial, commercial, and residential building permits for new building and improvements.
†Includes single-family and multifamily dwellings.
Source: Chamber of Commerce.

Negotiated contracts, in the absence of competition, allow the contractor to charge a small premium compared with a competitively bid project. However, few contractors greatly overcharge the owner on a negotiated project because doing so would most likely encourage the owner to use competitive bids on future projects.

Construction work historically has been classified by the government into three major categories: general building contractors, heavy construction, and specialized trades. Heavy construction is further divided into road construction (including paving) and other heavy construction such as elevated highways, sewer construction, tunnels, and bridges. Special trades are also subdivided into numerous types of construction specialties, including such work as electrical, plumbing, heating, excavation, demolition, painting, carpentry, roofing, and concrete and asphalt work other than road paving.

Major projects such as buildings and highways require many types of specialized construction work. Most larger construction firms have the capability of performing a variety of construction tasks associated with either building construction or heavy construction. Such firms are considered to be *general contractors*. In contrast, smaller firms tend to be more specialized, with their services limited to one or a few trades. Because of the complexity and variety of work in large construction projects, most prime contractors are general contractors. However, even general contractors will require the services of specialty firms to complete some parts of the project work (outsourcing). When other construction firms are hired by a prime contractor, such firms are called *subcontractors*. In most states, subcontractors have no formal nor legal relationship with the project owner or governmental unit. Their relationship is strictly with the prime contractor, and they are paid by the prime contractor. The work that subcontractors perform, however, must meet the same requirements specified in the prime contractor's contract. The prime contractor is responsible for the quality and timeliness of all work completed on the project, including the work of subcontractors. It is in the prime contractor's best interest to select the lowest-priced subcontractor for specialty work. However, the prime contractor must balance this cost issue against the need to select subcontractors who are competent and reliable to ensure that the work will be completed on time and meet the required specifications.

Most construction contracts contain provisions that allow the owner or governmental unit to withhold a percentage (usually 5 percent) of the prime contractor's progress payments in the form of a *retainage*. The retainage provides an incentive for the prime contractor to complete the remainder of the project in a timely fashion. This retainage is released to the prime contractor when the entire project has been completed to the owner's satisfaction. Prime contractors typically withhold the same retainage from their monthly progress payments to their subcontractors.

For publicly funded construction projects, bidders are required to provide *bid security* in the form of a bond or cashiers' check along with the bid. This security (usually 5 to 10 percent of the bid amount) provides assurance that if the bidder is awarded the contract, the bidding firm will enter into a contract for completion of the project at the bid price. If the bidder does not sign the contract, the firm loses its bid security. This money is then effectively used by the governmental unit to offset the higher bid of another firm. Once the contract is signed, the prime contractor is also required to provide a performance bond for the amount of the contract. This performance bond ensures the timely, quality completion of the project under the terms specified in the contract. If the prime contractor fails to complete a project within the stated time frame, the governmental unit may (if state law permits) withhold funds from the contractor's final payment as compensation for any financial losses incurred due to the delay. If the prime contractor should become bankrupt before the project is completed, the performance bond is used to hire another contractor to complete the work. In addition to retainage, bid security, and performance bonds, many projects require the prime contractor to provide a maintenance bond on the project's completion. The maintenance bond provides a guarantee that the contractor will correct any defects in the work during the specified warranty period. Should the contractor fail to repair defects that result from defective materials or workmanship within the warranty period, the owner or governmental unit will cash the maintenance bond and use the money to hire another contractor to complete the needed work.

In order for QA to obtain bonding, Mark and Doris Halvensen had to consent to a lien being placed on their personal home by the bonding agent. This lien provides collateral to the bonding company in the event QA fails to satisfactorily complete its construction contract commitments. If Mark and Doris were to transfer their ownership to their sons, this collateral requirement would apply to both Don and Greg.

Many publicly funded projects place additional constraints on bidders, including minimum wage scales, Disadvantaged Business Enterprise (DBE) and/or Minority Business Enterprise (MBE) participation, and resident employee requirements. Minimum wage scales, typically required on federally funded projects, define the minimum hourly wage that must be paid to employees working on the project, regardless of union affiliation. Minimum DBE and MBE participation is intended to enhance the competitiveness of qualified firms by requiring that a specified percentage of the contract work be subcontracted to such firms, if such firms are available to do the work. Resident employee requirements are intended to ensure that a specified portion of the public funds spent on the construction project remains in the local community in which the work is being done in the form of wages to local employees.

Construction timing is just as critical to the contractor as it is to the owner or governmental unit. Contractors rarely will fail to bid on a project that is within their capability. This means that a firm may submit bids on more projects than it could actually complete in a timely manner. Being too successful in bidding can become a contractor's worst nightmare (called the *winner's curse*). Contractors must be extremely competent in planning work activity when involved in multiple projects. Furthermore, luck also can affect project completion of outdoor work, since weather delays are common. One potential solution to time constraints is to use subcontractors to complete tasks, although the subcontractors may not be available when needed. Another alternative is to use overtime (work exceeding 40 hours per week requires overtime wages be paid at one-and-a-half times the normal wage rate), including work on weekends, although this alternative also may be limited by weather conditions. Both alternatives will reduce the contractor's profitability and must be compared with the penalty assessed for not meeting required deadlines. Because of the possibility of being overloaded if the firm wins too many contracts, many firms will *overbid* (submit a higher bid than necessary) on some contracts. Then, if the firm wins the contract, the bid price already contains some margin for error.

The state of Wisconsin recently initiated a pilot *design-build construction system* that is being monitored very closely by many other states. Under the program, the Wisconsin State Highway Department establishes results-oriented parameters for construction of a road. An example would be to design a road for 5000 trucks per day with a life expectancy of 15 years before any maintenance is required. The state accepts bids from contractors for the complete design of all details of the project including the methods to be used and materials needed, its construction, and any needed maintenance (in the form of a maintenance bond) of the road for the life of the contract warranty period. To date, Wisconsin has completed at least two of these projects and has several more under consideration. Wisconsin believes that this process will save the state money, as well as expedite the process of designing and constructing the state's road system. Many contractors are concerned that if this design-build system receives wider adoption, it will lessen the competition for all governmental road projects. Small companies will be unable to hire the design and engineering staff necessary to bid for such work and also will be at a disadvantage in obtaining bonding for a project with a higher level of risk to the contractor.

QUALITY ASPHALT'S COMPETITORS, CUSTOMERS, AND GEOGRAPHIC SCOPE

QA's 1995 dollar sales were divided among its customer groups in the following proportions: residential, 15 percent; small commercial, 25 percent; large commercial, 30 percent; and governmental, 30 percent. Although the percentages in each category varied somewhat from year to year, 1995 was a reasonably representative year. On residential and small commercial paving projects in the Williston area, QA competed with Clark Blacktop, Bilton Paving, and Acer Paving. Each of these three firms employed fewer than 10 people. Because these smaller firms focused on small private paving work, they did not compete head-to-head with Svenson, whose focus was on road paving and large commercial and industrial work. However, in late 1995, a large excavation contractor purchased 50 percent interest in Bilton Paving. Greg was sure that this substantial influx of cash would likely be used to improve Bilton's equipment and expand the scope of its business activity. He also suspected one of the other two smaller asphalt paving companies of occasionally skimping on the thickness of the rock base and asphalt pavement used for driveways in order to cut costs. If true, this practice could have an adverse effect on the residential and small commercial asphalt paving business in Williston, since low-quality pavement has a poor appearance and does not wear well. Dissatisfied customers might attribute their problems to the nature of asphalt rather than to the paver.

Approximately 85 percent of QA's 1995 sales derived from paving projects within 40 miles of its plant site. Paving work in New Brighton accounted for 10 percent of this amount. (Refer to the map in Exhibit C.) During the 1992–1993 period when Svenson pressured QA with its low bidding practices, QA was forced to seek more work outside its traditional geographic area. During this time, QA completed two projects in the Mt. Pias area. However, both projects barely broke even because of the distance from QA's asphalt plant. QA incurred higher expenses from transporting its work crews and equipment over 90 miles to the project site and from having to purchase its asphalt mix from Capital Asphalt and Concrete, a Mt. Pias company. In another attempt to gain additional business in 1993, QA actually had moved its asphalt plant 70 miles west of New Brighton in order to supply asphalt to another paving contractor. The cost required to move its asphalt plant was more expensive than QA anticipated, again resulting in a venture that barely broke even. Material problems and labor overtime from such distant work sites contributed to QA's very poor financial performance in 1993.

Although QA recently completed a parking lot paving project for a restaurant in Hartford, QA has not had much success in obtaining contracts for publicly funded projects in Hartford, primarily for two reasons. Hartford enacted a city code requiring 15 percent local labor participation for all city construction projects. During the 1990s, Packer Paving acquired controlling interest in Hopkins & Com-

pany, the only firm in Hartford that produced asphalt and the dominant firm in Hartford (just as Svenson, also owned by Packer Paving, was the dominant firm in New Brighton).

Greg and his sales assistant, Steve Lorens, performed all of QA's sales and bidding activities, as well as arranging for the acquisition of construction materials and any needed subcontractors. Steve Lorens' focus was entirely on the residential and small commercial customer markets, while Greg's efforts were directed toward large-project commercial and industrial sales and bidding on publicly funded projects. About 85 percent of the bids prepared were for residential and small commercial customer projects, which accounted for 60 percent of QA's total contracts and 40 percent of QA's sales.

QA's advertising and promotion have been directed toward the residential and smaller commercial customer groups. The advertising has consisted of large, strategically located ads in all area telephone directories. Additional promotion efforts have included the sponsorship of selected local civic activities such as community fund raisers, church events, and donations to the local softball league. The firm's logo appears on all the firm's equipment and vehicles. Greg and Steve believe the advertising and promotion activities have proven to be very effective. Many of the firm's residential and smaller commercial customers indicated that they called QA because of the size and text of QA's advertisement in the yellow pages. Steve has been responsible for writing the text and arranging for placement of the telephone directory advertising each year.

Since 1989 when he was hired, Steve has been kept busy responding to residential and small commercial customer telephone inquiries. Steve used a personal selling approach for these customers. Not only were site inspections needed to produce estimates of the materials, equipment, and labor needed for the potential project, but they were useful in promoting goodwill for the firm and for asphalt paving in general. Very few of these customers understood the nature of paving work. Since cost estimates were made on the spot, the price the customer would have to pay was provided immediately. John then spent time with the prospective customer explaining how the work would be done and how long the customer would be inconvenienced while the driveway parking lot was being paved and also answered any questions the potential customer had. Since there was usually some "sticker shock," Steve explained how the cost would likely compare with concrete paving and how asphalt pavement compared in terms of its appearance and durability.

All prices for proposed work were submitted to residential and commercial customers on proposal forms that also included the firm's payment terms. QA offered payment terms of a 2 percent discount if the bill was paid within 10 days of completion of the work. The entire payment was due within 30 days of completion. If not paid within the 30 days, a service fee of 1.75 percent per month (21 percent per year) was charged. In addition to the service fee, all proposals stated that the customer would be required to reimburse the firm for any legal fees involved in the collection of past due accounts. At the end of the fiscal year, QA used an attorney to assist in the collection of delinquent accounts. Most customers settled their accounts shortly after receiving a letter from the firm's attorney.

At the end of the 1995 construction season, Greg and Steve made arrangements to accept payment for construction work using either VISA or MasterCard. The necessary electronic transfer equipment had been ordered, and new project proposal forms were being printed indicating the use of credit cards as an alternative to the firm's other payment terms. The credit card companies have promised to wire payment within 48 hours of any such electronic sale transaction. To use this credit card service, QA will be assessed a fee amounting to 2.5 percent of the actual sale. Greg and Steve expect that credit card payment will be attractive to many of their customers and that the fee will be more than offset by the savings in the fees paid to the firm's attorney to collect past-due accounts. Pending legislation in the U.S. Congress also would permit many federal agencies to use credit cards to pay for maintenance work. If the legislation is passed, Greg and Steve hope that QA will benefit from being the only paving competitor in the area to offer a credit card payment option.

Through the efforts of Don and Greg, QA has developed a good working relationship with most of the local general building contractors, all of whom hire subcontractors for their paving work. Many of these building contractors negotiate directly with QA rather than using a bidding process for the paving work. QA believes it receives this preferential treatment because QA generally can do the work in a timely manner, whereas Svenson gives priority to road paving and larger commercial and industrial projects.

QA was qualified by the state DOT to bid as a prime contractor on state projects valued at a maximum of $4.5 million. However, because of the Halvensen's collateral value, QA's bonding company restricted QA's bidding to projects with a maximum value of $1 million. If the firm wanted to bid on projects larger than $1 million, the owners must schedule a personal interview with the principals of the bonding company to determine if special circumstances warrant a variance to this bonding limit. A waiver of this restriction was granted by the bonding company the one time it was requested to repair flood damage for the U.S. Army Corps of Engineers in 1994.

When QA is bidding to become the prime contractor on a project for which subcontractors will be required, Greg contacts firms in the needed specialty trade to determine which ones would be available to do the work and to obtain an estimate of their price for the subcontracted work. Greg and Don have continued to work with several specialty trade subcontractors with whom Mark Halvensen developed mutually beneficial and cooperative relationships.

QA and Svenson were the only two local firms that had the capacity to bid on larger projects in the local area. When bidding was required to obtain paving work, whether for publicly or privately funded projects, QA's policy was to bid on as much work as possible, until the firm had a large backlog of work. Such a work backlog was considered necessary to keep QA's field labor crews busy. However, a work backlog with many projects with deadlines and penalties for late completion could erode profitability if weather delays required crews to work considerable overtime. When the workload scheduled was more than a month, QA raised its bid price, a common industry practice when a firm did not especially want to be awarded the project. Greg and Don believed that QA should always bid on local paving projects for which they were qualified. Because of Svenson's larger resources, especially since the firm was acquired by Packer Paving, QA could not compete on price when Svenson really wanted the work. However, the company felt that allowing Svenson to bid for projects unopposed would be an invitation to firms outside Williston to bid for work in the Williston area. By bidding on all local projects, even if its bid price was high, QA might win a project at a price premium if there were no other bids on the project.

Large highway projects often attracted bids from large heavy construction firms from other parts of the state and from nearby states, not only from firms in the vicinity of the project site. When successful, many of these large nonlocal construction firms would set up their own high-volume, portable asphalt plants. Once a remote asphalt plant was in operation, any extra asphalt capacity not needed for the highway project would then be available to pave other projects in the local area. To get such work, the nonlocal construction firm was likely to enter a bid just marginally above its variable production cost. Such bidding activity would reduce the number of bids awarded to either QA or Svenson. This, in turn, would force Svenson to compete for work on smaller projects that it would normally not pursue. Ultimately, QA's work volume and its profitability could be adversely affected by such a chain of events.

Packer Paving was the state's largest paving company with subsidiaries throughout the state, including Svenson with operations in New Brighton and Williston and Hopkins in Hartford. Packer Paving had the ability to move either portable asphalt or concrete plants anywhere in the state to complete a project. However, Packer Paving's policy was not to compete with its subsidiary paving firms unless the project was very large. Similarly, its subsidiaries were restricted from competing for projects within the service area of another Packer Paving subsidiary. This corporate policy precluded Svenson from bidding on work in Hartford and Hopkins from bidding on work in either New Brighton or Hartford. Both subsidiaries, however, could bid for jobs in the Smithtown–Mt. Pias area because Packer did not have a subsidiary located in that portion of the state.

QUALITY ASPHALT'S ACTIVITIES AND OPERATION

QA's asphalt plant, rock inventory, equipment storage, and office were located on a 1-acre gravel-surfaced site in the industrial park on the outskirts of Williston. The company leased its premises from Mark and Doris Halvensen on an annual net lease basis, paying $48,000 during the fiscal year ending September 30, 1995. In 1995, QA and Svenson were the only two firms in the Williston area that pro-

duced asphalt. While Svenson also sold its asphalt mix to other local paving contractors, QA produced its mix only for its own use. Svenson, headquartered in New Brighton, employed 150 people and operated three asphalt production plants: its original and largest plant in New Brighton, one in Williston, and the newest plant located on leased land on Magna Mining's rock quarry property about 10 miles east of New Brighton. Together Svenson's three plants produced 10 times QA's annual asphalt volume of 50,000 tons in 1995.

QA's asphalt production facility consisted of a small drum-style asphalt plant and a 30-ton insulated (but not heated) storage silo. The insulated silo was purchased in 1991 to reduce waste (asphalt with a temperature below $250°F$) and thereby lower the material cost per ton paved. Some asphalt produced early in the day could be stored in the silo for use in the late afternoon. QA's drum-style asphalt plant operated as a continuous-flow system and, under ideal operating conditions, could produce 800 tons of asphalt a day. However, this continuous-flow system limited QA's ability to produce a variety of different asphalt mixes on the same day for different paving projects. This limitation required QA to carefully schedule small jobs that required the same paving mix on the same day. Many road paving projects require production capacities in excess of 1500 tons per day in order to complete construction within the project time frame. With its limited production capability, QA has been unable to bid on such projects. It may be noted that about 3000 tons of asphalt are required to pave a 4-inch layer of asphalt on a 1-mile stretch of two-lane highway with a standard width of 24 feet.

Greg would like to eliminate both these production limitations. One solution would be to buy a 200-ton heated asphalt silo, which would effectively increase QA's daily production capacity. By beginning asphalt production earlier in the day for a small job and then using the insulated silo to store this mix, asphalt production could then be changed to a different kind of mix for another, larger project. The heated silo would be used to store the extra mix from the second production to begin the morning's paving work until more of the second mix was made. Another way to overcome the capacity constraint would be to replace or augment the existing drum-style plant with a 1000 or more ton per day batch plant. A batch plant, producing each truckload of mix individually, would provide the ability to change the mix between truckloads.

QA's policy was to purchase major pieces of equipment at auction. A used 200-ton heated silo, purchased at auction, would cost about $120,000, including its setup. Depending on its condition and size, a used 1000-ton or larger batch plant would cost between $1 million and $1.5 million, including transportation and setup costs. This policy of purchasing used equipment that could be repaired in-house was instituted by Mark Halvensen when QA was founded. Since many construction firms experience bankruptcy, especially during economic recessions, other firms often could acquire relatively new equipment at bargain prices. Because QA purchased its equipment used, repair and maintenance costs were high. However, high employee turnover also contributed to this expense because short-term employees often do not take care of the equipment as well as they should. As of 1995, QA did not have a preventative maintenance program.

In 1995, QA's paving-related equipment included eight tandem axle (16-ton load) dump trucks, three tractor trailers (20-ton load), two end loaders, two paving machines, and several other pieces of paving machinery. The trucks were used to deliver asphalt mix and to haul other materials required for paving preparation work to the paving site. The end loaders were used primarily at its facility site to move rock from inventory to the asphalt plant, in paving preparation to create the rock underlayment, and to assist in snow removal during the winter. QA also owned 10 pickup trucks that were used by the paving supervisors, the management, and the sales assistant. QA had a rotation program to replace its pickup trucks every 5 years. No such program existed to replace its production equipment or larger vehicles.

Within the last year, QA purchased equipment to broaden the scope of the work it can perform on paving projects. The new equipment included a shouldering machine for placing rock along the edge of new pavement, a concrete breaker attachment to break up old pavement into small pieces, and a small tractor backhoe. By limiting its dependence on other firms to perform such work as pavement breaking, culvert installation, and shoulder preparation, QA has been able to bid as a general contractor on more complicated asphalt paving projects. Doing more work in-house also shortened the time frame for completing projects. Not only could some crews be kept working on

days when the weather is unfavorable for paving, but a great deal of time was saved by not having to coordinate the work with subcontractors.

The total cost of QA's equipment and leasehold improvements as recorded on its 1995 balance sheet are summarized below. Overall, at the end of 1955, the firm's property and equipment were about 53 percent depreciated. This depreciation is somewhat misleading, since most of the equipment was purchased used. (Refer to Exhibit A for the firm's financial statements.)

Quality Asphalt's Property and Equipment

Construction equipment	$1,300,000
Transportation equipment	730,000
Office equipment	50,000
Leasehold improvements	25,000
Total property and equipment	$2,105,000

In addition to housing its asphalt plant and office on its 1-acre gravel-surfaced site, QA also had six stockpiles of various sizes of rock aggregate that occupied about three-fourths of the total area. QA's main supplier of rock has always been Barnes Stone (now controlled by Packer Paving), located within 4 miles of QA's site. The only two alternative sources of supply were Magma Mining on the outskirts of New Brighton (where Svenson had located its newest asphalt production facility) and Henderson Quarry near Hartford (owned by Packer Paving).

QA's rock supplies were delivered by dump truck and unloaded onto the appropriate pile on its site. As needed, rock was transferred from these stockpiles to the asphalt plant using an end loader. The rock stockpiles were separated from one another as much as possible to avoid any intermingling of different sizes of rock. Despite efforts to separate the rock piles from one another, contamination often occurred during heavy rains and from the tendency of rock to spill from the trucks and end loader as they moved through the plant site. The gravel surface of the site also tended to become bumpy from rock spillage and mud holes that develop from rain. When dry, loose chunks of mud often were thrown into the rock piles by truck tires, which further aggravated the rock pile contamination problem. The office area also was affected because mud was easily tracked inside, and on dry, windy days, dust blew inside the building.

QA has considered constructing a bin storage system for its rock inventory. Such a system would take up less space and reduce the contamination problem. In addition, the bin walls would provide support for a roof system that would protect the stockpiles from rain. Rock that was contaminated with water increased the time required to produce the asphalt mix, since the water had to be evaporated before the rock could be added to the asphalt cement. To purchase and install such a storage bin system has been estimated to cost $500,000. Consideration also has been given to using excess asphalt (left over from a day's paving project and which is still above 250°F) to gradually pave the site area. Asphalt that falls below 250°F cannot be used for paving and must be disposed of in accordance with government regulations at designated locations for a fee. On average, QA must dispose of between 3 and 15 tons of asphalt per day, of which about 20 percent is still hot enough to use for paving.

Greg, who was responsible for ordering the paving materials, had been concerned about Barnes Stone, the rock supplier. Since Packer Paving purchased controlling interest in Barnes Stone in 1993, Greg had noticed that not only had rock costs risen, but Svenson had been receiving preferential treatment when a particular rock product was in short supply. Because about 32,500 tons of different sizes and types of rock were required to produce QA's 50,000 tons of annual asphalt production in 1995, and because rock aggregate is bulky and QA's storage area is limited in size, QA cannot maintain a large safety stock of each type.

Both asphalt and concrete pavement used for publicly funded projects must meet the standards specified for the project. This requires that the paving mixtures be tested frequently. If test results fall outside the specified parameters, a penalty is assessed against the general contractor (and if subcontractors were being used, the general contractor would then penalize the appropriate subcontractor). QA has the ability to conduct some of the required tests but not all of them. As a result, QA must outsource some of its testing. QA has always outsourced such work to an independent testing firm located 70 miles from Williston. Svenson was the only firm in the area with the required capability to complete all its own testing. To add the equipment it would need to do all test-

ing internally would cost QA approximately $100,000. In addition, a qualified individual would be required to perform the tests. QA's sales assistant, Steve Lorens, was the only employee with the necessary qualifications of both knowledge of asphalt production and statistics.

In addition to overcoming its asphalt production limitation in Williston, Greg would like the firm to expand geographically by purchasing another asphalt plant to be located in the Smithtown–Mt. Pias area. Although QA had not bid on any work in this area since 1993, Greg believed the asphalt paving market in this part of the state had tremendous growth potential. In the early 1990s, this area had only one larger-sized asphalt paving firm, Davidson Paving, which also did concrete paving but did not produce its own paving mixtures. Davidson purchased its asphalt and concrete mixes from Capital Asphalt and Concrete in Mt. Pias. Although Capital was the only asphalt producer in that part of the state, Capital had never been involved in asphalt paving. After failing to meet the completion date on a large paving project in 1994, Davidson was forced by its bonding company to sell off a considerable amount of equipment at auction in order to satisfy debt payments. Since then, Davidson had limited its activities to concrete paving of parking lots and municipal streets. Since no other firms in the area were large enough to bid for governmental asphalt paving work, most of the governmental agencies in the region had recently specified only concrete pavement, even though many of their engineers indicated a preference for asphalt.

When QA was preparing to begin a new project, Don scheduled the project using a simple type of Gantt chart showing when QA's various crews would be working on which projects. Greg was then responsible for getting any needed subcontractors to sign a contract with QA and for ensuring that the materials would be available in inventory when they were needed. QA generally had three or four projects being worked on at the same time, often at sites that were geographically separated by 30 or more miles. Don, who managed all field operations, was very skeptical of geographic expansion because he already spent a considerable amount of time traveling to the various sites to help resolve problems that had arisen. Although the field supervisors in many cases had the experience to make appropriate decisions, they often seemed unwilling to do so, especially when working on road projects that got behind schedule due to unfavorable weather. On an especially harrowing day, Don was heard to say: "Large projects tend to control the company rather than the company controlling the project."

Some of QA's field employees had suggested that the firm also should do concrete paving and sewer construction. Adding these two activities would give QA the ability to become a completely in-house general contractor on almost all municipal road construction projects in the Williston area. If QA decided to add concrete paving to its paving construction activities, there would be no need to produce its own concrete, since there are five firms in Williston that produce concrete mix for other firms and deliver it to the site. However, other equipment would be needed for concrete paving. A used concrete paving machine would cost $300,000 to $500,000, and a curb machine would cost about $75,000. One advantage to acquiring a curb machine is that both asphalt and concrete streets require concrete curbs.

If QA were to expand its activities to include concrete paving, the firm would face significantly more competition. Almost anyone with hand tools and a pickup truck can become a concrete contractor for sidewalks, driveways, and small parking lots. In 1995, Williston had four large concrete paving firms competing for road and parking lot construction, as well as 25 small firms competing for smaller projects. There were also 10 sewer contractors. Although QA had constructed street-level culverts that connect to storm sewers, QA lacked the capability of actually constructing the storm sewers. Sewer construction would require specialized equipment, estimated to cost about $500,000, that cannot be used in road construction.

EMPLOYEES AND PERSONNEL MANAGEMENT ACTIVITIES

In 1995, QA employed a total of 39 people, including Mark, Doris, Don, and Greg Halvensen. QA's 25 laborers were divided into five field crews: a dedicated paving crew, three full-time site preparation crews, and one multitask crew capable of handling site preparation and asphalt paving, as well as limited excavation, grading, and storm sewer and drain tile construction. Each of these five crews was headed by field supervisors. Additionally, QA employed a yard supervisor for the rock and equipment, an asphalt plant operator, a sales assistant (Steve Lorens), an office manager (John Richards), and an office worker (Janice Jeffries).

When paving and related types of work could not be done due to rain or cold weather, QA's crews were given time off without pay. When the paving operation was shut down for the winter season, the field laborers were placed on seasonal layoff, while the remaining personnel worked part time. During this 4-month period, the supervisors and asphalt plant manager engaged in equipment, vehicle, and facility maintenance and were on call for plowing snow. Although QA had an arrangement to plow snow for a few commercial and industrial customers, the firm had not made a major effort to expand this winter activity because snow removal was hard on the equipment.

The starting wage for the 25 field laborer positions at QA was $8 per hour in 1995, with a pay review scheduled at the end of a 90-day probation period. When positions became available, field laborers who had survived the probation period and had experienced the variety of work required for paving are promoted to other supervisory positions or to positions as equipment operators, if they had an appropriate license. A commercial driver's license was required to operate dump trucks and tractor trailers. All of QA's field supervisors were required to hold a valid commercial driver license. Operation of the liquid asphalt tanker required a license to haul hazardous materials because liquid asphalt was classified as a hazardous material by the DOT. No license was required to operate "off road" equipment.

Because of the low unemployment rate, QA has found it difficult to find and retain laborers. Employees often will seek other positions with industrial or commercial firms soon after they realize that shoveling hot asphalt on summer days is difficult work. John Richard's review of company employment records revealed that, on average, one laborer position turned over every week. Since about a month is needed for a new employee to become relatively proficient working on a paving crew, almost all of QA's work crews were constantly either short a laborer or had an inexperienced person to train. In 1995, only a few nonsupervisory employees had been with QA for more than 3 years. In contrast, the six supervisors and the asphalt plant manager had an average tenure of 7 years with QA.

None of the local asphalt paving firms had a

unionized labor force in 1995. Svenson had been unionized until it was purchased by Packer Paving. Under its new ownership, Svenson had published new terms of employment designed to bring wages and benefits in line with Packer's nonunion operations. The union that had represented Svenson's employees then voted to strike, but within 2 months most of the employees returned to work under the new labor conditions. As a result of this union-busting action, several of the unionized general contractors in the Williston area began to hire QA for paving work rather than Svenson. Nationally, 16.7 percent of the U.S. workforce was represented by unions in 1995. Workers represented by unions earned one-third more in 1995 than workers not represented by unions.

Average hourly earnings in 1995 for U.S. construction workers, of whom 18.8 percent were represented by unions, were $15.08. This earnings figure may be compared with the average hourly earnings of workers from all industries of $11.44. Throughout the year, construction workers averaged 38.8 hours of work per week, compared with the 34.6 average hours of work per week for all workers for all industries. It also may be noted that the minimum wage rate established by the federal government was $4.25 per hour in 1995, although some states had laws establishing higher minimum wage rates. During the 34 weeks of paving in QA's fiscal 1995 year, QA's field workers averaged almost exactly 40 hours per week, although some weeks included several hours of overtime work. If a project deadline was in danger of not being met, QA's policy was to reassign crews from other projects to expedite the delayed project's completion rather than to use overtime, which would significantly increase labor cost.

As part of QA's hiring process, and consistent with the statute of the state in which QA operates, all acceptable applicants were hired conditionally and required to submit to preemployment substance abuse testing. QA also required such testing (also permitted by state statute) for all employees who had been involved in a serious work accident or demonstrated unusual behavior that could endanger the life of other employees. Even though state law permitted random testing of employees for substance abuse, QA did not do so. The firm believes its policies have improved employee performance and the quality of their workforce.

Although no firms are required to provide fringe benefits for their employees, and small firms cannot usually afford to do so voluntarily, QA provided some employee benefits. The company had an employee health insurance program, available after the 90-day probation period. Under this program, the company contributed $80 per month to offset some of the insurance premium for its employees' health insurance plan and allowed its employees to have the remainder of the premium cost deducted from their weekly paychecks. Because the business was seasonal, the firm also offered to help its employees manage their yearly cash flow. A pay-ahead schedule was made available that allowed employees to have additional money deducted from their weekly pay checks during the summer to cover insurance premiums due in the winter when they were on seasonal layoff. The firm also provided a term life insurance policy for each employee who had been with QA for at least 1 year equal to their annual wage or salary. At the beginning of the year's paving season, QA also provided a wage or salary increase based on the increase in the cost of living for all employees who had been with the firm at least since the beginning of the previous year.

The Halvensens believed that employees needed to have a vested interest in the firm if QA was to be successful. Therefore, each December every employee who worked the entire season received a year-end bonus of 1 percent of the wage or salary earned during the year. Greg had suggested tying the bonus to the firm's profits rather than wages. He reasoned that such a change would encourage the employees to work more efficiently, thereby reducing material waste, which would lower the firm's construction cost, and increasing labor productivity, which would allow the firm to complete more revenue-generating projects. However, Mark and Doris vetoed his proposal because they did not want their employees, nor their competitors, to know QA's profitability.

ACCOUNTING AND OFFICE MANAGEMENT ACTIVITIES

QA's income statements (Exhibit A) were structured somewhat unusually in order to make it easier for Greg to prepare bids. General and administrative salaries included the compensation (wages and benefits) paid to Mark and Doris Halvensen, John Richards, and Janice Jeffries. In 1989, Mark began receiving a salary, rather than an hourly wage rate as Greg had joined the firm, taking over his father's sales responsibilities. The firm's contribution to Social Security (6.2 percent of all earnings) and Medicare (1.45 percent of all earnings) taxes for these four people were included in other G&A expenses. All remaining employees were paid an hourly wage rate. Construction labor included the compensation (wages and benefits) for all the firm's other employees, including Don and Greg Halvensen and Steve Lorens. QA's contributions to Social Security and Medicare taxes for these employees were included in other construction expenses. Other construction expenses also included equipment, maintenance and repair costs, fuel costs, and rental costs for equipment that QA required for a specific job but did not own.

Since joining QA, Greg had developed a strong working relationship with First State Savings, a locally owned bank. At mid-November, 1995, QA had 13 notes outstanding, all with First State Savings. Through Greg's efforts, none of the notes required monthly payments from the end of December until the end of April. All the notes were secured by the firm's vehicles and equipment, whose purchase the debt financed. The notes on more recent fixed-asset purchases carried interest rates ranging from 9.5 to 10.5 percent. The schedule of future principal repayments is shown in the table below. When Doris saw the principal repayment schedule, she expressed concern that the debt burden was too high. She said that if the number of local building permits continued to decline, QA's sales could drop even more, and if that happened, the firm's profitability would fall and QA might be unable to repay its debt obligations.

Quality Asphalt, Inc.
Principal Repayment Schedule

September 30, 1996	$126,000
September 30, 1997	$117,300
September 30, 1998	$108,000
September 30, 1999	$ 83,600
September 30, 2000	$ 30,100

John Richards and Janice Jeffries were responsible for all of QA's paperwork, including bookkeeping, compliance reporting, billing, and personnel record keeping. The firm outsourced its legal, accounting, financial reporting, and auditing work. QA must have its five largest projects audited at the end of every year. This special audit report must be submitted to the contract compliance office of the state highway department in order for QA to remain on the list of contractors qualified to bid on state-funded or state-administered projects.

During the construction season, Janice was responsible for tracking the construction materials ordered, by product type, in order to verify bills as they were received from suppliers. Time cards were used for payroll purposes. Each day all construction employees who were paid an hourly wage were required to record the number of hours they worked. The firm's receivables and payables, including payroll, were monitored using the Peachtree computerized accounting system that Greg and John selected in 1990.

Because QA engaged in both manufacturing (asphalt production) and construction activities, the firm was subject to both general industry and construction industry Occupational, Safety, and Health Administration (OSHA) regulations. In addition, the firm must comply with the requirements of many other regulatory agencies, including those of the Environmental Protection Agency (EPA), the Equal Employment Opportunity Commission (EEOC), the state department of transportation (DOT), the Federal Highway Administration (FHWA), and the Immigration and Naturalization Service (INS) for employee citizenship status checks. John was responsible for filing the necessary compliance reports and for keeping abreast of legal developments that were likely to affect the firm's operation. He also was responsible for hiring employees and for the substance abuse testing, since employment and medical records must be kept confidential.

Because of the pending conversion of all publicly funded projects to metric measurements, John planned to institute a metric training program for the firm's employees. Several state- and FHWA-funded projects had already been awarded using metric units exclusively. Conversion would require some minor equipment changes and changes to QA's record keeping and documentation. Don Halvensen was convinced that many laborers and several of the supervisors would resist the changeover to the metric system as long as possible. Furthermore, because the conversion would not apply to privately funded projects, the firm's employees must be "fluent" in both the English and metric systems. Otherwise, errors would most likely be made in preparing bids and in the actual construction work. If project costs were underestimated, the firm could lose money if it was awarded the project, and if project costs were overestimated, the firm could lose the opportunity to earn revenue. Measuring errors in the field operations could result in having to redo work, causing considerable waste of materials and labor time.

Although time cards were used for payroll purposes and construction material purchases were carefully monitored, QA had no internal job cost accounting system to determine the actual costs of various paving projects. As a result, cost estimates for bidding purposes tended to be based on "educated guesses." According to John, if the time cards recorded not only the number of hours worked but also the projects worked, much more accurate project cost information could be generated. However, Don did not believe the field personnel would cooperate simply because they were too exhausted at the end of a long day to want to do more paperwork. Steve Lorens requested that the firm buy a computer software package, such as Timberline, designed for construction contractors to integrate project estimation and job costing. Besides the estimated cost of $25,000 to set up such an integrated system, John was concerned that the new system would be incompatible with the present office software.

Greg used Microsoft Works computer spreadsheets to develop project bids. QA's bids and quotes for work that was not bid were based on the sum of three components. (Refer to the income statement in Exhibit A.) Greg considered all items included under cost of construction to be "variable costs." When these variable costs for the project had been estimated, a "fixed cost" overhead allocation was included. This fixed-cost component included all the items listed under general and administrative expenses. These total fixed costs were then allocated to the project based on the project's estimated asphalt tonnage as a percentage of the estimated total asphalt tonnage for QA for the year. Finally, the project price was adjusted based on Greg's overall assessment of the situation. The bid price would be raised or lowered to reflect QA's backlog of work or to match Greg's estimate of competitors' prices or the price Greg believed the market would bear.

As of 1995, QA did not have an objective that related to winning a specified percentage of bid projects, nor did it have a policy to include a specific profit margin percentage as part of the bid price. Greg was aware of the limitations of the system for preparing bids. He was concerned that without a job costing system, the firm could not really know if it had made a profit or suffered a loss on any given project. He believed that having such information would be valuable in establishing guidelines for pricing certain types of projects. Greg's approach to bidding was to bid each project "to make as much money as possible, given the limited costing information available." Don continued to oppose such changes primarily because he believed that implementation would be burdensome on all the construction-related employees. "Why do we need to do this now when we have operated fine without it for over 25 years?"

PLANNING FOR TOMORROW

As Greg sat alone in his office reflecting on QA's history and current activities and examining the financial statements, he became even more convinced that QA had to move forward. But how could he convince his brother and parents that growth was in all their best interests? If the economy remained strong in 1996, sales and profitability probably would both improve somewhat. But he was sure that such modest growth wouldn't be enough to support three generations of Halvensens in the future. But which opportunities would be best for the firm? Expansion would require more debt and more interest expense. Just how much could QA afford, and how would that limit its choices? Surely not taking advantage of opportunities would "pave the way" for Svenson to exert even more control in the Williston area in the future. But expansion probably also would intensify QA's rivalry with Svenson, at least in the short run. Could QA handle it? If Don continued to feel pressured in managing the field operations, then would doing more jeopardize QA's reputation for quality work and timely service? Even though their parents weren't as actively involved in the business as they had been, they still did pitch in when needed and still made all the major decisions. But would they continue to help as they had for the last 5 years, or would they finally retire completely? And if they did retire, who would "be in charge" with final say about the firm's direction? Of course, if they didn't have their parents' salaries to pay, they could afford to employ more people to help Don. Just what should he say tomorrow at the family's Thanksgiving "powwow"?

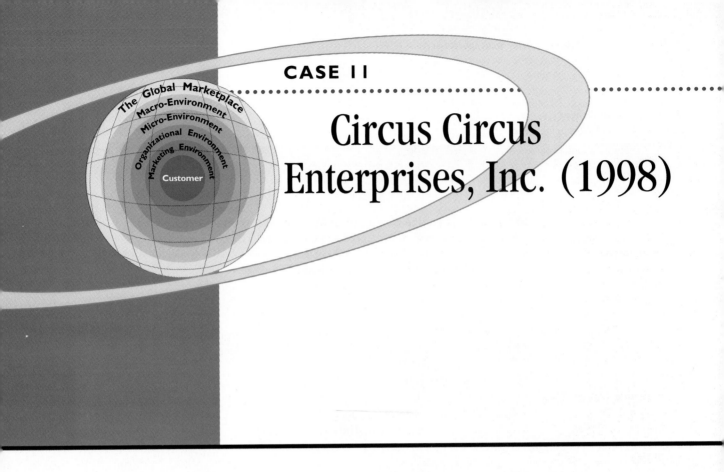

Circus Circus Enterprises, Inc. (1998)

This case was prepared by Professors John K. Ross III, Michael J. Keefe, and Bill J. Middlebrook of Southwest Texas State University.

We possess the resources to accomplish the big projects: the knowhow, the financial power and the places to invest. The renovation of our existing projects will soon be behind us, which last year represented the broadest scope of construction ever taken on by a gaming company. Now we are well-positioned to originate new projects. Getting big projects right is the route to future wealth in gaming; big successful projects tend to prove long staying power in our business. When the counting is over, we think our customers and investors will hold the winning hand.

Annual Report, 1997

Big projects and a winning hand. Circus Circus does seem to have both. And big projects they are, with huge pink and white striped concrete circus

The case was prepared for classroom purposes only, and is not designed to show effective or ineffective handling of administrative situations. Reprinted by permission of Dr. John K. Ross, III.

tents, a 600-foot-long river boat replica, a giant castle, and a great pyramid. The company's latest project, Mandalay Bay, will include a 3700-room hotel/casino, an 11-acre aquatic environment with beaches, a snorkeling reef, and a swim-up shark exhibit.

COMPANY HISTORY

Circus Circus Enterprises, Inc. (hereafter Circus), describes itself as in the business of entertainment and has been one of the innovators in the theme resort concept popular in casino gaming. Their areas of operation are the glitzy vacation and convention Mecca's of Las Vegas, Reno, and Laughlin, Nevada, as well as other locations in the United States and abroad. Historically, Circus's marketing of its products has been called "right out of the bargain basement" and has catered to "low rollers." Circus has continued to broaden its market and now

EXHIBIT A

**Directors and Officers:
Circus Circus Enterprises, Inc.**

Name	Age	Title
Directors		
Clyde T. Turner	59	Chairman of the Board and CEO, Circus Circus Enterprises
Michael S. Ensign	59	Vice Chairman of the Board and COO, Circus Circus Enterprises
Glenn Schaeffer	43	President and CFO, Circus Circus Enterprises
Yvett Landau		Vice President, General Counsel, and Secretary
Les Martin		Vice President and Chief Accounting Officer
William A. Richardson	50	Vice Chairman of the Board and Executive Vice President, Circus Circus Enterprises
Richard P. Banis	52	Former President and COO, Circus Circus Enterprises
Arthur H. Bilger	44	Former President and COO, New World Communications Group International
Richard A. Etter	58	Former Chairman and CEO, Bank of America–Nevada
William E. Bannen, M.D.	48	Vice President/Chief Medical Officer, Blue Cross-Blue Shield of Nevada
Donna B. More	40	Partner, Law Firm of Freeborn & Peters
Michael D. McKee	51	Executive Vice President, The Irving Company
Officers		
Clyde T. Turner		Chairman of the Board and Chief Executive Officer
Michael S. Ensign		Vice Chairman of the Board and Chief Operating Officer
Glenn Schaeffer		President, Chief Financial Officer, and Treasurer
William A. Richardson		Vice Chairman of the Board and Executive Vice President, Circus Circus Enterprises
Tony Alamo		Senior Vice President, Operations
Gregg Solomon		Senior Vice President, Operations
Kurt D. Sullivan		Senior Vice President, Operations
Steve Greathouse		Senior Vice President, Operations

Source: Annual Report 1998; Proxy statement, May 1, 1998.

aims more at the middle-income gambler and family-oriented vacationers as well as the more upscale traveler and player.

Circus was purchased in 1974 for $50,000 as a small and unprofitable casino operation by partners William G. Bennett, an aggressive cost cutter who ran furniture stores before entering the gaming industry in 1965, and William N. Pennington (see Exhibit A for board of directors and top managers). The partners were able to rejuvenate Circus with fresh marketing, went public with a stock offering in October 1983, and experienced rapid growth and high profitability over time. Within the 5-year period between 1993 and 1997, the average return on invested capital was 16.5 percent, and Circus had generated over $1 billion in free cash flow. Today, Circus is one of the major players in the Las Vegas, Laughlin, and Reno markets in terms of square footage of casino space and number of hotel rooms—despite the incredible growth in both markets. For the first time in company history, casino gaming operations in 1997 provided slightly less than half the total revenue, and that trend continued into 1998 (see Exhibit B). On January 31, 1998, Circus reported a net income of approximately $89.9 million on revenues of $1.35 billion.

EXHIBIT B
....
Circus Circus Enterprises, Inc.: Sources of Revenues as a Percentage of Net Revenues

	1998	1997	1996	1995
Casinos	46.7%	49.2%	51.2%	52.3%
Food & Beverage	15.9	15.8	15.5	16.2
Hotel	24.4	22.0	21.4	19.9
Other	10.5	11.0	12.2	14.2
Unconsolidated	7.3	6.5	3.5	.5
Less: Complimentary allowances	4.8	4.5	3.8	3.1

Source: Circus Circus 10-k, January 31, 1995–1998.

This was down slightly from 1997's more than $100 million net income on revenues of $1.3 billion. During the same year, Circus invested over $585.8 million in capital expenditures, and another $663.3 million was invested in fiscal year 1998.

CIRCUS CIRCUS OPERATIONS
....

Circus defines entertainment as pure play and fun, and it goes out of the way to see that customers have plenty of opportunities for both. Each Circus location has a distinctive personality. Circus Circus Las Vegas is the world of the Big Top, where live circus acts perform free every 30 minutes. Kids may cluster around video games while the adults migrate to nickel slot machines and dollar game tables. Located at the north end of the Vegas strip, Circus Circus Las Vegas sits on 69 acres of land with 3744 hotel rooms, shopping areas, two specialty restaurants, a buffet with seating for 1200, fast-food shops, cocktail lounges, video arcades, 109,000 square feet of casino space, and includes the Grand Slam Canyon, a 5-acre glass-enclosed theme park including a four-loop roller coaster. Approximately 384 guests also may stay at nearby Circusland RV Park. For the year ending January 31, 1997, $126.7 million was invested in this property for new rooms and remodeling, with another $35.2 million in fiscal year 1998.

Luxor, an Egyptian-themed hotel and casino complex, opened on October 15, 1993, when 10,000 people entered to play the 2245 slot and video poker games and 110 table games in the 120,000-square-foot casino in the hotel atrium (reported to be the world's largest). By the end of the opening weekend, 40,000 people per day were visiting the 30-story bronze pyramid that encases the hotel and entertainment facilities.

Luxor features a 30-story pyramid and two new 22-story hotel towers including 492 suites and is connected to Excalibur by a climate-controlled skyway with moving walkways. Situated at the south end of the Las Vegas strip on a 64-acre site adjacent to Excalibur, Luxor features a food and entertainment area on three different levels beneath the hotel atrium. The pyramid's hotel rooms can be reached from the four corners of the building by state-of-the-art "inclinators" that travel at a 39-degree angle. Parking is available for nearly 3200 vehicles, including a covered garage that contains approximately 1800 spaces.

The Luxor underwent major renovations costing $323.3 million during fiscal year 1997 and another $116.5 million in fiscal year 1998. The resulting complex contains 4425 hotel rooms, extensively renovated casino space, an additional 20,000 square feet of convention area, an 800-seat buffet, a series of IMAX attractions, five theme restaurants, seven cocktail lounges, and a variety of specialty shops. Circus expects to draw significant walk-in traffic to the newly refurbished Luxor and is one of the principal components of the Masterplan Mile.

Located next to the Luxor, Excalibur is one of the first sights travelers see as they exit interstate highway 15 (management was confident that the sight of a giant, colorful medieval castle would make a lasting impression on mainstream tourists and vacationing families arriving in Las Vegas). Guests cross a drawbridge, with moat, onto a cobblestone walkway where multicolored spires, turrets, and battlements loom above. The castle walls are four 28-story hotel towers containing a total of 4008 rooms. Inside is a medieval world complete with a Fantasy Faire inhabited by strolling jugglers, fire eaters, and acrobats, as well as a Royal Village complete with peasants, serfs, and ladies-in-waiting around medieval theme shops. The 110,000-square-foot casino encompasses 2442 slot machines, more than 89 game tables, a sports book, and a poker and keno area. There are 12 restaurants, capable of feeding more than 20,000 people daily, and a 1000-seat amphitheater. Excalibur, which opened in June 1990, was built for $294 million and primarily financed with internally generated funds. In the year ending January 31, 1997, Excalibur contributed 23 percent of the organization's revenues, down from 33 percent in 1993, yet 1997 was a record year, generating the company's highest margins and over $100 million in operating cash flow. In fiscal year 1998, Excalibur underwent $25.1 million in renovations and was connected to the Luxor by enclosed, moving walkways.

Situated between the two anchors on the Las Vegas strip are two smaller casinos owned and operated by Circus. The Silver City Casino and Slots-A-Fun primarily depend on the foot traffic along the strip for their gambling patrons. Combined, they offer more than 1202 slot machines and 46 gaming tables on 34,900 square feet of casino floor.

Circus owns and operates 10 properties in Nevada and 1 in Mississippi and has a 50 percent ownership in three others (see Exhibit C).

All of Circus' operations do well in the city of Las Vegas. However, Circus Circus 1997 operational earnings for the Luxor and Circus Circus Las Vegas were off 38 percent from the previous year. Management credits the disruption in services due to renovations for this decline.

However, Circus' combined hotel room occupancy rates had remained above 90 percent due, in part, to low room rates ($45 to $69 at Circus Circus Las Vegas) and popular buffets. Each of the major properties contain large, inexpensive buffets that management believes make staying with Circus more attractive. Yet, recently, results show a room occupancy rate of 87.5 percent, due in part to the building boom in Las Vegas.

The company's other big-top facility is Circus Circus Reno. With the addition of Skyway Tower in 1985, this big top now offers a total of 1605 hotel rooms, 60,600 square feet of casino, a buffet that can seat 700 people, shops, video arcades, cocktail lounges, midway games, and circus acts. Circus Circus Reno had several marginal years but has become one of the leaders in the Reno market. Circus anticipates that recent remodeling, at a cost of $25.6 million, will increase this property's revenue-generating potential.

The Colorado Belle and the Edgewater Hotel are located in Laughlin, Nevada, on the banks of the Colorado River, a city 90 miles south of Las Vegas. The Colorado Belle, opened in 1987, features a huge paddle wheel riverboat replica, buffet, cocktail lounges, and shops. The Edgewater, acquired in 1983, has a southwestern motif, a 57,000-square-foot casino, a bowling center, buffet, and cocktail lounges. Combined, these two properties contain 2700 rooms and over 120,000 square feet of casino. These two operations contributed 12 percent of the company's revenues in the year ended January 31, 1997, and again in 1998, down from 21 percent in 1994. The extensive proliferation of casinos throughout the region, primarily on Indian land, and the development of megaresorts in Las Vegas have seriously eroded outlying markets such as Laughlin.

Three properties purchased in 1995 and located in Jean and Henderson, Nevada, represent continuing investments by Circus in outlying markets. The Gold Strike and Nevada Landing service the I-15 market between Las Vegas and southern California. These properties have over 73,000 square feet of casino space, 2140 slot machines, and 42 gaming tables combined. Each has limited hotel space (1116 rooms total) and depends heavily on I-15 traffic. The Railroad Pass is considered a local casino and is dependent on Henderson residents as its market. This smaller casino contains only 395 slot machines and 11 gaming tables.

Gold Strike Tunica (formally Circus Circus Tunica) is a dockside casino located in Tunica, Mississippi, opened in 1994 on 24 acres of land located along the Mississippi River, approximately 20 miles south of Memphis. In 1997, operating income declined by more than 50 percent due to the increase in competition and lack of hotel rooms. Circus decided to renovate this property and add a 1200-

EXHIBIT C

Circus Circus Enterprises, Inc.: Properties and Percent of Total Revenues

Properties	Percent Revenues			
	1998	*1997*	*1996*	*1995*
Las Vegas				
Circus Circus Las Vegas	25*	24*	27*	29*
Excalibur	21	23	23	25
Luxor	23	17	20	24
Slots-A-Fun and Silver City				
Reno				
Circus Circus Reno				
Laughlin				
Colorado Bell	12†	12†	13†	16†
Edgewater				
Jean, Nevada				
Gold Strike	6‡	6‡	4‡	NA
Nevada Landing				
Henderson, Nevada				
Railroad Pass				
Tunica, Mississippi				
Gold Strike	4	4	5	3
50% ownership:				
Silver Legacy, Reno, Nevada	7.3	6.5§	3.5§	0.5§
Monte Carlo, Las Vegas, Nevada				
Grand Victoria Riverboat Casino,				
Elgin, Illinois				

*Combined with revenues from Circus Circus Reno.
†Colorado Bell and Edgewater have been combined.
‡Gold Strike and Nevada Landing have been combined.
§Revenues of unconsolidated affiliates have been combined. Revenues from Slots-A-Fun and Silver City, management fees, and other income were not separately reported.

room tower hotel. Total cost for all remodeling was $119.8 million.

Joint Ventures

Circus is currently engaged in three joint ventures through the wholly owned subsidiary Circus Participant. In Las Vegas, Circus joined with Mirage Re

sorts to build and operate the Monte Carlo, a hotelcasino with 3002 rooms designed along the lines of the grand casinos of the Mediterranean. It is located on 46 acres (with 600 feet on the Las Vegas strip) between the New York–New York casino and the soon to be completed Bellagio, with all three casinos to be connected by monorail. The Monte Carlo features a 90,000-square-foot casino contain

EXHIBIT D

Selected Financial Information

	FY98	FY97	FY96	FY95	FY94	FY93	FY92	FY91
Earnings per share	0.40	0.99	1.33	1.59	1.34	2.05	1.84	1.39
Current ratio	0.85	1.17	1.30	1.35	0.95	0.90	1.14	0.88
Total liabilities/ total assets	0.65	0.62	0.44	0.54	0.57	0.48	0.58	0.77
Operating profit margin	17.4%	17%	19%	22%	21%	24.4%	24.9%	22.9%

Source: Circus Circus Annual Reports and 10k's, 1991–1998.

ing 2221 slot machines and 95 gaming tables, along with a 550-seat bingo parlor, high-tech arcade rides, restaurants and buffets, a microbrewery, approximately 15,000 square feet of meeting and convention space, and a 1200-seat theater. Opened on June 21, 1996, the Monte Carlo generated $14.6 million as Circus's share in operating income for the first 7 months of operation.

In Elgin, Illinois, Circus is in a 50 percent partnership with Hyatt Development Corporation in The Grand Victoria. Styled to resemble a Victorian riverboat, this floating casino and land-based entertainment complex includes some 36,000 square feet of casino space, containing 977 slot machines and 56 gaming tables. The adjacent land-based complex contains two movie theaters, a 240-seat buffet, restaurants, and parking for approximately 2000 vehicles. Built for a total of $112 million, The Grand Victoria returned to Circus $44 million in operating income in 1996.

The third joint venture is a 50 percent partnership with Eldorado Limited in the Silver Legacy. Opened in 1995, this casino is located between Circus Circus Reno and the Eldorado Hotel and Casino on two city blocks in downtown Reno, Nevada. The Silver Legacy has 1711 hotel rooms, 85,000 square feet of casino, 2275 slot machines, and 89 gaming tables. Management seems to believe that the Silver Legacy holds promise; however, the Reno market is suffering, and the opening of the Silver Legacy has cannibalized the Circus Circus Reno market.

Circus engaged in a fourth joint venture to penetrate the Canadian market, but on January 23, 1997, it announced that it had been bought out by

Hilton Hotels Corporation, one of three partners in the venture.

Circus has achieved success through an aggressive growth strategy and a corporate structure designed to enhance that growth. A strong cash position, innovative ideas, and attention to cost control have allowed Circus to satisfy the bottom line during a period when competitors typically were taking on large debt obligations to finance new projects (see Exhibits D, E, F, and G). Yet the

EXHIBIT E

Twelve-Year Summary

	Revenues (in thousands)	Net Income
FY 98	$1,354,487	$ 89,908
FY 97	1,334,250	100,733
FY 96	1,299,596	128,898
FY 95	1,170,182	136,286
FY 94	954,923	116,189
FY 93	843,025	117,322
FY 92	806,023	103,348
FY 91	692,052	76,292
FY 90	522,376	76,064
FY 89	511,960	81,714
FY 88	458,856	55,900
FY 87	373,967	28,198
FY 86	306,993	37,375

Source: Circus Circus Annual Reports and 10k's, 1986–1998.

EXHIBIT F

················

Circus Circus Enterprises, Inc.: Annual Income
(Year Ended January 31, in thousands)

	1/31/98	1/31/97	1/31/96	1/31/95	1/31/94
Revenues					
Casino	$ 632,122	$ 655,902	$ 664,772	$ 612,115	$ 538,813
Rooms	330,644	294,241	278,807	232,346	176,001
Food and beverage	215,584	210,384	201,385	189,664	152,469
Other	142,407	146,554	158,534	166,295	117,501
Earnings of unconsolidated affiliates	98,977	86,646	45,485	5,459	—
	1,419,734	1,393,727	1,348,983	1,205,879	984,784
Less complimentary allowances	(65,247)	(59,477)	(49,387)	(35,697)	(29,861)
Net revenue	1,354,487	1,334,250	1,299,596	1,170,182	954,923
Costs and expenses					
Casino	316,902	302,096	275,680	246,416	209,402
Rooms	122,934	116,508	110,362	94,257	78,932
Food and beverage	199,955	200,722	188,712	177,136	149,267
Other operating expenses	90,187	90,601	92,631	107,297	72,802
General and administrative	232,536	227,348	215,083	183,175	152,104
Depreciation and amortization	117,474	95,414	93,938	81,109	58,105
Preopening expense	3,447	—	—	3,012	16,506
Abandonment loss		48,309	45,148	—	—
	1,083,435	1,080,998	1,021,554	892,402	737,118
Operating profit before corporate expense	271,052	223,252	278,042	277,780	217,805
Corporate expense	34,552	31,083	26,669	21,773	16,744
Income from operations	236,500	222,169	251,373	256,007	201,061
Other income (expense)					
Interest, dividends, and other income (loss)	9,779	5,077	4,022	225	(683)
Interest income and guarantee fees from unconsolidated affiliate	6,041	6,865	7,517	992	—
Interest expense	(88,847)	(54,681)	(51,537)	(42,734)	(17,770)
Interest expense from unconsolidated affiliate	(15,551)	(15,567)	(5,616)	—	—
	(88,578)	(58,306)	(45,614)	(41,517)	(18,453)
Income before provision for income tax	147,922	163,863	205,759	214,490	182,608
Provision for income tax	58,014	63,130	76,861	78,204	66,419
Income before extraordinary loss		—	—	—	116,189
Extraordinary loss	—	—	—	—	—
Net income	89,908	100,733	128,898	136,286	116,189
Earnings per share					
Income before extraordinary loss	0.95	0.99	1.33	1.59	1.34
Extraordinary loss		—	—	—	—
Net income per share	0.94	0.99	1.33	1.59	1.34

Source: Circus Circus Annual Reports and 10k's, 1994–1998.

Circus Circus Enterprises, Inc.: Consolidated Balance Sheets (in thousands)

	1/31/98	1/31/97	1/31/96	1/31/95	1/31/94
Assets					
Current assets					
Cash and cash equivalents	$ 58,631	$ 69,516	$ 62,704	$ 53,764	$ 39,110
Receivables	33,640	34,434	16,527	8,931	8,673
Inventories	22,440	19,371	20,459	22,660	20,057
Prepaid expenses	20,281	19,951	19,418	20,103	20,062
Deferred income tax	7,871	8,577	7,272	5,463	
Total current	142,863	151,849	124,380	110,921	87,902
Property, equipment	2,466,848	1,920,032	1,474,684	1,239,062	1,183,164
Other assets					
Excess of purchase price over					
fair market value	375,375	385,583	394,518	9,836	10,200
Notes receivable	1,075	36,443	27,508	68,083	
Investments in unconsolidated affiliates	255,392	214,123	173,270	74,840	
Deferred charges and other assets	21,995	21,081	17,533	9,806	16,658
Total other	653,837	657,230	612,829	162,565	26,858
Total assets	3,263,548	2,729,111	2,213,503	1,512,548	1,297,924
Liabilities and Stockholders Equity					
Current liabilities					
Current portion of long-term debt	3,071	379	863	106	169
Accounts and contracts payable					
Trade	22,103	22,658	16,824	12,102	14,804
Construction	40,670	21,144	—	1,101	13,844
Accrued liabilities					
Salaries, wages and vacations	36,107	31,847	30,866	24,946	19,650
Progressive jackpots	7,511	6,799	8,151	7,447	4,881
Advance room depoists	6,217	7,383	7,517	8,701	6,981
Interest payable	17,828	9,004	3,169	2,331	2,278
Other	33,451	30,554	28,142	25,274	25,648
Income tax payable					3,806
Total current liabilities	166,958	129,768	95,532	82,008	92,061
Long-term debt	1,788,818	1,405,897	715,214	632,652	567,345
Other liabilities					
Deferred income tax	175,934	152,635	148,096	110,776	77,153
Other long-term liabilities	8,089	6,439	9,319	988	1,415
Total other liabilities	184,023	159,074	157,415	111,764	78,568
Total liabilities	2,139,799	1,694,739	968,161	826,424	737,974
Redeemable preferred stock		17,631	18,530		
Temporary equity		44,950			
Commitments and contingent liabilities					
Stockholders equity					
Common stock	1,893	1,880	1,880	1,607	1,603
Preferred stock					
Additional paid-in capital	558,658	498,893	527,205	124,960	120,135
Retained earnings	1,074,271	984,363	883,630	754,732	618,446
Treasury stock	(511,073)	(513,345)	(185,903)	(195,175)	(180,234)
Total stockholders equity	1,123,749	971,791	1,226,812	686,124	559,950
Total liabilities and stockholders equity	3,263,548	2,729,111	2,213,503	1,512,548	1,297,924

Source: Circus Circus Annual Reports and 10k's, 1994–1998.

market is changing. Gambling of all kinds has spread across the country; no longer does the average individual need to go to Las Vegas or New Jersey. Instead, gambling can be found as close as the local quick market (lottery), bingo hall, many Indian reservations, the Mississippi River, and others. There are now almost 300 casinos in Las Vegas alone, 60 in Colorado, and 160 in California. In order to maintain a competitive edge, Circus has continued to invest heavily in renovation of existing properties (a strategy common to the entertainment/amusement industry) and continues to develop new projects.

New Ventures

Circus currently has three new projects planned for opening within the near future. The largest project, named Mandalay Bay, is scheduled for completion in the first quarter of 1999 and is estimated to cost $950 million (excluding land). Circus owns a contiguous mile of the southern end of the Las Vegas strip that it calls the Masterplan Mile and which currently contains the Excalibur and Luxor resorts. Located next to the Luxor, Mandalay Bay will aim for the upscale traveler and player and will be styled as a South Seas adventure. The resort will contain a 43-story hotel/casino with over 3700 rooms and an 11-acre aquatic environment. The aquatic environment will contain a surfing beach, swim-up shark tank, and snorkeling reef. A Four Seasons Hotel with some 400 rooms will complement the remainder of Mandalay Bay. Circus anticipates that the remainder of the Masterplan Mile eventually will be comprised of at least one additional casino resort and a number of stand-alone hotels and amusement centers.

Circus also plans three other casino projects, provided all the necessary licenses and agreements can be obtained. In Detroit, Michigan, Circus has combined with the Atwater Casino Group in a joint venture to build a $600 million project. Negotiations with the city to develop the project have been completed; however, the remainder of the appropriate licenses will need to be obtained before construction begins.

Along the Mississippi Gulf, at the north end of the Bay of St. Louis, Circus plans to construct a casino resort containing 1500 rooms at an estimated cost of $225 million. Circus has received all necessary permits to begin construction; however,

these approvals have been challenged in court, delaying the project.

In Atlantic City, Circus has entered into an agreement with Mirage Resorts to develop a 181-acre site in the Marina District. Land title has been transferred to Mirage; however, Mirage has purported to cancel its agreement with Circus. Circus has filed suit against Mirage, seeking to enforce the contract, while others have filed suit to stop all development in the area.

Most of Circus' projects are being tailored to attract mainstream tourists and family vacationers. However, the addition of several joint ventures and the completion of the Masterplan Mile also will attract the more upscale customer.

THE GAMING INDUSTRY

By 1997, the gaming industry had captured a large amount of the vacation/leisure time dollars spent in the United States. Gamblers lost over $44.3 billion on legal wagering in 1995 (up from $29.9 billion in 1992), including wagers at racetracks, bingo parlors, lotteries, and casinos. This figure does not include dollars spent on lodging, food, transportation, and other related expenditures associated with visits to gaming facilities. Casino gambling accounts for 76 percent of all legal gambling expenditures, far ahead of second-place Indian Reservations at 8.9 percent and lotteries at 7.1 percent. The popularity of casino gambling may be credited to a more frequent and somewhat higher payout as compared with lotteries and racetracks; however, as winnings are recycled, the multiplier effect restores a high return to casino operators.

Geographic expansion has slowed considerably because no additional states have approved casino-type gambling since 1993. Growth has occurred in developed locations, with Las Vegas, Nevada, and Atlantic City, New Jersey, leading the way.

Las Vegas remains the largest U.S. gaming market and one of the largest convention markets, with more than 100,000 hotel rooms hosting more than 29.6 million visitors in 1996, up 2.2 percent over 1995. Casino operators are building to take advantage of this continued growth. Recent projects include the Monte Carlo ($350 million), New York–New York ($350 million), Bellagio ($1.4 billion), Hilton Hotels ($750 million), and Project Paradise ($800 million). Additionally, Harrah's is adding a 989-room tower and remodeling 500 current rooms, and Caesar's Palace has expansion plans to add 2000 rooms. Las Vegas hotel and casino capacity is expected to continue to expand, with some 12,500 rooms opening within a year. According to the Las Vegas Convention and Visitor Authority, Las Vegas is a destination market, with most visitors planning their trip more than a week in advance (81 percent), arriving by car (47 percent) or airplane (42 percent), and staying in a hotel (72 percent). Gamblers are typically return visitors (77 percent), averaging 2.2 trips per year, liking to play the slots (65 percent).

For Atlantic City, besides the geographic separation, the primary differences in the two markets reflect the different types of consumers frequenting these markets. While Las Vegas attracts overnight resort-seeking vacationers, Atlantic City's clientele are predominantly day-trippers traveling by automobile or bus. Gaming revenues are expected to continue to grow, perhaps to $4 billion in 1997 split between 10 casino/hotels currently operating. Growth in the Atlantic City area will be concentrated in the Marina section of town, where Mirage Resorts has entered into an agreement with the city to develop 150 acres of the Marina as a destination resort. This development will include a resort wholly owned by Mirage, a casino/hotel developed by Circus, and a complex developed by a joint venture with Mirage and Boyd Corp. Currently, in Atlantic City, Donald Trump's gaming empire holds the largest market share, with Trump's Castle, Trump Plaza, and the Taj Mahal (total market share is 30 percent). The next closest in market share is Caesar's (10.3 percent), Tropicana and Bally's (9.2 percent each), and Showboat (9.0 percent).

There remain a number of smaller markets located around the United States, primarily in Mississippi, Louisiana, Illinois, Missouri, and Indiana. Each state has imposed various restrictions on the development of casino operations within their states. In some cases, e.g., Illinois, where there are only 10 gaming licenses available, this has severely restricted growth opportunities and hurt revenues. In other states, e.g., Mississippi and Louisiana, revenues are up 8 and 15 percent, respectively, in riverboat operations. Native American casinos continue to be developed on federally controlled Indian land. These casinos are not publicly held but do tend to be managed by publicly held corpora-

tions. Overall, these other locations present a mix of opportunities and generally constitute only a small portion of overall gaming revenues.

MAJOR INDUSTRY PLAYERS

Over the past several years there have been numerous changes as mergers and acquisitions have reshaped the gaming industry. As of year end 1996, the industry was a combination of corporations ranging from those engaged solely in gaming to multinational conglomerates. The largest competitors, in terms of revenues, combined multiple industries to generate both large revenues and substantial profits (see Exhibit H). However, those engaged primarily in gaming also could be extremely profitable.

In 1996, Hilton began a hostile acquisition attempt of ITT Corporation. As a result of this attempt, ITT merged with Starwood Lodging Corporation and Starwood Lodging Trust. The resulting corporation is one of the world's largest hotel and gaming corporations, owning the Sheraton, The Luxury Collection, the Four Points Hotels, and Caesar's, as well as communications and educational services. In 1996, ITT hosted approximately 50 million customer nights in locations worldwide. Gaming operations are located in Las Vegas, Atlantic City, Halifax and Sydney (Nova Scotia), Lake Tahoe, Tunica (Mississippi), Lima (Peru), Cairo (Egypt), Canada, and Australia. In 1996, ITT had net income of $249 million on revenues of $6.579 billion. In June 1996, ITT announced plans to join with Planet Hollywood to develop casino/hotels with the Planet Hollywood theme in both Las Vegas and Atlantic City. However, these plans may be deferred as ITT becomes fully integrated into Starwood and management has the opportunity to refocus on the operations of the company.

Hilton Hotels owns (as of February 1, 1998) or leases and operates 25 hotels and manages 34 hotels partially or wholly owned by others along with 180 franchised hotels. Eleven of the hotels are also casinos, 6 of which are located in Nevada, 2 in Atlantic City, with the other 3 in Australia and Uruguay. In 1997, Hilton had net income of $250.0 million on $5.31 billion in revenues. Hilton receives some 98 percent of total operating revenues from gaming operations and continues to expand in the market. Recent expansions include the Wild Wild West theme hotel/casino in Atlantic City, the

EXHIBIT H
....
Major U.S. Gaming, Lottery, and Parimutuel Companies:
1996 Revenues and Net Income (in millions)

	1997 Revenues	1997 Income	1996 Revenues	1996 Net Income
Starwood/ITT	—	—	$6597.0	$249.0
Hilton Hotels	5316.0	250.0	3940.0	82.0
Harrah's Entertainment	1619.0	99.3	1586.0	98.9
Mirage Resorts	1546.0	207	1358.3	206.0
Circus Circus	1354.4	89.9	1247.0	100.7
Trump Hotel and Casino, Inc.	1399.3	−42.1	976.3	−4.9
MGM Grand	827.5	111.0	804.8	74.5
Aztar	782.3	4.4	777.5	20.6
Int. Game Technology	743.9	137.2	733.5	118.0

Source: Individual companies annual reports and 10k's, 1996 and 1997.

completed acquisition of all the assets of Bally's, and construction on a 2900-room Paris Casino resort located next to Bally's Las Vegas.

Harrah's Entertainment, Inc., is primarily engaged in the gaming industry with casino/hotels in Reno, Lake Tahoe, Las Vegas, and Laughlin, Nevada, Atlantic City, New Jersey, riverboats in Joliet, Illinois and Vicksburg and Tunica, Mississippi, Shreveport, Louisiana, Kansas City, Kansas, two Indian casinos, and one in Auckland, New Zealand. In 1997, it operated a total of approximately 774,500 square feet of casino space with 19,835 slot machines and 934 tables games. With this and some 8197 hotel rooms, the company had a net income of $99.3 million on $1.619 billion in revenues.

All of Mirage Resorts' gaming operations are currently located in Nevada. It owns and operates the Golden Nugget-Downtown, Las Vegas, the Mirage on the strip in Las Vegas, Treasure Island, and the Golden Nugget-Laughlin. Additionally, it is a 50 percent owner of the Monte Carlo with Circus Circus. Net income for Mirage Resorts in 1997 was $207 million on revenues of $1.546 billion. Current expansion plans include the development of the Bellagio in Las Vegas ($1.6 billion estimated cost) and the Beau Rivage in Biloxi, Mississippi ($600 million estimated cost). These two properties would add a total of 265,900 square feet of casino space to the current Mirage inventory and an additional 252 gaming tables and 4746 slot machines.

An additional project is the development of the Marina area in Atlantic City, New Jersey, in partnership with Boyd Gaming.

MGM Grand Hotel and Casino is located on approximately 114 acres at the northeast corner of Las Vegas Boulevard across the street from New York–New York hotel and casino. The casino is approximately 171,500 square feet in size and is one of the largest casinos in the world, with 3669 slot machines and 157 table games. Current plans call for extensive renovation costing $700 million. Through a wholly owned subsidiary, MGM owns and operates the MGM Grand Diamond Beach Hotel and a hotel/casino resort in Darwin, Australia. Additionally, MGM and Primadonna Resorts, Inc., each own 50 percent of New York–New York hotel and casino, a $460 million architecturally distinctive themed destination resort that opened on January 3, 1997. MGM also intends to construct and operate a destination resort hotel/casino, entertainment, and retail facility in Atlantic City on approximately 35 acres of land on the Atlantic City Boardwalk.

THE LEGAL ENVIRONMENT
....

Within the gaming industry, all current operators must consider compliance with extensive gaming regulations as a primary concern. Each state or country has its own specific regulations and regulatory boards requiring extensive reporting and licensing requirements. For example, in Las Vegas, Nevada, gambling operations are subject to regulatory control by the Nevada State Gaming Control Board, the Clark County Nevada Gaming and Liquor Licensing Board, and city government regulations. The laws, regulations, and supervisory procedures of virtually all gaming authorities are based on public policy primarily concerned with the prevention of unsavory or unsuitable persons from having a direct or indirect involvement with gaming at any time or in any capacity and the establishment and maintenance of responsible accounting practices and procedures. Additional regulations typically cover the maintenance of effective controls over the financial practices of licensees, including the establishment of minimum procedures for internal fiscal affairs and the safeguarding of assets and revenues, providing reliable record keeping and requiring the filing of periodic reports, the prevention of cheating and fraudulent practices, and providing a source of state and local revenues through taxation and licensing fees. Changes in such laws, regulations, and procedures could have an adverse effect on many gaming operations. All gaming companies must submit detailed operating and financial reports to authorities. Nearly all financial transactions, including loans, leases, and the sales of securities, must be reported. Some financial activities are subject to approval by regulatory agencies. As Circus moves into other locations outside of Nevada, it will need to adhere to local regulations.

FUTURE CONSIDERATIONS

Circus Circus states that it is "in the business of entertainment, with ... core strength in casino gaming" and that it intends to focus its efforts in Las Vegas, Atlantic City, and Mississippi. Circus further states that the "future product in gaming, to be sure, is the entertainment resort" (Circus Circus 1997 Annual Report).

Circus was one of the innovators of the gaming resort concept and has continued to be a leader in that field. However, the megaentertainment resort industry operates differently than the traditional casino gaming industry. In the past, consumers would visit a casino to experience the thrill of gambling. Now they not only gamble but expect to be dazzled by enormous entertainment complexes that are costing billions of dollars to build. The competition has continued to increase at the same time growth rates have been slowing.

For years, analysts have questioned the ability of the gaming industry to continue high growth in established markets as the industry matures. Through the 1970s and 1980s, the gaming industry experienced rapid growth. Through the 1990s, the industry began to experience a shakeout of marginal competitors and consolidation phase. Circus Circus has been successful through this turmoil but now faces the task of maintaining high growth in a more mature industry.

Bibliography

"Circus Circus Announces Promotion," *PR Newswire,* June 10, 1997.

"Industry Surveys—Lodging and Gaming," *Standard and Poors Industry Surveys,* June 19, 1997.

"Casinos Move into New Areas," *Standard and Poors Industry Surveys,* March 11, 1993, pp. L35–L41.

Circus Circus Enterprises, Inc., Annual Report to Shareholders, January 31, 1989, January 31, 1990, January 31, 1993, January 31, 1994, January 31, 1995, January 31, 1996.

Circus Circus Enterprises, Inc., Annual Report to Shareholders, January 31, 1997.

Circus Circus Enterprises, Inc., Annual Report to Shareholders, January 31, 1998.

Corning, Blair. "Luxor: Egypt Opens in Vegas," *San Antonio Express News,* October 24, 1993.

Lalli, Sergio. "Excalibur Awaiteth," *Hotel and Motel Management,* June 11, 1990.

"Economic Impacts of Casino Gaming in the United States," by Arthur Anderson for the American Gaming Association, May 1997.

"Harrah's Survey of Casino Entertainment," Harrah's Entertainment, Inc., 1996.

"ITT Board Rejects Hilton's Offer as Inadequate, Reaffirms Belief that ITT's Comprehensive Plan Is in the Best Interest of ITT Shareholders," press release, August 14, 1997.

Mirage Resorts, Inc. *1997 and 1998 10k,* and retrieved from EDGAR Database, *http://www.sec.gov/Archives/edgar/data/.*

Hilton Hotels Corp. *1997 and 1998 10k,* retrieved from EDGAR Database, *http://www.sec.gov/Archives/edgar/data/.*

Aztar Corp. *1997 and 1998 10k,* retrieved from EDGAR Database, *http://www.sec.gov/Archives/edgar/data/.*

ITT Corp. *1997 10k,* retrieved from EDGAR Database, *http://www.sec.gov/Archives/edgar/data/.*

Harrah's Entertainment, Inc. *1997 and 1998 10k,* retrieved from EDGAR Database, *http://www.sec.gov/Archives/edgar/data/.*

MGM Grand, Inc. *1997 and 1998 10k,* retrieved from EDGAR Database, *http://www.sec.gov/Archives/edgar/data/.*

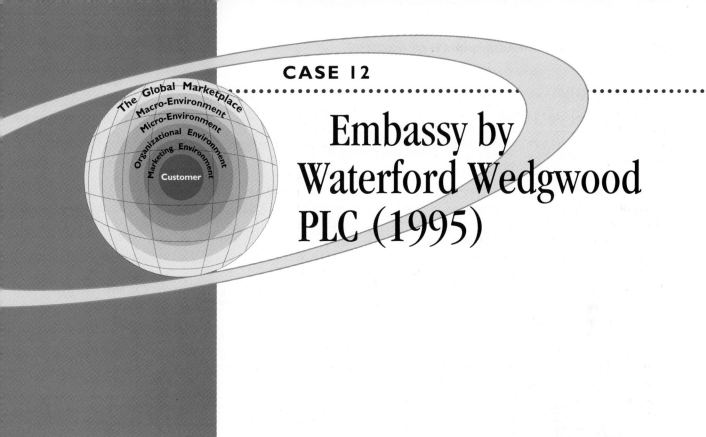

Embassy by Waterford Wedgwood PLC (1995)

This case was prepared by Julian W. Vincze, Professor of Marketing, Crummer Graduate School of Business, Rollins College.

The headline, "A New Brand Restores Sparkle to Waterford,"[1] caught Jane Mills' attention. As a bride-to-be, Jane had just registered her choices for Waterford crystal stemware and Wedgwood china at the bridal registries[2] of two local upscale department stores. Since the wedding was still several months away, Jane wondered if she had registered her choices too quickly. The article noted that in 1990, Waterford Wedgwood's future had looked grim. U.S. sales (Waterford's main market) were falling as the economy depressed and customers had turned away from prestige purchases. Jane recalled that in 1994 many large U.S. retailers had been in bankruptcy proceedings, and competition from low-cost producers in the former eastern European block was hot. But Jane now read that 1994 sales of Waterford crystal and

Wedgwood china were both up and that the company's share of market had increased seven percentage points from 1990 to a current 34 percent. After several years of losses, the company was profitable again. (See Exhibit A for details.) The article seemed to attribute this turnaround to the 1990 decision by Waterford to introduce Marquis, a midpriced brand and the first new brand for Waterford in 200 years. And now Waterford seemed to be hoping for the same impact on Wedgwood, with 1995 plans to introduce Embassy, a midpriced brand of porcelain dinnerware. Jane, an MBA student, decided to find out more about what had happened at Waterford Wedgwood, thinking it would be an interesting topic for discussion in her marketing strategy class.

WATERFORD WEDGWOOD HISTORY

Waterford Wedgwood PLC (WW), the Irish holding company, had two divisions—Waterford Crystal and Wedgwood Group. Waterford, with about 60

EXHIBIT A
················

Waterford Wedgwood PLC Key Financial Items (in 000s U.S. dollars)

	12/31/93	12/31/92	12/31/91	12/31/90
Sales	449,577	444,163	511,594	
Gross revenue	319,200	273,604	292,121	
Total operating expense	304,400	269,939	284,164	
Operating income	14,800	3,965	7,957	
Pretax income	10,100	−17,030	−2,630	
Total return on equity	9.56	−14.45	−3.75	−39.88
Operating margin %	4.64	1.45	2.72	3.23
Return on assets %	5.68	−4.70	0.17	−4.92
Quick ratio	1.36	1.13	1.24	0.85
Current ratio	2.93	2.76	2.95	1.83
Inventory-days held	185.18	222.52	222.69	233.79
Inventory turn ratio	1.94	1.62	1.62	1.54

Source: W/D Partners Worldscope.

percent of WW's revenue and world renowned for quality crystal, dated back to 1783 and the southeast Ireland port city of Waterford, where its main factory and headquarters still remain. Wedgwood, with about 40 percent of WW's revenue and based in Barlaston, England, and also world renowned, was acquired in 1986 and dated from 1759. The Wedgwood Group consisted of Josiah Wedgwood and Sons, Ltd. (its main operation, suppliers of high-quality tableware and ornamentalware in fine bone china, fine earthenware, oven-to-tableware, Jasperware, and Black Basalt); Johnson Brothers, Ltd. (makers of fine earthenware and tableware); Coalport China, Ltd. (fine bone china tableware and ornamentalware); Masons Ironstone, Ltd., and William Adams and Son (Potter), Ltd.; Wedgwood Hotelware, Ltd. (suppliers of bone china to the hotel and catering industries); and Precision Studios, Ltd. (manufacturers of high-quality transfers for ceramic, glass, and enamel cookware). WW was a major international supplier of crystal and china, with about 32 percent of its 1993 sales from the United States, 54 percent from Europe (including the United Kingdom), 9 percent from the Far East, and the remaining 6 percent from other countries.

Consortium Takeover
·················

In 1990, a consortium led by Morgan Stanley & Co. and H. J. Heinz Company's chairman, Anthony O'Reilly, bought a 30 percent stake in WW (Dr. O'Reilly became chairman in 1993). Since that time, WW had undertaken severe cost-cutting measures that resulted in savings of 35 million Irish pounds through wage reductions, automation, cutting staff from 10,392 to 7000, and reducing overhead. For example, the crystal division's three Irish plants in Waterford, Kilbarry, Dungarvan, and Butlerstown, undertook a 3-year cost-cutting program that invovled 800 redundancies[3] and was expected to result in a further reduction of 300 workers.[4] Dr. Paddy Galvin, Waterford Crystal chairman and chief executive, said: "Gradual restructuring [at Waterford] will continue,"[5] although industry observers believed radical restructuring had been completed. At WW's annual meeting held in Dublin on June 15, 1994, when asked about the lack of dividend payments since 1988, Dr. O'Reilly responded by noting that key financial goals directed WW's actions. The goals were to recommence dividend payments as soon as prudent, to deliver above-average capital growth and sustain an above-average price-earnings ratio, to strengthen the balance sheet, and continually to enhance the quality of earnings. O'Reilly said: "Further advance is imperative for the Group [WW]. Its orientation is clear: strategic repositioning of our brands, their increased development and enhanced recognition, sustained development of multisourcing opportunities for all Group [WW] brands, and sustained development of cost-efficient manufacturing units in the Group." When asked where the Waterford Crystal business would go in the future, O'Reilly said: "The strategy is to build on the firm foundations laid, through the further enhancement of the prestige image of Waterford Crystal as a world brand in world markets through increasing and sustained investment; the continued development of multisourcing opportunities for our crystal brands; the capture of a greater market share for Marquis in the midprice segments of world crystal markets; the unremitting development of the Waterford manufacturing plants as cost-efficient producers of premium quality, world-beating crystal; and the penetration of new and underdeveloped markets by Waterford brands."[6]

Launch of Marquis

The decision in 1990 to launch Marquis was a calculated risk because it was the first time outsourcing of production would be used by Waterford. The plants that produced Marquis were located in Germany (former East German location), Slovenia, Slovakia, and the Czech Republic. Also, Marquis was introduced to sell at about 20 percent less than traditional Waterford. Redmond O'Donoghue, Waterford's head of marketing, noted that Marquis sales were not intended to cannibalize existing, more expensive Waterford brands but were aimed at garnering added new sales and extra market share at the expense of competing brands (especially in the United States). The Marquis price range was not cheap; for example, in the American market, a stemware glass from Marquis would be priced at $30 retail, while regular Waterford prices would be $40 to $50. Christopher McGillivary, chief executive officer of Waterford's U.S. operations, suggested that the challenge would be to lure customers from the competition, which were such heavyweights as Brown-Foreman Corp. (U.S. maker

of Lenox crystal and china) and Hoya Corp. (Japan) and Baccarat (France).

Marketing Strategy

As a result of marketing research that involved focus groups in three countries and reviewing 30 hours of taped interviews with consumers, Waterford concluded that customers, although price conscious, were still willing to pay for sensible consumption. "Status isn't gone; it has just been redefined," said Mr. O'Donoghue.[7] Waterford decided on a three-tier market strategy with the old-line Waterford at the top, Marquis a rung lower, and a third lower tier "which we didn't want to be in," noted O'Donoghue.[8] The results were better than expected, and within 2 years, Marquis had sold more than US$13 million, had become the number six brand in the U.S. market, and had increased the number of bridal registrations from 613 to 10,376. In the same period, Waterford bridal registrations remained virtually constant at 12,475. "Bridal registrations are hugely important to us—they are inevitably the beginning of a crystal collection," says Mr. O'Donoghue.[9]

"I admit I was skeptical at first, but Marquis has been more successful than I would have ever guessed," said Susan Azar, crystal buyer for Dayton Hudson Corp.'s Marshall Field department stores. Ms. Azar expects that Marshall Field's combined sales of Waterford and Marquis will be up 30 percent in 1994. Marquis was given a distinctly different design—one that was simpler and lighter looking than traditional Waterford—while the company freshened up the original Waterford products by introducing colored crystal, new limited-edition sculpted pieces, and new designs such as the Doors of Dublin bowl, which reflected Irish tradition. Mr. O'Donoghue attributed the success of Marquis to keeping it sufficiently different from traditional Waterford while still allowing the new brand to benefit by association with the Waterford name.[10]

Restructuring

The downsizing and cost-cutting efforts (restructuring) had begun shortly after the consortium's buy-into WW and at about the same time as the decision to launch Waterford's new brand, Marquis. By September of 1993, the crystal division had installed more efficient production processes aimed at further lowering Waterford's cost base and boosting margins to the 50 percent required to sustain manufacturing. Dr. Galvin said: "We are well on the way to making crystal manufacturing more competitive, but we still have to complete the turn-around. Now that we are back in profit, it means we can approach the future with more enthusiasm and the workers have had the burden of uncertainty lifted." But Dr. Galvin was very cautious about the future and said: "Can anybody seriously suggest that we are already out of the woods?" since over the previous 5 years accumulated losses totaled 137 million Irish pounds.[11]

WEDGWOOD STRUGGLES

During this same 1990–1993 period, the Wedgwood fine china division also had struggled to cut costs by closing three plants and restructuring.[12] Profits remained level at approximately 8.6 million Irish pounds,[13] and Wedgwood was the U.K. market leader with about 20 percent market share, followed closely by Royal Doulton, then several larger firms, and finally, three or four dozen small firms. In the U.S. market, which accounted for 13.4 percent of Wedgwood's gross revenue, versus the United Kingdom's 61.3 percent, Wedgwood also was the market leader, although Japanese brands such as Noritake were fighting for leadership. In the Japanese market, Wedgwood was the leading import brand, although sales recently had turned downward. The distribution channels for tableware and giftware were dominated by department stores but included variety stores; specialist china or china and glass stores; hardware, cookware, and kitchenware shops; superstores; specialty gift shops; tourist shops; craft fairs; and even home shopping sources and supermarkets. Media advertising of china and earthenware products traditionally had been relatively limited, with the bulk of expenditures occurring by department stores via newspaper ads and/or color supplements. In the United States, restrictive consumer legislation had tightened controls on the amount of lead permitted to be released by tableware. In California, legislation known as Proposition 65 was even more restrictive than federal and other state laws. There, labeling regulations required products to carry the appropriate lead leaching warnings. In a recent lawsuit, California's state attorney alleged that Wedgwood, Royal Doulton, Noritake, and others had not complied with Proposition 65. The manufacturers, without admitting guilt or liability, paid US$1.2 million for expenses and penalties and agreed to establish a lead-reduction program.[14]

Embassy by Wedgwood

Introducing the new porcelain brand Embassy might prove more difficult for Wedgwood than Marquis had been for Waterford. True, both Embassy and Marquis were aimed at being priced about 20 percent below the traditional premium pricing of their parent brand—hence the midprice description. For example, Embassy was expected to be priced at about US$80 for a five-piece place setting, compared with US$100 to US$400 for a Wedgwood china setting. However, Wedgwood had produced only premium china for almost 250 years, and a porcelain brand was clearly a step down in quality and prestige. Adrian O'Carroll, an analyst at Dillon Read, Ltd., in London, said: "Marquis was still a crystal. But with Embassy, Wedgwood is talking about introducing something completely different from fine china."[15] Mr. O'Carroll said that the porcelain line Embassy may have its greatest chance of success in continental Europe, where the Wedgwood name is not as closely associated with fine china as it is in Britain and where porcelain tableware is popular. One key aspect of the Embassy launch will not be known for some time: Waterford is counting on customers who buy Marquis and Embassy to eventually trade up to the more expensive Waterford crystal and Wedgwood china lines as their buying power increases.

Dr. O'Reilly said: "We believe that it will move Wedgwood into a new era. The objective is to capture further market share in the international ceramics market. The strategy is to penetrate the midprice sector of the tableware market through a distinctive range of new designs—less formal, more affordable, and more accessible. The tactics will involve a judicious outsourcing campaign, vigorously overseen to ensure that the quality and technical standards, traditional in the Wedgwood brand product, are fully upheld." O'Reilly confirmed that further investment would be made to enhance internal systems at Wedgwood to improve management information and logistical support to both manufacturing and marketing. He said: "This new brand will be endorsed by the Wedgwood heritage, values, and quality and will develop a character of its own, distinct from Wedgwood's formal fine bone china pedigree, yet reflecting its core brand values. It will reflect the growing trend toward a less formal lifestyle, embodying a new style of design: more loose, fresher, lower-priced certainly, and widening the perception of Wedgwood to embrace both the 'traditional classic' and the 'contemporary classic,' whilst improving the operating margin from sales. It will be supported by an array of giftware products calculated to achieve deeper market penetration and profitability."[16]

Jane's Puzzlement

After gathering all the information she could readily find on WW, Jane was faced with a dilemma. She knew that if she were to begin an in-class discussion of the WW situation and describe the launch of Marquis in 1990 with its subsequent success and then note WW's plans for launching Embassy by Wedgwood, someone was bound to ask her what she thought of WW's plans. The professor might even ask her if she approved of WW's plans for Embassy. Jane knew that she had to form a firm opinion either for or against launching Embassy.

Questions

1. What are the key differences between the Waterford situation in 1990 when the decision was made to launch Marquis and the 1995 situation Wedgwood faced in deciding whether to launch Embassy?

2. What other issues were important to Waterford Wedgwood corporate officers in early 1995?

3. If you agree that Embassy should be launched during 1995, then detail your reasons for this viewpoint.

4. If you believe that launching Embassy in 1995 is inappropriate, then detail your reasons for this viewpoint.

5. What, if any, other action options are available to Waterford Wedgwood?

Endnotes

1. Judith Valente, "A New Brand Restores Sparkle to Waterford," *Wall Street Journal,* November 10, 1994.
2. Bridal registration is a U.S. system where a couple getting married register their favored crystal and dinnerware design with a department store to ensure that they receive that particular design and no other as wedding presents. The system is usually computerized and means that the retailer will know what items have already been purchased for the couple and thus eliminates the possibility of the couple receiving the same present twice.
3. Redundancies are employee positions that are determined to be no longer necessary—thus the employee is laid off or dismissed. Downsizing and re-engineering are terms sometimes used in the United States for a similar exercise of redesigning the workforce and working processes.
4. Mary Canniffe, "O'Reilly Says Results Justify Strategy," *The Irish Times,* September 2, 1994.
5. Mary Canniffe, "Waterford Wedgwood in Good Shape," *The Irish Times,* September 2, 1994.
6. "Waterford Wedgwood PLC: Chairman's AGM Statement," *PR Newswire,* June 15, 1994.
7. Judith Valente, "A New Brand Restores Sparkle to Waterford," *Wall Street Journal,* November 10, 1994.
8. Brendan McGrath, "Waterford Steps Up Marketing Drive: Plans Involve New Technology, Fewer Jobs, and an Aggressive Marketing Campaign," *The Irish Times,* September 24, 1993.
9. *Ibid.*
10. Judith Valente, "A New Brand Restores Sparkle to Waterford," *Wall Street Journal,* November 10, 1994.
11. Brendon McGrath, "Waterford Steps Up Marketing Drive," *The Irish Times,* September 24, 1993.
12. "Key Note Report: China and Earthenware—An Industry Sector Analysis," 1994 Key Note, Ltd., February 1, 1994.
13. Victor Kuss, "Waterford Breaches Pain Barrier," *The Irish Times,* April 1, 1994.
14. "Key Note Report: China and Earthenware—An Industry Sector Analysis," 1994 Key Note, Ltd., February 1, 1994.
15. Judith Valente, "A New Brand Restores Sparkle to Waterford," *Wall Street Journal,* November 10, 1994.
16. "Waterford Wedgwood PLC: Chairman's AGM Statement," *PR Newswire,* June 15, 1994.

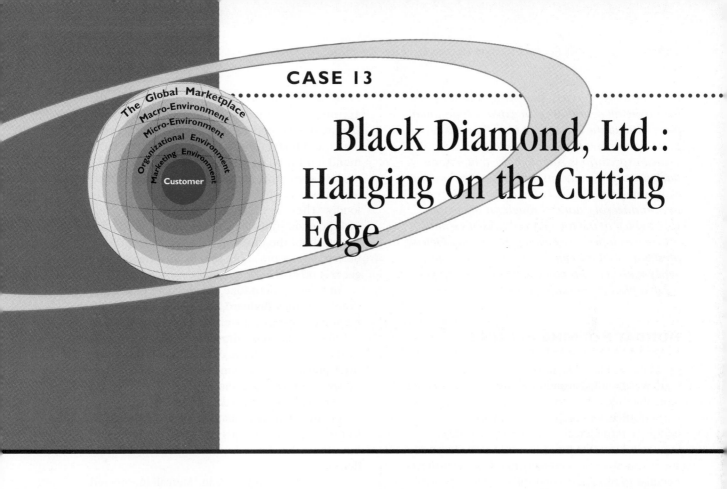

Black Diamond, Ltd.: Hanging on the Cutting Edge

This case was prepared by Steven J. Maranville, Assistant Professor of Strategic Management, University of St. Thomas and Madeleine E. Pullman of Southern Methodist University.

Jeff Jamison looked above at the glistening ice and snow of the frozen waterfalls. He had waited 3 weeks for the ice to get to this perfect condition, thick enough to support body weight, and the correct consistency for holding the picks of the two axes in his hands and the tooth-covered crampons on his feet. On this day in early January of 1993, he was trying out a new axe, the Black Prophet, a state-of-the-art climbing tool with a light weight, composite handle, and innovative head design produced by Black Diamond Equipment, Ltd. Everyone in the mountaineering world was talking about the Black Prophet's novel design and waiting for the tool to enter the stores in the coming months. Jeff was lucky

enough to have a connection with one of Black Diamond's sales representatives, giving Jeff access to the new Black Prophet before its formal release to the market.

At the top of the last pitch of the climb, he sunk the Black Prophet into the ice and suddenly felt a disconcerting snap. Jeff watched with trepidation as pieces of the broken axe plummeted thousands of feet to the canyon floor. As panic swept in, Jeff realized that he would be forced to descend with only one axe, a doable but challenging feat. During the long, arduous descent, all Jeff could think about was how could a tool like that one have left Black Diamond's factory.

The following Monday, January 4, 1993, Mellie Abrahamsen, Black Diamond's new quality assurance manager, a recent MBA graduate from the University of Utah, entered her office and turned on her computer to scan her e-mail. The news of the axe incident was echoing from all over the plant. Research & Development, Produc-

tion, Customer Service, Marketing, and the president were all demanding an explanation and a plan. With all the excitement over the new design, preseason orders for the Black Prophet had exceeded expectations. Although the tool was on back order for many customers, the first production run of the axe had already been shipped to mountaineering stores throughout the world. Highlighted at the top of Abrahamsen's e-mail listing was a priority message from Peter Metcalf, president of Black Diamond, calling an emergency meeting with all department heads to develop a plan for handling the crisis.

MONDAY MORNING MEETING

By 9:00 A.M., Black Diamond's top management team was huddled around the square butcher-block table that filled the center of Metcalf's congested corner office. As Abrahamsen approached, she could see into Metcalf's office through the two large windows that faced the shop floor. Because she was new to the company, many of the artifacts peculiar to Black Diamond still caught her attention.

Metcalf's office walls were decorated with framed photographs of mountain-climbing and skiing adventures. The management team members sitting around the table were dressed casually; many were wearing Black Diamond sportswear—tee-shirts and sweaters with the Black Diamond insignia. Abrahamsen squeezed through the office and found a seat next to Metcalf, from which she had a view out the windows.

Metcalf anxiously spoke to the group. "This incident is a devastating blow. Thank goodness the guy didn't get hurt, but now every one of our axes out there is suspect. If we have to issue a recall on the product, that will kill our axe business. If we have to discontinue our axe program, all the European competitors will step in and copy the technology that we worked so long to perfect. Yet, think of the liability implications of an accident from this tool! How could this have happened? I thought this axe had the latest and greatest technology! We've never had problems like this with our regular mountaineering axes."

Cranor, the marketing manager, added to Metcalf's fervent speech. "If customers see this axe as being of poor quality, we'll be forced to cease the axe program. But worse, if customers think Black Diamond is a company that markets unsafe products, our whole business is in jeopardy! Black Diamond must not lose its leadership image."

"My sales representatives are having a fit," Stan Smith, manager of customer service, proclaimed loudly. "They have huge back orders for the axe, and the retail shops have several customers a day asking about the tool. You folks know how this industry is—rumors about tool failures and accidents get around fast."

In a despondent tone, the designer of the Black Prophet, Chuck Brainard, said, "I can't believe this nightmare. Just as we were sitting on top of the world with the most innovative design to enter the market in years—all the competition taken by surprise, and a good ice climbing season ahead—a major stroke of bad luck hits."

"I can't help but think" said Stan Brown, the production manager, "that the cause of the axe's failure is in its design. It's great to be innovative, but I think the design is so innovative that it just doesn't work."

"Now wait a minute, Stan," Metcalf interjected, "I don't want this to deteriorate into finger pointing."

Brainard spoke, "No, no, that's all right Peter. Stan might be right. Maybe we did go too far."

Metcalf went on: "We don't know all the facts. So let's stay focused and not jump to conclusions. This is a companywide problem."

Trying to refocus the group, Cranor said, "We tried to cut the lead time on this project so that we would have at least a year of sales before the French, Swiss, and other U.S. competitors could copy our concept and steal our market share. We have the reputation as the quality and innovative design company. This incident is potentially very damaging to our reputation as the market leader for innovation."

"We've got to nip this one in the bud and find a way to reassure our customer base," contended Smith. "I need an answer as soon as possible."

John Bercaw, manager of research and development, said, "Stan, I appreciate the urgent need that you're feeling with regard to handling customer concerns, but we need more than a quick fix. We need to find out why the failure occurred and put systems in place to prevent this from happening again."

"I agree," Metcalf applauded. "As I said, this is a companywide problem."

Brainard attempted to clarify the situation: "As I see it, the possible sources of the failure are design, materials, and/or assembly."

"I can speak about the development phase of the project," stated Bercaw. "We worked hard to develop this axe and cut down on the lead time between the conceptualization and production of the final tool. Peter, you know we've been under tremendous pressure to have this new axe into the production phase and on the market in under 2 years."

Metcalf nodded. "That's been our strategy," he said, "being the firstest with the mostest."

Bercaw continued: "This project has been a real struggle; we've been working with all sorts of new technologies like composite construction and modular tool design. The vendors normally don't make tools for these types of applications. They've had a hard time meeting our specifications, and many of the vendors don't want to work on our products because of potential liability implications."

"What about the assembly?" asked Metcalf.

Brown spoke, "Well, the shop worked like crazy to get those axes out for the winter season, and I put my best people on the rush assembly. The shop has been really taxed, what with the increasing growth rate for all our climbing and mountaineering products. We're always scrambling to meet the back orders. We need more people and new machines to keep up with this demand and improve our quality."

Metcalf persisted: "Do you know of anything in particular that may have been out of the ordinary during assembly?"

Brown replied: "I'd have to talk to Brian, our lead assembler, to see if he has any clues about why that axe could have failed in the field."

Metcalf turned to his left, where Black Diamond's newest management team member was sitting. "I realize that this is all new to you and that you came in after the fact, so I doubt the Quality Assurance Department can do much about this situation now."

Caught somewhat by surprise, Abrahamsen pulled her thoughts together. "Since this job is a newly created position, I wasn't here during the design development and testing phase. I would like to see the procedures and testing information on the production lot of axes. Black Diamond wants to be ISO 9000-certified, and we would need to have all those documents for ISO 9000 certification anyway, so this is a good starting place. Meanwhile, I think we should bring all the field axes back for inspection to reinforce customer confidence and prevent what happened on Saturday from happening again."

Looking out of his office's windows, Metcalf pointed to the shop floor and remarked, "Isn't that Brian walking through the shop? Ask him to come in."

Brian Palmer, the lead assembler, entered Metcalf's office. There was no place to sit, so he remained standing. Metcalf explained to Brian the purpose for bringing him into the meeting. Brian indicated that he had heard about the climbing incident involving the Black Prophet.

Metcalf continued: "Brian, we're not on a witch hunt; we're trying to understand the full range of factors that could have contributed to the tool's failure. What can you tell us about the assembly?"

Brian spoke frankly: "I personally put together all those axes. We didn't have any procedures, because it was the first time we had made a production lot. Normally when we work on a new product, we go through a learning curve trying to figure out the best assembly method. We make so many different types of products in the shop, it's really like a craft shop. And I'm not even sure if I have the most up-to-date prints right now. The vendor had a lot of trouble casting all those parts to the exact dimensions. But I was able to find enough parts that seemed to fit, and with a little extra elbow grease, I hammered the pieces together. I had to work overtime to meet the deadline and get all the preliminary orders out to the customers. But that's what matters—pleasing the customer."

"But is creating a defective axe really pleasing the customer?" questioned Abrahamsen. "What good is it to be first to market if the product fails in the field. Sure, we have to get to market fast, but we also have to make the axe right the first time. The way we deal in the short term with the Black Prophet situation will have some long-term implications for Black Diamond's strategy. I think we should examine the new product introduction process as well as the ongoing production processes to see how we can prevent this type of thing from happening in the future."

THE MARKET FOR MOUNTAINEERING EQUIPMENT

The established customer for mountaineering products, including mountaineering skis, had traditionally been the serious international mountaineer—professionals as well as expert amateurs. Some dedicated mountaineers worked as professional guides and explorers; nonprofessionals had other jobs, but both professionals and amateurs spent their vacations and weekends climbing in their local areas and traveling throughout the world attempting to conquer remote peaks. This traditional customer base had been primarily in North America, eastern and western Europe, Japan, and Korea, although limited numbers of participants were from other countries.

Mountaineering was as popular in Europe as basketball was in the United States, with mountaineering stars earning high incomes through competitions, product endorsements, and other media exposure. Because of the long history of climbing in Europe, the European market was the biggest segment in the world climbing market, with 10 percent of the market in France alone. Not only did the adult urban European population prefer to spend vacations in mountain villages, but increasingly, younger generations of Europeans were forsaking crowded beaches for mountain holidays revolving around mountain sports.

Starting in the 1980s, media exposure had brought mountain sports to previously ignored market segments throughout the world. Rock climbing and mountaineering images had become popular for advertising many types of products and for adding "color" to music videos and movie plots. Because of this exposure, teenage and recreational customers—predominantly in the U.S. market—were high-growth segments, with noticeable growth in the mid-1980s erupting into an explosive growth rate of 40 percent in the early 1990s. Customers in this growing market segment had no intention of traveling the world looking for untouched and ever more challenging peaks; instead, this recreational segment climbed and skied purely for fun in their local and national resort areas.

Customarily, people wishing to learn mountain sports would employ guide services and schools for acquiring the necessary skills. The newer converts, however, were bypassing this conventional route by going to indoor climbing gyms or learning skills from friends. Many industry experts speculated that this breakdown of the conventional training methods would contribute to an increased lack of knowledge regarding mountaineering safety and lead to increased accident rates. In turn, accidents would increase the chances of litigation for all firms involved in the industry. These trends were a concern to mountain-sports firms worldwide.

COMPETITION IN THE MOUNTAINEERING EQUIPMENT INDUSTRY

Located in Salt Lake City, Utah, Black Diamond Equipment, Ltd., was a major player in the burgeoning international mountaineering industry, on both domestic and global fronts. Black Diamond manufactured and distributed a full range of products for mountain sports, from rock-climbing gear to mountaineering and backcountry skis, and faced few domestic or global competitors whose business was on a similar scale. (Exhibit A is a company/product profile of the mountaineering industry.)

The industry that served the mountaineering market consisted of three groups: retailers, wholesalers, and manufacturers.

Retailers

The retail businesses serving the market's diverse variety of mountaineering customers were one of three types. The first group, the "core" mountaineering shops, were small retail operations specializing in products specific to mountaineering such as ropes, climbing protection, climbing axes, expedition clothing, packs, harnesses, and information guides for local and national areas. Because these shops were usually located in mountain areas such as the Rocky Mountains or the Alps, the shop personnel were experts in the special tools and applications for their regions. In addition, these shop personnel often had personal knowledge of other international locations.

These shops usually carried products made in their region with specialized products from other countries. The core shops competed on the basis of the expertise of their personnel and their stock of technically appropriate tools. These retailers specialized in high-quality, cutting-edge-technology products. Prices were relatively high. The majority of their customers were highly skilled mountaineers. Black Diamond operated a small retail shop in this category located next to its Salt Lake City manufacturing facility. Black Diamond's full product range sold well in this type of shop.

Because of their remote locations, many core shops made effective use of catalogues as a direct-marketing tool. Several mail-order companies, including Black Diamond's mail-order division, competed in this core area, selling products both nationally and internationally.

The second group, "mom and pop" stores, also consisted of small retail outlets, but they sold all types of equipment from camping and backpacking equipment to bikes and skis. The product mix varied depending on the geographic location. Most of these stores carried a limited assortment of climbing products—usually ropes, harnesses, and carabiners, small clips used in all climbing applications to attach the climber to rock or snow. The personnel in mom and pop stores usually had limited technical knowledge of the products being sold.

The third group consisted of sporting goods and department store chains, ranging in size from regional chains such as Eastern Mountain Sports (7 stores) to national chains such as Recreational Equipment, Inc. (REI) (40 stores). These stores, which were located in major cities with access to mass markets, had extensive outdoor clothing departments, tents, stoves, canoes and kayaks, sleeping bags, bikes, skis, etc. Products in each category were selected for volume sales. Thus, in the climbing department, the product line covered the needs of entry-level or intermediate recreational climbers. The expertise of department store personnel was, however, generally limited.

In the United States, REI was the dominant firm in this group of retailers. REI operated department stores in Seattle, Boston, Los Angeles, and Washington, D.C., with limited national competition on this level. Because of its large size and wide scope, REI could buy in volume for all its stores and offered very competitive prices. The Canadian retailer, Mountain Equipment Coop (MEC), served a similar market in Canada, with a large store in each of Canada's major cities. In France, Au Vieux Campeur owned multiple department stores in major French cities, serving a broad customer base.

Wholesalers

Retail outlets bought their product lines from wholesalers during semiannual outdoor equipment shows held throughout the world. The wholesaler category of firms consisted of companies that either manufactured their own products or subcontracted the manufacturing of their designs and distributed their own product lines and companies licensed to distribute the products of other companies in certain geographic areas, as well as various combinations of these two. Black Diamond was in this last category. The company distributed equipment designed and manufactured in its Utah plant, equipment manufactured for Black Diamond by other firms, and merchandise designed by Black Diamond and distributed under other manufacturers' names. In all, Black Diamond offered over 250 different items, covering most mountain sports (see Exhibit B).

REI was Black Diamond's biggest wholesale customer, making up almost 10 percent of Black Diamond's total sales. The next biggest customer, Lost Arrow—Japan, was a Japanese distributor comprising 5 percent of Black Diamond's sales. The other major wholesale customers were North American outdoor sports department store chains, mail-order companies, and Black Diamond's own retail shop and mail-order business. Combined, the top 20 percent of Black Diamond's retail customers—roughly 60 companies—accounted for about 80 percent of total sales.

Domestically, Black Diamond's wholesaling competition came from Omega Pacific, which manufactured and distributed its own metal products, and Blue Water, which wholesaled its own lines of ropes and harnesses. Neither of these companies, however, carried a product line as extensive as Black Diamond's.

The international wholesaling segment included strong competition from two U.K. firms, Denny Morehouse Mountaineering and Wild Country, and a French company, Petzl. These firms wholesaled a full range of mountaineering products manufactured by companies with strong international reputations. Additional competition came

EXHIBIT A
....
Mountaineering Industry Competitive Product Profile

Product Category/ Manufacturers	National Market Share, %	International Market Share, %
Carabiners		
Black Diamond	50	10
Omega	10	3
SMC	10	3
Wild Country	10	20
DMM	10	20
Petzl	5	30
MSR (REI)	5	4
Climbing protections		
Black Diamond	50	20
Metolius	20	10
Lowe	10	10
Wild Country	10	25
DMM50	10	25
Harnesses		
Black Diamond	50	20
Petzl	20	50
REI	20	
Blue Water	10	10
Wild Country	5	20
Plastic boots		
Scarpa*	40	30
Merrell	25	5
Koflach	25	40
Lowe	15	5
Adjustable ski poles		
Black Diamond	60	5
Life Link	40	5
Mountaineer skis		
Rossignol	30	50
Hagen*	20	10
Climbing accessories		
Black Diamond	55	15
Omega	25	10
Petzl	20	75
Gloves		
Black Diamond	50	5
Snow climbing axes		
Charlie Moser	50	10
Black Diamond	20	5

EXHIBIT A *(continued)*
....
Mountaineering Industry Competitive Product Profile

Product Category/ Manufacturers	National Market Share, %	International Market Share, %
Ice climbing axes		
Black Diamond	30	10
Charlie Moser	30	15
DMM	25	30
Grivel	15	30
Rock shoes		
Scarpa*	25	20
Sportiva	25	35
Boreal	25	35
Five Ten	15	5
Ropes		
Mamutt	30	50
PMI*	20	40
New England	20	
Blue Water	20	10

*European manufacturers producing Black Diamond designs.
Source: Estimates of industry representatives.

from more regional firms. Most countries had several smaller manufacturers of specific products such as carabiners or climbing axes that were successful in wholesaling their own products.

Several issues influenced sales in the international marketplace. First, the International Organization of Standards had mandated that by 1997 "personal protective equipment" would have to meet ISO 9000 quality certification standards in order to be sold in Europe. Companies with certification stamped their products with a symbol showing that the product's manufacturer had met the relevant ISO 9000 standards. This certification was intended to give the consumer more confidence in a product's quality. Most of the European mountaineering manufacturers had initiated the certification process and were well on their way to obtaining certification. In contrast, very few American companies, including Black Diamond, had even begun the certification process. (Exhibit C provides an overview of the ISO 9000 standards.)

Second, some European countries had a long history of climbing and mountaineering, and certain manufacturers, Grivel, for example, dated back to the late 1800s. Although several European companies had well-established worldwide reputations for quality and innovative products, others relied on home country support, producing lower-quality, lower-priced products. All mountainous European countries had small factories for carabiners, skis, axes, or shoes that produced, at relatively low cost, simple products in high volume for domestic consumption.

Third, the European market was predominantly ethnocentric in purchasing behavior. French climbers preferred to buy French products, while German climbers preferred German products. Because of the risks involved in climbing and mountaineering, customers chose equipment they knew the most about and had the most confidence in. Usually, these products were from the buyers' respective countries.

EXHIBIT B
·············
Black Diamond Product Categories

Climbing protection	Ropes and rope bags
Camming devices	Packs
Nuts	Hip packs
Stoppers	Backpacks
Pitons	Tents
Piton hammers	Snow and ice tools
Slings	Axes
Runners	Crampons
Daisy chains	Ice screws and
Etriers	hooks
Webbing	Ski tools
Belay devices	Skis
Carabiners	Bindings
Harnesses	Poles
Sport climbing	Climbing clothing
Alpine	Tee-shirts
mountaineering	Sweatshirts
Big wall	Shorts
Footwear	Pants
Mountaineering	Hats
boots	Belts
Ski boots	Chalk bags
Rock climbing shoes	

Manufacturers
·············

As a manufacturer, Black Diamond faced both domestic and international competition. Domestic manufacturing firms ran the gamut from small garage operations to large machine shops with 50 or more employees, and most produced either "software" or "hardware." The software firms worked with textile products such as ropes and harnesses. The majority of the software firms, including Blue Water, Sterling Rope, and Misty Mountain, were located in the southeastern United States. These more specialized manufacturing firms expanded their market by catering to the needs of nonmountaineering industries, such as construction safety, military applications, and spelunking. The hardware group manufactured or assembled metal products such as carabiners and other climbing tools and protection. This group of manufacturers included Friends, Rock Hardware, and Rock

Exotica. These firms had reputations as producers of innovative and high-quality equipment.

REI had recently started up a small manufacturing facility for carabiners. The manager of this REI facility had many years of engineering experience with Boeing Aircraft and had designed a highly automated manufacturing system capable of both production and quality testing.

Because Black Diamond had begun as a machine shop, the company had strong capabilities in metalworking. Specifically, the Salt Lake facility manufactured cold-forged metal parts associated with carabiners, axes, and other climbing accessories and protection. Hot-forging and casting were subcontracted by Black Diamond to manufacturers specializing in this area. Black Diamond was beginning to expand into simple soft goods, such as slings and other webbing products, and intended to continue developing its in-house sewing capabilities.

Black Diamond had plans to become vertically integrated. Management believed that in-house performance of operations related to core products would enhance Black Diamond's competitiveness. Consequently, Black Diamond had started reviewing some of its subcontracting practices to determine what functions could be brought in-house. In particular, the company wanted to bring in-house all sewing of climbing gear and some metal treatments such as heat-treating.

Other products, such as skis, ski poles, foot gear, and ropes, required very specific technologies, production skills, and economies of scale for competitive pricing and quality. Black Diamond entered into subcontracting agreements with international manufacturers to design and manufacture such products. The company also subcontracted the production of its harnesses to a technically sophisticated harness manufacturer located next door to the Salt Lake City facility that made the harnesses on a semiautomated assembly line. This process required minimal human involvement, in contrast to a "garment industry" sewing process by which one person sews the complete harness from start to finish.

By the late 1980s, European competition was becoming a more significant factor in the U.S. market. In particular, Petzl, a French company with a full range of products, had taken an aggressive position in the U.S. market. Petzl, like several of the Eu-

EXHIBIT C
....
ISO 9000 Standards

The ISO 9000 standards provide the requirements for documenting processes and procedures. The intent of the standards mandates an organization "do what they say and say what they do." The standards offer three quality system models—ISO 9001, ISO 9002, and ISO 9003—with increasing levels of stringency. 9003 covers documentation and procedure requirements for final inspection and testing, 9002 adds production and installation, and 9001 includes design and development. An organization chooses the appropriate standard depending on the strategically important functional areas requiring quality procedures. In most cases, manufacturers use 9001 for covering all areas.

In order to receive ISO 9000 certification, a company will spend several years complying with the requirements in the standards. This compliance usually requires extensive documentation of the existing quality program and training for all employees involved in processes related to quality. Individual auditors, who work for the international ISO registration organization, evaluate the company for requirement compliance. The certified companies are reevaluated every two years to ensure continuing compliance.

A brief overview of the 9001 requirements are provided below:
• The entire quality system must be defined and documented to ensure each product meets specifications.
• The contractual requirements for quality between company and the customer must be defined and documented.
• Procedures are required to ensure that critical processes are under control.
• Procedures are required for inspection at all levels and for identification of nonconforming parts or products.
• Procedures are required to prevent nonconforming parts from getting damaged in storage, delivery, or packing.
• Training is required for all personnel affecting quality.
• The quality system must be audited internally to ensure effectiveness and compliance.

ropean competitors, had a well-established reputation as a producer of high-quality, innovative products. Petzl had set up a manufacturing facility in the United States within 60 miles of Black Diamond's manufacturing facility and had sponsored several professional U.S. climbers. Black Diamond, of course, was making efforts to sell its own products in Europe but faced the problem of ISO 9000 certification.

Some international manufacturing activity went on in Korea and Japan. Products produced by these manufacturers were marketed and distributed through other international companies. The majority of these products were low-cost, mass-produced items such as carabiners.

The continuing growth of copyright violations and product privacy—especially prevalent within international markets—added a further dimension to global competition. Several U.S. and European companies had used machine shops in Korea and Japan as subcontractors, supplying dies and other technological knowhow. Consequently, unlicensed clones of more expensive items were expected to appear soon in the international market.

BLACK DIAMOND'S OPERATIONS
....

Black Diamond Equipment, Ltd., opened for business in 1989 after a group of former managers with employee support bought the assets of Chouinard Equipment from Lost Arrow Corporation during Chapter 11 bankruptcy proceedings. The bankruptcy resulted from four lawsuits related to climbing equipment accidents during the 1980s. Chouinard Equipment was the first U.S. company to develop and manufacture rock-climbing gear. From its inception and for the following decade, Chouinard Equipment had a reputation for innovation and quality unmatched by any national competitors.

After the purchase, the new owners chose a

EXHIBIT D
....
Black Diamond Logo

new name for the company that would reflect its roots yet would project a fresh beginning. The insignia of a diamond was Chouinard Equipment's previous logo. The new company decided to keep the diamond image and chose the name "black diamond" because of the different associations the name might evoke: "diamond in the rough," "rogue," "bad boy," and "unusual" (see Exhibit D for the Black Diamond Logo). Furthermore, a "black diamond" was used to identify the most difficult type of run in ski areas, and the company owners hoped the name would appeal to the "extreme" athlete, their primary targeted customer base. Black Diamond's management believed that "if you target the extremities, the recreational customer will follow."

The mission of Black Diamond was "to design, manufacture, and bring to market, in a profitable and on-time manner, innovative and technical products of high quality, high performance, and exemplary durability that are targeted toward our primary customers—climbers and backcountry skiers." The company was committed to 10 guiding principles:

1. Being the market leader, synonymous with the sports we serve and are absolutely passionate about

2. Having a truly global presence

3. Supporting the specialty retailer

4. Creating long-term partnerships with companies we do business with

5. Being very easy to do business with

6. Being a fierce competitor with the highest ethical standards

7. Developing sustainable, competitive advantage

8. Sharing the company's success with its employees

9. Creating a safe, personally fulfilling work environment for all employees

10. Championing the preservation of and access to our mountain environments

In 1991, the owner-employees relocated the business from Ventura, California, to Salt Lake City, Utah, where they would be closer to the targeted customer. Black Diamond began operations with a staff of roughly 40, covering all functional areas. (See Exhibit E for Black Diamond's organizational structure.) Black Diamond was 50 percent owned by employees; the remaining 50 percent of the stock was held by outside investors, predominately distributors, customers, and friends and family of the main employee stockholders. Of the 50 percent that was employee owned, 75 percent was held by Metcalf, the CEO; Cranor, head of marketing; and Kawakami, the chief financial officer.

In 1993, Black Diamond's annual sales were expected to be approximately $12 million with a gross profit margin of about 40 percent (grossing about $4.8 million) and with a net profit margin of about 10 percent (netting around $1.2 million). From 1990 through 1993, the climbing industry had experienced tremendous sales growth of 20 to 40 percent per year. The market demanded more innovative products and faster delivery. Black Diamond struggled to keep up with the exploding customer demand by hiring more employees and upgrading shop machinery to increase productivity. Slowly, the original machinery was being replaced by automated machining centers and testing devices. By 1993, the company employed more than 100 people.

Like other metalworking shops, Black Diamond specialized in certain types of metalworking; the areas of specialization consisted of cold-forging metal parts, stamping and forming, computer numerically controlled (CNC) machining, and assembly or fabrication. Forging, stamping, and forming, along with the assembly processes, had been done for 20 years by the original Chouinard Company, and these processes were considered to be Black Diamond's

EXHIBIT E
·········
Black Diamond Organizational Structure

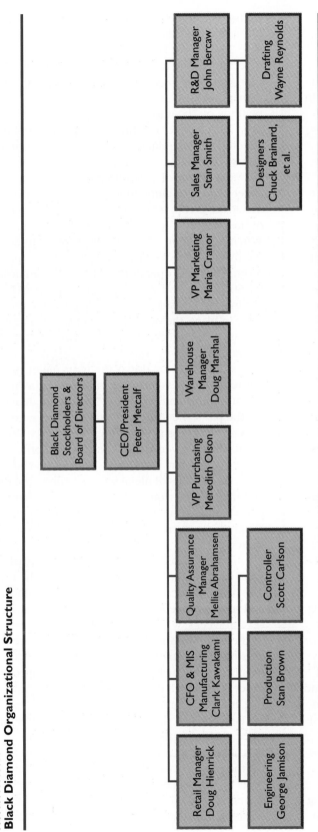

technical core. These core processes used the same multiton presses that forced metal stock into a die or mold to obtain the desired shape.

Since moving to Salt Lake City, the company had expanded into CNC machines—large programmable machine tools capable of producing small to medium-sized batches of intricate parts—in an effort to reduce costs and to move more production processes in-house. These machines were expensive, although they provided the advantages of capacity and product flexibility. Many of Black Diamond's processes, however, required machinery that was too costly to justify purchase for the manufacturing of a limited number of parts. Consequently, Black Diamond subcontracted with other vendors for aluminum hot-forging, investment casting, laser-cutting steel, preshearing metals, anodizing, heat treating, welding, screw machining, wire forming such as springs, and aluminum extrusion. These processes were subcontracted to achieve economies of scale (e.g., aluminum extrusion) or because the specialized equipment and skills required were beyond Black Diamond's capabilities (e.g., hot-forging).

Black Diamond's production facility was divided into several functional areas: the machine shop, which built prototypes and constructed and maintained tool and die apparatus; the punch press room, where parts were pressed out at a rate of one per second by several multiton presses; a room with assorted machines, each operated by one person doing drilling, milling, grinding, or operating CNC machines; a tumbling and polishing room, where large batches of parts were polished; the assembly room, where parts were assembled by individuals or teams; and finally, a room for materials and shipping.

Supported by a material requirements planning (MRP) system, materials were ordered several months in advance for a full batch of products—for example, 5000 carabiners or 500 axes. When fairly common parts such as springs and aluminum rod stock were involved, the orders arrived on time and met standard quality requirements. The more complex and customized parts, such as investment-cast axe parts, were difficult for vendors to make to specifications and thus often did not meet the assembly deadline.

When the parts arrived in the materials supply area, one person was responsible for spot-checking the order to see if the parts met specifications. For example, when 500 axe heads arrived, the inspector would randomly select 15 parts and would measure 20 different key dimensions on each part to determine if the tolerances met specifications. If one dimension was out of tolerance, the quality manager was summoned for an evaluation. Depending on the impact on other assembly processes, a larger meeting, involving all potentially affected parties, might be necessary to determine a course of action.

Most of Black Diamond's products began as a sheet of steel or aluminum rod. After receiving the metal, the incoming inspector would pull a sample of the metal to check hardness and dimensions. When production on an order was ready to begin, the metal was moved from a hallway to the press room. The press operator would receive an order for 5000 parts and would set up the press to begin cutting and smashing parts to shape. Once the dies were in place, the operator would smash a few sample parts and check with an inspector for approval.

As the dies wore down, the parts might turn out to have excess metal, or the logo engraving might be substandard. Depending on the demand for the parts, the inspector might feel pressure to pass on these cosmetically imperfect parts. Once approval was given, the operator would proceed to press out as many parts as possible in the shortest time. Often chips of metal would settle in the die and these chips would be imbedded into many parts before being discovered by the operator. When this occurred, thousands of parts needed to be scrapped.

After the smashing process, the parts usually were sent out for heat-treating to harden the metal. The heat-treatment plant was located in California, and so this procedure had a turnaround time of several weeks. When the parts returned, they went to the tumbling and drilling rooms for further processing. When color was needed, the parts would be shipped out again for anodizing, an electrolytic process by which metal is covered with a protective and/or decorative oxide film.

Finally, when the main body of a part was finished, the materials department would issue batches of all the other components needed to finish the product batch under production. All these parts would proceed to a group of assemblers, seated around tables, who were responsible for assembling the final product. The assembly room was the epitome of a craft shop environment. Large and expensive products such as axes were assembled in small batches by one individual, while products such as carabiners were assembled in larger batches by teams of people who often rotated jobs. The finished products would go through individual testing and inspection before passing to the shipping area. During inspection, one inspector might evaluate thousands of parts in a day.

Originally, the company had one employee responsible for quality assurance, and several shop employees performed quality control functions. The quality assurance person worked for the R&D department and focused on testing new products, prototypes, and work in production. As the company grew and ISO 9000 certification loomed in the future, several members of the management team decided that quality issues needed more prominent attention. Not only was testing required, but a plantwide program to ensure that defects did not occur in the first place was needed.

Black Diamond's original quality assurance officer had left the company to guide climbing expeditions, after which Black Diamond's management created a stand-alone Quality Assurance Department and hired Mellie Abrahamsen as the manager. At the time of Abrahamsen's hiring, the organization lacked a companywide quality assurance program. The members of R&D and the shop functioned along craft-shop lines. Product designers built prototypes on the shop floor, iterating between field testing and lab testing until they felt the design was ready. When the new design went into production, the shop personnel used trial and error to develop an assembly procedure. Out-of-tolerance parts often were accepted by shop personnel, who invented creative ways of adapting the parts or the procedures for assembling the products.

Implementing a quality control program would mean the introduction of formal testing and assembly procedures for both designers and shop workers. As Andrew McLean, a head designer, said: "We are like artists here, and you just can't restrain or rush creativity and get good results." Chuck Brainard complained: "If we have to write procedures for every step of production, we'll be changing those things a million times."

Like most machine-shop workers, Black Diamond's shop employees labored under comparatively unglamorous working conditions, involving, for example, noise, grease, and monotony. Many shop workers lacked a high school education, and some could not read or write in English. Although the shop workers were the lowest-paid employees at Black Diamond, the company offered a generous profit-sharing bonus to all workers and tried to involve all of them in monthly meetings concerning the financial performance of the company. Despite these measures, the shop had a high rate of job turnover.

Because quality control programs require training in procedure writing, blueprint reading, and statistical techniques, the shop employees needed elementary math and language training before they could learn more complicated subjects. Stan Brown acknowledged that the workers needed training but said: "I can't let those people miss too much work for training; we really need everyone working nonstop to get products out the door."

Many of the professional employees at Black Diamond were avid climbers and users of the products, taking great pride in trying to make the very best products available. Marketing was concerned about keeping up the company's innovative image with new products every season. Production worried about vendor costs, delivery of parts, and the shop's ability to meet sales forecasts. R&D attempted to simultaneously develop buildable new products, reduce lead time for new product development, and improve existing products. Customer service tried to keep retailers pacified with partial deliveries and promises.

Finally, quality assurance was charged with implementing quality control procedures, conducting training, testing products, and resolving problems attributed to parts or products not meeting specifications. All functional areas faced the problems inherent in trying to achieve the simultaneous goals of meeting customer demand and ensuring the highest-quality products, and the different areas often clashed on the best means and methods of achieving these goals.

THE BLACK PROPHET

The concept for the Black Prophet axe was developed originally to round out Black Diamond's product line of axes. The product line had two other axes: the Alpamayo, a glacier-walking and snow-climbing axe, and the X-15, a versatile axe for both

EXHIBIT F
The Black Prophet

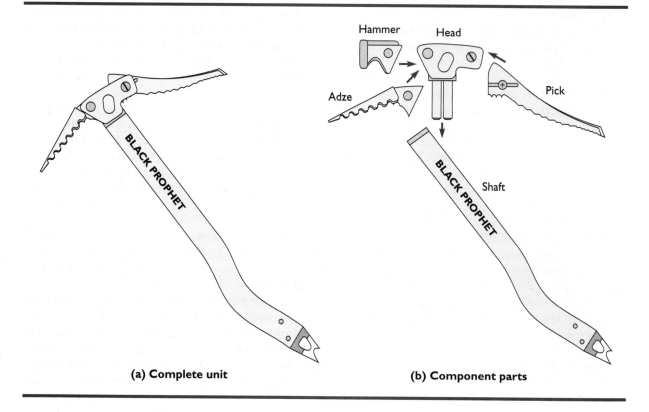

(a) **Complete unit**   (b) **Component parts**

snow and ice climbing. The Black Prophet was designed specifically for ice climbing and incorporated an innovative ergonomic shape to reduce arm fatigue, a composite, rubber-bounded shaft construction for gripability and weight reduction, and interchangeable modular components allowing the use of different types of tools—a hammer head, picks, or an adze—for miscellaneous ice applications. (Exhibit F is a drawing of the Black Prophet and its component parts.)

Designing and producing the axe entailed several years of working with different vendors to develop the appropriate production process for each component. The axe was designed as a prototype and field tested with different constructions until R&D agreed on a specific configuration. This configuration was then reviewed by sales representa-

tives considered to be mountaineering experts and by other company members at the quarterly meetings. If the tool did not pass the scrutiny of those examiners, R&D would begin a new phase of prototype development and field tests. This development process would continue until a company-wide consensus was reached.

The axe required five parts: shaft, head, hammer, pick, and adze. Three parts were cast metal, requiring a casting subcontractor with the ability to meet strict specifications. The composite shaft was produced by a composite and bonding manufacturer. The ice pick was manufactured in Black Diamond's plant. Black Diamond received the parts from each vendor, inspected them for conformance to specifications, and assembled the axes.

The Black Prophet, which cost approximately

$80 to produce, sold as an axe with two tool accessories. The total retail price was $200; the wholesale price was $140. The initial shipment of Black Prophets for winter season 1993 was approximately 200 axes. The company expected yearly sales of the axe to reach at least 2500 units, making a significant contribution to winter sales.

Management expected the Black Prophet to be one of Black Diamond's top 10 selling winter products, and the entire company regarded it as a very big image item on the world mountaineering scene. Every competitor in this industry had an axe for glacier walking. Axes were especially popular in Europe, where Black Diamond foresaw superb potential for the new axe.

The axe had been well received at the previous year's outdoor product show. At that time, no other axes like it were in the wings, and the climbing industry anticipated the Black Prophet's arrival with great excitement. All major U.S. and European industry magazines had published articles about the Black Prophet, and famous mountaineers had called Black Diamond requesting Black Prophets for their upcoming expeditions.

THE DILEMMA

As the Monday morning meeting continued, Black Diamond's top management team members struggled to find answers to the questions raised by the axe crisis. They knew that the situation required both short- and long-term solutions. In the short term, management needed to address the pressure for immediate delivery confronting customer service. Should management recall all the Black Prophet axes currently on the market? A recall would come with high shipping, testing, and opportunity costs. Or should Black Diamond basically ignore the incident, assuming the accident was a one-time freak, and continue to sell the axes while refuting any rumors about the axe's questionable performance? The possibility of lawsuits had to be considered. For any accident causing injury, legal fees could be expected to run $500,000, and a catastrophic accident could bring a suit for several million dollars. While Black Diamond's insurer would pay legal expenses and any settlement involved, with a cap of $1 million, Black Diamond could ex-

pect to pay at least $25,000—the company's insurance deductible—for each legal action. In addition, there would be the costs of lost time by the employees who had to go to court (such costs might involve one or two managers' salaries for a year—at $40,000 to $60,000 per person). Several catastrophic accident cases won by the plaintiffs in a single year could put the company into bankruptcy.

Another option was to continue the sale of Black Prophets—including the axes already released as well as those in production—but require all units to be sold with a cautionary label? Or should Black Diamond just quietly and quickly sell those Black Prophets already in retail outlets and only undertake a critical view of the axes still in production?

Management's response to the short-term issue of customer service would have major implications for Black Diamond's competitive strategy. Would Black Diamond be able to meet the market's rapidly growing demand for all products while improving—or at the very least maintaining—product quality? Would Black Diamond be able to maintain an image as the recognized industry leader in the manufacture of innovative tools and equipment? Would Black Diamond be able to balance the realities of increased risk associated with innovative product design and of increased liability corresponding to the greater potential for accidents, while still establishing a dominant competitive position? Even though various members held strong—and in some cases, divergent—opinions, the management team was willing to consider enterprising alternatives.

Nevertheless, management also knew that a more long-term plan needed to be put into place. "When crises strike," Metcalf said, "there will always be some degree of needing to react to the surprise of the situation. But we need to institute a system of managing crises proactively—that means organizing the business to prevent the preventable crises."

Even though the management team thought the Quality Assurance Department should be a constructive resource in this long-term effort, the department was so new that no one had a clear idea of the Quality Assurance Department's role. Abrahamsen also questioned her role:"I was hired to implement a plantwide quality control program and to specifically work on ISO 9000 certification. Representing QA, I'm supposed to improve the efficiency of the company by reducing or eliminating defects in the whole production chain, but I'm not sure that a TQM [total quality management] approach will completely solve Black Diamond's problems. Perhaps the whole process of new product development and on-going operations would be more effective if a BPR [business process reengineering] approach were used. Either way, my challenge is to get all these other employees and departments to change the way they do things so they're both more efficient and effective."

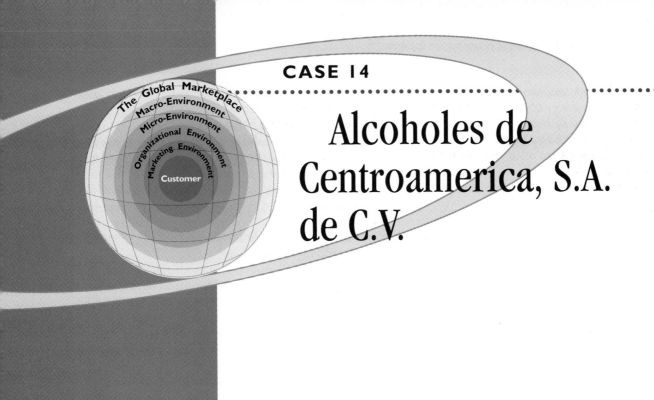

Alcoholes de Centroamerica, S.A. de C.V.

This case was prepared by Richard L. Priem, Associate Professor, The University of Texas at Arlington College of Business Administration and K. Matthew Gilley of James Madison University.

On a summer afternoon in 1995, Sr. Emin Barjum watched the faded-yellow Toyota pickup truck pull away from his loading dock in Tegucigalpa, Honduras. Sr. Barjum, founder and president of the Honduran liquor manufacturer Alcoholes de Centroamerica *(ALDECA), wondered if his plan would work. The truck was laboring under a load of* Yuscaran, *a competitor's brand of* aguardiente. *Sr. Barjum had purchased the* Yuscaran *for delivery to his most important cus-*

We thank Emin and Tony Barjum for their cooperation during the field research for this case, which was written solely for the purpose of student discussion. All data are based on field research and all incidents and individuals are real. The names of some ALDECA competitors have been disguised. All other rights reserved jointly to the authors and the North American Case Research Association (NACRA). Copyright © 1999 by the *Case Reseach Journal* and Richard L. Priem and K. Matthew Gilley.

tomers, the large liquor distributors in San Pedro Sula, a major industrial city in northern Honduras.

Sr. Barjum was doing this because Grupo Cobán, *a large conglomerate that had been able to establish a virtual monopoly in the* Guatemalan aguardiente *market, was planning to expand its business into Honduras. As an initial step in this process,* Grupo Cobán *had begun offering incentives to the largest San Pedro Sula liquor distributors in exchange for carrying its brands. Sr. Barjum was attempting to send a subtle message to these distributors. He wanted them to believe that ALDECA, which accounted for up to 80 percent of their business, could distribute its own brands, as well as those of the competition, directly to retailers. Sr. Barjum felt that this warning would provide leverage in his dealings with the distributors and might discourage them from doing business with* Grupo Cobán. *To make his message even stronger, Sr. Barjum was provid-*

ing the Yuscaran *to his distributors at a very low price. The distributors did not realize that ALDECA was actually losing money on each bottle of* Yuscaran *it delivered to the San Pedro Sula.*

Sr. Barjum also faced other problems in August 1995. In addition to the Grupo Cobán *threat, the market for* aguardiente *was shrinking slowly, because Honduran preferences were shifting to lighter alcohols like wine and beer. Also,* Licorera de Boaco, *a Nicaraguan distillery with production facilities in Honduras, had proposed a merger. After a year of study, a decision had to be made soon. The merger would give ALDECA additional capacity and could help fight the* Grupo Cobán *threat, but it would result in less direct control over marketing and operations. Was the additional capacity worth the loss of control? What other strategies might work? Sr. Barjum went back inside his office to speak with his son, Salomon "Tony" Barjum, about their company's future.*

HISTORY OF *ALCOHOLES DE CENTROAMERICA*

Emin Barjum returned home in 1965 to Tegucigalpa, the capital city of Honduras, after receiving a B.B.A. from the University of Pennsylvania and an M.B.A. from the University of California at Berkeley. He began looking for business opportunities while working for the Honduran government's Economics Ministry. Sr. Barjum noticed that there was a lack of good-quality industrial alcohol in Honduras. To fill this gap, he founded ALDECA in 1967, with initial financing from the Barjum family and a group of friends. The plant was designed with the help of a Mexican consulting firm. Because the minimum efficient scale was greater than the local demand for industrial alcohol, Sr. Barjum had to go into the liquor business to make the project feasible. He obtained technical advice on fermentation, distillation, and other aspects of alcohol manufacturing from a retired Cuban distiller who lived in Miami, Florida. ALDECA then began producing small quantities of rum, vodka, gin, Scotch, and an inexpensive liquor called *aguardiente.*

With production established, Sr. Barjum began marketing his liquor by loading as many cases as possible into his car and driving northward from Tegucigalpa. Those early sales trips were very difficult because Honduras had only 1000 kilometers of roads (barely 100 kilometers were paved). At first, Sr. Barjum sold only a few cases per trip. However, his marketing efforts soon began showing results. He persuaded the owners of many northern cantinas to begin carrying ALDECA's rum and *aguardiente.* Sr. Barjum was successful in part because he was the only distillery owner who called directly on customers; other distilleries used salespeople. ALDECA's sales grew each year.

When Sr. Barjum began producing alcohol, there were about sixteen distilleries in Honduras, most of which were relatively small in terms of output and market share. Sr. Barjum believed that "it was easier for us to compete then, since we had many small competitors instead of a few very large ones." ALDECA's entry into the market changed liquor manufacturing in Honduras. Most of the competitors had been using raw sugar in the fermentation process, which was quite expensive. ALDECA, however, produced lower-priced products made with black-strap molasses. In 1995, only eight distilleries remained in Honduras; the rest had gone out of business. About half the survivors were forced to change to molasses to remain cost competitive.

ALDECA prospered until 1972, when a large Nicaraguan distillery, Licorera de Boaco, entered the Honduran rum market. Hondurans preferred internationally produced rums, and sales of ALDECA's rum declined rapidly. As a result, ALDECA changed its focus to *aguardiente* production. By the early 1990s, the company had developed a presence in the *aguardiente* market throughout the country and had captured approximately 50 percent of the market share (see Exhibit C for details). However, northern Honduras was ALDECA's most important market, comprising nearly 85 percent of its sales.

THE HONDURAN *AGUARDIENTE* INDUSTRY

The Product, Its Consumers, and Place of Consumption

Aguardiente is a clear, inexpensive, very strong liquor that is generally purchased by the glass in small cantinas by poor, uneducated males between the ages of 26 and 45. The small, family-owned cantinas usually have a maximum of six tables and a small bar. "The cantinas are traditionally the place where men meet after work to have a few drinks," states Sr. Barjum. "They are basically a haven for men." Women traditionally avoided consumption of *aguardiente* because those women who drank it were considered immoral. The serving size is typically 125 milliliters (approximately one-half cup), and the average consumer drinks three servings per cantina visit. About 60 percent of *aguardiente* consumers drink it straight, while roughly 40 percent follow it with lemon, salt, or a sip of a soft drink.

The product is traditionally sold to the cantinas in 750-milliliter and 1-liter bottles, from which the bartenders pour drinks for their customers. A trend is developing, however, toward smaller, 125-milliliter bottles. Some customers prefer the small bottles because, when they purchase one, they are guaranteed that the bartender did not "water down" the product. However, production of *aguardiente* in the smaller bottles is quite expensive, and price is an important factor in the purchase decision. The "best" combination of taste (smoothness) and strength (alcohol content) typically determine a consumer's brand preference.

The Competitors

There were three major players in the Honduran *aguardiente* market in the mid-1990s: ALDECA, which sold approximately 2.5 million liters of its brands per year; Destilleria Buen Gusto, which sold approximately 2.5 million liters of *Yuscaran* per year; and Licorera de Boaco, which sold 700,000 liters of its brands per year. There were several smaller competitors in Honduras, as well as many black-market operations.

Although ALDECA commanded nearly half the legal Honduran *aguardiente* market, the company did not fare well "brand-to-brand" with Destilleria Buen Gusto's Yuscaran brand. A recent ALDECA marketing survey revealed that, in the city of San Pedro Sula (within ALDECA's core northern market), 57 percent of the respondents preferred Yuscaran over ALDECA's Caña Brava. Sr. Barjum notes that, "If we combine all of our brands, then we win. But, brand against brand, they have a better share."

The General Environment in Honduras

Honduras is located in Central America between Guatemala, El Salvador, and Nicaragua. Although the Honduran political environment has been stable in recent years, more than 150 internal rebellions, civil wars, and governmental changes have occurred in Honduras since 1900. Its 6 million people live in a country that is approximately the size of Louisiana (see Exhibit A) and depend primarily on agriculture for employment. In the mid-1990s, Honduras was among the poorest countries in the western hemisphere, with per capita income of approximately $630 (U.S.). The country suffered from high population growth, high unemployment (15 percent) and underemployment (36 percent), high interest rates (approximately 36 percent), and high inflation (averaging 22 percent between 1990 and 1994). A weak infrastructure also was a problem. For example, there were only 1700 kilometers of paved roads in 1995, and water and electric service were very unreliable.

A lack of hard currency for foreign exchange also was a problem. In 1994, the Honduran Central Bank mandated that commercial banks, exchange houses, and businesses could not retain foreign currency. Rather, they were required to sell foreign currency to the Central Bank within 24 hours of its acquisition in exchange for *lempiras,* the Honduran currency. The Central Bank then auctioned the foreign currency on the open market, but quotas limited the amount anyone could purchase per day. It took businesses quite some time, therefore, to obtain the currency necessary for foreign transactions.

ALCOHOLES DE CENTROAMERICA IN 1995

Personnel

In 1995, Sr. Barjum was joined by his son, Tony, who was "learning the business" after completing a B.B.A. and an M.B.A. at The University of Texas at Arlington. Sr. Barjum's daughter, Patricia, provided some marketing advice to ALDECA as needed. Other top managers at ALDECA included Armando Leonel Aguilar, production manager; Ileana Zelaya, head of laboratory; Lesbia Argentina Nunez de Flores, head of accounting; and Julio Valladares, sales

CENTRAL AMERICA

manager. Exhibit B highlights the education and experience of ALDECA's top managers. The remainder of the 84 employees filled clerical and production positions. ALDECA had little trouble filling these lower-level positions because of the high Honduran unemployment and underemployment rates, as well as ALDECA's higher-than-average pay scale.

The importance of having a qualified, in-house chemical engineer was highlighted in the early 1990s when Sra. Zelaya discovered a virus living in the fermentation tanks. The elimination of this virus enhanced the efficiency of the fermentation process and increased ALDECA's production capacity by nearly one-third.

Product Lines
....

ALDECA produced seven brands of *aguardiente:* Caña Brava (its highest-quality and best-selling brand), Tic-Tac, Catrachito, Costeño, Torero, Favorito, and Bambu (see Exhibit D for details). The multibrand strategy was developed in part, Sr. Barjum noted, because "each cantina will carry only two or three brands. That's one of the reasons we're trying to get a lot of brands into the market, to confuse the markets. That way, our brands could stock a whole cantina."

ALDECA also manufactured small amounts of vodka and wine on a manual production line. A separate Barjum-controlled company produced a

EXHIBIT B

ALDECA's Top Management Team

Name and Position	Age	Years at Company	Education	Experience
Emin Barjum Owner and general manager	53	28	M.B.A., University of California at Berkeley and B.B.A., University of Pennsylvania	Company president
Salomon "Tony" Barkum Assistant general manager	23	1	M.B.A. and B.B.A., The University of Texas at Arlington	Started here
Armando Leonel Aguilar Production manager	26	2	Chemical engineer and M.B.A., Honduras University	Assistant production manager at a sugar mill
Ileana Zelaya Head of laboratory	24	1	Chemical engineer, Currently getting M.B.A., Honduras University	Head of lab at another company
Lesbia Argentina Nunez de Flores Head of accounting	41	21	CPA, Honduras University	Started here
Julio Valladares Sales manager	40	4	High school graduate	10 years in sales (liquor)

line of cosmetics (perfumes, deodorants, and lotions) made from excess alcohol. *Aguardiente* production, however, remained ALDECA's specialty.

Production Process

ALDECA produced all its alcohol from black-strap molasses, which was obtained from a few large

EXHIBIT C

Liters of *Aguardiente* Sold by ALDECA, 1987–1994

1987	1,944,000
1988	2,177,000
1989	2,342,000
1990	2,449,000
1991	2,801,000
1992	2,711,000
1993	2,554,000
1994	2,445,000

sugarcane plantations in northern Honduras. Sr. Barjum signed contracts with these producers each year at the beginning of the harvest to ensure that ALDECA had enough molasses to last the entire year. However, since the molasses producers often promised more than they could manufacture, shortages were common toward the end of the year. ALDECA's attempts to resolve this problem were ineffective. Transportation costs prohibited the company from acquiring molasses from other countries, and large-capacity tanks, pipelines, and pumps would be very costly. Furthermore, it was impossible for ALDECA to build additional storage tanks in its current location because the land adjacent to the distillery had become developed in recent years.

Upon receiving the molasses from the manufacturers, ALDECA mixed the molasses with yeast and stored it in tanks, where it was allowed to ferment. After ALDECA's chemical engineer, Ileana Zelaya, determined that the mixture had achieved the proper level of fermentation, the molasses was .

EXHIBIT D
ALDECA *Aguardiente* **Prices, 1990–1995 (In** *lempiras* **per 12-Bottle Case)**

	1990	1991	1992	1993	1994	1995
Caña Brava	104	Not available	116	122	152	156
Tic-Tac	86	Not available	98	110	132	138
Catrachito	91	Not available	103	110	128	124
Costeño	95	Not available	107	114	129	115
Torero	99	Not available	111	117	135	124
Favorito	85	Not available	97	104	121	115
Bambu	85	Not available	97	104	116	93

pumped into distilling units, where it was converted into alcohol. The alcohol was then pumped into large vats, where it awaited the bottling process.

Following a standard practice in Honduras, ALDECA recycled all its bottles. The bottling process began at an enormous bottle-washing machine. Once the used bottles were washed, they were moved one by one through the filling machine, to the capping machine, and on to the labeling machine. They were then placed in boxes of twelve and were stored for shipment.

Although it may appear that ALDECA's production process was highly automated, it was still relatively labor-intensive. The bottles returned by the distributors were loaded manually into the bottle washer. After each bottle was filled, it was visually inspected for purity. Then, each bottle cap was started by hand before being tightened by the capping machine. Next, safety seals were secured by hand. Finally, the full bottles were boxed and stored manually.

In 1995, ALDECA was still using most of the same equipment with which it had begun production. Despite its age, the equipment remained simple, safe, efficient, flexible, and trouble-free. The bottling line was seldom interrupted by mechanical failures, and the interruptions that took place were usually solved within a few minutes.

Marketing

Marketing ALDECA's *aguardiente* was difficult. Nearly all *aguardiente* consumers were illiterate,

so common vehicles for advertising, such as newspapers and magazines, were ineffective. Advertising on television also was ineffective because the customers generally had no access to television. ALDECA used some radio advertising, since many cantinas (and some customers) had radios.

Most of ALDECA's marketing efforts, however, involved point-of-sale advertising. Each year, ALDECA developed a poster featuring a female model in a bathing suit. A 12-month calendar appeared at the bottom of the poster so that, according to Sr. Barjum, "the cantina owners will leave the poster on the wall all year." One year, ALDECA's advertising company failed to put the year itself on the calendar. As a result, that particular calendar remained on the walls of many cantinas for several years, even though the day/date designations were wrong! ALDECA also distributed to the cantinas, free of charge, disposable plastic cups with ALDECA's various product logos on the front and the serving sizes marked on the sides. Less successful marketing campaigns, such as neon signs for distributors and metal signs for cantinas, had been attempted at various times in the past.

ALDECA tried to improve the effectiveness of its advertising campaigns by hiring a well-respected local marketing firm to evaluate and revise its advertising. ALDECA gave this firm detailed information that included consumer demographics as well as frequency, amount, and location of consumption. The marketing firm then developed a multimedia campaign (television, radio, and print) that focused on a man consuming *aguardiente* at home. Sr. Barjum was disappointed with the result of the marketing firm's work because "we had given them all the marketing information we had, but they came out with a campaign which was completely out of the environment where people drink *aguardiente.*"

New product testing and introduction were handled through ALDECA's sales department. A sales representative typically visited the cantinas with the new *aguardiente* and offered the cantina owners several free bottles in exchange for permission to conduct a brief taste test. The free bottles were provided to the cantina owner as a show of goodwill and to offset revenues lost by the cantina during the test. The salesperson then offered cantina patrons free samples of the new product and asked for their opinions on how the new product compared to their favorite brands. A follow-up sales call was made later to secure the cantina's order.

Financial Performance

A cursory look at ALDECA's sales figures might lead one to believe that its bottom line had been suffering. Total factory sales dropped from 22 million *lempiras* in 1991 to 12 million *lempiras* in 1994. This drop, however, reflected an intentional response by ALDECA to changes in the taxation of *aguardiente* by the Honduran government. Until April 1992, the factory price of ALDECA's *aguardiente* included a flat tax of 4.5 *lempiras* per liter. In April 1992, the Honduran government implemented a new tax system requiring that tax be paid on a *percentage* of the selling price at the factory.

To remain competitively priced, ALDECA altered its transfer pricing. The company began selling its *aguardiente* to an in-house distributor at a lower price, thereby reducing the effect of taxes on the final price to wholesalers. The in-house distributor then provided ALDECA with the dividends shown at the bottom of ALDECA's income statement. Exhibits E and F provide more detailed information about ALDECA's financial performance.

The Honduran *Aguardiente* Market in 1995

In the early 1990s, demand for *aguardiente* began to shrink after 15 years of relative stability. As a result, ALDECA only produced 2.4 million liters in 1994, compared with 2.8 million liters in 1991. Sr.

Barjum explains the possible reason for this decline:

> We feel that there is a market for softer, or less alcoholic, beverages, like wine or beer. We found out that the demand for beer in Honduras is 260 million 12-ounce bottles per year. Wine imports have increased considerably. We don't have the exact figures because they aren't published, but we feel certain that these products have been taking some overall market share.

There were indications that demand for *aguardiente* was declining throughout Central America. As a result, competition within the industry was becoming more intense by the mid-1990s, as distilleries looked for ways to maintain profitability. Because of this, ALDECA was faced with a potential new competitor from Guatemala, as well as a merger offer from another Honduran distillery.

A New Threat

A Guatemalan conglomerate, Grupo Cobán, had recently made attempts to enter the Honduran *aguardiente* market. Sr. Barjum believed that Grupo Cobán was a major threat to ALDECA because it "has a monopoly on the Guatemalan *aguardiente* market, producing 15 million liters per year. It has total control in Guatemala. It owns a bank and a sugar mill. It also has an interest in the Pepsi Cola manufacturing facilities in Guatemala, as well as beer. In addition, it has a cost advantage with respect to raw materials; both molasses and fuel oils are cheaper in Guatemala."

Grupo Cobán purchased a small distillery in Honduras, as well as the rights to use several brands of *aguardiente* that have been popular there. Sr. Barjum explains:

> They [*Grupo Cobán*] have purchased relatively new facilities. That is a disadvantage because they had to put up a lot of money for them. Right now, they are testing the market and testing what competitive reactions will be. If they give credit to distributors, for example, what are we going to do? If they give away bottles, how will we react? They are at that stage. They have not really come in full-strength. I think they are just at the initial testing stage.

EXHIBIT E
••••••••••••••
Alcoholes de Centroamerica Balance Sheet, 1990–1995 (In *lempiras*)

Activo Circulante	(Short-Term Assets)	1990	1991	1992	1993	1994
Caja Chica	(Petty cash)	500	500	500	500	500
Caja General	(Cash on hand)	8,266	133,771	128,265	3,586	17,111
Cuentas de Banea	(Bank accounts)	1,580,559	1,299,762	2,231,299	1,574,759	1,088,872
Total	(Total Cash)	1,589,325	1,434,033	2,360,064	1,578,845	1,106,483
Cuentas a Cobrar	(Accounts receivable)	505,077	453,648	1,370,009	1,723,785	2,500,668
Provision Cuentas in Cobrables	(Loss provision for A/R)	58,914	58,914	137,000	172,378	250,066
Total	(Total A/R)	446,163	394,734	1,233,009	1,551,407	2,250,602
Anticipos	(Employee advances)	159,795	59,588	80,127	48,003	220,489
Prestamos a Cobrar	(Loans receivable)	36,489	37,916	79,604	451,794	329,723
Reparos a Cobrar	(Dividends receivable)	1,308	1,308	1,308	1,308	1,308
Total	(Total)	197,592	98,812	161,039	501,105	551,520
Materias Primas	(Raw materials)	247,656	449,741	486,839	626,792	569,605
Envases	(Containers)	330,825	388,210	721,474	835,297	1,300,724
Timbres y Casquetes	(Caps, labels, etc.)	6,079	9,754	0	0	0
Combustibles	(Fuel)	16,661	30,416	16,606	28,003	47,960
Producto En Proceso	(Work in progress)	130,471	171,738	215,949	190,000	192,097
Producto Terminado	(Finished goods inventory)	35,663	245,240	49,522	53,995	104,000
Total Inventarios	(Total Inventory)	767,355	1,295,099	1,490,390	1,734,087	2,214,386
Accesorarios	(Accessories)	35,996	29,487	114,846	118,433	127,897
Inv. En Transito	(Goods in transit)	0	0	0	1,837	0
Seguros Diferidos	(Prepaid insurance)	6,162	2,942	11,917	9,963	11,033
Publicidad Diferida	(Prepaid advertising)	4,924	0	9,057	18,911	5,234
Misc. Diferidos	(Prepaid misc.)	33,507	15,393	4,623	5,511	5,632
Impuestos Pagados	(Prepaid taxes)	8,233	9,094	26,662	5,300	25,562
Depositos Garanta	(Guaranteed deposits)	31,525	140,394	6,180	6,180	6,580
Envases En Circulacion	(Bottles in circulation)	179,989	266,131	353,205	370,306	350,222
Inversiones	(Short-term investments)	714,983	714,911	798,191	758,926	406,240
Total	(Total Other)	1,015,319	1,178,352	1,324,681	1,295,367	938,400
Total/Activo Circulante	(Total short-term assets)	4,015,754	4,401,030	6,569,183	6,660,811	7,061,391

EXHIBIT E (*continued*)

Activo Fijo	(Long-Term Assets)	1990	1991	1992	1993	1994
Terrenos	(Land)	297,004	297,004	297,004	317,246	317,246
Edificios	(Buildings)	485,880	485,880	485,880	595,949	595,949
Desp. Acum. Edificios	(Accumulated depr.—bldgs.)	151,411	163,486	175,561	197,195	224,160
Total	(Total)	631,473	619,398	607,323	716,000	689,035
Maquinaria	(Machinery)	1,582,256	1,824,121	2,180,582	2,386,341	2,884,602
Depr. acum.—maquinaria	(Accumulated depr. —mach.)	1,024,297	1,120,029	1,246,176	1,410,718	1,603,770
Total	(Total)	557,959	704,092	934,406	975,623	1,280,832
Otras instalaciones	(Other installations)	193,708	248,695	285,469	398,005	455,890
Depr. acum. — instalaciones	(Accumulated depr. —install.)	141,288	156,841	173,404	195,991	228,021
Total	(Total)	52,420	91,854	112,065	202,014	227,869
Mobiliario y equipo oficina	(Office equipment)	187,016	124,292	175,752	220,418	231,584
Depr. acum. —mobil. y equipo oficina	(Accumulated depr.—off. equip.)	114,983	92,025	102,134	118,466	138,593
Total	(Total)	72,033	32,267	73,618	101,952	92,991
Vehiculos	(Vehicles)	464,976	428,404	658,497	644,147	732,647
Depr. acum. —vehiculos	(Accumulated depr.—veh.)	353,718	353,298	416,043	446,155	516,949
Total	(Total)	111,258	75,106	242,454	197,986	215,698
Otros activos fijas	(Other L/T assets)	2,657	2,657	2,657	2,657	2,657
Depr. accu. —other activos fijas	(Accumulated depr. —L/T assets)	2,451	2,451	2,451	2,451	2,451
Total	(Total)	206	206	206	206	206
Total/activos fijas	(Total L/T assets)	1,425,349	1,522,923	1,970,072	2,174,188	2,506,631
Activos	(Total assets)	5,441,103	5,923,953	8,539,255	8,854,592	9,568,022

Pasivo Circulante	Liabilities	1990	1991	1992	1993	1994
Pasivo circulante	(Accounts payable)	210,435	137,030	73,186	113,791	214,013
Documentos por pagar	(Documents payable)	0	0	0	0	0
Prestamos por pagar	(Loans payable)	483,325	0	0	166,672	0
Imp. S ventas recaudado	(Taxes payable)	202,211	247,576	1,779,839	1,695,078	1,845,644
Retencion empleados	(Employee benefits payable)	3,266	4,580	6,796	4,545	9,192
Imp. S renta a pagar	(Income taxes payable)	346,005	427,230	4,206	2,958	(12,861)

(*continues*)

EXHIBIT E (*continued*)

Pasivo Circulante	Liabilities	1990	1991	1992	1993	1994
Dividendos por pagar	(Dividend payable)	3,476	3,476	454,781	3,476	3,476
Depositos de clientes	(Client deposits)	160,241	160,241	160,241	160,241	160,241
Total pasivo circulante	(Total liabilities)	1,408,959	980,133	2,479,049	2,146,761	2,219,705

Capital y Reservas	Equity	1990	1991	1992	1993	1994
Capital social	(Owner's equity)	2,000,000	2,000,000	2,000,000	2,000,000	2,000,000
Reserva legal	(Legal reserves)	441,543	17,127	611,690	688,818	774,696
Otras reservas	(Other reserves)	0	0	0	0	0
Utilidades no distribuidas	(Retained earnings)	522,553	915,001	1,556,925	2,476,507	4,573,621
Perdidas y ganancias	(Net income)	1,068,048	1,511,692	1,891,591	1,542,506	0
Total capital y reservas	(Total equity)	4,032,144	4,934,820	6,060,206	6,707,831	7,348,317
Total pasivo, capital, y reservas	(Total liabilities and equity)	5,441,103	5,923,953	8,539,255	8,854,592	9,568,022

Grupo Cobán's initial attempts to enter the Honduran market came in the form of enticements to ALDECA's distributors. Grupo Cobán executives offered one particularly attractive incentive; for initial orders, and for orders expanding a distributor's volume, Grupo Cobán would provide the reusable bottles free of charge. Normally, distributors wishing to carry a new manufacturer's *aguardiente* were required to either pay for the bottles up front or to provide acceptable used bottles for exchange. This represented a large initial cost for the distributors. Grupo Cobán's incentive shifted this cost from the distributor to the manufacturer. After the initial order was sold, the distributor would simply exchange the empty bottles to cover the bottle cost for the next order. However, while the bottles of most *aguardiente* manufacturers were interchangeable, thus minimizing the distributors' switching costs, Grupo Cobán's bottles were unique. Therefore, the distributors could only recover the value of these bottles by reordering Grupo Cobán brands.

Recently, Grupo Cobán invited ALDECA's four largest distributors in the San Pedro Sula area to visit Grupo Cobán's facilities in Guatemala. Two of the four declined that offer. The two distributors that accepted the offer reported some of the details of the meetings to Sr. Barjum. They were informed that Grupo Cobán was in the initial marketing stages in Honduras, confirming Sr. Barjum's suspicions. Later, Grupo Cobán was planning to introduce two new *aguardiente* brands into the Honduran market, each having a traditional Honduran name.

Unknown to ALDECA's distributors, Grupo Cobán had a history of entering markets in this way and then bypassing local distributors after its brands became established. Several of ALDECA's distributors indicated that they were considering Grupo Cobán's proposal, and Sr. Barjum was very concerned. He had been gathering and analyzing information on Grupo Cobán's entry into the Honduran market and identified several alternative courses of action for ALDECA. He explains:

EXHIBIT F

Alcoholes de Centroamerica Income Statements, 1990–1995 (In *lempiras*)

Ventas	Sales		1990	1991	1992	1993	1994	1995 Through 4/30
Aguardientes y rones	(Aguardiente and rum)		16,166,341	20,412,604	13,309,216	8,638,207	9,448,812	3,759,387
Otras bebidas	(Other drinks)		87,702	157,122	182,237	131,180	123,080	74,440
Vinos	(Wines)		49,720	38,880	97,268	118,564	95,642	56,230
Otros productos	(Other products)		860,260	155,764	1,062,047	1,262,978	1,959,433	844,051
Otros ingresos	(Other income)		438,591	512,147	364,106	454,011	484,937	225,735
Total ventas	(Total income)		17,602,614	22,276,507	15,014,874	10,604,940	12,111,904	4,959,844
Devoluciones y rebajas S/ventas	(Returned sales)		29,154	15,979	11,369	12,321	7,913	1,957
Total ventas e ing netos	(Net sales)		17,573,460	22,260,528	15,003,505	10,592,619	12,103,991	4,957,887
Costo de ventas	(Cost of goods sold)		13,826,979	16,957,738	8,591,248	4,898,314	6,397,587	2,798,326
Utilidad bruta	(Gross income)		3,746,481	5,302,790	6,412,257	5,694,305	5,706,404	2,159,561
Gastos de Fabricacion	**(Manufacturing Costs)**							
Salarios	(Salaries)		212,244	330,425	403,930	407,991	437,602	134,938
Sueldos	(Wages)		93,656	132,244	126,339	110,098	166,959	85,331
Vacaciones	(Vacation)		12,390	15,751	20,265	21,782	27,876	10,820
Prestaciones sociales	(Severance pay)		39,000	16,057	57,873	55,215	50,972	38,184
Depr. maquinaria	(Depr. of equip.)		76,369	95,731	126,147	164,541	193,052	64,350
Depr. otras instalaciones	(Depr. of installations)		10,304	15,553	16,562	22,587	32,030	10,677
Mantenimiento	(Maintenance)		155,334	225,031	232,628	177,324	223,830	39,741
Combustibles	(Fuels)		4,110	70	8,128	2,776	64,275	13,328
Miscelanea	(Misc.)		6,027	13,768	14,286	13,413	17,488	5,360
Materiales	(Materials)		30,671	48,230	10,909	14,725	5,586	1,171
Herramientas	(Tools)		2,668	8,066	3,877	1,573	4,316	181
Energia electrica	(Electricity)		75,737	145,582	183,817	215,922	213,482	72,745
Agua	(Water)		71	3,382	10,206	11,279	4,145	2,114
Vigilancia	(Security)		64,408	155,468	199,906	218,460	220,762	96,396
Regalias	(Licensing fees)		38,282	28,569	48,144	36,882	6,019	0
Marcas de registros	(Brand registration fee)		2,499	1,419	2,501	22,187	3,338	1,171
	(Total)		823,770	1,235,346	1,465,518	1,496,755	1,671,732	576,507

(continues)

EXHIBIT F (*continued*)
....
Alcoholes de Centroamerica Income Statements, 1990–1995 (In *lempiras*)

Gastos de Ventas	(Selling Expenses)	1990	1991	1992	1993	1994	1995 Through 4/30
Sueldos	(Wages)	8,423	20,256	43,616	46,400	49,050	12,700
Comisiones	(Commissions)	76,713	0	0	0	0	0
Vacaciones	(Vacations)	466	566	1,566	1,833	2,300	800
Prestaciiones sociales	(Severance pay)	0	0	0	0	0	0
Depr: vehiculos	(Depreciation of vehicles)	34,069	32,296	62,475	77,954	70,791	23,597
Combustibles	(Fuels)	62,499	103,425	89,378	112,819	126,278	38,182
Mantenimiento	(Maintenance)	39,855	125,614	129,591	77,034	108,265	58,199
Seguros	(Insurance)	25,981	37,705	37,716	33,701	38,014	39,733
Otros gastos vehiculos	(Other vehicle expense)	23,966	24,634	32,441	31,864	38,950	11,484
Fletes	(Transportation fees)	187,674	265,800	103,092	155,563	225,189	93,456
Cuentas incobrables	(Bad dept exp.)	0	0	93,197	35,377	77,688	0
Gastos de viaje	(Travel expense)	11,438	16,479	23,473	28,001	20,175	2,405
Promocion	(Advertising)	254,662	351,225	520,997	506,214	622,613	43,151
Otros gastos de venta	(Other selling expenses)	48,258	77,305	61,251	54,486	43,542	7,878
Miscelaneos	(Misc. expenses)	475	599	2,682	586	484	136
Impuestos distr. S/ventas	(Taxes)	23,436	46,990	55,088	54,982	60,353	21,218
Total	(Total)	797,915	1,102,894	1,256,563	1,216,814	1,483,692	352,939

Gastos Admin. y Grales	(Administrative Expenses)						
Sueldos	(Wages)	189,707	219,926	238,788	246,322	284,979	115,513
Vacaciones	(Vacations)	6,663	5,341	5,305	5,169	8,172	1,689
Prestaciones sociales	(Severance pay)	27,066	0	0	0	566	0
Benef. empleados	(Empl. benefits)	96,926	133,039	133,962	168,490	195,830	52,610
Depr: edificios	(Building exp.)	12,075	12,075	12,075	21,634	26,965	8,988
Depr: mobiliario	(Depr. —furniture)	12,880	9,360	10,108	16,331	20,127	6,709
Mantenamiento	(Maintenance)	11,426	22,565	23,931	15,676	28,142	10,106
Seguro	(Insurance)	22,232	28,731	34,626	29,532	29,532	24,359

Concepto	(Description)						
Arrendamiento equipos	(Lease-buyback expense)	0	39,193	53,123	60,979	20,060	0
Gastos de viaje	(Travel exp.)	10,072	38,254	25,892	34,928	34,905	0
Honorarios profesionales	(Legal fees)	56,308	19,210	20,870	33,625	52,524	15,061
Dietas y gastos de repres.	(Representation fees)	30,900	78,600	63,600	56,000	47,600	32,100
Papeleria y utiles	(Office supplies)	16,779	29,493	17,634	20,717	21,037	22,133
Correro, telgrafo, telefono	(Telephone and mail)	11,827	38,008	19,907	25,771	18,157	11,909
Donaciones	(Donations)	11,028	21,235	17,850	46,650	35,989	22,300
Miscelaneos	(Miscellaneous)	13,192	41,104	44,719	39,444	43,496	19,551
Otros impuestos distritales	(Taxes)	0	11,813	10,639	11,089	11,043	5,776
Otros gastos	(Other expenses)	0	0	0	0	0	0
Total	(Total)	370,082	911,223	777,388	787,998	715,848	507,805
Gastos financieros	(Financial exp.)						
Interese pagados	(Interest paid)	83,887	6,722	53,852	51,884	56,668	75,589
Gastos bancarias	(Bank comms.)	(9,728)	0	1,169	50,386	10,462	103,185
Total	(Total)	74,159	6,722	55,021	102,270	67,130	178,774
Gastos no deducibles	(Nondeductible expenses)						
Aportaciones INFOP	(Training institute tuition)	1,911	11,369	9,168	9,157	7,791	5,819
Multas, reparos, y otros	(Penalties)	0	128	352	423	989	378
Total	(Total)	1,911	11,497	9,520	9,580	8,780	6,197
Total gastos	(Total expenses)	1,375,598	4,084,866	3,555,498	3,621,929	3,129,998	2,314,461
Utilidad antes del I/S/renta	(Net income before taxes)	783,963	1,621,538	2,138,807	2,790,328	2,171,792	1,432,020
Impuestos S renta estimado	(Taxes)	0	597,306	809,715	1,071,835	823,073	523,876
Utilidad despues del I/S/renta	(Net icnome after taxes)	783,963	1,024,232	1,329,092	1,718,493	1,349,719	908,144
Dividendos recibidos	(Dividends received)	423,000	693,365	213,414	173,098	161,973	159,904
Utilidad neta	(Net income)	1,206,963	1,717,597	1,542,506	1,891,591	1,511,692	1,068,048

We can respond in-kind. To a certain extent, we can give credit to the wholesalers. We can also lower our prices. But, I'm trying to figure out some unique way to respond. One way might be to go to our distributors and tell them that they cannot take on different brands. If they choose to go with *Grupo Cobán,* then they can forget about us; we will begin selling directly to the cantinas. But, that would require a lot of changes in our marketing department. We don't have too much experience with retailing.

An Opportunity

ALDECA also had the opportunity to merge with another Honduran distillery, Licorera de Boaco, which had recently approached Sr. Barjum with a merger proposal. Licorera de Boaco also was concerned about Grupo Cobán's entry into the Honduran *aguardiente* market and felt that a merger was the best way to handle the situation. According to Sr. Barjum:

> We have been off and on for about two years with the possibility of closing down our plant and manufacturing all of our products in their facility, under our supervision, but using their technical procedures. We would give them all of our equipment, but we would keep the land and buildings. But, we are used to making decisions without talking too much with our board of directors. This merger would mean that any decision would have to be mutually agreed upon. They have been in the market for about fifteen years and haven't really been successful. They have good marketing and distribution, but they have not done a good job with the product.

In 1995, ALDECA was running at 80 percent of capacity. ALDECA's plot of land was surrounded by other development and was too small for additional construction. Any large increase in output would require a shift in production to a different location. Licorera de Boaco, however, had the ability to produce three times more alcohol than ALDECA, and it had the potential to produce it at 15 to 20 percent lower cost. Sr. Barjum notes:

> If we united with *Licorera de Boaco,* that would mean that we would have larger storage facilities, or we could build larger storage facilities because they have more land than we have. That would give us an advantage of being able to get better prices for molasses because, at certain times of the year, the sugar mills are really pressed for storage. At that time, you will find two or three of them competing with each other. The thing is, though, I'll be frank with you. If I'm going to merge, I don't want more problems than I had to begin with. I'm going to have to look closely at their operation from the start and see what problems they are having. It is going to be more difficult for us, because I'm going to have their production problems. Tony cannot take care of that, because he is just starting to learn. I'll have to worry about that myself. I'll also have to be concerned with their marketing problems.

A major marketing problem was that Licorera de Boaco had not been able to establish a strong brand name for its *aguardiente.* If ALDECA chose not to merge, however, Licorera de Boaco might have continued to try to build strong brands itself. Says Sr. Barjum:

> They have their own sugar mill, they have 85 percent control of the Nicaraguan market, they have the technical know-how, and they have banks in the United States. So, they are a very powerful company. They also own the franchise for MasterCard in Central America. Financially, I think they may be more powerful than *Grupo Cobán,* and we are in the middle. We are like the cheese between the two slices of bread . . . everyone is trying to get us. So that's one of the reasons we thought about the possible merger with these people. But, that would mean we would have to close down shop here. Some of our personnel would be taken over there, and some of them would not. So, we would have to pay approximately 1.2 million *lempiras* in workers' compensation.

Some of the conditions of the merger proposal were as follows:

1. ALDECA would shift all of its production equipment to the Licorera de Boaco distillery.

2. The consolidated firm would have exclusive rights to the brand names of both ALDECA and Licorera de Boaco for 99 years.

3. The board of directors of the new firm would have seven members, three from ALDECA and four from Licorera de Boaco.

EXHIBIT G
. . . .
ALDECA's Merger Analysis

ALDECA sales (2,491,000 its/year)	L.	28,694,112.00
Licorera de Boaco direct costs (If produced 2,491,000 its.)		
Alcohol	L.	5,762,513.33
Bottle caps	L.	498,200.00
Labels	L.	163,990.83
Flavorings	L.	207,583.33
Security seal	L.	78,560.00
Direct labor	L.	398,560.00
Indirect expenses	L.	1,668,970.00
Total costs	L.	8,778,377.49
Profit margin distillery	L.	4,151,666.67
Sale price at the factory (2,491,000 its.)	L.	12,930,365.83
Add:		
44% Elaboration tax	L.	5,689,360.97
20% Consumption tax	L.	2,586,073.17
10% Sales tax	L.	2,120,580.00
Cost to distribution co.	L.	23,326,379.96
Dist. gross margin	L.	5,367,732.04
Less:		
Advertising (L.4.00/box)	L.	830,333.33
Administration costs	L.	600,000.00
Sales exp.	L.	360,000.00
Transportation (L.4.00/box)	L.	830,333.33
Other costs	L.	400,000.00
Total costs	L.	3,020,666.66
NI distribution co.	L.	2,347,065.37
NI liquor manufacturing	L.	4,151,666.68
ALDECA contribution	L.	6,498,732.04
Licorera de Boaco Contr. (their NI)	L.	1,100,000.00
Total	L.	7,598,732.04
45% Participation ALDECA	L.	3,419,429.42
1994 ALDECA	L.	3,592,181.26

Details of the proposed equity arrangement for the merged company are provided in Exhibit G. Additional portions of ALDECA's initial merger analysis are shown in Exhibit H.

SR. BARJUM'S VIEW OF THE FUTURE
. . . .

Sr. Barjum sat in his office with his son, Tony, late into the night trying to come to some conclusions about their situation. "I am reacting on a day-to-day basis," Sr. Barjum explained. "I have not determined where I want the company to go in, say, five years. How are we going to meet the new competition that is coming into the country? Maybe the way we've operated in the past is not correct for today."

They decided to call a meeting of their most important distributors to discuss the issue. Tony wanted to tell the distributors directly of Grupo Cobán's usual form of market entry and then give

EXHIBIT H
....
Consolidation Analysis

1. The equity structure of Licorera de Boaco S.A. and Distribuidora de Boaco S.A. is as follows:

Investor #1	10.2%
Investor #2	5.3%
Investor #3	5.3%
Familia Cortez	79.2%

Note: Investor #3 is the general manager of Licorera and Distribuidora de Boaco.

2. Distribuidora de Boaco S.A. has 39% ownership of Distribuidora Puerto Barrias S.A., a large distribution company which had sales of 53 million lempiras last year.

Consolidation Proposal

1. ALDECA will transfer to Licorera de Boaco all its production machinery and equipment, including storage tanks and the electrical plant.
2. ALDECA will give Licorera de Boaco the exclusive authorization to produce and distribute its brand name products (a period of 99 years).
3. The owners of the brands that Licorera de Boaco currently manufactures and distributes would give the same authorization to the consolidation firm.
4. ALDECA would receive stock totaling 45% of the capital of Licorera de Boaco and Distribuidora de Boaco. The new capital structure would be the following:

Familia Cortez	45.0%
ALDECA	45.0%
Investor #1	5.0%
Investor #3	5.0%

5. The capital structure of Distribuidora Puerto Barrias will not be altered.
6. The board of directors will be chosen as follows:

Familia Cortez	3 directors
ALDECA	3 directors
Investor #1	1 director

7. The bylaws and articles of the corporation would be modified so that important decisions could be adopted with 90% of the stockholders approving a motion (for the General Assembly) and only with the vote of 6 of the 7 directors for the decisions pertaining to the Administrative Council.
8. The administration of Distribuidora de Boaco will correspond to Emin Barjum (CEO ALDECA).
9. The consolidated operations would yield the estimated income before taxes (taking into account current sales prices and costs):

For the fabrication and distribution of ALDECA products:	L. 6.5 million
For the fabrication and distribution of L. de Boaco products:	L. 1.1 million
Total	L. 7.6 million

Note: The contribution by ALDECA seems substantially superior due to the fact that it has been calculated as a marginal contribution, the fixed costs are absorbed by the production of Licorera de Boaco products.

The income before taxes of ALDECA in 1994 was of L. 3.6 million, with distributorship alcohol manufacturing and sales.

Advantages:
- Currently ALDECA has very little capability of increasing its production capacity without a substantial investment in equipment and buildings. The production capacity of ALDECA is 5000 liters of ethyl alcohol (12,500 liters of liquor) in 24 hours (currently operating at 80% of capacity).

EXHIBIT H (*continued*)

Consolidation Analysis

- The production capability of Licorera de Boaco is 15,000 liters of ethyl alcohol (37,500 liters of liquor) in 24 hours.
- Due to superior technology, the direct fabrication costs of Licorera de Boaco are 10% lower than ALDECA's costs.
- The consolidation would strengthen ALDECA's competitive situation against Grupo Cobán, which currently bought a distillery in the north part of the country. (They not only want to produce rum, but also *aguardientes,* attacking ALDECA's core market.)
- The consolidated sales would represent 40% of the liquor market in Honduras.
- ALDECA would have a 17.5% (45% of 39%) direct participation in Distribuidora Puerto Barrias' operations.
- The very valuable location where ALDECA is currently located could be developed for housing or commercial purposes.

Disadvantages:
- Administrative autonomy would be lost.
- Would have to lay off many workers and pay approximately L. 900,000 as compensation. (This cost will be recovered by asking Licorera de Boaco to pay ALDECA L. 6.00 for every box of liquor produced for a period of 2–3 years.)
- The merger agreement would have to be drafted carefully, with a lot of emphasis on detail, to protect both parties, to avoid paralyzing the operations due to disagreement, etc.
- There is always risk of bad faith in the actions of the other party.

Financial:
ALDECA

Machinery and equipment	L. 1,281,000.00
Other installments	L. 228,000.00
Replacement parts and accessories	L. 129,000.00
Total	L. 1,638,000.00

Owners equity and retained earnings

Licorera de Boaco	L. 4,720,000.00
Distribuidora de Boaco	L. 4,054,000.00
Total	L. 8,774,000.00

them an ultimatum: "Our brands or theirs, but not both." But what if the distributors did not believe that ALDECA could enforce the ultimatum? Sr. Barjum favored discussing the problem with the distributors and explaining to them some of the options that ALDECA was considering, like distributing *aguardiente* directly to the cantinas themselves. The implied threat should be enough to persuade the distributors to avoid Grupo Cobán's brands. Sr. Barjum hoped that the distributors did not know that ALDECA could only ship competitors' products, like the pickup-load of Yuscaran, at a loss.

References

Panet, J-P., Hart, L., and Glassman, O. 1994. *Honduras and Bay Islands Guide,* 2d ed. Washington: Open Road Publishing.
United Nations Economic Commission for Latin America and the Caribbean. 1996 *Report.*
U.S. Central Intelligence Agency. 1995. *World Fact Book.*
U.S. Department of Commerce. 1996. *National Trade Data Bank.*
U.S. International Trade Administration. 1995. *Country Commercial Guide: Honduras.*

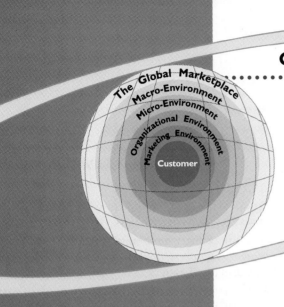

CASE 15

Frigidaire Company: Launching the Front-Loading Washing Machine

This case was prepared by Kay M. Palan and Timothy T. Dannels of Iowa State University.

The Frigidaire Company, Laundry Products Division, in Webster City, Iowa, was a high-volume manufacturer of washing machines and dryers. In October of 1996, after several years of intense development, Frigidaire introduced a new front-loading (horizontal axis) washing machine in the United States. This new machine was designed and developed to offer U.S. consumers an alternative laundry product that was superior to conventional, top-loading (vertical axis) washing machines in terms of energy consumption, water conservation, and washing performance. Although an eager and receptive market for the front-loading washer did not exist, Frigidaire intended to use the new product to expand its position in the marketplace and to establish itself as the industry leader in energy-saving, environmentally sound laundry products.

Despite a $20 million investment, exhaustive development efforts, and detailed marketing plans, however, Bill Topper, vice president and general manager of the Laundry Products Division, was concerned. Initial sales were sluggish; results for the first 3 months of sales were 30 to 40 percent below projected levels. Although this early dismal performance was not a cause for panic, it triggered some serious concerns for the Frigidaire management staff. As Bill Topper reviewed data for the first 3 months' performance, he pondered several questions that he would need to review with the key players in his management team—Chris Kenner, market manager; John Jergens, market planner; and Dave Modtland, manager of washer engineering and project leader. Could Frigidaire create and grow a market for horizontal-axis washing machines in the United States? How could Frigidaire best encourage product adoption?

THE FRIGIDAIRE COMPANY

The Frigidaire Company, owned by AB Electrolux of Sweden, was the fourth largest producer of household appliances in the United States, behind Whirlpool, General Electric, and Maytag (see Exhibit A for a summary of the U.S. appliance market). Frigidaire had 10 operating sites within the United States, with its corporate headquarters located in Dublin, Ohio. The company manufactured all major appliances—washers and dryers, refrigerators and freezers, ranges, dishwashers, and air conditioners—under the popular brand names of Frigidaire, White-Westinghouse, Gibson, Kelvinator, and Tappan. In addition, Frigidaire manufactured appliances for the General Electric Company (under the GE label) and for Sears (under the Kenmore label).

Laundry Products Division

The Laundry Products Division, located in Webster City, Iowa, produced washers, dryers, laundry centers (stacked, full-size washer-dryer combinations), and now, the front-loading washing machine. Transmission assemblies for washing machines were made at a smaller plant in nearby Jefferson, Iowa. The facility in Webster City had gradually been expanded and had the capacity to produce 6500 units a day (over 1.5 million units per year).

EXHIBIT A

1996 Major Appliance Market Share in the United States*

Company	Percent Market Share
Whirlpool	35.9
General Electric	30.4
Maytag	14.8
Frigidaire (Electrolux)	11.0
Amana (Raytheon)	6.4
Others	1.5
TOTAL	100.0

*Major appliances include dishwashers, ranges, washers/dryers, and refrigerators.
Source: *Appliance Magazine*, September 1997.

THE FRONT-LOADING WASHING MACHINE

Background

The U.S. laundry market was dominated by the top-loading (vertical axis) washing machine—it was estimated that over 95 percent of the washing machines in the United States were of this type. Top-loading machines were developed in the late 1940s and had been the primary method of washing clothes ever since. In contrast, the horizontal-axis, front-loading washer had experienced very little success with U.S. consumers. In 1945, Westinghouse started to market a front-loading machine. These machines were often referred to as "tumble action" washers because they simply tumbled clothes clean (versus cleaning with the "agitation motion" caused by the presence of an agitator in top-loaders). However, the early front-loading machines were plagued with many problems. Aside from the many mechanical problems that were reported (front-loaders were much more technologically complex than top-loaders), consumers perceived that front-loaders did not clean very well and even tangled clothes. Furthermore, front-loaders were more costly to purchase and service. Not surprisingly, in light of all these problems, the front-load market failed to materialize, and top-loading machines evolved as the dominant laundry product in the United States.

In Europe, however, high energy costs had driven the market toward front-loading technology because front-loading washers required less water and less energy to operate. In addition, Europeans believed that front-loading machines cleaned better and were gentler on clothes, relative to top-loading washers. The European market was dominated by front-loading machines.

Aware of the success of the front-loading washing machines in Europe, Sears and Magic Chef attempted, in 1981, to market front-loading washing machines in the United States by carrying foreign-made units. However, their attempts failed to produce significant results. Westinghouse, despite the disappointment associated with the original introduction of front-loading washers in the United States, continued to carry a front-loading machine, only to cease manufacturing in 1994 due to recurring service issues and customer complaints.

Despite these setbacks and problems, Bill Topper believed that the demand for front-loading machines in the United States would increase over the next several years. Initially, the management team believed that governmental influence would lead to a new market for this style of washing machine. It had been rumored for several years that the U.S. Department of Energy (DOE) was preparing to unleash new, rigid efficiency standards that would apply to household appliances. These regulations would lead to the design and introduction of new energy-efficient machines by all appliance makers and would create consumer demand for energy-efficient appliances. Furthermore, the team believed that the growth in environmental awareness and energy/water conservation in the United States would support the presence of an energy-efficient washing machine. After all, similar machines had been used in Europe for years for reasons of energy conservation, and it was felt that this trend would eventually drift into U.S. markets. Topper hoped that the company could stimulate this market by being the first domestic appliance manufacturer to successfully produce and sell a reliable, high-quality front-loading washing machine. If the front-loading washer functioned as intended, it would cost less to operate (use less water and energy), it would be gentler on clothes, and most important, it would clean better. Likewise, it would provide Frigidaire with much needed product differentiation in an industry where differentiation and competitive advantage were very difficult to attain.

With these considerations in mind, a $20 million project to design, develop, and produce a new and better front-loading washing machine was begun by Frigidaire in 1989. The project experienced a setback in 1994, however, when the government announced that the much-anticipated DOE changes would be delayed indefinitely. Industry speculations included the possibility that the delayed DOE regulations eventually might set energy-efficiency standards that could easily be met by either revolutionary vertical-axis designs or the more conventional top-loading machines currently available. Consequently, many appliance manufacturers had chosen to discontinue development of front-loading machines. Frigidaire, however, continued with the project because the management team believed that the benefits of differentiation, combined with increasing environmental awareness, ultimately would lead to a demand for the front-loading washer.

With the delay of the DOE regulations, the market manager, Chris Kenner, could no longer be assured that a ready-made market would exist for the front-loading washer. Instead, Kenner and his team were forced to focus on the difficulties and unknowns associated with market creation.

Exactly *who* would buy a front-loader?

How much would consumers pay for a front-loader?

How could loyal consumers of top-loading washers be converted to the use of front-loaders? Could consumers be converted?

What were the direct competitors doing with respect to the development and introduction of front-loaders?

The Product

Dave Modtland, manager of washer engineering and project leader for the front-loader, was tasked with overseeing the design of this revolutionary washing machine. The front-loading washing machine represented the first major technological innovation in several years in the industry. The horizontal-axis washer used tumble action—top-loading washers used an agitator that actually forced clothes to beat against each other, while the front-loader lifted and tumbled clothes in and out of the water without rough agitation. The new washer had more capacity than previous front-loaders and used approximately 20 less gallons of water per load than conventional top-loaders, or about 8000 gallons a year. Likewise, the front-loader saved on energy costs. Using national averages, water and energy savings were calculated to be at least $86 per year. Additional savings would be gained from reduced drying time due to the higher spin speeds achieved in front loaders. The front-loader also offered many features—automatic dispensing (of detergent, bleach, and fabric softener), an extra rinse option (i.e., for infant clothing), automatic water fill (fills to needed level and eliminates waste), and dryer clothes due to its high-rpm motor. Moreover, the front-loading washer offered versatility in installation—it could be installed under a counter, stacked with a dryer, or used in a free-

EXHIBIT B
....
Major Appliance Industry Brands by Company, 1996

Frigidaire	Maytag	Whirlpool	General Electric	Amana
Frigidaire	Maytag	Whirlpool	General Electric	Amana
Frigidaire Gallery	Jenn Aire	KitchenAid	GE Profile	Speed Queen
White-Westinghouse	Admiral	Roper	Hotpoint	
Gibson	Magic Chef	Estate	RCA	
Tappan	Norge	Kenmore (Sears)		
Kelvinator				
O'Keefe & Merrett				
Kenmore (Sears)				
GE (General Electric)				

Source: Frigidaire Product Planning Department, Webster City, Iowa.

standing position. The washer had a unique look, and the glass door allowed the viewing of machine operation. A matching clothes dryer complemented the new washer very well.

There were, however, some disadvantages associated with the front-loading washer. The washer was very heavy and more difficult to install (due to extra internal packing needed to protect critical components during shipment). Also, the front-loading washer was more costly to service than conventional top-loaders.

COMPETITION
•••••••••••••••••••••••••••••••••

The laundry market represented a very competitive and demanding environment. Frigidaire currently competed with four other major appliance manufacturers in the United States—Whirlpool, General Electric, Maytag, and Amana—all of whom managed several different brand names (see Exhibit B). At the present time, Frigidaire's market share for the home laundry market was about 7.9 percent, down from 9.2 percent in 1995. However, the Frigidaire brand name itself represented only about 2 percent of the washer market (see Exhibit C). The Laundry Division's market planner, John Jergens, believed the front-loader represented a tremendous opportunity for Frigidaire to expand its position in the marketplace.

Despite delayed DOE regulations, both Maytag

and Amana had announced plans to introduce their own versions of horizontal-axis machines in 1997; Frigidaire managers had noted, though, that news releases on Maytag's new washer indicated that it might not be front-loading. In addition, Whirlpool was in the process of developing a new-generation washing machine, which was rumored to be neither traditional vertical nor horizontal axis, and GE had recently released a new, redesigned vertical-axis machine. Because of the new products being

EXHIBIT C
....
1996 Washing Machine Market Share in the United States

Brand Name	Percent Market Share
Kenmore	29.0
Whirlpool	21.6
Maytag	14.7
GE	13.1
Amana	4.9
Roper	2.4
Frigidaire	2.3
Admiral	1.9
Others	10.1
TOTAL	100.0

Source: Industrial Marketing Research, Inc.

developed by competitors, Jergens felt that early presence in the marketplace would be vital to the success of the front-loader.

CUSTOMER ANALYSIS

Bill Topper and his management team knew that a key to market creation was to understand the needs and wants of potential consumers with respect to washing machines. Several pieces of information were available to the management team, including survey and focus group data and personal feedback from consumers who had tried early prototypes of the front-loader.

Survey Data

Results of a 1991 consumer/environmental profile suggested to Chris Kenner, marketing manager, that a potential market existed for the front-loader. Over half of surveyed households (53 percent) purchased energy-efficient appliances, while 28 percent used water-conservation devices in their homes; 46 percent of households reported considering environmental impact when purchasing products. Consumers in several geographic regions in the United States were rated above average for considering environmental issues when purchasing appliances; cities included Denver, Minneapolis–St. Paul, Houston, Washington, D.C., Salt Lake City, Seattle, San Francisco, Dallas–Fort Worth, and Hartford.

Kenner also reviewed information related to current Frigidaire users. The majority of Frigidaire brand purchasers were families (79.3 percent), followed by single females (14.5 percent), and single males (6.1 percent). Brand sales were highest in the East North Central (26.8 percent) and South Atlantic (22.0 percent) regions; New England posted the fewest brand sales (1.2 percent). Sales in the other regions of the United States varied from 4.9 to 12.2 percent. Sales of washing machines were subject to fluctuations—for example, sales tended to be lowest in January and April. However, Kenner did not find evidence of seasonal sales. Of more concern to Kenner was Frigidaire's low ranking in brand acceptability relative to major competitors (see Exhibit D).

EXHIBIT D

1996 Brand Acceptability among U.S. Households

Brand Name	Acceptability
Maytag	97%
General Electric	95%
Whirlpool	93%
Frigidaire	92%
Amana	87%

Source: Frigidaire Market Research Department, Webster City, Iowa.

Focus Groups

Chris Kenner also reviewed a 1993 market research focus study, which exposed consumers to the front-loading washer. Several concerns about the washer had been identified in the study:

1. Water leakage through the front door

2. Small load capacities

3. Cleaning performance without an agitator

4. Insufficient water savings and energy conservation to merit purchase

5. Difficult loading and unloading of the washer

6. Brand loyalty to current (i.e., familiar and proven) washing technologies

Another study, conducted by Kenner's Market Research Department, had shown that pricing of the front-loader was a potential problem. Consumer interest in the washer did not increase significantly until the price was reduced to $599 or less. Many consumers reported that a lower price and/or a manufacturer's rebate would offer the best incentive for purchase. Even with an incentive, 35 percent of those consumers surveyed indicated that they would not buy the washer.

Consumer Feedback

In 1995, Bill Topper had implemented a controlled sales program in Iowa, Wisconsin, and California. The purpose of the program was to obtain consumer feedback on the new washer prior to national introduction. Several hundred units were sold to target consumers; they were given large rebates and were asked to work with the design and marketing teams to identify the strengths and weaknesses of the product. Engineers and other manufacturing personnel stayed in close contact with these consumers—reading surveys, answering telephone calls, and visiting actual homes to discuss performance and problems. Problems were identified and corrected, and more important, Frigidaire found that many of the customers reported high levels of satisfaction with the close personal contact and attention they received from manufacturing personnel.

Market Segmentation

Using historical data obtained on previous buyers of front-loading machines (White-Westinghouse), Kenner and his marketing group identified six target segments of potential customers. Although the information was dated, the profiles were used to estimate demand potential and sales forecasts for the new washers. The six segments, representing only 16.7 percent of U.S. households, had generated nearly half the demand for the previous White-Westinghouse front-loading machines. Frigidaire's marketing department calculated that the same segments would produce a potential demand of 134,000 units per year for the new front-loading machine (the estimate included a conversion factor that assumed a 14-year life for each horizontal washer). The segmentation data is summarized in Exhibit E.

MARKETING PLAN FOR HORIZONTAL-AXIS, FRONT-LOADING WASHER

Bill Topper and his management team concluded that in order for the front-loading machine to be successful, the company would have to implement a marketing plan that would (1) overcome consumers' negative perceptions about the Frigidaire brand name and about the front-loading technology, (2) take advantage of the environmental and energy concerns of consumers, and (3) provide close personal contact and attention to customers.

Product Introduction

The front-loader washer initially would be marketed under the Frigidaire Gallery brand name, a new professional series line recently launched by Frigidaire. This tactic allowed the new washer to take advantage of the market synergies created by the recent large-scale Gallery introduction. Introduction focused on one model, available in either white or almond. This approach streamlined production, inventory levels, and distribution.

The management team believed that it was imperative to convey the potential benefits of the front-loader to consumers, dealers, and within the company itself. Failure to do so would hamper successful introduction of the washer. Consequently, Kenner and his marketing department developed a summary of benefits to guide product introduction:

Consumer Benefits	Dealer Benefits	Frigidaire Benefits
Better washing performance	High profit potential	Increased market share
Gentler on clothes	Improved product offering	Increased profitability
Saves energy, saves water	Improved visibility/traffic	Improved product offering
Flexible installation	New laundry room options	First-mover advantages

Although the initial product introduction involved only one model, the engineering department, under the direction of Dave Modtland, continued to develop additional features and product offerings. Negotiations were underway with GE and Whirlpool to possibly manufacture front-loading washers for these major appliance companies. Commercial versions and coin-operated machines also were under development. Finally, a line of horizontal machines, with varying features and price points, was planned for future introduction. Eventual plans called for an ultra-high-end model and a low-end model that could compete with traditional top-loader price points.

Pricing

Topper wanted to competitively price the new washing machine—not so high that consumers would not even consider the washer but also not so low that profit objectives could not be attained.

Consequently, a suggested retail price range for the new horizontal-axis machine was established at $749 to $849, with a target retail selling price of $799. Built into the price was a very appealing profit margin for dealers (30 percent) relative to dealer margins for top-loading washing machines (10 percent). Frigidaire's profit margin was set at about 26 percent). Frigidaire's profit margin accounted for all variable and fixed costs allocated to the front-loading washer. The price also allowed for a 12 percent return on investment (ROI) to be obtained.

Even at this price, however, the management team knew that the front-loader faced a tough challenge. There were (and would continue to be) many conventional washing machines on the market that cost much less than the front-loading washer; most top-of-the-line washers sold for less than the front-loader would sell for. In fact, only about 0.8 percent of the available washing machines on the market were priced above $700. Thus, at the targeted retail selling price of $799, consumers had the very attractive option of purchasing a conventional top-loading machine *and* a dryer or just a front-loading washer.

Merchandising

The front-loader washing machine would be marketed through existing distribution channels, catalogues, and the Internet (*www.frigidaire.com*). In addition, a dedicated sales manager was assigned to the new washer to help push it through the new distribution channels. High priority also would be given to the dealers. According to Chris Kenner:

> A critical step in growing this market is to educate and convince dealers of the benefits of front-load technology.

Consequently, several steps were implemented to educate dealers about the new washer and to assist dealers in sales of the washer.

First, the manufacturing facility in Webster City hosted an open house and training for dealers and district managers as a kickoff for the front-loading washing machine introduction. Dealers and district managers also received free sales and training kits to help stimulate sales. Those who could not attend the training at the Webster City facility received a free formal introduction presentation at their own facilities. Dealers and retailers also received a free floor plan to assist in the visual display of the new washer. Retailers were equipped with a variety of sales aids to enhance in-store sales efforts; for example, a sliding rule showing energy and water savings was made available to retailers.

An Inside Line Consumer Direct program was established for fully trained, certified retailers. These retailers had access to an upscale consumer database to capitalize on target markets.

Financial incentives were initiated. Dealers would earn a higher profit margin for the front-loader than for conventional washers. Discounted pricing would be implemented throughout the first year of sales, creating an even larger profit margin. District managers would receive premium commissions for their sales efforts and results. Both retail sales personnel and district managers were enrolled in the Earn a Free Washer sales contest program—free front-loading washers would be awarded based on number of units sold.

Consumer-oriented strategies aimed at assisting dealers and district managers also were implemented. Free financing for 6 months (no pay, no interest) was made available to consumers; moreover, because installing a front-loading washer was more difficult and costly than that required for conventional machines, an installation allowance would be provided to purchasers. The front-loading washer carried a full 2-year warranty, the longest available in the industry, and consumers were promised a 30-day money back guarantee if they were not fully satisfied with the cleaning performance—The Cleaner/Gentler Promise. Consumer promotions included free "low suds" detergent samples of Wisk (Frigidaire and Lever Brothers were partners in developing and marketing this low-sudsing detergent), and those customers who purchased both a new front-loading washer and a matching dryer received a free Braun steam iron.

There was a contest for consumers, too. A Watch & Win program enabled interested customers to watch an "infomercial" videotape about the front-loading washer and then answer some questions about the washer on a contest entry form. Completing the entry form provided a chance for the consumer to win free Frigidaire Gallery appliances. But the contest actually had a broader aim, which was to educate consumers about the benefits of the new washing machine.

EXHIBIT E
....
Potential Market Segments for Front-Loading Washing Machines

Segment	Age Group	Ethnic Background	Affluence	Psychographics	Ecological Orientation	Motivation to Buy	Expected Demand
Urban Gold Coast Elite urban singles and couples	25–34 35–54	White, Asian	High	Egocentric, amicable, conforming, self-assured Not style-conscious, impulsive, or cautious	Below Average	Space Savings	0.51%
Gray Power Affluent retirees in sunbelt cities	65+	White	Middle	Cautious, egocentric, broad-minded, reserved, brand loyal Not experimenters, ad-believers, or conformists	Low	Energy Savings	2.09%
A. *Money & Brains* Sophisticated townhouse couples	55–64 65+	White, Asian	High	Amicable, broad-minded, efficient, intelligent, creative Not reserved, impulsive, or economy-minded	Above Average	Space Savings Performance Environment	3.08%
B. *Young Literan* Upscale urban singles and couples	25–34 35–54	White, Asian	Middle				
C. *Bohemian Mix* Bohemian singles and couples	Under 24 25–34	Ethnic Diversity	Middle				

EXHIBIT E *(continued)*

Potential Market Segments for Front-Loading Washing Machines

Segment	Age Group	Ethnic Background	Affluence	Psychographics	Ecological Orientation	Motivation to Buy	Expected Demand
A. *Kids & Cul-de-Sacs* Upscale suburban families	35–54	White, Asian	High	Amicable, intelligent, efficient, reserved, style-conscious, cautious	Above Average	Performance Fashion	4.76%
B. *Winner's Circle* Executive suburban families	35–54 55–64	White, Asian	High	Not conformists, brand loyal, impulsive, or economy-minded			
A. *Executive Suites* Upscale white-collar couples	25–34 55–64	White, Asian	High	Amicable, efficient, brand loyal, intelligent, cautious, creative, style-conscious	Below Average	Performance Fashion	4.75%
B. *Pools & Patios* Established empty nesters	55–64 65+	White, Asian	High	Not experimenters, conformists, ad-believers, economy-minded, or impulsive			
C. *Second City Elite* Upscale executive families	35–54 55–64	White	High				
Blue Blood Estates Elite super-rich families	35–54	White, Asian	High	Amicable, cautious, intelligent, refined, efficient, self-assured, frank, brand loyal Not experimenters, impulsive, ad-believers, or economy-minded	Above Average	Performance Fashion	0.78%

Source: Claritas, PRIZM Profiles, 1994.

Marketing Communications
● ●

The management team believed that the benefits of the front-loader were best conveyed to potential customers through personal communications. Although mass media reached a large number of consumers quickly, explaining the front-loading machine necessitated a complex message. Plus Frigidaire's experience with the controlled sales program had revealed that personal contact with consumers was crucial to creating satisfied customers. Consequently, mass-media advertising was limited to a brief television advertisement, to be aired in national markets in early 1997. The primary thrust of the communications plan rested on the ability of retailers and dealers to communicate and educate consumers on the benefits of the front-loader at the point of sale. Besides training all salespeople, floor displays and literature were designed to enhance and complement sales efforts. All communications emphasized a performance-driven product that resulted in superior cleaning, delicate handling, better efficiency, and flexible installation.

To promote postpurchase satisfaction, a Use and Care video was issued with every purchased front-loading washing machine to educate the buyer and to prevent service calls related to the installation and/or use of the product. The Watch & Win contest provided an incentive to purchasers to watch the video if they had not done so prior to purchase. Also, a 1-800 customer line was established to address customer complaints, concerns, or comments.

An After-Sales Call program would be established, although not until 1998. This would be a continuation of the earlier experiment that allowed customers to talk directly to the manufacturing personnel who had actually built their washing machine. The management team believed that this interaction not only would result in satisfied customers but also would pinpoint product problems and areas for product improvement.

EARLY SALES PERFORMANCE AND CONCERNS
● ●

The front-loading washer was released to the public on October 1, 1996. The initial project release date had been May 1995; however, due to several late design changes and some unanticipated component failures, the introduction was delayed. The development of the washer had taken considerably longer to complete than any other machine Frigidaire had ever produced. The primary reason for the delay was that the front-loader represented a much more complex design than the top-loading machine, and it was mandatory that this machine be "perfect"—it could not have the problems that so many of the early front-loading machines had. Despite these setbacks, the front-loader was a design success—it met initial design specifications and, more important, met the high quality and reliability standards established during the infant stages of the development process.

Unfortunately, initial sales volumes for the horizontal-axis machine were sluggish. Based on the target market analysis, previous sales, industry projections, brand positioning factors, and future DOE regulations, Bill Topper and his team had developed a sales volume forecast for the front-loading washer for 1996 through 1999. The forecast incorporated Frigidaire's plans to sell the washer not only under its own brand name but also under Sears' Kenmore label and other private-label agreements being negotiated; international sales also were projected. However, because the forecast was based on several market variables that were not yet truly understood, Topper believed sales tracking would be critical to the determination of market reaction. Details of the forecast are located in Exhibit F.

Sales for October, November, and December of 1996, the first three months that the front-loading

EXHIBIT F
● ● ● ● ● ● ● ● ● ● ● ● ●
Sales Volume Forecast—Horizontal-Axis Washer (000s of units)

Brand	1996	1997	1998	1999
Frigidaire	60	70	100	120
Kenmore	20	30	30	30
Private Label	10	10	10	10
International	8	12	20	30
TOTAL	98	122	160	190

Source: Frigidaire Marketing Department, Webster City, Iowa.

EXHIBIT G
. . . .
**Horizontal-Axis Front-Loading Washing Machine Sales,
October 1, 1996–December 27, 1996**

Month	Monthly Production Budget	Monthly Sales Forecast	Monthly Sales	Sold/ Forecast (%)
October	5750	4503	4876	108.28
November	4750	3456	2433	70.40
December	4500	2483	1894	76.28
TOTAL	15,000	10,442	9203	88.13

Notes: (1) Production budget = (units produced/day) × (# of available work days per month). Current production schedule is to build 250 units/day (equivalent to 60,000 units/year). (2) Monthly sales forecast is the original forecast.
Source: Frigidaire Marketing Department, Webster City, Iowa.

machine was on the market, were up to 30 percent below projected levels (see Exhibit G). In fact, sales projections for the first year had been decreased from 98,000 units to 60,000 units because Frigidaire had been unable to finalize negotiations with Sears to manufacture the horizontal-axis washer under the Kenmore name.

The reasons for this unanticipated dismal performance were unclear. Some managers believed the retail price was to blame for slow sales; as a result of the delayed introduction (delayed from May 1995 to October 1996), the target retail price had been increased from $799 to $999. The delay, everyone agreed, had been necessary to correct quality and reliability problems. However, costs increased, driving the retail price higher. In addition, it was speculated that Maytag's competing front-loading washer, due out in 1997, would be priced in the range of $1200 to $1300. Because of Maytag's high association with quality, Frigidaire managers worried that their washer priced at $799 would be perceived as inferior relative to Maytag. Consequently, the price was increased to $999 in order to still be competitive with Maytag's product

and at the same time to be close enough to Maytag's price that consumers would perceive Frigidaire as a quality washing machine. Managers reasoned that if a price adjustment was necessary, it would be easier to decrease the price than to increase it. However, other factors also may have been responsible for the lackluster sales. For example, managers questioned the decision to limit mass-media advertising, especially in light of the fact that Maytag was known to effectively use television and print media to mass advertise its products. It also was possible that demand for the front-loading washer had been overestimated.

In response to the initial sales volumes, the management team began to review its marketing strategies and objectives. The dominant question on their minds was, "How do we develop a market that has failed to take off for over 50 years?" Bill Topper knew they had to do something quickly to create a market for the front-loading washer if Frigidaire wanted to establish itself as the dominant player and industry leader in this new sector of the laundry market.

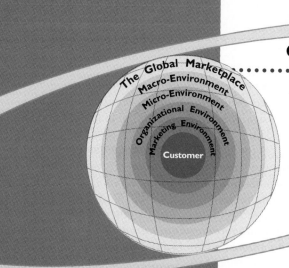

The Global Marketplace
Macro-Environment
Micro-Environment
Organizational Environment
Marketing Environment
Customer

The U.S. Internal Revenue Service: An Agency under Siege

This case was prepared by James W. Camerius, Professor of Marketing, Northern Michigan University and James W. Clinton, Professor of Management, University of Northern Colorado.

The U.S. Internal Revenue Service (IRS), in the spring of 1998, faced an uncertain future. The Republican party's leadership, Speaker Newt Gingrich of the House of Representatives and Senate Majority Leader Trent Lott, in a proposal known as the Tax Code Termination Act, sought the elimination of the country's tax code by December 31, 2001, which would significantly curtail the role of the Internal Revenue Service, administrator of the code.[1] Lott has said that "some call the IRS a 'necessary evil.' I know I agree with the second part of that description. I have not yet made [up] my mind about the first part."[2]

Senate hearings held during the fall 1997 session of Congress uncovered numerous examples of arrogant behavior by tax collectors that drove some taxpayers to commit suicide. The hearings were of critical significance to the agency because

Reprinted by permission of James W. Camerius, Professor of Marketing, Northern Michigan University, and James W. Clinton, Professor of Management, University of Northern Colorado.

the Congress appropriates funds for the agency's operations, can determine the scope of the agency's mission, and could, if it chose, initiate actions that might ultimately lead to its demise. The IRS also has been accused of squandering hundreds of millions of dollars on a computer information system that did not work and which was canceled by the Secretary of the Treasury.[3] A new commissioner was appointed in the fall of 1997 with the understanding that he reverse the negative image held of the agency by taxpayers and members of Congress, reduce waste, and make the agency's operations more efficient. Critics' condemnation of the agency indicated that the new commissioner had only a limited amount of time in which to successfully reform the agency.

MISSION

The IRS collected most of the revenues obtained by the U.S. federal government, nearly $1.5 trillion in 1997, necessary to fund the functions and operations of the government, such as Social Security and national defense.[4] At the same time, however, the agency was responsible for assisting taxpayers in filing their tax forms. The IRS, therefore, had competing tasks of collecting taxes and ensuring that those who owed taxes paid what was owed while also providing tax advisory services to those same taxpayers. These competing roles, enforcement versus service, complicated attainment of the agency's primary mission, the collection of taxes.

HISTORY

On June 16, 1909, President William Howard Taft, twenty-seventh President of the United States, recommended to Congress that the U.S. Constitution be amended to legalize the collection of federal income taxes. On February 12, 1913, after ratification by three-fourths of the states, the 16th Amendment to the Constitution was enacted, legalizing the income tax. The Bureau of Internal Revenue was created to collect personal and corporate income taxes. In 1953, Secretary of the Treasury George Humphrey changed the name of the agency to the Internal Revenue Service.[5]

The income tax originally was set at only 1 percent of the first $20,000 and by increments rose to 7 percent for income above $500,000.[6] Currently, taxpayers earning over $271,050 pay a tax of 39.6 percent on income over this amount. By 1939, only 5 percent of the population paid an income tax. Payroll tax deductions were introduced during World War II, enabling the government to obtain tax revenues throughout the year, without waiting until the end of the year for taxpayers to file their tax returns.[7] Initially, tax returns were required to be filed by March 15. This was later changed to April 15.

The IRS operated under the supervision of the Secretary of the Treasury and was directed by the Commissioner of Internal Revenue. Charles Rossotti was appointed commissioner in the fall of 1997. Rossotti was the first non-tax lawyer appointed to the post.[8] Rossotti brought to the agency technological and management experience derived from his founding and leadership of American Management Systems, a company that specialized in the development of computer systems.

PROBLEMS AND ISSUES

The IRS has been criticized for (1) inefficient use of resources, (2) heavy-handed treatment of taxpayers, (3) a tax code too complex for most taxpayers to understand, (4) too many special provisions and exceptions that favored a limited number of individuals and corporations, and (5) using the tax code to carry out the government's social objectives. Critics have recommended elimination of the existing tax code and replacement of the code with one of three alternatives: (1) a flat tax that exempted low-income wage earners, (2) a sales tax collected directly at the source, or (3) a value-added tax on business transactions.[9]

Between 1986 and 1996, the IRS spent $400 million to modernize its computer systems. For many reasons, including the incompatibility of both software and hardware, the effort was a complete failure.[10] Whereas credit card companies, insurance companies, and mutual funds can access customer files in real time, the IRS, despite substantial expenditures, has been unable to achieve a comparable level of efficiency. Evidence of the agency's failure to successfully modernize its computer systems was reflected in the fact that in 1981, the IRS spent 41 cents for every $100 collected; in 1997, the IRS spent 49 cents to collect the same amount.[11] Mismanagement of the computer modernization process led to cancellation of the modernization program.

Not all the population who owed taxes paid the IRS, either failing to file a return or fraudulently claiming deductions from their taxes to which they were not entitled. And the problem was getting worse. In 1982, the IRS estimated that collections fell $51.9 billion short of what they should have been. In 1992, the latest year for which data were available, the gap widened to $95.3 billion.[12] The absence of a modern computer information system limited the agency's ability to identify either delinquent taxpayers or those who had failed to file a tax return.

President William Clinton blasted Republican party proposals to eliminate the existing tax code without presenting a workable alternative. He noted that deductions for mortgage interest and other middle-class tax cuts would be wiped out and place unnecessary hardship on middle-income taxpayers.[13] House Majority Leader Richard Armey, on the other hand, believed that the existing tax code influenced taxpayer decisions on economic behavior and was nothing more than an instrument of social engineering.[14]

Fifteen million households received a cash payment from the IRS through the Earned Income Tax Credit (EITC) Program, which was intended to assist low-income families. At present, families who earned up to $29,000 were eligible for the credit, and it was estimated that by 2007, families earning up to $39,000 would be eligible for the cash payment. This redistribution-of-income program (averaging $1151 per check) was marked by a rate of fraud, according to recent data, of one out of every five returns.[15]

Under current federal tax laws, spouses who signed a joint tax return were held responsible for the full amount of the couple's tax liability. Women testified at a Senate hearing of being unaware that their present or former spouses had not paid the IRS but were nevertheless being pursued by the IRS for payment, which they perceived as unfair.[16] At the same hearing, taxpayers told of paying money to the IRS that they did not owe but which they paid to avoid bankruptcy or greater economic loss. An IRS agent testified that IRS managers manipulated tax-collection data to improve the appearance of their job performance. The Arkansas-Oklahoma office of the IRS was determined to have used quotas, including the seizure of property, to evaluate job performance. IRS managers indicated that they were under pressure to seize taxpayer assets, although a review of the seizures indicated that almost one-third were unwarranted.[17]

Some taxpayers were threatened with loss of their homes, their jobs, and their wages. Some were threatened with prison. Some taxpayers, in response to IRS threats, committed suicide, filed for bankruptcy, developed major medical problems, were forced into foreclosure of property that was sold at distress prices, and incurred large legal bills to appeal agency rulings. The agency's new commissioner conceded that the agency "put too much emphasis on revenue and other statistical goals and not enough on quality customer service and taxpayer rights."[18]

A General Accounting Office (GAO) study found that random audits by the IRS were skewed to focus on residents of southern states and those with incomes below $25,000. The IRS responded that certain groups with questionable deductions were concentrated in southern states and that certain low-income individuals claiming an earned income tax credit, an area in which a significant fraud had been uncovered, were the targets of the audits.[19]

The IRS tax code was about 3000 pages long, up from an original 16 pages in 1913. Supplemental IRS regulations and rulings and decisions by tax courts added an additional 39,000 pages. The code was complex and constantly modified by Congress. The Tax Relief Act of 1997 contained 821 changes to the code, and each one of these required the agency to issue bulletins, rulings, regulations, etc. to clarify the intent of the changes.[20] In some cases it cost the IRS more to collect certain taxes than the amount of tax actually collected. Some taxes were not paid because the filers did not understand the IRS regulations.

The complexity of the code has forced an increasing number of taxpayers to seek assistance from private tax preparers to complete their tax returns. H&R Block, a national tax-preparer company, reported that its U.S. offices prepared 2.2 million tax returns in January 1998, an increase of 10 percent over 1997.[21] Since the IRS administered tax laws passed by Congress, it was apparent that Congress, and not the IRS, was primarily responsible for the complexity of the code. The Taxpayer Relief Act of 1997, a mislabeled statute if there ever was one, incorporated changes, finely tuned with respect to tax rates, effective dates, and income thresholds, that triggered different tax rates, driven by the objective of identifying a cap of $90 billion in tax cuts that would permit a balanced budget based on projected revenues to be collected by the IRS.[22]

Critics of the tax code believed that some businesses and some corporations have discovered loopholes in the tax code that enabled them to pay less than their fair share. President Clinton, responding to the need to close some of these loopholes, has proposed reforms that would impact the banking industry, multinational companies, real estate investment trusts, and estate planning. The proposals were expected to bring in $8.4 billion in additional revenues.[23]

Contributing to criticism of the IRS was a belief by many that government was too big, too expensive, and too intrusive into the private affairs of its citizenry. Advocacy groups formed across the country to curtail government influence and the government's right to collect taxes. Former President

Ronald Reagan added momentum to the antigovernment movement with his promotion of self-reliance and a reduction in the role of government in the lives of its citizens. While millions of Americans were beneficiaries of government support payments, many more millions experienced only the pain of contributing a significant portion of their salaries and/or income to the IRS, the one federal agency transparently responsible for the diminished size of their paychecks and the one federal agency whose directives and deadlines they were forced to comply with under penalty of fine, imprisonment, seizure of assets, etc., none of which was guaranteed to engender feelings of endearment.

SCOPE OF OPERATIONS

The IRS employed more than 100,000 employees in 1997. As of February 27, 1998, the IRS approved $36.8 billion in refunds, an increase of 12 percent over 1997. A week earlier, the IRS reported that it had received 10.7 million returns filed through electronic means, an increase of 19 percent over 1997.[24] The increase in the number of electronic returns filed was reported to have speeded up both the filing and the refund process. Taxpayers, through a new system known as TeleFile, could file their returns by phone. This system was used by 3.8 million filers, an increase of 25 percent above the previous year.

Taxpayer appeals of IRS decisions outstanding before the federal tax court involved $33.2 billion, as of September 30, 1997, up from $32.2 billion for the same date in 1995.[25] One of the reasons for the number of appeals was alleged to be the complexity and ambiguity of the tax code, which motivated large corporations to appeal IRS decisions, in the hope that the tax court would interpret the code in a more favorable manner.

The IRS projected audits of only 1.09 percent of individual income tax returns in 1998, down from 1.67 percent in 1996. Critics said that more, rather than fewer, audits were necessary to discourage cheating. In 1997, the IRS audited 2.67 percent of 2.6 million corporate income tax returns, including a 47 percent rate of companies with assets of $250 million or more.[26]

CONGRESSIONAL AND AGENCY RESPONSES

As noted earlier, the President appointed a new commissioner with a background in management systems to overhaul the agency's data-processing systems. The consulting firm of Booz-Allen and Hamilton was hired to evaluate the agency's plan for reorganization.[27]

Congress was considering new legislation that would eliminate inequities associated with "innocent spouses" being required to pay the tax bills of former spouses.[28]

The agency, under its new director, planned a renewed effort at modernizing the IRS's computer systems, reorganizing its assets to improve efficiency, and developing a new and improved organizational culture committed to be more flexible and compassionate in addressing those situations which placed questionable and excessive pressures on taxpayers. Commissioner Rossotti has said that periodic reviews would be conducted to ensure that employees were not evaluated on the basis of quotas and that all IRS employees complied with the provisions contained in a taxpayers' bill of rights.[29]

Commissioner Rossotti proposed to restructure the IRS to account for differences in taxpayer groups. He would centralize decision making of the four existing regional offices at the national office and group functions into four customer groups: (1) individual taxpayers with only wage or investment income, representing about 140 million taxpayers, (2) small business owners, (3) large corporations, and (4) tax-exempt organizations.[30]

The IRS began conducting surveys to obtain feedback from taxpayers concerning IRS responsiveness and service. The IRS also sought volunteers to serve on citizen advocacy panels to evaluate how well the agency treated taxpayers.[31]

The IRS offered extended walk-in service to taxpayers at more than 150 locations and planned to provide assistance to low-income and elderly taxpayers at those locations as well. The IRS planned to appoint an outside group to evaluate the effectiveness of IRS inspectors responsible for detecting fraud and abuse in IRS operations.[32]

Commissioner Rossotti has directed that before IRS agents can seize taxpayer property for nonpayment of taxes, the proposed action must first be reviewed by a senior-level IRS manager. When taxpayers claim that an IRS decision would impose hardship, a taxpayer advocate from the IRS will review the claim. The IRS was conducting an internal audit of 12 of its 33 districts to determine if quotas related to seizure of taxpayer assets were in effect and, if found, eliminated.[33]

The National Commission on Restructuring the Internal Revenue Service was convened and met throughout 1996 to make recommendations to Congress concerning improvements to the IRS's operations. Recommendations included the appointment of an 11-member board, composed primarily of private citizens, to oversee the IRS. The commission also recommended that taxpayers be given the opportunity to recover costs and fees incurred by the taxpayers due to IRS negligence. Following the recommendations of the commission, Congress was in the process of passing legislation to guarantee taxpayers rights that would protect them from inappropriate behavior by IRS employees.[34]

The Oversight Board, an entity seen as a necessity by Congress, critics, and the present commissioner, would be specifically tasked to review and approve (1) the IRS's strategic plans, including both mission and objectives, and (2) standards of performance relative to these strategic plans.[35]

AN UNRESOLVED AND UNCERTAIN FUTURE

The future of the IRS was unresolved: The President leaned toward the status quo; members of the opposition party were actively seeking to either eliminate the agency or drastically curtail its scope of operations. Concurrently, Congress and the President were being lobbied to replace the tax code with a national sales tax. Advocates of a national sales tax asserted that such a tax would replace the individual and corporate income tax, the capital gains tax, and estate and gift taxes without reducing tax collections. National sales tax advocates also said that because the tax exempted low-income households, the number of tax returns filed could drop by as much as 80 percent.[36]

Senator Roth, chairman of the Senate committee reform hearings on the IRS, believed that reform of the IRS should

1. Establish an oversight board that was immune to political and internal (IRS) influence

2. Change the organization's culture so as to improve morale, efficiency, and service

3. "Address the balance of power between the taxpayer and the agency [to include] . . . burden of proof rules . . . how interest and penalties are assessed [and] how liens and seizures are used . . .

4. Resolve taxpayer cases quickly and conclusively

5. Increase accountability of IRS employees

6. Develop simplified and consistent administrative processes

As the agency's stakeholders, that is, the agency itself, the President and the Congress, individual and corporate taxpayers, and advocates for reform or elimination of the agency, continued to assert their special interests, it was clear that the agency was going to change. What was not clear, however, was the degree of change and the rate of change necessary for the IRS to survive as an organization.[37]

Endnotes

1. "Gingrich on Taxes: Wait for GOP Rule," *Rocky Mountain News,* March 8, 1998, p. 38A.
2. Tom Herman, "Tax Report," *Wall Street Journal,* February 4, 1998, p. A1.
3. "IRS Gives Technology Another Try," Edupage Editors, *educom@educom.unc.edu,* May 27, 1997.
4. Ralph Vartabedian, "Simplifying Tax Code: A Monumental Task," *The Denver Post,* January 25, 1998, p. 4L.
5. "IRS Identity and Principle of Interest," *http://www.mindspring.com.*
6. "Scrap the Income Tax," National Center for Policy Analysis, *Policy Digest, http://pages.map.com,* October 6, 1997.
7. *Ibid.*
8. Jeffrey H. Birnbaum, "Washington's Most Dangerous Bureaucrats," *Fortune,* September 29, 1997, pp. 118–126.
9. Vartabedian, *op. cit.*
10. "IRS Gives Technology Another Try," *op. cit.*
11. "More Resources Haven't Helped IRS," National Center for Policy Analysis, *Policy Digest, http://pages.map.com,* December 3, 1997.
12. *Ibid.*
13. Jackie Calmes, "Clinton Calls GOP Tax-Code Proposal Irresponsible, Says It Threatens Chaos," *Wall Street Journal,* March 3, 1998, p. A2.
14. *Ibid.*

15. "Rebate Rising," Editorial, *Wall Street Journal,* December 1, 1997, p. A22.

16. Tabassum Zakaria, "Taxpayers Detail Wrongs at Hands of IRS," YAHOO, Reuters, *http://www.yahoo.com,* September 24, 1997.

17. Dave Skidmore, "Rubin Disturbed by IRS Violations," *http://www.abcnews.com,* December 13, 1998.

18. "Tax Chief Reports Fresh Problems with IRS," YAHOO, Reuters, *http://www.yahoo.com,* January 13, 1998.

19. David Pace, "South, Poor Targets of Tax Audits," *Rocky Mountain News,* March 1, 1998, p. 50A.

20. Vartabedian, *op. cit.*

21. Tom Herman, "Tax Report," *Wall Street Journal,* March 4, 1998, p. A1.

22. Albert B. Crenshaw, "Tax Cuts Raise Hackles," *Denver Post,* March 8, 1998, pp. 1A, 24A.

23. Jacob M. Schlesinger, "Tax-Loophole Hunt Focuses on Insurers, Multinationals," *Wall Street Journal,* February 3, 1998, p. A10.

24. Herman, *op. cit.*

25. *Ibid.*

26. *Ibid.*

27. *Ibid.*

28. *Ibid.*

29. Glenn Somerville, "IRS Chief Pledges Reform for Agency," YAHOO, Reuters, *http://www.yahoo.com,* January 24, 1998.

30. *Ibid.*

31. Jacob M. Schlesinger, "Help Wanted: Hated Bureaucracy Seeks Real People to Raise Image," *Wall Street Journal,* February 27, 1998, p. B1.

32. Herman, *op. cit.*

33. Skidmore, *op. cit.*

34. Michael Briggs, "Senator Mosely-Braun Backs Internal Revenue Service Reform," *http://www.sen ate.gov,* November 6, 1997.

35. "Summary of Oversight Proposal," *Politics: The Bully Pulpit, http://www.delphi.com/bully/inside.html.*

36. "Cato Study Shows How National Sales Tax Would Work," *http://pages.map.com.bkpowell/cato_natl salestax.html,* April 20, 1997.

37. "Internal Revenue Service: Reform Hearings," *http://www.senate.gov/roth/speeches/irs.htm,* January 28, 1998.

CASE 17

Outback Goes International

The Global Marketplace
Macro-Environment
Micro-Environment
Organizational Environment
Marketing Environment
Customer

This case was prepared by Marilyn L. Taylor of the Bloch School of Business and Public Administration, University of Missouri at Kansas City, George M. Puia of the College of Business Administration, Indiana State University, Krishnan Ramaya of the School of Business Administration, University of Southern Indiana, and Madelyn Gengelbach of the Bloch School of Business and Public Administration, University of Missouri at Kansas City.

In early 1995, Outback Steakhouse enjoyed the position as one of the most successful restaurant chains in the United States. Entrepreneurs Chris Sullivan, Bob Basham, and Tim Gannon, each with more than 20 years' experience in the restaurant industry, started Outback Steakhouse with just two stores in 1988. In 1995, the company was the fastest growing U.S. steakhouse chain with over 200 stores throughout the United States.

Outback achieved its phenomenal success in an industry that was widely considered as one of the most competitive in the United States. Fully 75 percent of entrants into the restaurant industry failed

This case was developed with support from the Ewing Marion Kauffman Foundation and was presented to North American Case Research Association.

within the first year. Outback's strategy was driven by a unique combination of factors atypical of the foodservice industry. As Chairman Chris Sullivan put it, "Outback is all about a lot of different experiences that has been recognized as entrepreneurship." Within 6 years of commencing operations, Outback was voted as the best steakhouse chain in the country. The company also took top honors along with Olive Garden as America's favorite restaurant. In December 1994, Outback was awarded *Inc.'s* prestigious Entrepreneur of the Year award. In 1994 and early 1995, the business press hailed the company as one of the biggest success stories in corporate America in recent years.

In late 1994, Hugh Connerty was appointed president of Outback International. In early 1995, Connerty, a highly successful franchisee for Outback, explained the international opportunities facing Outback Steakhouse as it considered its strategy for expansion abroad:

> We have had hundreds of franchise requests from all over the world. [So] it took about two seconds for me to make that decision [to become president of Outback International]. . . . I've met with and talked to other executives who have international divisions. All of them have the same story. At some point in time the light goes off and they say, "Gee we have a great product. Where do we start?" I have traveled quite a bit on holiday. The world is not as big as you think it is. Most companies who have gone global have not used any set strategy.

Despite his optimism, Connerty knew that the choice of targeted markets would be critical. Connerty wondered what strategic and operational changes the company would have to make to ensure success in those markets.

HISTORY OF OUTBACK STEAKHOUSE, INC.

Chris Sullivan, Bob Basham, and Tim Gannon met in the early 1970s shortly after they graduated from college. The three joined Steak & Ale, a Pillsbury subsidiary and restaurant chain, as management trainees as their first postcollege career positions. During the 1980s, Sullivan and Basham became successful franchisees of 17 Chili's restaurants in Florida and Georgia with franchise headquarters in Tampa, Florida.[1] Meanwhile, Tim Gannon played significant roles in several New Orleans restaurant chains. Sullivan and Basham sold their Chili's franchises in 1987 and used the proceeds to fund Outback, their start-from-scratch entrepreneurial venture. They invited Gannon to join them in Tampa in the fall of 1987. The trio opened their first two restaurants in Tampa in 1988.

The three entrepreneurs recognized that in-home consumption of meat, especially beef, had declined.[2] Nonetheless, upscale and budget steakhouses were extremely popular. The three concluded that people were cutting in-home red meat consumption but were still very interested in going out to a restaurant for a good steak. They saw an untapped opportunity between high-priced and budget steakhouses to serve quality steaks at an affordable price.

Using an Australian theme associated with the outdoors and adventure, Outback positioned itself as a place providing not only excellent food but also a cheerful, fun, and comfortable experience. The company's Statement of Principles and Beliefs referred to employees as "Outbackers" and highlighted the importance of hospitality, sharing, quality, fun, and courage.

Catering primarily to the dinner crowd,[3] Outback offered a menu that featured specially seasoned steaks and prime rib. The menu also included chicken, ribs, fish, and pasta entrees in addition to the company's innovative appetizers.[4] CFO Bob Merritt cited Outback's food as a prime reason for the company's success. As he put it:

> One of the important reasons for our success is that we took basic American meat and potatoes and enhanced the flavor profile so that it fit with the aging population. . . . Just look at what McDonald's and Burger King did in their market segment. They [have] tried to add things to their menu that were more flavorful. [For example] McDonald's put the Big Mac on the menu. . . . as people age, they want more flavor . . . higher flavor profiles. It's not happenstance. It's a science. There's too much money at risk in this business not to know what's going on with customer taste preferences.

The company viewed suppliers as "partners" in the company's success and was committed to work with suppliers to develop and maintain long-term relationships. Purchasing was dedicated to obtaining the highest-quality ingredients and supplies. Indeed, the company was almost fanatical about quality. As Tim Gannon, vice president and the company's chief chef, put it, "We won't tolerate less than the best." One example of the company's quality emphasis was its croutons. Restaurant kitchen staff made the croutons daily on site. The croutons had 17 different seasonings, including fresh garlic and butter. The croutons were cut by hand into irregular shapes so that customers would recognize they were handmade. At about 40 percent of total costs, Outback had one of the highest food costs in the industry. On Friday and Saturday nights, customers waited up to 2 hours for a table. Most felt that Outback provided exceptional value for the average entree price of $15 to $16.

Outback focused not only on the productivity and efficiency of "Outbackers" but also on their long-term well-being. Executives referred to the company's employee commitment as "tough on results, but kind with people." A typical Outback restaurant staff consisted of a general manager, an assistant manager, and a kitchen manager plus 50 to 70 mostly part-time hourly employees. The company used aptitude tests, psychological profiles, and interviews as part of the employee selection process. Every applicant interviewed with two managers. The company placed emphasis on creating an entrepreneurial climate where learning and personal growth were strongly emphasized. As Chairman Chris Sullivan explained:

> I was given the opportunity to make a lot of mistakes and learn, and we try to do that today. We try to give our people a lot of opportunity to make some mistakes, learn, and go on.

In order to facilitate ease of operations for employees, the company's restaurant design devoted 45 percent of restaurant floor space to kitchen area. Wait staff were assigned only three tables at any time. Most Outback restaurants were only open 4:30 to 11:30 P.M. daily. Outback's wait staff enjoyed higher income from tips than in restaurants that also served lunch. Restaurant management staff worked 50 to 55 hours per week in contrast to the 70 or more common in the industry. Company executives felt that the dinner-only concept had led to effective utilization of systems, staff, and management. "Outbackers" reported that they were less worn out working at Outback and that they had more fun than when they worked at other restaurant companies.

Outback executives were proud of their "B-locations [with] A-demographics" location strategy. They deliberately steered clear of high-traffic locations targeted by companies that served a lunch crowd. Until the early 1990s, most of the restaurants were leased locations, retrofits of another restaurant location. The emphasis was on choosing locations where Outback's target customer would be in the evening. The overall strategy payoff was clear. In an industry where a sales-to-investment ratio of 1.2:1 was considered strong, Outback's restaurants generated $2.10 for every $1 invested in the facility. The average Outback restaurant unit generated $3.4 million in sales.

In 1995, management remained informal. Headquarters were located on the second floor of an unpretentious building near the Tampa airport. There was no middle management—top management selected the joint-venture partners and franchisees who reported directly to the president. Franchisees and joint-venture partners, in turn, hired the general managers at each restaurant.

Outback provided ownership opportunities at three levels of the organization: at the individual restaurant level, though multiple-store arrangements (joint-venture and franchise opportunities), and through a stock ownership plan for every employee. Health insurance also was available to all employees, a benefit not universally available to restaurant industry workers. Outback's restaurant-level general managers' employment and ownership opportunities were atypical in the industry. A restaurant general manager invested $25,000 for a 10 percent ownership stake in the restaurant, a contract for 5 years in the same location, a 10 percent share of the cash flow from the restaurant as a yearly bonus, opportunity for stock options, and a 10 percent buyout arrangement at the end of the 5 years. Outback store managers typically earned an annual salary and bonus of over $100,000 as compared with an industry average of about $60,000 to $70,000. Outback's management turnover of 5.4 percent was one of the lowest in its industry, in which the average was 30 to 40 percent.

Community involvement was strongly encouraged throughout the organization. The corporate office was involved in several nonprofit activities in the Tampa area and also sponsored major national events such as the Outback Bowl and charity golf tournaments. Each store was involved in community participation and service. For example, the entire proceeds of an open house held just prior to every restaurant opening went to a charity of the store manager's choice.

Early in its history the company had been unable to afford any advertising. Instead, Outback's founders relied on their strong relationships with local media to generate public relations and promotional efforts. One early relationship developed with Nancy Schneid who had extensive experience in advertising and radio. Schneid later became Outback's first vice president of marketing. Under her direction, the company developed a full-scale national media program that concentrated on television advertising and local billboards. The company avoided couponing, and its only printed advertising typically came as part of a package offered by a charity or sports event.

Early financing for growth had come from limited-partnership investments by family members, close friends, and associates. The three founders' original plan did not call for extensive expansion or franchising. However, in 1990, some friends, disappointed in the performance of several of their Kentucky-based restaurants, asked to franchise the Outback concept. The converted Kentucky stores enjoyed swift success. Additional opportunities with other individuals experienced in the restaurant industry arose in various parts of the country. These multistore arrangements were in the form of franchises or joint ventures. Later in 1990, the company turned to a venture capital firm for financing for a $2.5 million package. About the same time, Bob Merritt joined the company as CFO. Merritt's previous IPO[5] experience helped the company undertake a quick succession of three highly successful public equity offerings. During 1994, the price of the company's stock ranged from $22.63 to a high of $32.00. The company's income statements, balance sheets, and a summary of the stock price performance appear as Exhibits A, B, and C, respectively.

OUTBACK'S INTERNATIONAL ROLLOUT

Outback's management believed that the U.S. market could accommodate at least 550 to 600 Outback steakhouse restaurants. At the rate the company was growing (70 stores annually), Outback would near the U.S. market's saturation within 4 to 5 years. Outback's plans for longer-term growth hinged on a multipronged strategy. The company planned to roll out an additional 300 to 350 Outback stores, expand into the lucrative Italian dining segment through its joint venture with the successful Houston-based Carrabbas Italian Grill, and develop new dining themes.

At year-end 1994, Outback had 164 restaurants in which the company had direct ownership interest. The company had 6 restaurants that it operated through joint ventures in which the company had a 45 percent interest. Franchisees operated another

44 restaurants. Outback operated the company-owned restaurants as partnerships in which the company was general partner. The company owned from 81 to 90 percent. The remainder was owned by the restaurant managers and joint-venture partners. The 6 restaurants operated as joint ventures also were organized as partnerships in which the company owned 50 percent. The company was responsible for 50 percent of the costs of these restaurants.

The company organized the joint venture with Carrabbas in early 1993. The company was responsible for 100 percent of the costs of the new Carrabba's Italian Grills, although it owned a 50 percent share. As of year-end 1994, the joint venture operated 10 Carrabba's restaurants.

The franchised restaurants generated 0.8 percent of the company's 1994 revenues as franchise fees. The portion of income attributable to restaurant managers and joint-venture partners amounted to $11.3 million of the company's $72.2 million 1994 income.

By late 1994, Outback's management also had begun to consider the potential of non-U.S. markets for the Outback concept. As Chairman Chris Sullivan put it:

> . . . we can do 500 to 600 [Outback] restaurants, and possibly more over the next 5 years. . . . [However] the world is becoming one big market, and we want to be in place so we don't miss that opportunity. There are some problems, some challenges with it, but at this point there have been some casual restaurant chains that have gone [outside the United States] and their average unit sales are way, way above the sales level they enjoyed in the United States. So the potential is there. Obviously, there are some distribution issues to work out, things like that. But we are real excited about the future internationally. That will give us some potential outside the United States to continue to grow as well.

In late 1994, the company began its international venture by appointing Hugh Connerty as president of Outback International. Connerty, like Outback's three founders, had extensive experience in the restaurant industry. Prior to joining Outback, he developed a chain of successful Hooter's restaurants in Georgia. He used the proceeds from the sale of these franchises to fund the development of his franchise at Outback restau-

EXHIBIT A
....
Consolidated Statements of Income

	Years Ended December 31,		
	1994	*1993*	*1992*
Revenues	$451,916,000	$309,749,000	$189,217,000
Costs and expenses			
Costs of revenues	175,618,000	121,290,000	73,475,000
Labor and other related expenses	95,476,000	65,047,000	37,087,000
Other restaurant operating expenses	93,265,000	64,603,000	43,370,000
General and administrative expenses	16,744,000	12,225,000	9,176,000
(Income) from oper. of unconsol. affl.	(1,269,000)	(333,000)	
	379,834,000	262,832,000	163,108,000
Income from operations	72,082,000	46,917,000	26,109,000
Nonoperating income (expense)			
Interest income	512,000	1,544,000	1,428,000
Interest expense	(424,000)	(369,000)	(360,000)
	88,000	1,175,000	1,068,000
Income before elimination			
Minority partners interest and income taxes	72,170,000	48,092,000	27,177,000
Elimination of minority partners' interest	11,276,000	7,378,000	4,094,000
Income before provision for income taxes	60,894,000	40,714,000	23,083,000
Provision for income taxes	21,602,000	13,922,000	6,802,000
Net income	$39,292,000	$26,792,000	$16,281,000
Earnings per common share	$0.89	$0.61	$0.39
Weighted average number of			
common shares outstanding	43,997,000	43,738,000	41,504,000
Pro forma:			
Provision for income taxes	22,286,000	15,472,000	8,245,000
Net income	$38,608,000	$25,242,000	$14,838,000
Earnings per common share	$0.88	$0.58	$0.36

rants in northern Florida and southern Georgia. Connerty's success as a franchisee was well recognized. Indeed, in 1993 Outback began to award a large crystal trophy with the designation "Connerty Franchisee of the Year" to the company's outstanding franchisee.

Much of Outback's growth and expansion were generated through joint-venture partnerships and franchising agreements. Connerty commented on Outback's franchise system:

Every one of the franchisees lives in their areas. I lived in the area I franchised. I had relation-

ships that helped with getting permits. That isn't any different than the rest of the world. The loyalties of individuals that live in their respective areas [will be important]. We will do the franchises one by one. The biggest decision we have to make is how we pick that franchise partner.... That is what we will concentrate on. We are going to select a person who has synergy with us, who thinks like us, who believes in the principles and beliefs.

Outback developed relationships very carefully. As Hugh Connerty explained:

EXHIBIT B
Consolidated Balance Sheets

	December 31,				
	1994	1993	1992	1991	1990
Assets					
Current assets					
Cash and cash equivalents	$18,758,000	$24,996,000	$60,538,000	17,000,700	2,983,000
Short-term municipal securities	4,829,000	6,632,000	1,316,600	1,020,800	319,200
Inventories	4,539,000	3,849,000	2,166,500	794,900	224,100
Other current assets	11,376,000	4,658,000	2,095,200	18,816,400	3,526,300
Total current assets	39,502,000	40,135,000	66,116,700		
Long-term municipal securities	1,226,000	8,903,000	7,071,200		
Property, fixtures, and equipment, net	162,323,000	101,010,000	41,764,500	15,479,000	6,553,200
Investments in and advances to unconsolidated affiliates	14,244,000	1,000,000			
Other assets	11,236,000	8,151,000	2,691,300	2,380,700	1,539,600
	$228,531,000	$159,199,000	$117,643,700	36,676,100	11,619,100
Liabilities and stockholders' equity					
Current liabilities					
Accounts payable	$10,184,000	$1,053,000	$3,560,200	643,800	666,900
Sales taxes payable	3,173,000	2,062,000	1,289,500	516,800	208,600
Accrued expenses	14,961,000	10,435,000	8,092,300	2,832,300	954,800
Unearned revenue	11,862,000	6,174,000	2,761,900	752,800	219,400
Current portion of long-term debt	918,000	1,119,000	326,600	257,000	339,900
Income taxes payable			369,800	1,873,200	390,000
Total current liabilities	41,098,000	20,843,000	16,400,300	6,875,900	2,779,600
Deferred income taxes	568,000	897,000	856,400	300,000	260,000
Long-term debt	12,310,000	5,687,000	1,823,700	823,600	1,060,700
Interest of minority partners in consolidated partnerships	2,255,000	1,347,000	1,737,500	754,200	273,000
Total liabilities	56,231,000	28,774,000	20,817,900	8,753,700	4,373,300

EXHIBIT B *(continued)*
Consolidated Balance Sheets

	1994	1993	December 31, 1992	1991	1990
Stockholders' equity					
Common stock, $0.01 par value, 100,000,000 shares authorized for 1994 and 1993; 50,000,000 authorized for 1992 42,931,344 and 42,442,800 shares issues and outstanding as of December 31, 1994 and 1993, respectively. 39,645,995 shares issued and outstanding as of December 31, 1992.	429,000	425,000	396,500	219,000	86,300
Additional paid-in capital	83,756,000	79,429,000	74,024,500	20,296,400	4,461,100
Retained earnings	88,115,000	50,571,000	22,404,800	7,407,000	2,698,400
Total stockholders' equity	172,300,000	130,425,000	96,825,800	27,922,400	7,245,800
	$228,531,000	$159,199,000	$117,643,700	36,676,100	11,619,100

EXHIBIT C
....
Selected Financial and Stock Data

Year	Systemwide Sales	Co. Revenues	Net Income	EPS	Co. Stores	Franchises and JVS	Total
1988	2,731	2,731	47	0.01	2	0	2
1989	13,328	13,328	920	0.04	9	0	9
1990	34,193	34,193	2,260	0.08	23	0	23
1991	91,000	91,000	6,064	0.17	49	0	49
1992	195,508	189,217	14,838	0.36	81	4	85
1993	347,553	309,749	25,242	0.58	124	24	148
1994	548,945	451,916	38,608	0.88	164	50	214

OUTBACK Stock Data	High	Low
1991		
Second quarter	$4.67	$4.27
Third quarter	6.22	4.44
Fourth quarter	10.08	5.5
1992		
First quarter	13.00	9.17
Second quarter	11.41	8.37
Third quarter	16.25	10.13
Fourth quarter	19.59	14.25
1993		
First quarter	22.00	15.50
Second quarter	26.16	16.66
Third quarter	24.59	19.00
Fourth quarter	25.66	21.16
1994		
First quarter	29.50	23.33
Second quarter	28.75	22.75
Third quarter	30.88	23.75
Fourth quarter	32.00	22.63

... trust ... is foremost and sacred. The trust between [Outback] and the individual franchisees is not to be violated.... Company grants franchises one at a time.[6] It takes a lot of trust to invest millions of dollars without any assurance that you will be able to build another one.

However, Connerty recognized that expanding abroad would present challenges. He described how Outback would approach its international expansion:

> We have built Outback one restaurant at a time.... There are some principles and beliefs we live by. It almost sounds cultish. We want international to be an opportunity for our suppliers. We feel strongly about the relationships with our suppliers. We have never changed

suppliers. We have an undying commitment to them and in exchange we want them to have an undying commitment to us. They have to prove they can build plants [abroad]. . . .

He explained:

It think it would be foolish of us to think that we are going to go around the world buying property and understanding the laws in every country, the culture in every single country. So the approach that we are going to take is that we will franchise the international operation with company-owned stores here and franchises there so that will allow us to focus on what I believe is our pure strength, a support operation.

U.S RESTAURANTS IN THE INTERNATIONAL DINING MARKET

Prospects for international entry for U.S. restaurant companies in the early 1990s appeared promising. Between 1992 and 1993 alone, international sales for the top 50 restaurant franchisers increased from US$15.9 billion to US$17.5 billion. Franchising was the most popular means for rapid expansion. Exhibit D provides an overview of the top U.S. restaurant franchisers, including their domestic and international revenues and number of units in 1993 and 1994.

International expansion was an important source of revenues for a significant number of players in the industry. International growth and expansion in the U.S. restaurant industry over the 1980s and into the 1990s was driven largely by major fast-food restaurant chains. Some of these companies, for example, McDonald's, Wendy's, Dairy Queen, and Domino's Pizza, were public and free-standing. Others, such as Subway and Little Caesars, remained private and free-standing. Some of the largest players in international markets were subsidiaries of major consumer products firms such as PepsiCo[7] and Grand Metropolitan PLC.[8] Despite the success enjoyed by fast-food operators in non-U.S. markets, casual dining operators were slower about entering the international markets. (See Appendix A for brief overviews of

the publicly available data on the top 10 franchisers and casual dining chains that had ventured abroad as of early 1995.)

One of the major forces driving the expansion of the U.S. foodservice industry was changing demographics. In the United States, prepared foods had become the fastest-growing category because they relieved the cooking burdens on working parents. By the early 1990s, U.S. consumers were spending almost as much on restaurant fare as for prepared and nonprepared grocery store food. U.S. food themes were very popular abroad. U.S. food themes were common throughout Canada as well as western Europe and East Asia. As a result of the opening of previously inaccessible markets such as eastern Europe, the former Soviet Union, China, India, and Latin America, the potential for growth in U.S. food establishments abroad was enormous.

In 1992 alone, there were more than 3000 franchisers in the United States operating about 540,000 franchised outlets—a new outlet of some sort opened about every 16 minutes. In 1992, franchised business sales totaled $757.8 billion, about 35 percent of all retail sales. Franchising was used as a growth vehicle by a variety of businesses, including automobiles, petroleum, cosmetics, convenience stores, computers, and financial services. However, foodservice constituted the franchising industry's largest single group. Franchised restaurants generally performed better than free-standing units. For example, in 1991 franchised restaurants experienced per-store sales growth of 6.2 percent versus an overall restaurant industry growth of 3.0 percent. However, despite generally favorable sales and profits, franchisor-franchisee relationships often were difficult.

Abroad, franchisers operated an estimated 31,000 restaurant units. The significant increase in restaurant franchising abroad was driven by universal cultural trends, rising incomes, improved international transportation and communications, rising educational levels, increasing numbers of women entering the workforce, demographic concentrations of people in urban areas, and the willingness of younger generations to try new products.[9] However, there were substantial differences in these changes between the United States and other countries and from country to country.

EXHIBIT D
Top 50 U.S. Restaurant Franchises Ranked by Sales

Rank	Firm	Total Sales		International Sales		Total Stores		International Stores	
		1994	1993	1994	1993	1994	1993	1994	1993
1	McDonald's	25986	23587	11046	9401	15205	13993	5461	4710
2	Burger King	7500	6700	1400	1240	7684	6990	1357	1125
3	KFC	7100	7100	3600	3700	9407	9033	4258	3905
4	Taco Bell	4290	3817	130	100	5615	4634	162	112
5	Wendy's	4277	3924	390	258	4411	4168	413	377
6	Hardee's	3491	3425	63	56	3516	3435	72	63
7	Dairy Queen	3170	2581	300	290	3516	3435	628	611
8	Domino's	2500	2413	415	275	5079	5009	840	550
9	Subway	2500	2201	265	179	9893	8450	944	637
10	Little Caesar	2000	2000	70	70	4855	4754	155	145
Average of firms 11-20		1222	1223	99	144	2030	1915	163	251
Average of firms 21-30		647	594	51	26	717	730	37	36
Average of firms 31-40		382	358	7	9	502	495	26	20
Average of firms 41-50		270	257	17	23	345	363	26	43

Non-Fast Food in Top 50

Rank	Firm	Total Sales		International Sales		Total Stores		International Stores	
		1994	1993	1994	1993	1994	1993	1994	1994
11	Denny's	1779	1769	63	70	1548	1515	58	63
13	Dunkin Donuts	1413	1285	226	209	3453	3047	831	705
14	Shoney's	1346	1318	0	0	922	915	0	0
15	Big Boy	1130	1202	100	0	940	930	90	78
17	Baskin-Robbins	1008	910	387	368	3765	3562	1300	1278
19	T.G.I. Friday's	897	1068	114	293	314	NA	37	NA
20	Applebee's	889	609	1	0	507	361	2	0
21	Sizzler	858	922	230	218	600	666	119	116
23	Ponderosa	690	743	40	38	380	750	40	38
24	Int'l House of Pancakes	632	560	32	29	657	561	37	35
25	Perkins	626	588	12	10	432	425	8	6
29	Outback Steakhouse	549	348	0	0	NA	NA	NA	NA
30	Golden Corral	548	515	1	0	425	425	2	1
32	TCBY Yogurt	388	337	22	15	2801	2474	141	80
37	Showbiz/Chuck.E Cheese	370	373	7	8	332	NA	8	NA
39	Round Table Pizza	357	340	15	12	576	597	29	22
40	Western Sizzlin	337	351	3	6	281	NA	2	NA
41	Ground Round	321	310	0	0	NA	NA	NA	NA
42	Papa John's	297	NA	0	NA	632	NA	0	NA
44	Godfather's Pizza	270	268	0	0	515	531	0	0
45	Bonanza	267	327	32	47	264	NA	30	NA
46	Village Inn	266	264	0	0	NA	NA	NA	NA
47	Red Robin	259	235	27	28	NA	NA	NA	NA
48	Tony Roma's	254	245	41	36	NA	NA	NA	NA
49	Marie Callender	251	248	0	0	NA	NA	NA	NA

Note: NA: Not ranked in the top 50 for that category.

Source: "Top 50 Franchises," *Restaurant Business,* November 1, 1995, pp. 35–41.

FACTORS AFFECTING COUNTRY SELECTION

Outback had not yet formed a firm plan for its international rollout. However, Hugh Connerty indicated the preliminary choice of markets targeted for entry:

> The first year will be Canada.... Then we'll go to Hawaii.... Then we'll go to South America and then develop our relationships in the Far East, Korea, Japan, ... the Orient. At the second year we'll begin a relationship in Great Britain and from there a natural progression throughout Europe. But we view it as a very long-term project. I have learned that people think very different than Americans.

There were numerous considerations that U.S. restaurant chains had to take into account when determining which non-U.S. markets to enter. Some of these factors are summarized in Exhibit E. Issues regarding infrastructure and demographics are expanded below. Included are some of the difficulties that U.S. restaurant companies encountered in various countries. Profiles of Canada, South Korea, Japan, Germany, Mexico, and Great Britain appear as Appendix B.

Infrastructure

A supportive infrastructure in the target country is essential. Proper means of transportation, communication, basic utilities such as power and water, and locally available supplies are important elements in the decision to introduce a particular restaurant concept. A restaurant must have the ability to get resources to its location. Raw materials for food preparation, equipment for manufacture of food served, employees, and customers must be able to enter and leave the establishment. The network that brings these resources to a firm is commonly called a *supply chain.*

The level of economic development is closely linked to the development of a supportive infrastructure. For example, the U.S. International Trade Commission said:

> Economic conditions, cultural disparities, and physical limitations can have substantial impact on the viability of foreign markets for a franchise concept. In terms of economics, the level

of infrastructure development is a significant factor. A weak infrastructure may cause problems in transportation, communication, or even the provision of basic utilities such as electricity.... International franchisers frequently encounter problems finding supplies in sufficient quantity, of consistent quality, and at stable prices.... Physical distance also can adversely affect a franchise concept and arrangement. Long distances create communication and transportation problems, which may complicate the process of sourcing supplies, overseeing operations, or providing quality management services to franchisees.[10]

Some food can be sourced locally, some regionally or nationally, and some must be imported. A country's transportation and distribution capabilities may become an element in the decision of the country's suitability for a particular restaurant concept.

Sometimes supply-chain issues require firms to make difficult decisions that affect the costs associated with the foreign enterprise. Family Restaurants, Inc., encountered problems providing brown gravy for its CoCo's restaurants in South Korea. "If you want brown gravy in South Korea," said Barry Krantz, company president, "you can do one of two things. Bring it over, which is very costly. Or, you can make it yourself. So we figure out the flavor profile, and make it in the kitchen." Krantz concedes that a commissary is "an expensive proposition but the lesser of two evils."[11]

In certain instances, a country may be so attractive for long-term growth that a firm dedicates itself to creating a supply chain for its restaurants. An excellent illustration is McDonald's expansion into Russia in the late 1980s:

> ...supply procurement has proved to be a major hurdle, as it has for all foreign companies operating in Russia. The problem has several causes: the rigid bureaucratic system, supply shortages caused by distribution and production problems, available supplies not meeting McDonald's quality standards.... To handle these problems, McDonald's scoured the country for supplies, contracting for such items as milk, cheddar cheese, and beef. To help ensure ample supplies of the quality products it

EXHIBIT E
....
Factors Affecting Companies' Entry into International Markets

External Factors

Country market factors

Size of target market, competitive structure—atomistic, oligopolistic to monopolistic, local marketing infra-structure (distribution, etc.)

Country production factors

Quality, quantity, and cost of raw materials, labor, energy, and other productive agents in the target country as well as the quality and cost of the economic infrastructure (transportation, communications, port facilities, and similar considerations)

Country environmental factors

Political, economic, and sociocultural character of the target country—government policies and regulations pertaining to international business

Geographic distance—impact on transportation costs

Size of the economy, absolute level of performance (GDP per capita), relative importance of economic sectors—closely related to the market size for a company's product in the target country

Dynamics including rate of investment, growth in GDP, personal income, changes in employment. Dynamic economies may justify entry modes with a high break-even point even when the current market size is below the break-even point.

Sociocultural factors—cultural distance between home country and target country societies. Closer the cultural distance, quicker entry into these markets, e.g., Canada

Home country factors

Big domestic market allows a company to grow to a large size before it turns to foreign markets. Competitive structure. Firms in oligopolistic industries tend to imitate the actions of rival domestic firms that threatens to upset competitive equilibrium. Hence, when one firm invests abroad, rival firms commonly follow the lead. High production costs in the home country is an important factor.

Internal Factors

Company product factors

Products that are highly differentiated with distinct advantages over competitive products give sellers a significant degree of pricing discretion.

Products that require an array of pre- and postpurchase services makes it difficult for a company to market the product at a distance.

Products that require considerable adaptation.

Company resource/commitment factors

The more abundant a company's resources in management, capital, technology, production skills, and marketing skills, the more numerous its entry mode options. Conversely, a company with limited resources is constrained to use entry modes that call for only a small resource commitment. Size is therefore a critical factor in the choice of an entry mode. Although resources are an influencing factor, it must be joined with a willingness to commit them to foreign market development. A high degree of commitment means that managers will select the entry mode for a target from a wider range of alternative modes than managers with a low commitment.

The degree of a company's commitment to international business is revealed by the role accorded to foreign markets in corporate strategy, the status of the international organization, and the attitudes of managers.

Source: Franklin Root: Entry Strategies for International Markets. Lexington, MA: D.C. Heath (1987).

needed, it undertook to educate Soviet farmers and cattle ranchers on how to grow and raise those products. In addition, it built a $40 million food-processing center about 45 minutes from its first Moscow restaurant. And because distribution was [and still is] as much a cause of shortages as production was, McDonald's carried supplies on its own trucks.[12]

Changing from one supply chain to another can affect more than the availability of quality provisions—it can affect the equipment that is used to make the food served. For example:

> ...Wendy's nearly had its Korean market debut delayed by the belatedly discovered problem of thrice-frozen hamburger. After being thawed and frozen at each step of Korea's cumbersome three-company distribution channel, ground beef there takes on added water weight that threw off Wendy's patty specifications, forcing a hasty stateside retooling of the standard meat patty die used to mass-produce its burgers.[13]

Looking at statistics such as the number of ports, airports, quantity of paved roads, and transportation equipment as a percentage of capital stock per worker can give a bird's eye view of the level of infrastructure development.

Demographics

Just like the domestic market, restaurants in a foreign market need to know who their customers will be. Different countries will have different strata in age distribution, religion, and cultural heritage. These factors can influence the location, operations, and menus of restaurants in the country.

A popular example is India, where eating beef is contrary to the beliefs of the 80 percent of the population that is Hindu.[14] Considering that India's population is nearly 1 billion people, companies find it hard to ignore this market even if beef is a central component of the firm's traditional menu. "We're looking at serving mutton patties," says Ann Connolly, a McDonald's spokeswoman.[15]

Another area where religion plays a part in affecting the operation of a restaurant is the Middle East. Dairy Queen expanded to the region and found that during the Islamic religious observance of Ramadan, no business was conducted; indeed, the windows of shops were boarded up.[16]

Age distribution can affect who should be the target market. "The company [McDonald's in Japan] also made modifications [not long after entering the market], such as targeting all advertising to younger people, because the eating habits of older Japanese are very difficult to change."[17] Age distribution also can affect the pool of labor available. In some countries, over 30 percent of the population is under 15 years old; in other countries, over 15 percent is 65 or older. These varying demographics could create a change in the profile for potential employees in the new market.

Educational level may be an influence on both the buying public and the employee base. Literacy rates vary, and once again, this can change the profile of an employee as well as who comprises the buying public.

Statistics can help compare countries using demographic components such as literacy rates, total population and age distribution, and religious affiliations.

Income

Buying power is another demographic that can provide clues to how the restaurant might fare in the target country, as well as how the marketing program should position the company's products or services. Depending on the country and its economic development, the firm may have to attract a different segment than in the domestic market. For example, in Mexico:

> ...major U.S. firms have only recently begun targeting the country's sizable and apparently burgeoning middle class. For its part, McDonald's has changed tactics from when it first entered Mexico as a prestige brand aimed almost exclusively at the upper class, which accounts for about 5 percent of Mexico's population of some 93 million. With the development of its own distribution systems and improved economies of scale, McDonald's lately has been slashing prices to aid its penetration into working-class population strongholds. "I'd say McDonald's pricing now in Mexico is 30 percent lower, in constant dollar terms, than when we opened in '85," says Moreno [Fernando Moreno, now inter-

national director of Peter Piper Pizza], who was part of the chain's inaugural management team there.[18]

There are instances where low disposable income does not translate to a disinterest in dining out in a Western-style restaurant. While Americans dine at a fast-food establishment such as McDonald's one or two times per week, lower incomes in the foreign markets make eating at McDonald's a special, once-a-month occurrence. "These people are not very wealthy, so eating out at a place like McDonald's is a dining experience."[19] China provides another example:

> . . . at one Beijing KFC last summer, [the store] notched the volume equivalent of nine U.S. KFC branches in a single day during a $1.99 promotion of a two-piece meal with a baseball cap. Observers chalk up that blockbuster business largely to China's ubiquitous "spoiled-brat syndrome" and the apparent willingness of indulgent parents to spend one or two months' salaries on splurges for the only child the government allows them to rear.[20]

Statistics outlining the various indexes describing the country's gross domestic product, consumer spending on food, consumption and investment rates, and price levels can assist in evaluating target countries.

Trade Law

Trade policies can be friend or foe to a restaurant chain interested in expanding to other countries. Trade agreements such as NAFTA (North American Free Trade Agreement) and GATT (General Agreement on Tariffs and Trade) can help alleviate the ills of international expansion if they achieve their aims of "reducing or eliminating tariffs, reducing non-tariff barriers to trade, liberalizing investment and foreign exchange policies, and improving intellectual property protection. . . . The recently signed Uruguay Round Agreements [of GATT] include the General Agreement on Trade in Services (GATS), the first multilateral, legally enforceable agreement covering trade and investment in the services sector. The GATS is designed to liberalize trade in services by reducing or eliminating governmental measures that prevent services from being freely provided across national borders or that discriminate against firms with foreign ownership."[21]

Franchising, one of the most popular modes for entering foreign markets, scored a win in the GATS agreement. For the first time, franchising was addressed directly in international trade talks. However, most countries have not elected to make their restrictions on franchising publicly known. The U.S. International Trade Commission pointed out:

> Specific commitments that delineate barriers are presented in Schedules of Commitments [Schedules]. As of this writing, Schedules from approximately 90 countries are publicly available. Only 30 of these countries specifically include franchising in their Schedules. . . . The remaining two-thirds of the countries did not schedule commitments on franchising. This means that existing restrictions are not presented in a transparent manner and additional, more severe restrictions may be imposed at a later date. . . . Among the 30 countries that addressed franchising in the Schedules, 25 countries, including the United States, have committed themselves to maintain no limitations on franchising except for restrictions on the presence of foreign nationals within their respective countries.[22]

Despite progress, current international restaurant chains have encountered a myriad of challenges because of restrictive trade policies. Some countries make the import of restaurant equipment into their country difficult and expensive. The Asian region possesses "steep tariffs and [a] patchwork of inconsistent regulations that impede imports of commodities and equipment."[23]

OUTBACK'S GROWTH CHALLENGE

Hugh Connerty was well aware that there was no mention of international opportunities in Outback's 1994 Annual Report. The company distributed that annual report to shareholders at the April 1995 meeting. More than 300 shareholders packed the meeting to standing room only. During the question and answer period, a shareholder had closely questioned the company's executives as to why the company did not pay a dividend. The shareholder pointed out that the company made a considerable profit in 1994. Chris Sullivan responded that the company needed to reinvest the cash that might be used as dividends in order to achieve the targeted growth. His response was a pubic and very visible commitment to continue the company's fast-paced growth. Connerty knew that international had the potential to play a critical role in that growth. His job was to help craft a strategy that would ensure Outback's continuing success as it undertook the new and diverse markets abroad.

Endnotes

1. All three Outback founders credited casual dining chain legend and mentor Norman Brinker with his strong mentoring role in their careers. Brinker played a key role in all the restaurant chains Sullivan and Basham were associated with prior to Outback.
2. American consumption of meat declined from the mid-1970s to the early 1990s primarily as a result of health concerns about red meat. In 1976, Americans consumed 131.6 pounds of beef and veal, 58.7 pounds of pork, and 12.9 pounds of fish. In 1990, the figures had declined to 64.9 pounds of beef and veal, 46.3 of pork, and 15.5 of fish. The dramatic decrease was attributed to consumer attitudes toward a low-fat, healthier diet. Menu items that gained in popularity were premium baked goods, coffees, vegetarian menu items, fruits, salsa, sauces, chicken dishes, salad bars, and spicy dishes. [George Thomas Kurian, *Datapedia of the United States 1790-10000* (Maryland: Bernan Press, 1994), p. 113.]
3. Outback's original Henderson Blvd. (Tampa, Florida) restaurant was one of the few open for lunch. By 1995, the chain also had begun to open in some locations for Sunday lunch or for special occasions such as Mother's Day lunch.
4. Outback's signature trademark was its best-selling "Aussie-Tizer," the Bloomin' Onion. The company expected to serve 9 million Bloomin' Onions in 1995.
5. Merritt had worked as CFO for another company that had come to the financial markets with its IPO (initial public offering).
6. Outback did not grant exclusive territorial franchises. Thus, if an Outback franchisee did not perform, the company could bring additional franchisees into the area. Through 1994, Outback had not had territorial disputes between franchisees.
7. PepsiCo owned Kentucky Fried Chicken, Taco Bell, and Pizza Hut.
8. Grand Met owned Burger King.
9. Ref. AME 76 (KR).
10. "Industry and Trade Summary: Franchising," U.S. International Trade Commission, Washington, D.C., 1995, pp. 15-16.
11. "World Hunger," *Restaurant Hospitality,* November 1994, p. 97.
12. *International Business Environments and Operations,* 7th ed. 1995), pp. 117-119.
13. "U.S. Restaurant Chains Tackle Challenges of Asian Expansion," *Nation's Restaurant News,* February 14, 1994, p. 36.
14. *CIA World Factbook,* India, 1995.
15. "Big McMuttons," *Forbes,* July 17, 1995, p. 18.
16. Interview with Cheryl Babcock, professor, University of St. Thomas, October 23, 1995.
17. "Franchise Management in East Asia," *Academy of Management Executive,* 4(2) (1990), p. 79.
18. "U.S. Operators Flock to Latin America," *Nation's Restaurant News,* October 17, 1994, p. 47.
19. Interview with Cheryl Babcock, professor, University of St. Thomas, October 23, 1995.
20. "U.S. Restaurant Chains Tackle Challenges of Asian Expansion," *Nation's Restaurant News,* February 14, 1994, p. 36.
21. "Industry and Trade Summary: Franchising," U.S. International Trade Commission, Washington, D.C., 1995, p. 30.
22. *Ibid.*
23. "U.S. Restaurant Chains Tackle Challenges of Asian Expansion," *Nation's Restaurant News,* February 14, 1994, p. 36.

APPENDIX A: Profiles of Casual Dining and Fast-Food Chains*

This appendix provides summaries of the 1995 publicly available data on (1) the two casual dining chains represented among the top 50 franchisers that had operations abroad (Applebee's and T.G.I. Friday's/Carlson Companies, Inc.) and (2) the top ten franchisers in the restaurant industry, all of which are fast-food chains (Burger King, Domino's, Hardee's, International Dairy Queen, Inc., Little Caesar's, McDonald's, PepsiCo including KFC, Taco Bell and Pizza Hut, Subway, and Wendy's).

(1) CASUAL DINING CHAINS WITH OPERATIONS ABROAD

Applebee's

Applebee's was one of the largest casual chains in the United States. It ranked twentieth in sales and thirty-sixth in stores for 1994. Like most other casual dining operators, much of the company's growth had been fueled by domestic expansion. Opening in 1986, the company experienced rapid growth and by 1994 had 507 stores. The mode of growth was franchising, but in 1992 management began a program of opening more company-owned sites and buying restaurants from franchisees. The company positioned itself as a neighborhood bar and grill and offered a moderately priced menu including burgers, chicken, and salads.

In 1995 Applebee's continued a steady program of expansion. Chairman and CEO Abe Gustin set a target of 1200 U.S. restaurants and also had begun a slow push into international markets. In 1994 the company franchised restaurants in Canada and Curacao and signed an agreement to franchise 20 restaurants in Belgium, Luxembourg, and the Netherlands.

	1989	1990	1991	1992	1993	1994[a]
Sales ($m)	29.9	38.2	45.1	56.5	117.1	208.5
Net income ($m)	0.0	1.8	3.1	5.1	9.5	16.9
EPS ($)	(0.10)	0.13	0.23	0.27	0.44	0.62
Stock price close ($)	4.34	2.42	4.84	9.17	232.34	13.38
Dividends ($)	0.00	0.00	0.01	0.02	0.03	0.04
No. of employees	1,149	1,956	1,714	2,400	46,600	8,700

[a]1994: Debt ratio 20.1%; R.O.E. 19.2; cash $17.2m; current ratio 1.13; LTD $23.7

T.G.I. Friday's/Carlson Companies, Inc.

T.G.I. Friday's was owned by Carlson Companies, Inc., a large, privately held conglomerate that had interests in travel (65 percent of 1994 sales), hospitality (30 percent) plus marketing, employee training and incentives (5 percent). Carlson also owned a total of 345 Radisson Hotels and Country Inns plus 240 units of Country Kitchen International, a chain of family restaurants.

Most of Carlson's revenues came from its travel group. The company experienced an unexpected surprise in 1995 when U.S. airlines announced that it would put a cap on the commissions it would pay to book U.S. flights. Because of this change, Carlson decided to change its service to a fee-based arrangement and expected

*Unless otherwise noted, the information from this Appendix was drawn from "Top 50 Franchisers," *Restaurant Business,* November 1, 1995, pp. 35–41; and Hoover's Company profile Database 1996, Reference Press, Inc., Austin, TX (from American Online Service), various company listings.

sales to drop by US$100 million in 1995. To make up for this deficit, Carlson began to focus on building its hospitality group of restaurants and hotels through expansion in the United States and overseas. The company experienced significant senior management turnover in the early 1990s, and founder Curtis Carlson, age 80, had announced his intention to retire at the end of 1996. His daughter was announced as next head of the company.

T.G.I. Friday's grew 15.7 percent in revenue and 19.4 percent in stores in 1994. With 37 restaurants overseas, international sales were 12.7 percent of sales and 11.8 percent of stores systemwide. Carlson operated a total of 550 restaurants in 17 countries. About one-third of overall sales came from activities outside the U.S.

	1985	1986	1987	1988	1989	1990	1991	1992	1993	1994
Sales[a]	.9	1.3	1.5	1.8	2.0	2.2	2.3	2.9	2.3	2.3

[a]$b; no data available on income; excludes franchisee sales

(2) THE TOP TEN FRANCHISERS IN THE RESTAURANT INDUSTRY

Burger King

In 1994, Burger King was number two in sales and number four in stores among the fast-food competitors. Burger King did not have the same presence in the global market as McDonald's and KFC. For example, McDonald's and KFC had been in Japan since the 1970s. Burger King opened its first Japanese locations in 1993. By that time, McDonald's already had over 1000 outlets there. In 1994, Burger King had 1357 non-U.S. stores (17.7 percent of systemwide total) in 50 countries, and overseas sales (18.7 percent) totaled US$1.4 billion.

Burger King was owned by the British food and spirits conglomerate Grand Metropolitan PLC. Among the company's top brands were Pillsbury, Green Giant, and Haagen-Dazs. Grand Met's situation had not been bright during the 1990s, with the loss of major distribution contracts like Absolut vodka and Grand Marnier liqueur, as well as sluggish sales for its spirits in major markets. Burger King was not a stellar performer either and undertook a major restructuring in 1993 to turn the tide including reemphasis on the basic menu, cuts in prices, and reduced overhead. After quick success, BK's CEO James Adamson left his post in early 1995 to head competitor Flagston Corporation.

	1985	1986	1987	1988	1989	1990	1991	1992	1993	1994
Sales[a]	5,590	5,291	4,706	6,029	9,298	9,394	8,748	7,913	8,120	7,780
Net income[a]	272	261	461	702	1,068	1,069	616	412	450	
EPS ($)	14	16	19	24	28	32	33	28	30	32
Stock price close ($)	199	228	215	314	329	328	441	465	476	407
Dividend/ share ($)	5.0	5.1	6.0	7.5	8.9	10.2	11.4	12.3	13.0	14.0
Employees (K)	137	131	129	90	137	138	122	102	87	64

[a]Millions of Sterling; 1994: debt ratio 47.3%; R.O.E. 12.4%; Cash (Ster.) 986M; LTD (Ster.) 2322M. 1994 Segments sales (profit): North America: 62% (69%); U.K. & Ireland 10% (10%); Africa & Middle East 2% (1%); Other Europe: 21% (18%); Other Countries: 5% (2%). Segment sales (profits) by operating division: drinks 43% (51%); food 42% (26%); retailing 14% (22%); other 1% (1%).

Domino's
• • • • • • • •

Domino's Pizza was eighth in sales and seventh in stores in 1994. Sales and store unit growth had leveled off; from 1993 to 1994 sales grew 3.6 percent and units only 1.4 percent. The privately held company registered poor performance in 1993, with a 0.6 percent sales decline from 1992. Observers suggested that resistance to menu innovations contributed to the share decline. In the early 1990s the company did add deep dish pizza and buffalo wings.

Flat company performances and expensive hobbies were hard on the owner and founder Thomas Monaghan. He attempted to sell the company in 1989 but could not find a buyer. He then replaced top management and retired from business to pursue a growing interest in religious activities. Company performance began to slide, and the founder emerged from retirement to retake the helm in the early 1990s. Through extravagant purchases of the Detroit Tigers, Frank Lloyd Wright pieces, and antique cars, Monaghan put the company on the edge of financial ruin. He sold off many of his holdings (some at a loss), reinvested the funds to stimulate the firm, and once again reorganized management.

Despite all its problems, Domino's had seen consistent growth in the international market. The company opened its first foreign store in 1983 in Canada. Primary overseas expansion areas were eastern Europe and India. By 1994, Domino's had 5079 stores, with 823 of these in 37 major international markets. International brought in 17 percent of 1994 sales. Over the next 10 to 15 years the company had contracts for 4000 additional international units. These units would give Domino's more international than domestic units. International sales were 16.6 percent of total, and international stores were 16.5 percent of total in 1994.

	1985	1986	1987	1988	1989	1990	1991	1992	1993	1994
Sales[a]	1,100	1,430	2,000	2,300	2,500	2,600	2,400	2,450	2,200	2,500
Stores	2,841	3,610	4,279	4,858	5,185	5,342	5,571	5,264	5,369	5,079
Employees (K)	na	na	na	na	na	100	na	na	na	115

[a]$000,000

Hardee's
• • • • • • •

Hardee's was number 6 in sales and 11 in stores for 1994. In 1981, the large, diversified Canadian company Imasco purchased the chain. Imasco also owned Imperial Tobacco (Player's and du Maurier, Canada's top two sellers), Burger Chef, two drug store chains, the development company Genstar, and CT Financial.

Hardee's had pursued growth primarily in the United States. Of all the burger chains in the top 10 franchises, Hardee's had the smallest international presence, with 72 stores generating US$63 million (1.8 and 2.0 percent of sales and stores, respectively) in 1994.

Hardee's sales grew by about 2 percent annually for 1993 and 1994. A failed attempt by Imasco to merge its Roy Roger's restaurants into the Hardee's chain forced the parent company to maintain both brands. Hardee's attempted to differentiate from the other burger chains by offering an upscale burger menu, which received a lukewarm reception by consumers.

	1985	1986	1987	1988	1989	1990	1991	1992	1993	1994
Sales[a]	3,376	5,522	6,788	7,311	8,480	9,647	9,870	9,957	9,681	9,385
Net income[a]	262	184	283	314	366	205	332	380	409	506
EPS ($)	1.20	0.78	1.12	1.26	1.44	1.13	0.64	0.68	0.74	0.78
Stock price close ($)	13.94	16.25	12.94	14.00	18.88	13.81	18.25	20.63	20.06	19.88
Dividends ($)	0.36	0.42	0.48	0.52	0.56	0.64	0.64	0.68	0.74	0.78
Employees (K)	na	na	na	na	190	190	180	na	200	200

[a]$M—all $ in Canadian; 1994: debt ratio: 38.4%; R.O.E. 16.1%; current ratio: 1.37; LTD (M): $1927; 1994 Segment sales (operating income): CT Financial Services 47%; (28%); Hardee's 32% (11%); Imperial Tobacco 16% (50%); Shoppers Drug Mart 2% (9%); Genstar Development 1% (2%).

International Dairy Queen, Inc.
• •

Dairy Queen was one of the oldest fast-food franchises in the United States; the first store was opened in Joilet, Illinois, in 1940. By 1950, there were over 1100 stores, and by 1960, Dairy Queen had locations in 12 countries. Initial franchise agreements focused on the right to use the DQ freezers, an innovation that kept ice cream at the constant 23°F necessary to maintain the soft consistency. In 1970, a group of investors bought the franchise organization, but the group has been only partly successful in standardizing the fast-food chain. In 1994 a group of franchisees filed an antitrust suit in an attempt to get the company to loosen its control on food supply prices and sources. DQ franchises cost $30,000 initially plus continuing payments of 4 percent of sales.

The company's menu consisted of ice cream, yogurt, and brazier (hamburgers and other fast food) items. Menu innovations had included Blizzard (candy and other flavors mixed in the ice cream). The company also had acquired several companies, including the Golden Skillet (1981), Karmelkorn (1986), and Orange Julius (1987).

In 1994, Dairy Queen ranked number 7 in sales and 6 in stores. By that same year, the company had expanded its presence into 19 countries with 628 stores and US$300 million in international sales. 1994 was an excellent year for DQ; sales were up 22.8 percent over 1993. This dramatic change (1993 scored an anemic 3.0 percent gain) was fueled by technology improvements for franchisees and international expansion. In 1992 Dairy Queen opened company-owned outlets in Austria, China, Slovenia, and Spain. DQ announced in 1995 that they had a plan to open 20 stores in Puerto Rico over a 4-year period.

	1985	1986	1987	1988	1989	1990	1991	1992	1993	1994
Sales[a]	158	182	210	254	282	287	287	296	311	341
Net income[a]	10	12	15	20	23	27	28	29	30	31
EPS ($)	0.33	0.42	0.51	0.70	0.83	0.97	1.05	1.12	1.79	1.30
Stock price close ($)	5.20	7.75	8.00	11.50	14.75	16.58	21.00	20.00	18.00	16.25
Dividends ($)	-0-	-0-	-0	-0-	-0-	-0-	-0-	-0-	-0-	-0-
Employees (K)	430	459	503	520	549	584	592	672	538	564

[a]$M; 1994: debt ratio 15.3%; R.O.E. 24.4%; current ratio 3.04; LTD $23M. 1994 restaurants: U.S. 87%; Canada 9%; other 4%; restaurants by type: DQs franchised by company, 62%; franchised by territorial operators, 27%; foreign, 3%; Orange Julius, 7%; Karmelkorn, 1%; Golden Skillet less than 1%; sales by source: good supplies and equipment to franchises, 78%; service fees, 16%; franchise sales and other fees, 3%; real-estate finance and rental income, 3%.

Little Caesar's
• • • • • • • • • • • • •

Little Caesar's ranked 10 in sales and 8 in stores for 1994. Sales growth had slowed to a halt; a 1992–1993 increase of 12.2 percent evaporated into no increase for 1993–1994.

These numbers were achieved without a significant overseas presence. Of the top 10 franchises, only Hardee's had a smaller number of stores in foreign lands. Little Caesar's received 3.5 percent of sales from foreign stores. Only 3.2 percent of the company's stores were in non-U.S. locations, namely, Canada, Czech and Slovak Republics, Guam, Puerto Rico, and the United Kingdom.

	1985	1986	1987	1988	1989	1990	1991	1992	1993	1994
Sales	340	520	725	908	1,130	1,400	1,725	2,050	2,150	2,000
No. of stores	900	1,000	1,820	2,000	2,700	3,173	3,650	4,300	5,609	4,700
Employees	18,000	26,160	36,400	43,600	54,000	63,460	73,000	86,000	92,000	95,000

McDonald's
• • • • • • • • •

At the top in 1994 international sales and units, McDonald's, Inc., was the most profitable retailer in the United States during the 1980s and into the 1990s. The company opened its first store in California in 1948, went public in 1965, and by 1994 had over 20 percent of the U.S. fast-food business. McDonald's opened its first international store in Canada in 1967. Growing domestic competition in the 1980s gave impetus to the company's international expansion. By 1994 there were over 15,000 restaurants under the golden arches in 79 countries. The non-U.S. stores provided about one-third of total revenues and half the company's profits. McDonald's planned to open 1200 to 1500 new restaurants in 1995—most outside the United States. International markets had grown into an attractive venue for the burger giant because there was "less competition, lighter market saturation, and high name recognition" in international markets.

The company's growth was fueled by aggressive franchising. In the early 1990s, two-thirds of the McDonald's locations were franchised units, and franchisees remained with the company an average of 20 years. McDonald's used heavy advertising ($1.4 billion in 1994) and frequent menu changes and other innovations (1963, Filet-O-Fish sandwich and Ronald McDonald; 1968, Big Mac and first TV ads; 1972, Quarter Pounder, Egg McMuffin (breakfast); 1974, Ronald McDonald House; 1975, drive thru; 1979, Happy Meals; 1983, Chicken McNuggets; 1986, provided customers with list of products' ingredients; 1987, salads; 1980s, "value menus"; 1991, McLean DeLuxe, a low-fat hamburger (not successful) and experimentation with decor and new menu items at local level; 1993; first restaurants inside another store (Wal-Mart). The company planned to open its first restaurants in India in 1996 with menus featuring chicken, fish sandwiches, and vegetable nuggets. There would be no beef items.

From 1993–1994, McDonald's grew 10.2 percent in sales and 8.7 percent in stores. Because of its extensive experience in international markets, international sales had grown to 42.5 percent of total revenues and half its profits. Indeed, McDonald's was bigger than the 25 largest full-service chains put together.

	1985	1986	1987	1988	1989	1990	1991	1992	1993	1994
Sales[a]	3,695	4,144	4,894	5,566	6,142	6,640	6,695	7,133	7,408	8,321
Net income[a]	433	480	549	656	727	802	860	959	1,083	1,224
EPS ($)	0.56	0.63	0.73	0.86	0.98	1.10	1.18	1.30	1.46	1.68
Stock price close ($)	9.00	10.16	11.00	12.03	17.25	14.56	19.00	24.38	28.50	29.25
Dividends ($)	0.10	0.11	0.12	0.14	0.16	0.17	0.18	0.20	0.21	0.23
Employees (K)	148	159	159	169	176	174	168	166	169	183

[a]$M; 1994: debt ratio 41.2%; R.O.E. 20.7%; cash: $180M; current ratio: 0.31; LTD $2.9M; market value: $20B.

PepsiCo: KFC and Taco Bell (also Includes Pizza Hut; Latter Is Not in the Top 50)
• •

Pepsico owned powerful brand names such as Pepsi-Cola and Frito-Lay and also was the world's no. 1 fast-food chain—with its ownership of KFC, Taco Bell, and Pizza Hut. KFC was third in sales and stores of the top 50 franchises in 1994. Active in the international arena since the late 1960s, KFC had been a major McDonald's competitor in non-U.S. markets. In 1994, the company had US$3.6 billion in sales and 4258 stores in other countries. McDonald's had been commonly number one in each country it entered, but KFC had been number two in international sales and had the number one sales spot in Indonesia. In 1994, KFC international revenues were 50.7 percent of sales with 45.3 percent of stores in international locations.

Taco Bell was fourth in sales and fifth in stores of the top 50 franchises in 1994. This ranking had been achieved with minimal international business to date. Taco Bell had US $130 million sales and 162 stores internationally. The company attempted to enter the Mexican market in 1992 with a kiosk and cart strategy in Mexico City. The venture did not fare well, and Taco Bell soon pulled out of Mexico. In 1994, international revenues were 3.0 percent of sales and 2.9 percent of stores were international locations.

	1985	1986	1987	1988	1989	1990	1991	1992	1993	1994
Sales[a]	8,057	9,291	11,485	13,007	15,242	17,803	19,608	21,970	25,021	28,474
Net income[a]	544	458	595	762	901	1,077	1,080	1,302	1,588	1,784
EPS ($)	0.65	0.58	0.76	0.97	1.13	1.35	1.35	1.61	1.96	2.22
Stock price close ($)	8.06	8.66	11.11	13.15	21.31	26.00	22.88	31.40	40.88	36.25
Div./share ($)	0.15	0.21	0.22	0.25	0.31	0.37	0.44	0.50	0.58	0.68
Employees (K)	150	214	225	235	266	308	338	372	423	471

[a]$M; 1994: debt ratio 48.1%, R.O.E. 27.0%; cash(M) $1,488; current ratio 0.96; LTD (M) $8.841. 1994 segment sales (operating income): restaurants: 37% (22%); beverages 34% (37%); snack foods 29% (41%).

Subway

• • • • • •

Founded more than 29 years ago, Subway remained privately held in 1994. The company had experienced explosive growth during the 1990s. It ranked ninth in sales and second in stores for 1994. Sales grew 13.6 percent from 1993 to 1994 and 26 percent from 1992 to 1993. Stores grew 17.1 percent from 1993 to 1994 and 15.3 percent from 1992 to 1993. In 1994, Subway overtook KFC as the number two chain in number of stores behind McDonald's. The company attributed its growth at least partially to an exceptionally low-priced and well-structured franchise program. In addition, store sizes of 500 to 1500 square feet were small. Thus the investment for a Subway franchise was modest.

The company's growth involved a deliberate strategy. The formula involved no cooking on site, except for the baking of bread. The company promoted the "efficiency and simplicity" of its franchise and advertised its food as "healthy, delicious, [and] fast." The company advertised regularly on TV with a $25 million budget and planned to increase that significantly. All stores contributed 2.5 percent of gross sales to the corporate advertising budget. Subway's goal was to equal or exceed the number of outlets operated by the largest fast-food company in every market that it entered. In most cases the firm's benchmark was burger giant McDonald's.

International markets played an emerging role in Subway's expansion. In 1994, international sales were 10.6 percent of sales, compared with 8.9 percent the previous year. International stores were 9.5 percent of total in 1994 and 7.5 percent in 1993. Subway boasted a total of 9893 stores in all 50 states and 19 countries.

Wendy's

• • • • • • •

Wendy's was number five in sales and number nine in stores for 1994. In 1994, after 25 years of operation, Wendy's had grown to 4411 stores. This growth had been almost exclusively domestic until 1979, when Wendy's ventured out of the United States and Canada to open its first outlets in Puerto Rico, Switzerland, and West Germany. Wendy's granted J.C. Penney the franchise rights to France, Belgium, and Holland and had one store opened in Belgium by 1980.

Wendy's still saw opportunities for growth in the United States. Industry surveys had consistently ranked Wendy's burgers number one in quality but poor in convenience (Wendy's had one store for every 65,000 people, while McDonald's, in contrast, had one for every 25,000). Growth was driven primarily by franchising. In 1994, 71 percent of the stores were operated by franchisees and 29 percent by the company. Company restaurants provided 90 percent of total sales, while franchise fees provided 8 percent. The company had made menu and strategic changes at various points in history. For example, in 1977 the company first began TV advertising; 1979 introduced its salad bar; 1985 experimented with breakfast; 1986 and 1987 introduced Big Classic and SuperBar buffet (neither very successful); 1990: grilled chicken sandwich and 99 cent Super Value Menu items; and 1992 packaged salads.

Wendy's planned to add about 150 restaurants each year in foreign markets. With a presence of 236 stores in 33 countries in 1994, international was 9.1 percent of sales and 9.4 percent of stores in 1994.

	1985	1986	1987	1988	1989	1990	1991	1992	1993	1994
Sales[a]	1,126	1,140	1,059	1,063	1,070	1,011	1,060	1,239	1,320	1,398
Net income[a]	76	(5)	4	29	24	39	52	65	79	97
EPS ($)	0.82	(0.05)	0.04	0.30	0.25	0.40	0.52	0.63	0.76	0.91
Stock price close ($)	13.41	10.25	5.63	5.75	4.63	6.25	9.88	12.63	17.38	14.38
Div./share ($)	0.17	0.21	0.24	0.24	0.24	0.24	0.24	0.24	0.24	0.24
Employees (K)	40	40	45	42	39	35	39	42	43	44

[a]$M; 1994: debt ratio 36.6%; R.O.E. 5.2%; current ratio 0.98; LTD(M) $145.

APPENDIX B: Country Summaries*

CANADA

• •

In the 1990s, Canada was considered an ideal first stop for U.S. business seeking to begin exporting. Per capita output, patterns of production, market economy, and business practices were similar to the United States. U.S. goods and services were well received in Canada; 70 percent of all Canadian imports were from the United States. Canada's market conditions were stable, and U.S. companies continued to see Canada as an attractive option for expansion.

Canada had one of the highest real growth rates among the OECD during the 1980s, averaging about 3.2 percent. The Canadian economy softened during the 1990s, but Canadian imports of U.S. goods and services were expected to increase about 5 percent in fiscal year 1996.

Although Canada sometimes mirrored the United States, there are significant cultural and linguistic differences from the United States and between the regional markets in Canada. These differences were evident in the mounting friction between the English- and French-speaking areas of Canada. The conflict had potential for splitting of territory between the factions, slicing Canada into two separate countries. The prospect of this outcome left foreign investors tense.

GERMANY

• •

In the mid-1990s, Germany was the largest economy in Europe, and the fifth largest overall importer of U.S. goods and services. Since reunification in 1990, the eastern part of Germany had continued to receive extensive infusions of aid from western Germany, and these funds were only just beginning to show an impact. The highly urbanized and skilled western German population enjoyed a very high standard of living with abundant leisure time. In 1994, Germany emerged from a recession and scored a GDP of US$2 trillion.

A unique feature of Germany was the unusually even distribution of both industry and population—there was no single business center for the country. This was a challenge for U.S. firms. They had to establish distribution networks that adequately covered all areas of the country. In Germany there was little opportunity for regional concentration around major population centers as in the United States.

The country was a good market for innovative high-tech goods and high-quality food products. Germans expected high-quality goods and would reject a less expensive product if quality and support were not in abundance. Strongest competition for U.S. firms were the German domestic firms not only because of their home-grown familiarity of the market but also because of the consumers' widely held perception that German products were "simply the best."

A recurring complaint from Germans was the prevalent "here today, gone tomorrow" business approach of American firms. Germans viewed business as a long-term commitment to support growth in markets and did not always receive the level and length of attention necessary from U.S. companies to satisfy them.

Conditions in the former area of East Germany were not the doomsday picture often painted, nor were they as rosy as the German government depicts. It would take 10 to 15 years for the eastern region of the country to catch up to the western region in terms of per capita income, standard of living, and productivity.

JAPAN

• •

Japan had the second largest economy in the world. Overall economic growth in Japan over the past 35 years had been incredible: 10 percent average annual growth during the 1960s, 5 percent in the 1970s and 1980s.

*Note that the material in this Appendix is adapted from the Department of Commerce *Country Commercial Guides* and the *CIA World Fact Book.*

Growth ground to a halt during the 1990s due to tight fiscal policy. The government tightened fiscal constraints in order to correct the significant devaluation of the real estate markets. The economy posted a 0.6 growth in 1994 largely due to consumer demand. The overall economic outlook remained cloudy, but the outlook for exports to Japan remained positive.

Japan was a highly homogeneous society with business practices characterized by long-standing close relationships among individuals and firms. It took time for Japanese businessmen to develop relationships, and for non-Japanese businesspeople the task of relationship building in Japan was formidable. It was well known that Japan's market was not as open as the United States, but the U.S. government had mounted multifaceted efforts to help U.S. businesspeople to "open doors." While these efforts were helpful, most of the responsibility in opening the Japanese market to U.S. goods or services remained with the individual firm. Entering Japan was expensive and generally required four things: (1) financial and management capabilities and a Japanese-speaking staff residing within the country, (2) modification of products to suit Japanese consumers, (3) a long-term approach to maximizing market share and achieving reasonable profit levels, and (4) careful monitoring of Japanese demand, distribution, competitors, and government. Despite the challenges of market entry, Japan ranked as the second largest importer of U.S. goods and services.

Historically, Japanese consumers were conservative and brand conscious, although the recession during the 1990s nurtured opportunities for "value" entrants. Traditional conformist buying patterns were still prominent, but more individualistic habits were developing in the younger Japanese aged 18 to 21. This age cohort had a population of 8 million people and boasted a disposable income of more than US$35 billion.

Japanese consumers were willing to pay a high price for quality goods. However, they had a well-earned reputation for having unusually high expectations for quality. U.S. firms with high-quality, competitive products had to be able to undertake the high cost of initial market entry. For those who were willing, Japan could provide respectable market share and attractive profit levels.

MEXICO

Mexico had experienced a dramatic increase in imports from the United States since the late 1980s. During 1994, the country experienced 20 percent growth over 1993. In 1994, Mexico's peso experienced a massive devaluation brought on by investor anxiety and capital flight. Although the Mexican government implemented tight fiscal measures to stabilize the peso, its efforts could not stop the country from plunging into a serious recession.

Inflation rose as a result of the austerity policies, and it was expected to be between 42 and 54 percent in 1995. Negative economic growth was anticipated in 1995 as well. The U.S. financial assistance package (primarily loans) provided Mexico with nearly US$50 billion and restored stability to the financial markets by mid-1995. The government was taking measures to improve the country's infrastructure. Mexico's problems mask that its government had, on the whole, practiced sound economic fundamentals.

Mexico was still committed to political reform despite the current economic challenges. After ruling the government uninterrupted for 60 years, the PRI party had begun to lose some seats to other political parties. Mexico was slowly evolving into a multiparty democracy.

Despite the economic misfortunes of recent years, Mexico remained the United States' third largest trading partner. Mexico still held opportunities for U.S. firms able to compete in the price-sensitive recessionary market. Mexico had not wavered on the NAFTA agreement since its ratification, and in the mid-1990s, 60 percent of U.S. exports to Mexico entered duty-free.

SOUTH KOREA

South Korea had been identified as one of the U.S. Department of Commerce's 10 "Big Emerging Markets." The country's economy overcame tremendous obstacles after the Korean War in the 1950s left the country in ruins. The driving force behind South Korea's growth was export-led development and energetic emphasis on entrepreneurship. Annual real GDP growth from 1986 to 1991 was over 10 percent. This blistering pace created inflation, tight labor markets, and a rising current account deficit. Fiscal policy in 1992 focused on curbing inflation and reducing the deficit. Annual growth, reduced to a still enviable 5 percent in 1992, rose to 6.3 percent in 1993. Fueled by exports, 1994s growth was a heady 8.3 percent. South Korea's GDP was larger than those of Russia, Australia, and Mexico.

The American media had highlighted such issues as student demonstrations, construction accidents, and North Korean nuclear problem and trade disputes. Investors needed to closely monitor developments related to North Korea. However, the political landscape in South Korea had been stable enough over the 1980s to fuel tremendous economic expansion. The country was undertaking significant infrastructure improvements. Overall, South Korea was a democratic republic with an open society and a free press. It was a modern, cosmopolitan, fast-paced, and dynamic country with abundant business opportunities for savvy American businesses.

There had been staggering development of U.S. exports to South Korea: US$21.6 billion in 1994 and over US$30 billion expected in 1995. While South Korea was 22 times smaller than China in terms of population, it imported two times more U.S. goods and services than China in 1994.

Although South Korea ranked as the United States' sixth largest export market, obstacles for U.S. firms still remained. Despite participation in the Uruguay Round of GATT and related trade agreements, customs clearance procedures and regulations for labeling, sanitary standards, and quarantine often served as significant nontariff barriers.

UNITED KINGDOM (OR GREAT BRITAIN)

The United Kingdom (U.K.) was the United States' fourth largest trading partner and the largest market for U.S. exports in Europe. Common language, legal heritage, and business practices facilitated U.S. entry into the British market.

The United Kingdom had made significant changes to their taxation, regulation, and privatization policies that changed the structure of the British economy and increased its overall efficiency. The reward for this disciplined economic approach had been sustained, modest growth during the 1980s and early 1990s. GDP grew 4.2 percent in 1994, the highest level in 6 years. The United Kingdom trimmed its deficit from US$75 billion in fiscal 1994 to US$50 billion in fiscal 1995.

The United Kingdom had no restrictions on foreign ownership and movement of capital. There was a high degree of labor flexibility. Efficiencies had soared in the United Kingdom, and in the mid-1990s, the country boasted the lowest real per unit labor cost of the Group of Seven (G7) industrialized countries.

The United Kingdom's shared cultural heritage and warm relationship with the United States translated into the British finding U.S. goods and services as attractive purchases. These reasons, coupled with British policy emphasizing free enterprise and open competition, made the United Kingdom the destination of 40 percent of all U.S. investment in the EU.

The U.K. market was based on a commitment to the principles of free enterprise and open competition. Demand for U.S. goods and services was growing. The abolition of many internal trade barriers within the European Common market enabled European-based firms to operate relatively freely. As a result, U.S. companies used the United Kingdom as a gateway to the rest of the EU. Of the top 500 British companies, one in eight was a U.S. affiliate. Excellent physical and communications infrastructure combined with a friendly political and commercial climate were expected to keep the United Kingdom as a primary target for U.S. firms for years to come.

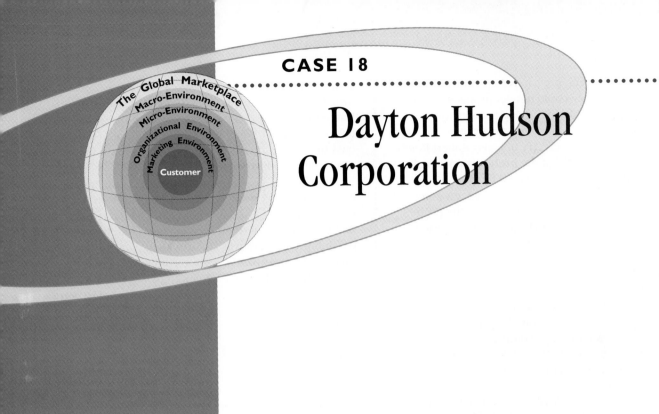

Dayton Hudson Corporation

This case was prepared by Jan Zahrly, Marshall Foote, Troy Gleason, Aaron Martin, Brent Olson, and Brian Wavra of the University of North Dakota.

Robert J. Ulrich assumed the chairman and CEO positions of Dayton Hudson Corporation (DHC) in July of 1994 with a multitude of problems. Media coverage was negative and getting worse. Analysts' assessments were negative. Investigations by the U.S. Labor Department, earnings down seriously, key executives resigning, and merger offers from major competitors were some of the problems Ulrich had to face. And each of the divisions seemed to be cannibalizing customers from the others. Ulrich joined the company in 1967 as a merchandise trainee and was one of the managers who built Target into a powerhouse, but so far he had not been able to turn the company around.

When would investors and Wall Street analysts give up on DHC? When would the company give

up on itself and sell out or merge or divest its poorly performing division?

DHC is the fourth largest discount and fashion retailer in the United States behind Wal-Mart, Sears, and Kmart. J.C. Penney closely trails Dayton Hudson in sales. DHC has retail operations in all segments of the discount and clothing industry. These range from a national upscale discount store chain (Target) to Mervyn's, a moderate-priced family department store chain specializing in nondurable goods. DHC also includes a Department Store Division (DSD), which is a centrally operated full-line, full-service chain of department stores emphasizing fashion leadership (under the names of Dayton's, Hudson's, and Marshall Field's).

A PLETHORA OF PROBLEMS

Dayton Hudson Corporation's problems were so many that stockholders and analysts were begin-

This case was written solely for the purpose of stimulating student discussion. Presented at the North American Case Research Association annual meeting, Orlando, November 1995. Reprinted by permission of the authors.

ning to group them into categories. First and foremost, the company could not get profits up. This was reflected in the stock price. Second, the problems with the U.S. Labor Department were not only serious but public. Secretary of Labor Robert Reich insisted on talking about the problems on TV talk shows, and news shows covered the sweatshop raids. Finally, the profit and labor problems contributed to personnel problems. Again, the problems became public knowledge when a division CEO resigned unexpectedly.

Profitability Problems

On May 16, 1995, DHC announced that first-quarter earnings fell 72 percent from the previous year's first-quarter earnings. The company blamed weakness in its Mervyn's division and weaker than projected sales in its other department stores for the steep decline in profits.

On March 14, 1996, DHC announced that net earnings for fiscal year 1995 were down 28 percent from the year before. The company cited a "tough Christmas season" and a bad year in general. Company spokesperson Jill Schmidt contended that DHC did not plan any reorganization. "Right now, there are no plans to sell anything. We're sticking with the plans in place," Schmidt stated.

Apparently, J.C. Penney did not believe the public statements of DHC and approached the firm

about a merger in February 1996. Penney confirmed that it offered $6.8 billion for DHC, but the Dayton Hudson board promptly rejected the unsolicited offer and offered no counterproposal to discuss the possibilities of a merger. See Exhibit A for comparative industry data.

The Mervyn's division continued to lag the industry, with 1995 profits down 51 percent from the previous year. Executives at DHC maintained that discount and fashion retailing was in an industry slump, and there was some evidence to support this argument. Apparel sales were up only 2 percent in the first half of 1995, and much of that was due to special sales. Analysts noted that the industry is saturated and some firms such as Target and Sears are expanding.

Legal Problems

In August of 1995, DHC found itself in trouble with the U.S. Labor Department when an El Monte, California, sweatshop was raided. Dozens of Thai nationals, illegal aliens, were discovered working in a shop manufacturing clothing. They were enclosed behind barbed wire and were making less than $1 an hour. Also discovered were boxes of clothing with shipping labels for Montgomery Ward and Mervyn's stores.

"Two retail stores, from initial evidence, appear to have been dealing directly with the contractors"

EXHIBIT A

**Comparative Sales and Earnings Data, 1995:
Discount and Fashion Retailing Industry
(Sales and Profits in Millions of $)**

	Sales	Profits	Return on Equity
Wal-Mart	$90,524	$2827.6	20.1
Sears	$34,925	$1025.0	25.1
Kmart	$34,572	$ 8.0	−.2
DHC	$22,564	$ 362.0	11.3
J.C. Penney	$22,019	$ 940.0	16.9
Industry average			12.9

Source: *Business Week Corporate Scoreboard,* March 4, 1996.

who managed the sweatshop according to California Labor Commissioner Victoria Bradshaw.

Robert Reich, Secretary of Labor, forced a meeting in September 1995 with executives from DHC, Sears, and Montgomery Ward to discuss ways the firms could counter the use of sweatshops. DHC was later excluded from a list of "Fair Labor Fashions Trendsetters" issued by the Labor Department in December 1995. The list of 31 retailers included firms that were actively working to guarantee that clothing sold by the retailers was made in shops and factories that comply with federal wage, labor, and immigration laws. Secretary Reich wanted the retail industry to take an active role in enforcing fair labor and wage laws and was using public pressure to get retailers to comply.

The negative publicity about Mervyn's contracting directly with sweatshops for clothing hurt DHC's image of being a socially responsible firm. Hoover's *Handbook of American Business* in 1993 listed DHC as fifth in the nation for job creation. Hoover's *Handbook* also noted that, "Dayton Hudson has a long history as a great place to work. . . ." Because of its high-quality work atmosphere, job-creation activities, and corporate charitable policies (5 percent of net income goes to local charities), DHC was included in The 100 Best Companies to Work for in America in 1993.

The corporation was recognized in 1993 for its good treatment of working parents, minorities, and those with disabilities. DHC was listed in The 100 Best Companies for Minorities: Employers Across America Who Recruit, Train and Promote Minorities. Dayton Hudson also was named to The 100 Best Companies for Working Women by *Working Mother* magazine and The 50 Best Companies for Hispanic Women, compiled by the *Vista* magazine section of the *Dallas Morning News*. Overall, DHC, through its generous contributions and attitudes toward hiring, had made itself one of the more identifiable good corporate citizens—until the news of the sweatshop raid become public.

Personnel Problems

In March 1996, Stephen Watson abruptly resigned as president of the Department Store Division. He had been popular with subordinates but had clashed with Chairman Ulrich. Watson was quoted as saying he resigned because he believed the Department Store Division will soon "no longer need" a chief executive officer. He was apparently referring to the intervention of Ulrich.

At the same time Watson's resignation was announced, Linda Ahlers, one of the few women in Ulrich's inner circle, was named as the new CEO of the Department Store Division. Many outsiders and analysts believe that Ahlers "does not have much of a chance," even though she has been with Target for 19 years and has been very successful. The department stores' profits were down by 32 percent in 1995 (compared with profits in 1994), Ahlers is under pressure to cut millions of dollars in costs, and the department stores' product line is being rejected by customers after a 1994 strategy shift to "value" products.

COMPANY HISTORY

The history of DHC dates back to the late 1800s when the J. L. Hudson Company was founded in Detroit, Michigan. The Dayton Company was founded in Minneapolis, Minnesota, in 1902 and later became the Dayton Corporation. In 1956, Dayton's opened the world's first fully enclosed, two-level shopping center in suburban Minneapolis, named Southdale. Meanwhile, Hudson's opened the Northland Center in Detroit, the world's largest shopping center at the time.

The shopping centers gained national attention from other retailers. Dayton's and Hudson's each realized they had market potential, and both grew externally through acquisitions and mergers during the 1960s, 1970s, and 1980s. Dayton's also developed internal growth ventures, hoping to capitalize on low-margin merchandising. The 1962 venture was the opening of three Target stores in the Minneapolis area. Dayton's entered the specialty book retailing market in 1966 through the creation of the B. Dalton Bookseller stores.

In 1969, the Dayton Corporation and the J. L. Hudson Company merged to form the Dayton Hudson Corporation (DHC), making the corporation the fourteenth largest general merchandise retailer in the United States. DHC continued its strategy of growth. Department store expansion moved to the West through mergers and acquisitions of specialty stores and fashion retailers. In 1977, Target stores became the corporation's top revenue producer.

DHC merged with Mervyn's, a West Coast department store chain, in 1978 and became the country's seventh largest general-merchandise retailer. At the same time, DHC began to shed its less profitable operations by selling regional shopping centers and entire divisions. DHC bought and sold stores in an attempt to strengthen its core business, general and fashion retailing. In 1984, Hudson's and Dayton's department stores combined to form the Dayton Hudson Department Store Company, the largest individual department store company in the nation. B. Dalton Bookseller was sold in the same year.

In 1990, DHC made its final major acquisition. It acquired Marshall Field's, a Midwest upscale department store chain founded in Chicago in 1852. Mervyn's initiated a major entry into South Florida by acquiring six Jordan Marsh stores and five Lord & Taylor stores. Target expanded into key Florida markets also and opened its first of many smaller market store formats. By 1993, the Mervyn's stores were losing market share due to heavy competition.

On January 7, 1994, Retailers National Bank, a national credit card bank and a wholly owned subsidiary, was chartered. The bank acquired the outstanding accounts receivable of the Department Store Division and Target. The bank now issues the DSD-named credit cards and a Target credit card.

INDUSTRY TRENDS

The general and fashion retailing industry is characterized by intense competition. For most of the 1970s and through the mid-1980s, retailers achieved earnings and growth by adding new units and expanding existing stores. Strong economic growth and vigorous consumer spending made this possible and feasible. With high volume, retailers were able to reduce operating costs as a percentage of sales, producing solid profits year after year.

In the wake of the recession of the early 1990s, however, the retail landscape changed. Slow economic growth, a decrease in consumer spending for nondurable goods, and a surfeit of retail space put American retailers to the test. Successful department stores and general merchandise chains were following corporate-level strategies of growth through acquisitions. At the same time, less successful companies were following retrenchment strategies. Successful business-level strategies were differentiation and niche.

Retailers and customers alike grew accustomed to innovations in retailing. Upstart competitors were appearing in virtually every segment of retailing. Outlet malls, for example, with their selection of brand-name apparel at value prices were luring customers away from department stores and off-price retailers. Superstores, carrying a wider variety of goods than the traditional department store, emerged. Specialty stores evolved into "category killers" that carry a single dominant product. Examples are stores that carry many varieties of office supplies or many computer products. Specialty retail stores do not attempt to carry many different products; they want to carry all products related to a particular product or service.

Catalog retailing is expanding, and at-home shopping is growing. Most of these new formats are competing on price or convenience. Different types of competition are becoming more powerful in the marketplace. Technological advances such as television, computer on-line services, and computer databases have opened new doors to reach consumers in their homes. Companies such as The Home Shopping Network (QVC), American On-Line, and Eddie Bauer are all cashing in on this new technology.

While some consumers remain loyal to the stores they patronize, customer loyalty, in general, is eroding throughout the industry. The once powerful and extremely profitable department stores have reached a mature stage in the industry. The only segment of the retail industry that is currently in the growth stage is the discount merchandise retailer.

> The retail lifecycle is a natural evolutionary process, and executives can do very little to counteract it. What they can do is to plan more efficiently in order to sustain profitability in the different stages. Such planning implies continuous rethinking and revision of operations. This, in turn, means that retailing will continue to be an area of turbulence and uncertainty for some time to come.

DAYTON HUDSON CORPORATION DIVISIONS

In 1995, DHC had three divisions, all involved in general merchandise and fashion retailing. Credit operations were consolidated in a wholly owned subsidiary, the Retailer's National Bank.

Target

In 1962, the Target division was created and focused on discount prices. During the 1970s, Target expanded rapidly with internal development of stores and external acquisitions. In 1977, Target became Dayton Hudson's top revenue-producing division. One year later, Target made its first entry into a shopping mall in Grand Forks, North Dakota.

Target was the first mass merchant to use a promotional toy in 1986. More than one and one-half million Kris Kringles were sold during the 1986 holiday season. During the 1990s, Target introduced several new strategies, including establishing local flexibility through micro-marketing, initiating a total quality system, and focusing on efficiency through use of advanced communication technology and reduced inventory levels.

Target executives characterize the firm as an upscale discounter in the general merchandise retail industry. The discount segment of the industry is experiencing intense growth. Target is trying to position itself by focusing on the quality of service it offers its consumers. Target stores are described as having high quality at low prices, maintaining clean and attractive stores, stocking plenty of products to avoid stockouts, and offering fast, friendly, and accurate checkout procedures. Many consumers have realized that there is not much difference in the brands they can purchase at Target compared with those they might purchase at Nordstrom's or Dayton's.

The broad product mix is one of the reasons Target has been so successful. Target's emphasis is on basic, family-oriented merchandise. An aggressive fashion strategy enables Target to compete as a lifestyle trend merchandiser in all categories. Apparel and domestics represent approximately one-third of the product assortment. The targeted customer is 25 to 44 years old, typically married with children, and in a two-wage earner family with income and education levels higher than the market median.

The perceived value to the consumer has been a key differentiation factor. Another less obvious differentiation factor is the millions of dollars Target and its employees annually donate to local non-profit organizations. Through these numerous contributions, Target has established goodwill in the communities in which it operates.

At year-end 1995, Target had 611 stores throughout the United States. The only region Target does not operate in is the Northeastern part of the country. Exhibit B lists the number of stores in each division.

Target's performance is the strength of DHC. Even though Target is a discounter and most of the products it sells make low profit margins, it is still the most profitable division of the company.

EXHIBIT B

Number of Stores (Year End): Dayton Hudson Corporation

	1995	1994	1993
Target	611	554	506
Mervyn's	286	276	265
Department stores	63	63	63
Dayton's (19)			
Hudson's (21)			
Marshall Field's (23)			
Total	960	893	834

Source: Hoover's Handbook, 1994, 1995, 1996.

	1992	1993	1994
Revenues ($ in mil.)	10,393	11,743	13,600
Operating profit ($ in mil.)	574	662	732
Net profit margin	5.52	5.63	5.38

Source: Dayton Hudson 1994 Annual Report.

Mervyn's
• • • • • • •

Mervyn's is a moderate-priced family department store specializing in soft goods. Based in the San Francisco Bay area, Mervyn's was founded in 1949 and was purchased by DHC in 1978. Retailer Mervyn Morris started the chain with the objective of mirroring J.C. Penney Co. but offering national brands and customer credit. Mervyn's still views its typical stores as smaller versions of J.C. Penney and Sears stores without the hardware and appliance departments.

By year-end 1995, approximately 70 percent of Mervyn's senior management team was new to Mervyn's. The single purpose of the new management was a turnaround. Mervyn's profitability was below industry averages for several years. One key addition to the management team was Paul Sauser, formerly senior vice president of merchandising at Target, now Mervyn's president and chief operating officer. Sauser, a highly regarded retail executive, was brought in to help implement Mervyn's turnaround. Mervyn's turnaround included a new pricing strategy, shrinking inventory, sprucing up stores, tailoring merchandise assortments to match the needs of the local customers, and polishing Mervyn's image among customers. The stores were being renovated with wider aisles, knowledgeable associates, less crowding, and improved store graphics.

Mervyn's recent pricing strategy is an improvement on the previous strategy, which created large price differentials on many sale items. For example, a cotton blanket was regularly priced at $35 but carried a $17.50 sale price 1 week per month. Consequently, virtually all the purchases occurred when specific items were sale priced. Under the new pricing strategy, the blanket's promotional price is $17.99, with a regular price of $25.

Another element of the turnaround was an improvement in its image. This key element involved a return of women's career apparel and dresses,

which Mervyn's dropped in 1991. Mervyn's reintroduced its female business apparel product line, which sparked sales of more than $90 million in 1993. Approximately 50 percent of its offered merchandise is nationally known name brands. The key customer is a 25- to 44-year-old female, typically married with children, working outside the home. The customer tends to have a moderate household income and some college education.

Mervyn's operates in 15 states in the Northwest, West, Southwest, Southeast, and Michigan. The vast majority of stores are located in California, where Mervyn's derives about 50 percent of its revenues. Other major states Mervyn's operates in are Arizona, Florida, Colorado, and Michigan. Mervyn's faces additional threats because of its strong presence in the struggling California economy. Even though Mervyn's profits and profit margin were increasing by 1994, they continued to lag the industry and depress company profits.

	1992	1993	1994
Revenues ($ in mil.)	4,510	4,436	4,561
Operating profit ($ in mil.)	284	179	206
Net profit margin	6.29	4.03	4.52

Source: Dayton Hudson 1994 Annual Report.

"Mervyn's was our major disappointment" the fourth largest U.S. retailer noted in its 1993 year-end earnings report. By 1995, the annual report noted that Mervyn's had "solid improvement" because of improved markdowns, reduced initial retail prices, and improved inventory management.

Department Store Division
• • • • • • • • • • • • • • • • • • • •

The Department Store Division (DSD) operates stores under the Dayton's, Marshall Field's, and Hudson's names. The division has goals of fashion leadership, quality merchandising, customer service, and dedication to the communities in which it operates.

The Department Store Division focuses on trends in the marketplace and new fashions and products. The emphasis placed on product mix is a strength when competing with rivals. The DSD relies on a broad assortment of trend-right, quality softlines and hardlines, national brands, and private labels to fulfill customer interest and to sustain a competitive advantage. The DSD also invests in fashion and basic merchandise in the moderate to better price range to renew focus on "value" offerings across the price spectrum. This broadened their customer base by lowering opening price points in many departments. An example of this value-priced merchandise is its Field Gear line, introduced in 1993. While customers could still purchase higher-priced items like Ralph Lauren and Pierre Cardin, they also could choose from the Field Gear line that prices button-down shirts at $32.

The department stores' target consumer is married, with a median age of 43, and median family income of $50,000. Approximately 40 percent have children living at home. Over half have attained at least an undergraduate degree; two-thirds hold white-collar positions.

The DSD is in the business of selling image and maintaining a certain image. Service, human resources management, and community involvement are elements that relate to its image. The division upholds the quality of store appearance and remodels when changes are needed or anticipated. The overall image of the DSD is that of a full-service department store, fulfilling the needs and wants of its consumer.

The DSD places a heavy emphasis on full-color tabloids, direct mail, and occasionally television and radio. Also, a strong special store events calendar tied to key merchandising trends and/or community events aids in specialty pricing. Finally, a strong emphasis on primary and secondary holiday advertising and promotions is utilized.

The net profit margin for the DSD has been increasing over the last 3 years. This trend is due to the increase in inventory turnover and the fact that the department stores can offer a higher price for products. Higher productivity also has resulted from the introduction of new systems that track and control the purchase and delivery of merchandise.

	1992	1993	1994
Revenues ($ in mil.)	3,024	3,054	3,150
Operating profit ($ in mil.)	228	268	270
Net profit margin	7.54	8.77	8.57

Source: Dayton Hudson 1994 Annual Report.

The DSD's major markets are located in Chicago, Minneapolis–St. Paul, and Detroit. The division continues to grow. A new Dayton's is planned for Minneapolis in 1997, as well as a new Marshall Field's in Columbus, Ohio. The recently resigned CEO of the division, Stephen Watson, said, "We wouldn't build them if we couldn't pencil in a good return."

FINANCIAL POSITION

DHC has two main financial objectives: to produce an average 15 percent annual fully diluted earnings per share growth and to achieve an 18 percent return on equity. See Exhibits C and D for financial statements.

DHC had average returns on equity but lower than industry returns on assets for 1994. The industry average return on equity was 17.4 percent. However, this number is inflated due to Wal-Mart's return on equity of 25.3 percent. The industry, without Wal-Mart, had a return on equity of 15.4 percent.

	ROE	ROA
Dayton Hudson Corp.	15.2%	3.9%
Industry avg.	17.4%	6.6%
Industry avg. w/o Wal-Mart	15.4%	5.1%

Source: Standard & Poor's Industry Surveys, 1994.

CURRENT SITUATION

Target has a strong market position in the industry. The department stores and Target carry recognizable brand-name products that give the stores credibility. Target and the department stores have a strong market image in the markets in which they operate.

However, one of DHC's main strengths could pose a problem to another aspect of its business. This is the phenomenal growth of Target. Target's growth in stores and customers may lead to cannibalization of the DSD. "After all, why should I shop in Dayton's when I can get almost the same thing for less money in Target?" said a recent Target customer who was applying for a Target credit card.

A similar problem that may arise could be the cannibalization of Target by the DSD. Since the

EXHIBIT C
....
Dayton Hudson Corporation:
Consolidated Balance Sheets
(Numbers in Millions)

	1/95	1/94	1/93
Assets			
Current assets			
Cash and cash equivalents	$ 147	$ 321	$ 117
Accounts receivable	1810	1536	1514
Merchandise inventories	2227	2497	2618
Other	225	157	165
Total current assets	4959	4511	4414
Property and equipment			
Land	1251	1120	4342
Buildings and improvements	5208	4753	4342
Fixtures and equipment	2257	2162	2197
Construction in progress	293	248	223
Accumulated depreciation	(2624)	(2336)	(2197)
Net property and equipment	6385	5947	5563
Other	353	320	360
Total assets	$11,697	$10,778	$10,337

	1/95	1/94	1/93
Liabilities and shareholders' investment			
Current liabilities			
Notes payable			$ 23
Accounts payable	$1961	$1654	1596
Accrued liabilities	1045	903	849
Income tax payable	175	145	125
Current portion long-term debt	209	373	371
Total current liabilities	3390	3075	2964
Long-term debt	4488	4279	4330
Deferred income taxes	582	536	450
Convertible preferred stock	360	368	374
Loan to ESOP	(166)	(217)	(267)
Common shareholders' investment			
Common stock	72	72	71
Additional paid-in capital	89	73	58
Retained earnings	2882	2592	2357
Total common shareholders' investment	3043	2737	2486
Total liabilities and common shareholders' investment	$11,697	$10,778	$10,337

Source: Dayton Hudson Annual Report 1994.

EXHIBIT D
....
**Dayton Hudson Financial
and Operating Data
(Numbers in Millions Except Share Data)**

	1/95	1/94	1/93
Revenues	$21,311	$19,233	$17,927
Cost of sales, buying	15,636	14,164	13,129
Selling, publicity and administration	3,631	3,175	2,978
Depreciation	531	498	459
Interest expense, net	426	446	437
Earnings from continuing operations, net of tax	714	607	611
Income taxes	280	232	228
Net earnings	434	375	383
Earnings per share	$5.52	$4.77	$4.82

Source: Dayton Hudson Annual Report 1994.

DSD is introducing lower-priced product lines to attract a wider consumer base, it might take consumers away from Target. The department stores also use sales, with significant advertising, to attract the budget-conscious shopper.

DHC is considering the introduction of a single consolidated credit card. Currently, the corporation has three cards. The first one can be used in all the DSD stores as well as Target. A second card is a Mervyn's card and can be used only at Mervyn's. The third card is a Target signature card that is limited to use at Target stores.

DHC says that it is committed to the creation of value for its shareholders, despite a disappointing performance during the past 10 years. The stock price has remained flat for the last 5 years, and earnings are "up just 5 percent in 4 years despite 45 percent growth in sales." High and low stock prices for the last 5 years are listed below.

	1991	1992	1993	1994	1995
Stock price high	80.25	79.25	85.00	86.88	81.00
Stock price low	53.73	58.00	62.63	64.88	63.00

Source: Hoover's *Handbook,* 1996.

Ulrich had his hands full. Stockholders and analysts were truly frustrated with the downward cycle of profits as well as the stock price in light of the recent bull market. The image of the firm was tarnished. Top executives were leaving suddenly. Mervyn's was a burden. Hungry competitors were circling the firm. Divisions were cannibalizing each other. Would things ever get better?

Bibliography

Bass, S. J., Bates, A. D., and Davidson, W. R. "The Retail Life Cycle," *Harvard Business Review,* Nov.–Dec. 1976, p. 75.

Chandler, S. "An Endangered Species Makes a Comeback," *Business Week,* November 27, 1995, p. 96.

Chandler, S. "Look Who's Sweating Now," *Business Week,* October 16, 1995, pp. 96–98.

Chandler, S. "Speed Is Life at Dayton Hudson," *Business Week,* March 27, 1995, pp. 84–85.

Chandler, S. "Under the Gun at Dayton Hudson," *Business Week,* May 20, 1996, pp. 69–70.

Chandler, S. "Why Clothiers Are Feeling Pinched," *Business Week,* September 18, 1995, p. 47.

"Corporate Scoreboard," *Business Week,* March 4, 1996, pp. 99–122.

Dayton Hudson Corporation. Annual Reports, 1994, 1993, Minneapolis, MN.

Dayton Hudson Corporation. *Dayton Hudson: 1994 at a Glance,* 1994, Minneapolis, MN.

Dayton Hudson Corporation. *History,* 1994, Minneapolis, MN.

Dayton Hudson Corporation. *Investor's Factbook,* 1994, Minneapolis, MN.

"Dayton Hudson Earnings Fall," *Grand Forks Herald,* May 17, 1995, p. D7.

"Dayton Hudson Executive Resigns," *Grand Forks Herald,* March 26, 1996, p. D7.

"Dayton Hudson Plans No Changes Despite Profit Dip," *Grand Forks Herald,* March 15, 1996, p. D5.

"Dayton Is Against Sweatshops," *Grand Forks Herald,* December 6, 1995, p. D7.

Department Store Division of Dayton Hudson Corporation. *Three Great Stores, One Great Company,* 1991, Minneapolis, MN.

Fearnley-Whittingstall, S. "Outlook for Field's Northbrook Opening," *Womens Wear Daily,* October 13, 1993, p. 20.

Hoover, G., Campbell, A., and Spain, P. J. "Dayton Hudson Corporation," *Hoover's Handbook of American Business.* Austin, TX: Reference Press, 1995, 1994, 1993.

Keeton, L. E., and Patterson, G. A. "Dayton's First-Period Profit Sank 72%: Net Fell at Penney but Rose at Wal-Mart," *Wall Street Journal,* May 17, 1995, p. A8.

"National Retailers Investigated in Forced Labor Case," *Grand Forks Herald,* August 10, 1995, p. A3.

Patterson, G. A. "Mervyns Effort to Revamp Results in Disappointment," *Wall Street Journal,* March 29, 1994, p. B4.

Spain, P. J., and Talbot, J. R. "Dayton Hudson Corporation," *Hoover's Handbook of American Business.* Austin, TX: Reference Press, 1996.

Standard & Poor's. *Standard & Poor's Industry Surveys.* New York, 1993, 1994.

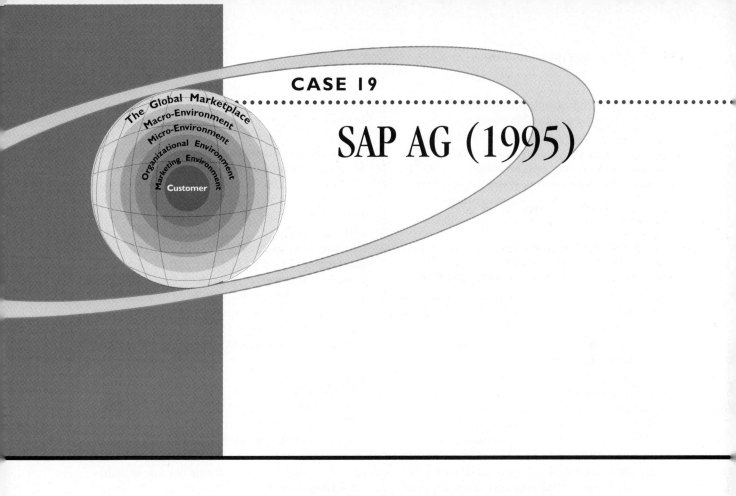

SAP AG (1995)

*This case was prepared by Julian W. Vincze, Professor of Marketing,
Crummer Graduate School of Business, Rollins College.*

HONEYMOON OVER?

SAP AG, located in Walldorf, Germany, has become recognized as the world's leader for client-server business applications software. With fiscal year 1994 revenues exceeding US$1 billion, a 66 percent increase over 1993, SAP became the first business applications software manufacturer in history to reach the billion dollar revenue level.[1] SAP's phenomenal growth was attributed to the demand for its R/3 System, designed for client-server networks of personal computers (PCs), which was an adaptation of its prior successful R/2 System, designed for mainframe computers. SAP software had over the last few years enjoyed extraordinary success as major companies throughout the globe became customers. However, recently, SAP had been

This case is intended to be used as a basis for class discussion rather than as an illustration of either effective or ineffective handling of the situation. This case was prepared by Julian W. Vincze, Crummer Graduate School of Business, Rollins College. Copyright © 2000 Julian W. Vincze.

receiving criticism from users in both the United Kingdom and Germany over the large costs of implementation and chronic project overruns. Dennis Keeling, a well-known accounting software analyst, said: "SAP never realized R/3 would take off so fast and was not aware of some of the complexities of implementing it. The honeymoon is over."[2]

ESTABLISHING SAP AG

SAP was formed in 1972, when four young employees of IBM in Germany, Dieter Hopp, Hasso Plattner, Hans Werner Hector, and Klaus Tschira, quit because funding for their proposal was turned down. They began by working long hours on borrowed computers and grew a customer at a time. "We had a vision, and we stuck to it," said Hasso Plattner, vice chairman and technology chief of SAP (and member of the board of directors).[3] Although SAP is headquartered in a small town near Heidelberg, the corporate culture is not traditional. Instead, it typifies the entrepreneurial spirit of its founders; for example, employees wear sandals and can choose their own hours. Mr. Plattner recalls that early in his career he interviewed at Siemens, the huge electronics company, before taking a lesser job with IBM's German subsidiary. He said: "I knew right during the interview that I could never work for Siemens. It was like the post office."[4]

MARKET SHARE GROWTH

When Mr. Plattner and the others began SAP, their idea was to offer standardized computer programs for accounting, finance, and other business applications. Their first product, the R/2 System, was directed at mainframe computer users and met with respectable success. SAP's growth over the period 1972–1991 was an exercise in determination and ingenuity. With the introduction of its R/3 System in 1991, however, SAP made the jump from mainframes to PCs. By 1995, its R/3 package accounted for more than half of total sales. SAP was a closely held organization, which had at least 81 percent of ordinary share capital (and 74 percent of voting rights) in the hands of SAP directors or members of their families (who were involved in a joint voting rights pool).[5] In response to rapid growth, SAP had continually added new employees worldwide to support the demands of its expanding multinational enterprise. By year end 1994, SAP had 28 international subsidiaries, the largest of which was its U.S. subsidiary, employed a total of 5044 individuals, and serviced more than 4300 client companies located in 41 countries who used SAP software to manage complex financial, manufacturing, sales, and human resources requirements. "The 1994 figures are impressive proof that we have gained the leading position in the worldwide market for standard applications software," said Dieter Hopp, chairman of the executive board. "The high level of investment in our systems is paying off, both for our customers and for the company."[6]

FINANCIAL RESULTS

1994 was an outstanding year for SAP in every respect. The total revenue figure of US$1.1 billion consisted of the following categories: product sales revenues of $805 million, consulting and training revenues of $305 million, and other revenues of $20 million. For the first time, SAP's domestic revenues were less than from outside Germany as follows: German revenues up 19 percent to $412 million, while outside revenues, which represent 64 percent of total revenues, were up 48 percent. Klaus P. Besier, chief executive officer and president of SAP America, said: "It was an incredible year for SAP. . . . R/3 was one of the first client-server applications suites [systems] to come to market, and the subsequent growth has exceeded even our ambitious expectations."[7] SAP's financial success was evident in that total revenue had doubled every 2 years or so, while profits had been increasing at double-digit rates for a number of years—up a remarkable 92 percent in 1994.[8] (For more detailed results, the reader should refer to Exhibits A and B.)

PRODUCT POLICY

After approximately 20 years of first development and then fine-tuning, SAP's R/2 System for mainframe computer users in accounting, finance, sales, and other business applications became an industry standard and the basis of SAP's growth into a global competitor. However, SAP recognized the trend toward using PCs in business networks and in the early 1990s allocated sufficient resources to convert the R/2 System for mainframe computers into the R/3 System for client-server business applications. The R/3 System was compatible with most popular hardware, software, and database platforms and hit the market at the height of the downsizing frenzy. "R/3 was written from the bottom up more than 3 years ago and cost us US$200 million," said Trevor Salomon, SAP's business development manager. "It is not just a mainframe port."[9] R/3's three-tier architecture puts the end-user software on the client PC, the application software on one server, and the associated database on a separate server. "Unlike other client-server products, we have a dedicated application server so you can increase the number of applications and modules but you still only need the one database," said Mr. Salomon.[10]

Release 2.2 Announced

In mid-1994, SAP announced a significant new release of the R/3 System.[11] Release 2.2 incorporated functionality that had not been slated for delivery

EXHIBIT A

Software Success Story

SAP Leads the Market...
Leading vendors of client/server applications based on 1994 world-wide sales, in millions of dollars

	1993	1994
SAP	$180	$603
Lotus	190	270
Oracle	118	149
Microsoft	69	120
PeopleSoft	38	105
Computer Associates	71	90

Benefiting from Strong Growth...
Sales, in billions of dollars

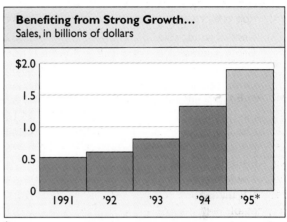

*Projection

From a Variety of Regions...
Breakdown of 1994 sales

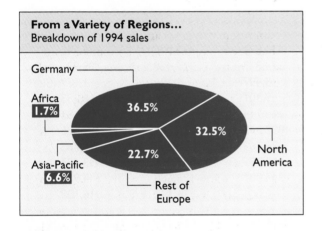

Especially North America
Sales, in millions of dollars

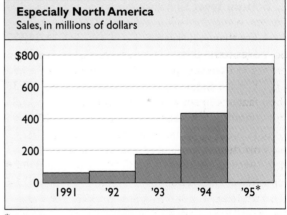

*Projection

Note: Sales figures converted from German marks at current exchange rate.
Sources: SAP, International Data Corp., Paribas Capital Markets.

until 1995. Release 2.2 completed the line of R/3 client-server software by including new business processes and industry-specific capabilities that addressed information management requirements of manufacturing logistics, sales and distribution, and finance departments. In addition, the manufacturing applications were enhanced to provide extended functionality for both repetitive and discrete manufacturers. Release 2.2 also had logistics application enhancements for the packaged-goods industry, corporate resource planning, and integrated supply-chain management. Additionally, Release 2.2 included a powerful component for in-

tegrated credit management and significantly extended electronic data information functionality.

For example, human resources (HR) applications could now be linked to optical archiving, which was necessary for payroll accounting functions within U.S. companies. Another enhancement of R/3 Release 2.2 was a new configuration management component within the logistics application that provided a turn-key solution for companies whose product lines included a wide range of product variations such as automobile parts manufacturers. The configuration management function enabled manufacturers to optimize

EXHIBIT B
. . . .

Income Statement (in 000s DM)	1994	1993	1992	1991
Net sales revenue	1,831,143	1,101,734	831,178	707,103
Cost of goods sold	420,820	299,089	205,683	173,847
Gross income	1,321,661	740,860	561,725	486,112
Depreciation and amortization	88,662	61,785	63,770	47,144
Other operating expenses	1,413,568	917,520	719,975	556,678
Operating income	417,575	184,214	111,203	150,425
Interest income	25,161	31,618	29,962	9,989
Other misc. income	16,087	32,838	25,849	14,481
Reserves (increase/decrease)	−260	−227	−2,080	0
Interest expense	1,749	1,272	1,178	633
Pretax income	457,334	247,625	167,916	174,262
Income taxes	176,160	101,311	40,675	50,983
Minority interests	920	546	899	421
Net income	280,254	145,768	126,342	122,858

Balance Sheet Summary	1994	1993	1992	1991
Cash and equivalents	347,225	433,873	433,006	145,745
Net receivables	623,181	374,717	223,420	199,931
Inventories	4,936	5,497	2,126	1,177
Prepaid expenses	13,385	9,301	13,358	8,285
Other current assets	17,831	14,144	14,934	6,487
Total current assets	1,006,558	837,532	686,844	361,625
Miscellaneous investments	162,610	28,763	20,368	12,763
Property, plant, and equipment	827,835	663,395	549,456	429,657
Accumulated depreciation	313,352	244,007	194,660	144,918
Other misc. assets	51,072	40,004	36,142	16,188

Total Assets	1,749,729	1,306,185	1,080,079	667,221
Accounts payable	115,916	53,553	43,358	33,501
Current notes payable	47,189	25,442	17,341	13,598
Income taxes payable	41,849	33,642	26,206	16,252
Other current liabilities	41,447	28,426	18,765	13,003
Total current liabilities	246,401	141,063	105,670	76,354
Long-term debt	21,946	1,000	1,000	1,000
Provisional risks/charges	222,659	135,743	63,607	74,603
Deferred taxes and other liabilities	22,339	19,362	12,349	7,366
Total liabilities	513,345	297,168	182,626	159,323
Reserves and minority interests	2,588	1,199	622	543
Common stock	506,153	100,000	100,000	85,000
Capital surplus	137,837	528,976	528,976	243,976
Retained earnings	589,806	378,842	267,855	178,379
Common shareholders equity	1,233,796	1,007,818	896,831	507,355

Total liability & equity	1,749,729	1,306,185	1,080,079	667,221

their entire business process chain—from sales to production—and to monitor the process through a powerful order-control function. It also allowed manufacturers to react flexibly to customer orders, to reduce lead times between order and delivery, and to constantly improve product quality. For manufacturers who produced hundreds or thousands of standardized products per day, a new repetitive manufacturing component allowed users to create plans based on quantities and periods. Called the *MRP II planning run procedure,* it was a user-friendly planning table that plotted production quantities per period, allocated production lines, and carried out interactive resource leveling so that users had more flexibility in scheduling than was available traditionally with order/batch manufacturing methods. And MRP II had extensive simulation options that allowed plans to be easily altered as conditions changed. It also had a cross-application function for managing bill-of-material "explosion" numbers, which make it possible to track the paths of individual parts (often a federal government supplier requirement).

Packaged-goods industry users of Release 2.2 would be able to increase the efficiency of their sales activities through flexible customer hierarchies for graded rebate agreements and enhanced pricing functions for promotions and sales campaigns, while the credit management component allowed fully dynamic credit control from order acceptance to invoicing. The new activity-based costing module supported business reengineering processes and had additional functions for electronic banking based on international standards and enhanced U.S. tax processing. But perhaps the most significant aspect of R/3 Release 2.2 was that it would be available in the Microsoft Windows 3.1 help system WinHelp. This feature would allow users on-line access to over 100 manuals contained in the R/3 System documentation library. Access was simplified by pull-down menus and key word retrieval functions. This on-line documentation would give users an intelligent applications link for moving directly from any business process to the appropriate chapter in the R/3 System documentation for assistance.

CHANGED STRATEGY

During SAP's earlier growth periods it had used a marketing strategy that had relied heavily on tech-

nically up-to-date product features, explained appropriately to potential customers by its direct sales teams and backed up by technical experts and brochures with detailed and thorough explanations of product features, all priced at the high end of competitiveness. This could be described as a direct sales approach, which is standard in the industry. SAP's growth outside Germany followed a similar direct sales approach but adapted to a network of international subsidiaries. For example, the SAP American subsidiary was headquartered in Philadelphia, had a Technology Development Center in Foster City, California, a number of regional headquarters such as the one in Westchester, Illinois (Midwestern region), and within each region sales offices such as the Minneapolis office that opened March 1 of 1995. SAP's Minneapolis office opened with 25 employees, including consultants and support staff, but had plans for expansion to 50 employees by year's end. The office featured a classroom for hands-on training and two state-of-the-art demonstration rooms with multimedia capabilities. Demonstrations included a range of hardware platforms loaded with SAP's software to educate customers and sales partners on core business needs and processes and how SAP products affected those processes. "The new office offers Minneapolis-based SAP customers greater local service and support," said Scott Martin, district director. "We are aggressively responding to the needs of our customers in the Midwestern region by offering, in Minneapolis, resources that will complement those available through our regional headquarters."[12]

However, in 1994 SAP announced a change in its sales strategy. The new sales strategy was to concentrate on larger customers. SAP's own sales teams in its German language region (and later worldwide) would continue to service existing clients and group customers, but in the future SAP would concentrate its sales efforts on companies with between DM200 million and DM250 million in sales revenue. This meant that small and medium-sized companies would be serviced indirectly and in cooperation with sales partners. SAP would designate and certify sales partners who would cease selling their own software (or software from SAP's competitors) in order to concentrate on selling and providing services for SAP's R/3 System.[13] Customers with between DM50 million and DM200 million in sales and a workforce of between 100 and 1500 would be serviced by certified sales partners who had already been working closely with SAP and who would receive a 40 percent margin on sales made to ultimate customers. SAP believed that customer organizations would benefit because they would have a one-stop shop for software solutions and support from a SAP sales partner experienced in working with small and medium-sized firms. Mr. Hopp observed that SAP would only consider as partners those companies which could show they had already made a name for themselves with standard solutions, that had a satisfied customer base, that had their own sales and service structure, that had sufficient competent staff, and of special importance, that had a sound financial base. SAP would provide its sales partners with support, marketing, sales activities, free initial employee training, and a free R/3 System. And although SAP was not planning on capital linkups with its sales partners, it was reported to be investing DM26 million in this program in order to attract partners who were capable of reaching previously unserviced customer areas both geographically and in terms of business activities.[14]

DIFFICULTIES EXPERIENCED

Although SAP had enjoyed recent successes as major companies throughout the globe signed up for its R/3 System, it also had been criticized by U.K. and German customers about the high costs of implementation and about chronic project overruns. SAP's response was to fight back, especially against accusations that the R/3 System was not capable of performing the tasks desired by users who wanted to unify all their disparate systems and downsize off the mainframe. SAP sued a German magazine for libel and issued a written denial of allegations that it received payoffs from computer hardware manufacturers when SAP recommended such hardware products to customers. However, some industry observers believed the real issue may have been rampant overenthusiasm about SAP's R/3 System. Chris Cadman, of Input, a U.K. market research company, said: "Everyone was carried away with euphoria."[15]

Because R/3 had a three-tier architecture (noted above) whereby end-user software was on the client PC and the application software on one server and the associated database on a separate server, this could prove to be a disadvantage to some users. Accounting software analyst Dennis

Keeling said: "It's not easy distributing the database, because R/3 has a centralized configuration, like a mainframe, even though it runs on Unix."[16] This feature made R/3 less scalable than many users expected and made it less suitable for deploying across multiple small departmental units of an organization. However, Chris Knight, European Information Technology manager at pharmaceutical company Syntex and chairman of the R/3 users' technical group (organized by SAP), noted that "few packages of this complexity could run well on a distributed database."[17] However, other industry observers believed that the major concern about the R/3 System was flexibility—or lack of it—and its impact on implementing the software. David Lyons, chairman of the SAP users' group and R/3 project manager at Unilever, said: "You have to accept that you must map the organization to the software, not vice versa."[18] Mr. Lyons believed that such adjustments were worth it, that the kind of business changes required were trivial, and that the real implementation issue was one of managing the business, not the system. Because R/3's database table structures were very sophisticated, implementors had to be certain to understand them; otherwise, mistakes were easily made. In addition, R/3, like many software products, worked best in organizations with a stable structure, something that in the current business environment of re-engineering and downsizing was not always possible.

Users also might encounter change-related problems when software was upgraded. Mr. Knight said: "That's our biggest problem. For example, moving from R/3 Release 2.1 [to 2.2] required a new version of Oracle. It took us 5 days to export, reorganize, and reimport the tables, which is unacceptable, even though we got more functionality."[19] With SAP due to launch R/3 Release 3.0 in the fall of 1995, current users realistically may be concerned with change-related costs and problems. Current R/3 users also were concerned that the goal of having a unified all-encompassing software application covering all activities of the firm was not easily achieved. Mr. Keeling noted: "They are running into problems because of the complexity of integrating the modules, which is not straightforward, and needs tremendous detailed analysis. This is often underestimated when the software is purchased."[20] However, perhaps it is the very complexity of implementing R/3 that has been one of the reasons for its popularity. R/3's complexity may have encouraged the sales partners and other consultants to push R/3 to corporate users in order to collect ongoing consulting fees.

However, regardless of the implementing complexities, SAP had come under attack from users for failing to provide them with adequate technical and implementation support. The question facing SAP was whether customers who had been euphoric over R/3 would now become disillusioned? And what would disillusioned customers do? SAP's competitors such as Dun & Bradstreet and Oracle Financials probably were eager to help out any disillusioned SAP customers, especially those who wanted to start with a small system and later build it into a much larger one.

Questions

1. What were the key success factors in SAP's growth strategy for the period 1971 through 1990?

2. What if anything changed in the key success factors when SAP introduced the first version of R/3 in 1991?

3. When SAP announced a change in strategy to target larger customers for its own sales teams and to certify what it called sales partners, who would then service small and medium-sized customers? How did this alter SAP's marketing mix? Was this a change in sales strategy or a change in marketing strategy?

4. What is the role of SAP's product policy component in its 1995 marketing strategy? Will this change in the foreseeable future?

5. Is the honeymoon over for SAP?

6. What marketing strategy or tactical actions would you recommend that SAP take in 1995 and in subsequent years?

Endnotes

1. "SAP Surpasses Billion Dollar Revenue Mark; Revenues up 66%, Net Income Jumps 92%," *Business Wire,* February 1, 1995.
2. Julia Vowler, "Germany: SAP's Honeymoon Comes to an End—SAP Software," *Computer Weekly,* April 6, 1995.
3. Greg Steinmetz, "German Firm Grows, Silicon-Valley Style," *Wall Street Journal,* April 11, 1995.
4. *Ibid.*
5. "Germany: SAP Announces 74 percent of Voting Rights Are Held in Pool," *Boersen Zeitung,* April 6, 1995.
6. "SAP Surpasses Billion Dollar Revenue Mark; 1994 Revenues Up 66 percent, Net Income Jumps 92 percent," *Business Wire,* February 1, 1995.
7. *Ibid.*
8. "Germany: SAP Likely to Be Dominant on Software Market in Future," *Top-Business,* March 1, 1995.
9. "Germany: SAP's Honeymoon Comes to an End—SAP Software," *Computer Weekly,* April 6, 1995.
10. *Ibid.*
11. "SAP Announces Significant New Release of Its Industry-Leading Client/Server Applications; Version 2.2 Incorporates Functionality Slated for 1995 but Available Today," *Business Wire,* August 29, 1994.
12. "SAP Open Minneapolis Office," *Business Wire,* March 1, 1995.
13. "Germany: SAP Almost Triples Profit in First Nine Months 1994," *Handelsblatt,* October 21, 1994.
14. "Germany: SAP Targets Small and Medium-Sized Firms in Bid for Further Growth," *Handelsblatt,* February 14, 1994.
15. "Germany: SAP's Honeymoon Comes to an End—SAP Software," *Computer Weekly,* April 6, 1995.
16. *Ibid.*
17. *Ibid.*
18. *Ibid.*
19. *Ibid.*
20. *Ibid.*

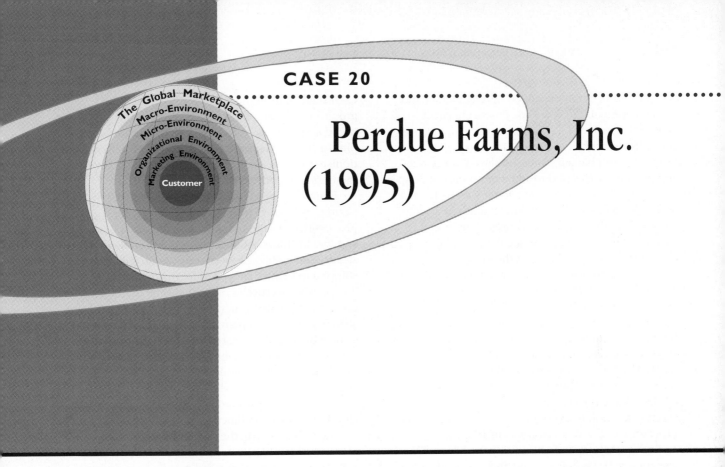

CASE 20

Perdue Farms, Inc. (1995)

This case was prepared by George C. Rubenson and Frank M. Shipper of the Franklin P. Perdue School of Business at Salisbury State University and Jean M. Hanebury of the College of Business Administration at Texas A&M University, Corpus Christi.

BACKGROUND/COMPANY HISTORY

I have a theory that you can tell the difference between those who have inherited a fortune and those who have made a fortune. Those who have made their own fortune forget not where they came from and are less likely to lose touch with the common man [Bill Sterling, "Just Browsin" column, *Eastern Shore News*, March 2, 1988].

Acknowledgments: The authors are indebted to Frank Perdue, Jim Perdue, and the numerous associates at Perdue Farms, Inc., who generously shared their time and information about the company. In addition, the authors would like to thank the anonymous librarians who routinely review area newspapers and file articles about the poultry industry—the most important industry on the DelMarVa Peninsula. Without their assistance, this case would not have been possible. Reprinted by permission of the authors.

In 1917, Arthur W. Perdue, a Railway Express agent and descendant of a French Huguenot family named Perdeaux, bought 50 leghorn chickens for $5 and began selling table eggs near the small town of Salisbury, Maryland. A region immortalized in James Michener's *Chesapeake,* it is alternately known as "the Eastern Shore" or the "DelMarVa Peninsula" and includes parts of *De*laware, *Mary*land and *Virgin*ia.

Initially, the business amounted to little more than a farm wife's chore for "pin money," raising a few "biddies" in a cardboard box behind the wood stove in the kitchen until they were old enough to fend for themselves in the barnyard. In 1920, however, when Railway Express asked "Mr. Arthur" to move to a station away from the Eastern Shore, at age 36 he quit his job as Salisbury's Railway Express agent and entered the egg business full time. His only child, Franklin Parsons Perdue, was born that same year.

241

"Mr. Arthur" soon expanded his egg market and began shipments to New York. Practicing small economies such as mixing his own chicken feed and using leather from his old shoes to make hinges for his chicken coops, he stayed out of debt and prospered. He tried to add a new chicken coop every year. By the time young Frank was 10, he had 50 chickens or so of his own to look after, earning money from their eggs. He worked along with his parents, not always enthusiastically, to feed the chickens, clean the coops, dig the cesspools, and gather and grade eggs. A shy, introverted country boy, he went for 5 years to a one-room school, eventually graduated from Wicomico High School, and attended the State Teachers College in Salisbury for 2 years before returning to the farm in 1939 to work full time with his father.

By 1940, it was obvious to father and son that the future lay in selling chickens, not eggs. But the Perdues made the shift to selling broilers only after careful attention to every detail—a standard Perdue procedure in the years to come. In 1944, "Mr. Arthur" made his son Frank a full partner in what was then A. W. Perdue and Son, Inc., a firm already known for quality products and fair dealing in a toughly competitive business. In 1950, Frank took over leadership of Perdue Farms, a company with 40 employees. By 1952, revenues were $6 million from the sale of 2.6 million broilers.

By 1967, annual sales had increased to about $35 million but it was becoming increasingly clear that additional profits lay in processing chickens. Frank recalled in an interview for *Business Week* (September 15, 1972) ". . . processors were paying us 10 cents a live pound for what cost us 14 cents to produce. Suddenly, processors were making as much as 7 cents a pound."

A cautious, conservative planner, Arthur Perdue had not been eager for expansion, and Frank Perdue himself was reluctant to enter poultry processing. But economic forces dictated the move, and in 1968, Perdue Farms became a vertically integrated operation, hatching eggs, delivering the chicks to contract growers, buying grain, supplying the feed and litter, and finally, processing the broilers and shipping them to market.

The company bought its first plant in 1968, a Swift and Company operation in Salisbury, renovated it, and equipped it with machines capable of processing 14,000 broilers per hour. Computers were soon employed to devise feeding formulas for each stage of growth so that birds reached their growth potential sooner. Geneticists were hired to breed larger-breasted chickens, veterinarians were put on staff to keep the flocks healthy, and nutritionists handled the feed formulations to achieve the best feed conversion.

From the beginning, Frank Perdue refused to permit his broilers to be frozen for shipping, a process that resulted in unappetizing black bones and loss of flavor and moistness when cooked. Instead, Perdue chickens were (and some still are) shipped to market packed in ice, justifying the company's advertisements at that time that it sold only "fresh, young broilers." However, this policy also limited the company's market to those locations which could be serviced overnight from the Eastern Shore of Maryland. Thus Perdue chose for its primary markets the densely populated towns and cities of the East Coast, particularly New York City, which consumes more Perdue chickens than all other brands combined.

During the 1970s, the firm entered the Baltimore, Philadelphia, Boston, and Providence markets. Facilities were expanded rapidly to include a new broiler processing plant and protein conversion plant in Accomac, Virginia, a processing plant in Lewiston, North Carolina, a hatchery in Murfreesboro, North Carolina, and several Swift and Company facilities including a processing plant in Georgetown, Delaware, a feedmill in Bridgeville, Delaware, and a feedmill in Elkin, North Carolina.

In 1977, "Mr. Arthur" died at the age of 91, leaving behind a company with annual sales of nearly $200 million, an average annual growth rate of 17% compared to an industry average of 1% a year, the potential for processing 78,000 broilers per hour, and annual production of nearly 350 million pounds of poultry per year. Frank Perdue, who says without a hint of self-deprecation that "I am a B-minus student. I know how smart I am. I know a B-minus is not as good as an A," said of this father simply, "I learned everything from him."

Stew Leonard, owner of a huge supermarket in Norwalk, Connecticut, and one of Perdue's top customers, describes Frank Perdue as "What you see is what you get. If you ask him a question, you will get an answer." Perdue disapproves of the presence of a union between himself and his associates and adds: "The absence of unions makes for a better relationship with our associates. If we treat our associates right, I don't think we will have a union." On conglomerates, he states: "Diversification is the most dangerous word in the English language." His business philosophy is: "I'm interested in being the best rather than the biggest. Expansion is OK if it has a positive effect on product quality. I'll do nothing that detracts from product quality."

Frank Perdue is known for having a temper. He is as hard on himself, however, as he is on others, readily admitting his shortcomings and even his mistakes. For example, in the 1970s he apparently briefly discussed using the influence of some unsavory characters to help alleviate union pressure. When an investigative report in the late 1980s asked him about this instance, he admitted that it was a mistake, saying "... it was probably the dumbest thing I ever did."

In 1981, Frank Perdue was in Massachusetts for his induction into the Babson College Academy of Distinguished Entrepreneurs, an award established in 1978 to recognize the spirit of free enterprise and business leadership. Babson College President Ralph Z. Sorenson inducted Perdue into the academy, which, at that time, numbered 18 men and women from four continents. Perdue had the following to say to the college students:

> There are none, nor will there ever be, easy steps for the entrepreneur. Nothing, absolutely nothing, replaces the willingness to work earnestly, intelligently toward a goal. You have to be willing to pay the price. You have to have an insatiable appetite for detail, have to be willing to accept constructive criticism, to ask questions, to be fiscally responsible, to surround yourself with good people and most of all, to listen.

The early 1980s proved to be a period of further growth as Perdue diversified and broadened its market. New marketing areas included Washington, D.C., Richmond, Virginia, and Norfolk, Virginia. Additional facilities were opened in Cofield, Kenly, Halifax, Robbins, and Robersonville, North Carolina. The firm broadened its line to include value-added products such as Oven Stuffer roasters and Perdue Done It!, a new brand of fresh, prepared chicken products featuring cooked chicken breast nuggets, cutlets, and tenders. James A. (Jim) Perdue, Frank's only son, joined the company as a management trainee in 1983.

The latter 1980s also tested the mettle of the firm, however. Following a period of considerable

expansion and concentric diversification, a consulting firm was brought in to recommend ways to cope with the new complexity. Believing that the span of control was too broad, the consulting firm recommended that strategic business units, responsible for their own operations, be formed. In other words, the firm should decentralize.

Soon after, the chicken market leveled off and eventually began to decline. At one point the firm was losing as much as $1 million a week, and in 1988 Perdue Farms experienced its first year in the red. Unfortunately, the decentralization had created duplication of duties and enormous administrative costs. MIS costs, for example, had tripled. The firm's rapid plunge into turkeys and other food processing, where it had little experience, contributed to the losses. Waste and inefficiency had permeated the company. Characteristically, Frank Perdue took the firm back to basics, concentrating on efficiency of operations, improving communications throughout the company, and paying close attention to detail.

On June 2, 1989, Frank celebrated 50 years with Perdue Farms, Inc. At a morning reception in downtown Salisbury, the governor of Maryland proclaimed it "Frank Perdue Day." The governors of Delaware and Virginia did the same.

The 1990s have been dominated by market expansion to North Carolina, Atlanta, Georgia, Pittsburgh, Pennsylvania, Cleveland, Ohio, Chicago, Illinois, and Florida. New product lines have included fresh ground chicken, fresh ground turkey, sweet Italian turkey sausage, turkey breakfast sausage, fun-shaped chicken breast nuggets in star and drumstick shapes, and BBQ and oven-roasted chicken parts in the Perdue Done It! line. A new Fit 'n Easy label was introduced as part of a nutrition campaign using skinless, boneless chicken and turkey products. By 1994, revenues had increased to about $1.5 billion, Frank Perdue was chairman of the executive committee and Jim Perdue was chairman of the board.

In January 1995, Perdue Farms became the third largest producer in the broiler industry when it bought Showell Farms, Inc., of Showell, Maryland, the twelfth largest producer in the United States with about 8000 employees and revenues of approximately $550,000.

Sitting in the small, unpretentious office that had been his dad's for 40 years, Jim looked out the window at the house where he had grown up, the broiler houses Frank built in the 1940s, his grandfather's homestead across the road where Frank was born, and a modern hatchery. "Dad would come home for dinner and then come back here and work into the early hours of the morning. There's a fold-out cot behind that credenza. He got by on 3 or 4 hours of sleep a night."

MISSION STATEMENT AND STATEMENT OF VALUES

From the beginning, "Mr. Arthur's" motto had been to ". . . create a quality product, be aware of your customers, deal fairly with people, and work hard, work hard, work hard." In a speech in September 1991 to the firm's lenders, accountants, and Perdue associates, Frank reiterated these values, saying

> If you were to ask me what was the biggest factor in whatever success we have enjoyed, I would answer that it was not technology, or economic resources, or organizational structure. It . . . has been our conscious decision that, in order to be successful, we must have a sound set of beliefs on which we premise all our policies and actions. . . . Central to these beliefs is our emphasis on quality. . . . Quality is no accident. It is the one absolutely necessary ingredient of all the most successful companies in the world.

The centrality of quality to the firm is featured in its mission statement and its statement of values. To ensure that all associates know what the company's mission, quality policy, values, and annual goals are, managers receive a fold-up, wallet-sized card with them imprinted on it (see Exhibit A).

SOCIAL RESPONSIBILITY

To realize its corporate statement of values, Perdue Farms works hard to be a good corporate citizen. Two areas in which this is especially clear are its code of ethics and its efforts to minimize the environmental damage it causes.

Code of Ethics

Perdue Farms has taken the somewhat unusual step of setting forth explicitly the ethical standards it expects all associates to follow. Specifically, the Code of Ethics calls on associates to conduct every aspect of business in the full spirit of honest and lawful behavior. Further, all salaried associates and certain hourly associates are required to sign a statement acknowledging that they understand the code and are prepared to comply with it. Associates are expected to report to their supervisor dishonest or illegal activities as well as possible violations of the code. If the supervisor does not provide a satisfactory response, the employee is expected to contact either the vice president for human resources or the vice president of their division. The code notes that any Perdue manager who initiates or encourages reprisal against any person who reports a violation commits a serious violation of the code.

Minimizing Environmental Damage

Historically, chicken processing has been the focus of special-interest groups whose interests range from animal rights to repetitive-motion disorders to environmental causes. Perdue Farms has accepted the challenge of striving to maintain an environmentally friendly workplace as a goal that requires the commitment of all its associates, from Frank Perdue down. Frank Perdue states it best: "We know that we must be good neighbors environmentally. We have an obligation not to pollute, to police ourselves, and to be better than EPA requires us to be."

For example, over the years, the industry had explored many alternative ways of disposing of dead birds. Perdue research provided the solution—small composters on each farm. Using this approach, dead birds are reduced to an end product that resembles soil in a matter of a few days. This has become a major environmental activity. Another environmental challenge is the disposal of hatchery wastes. Historically, manure and unhatched eggs that make up these wastes were shipped to a landfill. Perdue produces about 10 tons of this waste per day. However, Perdue has reduced the waste by 50% by selling the liquid fraction to a pet food processor who cooks it for protein. The other 50% is recycled through a rendering process. In 1990, Perdue spent $4.2 million to construct a state-of-the-art waste water treatment facility at its Accomac, Virginia, plant. This facility uses forced hot air heated to 120°F to cause

EXHIBIT A
....
Perdue: Fiscal Year 1994

Mission Statement

Our mission is to provide the highest-quality poultry and poultry-related products to retail and food service customers.

We want to be the recognized industry leader in quality and service, providing more than expected for our customers, associates, and owners.

We will accomplish this by maintaining a tradition of pride in our products, growth through innovation, integrity in the management of our business, and commitment to Team Management and the Quality Improvement Process.

Quality Policy

We shall produce products and provide services at all times which meet or exceed the expectations of our customers.

We shall not be content to be of equal quality to our competitors.

Our commitment is to be increasingly superior.

Contribution to quality is a responsibility shared by everyone in the Perdue organization.

Statement of Values

Our success as a company, and as individuals working at Perdue, depend upon:

- Meeting customer needs with the best-quality, innovative food and food-related products and services.
- Associates being team members in the business and having opportunities to influence, make contributions, and reach their full potential.
- Working together as business partners by implementing the principles of the QIP so that mutual respect, trust, and a commitment to being the best are shared among associates, customers, producers, and suppliers.
- Achieving the long-term goals of the company and providing economic stability and a rewarding future for all associates through well-planned, market-driven growth.

- Being the best in our industry in profitability as a low-cost producer, realizing that our customers won't pay for our inefficiencies.
- Staying ahead of the competition by investing our profits to provide a safe work environment; to pay competitive wages; to maintain up-to-date facilities, equipment, and processes; and to create challenging opportunities for associates.
- Serving the communities in which we do business with resources, time, and the creative energies of our associates.

FY 1994 Company Goals

1. PEOPLE—Provide a safe, secure, and productive work environment.
   - Reduce OSHA recordable incidents by 12%
   - Reduce per capita workers' compensation by 28%
   - Implement an associates satisfaction survey process
   - Provide an annual performance evaluation for all associates.

2. PRODUCTS—Provide the highest-quality products and services at competitive costs.
   - Develop an improved measurement of consumer satisfaction
   - Improve the "Customer Service Satisfaction Index"
   - Improve our quality spread over competition
   - Consistently achieve a plant weighted ranking score for product quality of 212 points
   - Increase sales from new products

3. PROFITABILITY—Lead the industry in profitability.
   - Achieve a 10% ROAE
   - Broiler Agrimetrics Index to be equal to the Southeast Best Eight Average
   - Turkey Agrimetrics Index to be equal to the Best Eight National Average
   - Increase market share by growing at a rate which exceeds the industry.

the microbes to digest all traces of ammonia, even during the cold winter months. In April 1993, the company took a major step with the creation of its Environmental Steering Committee. Its mission is "... to provide all Perdue Farms work sites with vision, direction, and leadership so that they can be good corporate citizens from an environmental perspective today and in the future." The committee oversees how the company is doing in such environmentally sensitive areas as waste water, storm water, hazardous waste, solid waste, recycling, biosolids, and human health and safety.

Jim Perdue sums it up as follows: "... we must not only comply with environmental laws as they exist today, but look to the future to make sure we don't have any surprises. We must make sure our policy statement is real and that there's something behind it and that we do what we say we're going to do."

MARKETING

In the early days, chicken was sold to groceries as a commodity; that is, producers sold it in bulk, and butchers cut and wrapped it. The consumer had no idea what company grew the chicken. Frank Perdue was convinced that higher profits could be made if Perdue's products were premium quality so that they could be sold at a premium price. However, the only way the premium quality concept would work was if consumers asked for it by name—and that meant the product must be differentiated and "branded" to identify what the premium qualities are—hence the emphasis over the years on superior quality, a higher meat-to-bone ratio, and a yellow skin (the result of mixing marigold petals in the feed), which is an indicator of bird health.

In 1968, Perdue spent $40,000 on radio advertising. In 1969, the company spent $80,000 on radio, and in 1970, it spent $160,000, split 50-50 between radio and television. The advertising agency had recommended against television advertising, but the combination worked. TV ads increased sales, and Frank Perdue decided that the old agency he was dealing with did not match one of the basic Perdue tenets: "The people you deal with should be as good at what they do as you are at what you do."

This decision set of a storm of activity on Frank's part. In order to select a new ad agency, Frank studied intensively and personally learned more about advertising than any poultry man before him. He began a 10-week immersion in the theory and practice of advertising. He read books and papers on advertising. He talked to sales managers of every newspaper and radio and television station in the New York City area, consulted experts, and interviewed 48 ad agencies. On April 2, 1971, Perdue Farms selected Scali, McCabe, Sloves as its new advertising agency. As the agency tried to figure out how to successfully "brand" a chicken—something that had never been done—it realized that Frank Perdue was their greatest ally. "He looked a little like a chicken himself, and he sounded a little like one, and he squawked a lot!" Ed McCabe, partner and chief copywriter of the firm, decided that Frank Perdue should be the firm's spokesperson. Initially, Frank resisted. In the end, however, he accepted the role, and the campaign based on "It takes a tough man to make a tender chicken" was born. Frank set Perdue Farms apart by educating consumers about chicken quality. The process catapulted Perdue Farms into the ranks of the top poultry producers in the country.

The firm's very first television commercial showed Frank at a picnic in the Salisbury City Park saying

> A chicken is what it eats.... And my chickens eat better than people do.... I store my own grain and mix my own feed.... And give my Perdue chickens nothing but pure well water to drink.... That's why my chickens always have that healthy golden yellow color.... If you want to eat as good as my chickens, you'll just have to eat my chickens.... Mmmm, that's really good!"

Additional ads, touting superior quality and more breast meat, read as follows:

> Government standards would allow me to call this a grade A chicken ... but my standards wouldn't. This chicken is skinny.... It has scrapes and hairs.... The fact is, my graders reject 30% of the chickens government inspectors accept as grade A.... That's why it pays to insist on a chicken with my name on it.... If you're not completely satisfied, write me and I'll give you your money back.... Who do you write in Washington? ... What do they know about chickens?

Never go into a store and just ask for a pound of chicken breasts.... Because you could be cheating yourself out of some meat.... Here's an ordinary one-pound chicken breast, and here's a one-pound breast of mine.... They weigh the same. But as you can see, mine has more meat, and theirs has more bone. I breed the broadest breasted, meatiest chicken you can buy.... So don't buy a chicken breast by the pound.... Buy them by the name ... and get an extra bite in every breast.

The ads paid off. In 1968, Perdue Farms held about 3% of the New York market. By 1972, one out of every six chickens eaten in New York was a Perdue chicken. Fifty-one percent of New Yorkers recognized the label. Scali, McCabe, Sloves credited Frank Perdue's "believability" for the success of the program. "This was advertising in which Perdue had a personality that lent credibility to the product." Today, 50% of the chickens consumed in New York are Perdue.

Frank had his own view. As he told a Rotary audience in Charlotte, North Carolina, in March 1989, "... the product met the promise of the advertising and was far superior to the competition. Two great sayings tell it all: 'nothing will destroy a poor product as quickly as good advertising' and 'a gifted product is mightier than a gifted pen!'"

Today, the Perdue marketing function is unusually sophisticated. Its responsibilities include deciding (1) how many chickens and turkeys to grow, (2) what the advertising and promotion pieces should look like, where they should run, and how much the company can afford, and (3) which new products the company will pursue. The marketing plan is derived from the company's 5-year business plan and includes goals concerning volume, return on sales, market share, and profitability. The internal marketing department is helped by various service agencies, including

- Lowe & Partners/SMS—advertising campaigns, media buys

- R. C. Auletta & Co.—public relations, company image

- Gertsman & Meyers—packaging design

- Group Williams—consumer promotional programs

- Various research companies for focus groups, telephone surveys, and in-home use tests

OPERATIONS

Two words sum up the Perdue approach to operations—*quality* and *efficiency*—with emphasis on the first over the latter. Perdue more than most companies represents the total quality management (TQM) slogan: "Quality, a journey without end." Some of the key events are listed in Exhibit B. The pursuit of quality began with Arthur Perdue in 1924 when he purchased breeding roosters from Texas for the princely sum of $25 each. For comparison, typical wages in 1925 were $1 for a 10-hour workday. Frank Perdue's own pursuit of quality is legendary. One story about his pursuit of quality was told in 1968 by Ellis Wainwright, the State of Maryland grading inspector, during startup operations at Perdue's first processing plant. Frank had told Ellis that the standards that he wanted were higher than the government grade A standard. The first 2 days had been pretty much disastrous. On the third day, as Wainwright recalls,

We graded all morning, and I found only five boxes that passed what I took to be Frank's standards. The rest had the yellow skin color knocked off by the picking machines. I was afraid Frank was going to raise cain that I had accepted so few. Then Frank came through and rejected half of those.

To ensure that Perdue continues to lead the industry in quality, it buys about 2000 pounds of competitors' products a week. Inspection associates grade these products, and the information is shared with the highest levels of management. In addition, the company's quality policy is displayed at all locations and taught to all associates in quality training (see Exhibit A).

Perdue insists that nothing artificial be fed or injected into its birds. The company will not take any shortcuts in pursuit of the perfect chicken. A chemical- and steroid-free diet is fed to the chickens. Young chickens are vaccinated against disease. Selective breeding is used to improve the quality of the chickens sold. Chickens are bred to yield more breast meat because that is what the consumer wants.

EXHIBIT B
....
Milestones in the Quality Improvement Process at Perdue Farms

1924	Arthur Perdue buys leghorn roosters for $25.
1950s	Adopts the company logo of a chick under a magnifying glass.
1984	Frank Perdue attends Philip Crosby's Quality College.
1985	Perdue recognized for its pursuit of quality in *A Passion for Excellence*.
	200 Perdue Managers attend Quality College.
	Adopted the Quality Improvement Process (QIP).
1986	Established Corrective Action Teams (CATs).
1987	Established Quality Training for all associates.
	Implemented Error Cause Removal Process (ECR).
1988	Steering Committee formed.
1989	First Annual Quality Conference held.
	Implemented Team Management.
1990	Second Annual Quality Conference held.
	Codified Values and Corporate Mission.
1991	Third Annual Quality Conference held.
	Customer Satisfaction defined.
1992	Fourth Annual Quality Conference held.
	"How to" implement Customer Satisfaction explained for team leaders and QITs.

Efficiency is improved through management of details. As a vertically integrated producer of chickens, Perdue manages every detail, including breeding and hatching its own eggs, selecting growers, building Perdue-engineered chicken houses, formulating and manufacturing its own feed, overseeing the care and feeding, operating its own processing plants, distributing via its own trucking fleet, and marketing. Improvements are measured in fractional cents per pound. Nothing goes to waste. The feet that used to be thrown away are now processed and sold in the Orient as a bar room delicacy.

Frank's knowledge of details is also legendary. He not only impresses people in the poultry industry but those in other industries as well. At the end of one day the managers and engineers of a new Grumman plant in Salisbury, Maryland, were reviewing their progress. Through the door, unannounced came Frank Perdue. The Grumman managers proceeded to give Frank a tour of the plant. One machine was an ink-jet printer that labeled parts as they passed. Frank said he believed he had some of those in his plants. He paused for a minute, and then he asked them if it clogged often. They responded yes. Frank exclaimed excitedly, "I

am sure that I got some of those!" To ensure that this attention to detail pays off, eight measurable items—hatchability, turnover, feed conversion, livability, yield, birds per worker-hour, utilization, and grade—are tracked.

Frank Perdue credits much of his success to listening to others. He agrees with Tom Peters that "nobody knows a person's 20 square feet better than the person who works here." To facilitate the transmission of ideas through the organization, it is undergoing a cultural transformation beginning with Frank (Exhibit C). He describes the transition from the old to the new culture and himself as follows:

> . . . we also learned that *loud and noisy* were worth a lot more than mugs and pens. What I mean by this is, we used to spend a lot of time calling companies to get trinkets as gifts. Gradually, we learned that money and trinkets weren't what really motivated people. We learned that when a man or woman on the line is going all out to do a good job, that he or she doesn't care that much about a trinket of some sort; what they really want is for the manager to get up from behind his desk, walk over to them and, in

EXHIBIT C
....
Perdue Farms, Inc., Cultural Transformation

Old culture

1. Top-down management
2. Poor communications
3. Short-term planning
4. Commitment to quality
5. Profitability focus
6. Limited associate recognition
7. Limited associate training
8. Short-term cost reduction
9. Annual goals as end target
10. Satisfied customers

New culture

1. Team management
2. Focused message from senior management
3. Long-range planning
4. Expanded commitment to quality
5. Focus on people, product, and profitability
6. Recognition is a way of life
7. Commitment to training
8. Long-term productivity improvements
9. Continuous improvement
10. Delighted customers

front of their peers, give them a hearty and sincere "thank you."

When we give recognition, now, we do it when there's an audience and lots of peers can see. This is, I can tell you, a lot more motivating than the "kick in the butt," that was part of the old culture—*and I was the most guilty!*

Changing the behavioral pattern from writing up people who have done something wrong to recognizing people for doing their job well has not been without some setbacks. For example, the company started what it calls the "Good Egg Award," which is good for a free lunch. Managers in the Salisbury plan were all trained and asked to distribute the awards by "catching" someone doing a good job. When the program manager checked with the cafeteria the following week to see how many had been claimed, the answer was none. A meeting of the mangers was called to see how many had been handed out. The answer was none. When the managers were asked what they had done with their award certificates, the majority replied they were in their shirt pocket. A goal was set for all managers to hand out five a week.

The following week, the program manager still found that very few were being turned in for a free lunch. When employees were asked what they had done with their awards, they replied that they had framed them and hung them up on walls at home or put them in trophy cases. The program was changed again. Now the "Good Egg Award" consists of both a certificate and a ticket for a free lunch.

Perdue also has a beneficial suggestion program that it calls "Error Cause Removal." It averages better than one submission per year per three employees. Although that is much less than the 22 per employee per year in Japan, it is significantly better than the national average in the United States of one per year per five employees. As Frank has said, "We're 'one up' . . . because with the help of the Quality Improvement Process and the help of our associates, we have *thousands* of 'better minds' helping us."

MANAGEMENT INFORMATION SYSTEMS (MIS)
....

In 1989, Perdue Farms employed 118 IS people who spent 146 hours per week on IS maintenance—"fix it"—jobs. Today, the entire department has been reduced to 50 associates who spend only 52 hours per week in "fix it" and 94 percent of their time building new systems or re-engineering old ones. Even better, a 6-year backlog of projects has been eliminated, and the average "build it" cost for a project has dropped from $1950 to $568—an overall 300% increase in efficiency.

According to Don Taylor, director of MIS, this is the payoff from a significant management re-orientation. A key philosophy is that a "fix it" mentality is counterproductive. The goal is to determine the root cause of the problem and re-engineer the program to eliminate future problems.

Developer-user partnerships—including a monthly payback system—were developed with five functional groups: sales and marketing, finance and human resources, logistics, quality assurance, and fresh poultry and plant systems. Each has an assigned number of IS hours per month and defines its own priorities, permitting it to function as a customer.

In addition, a set of critical success factors (CSFs) was developed. These include (1) automation is never the first step in a project; it occurs only after superfluous business processes are eliminated and necessary ones simplified; (2) senior management sponsorship—the vice president for the business unit—must sponsor major projects in their area; (3) limited size, duration, and scope; IS has found that small projects have more success and a cumulative bigger payoff than big ones, and all major projects are broken into 3- to 6-month segments with separate deliverables and benefits; (4) precise definition of requirements—the team must determine up front exactly what the project will accomplish; and (5) commitment of both the IS staff and the customer to work as a team.

Perdue considers IS key to the operation of its business. For example, IS developed a customer ordering system for the centralized sales office (CSO). This system automated key business processes that link Perdue with its customers. The CSO includes 13 applications including order entry, product transfers, sales allocations, production scheduling, and credit management.

When ordering, the Perdue salesperson negotiates the specifics of the sale directly with the buyer in the grocery chain. Next, the salesperson sends the request to a dispatcher who determines where the various products are located and designates a specific truck to make the required pickups and delivery, all within the designated 1-hour delivery window that has been granted by the grocery chain. Each truck is even equipped with a small satellite dish that is connected to the LAN so that a trucker on the New Jersey Turnpike headed for New York can call for a replacement tractor if his or her rig breaks down.

Obviously, a computer malfunction is a possible disaster. Four hours of downtime is equivalent to $6.2 million in lost sales. Thus Perdue has separate systems and processes in place to avoid such problems. In addition to maximizing on-time delivery, this system gives the salespeople more time to discuss wants and needs with customers, handle customer relations, and observe key marketing issues such as Perdue shelf space and location.

On the other hand, Perdue does not believe that automation solves all problems. For example, it was decided that electronics monitoring in the poultry houses is counterproductive and not cost-effective. While it would be possible to develop systems to monitor and control almost every facet of the chicken house environment, Perdue is concerned that doing so would weaken the invaluable link between the farmer and the livestock; that is, Perdue believes that poultry producers need to be personally involved with conditions in the chicken house in order to maximize quality and spot problems or health challenges as soon as possible.

RESEARCH AND DEVELOPMENT

Perdue is an acknowledged industry leader in the use of technology to provide quality products and service to its customers. A list of some of its technological accomplishments is given in Exhibit D. As with everything else he does, Frank Perdue tries to

EXHIBIT D

Perdue Farms, Inc., Technological Accomplishments

- Breed chickens with 20% more breast meat
- First to use digital scales to guarantee weights to customers
- First to package fully cooked chicken products on microwavable trays
- First to have a box lab to define quality of boxes from different suppliers
- First to test both its chickens and competitors' chickens on 52 quality factors every week
- Improved on-time deliveries 20% between 1987 and 1993

leave nothing to chance. Perdue employs 25 people full time in the industry's largest research and development (R&D) effort, including five with graduate degrees. It has specialists in avian science, microbiology, genetics, nutrition, and veterinary science. Because of its R&D capabilities, Perdue is often involved in USDA field tests with pharmaceutical suppliers. Knowledge and experience gained from these tests can lead to a competitive advantage. For example, Perdue has the most extensive and expensive vaccination program among breeders in the industry. As a result, Perdue growers have more disease-resistant chickens and one of the lowest mortality rates in the industry.

Perdue is not complacent. According to Dr. Mac Terzich, doctor of veterinary medicine and laboratory manager, Perdue really pushes for creativity and innovation. Currently, the company is working with and studying some European producers who use a completely different process.

HUMAN RESOURCES MANAGEMENT

When entering the Human Resources Department at Perdue Farms, the first thing one sees is a prominently displayed set of human resources corporate strategic goals (Exhibit E). Besides these human resources corporate strategic goals, Perdue sets annual company goals that deal with "people." Fiscal year 1995s strategic "people" goals center on providing a safe, secure, and productive work environment. The specific goals are included on the wallet-sized, fold-up card mentioned earlier (see Exhibit A).

Strategic human resources planning is still developing at Perdue Farms. According to Tom Moyers, vice president for human resources management, "Every department in the company has a mission statement or policy which has been developed within the past 18 months. . . . Department heads are free to update their goals as they see fit. . . . Initial strategic human resource plans are developed by teams of three or four associates. . . . These teams meet once or twice a year company-wide to review where we stand in terms of meeting our objectives."

To keep associates informed about company plans, Perdue Farms holds "state of the business meetings" for all interested associates twice a year. For example, during May 1994, five separate meetings were held near various plants in DelMarVa, the Carolinas, Virginia, and Indiana. Typically, a local auditorium is rented, overhead slides are prepared, and the company's progress toward its goals and its financial status are shared with its associates. Discussion revolves around what is wrong and what is right about the company. New product lines are introduced to those attending, and opportunities for improvement are discussed.

On joining Perdue Farms, each new associate attends an extensive orientation that begins with a thorough review of the *Perdue Associate Handbook*. The handbook details Perdue's philosophy

EXHIBIT E
Human Resources Corporate Strategic Goals

- Provide leadership to the corporation in all aspects of human resources, including safety, recruitment and retention of associates, training and development, employee relations, compensation, benefits, communication, security, medical, housekeeping, and food services.
- Provide leadership and assistance to management at all levels in communicating and implementing company policy to ensure consistency and compliance with federal, state, and local regulations.
- Provide leadership and assistance to management in maintaining a socially responsible community image in all our Perdue communities by maintaining positive community relations and encouraging Perdue associates to be active in their community.
- Provide leadership and assistance to management in creating an environment wherein all associates can contribute to the overall success of the company.
- Be innovative and cost-efficient in developing, implementing, and providing to all associates systems that will reward performance, encourage individual growth, and recognize contribution to the corporation.

on quality, employee relations, drugs and alcohol, and its code of ethics. The orientation also includes a thorough discussion of the Perdue benefit plans. Fully paid benefits for all associates includes (1) paid vacation, (2) eight official paid holidays, (3) health, accident, disability, and life insurance, (4) savings and pension plans, (5) funeral leave, and (6) jury duty leave. The company also offers a scholarship program for children of Perdue associates.

Special arrangements can be made with the individual's immediate supervisor for a leave of absence of up to 12 months in case of extended non-job-related illness or injury, birth or adoption of a child, care of a spouse or other close relative, or other personal situations. Regarding the Family and Medical Leave Act of 1993, although opposed by many companies because its requirements are far more than their current policies, the act will have little impact on Perdue Farms, since existing leave of absence policies are already broader than the new federal law.

Perdue Farms is a nonunion employer. The firm has had a long-standing open-door policy, and managers are expected to be easily accessible to other associates, whatever the person's concern. The open door has been supplemented by a formal peer-review process. While associates are expected to discuss problems with their supervisors first, they are urged to use peer review if they are still dissatisfied.

Wages and salaries, which are reviewed at least once a year, are determined by patterns in the poultry industry and the particular geographic location of the plant. Changes in the general economy and the state of the business are also considered.

Informal comparisons of turnover statistics with others in the poultry industry suggest that Perdue's turnover numbers are among the lowest in the industry. Perdue also shares workers' compensation claims data with its competitors, and incidence rates (for accidents) are also among the lowest in the industry. Supervisors initially train and coach all new associates about the proper way to do their jobs. Once trained, the philosophy is that all associates are professionals and, as such, should make suggestions about how to make their jobs even more efficient and effective. After a 60-day introductory period, the associate has seniority based on the starting date of employment. Seniority is the determining factor in promotions where qualifications (skill, proficiency, dependability, work

record) are equal. Also, should the workforce need to be reduced, this date is used as the determining factor in layoffs.

A form of management by objectives (MBO) is used for annual performance appraisal and planning review. The format includes a four-step process:

1. Establish accountability, goals, standards of performance, and their relative weights for the review period.

2. Conduct coaching sessions throughout the review period, and document these discussions.

3. Evaluate performance at the end of the review period, and conduct an appraisal interview.

4. Undertake next review period planning.

The foundation of human resources development includes extensive training and management development plus intensive succession planning and career pathing. The essence of the company's approach to human resources management is captured in Frank Perdue's statement:

> We have gotten where we are because we have believed in hiring our own people and training them in our own way. We believe in promotion from within, going outside only when we feel it is absolutely necessary—for expertise and sometimes because our company was simply growing faster than our people development program. The number one item in our success has been the quality of our people.

FINANCE

Perdue Farms, Inc., is a privately held firm and considers financial information to be proprietary. Hence available data are limited. Stock is primarily held by the family and a limited amount by Perdue management. *Forbes* (December 5, 1994) estimates Perdue Farms revenues for 1994 at about $1.5 billion, net profits at $50 million, and the number of associates at 13,800. The January 1995 purchase of Showell Farms, Inc., should boost revenues to more than $2 billion and the number of associates to about 20,000.

The firm's compound sales growth rate has been slowly decreasing during the past 20 years, mirroring the industry, which has been experiencing market saturation and overproduction. However, Perdue has compensated by wringing more efficiency from its associates; for example, 20 years ago, a 1% increase in associates resulted in a 1.3% increase in revenue. Today, a 1% increase in associates results in a 2.5% increase in revenues (see Table 1).

Perdue Farms has three operating divisions: Retail Chicken (62% of sales, growth rate 5%), Foodservice Chicken and Turkey (20% of sales, growth rate 12%), and Grain and Oilseed (18% of sales, growth rate 10%). Thus the bulk of sales comes from the sector—retail chicken—with the slowest growth rate. Part of the reason for the slow sales growth in retail chicken may stem from Perdue Farm's policy of selling only fresh—never frozen—chicken. This has limited the company's traditional markets to cities that can be serviced overnight by truck from production facility locations, for example, New York, Boston, Philadelphia, Baltimore and Washington, which are pretty well saturated (developing markets include Chicago, Cleveland, Atlanta, Pittsburgh, and Miami). On the other hand, foodservice and grain and oilseed customers are nationwide and include export customers in eastern Europe, China, Japan, and South America. Perdue Farms has been profitable every year since its founding, with the exception of 1988. Company officials believe the loss in 1988 was caused by a decentralization effort begun during the early eighties. At that time, there was a concerted effort to push decisions down through the corporate ranks to provide more autonomy. When the new strategy resulted in higher costs, Frank Perdue responded quickly by returning to the basics, reconsolidating and downsizing. Now the goal is to constantly streamline in order to provide cost-effective business solutions.

Perdue Farms has a conservative approach to financial management, using retained earnings and cash flow to finance asset replacement projects and normal growth. When planning expansion projects or acquisitions, long-term debt is used. The target debt limit is 55% of equity. Such debt is normally provided by domestic and international bank and insurance companies. The debt strategy is to match asset lives with liability maturities and have a mix of fixed-rate and variable-rate debt. Growth plans require about $2 in projected incremental sales growth for each $1 in invested capital.

THE U.S. POULTRY INDUSTRY

U.S. annual per capita consumption of poultry has risen dramatically during the past 40 years from 26.3 pounds to almost 80 pounds in 1990. Consumption continued to grow through 1994 according to a broiler industry survey of the largest integrated broiler companies. Output of ready-to-cook product increased 5.8% in 1991, 5.3% in 1992, 6.0% in 1993, and 7.9% in 1994 to 508 million pounds per week.

Recent growth is largely the result of consumers moving away from red meat due to health concerns and the industry's continued development of increased-value products such as precooked or roasted chicken and chicken parts. Unfortunately, this growth has not been very profitable due to chronic overcapacity throughout the industry that has pushed down wholesale prices. The industry has experienced cyclic troughs before, and experts expect future improvement in both sales and profits. Still, razor-thin margins demand absolute efficiency.

Fifty-three integrated broiler companies account for approximately 99% of ready-to-cook production in the United States. While slow consolidation of the industry appears to be taking place, it is still necessary to include about 20 companies to get to 80% of production. Concentration has been fastest among the top four producers. For example, since 1986, market share of the top four has grown from 35% to 42% (see Table 2). Although the DelMarVa Peninsula (home to Perdue Farms, Inc.) has long been considered the

TABLE I

Annual Compound Growth Rate: Revenues and Associates

	Revenue Growth	Associate Growth
Past 20 years	13%	10%
Past 15 years	11%	8%
Past 10 years	9%	5%
Past 5 years	5%	2%

TABLE 2
....

Nation's Top Four Broiler Companies, 1995*

	Million Heads	Million Pounds
1. Tyson Foods, Inc.	26.70	88.25
2. Gold Kist, Inc.	13.40	44.01
3. Perdue Farms, Inc.	10.97†	42.64†
4. ConAgra, Inc.	10.50	37.91

*Based on average weekly slaughter; Broiler Industry Survey, 1995.
†Includes figures for Showell Farms, Inc., which Perdue acquired in January 1995.

TABLE 3
....

Integrated Broiler Producers Operating on the DelMarVa Peninsula*

	National Rank
Tyson Foods, Inc.	1
Perdue Farms Inc. (includes Showell Farms, Inc., which Perdue acquired in January 1995)	3
ConAgra, Inc.	4
Hudson Foods, Inc.	7
Townsend, Inc. (Millsboro, Delaware)	10
Allen Family Foods, Inc. (Seaford, Delaware)	14
Mountaire Farms of Delmarva, Inc. (Selbyville, Delaware)	26

*DelMarVa Poultry Industry, Inc., May 1995 fact sheet.

birthplace of the commercial broiler industry, recent production gains have been most rapid in the Southeast. Arkansas, Georgia, and Alabama are now the largest poultry producing states—a result of abundant space and inexpensive labor. The Southeast accounts for approximately 50% of the $20 billion U.S. chicken industry, employing 125,000 people across the region. Still, DelMarVa chicken producers provide about 10% of all broilers grown in the United States. This is due largely to the region's proximity to Washington, Baltimore, Philadelphia, New York, and Boston. Each weekday, more than 200 tractor trailers loaded with fresh dressed poultry leave DelMarVa headed for these metropolitan markets.

Seven integrated companies operate 10 feed mills, 15 hatcheries, and 13 processing plants on the DelMarVa Peninsula, employing approximately 22,000 people and producing approximately 10 million broilers each week (see Table 3).

THE FUTURE

Considering Americans' average annual consumption of chicken (almost 80 pounds per person in 1990), many in the industry wonder how much growth is left. For example, after wholesale prices climbed from 14 cents per pound in 1960 to about 37 cents per pound in 1989, the recession and a general glut in the market caused prices to fall back (see Figure 1). Although prices rebounded somewhat in 1993 and 1994, in real terms the price of chicken remains at an all-time low. A pound of chicken is down from 30 minutes of an

average worker's 1940 wage to only 4.5 minutes of a 1990 wage.

While much of this reduction can be justified by improved production efficiencies, prices are clearly depressed due to what some consider overcapacity in the industry. For example, in 1992, ConAgra, Inc., temporarily stopped sending chicks to 30 DelMarVa growers to prevent an oversupply of chickens, and several chicken companies have started to experiment with producing other kinds of meats—from pork to striped bass—to soften the impact (Kim Clark, *The Sun,* July 4, 1993).

The trend is away from whole chickens to skinless, boneless parts. Perdue has responded with its line of Fit 'n Easy products with detailed nutrition labeling. It is also developing exports of dark meat to Puerto Rico and chicken feet to China. Fresh young turkey and turkey parts have become an important product, and the Perdue Done It! line has been expanded to include fully cooked roasted broilers, Cornish hens, and parts. Recently, the company has expanded its lines to include ground chicken and turkey sausage.

Frank Perdue reflected recently that "... we have a very high share of the available supermarket business in the Middle Atlantic and Northeastern

FIGURE 1

....

Wholesale Price per Pound of Live Broilers as Received by Farmers.

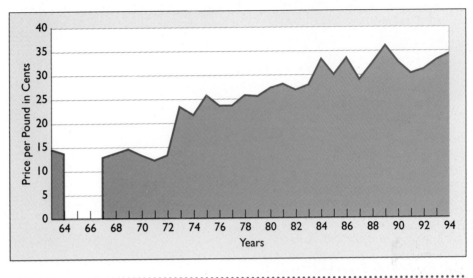

United States, and if we were to follow that course which we know best—selling to the consumer through the retailer—we'd have to consider the Upper Midwest—Pittsburgh, Chicago, Detroit, with 25 to 30 million people.

Public Sources of Information

Barmash, Isadore, "Handing Off to the Next Generation," *New York Times,* July 26, 1992, Business, p. 1.

Bates, Eric, and Bob Hall, "Ruling the Roost," *Southern Exposure,* Summer 1989, p. 11.

Clark, Kim, "Tender Times: Is Sky Falling on the Chicken Boom?" *The Sun,* July 4, 1993. Business, p. 4F.

"Facts About the DelMarVa Broiler Industry—1973," Industry Bulletin, February 25, 1974.

"Facts About the DelMarVa Poultry Industry," DelMarVa Poultry Industry, Inc., May 1995.

Fahy, Joe, "All Pain, No Gain," *Southern Exposure,* Summer 1989, pp. 35–39.

Flynn, Ramsey, "Strange Bird," *The Washingtonian,* December 1989, p. 165.

"The 400 Largest Private Companies in the U.S.," *Forbes,* December 5, 1994.

Gale, Bradley T., "Quality Comes First When Hatching Power Brands," *Planning Review,* July-August, 1992, pp. 4–48.

Goldoftas, Barbara, "Inside the Slaughterhouse," *Southern Exposure,* Summer 1989, pp. 25–29.

Hall, Bob, "Chicken Empires," *Southern Exposure,* Summer 1989, pp. 12–19.

"Golden Jubilee! Company Honors Frank Perdue for His 50 Years of Service," *Perdue Courier* (Special Edition), July 1989.

"In the Money: Downhome Retailer is Nation's Richest, *Forbes* says," *Washington Post,* October 14, 1986.

MacPherson, Myra, "Chicken Big," *Washington Post, Potomac Magazine,* May 11, 1975, p. 15.

"Nation's Broiler Industry," *Broiler Industry,* January 1995.

"Perdue Chicken Spreads Its Wings," *Business Week,* September 16, 1972, p. 113.

Perdue Farms Incorporated—Historical Highlights, Perdue Farms, Inc., publication, September 1992.

Perdue, Frank, Speech at Babson College, April 28, 1981.

Perdue, Frank, Speech to firm's leaders, accountants, and Perdue Associates, September 1991.

Poultry industry file, Miscellaneous newspaper clippings from 1950 to 1994, The Maryland Room, Blackwell Library, Salisbury State University.

Santosus, Megan, "Perdue's New Pecking Orders," *CIO,* March 1993, pp. 60–68.

Scarupa, Henry, "When Is a Chicken Not a Football?" *The (Baltimore) Sun Magazine,* March 4, 1973, pp. 5–12.

"Silent Millionaires in America," *Economist,* 270 (7072), March 17, 1979.

Sterling, Bill, "Just Browsin'," *Eastern Shore News,* March 2, 1988.

"The Perdue Story. And the Five Reasons Why Our Consumers Tell It Best," Perdue Farms, Inc., publication, October 1991.

Thornton, Gary, "Data from Broiler Industry," Elanco Poultry Team, partner with the poultry industry, December 1993.

Yeoman, Barry, "Don't Count Your Chickens," *Southern Exposure,* Summer 1989, pp. 21–24.

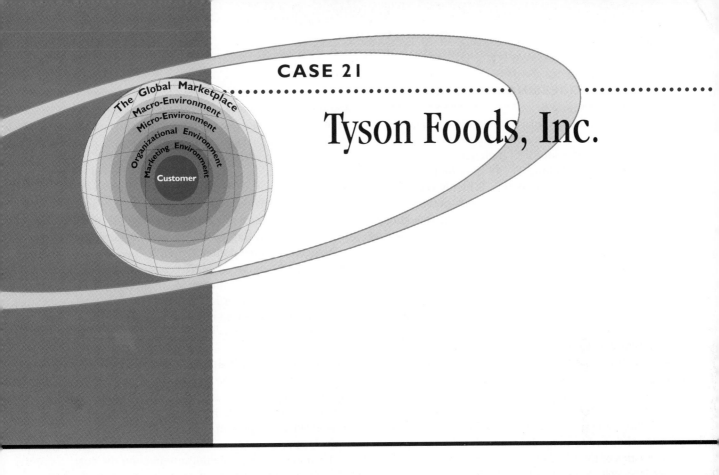

CASE 21

Tyson Foods, Inc.

This case was prepared by Loretta Ferguson Cochran of Clemson University.

Tyson's Real Asset: The people of Tyson are the people who work in the plants, in the feed mills, and in the offices. We live in the deep South, on the East Coast and overseas—everywhere we have operations. We are as diverse as our work.

We work in live swine production. We catch fish in the Bering Sea. We load pallets of product to be shipped to customers in places such as Hong Kong and Russia, as well as 41 other countries.

Every day, all 55,800 of us work not only to keep the company number one in the poultry category, but to expand other growing areas such as our beef, pork, fish, corn and flour operations.

We take responsibility for our work. Together we manage both people and capital. But most important is how we build our company by taking chances, doing new things, working as a

team, sharing credit and keeping an eye on the bottom line.

We are always challenging ourselves. Our philosophy is that if we're doing things the same way we did yesterday, chances are there's room for improvement.

We continue to believe that our people are our number one asset. We believe that if we take care of our people, they will take care of our customers, which ultimately take care of our shareholder. It's simple, but it works [Don Tyson, 1994 Annual Report].

Tyson Foods, Inc., is the world's largest fully integrated producer, processor, and marketer of poultry-based food products. In addition, it is a significant producer and marketer of other "center-of-the-plate" (entrée) and convenience food items.[1] Tyson's stated strategy is to "segment, concentrate, and dominate." According to Don Tyson, CEO, "We [Tyson Foods, Inc.] find something we can do, focus on it, and aim to be no. 1."[2]

POULTRY PROCESSING INDUSTRY

Poultry production is a major component of agricultural production throughout the world, with poultry serving as a source of high-quality protein for the world population.[3] The poultry industry, unlike most agricultural production, is highly vertically integrated. Beginning in the 1950s, poultry farmers combined feed mills, processing plants, and further-processing plants to create efficient operation complexes.[4]

There are three distinct processed poultry meat products produced by the industry. First, *fresh carcass products* are those which are packaged as the whole bird and as parts (e.g., a package of chicken legs). Second, *formed products,* both whole and chopped, consist of deboned meat shaped into a specific form and held in place while being cooked into that shape. Whole products are those where the whole muscle is left intact or left in large pieces to retain the intact muscle tissue texture, and chopped products are those where the meat is finely chopped to the point where it loses the characteristics of muscle tissue. Third, *emulsified products* are meat products where the meat has been pureed into a batter and forced into a product casing to form items such as frankfurters and bologna. These items are typically cooked, smoked, or cured.[5]

Poultry producers sell direct to large grocery and restaurant chains such as Winn Dixie and McDonald's but use food wholesalers to reach smaller chains and sole proprietorships.

Processed poultry meats have emerged as a low-fat alternative (substitute) for red meats. Prior to the 1970s, consumer demand was for commodity chicken, marketed and distributed through grocery store outlets. In the middle to late 1970s, demand began to shift to more convenience products, such as formed patties. Presently, the slow growth in whole fryers and parts has continued, and the demand is continuing to strengthen for processed parts and formed products that are available as prepared food in restaurants and as ready-to-eat products in grocery stores.

Industry Sales and Profits

The industry shipments for poultry processing (SIC 2015) are listed in Exhibits A through C. Poultry consumption per person each year is listed in Exhibits D and E.

Feed prices have a significant effect on the cost of poultry raising and therefore the profitability of poultry farmers and processors. Given the latest bumper (feed) crops, feed prices have declined recently, which should widen profit margins on poultry, even if selling price per pound falls slightly.[11]

EXHIBIT A
Poultry Processing Shipments (in Millions of Dollars)[6]

1987	1988	1989	1990	1991
14,912	16,598	20,283	20,928	21,703

EXHIBIT B
Poultry Processing Shipments (Percent Change)[7]

87–88	88–89	89–90	90–91
11.3	22.2	3.2	3.7

EXHIBIT C
Product Shipments, Exports & Imports (Millions of Dollars)[8]

Product Shipments		Value of Exports		Value of Imports	
1990	1991	1990	1991	1990	1991
20,353	21,246	717	879	32	37
Percent change	4.4%	Percent change	22.6%	Percent change	15.6%

EXHIBIT D
Per Capita Consumption of Chicken and Turkey (in Pounds)[9]

	1983	1984	1985	1986	1987	1988	1989	1990	1991	1992
Chicken	50.7	52.4	54.1	55.4	58.5	58.7	60.6	63.0	65.6	68.4
Turkey	11.8	11.8	11.6	12.9	14.7	15.7	16.6	17.6	18.0	18.0

EXHIBIT E
Per Capita Consumption (Percent Change)[10]

	83–84	84–85	85–86	86–87	87–88	88–89	89–90	90–91	91–92
Chicken	3.35	3.24	0.4	5.6	0.34	3.24	4.0	4.13	4.27
Turkey	0	−0.02	11.2	14.0	6.8	5.7	6.02	2.3	0

Seventy percent of the industry cost of producing a ready-to-cook chicken is from the feed ingredients. It is the single most influential factor on poultry industry cycles.[12] Vertically integrated firms are able, to some extent, to control the influence of feed suppliers by producing their own feed. However, floods and droughts are beyond their control and raise their feed costs as well.

Competitors

Exhibit F includes 1993 market share, revenues, and net income amounts (in millions of dollars) for the top 10 companies in poultry processing.[13] The revenue and net income figures are for the entire corporation, which often includes more than poultry processing. Market share is based on 289.5 million pounds of ready-to-cook poultry product produced per week in 1993.

The top four producers capture less than 40 percent of the market, which indicates a moderate level of fragmentation in the industry. In addition, half the firms listed in Exhibit F are privately held. Poultry processing is fragmented in part due to the way vertical integration of the industry developed. When firms began integration, there were significantly fewer barriers to entry than today. As the product experienced moderate growth, firms became more automated and efficient. Smaller firms tend to have less extensive vertical integration, while the larger firms maintain a high degree of vertical integration.

EXHIBIT F
· · · · · · · · · · · · · · ·
Competitor Information

Company	Percent of Market Share	Sales ($ million)	Net Profit ($ million)	Operating Margin (Percent)
Tyson Foods	15.4%	4,707.4	180.33	11.7%
ConAgra	9.4%	21,519	399.5	5.6%
Gold Kist	6.7%	1,561	*	*
Perdue Farms	5.6%	1,020	*	*
Pilgrim's Pride	4.2%	887.87	22.3	6.32%
Hudson Foods	3.5%	920.5	15.9	6.2%
WLR Foods	3.0%	617	14.6	9.0%
Foster Farms	2.9%	1,160	*	*
Wayne Poultry	2.9%	11	*	*
Townsends	2.1%	270	*	*
Others	44.3%			

*Data unavailable for private firms, and their sales figures are estimates.

Competition tends to focus on price and quality, with name recognition being an avenue for capturing market share. Usefulness of name recognition was evidenced when Tyson acquired Holly Farms in 1988. This acquisition was important because Holly Farms held 19 percent of the brand-name chicken grocery market. Name recognition is vital in obtaining shelf space and subsequent market share for branded products. The Holly Farms acquisition also was necessary to increase Tyson's supply of chickens and processing capacity due to Tyson's rapid growth in supplying the fast-food industry.

Geographic competition is also present for the best contract growers.[14] Contract growers are individuals with broiler houses that raise company-provided chicks to market-size broilers. These growers are served by a company representative that checks on chick development. The growers own the houses and pay utilities, but the company supplies the feed and supplements for the birds. The growers are paid for the broilers by a formula that includes weight, feed conversion, mortality rate, and other factors. Within a geographic region, there can be several broiler complexes from various companies. These complexes are made up of a hatchery, a feed mill, and a processing plant. Each complex has affiliated with it egg and broiler producers. The competition arises for the best contract producers to affiliate with the complex.

This sort of geographic association supports poultry as a regional industry in terms of ownership, with broiler production predominately in the southern region. Exhibit G outlines the top five states in 1992 in terms of production.[15]

Historically, each division of the poultry industry (broilers, layers, turkeys) functioned as a sector industry with independent hatcheries, feed suppli-

EXHIBIT G
· · · · · · · · · · · · · ·
Geographic Regions of Production

State	Percentage
Arkansas	15.3%
Alabama	13.5%
Georgia	13.2%
North Carolina	9.9%
Mississippi	7.5%
Total percent of market accounted for	88.2%

EXHIBIT H
················
An Example of Vertical Integration: Tyson Foods

Step	Description
Foundation breeder flock	Pedigree flocks that yield the highly productive line of breeder hens and roosters
Hatchery supply flock	Breeder houses where roosters and hens produce broiler eggs
Commercial hatchery	Environmentally controlled nurseries where eggs hatch
Feed mill	Hammer and grinding mills where train loads of grain are mixed and trucked to nearby farms
Broiler growout farms	Long, narrow houses (company owned) where flocks of chickens are raised
Processing plant	Automated factories where birds are processed into poultry staples and by-products
Distribution channels	Massive freezer warehouses and trucking fleets deliver products

Note: Independently owned farms are strategic alliances, not part of the company's vertical integration.

ers, and processors.[16] For example, broiler growers would buy chicks and feed from different suppliers than would layer and turkey growers. Individual farmers negotiated price with processors, who then handled the sale of their products to retailers. A development in the poultry industry, along with more reliable scheduling and product commitments, was the evolution of binding contracts between producers, feed suppliers, and processors—particularly in the broiler segment. In the broiler segment, individual producers own the birds but agree to do business with a specific feed supplier and a specific processor. Over the past 40 years, these relationships between hatcheries, feed suppliers, and processors have developed into the vertical integration that is present in today's poultry processing industry; as strategic alliances have emerged between companies and contract growers[17] (Exhibit H and Figure 1), the company owns a hatchery, a feed mill, and a processing plant. Vertical integration dominates the industry, since over 95 percent of commercial broilers are produced by vertically integrated firms.[18]

Strategic alliances have developed between the contract growers and the affiliated company. The broilers from the hatchery are grown by independent contract farms or by company-owned farms. Company-owned farms account for a very small percentage of chickens grown. The company is not the grower; it just facilitates broiler production.

Vertical integration has been advantageous for companies by consolidating the marketing, sales, quality standards, and administrative functions that were present in each sector before integration. It has had a positive effect on demand and profitability by maintaining efficient processes and lowering costs. Establishing quality standards between a company and a supplier in today's market is important for those companies which adhere to universal product standards such as ISO 9000, since the quality standards extend to suppliers. These types of supplier-customer relationships existed years ago in the poultry industry and have improved the process of growing a uniform bird.

Economies of scale also have been experienced in scheduling, distribution, coordinating facilities, and controlling production. Many of the costs of vertical integration have been avoided so far partially because past integration developed through acquisitions was perceived as beneficial to both companies and therefore not opposed by the stakeholders. The level of vertical integration is different from economies of scale. Purchase and development of feeds, chicks, and other necessary materials for production enjoy a reduction in per unit cost when done in larger amounts. Vertical

FIGURE I

Vertical Integration of the Poultry Processing Industry

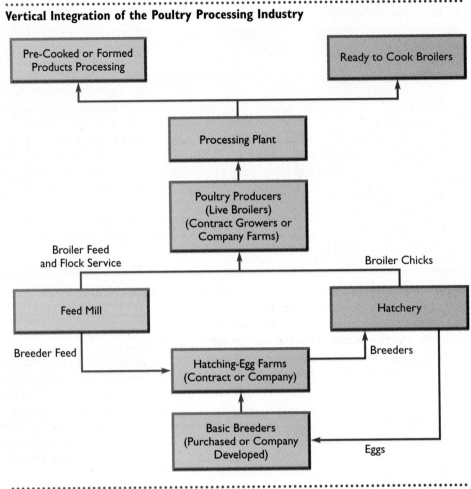

integration allows for firms to own everything from the feed mill and processing plant to the distribution process and facilities.[19] This integration allows for lower costs than if the units were operating separately, with each demanding a markup in price.

Global Issues

Three countries account for over 55 percent of the broiler exports in the world for 1992: United States (26 percent), France (16 percent), and Brazil (15 percent).[20] In 1992, Japan and Hong Kong were the largest importers of U.S. poultry: Japan ($130 million), Hong Kong ($127 million), Canada, ($90 million), and Mexico ($71 million). One way larger processors are penetrating foreign markets is to buy into foreign poultry processing concerns. Tyson holds a majority interest in Trasgo, S.A. de

C.V., Mexico's third largest poultry processor.[21] Cargill has found its way to Europe with Cargill France, which has opened a processing plant in France to supply McDonald's with chicken products.

The effect of the North American Free Trade Agreement and General Agreement on Tariffs and Trade on expanding markets may be twofold. First, these agreements may open up international markets and relieve some international subsidies on poultry products. In addition, both agreements contain new labeling regulations that mandate extensive disclosure requirements. These agreements, along with the enforcement of the Nutrition Labeling and Education Act by the Food and Drug Administration, may benefit the poultry processing industry by highlighting the "healthier" nature of poultry over other meat products and possibly by giving U.S. firms an advantage because of previous experience with this type of regulation.[22]

Safety Issues

New regulations on handling, cooking, and inspecting poultry have been created in response to recent attention by the media to the poor standards of inspection and unsafe working conditions in the poultry processing industry. The enforcement of laws regulating labor conditions has included the imposition of fines and jail sentences on those responsible for the labor law violations.

Performance of firms with respect to these safety and health standards varies considerably across the industry. For example, a Reidsville, N.C., Equity Meats facility has above-standard programs for safety and health, while the Imperial Foods Hamlet operation had no safety program. The Hamlet facility burned in 1991 with locked exit doors and no sprinkler system, killing 25 workers and injuring 55 others.[23] Members of the management team were held responsible for the incident with fines and jail terms.

Technological Trends

The poultry processing industry is much more capital-intensive than in the past. With broilers now grown to a uniform size and shape, highly automated processing facilities have emerged to set new industry production and quality standards. Line speeds of 140 chickens per minute are normal for plants that are automated and efficient.[24] Other processing developments include feather-plucking technology and improved disinfectant bird bathing processes.

Technological advances are used in product development as well. A technological development currently being tested is a meat analogue product that is made from washed poultry meat. This is finely ground meat that is mixed with buffers that remove soluble protein fraction from the muscle tissue. The insoluble protein fraction that remains is formed and cooked into the designed shape. The resulting product is high in protein, low in fat, and can be flavored in such a way as to serve as a substitute product for other meats such as lobster and crab.[25]

Labor Unions

Labor unions such as Laborers' International Union of North America (LIUNA) and United Food and Commercial Workers International Union (UFCW) are organizing poultry facilities all across the South, with membership growing at a rapid rate. The large poultry processor, Tyson, has only 7 plants companywide, of 63, that are unionized. In contrast, Hudson Foods has 7 of its total of 14 plants unionized. Unionized labor could have a significant impact on the availability and cost of labor, which will drive up prices.

Other Products

An emerging substitute for chicken appears to be ostrich.[26] As chicken is viewed as the healthful alternative to red meat, ostrich surpasses it. Exhibit I outlines the nutritional information on various types of meat for a 3-oz serving. As ostrich has increased in availability, prices have been falling. If this trend continues, ostrich could compete directly with poultry as the healthful bird. Consumer reaction to ostrich has been less than favorable, but growers remain optimistic. According to growers, the biggest challenge on the horizon is finding a way to convince consumers to taste ostrich meat.

TYSON FOODS, INC.

Tyson Foods and its subsidiaries produce, market, and distribute various food products. These products serve the function of providing nourishment. Their product mix consists of value-enhanced poultry, fresh and frozen poultry, value-enhanced beef and pork products, fresh and frozen pork products,

EXHIBIT I

Comparison of Various Meat Products

Meat	Calories	Cholesterol	Fat
Ostrich	82.5	50.7 g	0.5 g
Chicken	140	73 g	3 g
Beef	240	77 g	15 g
Pork	275	84 g	19 g

value-enhanced seafood products, fresh and frozen seafood products, and flour and corn tortillas, chips, and other Mexican food–based products. Other products and processes include live swine, animal feed, and pet food. Value-enhanced products are ones that have added value in some fashion (deboned, seasoned, cooked, etc.) for a food-service firm or have been processed (patties, frankfurters, etc.) and packed for the retail shelf.

The vertically integrated operations consist of breeding and rearing chickens and hogs, harvesting seafood, and then processing, further processing, and marketing these food products and beef products.[27] Poultry production and subsequent processing, marketing, and distribution capture the largest amount of revenue generated for Tyson Foods. The breakdown of Tyson's Business Units in terms of sales mix for 1994 is shown in Figure 2.

Markets served by Tyson products, as outlined in Figure 3, include food service, retail, wholesale club, international, and other. Food-service customers include hotels, cafeterias, fast-food chains, and food-service distributors. Retail products on supermarket shelves include Tyson Holly Farms Fresh Chicken, a variety of Weaver brand products, Louis Kemp Crab and Lobster, and several ready-to-eat roasted chicken and "complete" meal kits. Annual sales are highlighted with gross margin in the following graph (Figure 4).

Company Characteristics

The following is a brief overview of Tyson Foods, Inc. The data are taken from the 1994 annual report year ending October 31, 1994, and from Moody's Company Data Report on Tyson Foods from October 1994.[28,29]

FIGURE 2

1994 Sales Mix (by Percentage)

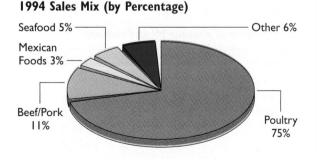

FIGURE 3

1994 Markets Served (by Percentage)

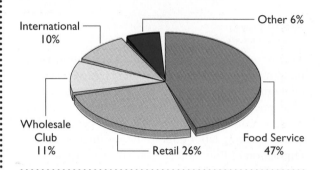

Tyson's was incorporated in Delaware in 1986 to change from the company originally incorporated in Arkansas on October 7, 1947. The company is headquartered in Springdale, Arkansas, with production and distribution operations as shown in Figure 5.

In addition, there are facilities or joint ventures in a number of international locations (Figure 6). The diverse international locations are due principally to operations of Trasgo and Cobb-Vantress. All company subsidiaries are listed in Exhibit J.

Exhibit K outlines Tyson's acquisition history and current subsidiaries.[30] As noted, Tyson has shifted the focus of its acquisition history. Prior to the 1990s, acquisition efforts were horizontal and vertical as a part of the poultry processing industry. From 1990 forward, Tyson purchases have consisted of diversification opportunities.

Sales for 1994 peaked at a historic $5,110,270,000. Due to a one-time special charge of $214 million (pretax) related to the assets of Arctic Alaska seafood operations, net income was a loss of $2,128,000. The special charge was taken in the third quarter of fiscal 1994 to write-down the goodwill and impaired asset values of the Arctic Alaska Fisheries portion of the Seafood Division. The write-down was necessary due to unanticipated production overcapacity, intense competition for a decreasing number of fish, shorter fishing seasons, and less production per vessel. Total assets are at $3,668,000,000, and long-term debts are $1,381,481,000.

Tyson, along with rest of the poultry processing industry, is heavily automated, especially in value-added further-processing facilities. Value-added

FIGURE 4

Tyson Foods, Inc., Sales (in Thousands)

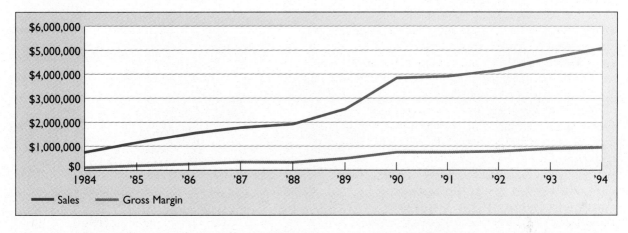

products, such as chicken nuggets sold to fast-food chains, require processing beyond whole-fryer commodity chicken. Additional processing is necessary to add ingredients and shape the products. Value-added further-processed products are those which are packed product ready for the retail consumer. Tyson frozen and children's meals are examples of these products.

One distinctive competence is Tyson's commitment to making the customer aware of each product's advantages. From the beginning, Tyson's target has been to convince customers that precooked products are more practical than dishes from scratch. In this way, Tyson has been instrumental in facilitating the market acceptance of the value-added products that provide today's growth.

FIGURE 5

Location of Tyson Foods' U.S. Operations

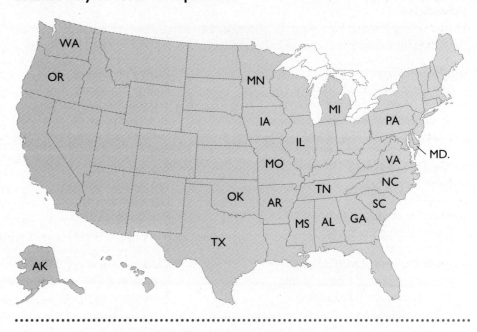

FIGURE 6
International Locations

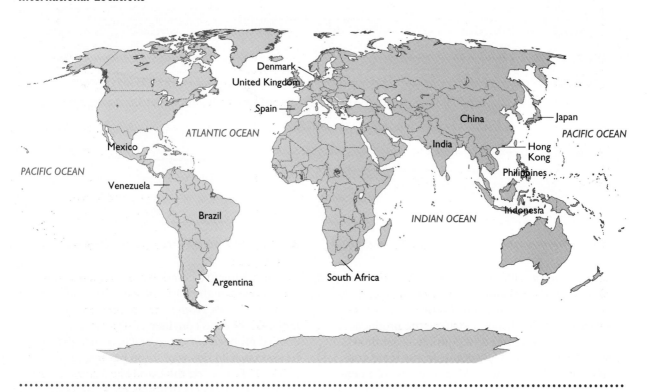

EXHIBIT J
Subsidiaries

Subsidiary	Description
AAFC Holdings, Ltd. (Canada)	Poultry processing
AAFC Intl., Inc. (Virgin Islands)	Poultry processing
Arctic Alaska Fisheries Corp.	Seafood division
Global Employment Services	Internal employment services
Southeast Health Plan of AR	Internal self-insured employee health plan
Trasgo, S.A. de C.V. (Mexico)	Poultry processor
Tyson Breeders, Inc.	Breeder flock
Tyson Export Sales	Export sales division
Tyson Farms, Inc.	Complex division
Tyson Foods, Inc.	Processing division
Tyson Holding Company	Acquisition division
Tyson Marketing	U.S. marketing division
Tyson Marketing, Ltd. (Canada)	Canadian marketing division
We Care Workers' Compensation	Internal workers' compensation
WLR Acquisition Corp. (failed)	Failed takeover division

EXHIBIT K
....
Acquisition History

Date	Acquired	Price	Description
March 1963	Garrett Poultry Co.	$300,000	Poultry producer
September 1966	Washington Creamery	$1,500,000	Poultry distributor
November 1967	Franz Foods Producers	53,196 shares, common stock	Poultry producer and processor
1969	Prospect Farms	*	Poultry producer
April 1972	Ocoma Foods	*	Poultry processor
July 1972	Krispy Kitchens	*	Poultry processor
August 1973	Cassady Broiler Co.	*	Poultry processor
February 1974	Vantress Pedigree	*	Genetic research and breeding farm
July 1978	Wilson Foods Poultry Division	*	Poultry producer and processor
January 1981	Honeybear Foods	$3,100,000 cash and stock	Poultry producer
1983	Mexican Original	*	Flour/corn tortillas
October 1984	90% of Valmac Industries	$70,723,815	Poultry producer and processor
December 1985	Heritage Valley Processing Division	$9,400,000	Poultry processor
May 1986	Lane Processing	$107,000,000	Poultry processor
July 1989	Holly Farms	$1.5 billion	Integrated poultry producer and processor
June 1991	Arkansas-California Livestock Company	100,000 shares class A stock	Beef and swine producer
October 1992	Arctic Alaska Fisheries	242,700,000 cash and stock	Seafood producer and processor
October 1992	Louis Kemp Seafood	$19,300,000	Seafood processor
November 1992	Swine plants	*	Swine processor
December 1992	Brandywine Foods	*	Swine processor
January 1994	Georges Food service	*	Beef processor for food service
April 1994	Majority ownership of Trasgo, S.A. de C.V.	*	Poultry producer and processor
July 1994	Culinary Foods	*	Processor of value-added specialty frozen foods
August 1994	Increased to 100% ownership of Cobb-Vantress	*	Supplier of breeding stock for broilers

*Some information was unavailable. Acquisitions were made in cash unless otherwise noted.

Tyson serves as the industry leader in technology and processing innovation and change. Tyson is very protective of its processes and discourages facility tours of any kind. Automated hatcheries and capital-intensive processing facilities highlight the technology commitment Tyson has made. The company's shift from internal combustion to electric forklifts is eliminating emissions problems. These forklifts operate in their processing plants and distribution facilities, saving Tyson a "significant" amount in maintenance costs.[31]

Tyson's corporate philosophy is one of growing shareholder value. The return on a $100 investment in Tyson Foods (including dividend reinvestment) for a 10-year period ending October 1, 1994, yielded 34.2 percent. The 10-year compounded annual growth rates for the period ending October 1, 1994, for three indices pale in comparison: 16.9 percent for the Dow Jones Industrial Average, 16.4 percent for the Wilshire 5000, and 14.6 for the Standard & Poor's 500. In addition, Tyson closed 1994 with record sales of $5.1 billion.

Tyson has chosen to focus on the needs of its customers, with the largest segment being the food-service industry. Tyson has responded positively with product and service improvements to customer concerns over labor shortages, food costs, and food safety. For example, food-service customers, such as institutional food, needed products that require the least amount of labor and time to prepare. Further-processed products have allowed Tyson to reduce these customers' preparation times and manpower needs.

Recent Tyson acquisitions include Culinary Foods and Georges Food Service, Inc., both of which are important to diversification by expanding sales and service in the growth market of the food-service industry. Tyson also purchased Upjohn's interest in Cobb-Vantress, becoming the sole owner. It is a world leader in supplying broiler breeding stock, with 90 percent of its sales outside the United States.

Tyson's philosophy is simple: to increase shareholder value. The strategy is to "segment, concentrate, and dominate." Through acquisitions and internal expansion, Tyson first segments the particular product market and then concentrates on technology innovation and acquisitions to dominate that market segment as the largest competitor. This vision of domination in the center-of-the-plate

food markets should place Tyson in a position of industry leader.

Examples of attempting this strategy through horizontal integration in poultry using acquisition are Holly Farms and WLR. Holly Farms was a competitor until Tyson won a bidding war with ConAgra over the acquisition of Holly Farms. Tyson failed in its recent bid for WLR, a competitor, but it has not stopped looking for other acquisitions.

Tyson's mission has evolved with the company. Prior to the 1970s, most of the company's sales were from commodity chicken, marketed and distributed through grocery store outlets. John Tyson maintained a production-oriented strategy during the early days. The 1950s and 1960s were a time for the company to focus on expanding production facilities and competitive technological innovation and to complete vertical integration in the broiler industry. In 1964, Don Tyson offered a signal to the company's changing focus. He concluded that the best way for the company to grow was to buy assets with profit-making potential at values under its own earnings per share. At first, these acquisitions were within the poultry industry; however, by the late 1980s and early 1990s, Tyson had expanded into related fields of swine and beef. By doing so, Tyson established a product diversification plan centered around new product introduction.[32] The 1970s were a time of growth and poultry processing integration. During this time, Tyson emerged, surviving the changes in the poultry business, as an industry leader in new product introduction. By 1979, the company had 24 specialty poultry products. In addition, the processing plants were industry leaders in technological improvements.

All along, Tyson has achieved the majority of its vertical integration through successful acquisitions. The company has been successful in gaining the cost and productivity savings and efficiencies out of these acquired concerns that are evident in their poultry processing concerns. According to Don Tyson, efficiency and improved product quality in processing are a direct result of putting killing facilities and processing plants together.[33] Through successful vertical integration, including ownership of feed producers, feed costs at Tyson account for only 40 percent of the production costs. Tyson maintains freezer/warehouse facilities that use an inventory system tied into the Springdale mainframe and subsequently linked to processing levels and activities. The status and location of any product are always available. This information integration is a skill the company continues to improve. In 1980, Tyson consolidated its further-processing efforts into a product line that consisted of chicken that was quick and easy to prepare. Presently Tyson holds the philosophy that change is necessary for improvement and dominance in the marketplace.

Value-Added Chain

Tyson has achieved success through vertical integration with timely acquisitions and synergistic results from these acquired businesses. Tyson has a level of vertical integration untouched even by other poultry companies. As noted previously in Exhibit H and Figure 1, seven levels are incorporated into the poultry processing business. First, Tyson has the foundation breeder flocks from which the breeder hens and roosters are obtained. Next, the hatchery supply flock is responsible for the broiler eggs. Then, in the controlled hatchery environment, the eggs hatch. The feed mills supply both the hatcheries and the grower farms. Next, the automated plants process the broilers. The warehouse and truck fleet system delivers the product either to the customer or to a further-processing facility. One exception to this model is the broiler growout farm. Broilers are typically grown by contract farmers that are in a strategic alliance with Tyson and are not part of the company's vertical integration. An additional level not shown is the recently completed purchase of Up-john's 50 percent stake in Cobb-Vantress, Inc. Cobb-Vantress is a genetic engineering firm where varieties of broilers are developed that will grow uniformly and quickly, which produces a bird that is genetically efficient.

An example of how Tyson has made these acquisitions work is present in Cobb-Vantress. Tyson is able to take the birds that are developed but not qualified for breeding stock and absorb them into Tyson's processing volume. Tyson is a primary but not sole customer of Cobb-Vantress at the present time. Tyson has been able to capitalize on the benefits of vertical integration and has negated much of the costs by creating a highly efficient operation along with greatly improving the quality of the product. Tyson facilities are top of the line and pris-

tine compared with the industry average and Tyson's closest competitors.

The complete vertical integration has developed an unparalleled advantage for Tyson in that it has controlled the majority of the factors that affect poultry prices and at the same time made them efficient and productive through automation. Complexes have a feed mill and processing facility, typically with a warehouse and freezer unit connected. Normally, growers are within a 60-mile radius of the facility. Exhibit K highlighted the company's acquisition history.[34]

Management

Several principal, long-time senior managers have been with Tyson since the early days in the 1960s. The members of general management are identified in Exhibit L.

Tyson, Tollett, and Wray are the key players within the company and have been together for over 30 years. Tollett and Wray are the balancing forces that complement Tyson's aggressive ideas for future growth. Tyson sets the corporate direction and long-term goals. These men are committed to Don Tyson's vision of "segment, concentrate, and dominate" as the way to increase shareholder wealth through acquisition.

There are 900 million shares of class A common stock authorized outstanding. These shares have one vote per share. Don Tyson, founder John Tyson's son, controls 99.9 percent of the 900 million shares of class B stock. These shares have 10 votes per share and can be converted to class A stock.

Growth

Growth at Tyson is a result of the desire to evolve into a company that produces chicken-based foods that are free from market swings. Regardless of the acquisition source, as long as it is within a select field of expertise, the company will try it if Tyson can grow it. "Segment, concentrate, and dominate" is the phrase that holds the company's focus. An example of segmentation is the growth of the poultry business. By initially segmenting the meat-processing concerns, Tyson focused on the poultry production and its efficiencies.

Recent success for Tyson has been based on a decreasing focus on commodity products and

EXHIBIT L
....
Tyson Management

Individual	Company History
Don Tyson	1952 to present—has been president and CEO, then chairman of the board and CEO, presently chairman of the board; will step down in April 1995, to become sr. chairman.
Leland Tollett	1961 to present—was vice president, then COO, then president and COO, presently vice chairman, president, and CEO; in April 1995, will become chairman.
Donald Wray	1959 to present—was vice president of marketing, then executive VP sales and marketing, then senior VP processing sales and marketing, then sr. VP sales and marketing and is presently COO.
Gerald Johnston	1970 to present—was vice president and presently is executive VP finance.
David Purtle	1971 to present—was group vice president operations and is currently senior VP operations.
Wayne Britt	1973 to present—was secretary/treasurer vice president, then treasurer VP, now senior VP of international sales and marketing.

movement into further-processed and value-added poultry. Tyson desires to meet customer wants with top-quality products. New product development is the one area of the company not subject to strict budgetary controls present throughout the corporation. Due to management's style of risk taking and financial support, the new product development groups have been able to introduce products with development times well below the industry average. The goal is to make Tyson a recognized household name with brand loyalty second to none.

New products have a relatively short and fairly predictable product life cycle. Tyson is aware of these factors and therefore has a range of products in development at different stages of the process. Tyson is committed to sticking with what it does best and to not competing with current customers. For example, it sold off its fast-food venture because Tyson would be in direct competition with one of its largest customer bases in the fast-food market.

The purchase of Prospect Farms in 1969 was Tyson's first attempt at growth into value-added products on a large scale. Tyson was able to enter into food-service products where sales were relatively uninfluenced by fluctuations in the chicken market. Consumer demand for value-added food-service products began to include the retail mar-

kets. Not all market-development efforts have succeeded. The Looney Tunes line of children's meals was pulled in 1994. This was done in part because the customers that the product was targeted for were too young to operate the microwave. However, top management accepts that when going for the advantage of reaching a new market first, there will be some missteps.

Tyson had the beginnings of a vertically integrated system in the late 1960s, which was just in time to watch firms fail during extreme market swings. Major acquisitions were made when firms were financially depressed or overextended. Companies were purchased when it was easier and cheaper to buy than to build. Tyson sticks close to what it knows and guides acquisitions with an axiom of "never acquire a business you don't know how to run."[35] For the most part, these purchases have facilitated dramatic growth in sales.

Not all acquisition targets are success stories. The 1994 attempt to acquire WLR resulted in failure due to WLR's purchase of Cuddy Farms (turkey), which pushed WLR above the limit in terms of cost for Tyson. In addition, not all purchases have led to increased profits. The Arctic Alaska Fisheries acquisition resulted in a $191 million special charge for excess of investment over net assets acquired in addition to the $23 million for impaired long-lived assets. These charges have resulted in a special charge, after tax, of $205 million, or $1.38 per share, in 1994. In addition, government restrictions and legal troubles are on the horizon for Arctic. Seafood is a related product to Tyson's core business of poultry; therefore, this business unit, as problematic as it seems, is a part of the company's growth strategy. Management has taken an early and preemptive financial charge in the hope of initializing a recovery of the seafood company.

In concert with the corporate strategy of "segment, concentrate, dominate," marketing has specific sales approaches for a wide range of products and customers. In food service, for example, 23 purchase points have been identified—separate markets being served that each require a different marketing effort. These purchase points include food-service and grocery purchase points for commodity, processed, and further processed products.

As a function of operations, Tyson has a staff of employees that work closely with independent food-service distributors and brokers. The company helps train these individuals to sell Tyson products and know every detail about each product at no charge to the distributor. In addition, Tyson is one of only a few companies that offers food-service customers such as restaurants 3-year contracts with price protection.

Tyson will not introduce a product or enter a market if a company using Tyson products is already established there. Tyson is not in the food-service industry, since the largest portion of its sales go to that industry. Food-service companies include hotels, cafeterias, most fast-food chains, and major food-service distributors. The food-service distributors are the intermediaries for smaller institutional customers. The only rule is to respect the customer. This noncompete attitude has been a key to the successfulness of the company's growth through integration. However, Tyson will not necessarily abandon its established distribution methods (customers) when a current competitor becomes a customer. For example, the chicken-based frozen entrees market is not a policy conflict. Tyson marketed its own brand of frozen entrees before it began providing chicken ingredients to other companies for their frozen dinners.

Tyson Foods has made purchases in the swine and beef businesses. The swine operation is the largest hog farming operation in the country. Tyson has attributed increased efficiencies by using the poultry freezer and distribution system in the swine production.

Differentiation

Tyson's competitive strategy has shifted over the years from low cost to differentiation and low cost.

EXHIBIT M

ConAgra

Year	Operating Margin	Net Profit Margin	Return on Assets	Return on Equity	Current Ratio	Quick Ratio
1994	5.7%	1.9%			1.06	0.48
1993	5.6%	1.8%	2.21%	17.2%	1.08	0.48
1992	5.7%	1.8%	2.15%	16.7%	1.05	0.48
1991	5.3%	1.6%	4.06%	20.1%	1.1	
1990	4.1%	1.5%	5.36%	22.4%	1.1	
1989	4.8%	1.7%	5.27%	22.5%	1.1	
1988	4.1%	1.6%	6.22%	20.1%		
1987	4.4%	1.7%				
1986	4.6%	1.8%				
1985	4.4%	1.7%				
1984	4.1%	2.0%				

EXHIBIT N
· · · · · · · · · · · · · · · ·
Hudson Foods

Year	Operating Margin	Net Profit Margin	Return on Assets	Return on Equity	Current Ratio	Quick Ratio
1994	7.1%	2.6%			1.87	0.69
1993	6.2%	1.7%			2.22	0.82
1992	3.2%	0.3%			1.61	0.66
1991	4.9%	1.1%	2.6%	6.5%		
1990	4.7%	1.3%	3.0%	7.3%		
1989	9.0%	3.7%	8.1%	23.6%		
1988	2.7%	0.7%	1.4%	4.9%		
1987	8.6%	3.0%	5.7%	20.8%		
1986	13.7%	6.0%				
1985	12.0%	4.6%				

This strategy has been consistent with the market and demand shifts. The strategy of differentiation is in line with the "segment, concentrate, and dominate" theme through the development of additional markets where the synergism found in the integration of the poultry processing industry can be enjoyed. Tyson competed on price in the 1950s when the main products were commodity chicken. Now Tyson's products are increasingly further-processed and value-added by the company through the increased processing (items that are higher priced with larger margins). However, Tyson's vertical integration has afforded it the advantage of also being the lowest-cost producer of value-added products.

EXHIBIT O
· · · · · · · · · · · · · · · ·
Tyson

Year	Operating Margin	Net Profit Margin	Return on Assets	Return on Equity	Current Ratio	Quick Ratio	Debt Ratio	Asset Turnover
1994	11.7%	4.0%	−58%	NEG	2.34	0.94	0.40	1.39
1993	11.7%	3.8%	5.5%	13.3%	1.54	0.26		1.45
1992	11.5%	3.9%	6.1%	16.4%	1.46	0.33		1.59
1991	12.0%	3.7%	5.8%	17.7%	1.20			1.48
1990	11.8%	3.1%	4.6%	18.1%	1.21			1.53
1989	11.6%	4.0%	11.3%	22.5%	1.60			0.98
1988	10.0%	3.4%	10.1%	23.9%	2.40			2.18
1987	11.5%	3.8%	8.9%	25.1%	1.23			2.21
1986	10.5%	3.3%	6.6%	24.7%	1.20			1.98
1985	10.5%	3.1%	7.4%	22.5%	1.23			2.41
1984	7.7%	2.4%	6.1%	21.5%	1.34			2.52

FIGURE 7

Operating Margin

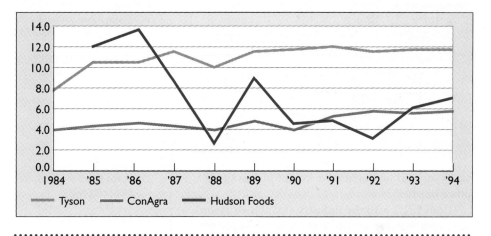

Financial Information

The brand recognition of "quality" in Tyson products is its differentiation angle. In addition to Tyson's channel dominance and low-cost advantage, this differentiation into convenience chicken products has introduced another barrier to entry for competitors. The initial investment for a new competitor would be enormous. Potential problems arise when competitors such as ConAgra have the resources to compete and copy Tyson's products. ConAgra and Tyson have a long-standing rivalry that discourages other companies from entering the poultry market.

With the exception of the special charge in 1994, Tyson's financial data indicate that not only is it a leading producer, it is a leading firm in terms of financial strength. Tyson's profitability ratios, in the following graphs and exhibits (Exhibits M, N, and O and Figures 7 and 8), are contrasted with those of two competitors: ConAgra and Hudson Foods. As a performance measure of profitability, operating margin attempts to standardize sales. Net profit margin also indicates the advantage of integration

FIGURE 8

Net Profit Margin

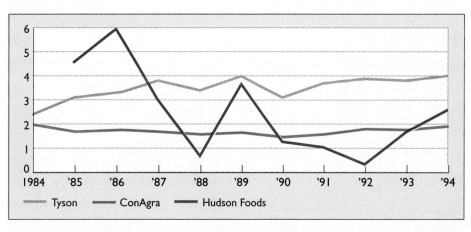

EXHIBIT P
. . . .
Industry Ratios

Industry (SIC 2015), 1993	Upper Quartile	Median	Lower Quartile
Quick ratio	1.1	0.8	.05
Current ratio	2.2	1.4	1.1
ROA	10.2	5.6	1.4
ROE	24.6	10.9	3.4

for Tyson and highlights the weight of ConAgra's other businesses.

Compared with the industry (Exhibit P) Tyson's net profit margins are on target, since the industry net profit is 2.6 percent (1993).[36] Return on equity is in the median range for the industry.

Endnotes

1. Tyson Foods, "Tyson Foods Reports Record First Quarter Sales and Earnings: First Quarter 1995 Operating Results," January 30, 1995.
2. Schwartz, M., *Tyson, From Farm to Market.* Fayetteville, AR: University of Arkansas Press, 1991.
3. Scanes, C. G., and M. Lilburn, "Poultry Production," in *Encyclopedia of Agricultural Science,* Vol. 3. New York: Academic Press, 1994, pp. 441–450.
4. Kemp, G., "International Poultry Show: Poultry Marketing and Packaging Trends," *Quick Frozen Goods International* 35(4), 1994, p. 95.
5. Scanes and Lilburn, *op. cit.*
6. U. S. Industrial Outlook 1994—Other Consumer Nondurables.
7. *Ibid.*
8. *Ibid.*
9. U.S. Statistics, *Dairy and Poultry Statistics,* Washington, DC: GPO, 1993.
10. *Ibid.*
11. Tyson Foods, *ValueLine Investment Survey,* Vol. I, No. 10, Part 3. New York: Value Line Publishing, 1994, p. 1489.
12. Schwartz, *op. cit.*
13. Poultry and Egg Marketing from National Broiler Council, as cited in Gale Research, Inc., Market Share Reporter, 1995.
14. Scanes and Lilburn, *op. cit.*
15. *Ibid.*
16. *Ibid.*
17. *Ibid.*
18. *Ibid.*
19. *Ibid.*
20. *Ibid.*
21. Tyson Foods Company Report, August 1994. Source: Stephen's, Inc.
22. U.S. Industrial Outlook, 1994.
23. PRNewswire, October 18, 1994. "Laborers' Union Hams It Up in North Carolina," p. 1018DC019.
24. *Ibid.*
25. Sams, A. R., "Poultry Processing and Products," in *Encyclopedia of Agricultural Science,* Vol. 3. New York Academic Press, 1994, pp. 433–440.
26. McCarrell, P., "Ostrich Breeders Confront Chicken-and-Egg Situation," *Puget Sound Business Journal,* August 26, 1994.
27. Moody's, Moody's Company Data Report on Tyson Foods, Inc., 1995.
28. Tyson's 1994 annual report.
29. Moody's, *op. cit.*
30. Porter, M. E., *Competitive Advantage.* New York: Free Press, 1985.
31. Rice, J., "Electric Forklifts Slash Maintenance Costs at Tyson; Handle 3000-lb. Loads over Extended Lift Cycles," *Food Processing* 54(6), 1993, pp. 123–125.
32. Schwartz, *op. cit.*
33. *Ibid.*
34. Moody's, *op. cit.*
35. Schwartz, *op. cit.*
36. S&P Industry Surveys, 1994.

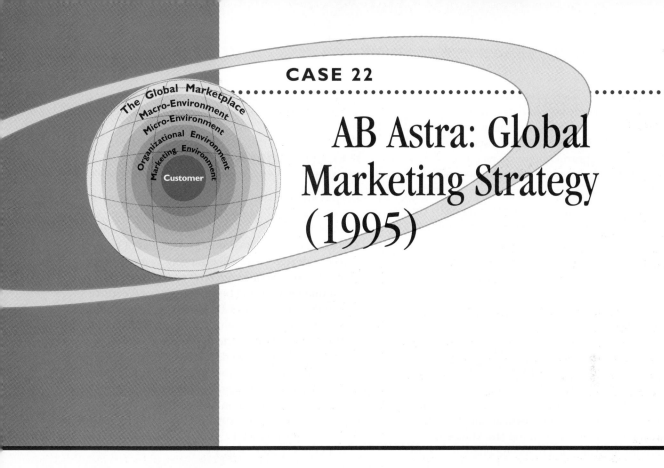

CASE 22

AB Astra: Global Marketing Strategy (1995)

This case was prepared by Julian W. Vincze, Professor of Marketing, Crummer Graduate School of Business, Rollins College.

HISTORY

Astra, a Swedish pharmaceutical company founded in 1913, grew modestly until the 1930s. At that time, the company's research program, which was started in the early 1930s, began to yield a series of original pharmaceutical products. Because of the unique aspects of these new products, Astra's revenues increased, and growth accelerated. During the 1950s and 1960s, Astra was able to build an international network of subsidiaries, agents, and licensees.[1] Thus, by the 1970s, Astra had become a player in the global pharmaceutical industry. During this same growth period, the company's operations had expanded to include a number of nonpharmaceutical areas. Then, in the late 1970s, Astra decided to reconcentrate its operations on pharmaceutical products. This reconcentration re-

quired the disposal of virtually all the nonpharmaceutical subsidiaries. By the late 1980s, Astra had grown to become the largest Nordic pharmaceutical company and had concentrated both research and manufacturing operations in Sweden. Although Sweden accounted for nearly 85 percent of 1987 sales revenues, Astra remained a global player servicing approximately 120 other international markets. When Hakan Mogren became chief executive officer of Astra in 1988 after running Sweden's largest candy company, he took over a company that by many measures had just completed an impressive 10-year period of rapid growth. Indicative of this growth spurt was a special attachment to the 1987 Annual Report entitled, "Astra 1978–1987: Growth with Quality." This attachment detailed Astra's rapid growth and profitability trends that were unparalleled in the history of the company. The summary to the five-page report read as follows:

> Astra, with its strong economic growth during the period 1978–1987, exemplifies a growth company in the classical sense of the term—a company that grows through successful marketing of its own innovations, practically without

the help of new share issues. Astra's growth potential is closely linked to its R&D investments—investments whose value is not reflected in the traditional financial statements.

These facts provide an overall picture of Astra's strong industrial growth—growth with quality.

- Astra's real growth in sales amounted during the period to an average of 7 percent annually (including divested operation, 3 percent annually).

- Despite an unchanged total number of personnel on the whole, the number of employees engaged in R&D increased by nearly 700.

- The rapid earnings trend resulted in real growth of stockholders' equity by 13 percent annually.

- The theoretical value of Astra's R&D investments amounted at year-end 1987 to about 3.5 billion Swedish kronor.

- Even if the value of R&D investments is added to stockholders' equity, Astra attained a stable real return of 12 percent on stockholders' equity annually, which may be compared with

the real rate of interest of 4 percent per year on Swedish bonds.[2]

HAKAN MOGREN TAKES CHARGE

Despite the unparalleled 10-year period of growth reported in 1987, when Hakan Mogren became CEO in 1988, he realized that Astra to a large extent had lost total control of its products. This loss of control had occurred by Astra's licensing away many of its marketing rights. Dr. Mogren reversed this passive marketing strategy and began buying back control of Astra's drug products. Dr. Mogren's change in marketing strategy had a dramatic impact. It resulted in sales quadrupling over the period 1988–1994 to reach the 28 billion Swedish kronor level in 1994 (a 24 percent increase to follow a 1993 surge of 45 percent), while pretax profits during the same period rose from 1.5 billion to 9.62 billion kronor (US$1.33 billion). The 1994 pretax profit increase of 23 percent followed a 1993 jump of 53 percent. (See Exhibit A for details.)

EXHIBIT A
The Profit Picture (in billions of Swedish kronor)

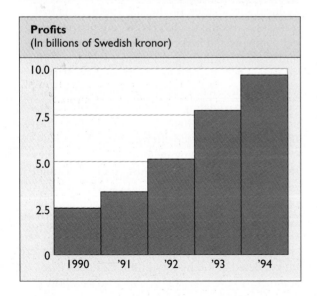

Profits
(In billions of Swedish kronor)

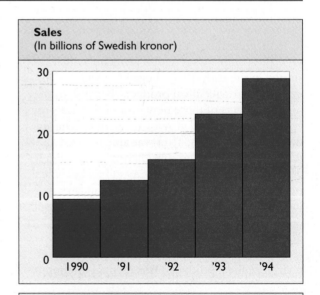

Sales
(In billions of Swedish kronor)

MAJOR PRESCRIPTION DRUGS:
Losec (antiulcer), Pulmicort Turbuhaler (antiasthma), Plendil (hypertension), Seloken (cardiovascular), Xylocaine (anesthetic)

R&D Expenditures for Growth

The results achieved were even more impressive when research and development (R&D) expenditures during the same period were taken into consideration. Astra, unlike many competitors in global pharmaceuticals, had continued to invest heavily in R&D even though depressed economic conditions existed in many of its global markets during the late 1980s and early 1990s. During much of this time, Astra's R&D expenditures were rising, on average, 25 percent a year. Astra maintained operations at three research laboratories in Sweden and one in Bangalore, India.

Often, with increased R&D expenditures, pharmaceutical firms experience a temporary lull in sales and profit growth. Yet Astra's results indicated that sales had climbed even faster than R&D expenditures, so Astra's percentage of sales spent on R&D had dropped to about 16 percent in 1994. And profit margins also had increased, thereby helping to ensure the flow of future products from R&D efforts. Peter Laing, a London-based drug analyst at Salomon Brothers, Inc., predicted "further development of products already in the market alone means that Astra is likely to remain one of the fastest-growing companies in the industry for at least the next 5 years."[3] For example, Mr. Laing forecasted a doubling of total Losec (ulcer drug) sales by 1998. While Dr. Mogren explained that he did not wish to specify in which product areas Astra expected the next big seller, one of the areas ought to be diseases of the central nervous system, where Astra had been less successful. The company had to withdraw two of its products, Zelmid and Roxiam, because of side effects.

Before coming to Astra, Dr. Mogren had worked in both the research and marketing fields. His marketing background perhaps turned out to be his most important asset, for he believed that Astra would not have been as successful if he had not changed its marketing strategy to take charge of its own sales instead of selling on license. Furthermore, Dr. Mogren did not acknowledge a dividing line between organic chemistry and biotechnology. While there were very few pure biotechnology companies, all drug companies used biotechnology as a tool. Astra had a large number of projects where biotechnology played a part. According to Mr. Mogren, Astra, in comparison with other pharmaceutical companies, had a good product balance. The strongest-selling products for Astra were the stomach/intestinal pharmaceuticals (gastrointestinal), which were supported by successful products in the other main pharmaceutical product areas of cardiovascular and respiratory drugs. For example, Astra's second-largest-selling product was the asthma preparation Pulmicort. Even local anesthetics, which constituted Astra's oldest product area, were growing by about 10 percent per year.[4]

REGAINING MARKETING CONTROL

Dr. Mogren believed that the modified marketing strategy had resulted in increased control over Astra's marketing of its own products and that it was the key factor that had lead to Astra's latest successful growth. Recent moves in the Japanese, European, and U.S. markets exemplified this changed marketing strategy of direct marketing control.

Japanese Market

In Japan, Astra had a long-standing joint venture with Fujisawa Pharmaceutical Co. to market all of Astra's products. Fujisawa was the operating partner of the joint venture, and Astra had become increasingly unhappy with the relatively low market shares being achieved. For example, Losec's Japanese market share had remained at only a fraction of the drug's penetration of about 40 percent in Europe and 20 percent in the United States. In addition, Astra found that Fujisawa had a conflicting licensing deal with the British company Fisons PLC so that Pulmicort, Astra's flagship antiasthmatic medication, had not been made available in the Japan marketplace. Responding to these concerns, Astra in 1994 assumed management control of the joint venture. In order to prepare for a marketing blitz in Japan after the takeover, Astra also bought back Japanese marketing rights to their successful hypertension drug Plendil, which they had previously sold to rival Ciba-Geigy AG.[5] Therefore, when the 1994 marketing blitz in Japan occurred, both Pulmicort and Plendil could be highlighted and received synergistic impact. However, Astra did not limit its aggressive marketing to Japan.

European Markets

Another initiative taken by Astra with a Japanese company related to a joint development program started in early 1994 with Takeda. The drug, TCV-

116, was discovered by Takeda and was one of the angiotension II antagonists. Drugs in this category are thought to be of benefit in the treatment of cardiovascular conditions, including congestive heart failure and hypertension. This collaborative agreement had given Astra the exclusive right to market TCV-116 in South Africa, Sweden, Norway, the Netherlands, Finland, Denmark, Belgium, and New Zealand. Moreover, Astra was given additional co-marketing rights for the rest of the world, excepting only the Japanese market.[6]

In another 1994 agreement, Astra and Mitsubishi Kasei Corporation agreed to joint development in Europe of Mitsubishi drugs. Mitsubishi Kasei licensed certain drugs to Astra for development and marketing in the European market. The agreement covered drugs developed by Mitsubishi Kasei within 7 years and was reported to include Mitsubishi Kasei's antiplatelet agents, its antihyperlipidemia agent, and its radical scavenger, all of which were in the clinical testing phase of development. The agreement covered all of Europe, including eastern Europe and Russia.[7]

U.S. Market

In the highly competitive U.S. market, Astra had been shielded by a long-time licensing agreement with Merck & Co. Under the agreement, Merck had operated a joint venture organization that held licenses for the U.S. marketing rights of most of Astra's products. However, this licensing pact had a clause that stipulated that once Merck's sales of Astra products reached a certain trigger level, then a separate new company could be formed to take over the marketing of those Astra products in the United States. Astra acted on this clause, and the new company, Astra Merck, Inc. (AMI), was created in 1994. Astra would no longer receive royalties for the antiulcer agent Prilosec, the vasodilator drug Plendil, or the cardiac arrhythmia treatment Tonocard. Instead, profits from AMI would be split equally between Merck and Astra.[8] In order to complete this transaction, Astra was required to pay Merck US$820 million for a 50 percent interest in AMI.[9] Astra financed the deal from its cash holdings, which were estimated to be around 1 billion U.K. pounds at the end of 1994.[10] Dr. Mogren insisted that "the AMI organization is extremely anxious to be independent from Merck."[11] As an example of this desire for independence, he noted the pact between AMI and Marion Merrill Dow,

Inc. This agreement was to copromote Losec and replaced a similar arrangement between Astra and Merck. Dr. Mogren said AMI management made the change because "Marion Merrill Dow can do it better and cheaper—and they're hungrier than Merck."[12]

Strategic Cooperation/Competition

The creation of AMI and its subsequent operations increased the competition between Merck and Astra in many ways. For example, prior to the establishment of AMI, Astra had previewed all its future products for Merck executives. This included providing Merck with progress reports on all Astra drugs under development. This type of direct communication between Astra and Merck's research staffs would no longer occur. Since all new products for AMI would in the future come from Astra, intense communication between the sales units of AMI and Astra would become necessary. Dr. Mogren said, "No one from Merck can look into our new products. So you can assume that people in AMI will work more closely with us than Merck."[13]

Astra's Separate U.S. Unit

Astra also had a separate, wholly owned U.S. unit that marketed its own as well as other manufacturers' local anesthetics products in the U.S. marketplace. Future plans were for this unit to eventually also market Astra's portfolio of respiratory drugs (both of which were excluded from the original licensing accord with Merck). Asked about the possibility of a future merger between AMI and this Astra-owned U.S. unit, Dr. Mogren answered by noting that Astra's own sales unit "should have sales increases for the next 8 years if we succeed with introduction of the respiratory product line. We want them to really concentrate on the therapeutic area, while AMI concentrates on our cardiovascular and gastrointestinal product lines." However, he acknowledged that it was still not clear "what might happen" in 8 years, "and we're free to negotiate with Merck or propose different alternatives for AMI later on. But it's not something we're worrying about now; the current AMI arrangement is fine for the time being."[14]

FDA Reviews

Astra's wholly owned sales unit also had been busy trying to secure the Food and Drug Administration's

(FDA's) permission to market its respiratory products. In early 1994 it had submitted an application for Pulmicort, a so-called corticosteroid delivered through Astra's patented dry-powder inhaler called Turbuhaler. However, the FDA review had not gone smoothly and remained pending while awaiting Astra's submission of further dose-uniformity data. Dry-powder inhalers had been growing in popularity among asthma patients. Industry observers believed that Astra had a significant lead over the competition and could establish the Turbuhaler in the U.S. market before rival devices could reach the market. However, if FDA approval were to be delayed into 1996, this market lead would be eroded. Nevertheless, the delay in Turbuhaler approval by the FDA was likely to only reinforce Dr. Mogren's conviction that Astra needed to focus on a small number of therapeutic areas. Skeptical about the wave of drug industry mergers announced in late 1994 and early 1995, Dr. Mogren said: "Our motto has always remained to get better in areas where we already are good. We're focusing on four therapeutic areas and are looking for new ones to enter, with the prerequisite that we have some really innovative [scientific] approach to offer."[15]

THE FUTURE

What does the future hold for Astra? Early in 1995, most industry observers seemed loath to argue with Astra's apparent success. However, early 1995 also had seen the merger or acquisition of several global players in the pharmaceutical industry. Was Astra large enough, when ranked as the twentieth largest pharmaceutical company, to withstand these consolidation forces? Or did it have to get into the acquisition mode to preserve its ranking as the fastest-growing pharmaceutical firm in the world?

Questions

1. Explain in detail what the change was in Astra's marketing strategy initiated by Dr. Mogren.

2. Did Dr. Mogren change any other components of Astra's corporate strategy? For example, did Astra attempt to be the low-cost producer in the industry? Did Astra compete on the basis of customer service?

3. What are Astra's competitive strengths and key success factors?

4. Was Astra's growth in the 1990s due only to the changed marketing strategy? If you believe that there were other factors that contributed to Astra's growth, what were those factors, and how did they affect revenue or profit growth?

5. What was Astra's product strategy component of its marketing mix? How did R&D fit into Astra's product strategy?

6. Does Dr. Mogren's statement at the end of the case—"Our motto has always remained to get better in areas where we already are good. We're focusing on four therapeutic areas and are looking for new ones to enter, with the prerequisite that we have some really innovative [scientific] approach to offer"—affect Astra's marketing strategy?

7. What are some of the difficulties faced by Astra as a company located in Sweden when competing with other players in the global pharmaceutical industry?

Endnotes

1. David F. Hawkins, "AB Astra," Publishing Division, Harvard Business School, 1992.
2. 1987 Annual Report, AB Astra.
3. Stephen D. Moore, "Aggressive Marketing Changes Put Astra on Fast Track," *Wall Street Journal,* February 27, 1995.
4. "Sweden: Astra Head Confident about Future Growth," *European Chemical News,* November 28, 1994.
5. Stephen D. Moore, "Aggressive Marketing Changes Put Astra on Fast Track," *Wall Street Journal,* February 27, 1995.
6. "Astra/Takeda Select Drug for Joint Project," *Chemical Business Newsbase,* December 16, 1994.
7. "Japan: Mitsubishi Teams up with Astra for Drug Development," *Chemical Business Newsbase,* May 12, 1994.
8. "Sweden: Astra-Merck Deal Opens U.S. Market," *Chemical Business Newsbase,* November 21, 1994.
9. "Sweden: Merck, Astra Set Ulcer Drug Pact," *Chemical Marketing Reporter,* November 7, 1994.
10. Mark Milner, "Swedish Drugs Firm Sets up U.S. Market Link with Pound 500 Million Deal," *The Guardian,* November 2, 1994.
11. Stephen D. Moore, "Aggressive Marketing Changes Put Astra on Fast Track," *Wall Street Journal,* February 27, 1995.
12. *Ibid.*
13. *Ibid.*
14. *Ibid.*
15. *Ibid.*

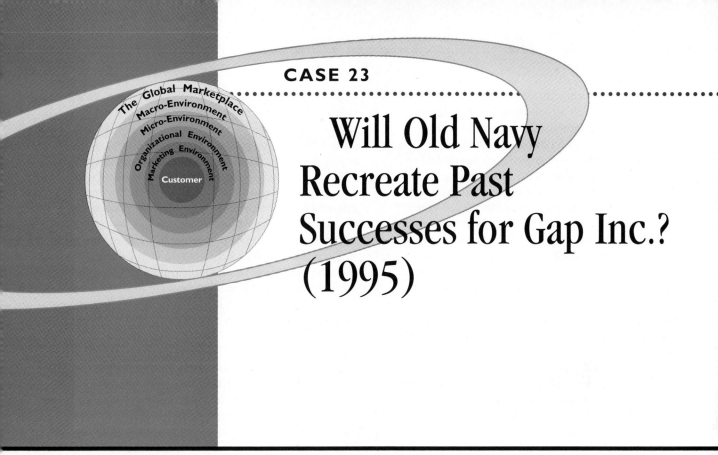

This case was prepared by Julian W. Vincze, Professor of Marketing, Crummer Graduate School of Business, Rollins College.

In the multi-billion-dollar apparel market, Gap Inc. recorded more than $3 billion in sales in 1994 through its various stores: the Gap, Banana Republic, GapKids, BabyGap, Gap Warehouse, and Gap Shoes. Increasingly, however, it had seen competitors take what was basically known as the Gap "look" and sell it for less to a mass middle market that did not want to pay for, or could not afford, the prices for Gap clothes.[1] In the United States there are 754 Gap, 178 Banana Republic, 283 GapKids, and 45 Gap Warehouse stores. Internationally, there are 103 Gap and GapKids stores.[2]

GAP'S HISTORY

Gap Inc. has headquarters located on the waterfront at the eastern edge of San Francisco Bay,

This case is intended to be used as a basis for class discussion rather than as an illustration of either effective or ineffective handling of the situation. This case was prepared by Julian W. Vincze, Crummer Graduate School of Business, Rollins College. Copyright © 2000 Julian W. Vincze.

where the fog rarely reaches. From the modest white Gap building there is a clear view across the blue-gray waters of the bay. Inside the building you find few people in the art gallery ambience of the Gap cafeteria. Instead, you find most of the people who are working their 60-hour weeks in their blond-wood offices drinking coffee out of shining blue Gap mugs, wearing informal Gap cotton at their white desks. Gap Inc. is sufficiently big (second only to Levi's in sales) and unusual (making big profits over the last few years) to have become a major international competitor. Established in 1969 by Donald Fisher, when he couldn't exchange a pair of Levi's at a San Francisco department store, Gap's name is purported to be based on a remark that his wife made about "the generation gap." Mr. Fisher opened his first store, selling flared Levi's, records, and tapes. However, with the hippie wave receding, he quickly dropped the music and began advertising "Four Tons of Levi's."[3] In the next 15 years, Gap stores spread across the United States, but by the seventies and early eighties, the Gap was filled with terry-cloth polo shirts, chocolate-colored fatigues, and T-shirts with zip-off sleeves, squeezed onto pipe rails. "Fall into the Gap" jingled television and radio advertisements, and people did—but lured by almost continuous discounting.[4]

The Gap's explosive growth can be traced to the 1983 hiring of Millard "Mickey" Drexler, who was given the task of taking the Gap upmarket when 1984's profits fell 43 percent. Mickey asked the company's designers why they never wore Gap clothes themselves. "We don't like them. They're junk," said Patricia DeRosa, now executive vice-president.[5] Mr. Drexler liquidated the "junk" and put new clothes on tables in the stores so that customers could easily touch them. The new stock was clever—both old-fashioned ("classic" American styling) and daring (rejecting conspicuous consumption for what the *Los Angeles Times* called "stealth wealth").[6] And the marketing was even more clever: using glitzy stars like Kim Basinger to sell ascetic white T-shirts. After this, Mickey just repeated the winning formula. As in a lot of family businesses (the Fisher family owned more than a third of the shares), decisions were highly centralized (and still are), with standard store layouts dictated to managers from headquarters every few months. Mickey Drexler was constantly visiting stores to ensure compliance to policies. For example, all customers were supposed to be subjected to the GAP-ACT. The GAP-ACT was a process that involved the following six steps: Step 1: Greet customers within 30 seconds; Step 2: Approach and ask, "Can I help you?"; Step 3: Provide product information; Step 4: Add-ons: Suggest more buys; Step 5. Close sale honestly; if it looks bad, say so; Step 6. Thank customer.

By the early nineties, the Gap was the success story of the decade. It had become almost totally self-sufficient, controlling design, manufacturing, marketing, and sales. The Gap did not franchise. All stores were company owned and operated. Stock prices peaked in early 1992, and Mr. Fisher, in an uncharacteristically immodest moment, predicted breakneck growth for another 5 years. But profits fell in 1992, to $211 million from the prior year's $230 million, and more important, sales per square foot—retail's benchmark—stalled, after rising at least 10 percent each year since the mid-eighties.[7] In reaction to this setback, the Gap re-launched Banana Republic—acquired in 1983 as a more cutting-edge complement to existing Gap stores. This re-launch of Banana Republic was viewed by many as simply a re-emphasis of Banana Republic's operations, which had been somewhat ignored by senior executives at Gap during the late 1980s and early 1990s—but sales expectations weren't reached. "It has a really unsavory name," said Alan Millstein, a New York fashion retail analyst, "and it's just a higher-priced Gap."[8] By 1993, as Gap stores continued to falter, with profits down an additional 8% in the first quarter and 24% in the second, Mr. Fisher said: "We are not pleased with these results." And neither was Wall Street, where Gap's share price had dropped 50 percent from its 1992 high. Mr. Millstein said: "Their salad days are over."[9]

Gap Uncool

For Christmas of 1994, 17-year-old Lucas Swanson told his family, "Please, no more gift certificates from the Gap."[10] Was he tired of Jeans? Sick of T-shirts? Not really! The high-school senior, wearing exactly that clothing, said he purchased his clothing from a secondhand store. "I just don't dig the Gap anymore," he said.[11] The Gap, which once offered the epitome of cool, with basic T-shirts and jeans that looked like designer clothing without the arrogance—no fancy labels, logos, or inflated price tags—may be suffering a "Gap-lash" of sorts. Once of enormous appeal for the middle-class and middle-aged, Gap attire and advertising have become the butt of jokes and the target of resentment by teens and Generation Xers. Hugh Gallagher, a writer of satire for Los Angeles's *Grand Royal* magazine, said: "Their clothes promote a straight, white, lame lifestyle, which is just how THEY [big government] want us to be."[12] Comic Ellen DeGeneres, of the popular ABC TV program "Ellen," in the ultimate put-down, calls her navy-and-khaki-clad neighbors "Gaps."[13]

Gap Inc. until recently could ignore comedic put-downs and snide essays in trendy publications because many on Wall Street had bet it would have strong, double-digit profit growth into the next century. But could Gap be losing its edge with its more important clientele: shoppers under age 30? In Leo Burnett Co.'s biannual "What's hot among kids" survey for 1992, about 90 percent of teens said Gap clothes were "cool," but by the summer of 1993, that figure was 83 percent, falling to 75 percent by winter of 1993 and to 66 percent in the two 1994 surveys. Moreover, sales at Gap stores open for at least a year increased by only 1 percent in 1994.[14] To Stanford University senior Jerry Chang, Gap's appeal is its simple, casual clothing. But he said: "I think the Gap has dropped out of mainstream college kids' lives. The Gap relies too much on its name and hasn't given us new and fresh styles."[15] Meanwhile, 24-year-old Brannigan Waycott, who remembers Gap stores in the 1980s as carrying a wider variety of clothes, said now "They're trying to appeal to a larger mass of people, like homogenized cheese or something."[16]

In fact, some industry observers believe the Gap has been struggling for the past 3 years to offer a more effective advertising and merchandise mix. They note that Gap cited "mixed reviews" when pulling the plug early on 1992's TV ad campaign featuring New York poet Max Blagg rambling about "jeans/that fit like a glove/like a lover coming back for more." Gap's 1993 print ad copy, "Commingle. It's how you marshal every fact and contraction, how you make the universe of choice suit you. Classic Gap, for individuals," was judged to be incomprehensible by many customers. Mickey Drexler has responded by stocking more trendy, fashionable items like leather vests and long crepe skirts. "We can't afford not to change," he said at the time.[17] To some industry observers, however, it is too late. The Gap has become part of the establishment and fair game for mockery. The Gap, once considered brilliant for convincing customers that unobtrusive clothing actually illuminated a person's unique look, in 1994 moved a group of seven New York artists to create an anti-Gap art exhibit. One of them, 23-year-old Daniel McDonald, declared, the Gap is "promoting individuality as a tool to sell totally banal clothing."[18]

Still Cool in the United Kingdom

After 6 years in the United Kingdom, little has disturbed the Gap's smooth expansion; there are 40 stores, and each sells more (of exactly the same) clothes than those back in America. But it's a very defensive empire, one that has a minimal press office in its most successful outpost—Britain—and which avoids dealing with the fashion press. Despite its apparently relentless growth and its famed in-house advertising, Gap Inc. remains secretive. "We rarely do any interviews at all," said Richard Crisman, the company's only spokesman located in Britain.[19] "The Gap is still very cool," said *GQ* fashion editor Jo Levin. "People enjoy carrying Gap car-

rier bags. Almost everyone I know shops at the Gap for something."[20]

ESTABLISHING MASS-MERCHANDISING DIVISION

The Gap first entered the mass-merchandising market in 1989 when it opened Gap Outlets. Merchandise in the Gap Outlets was made up of irregulars and Gap leftovers. With this move, the Gap initiated an attempt at a three-tiered retailing strategy, with its Banana Republic chain at the high end of the market, Gap in the middle, and Gap Outlets at the low end. However, growth of Gap Outlets was not as quick as expected, given that Gap Inc. saw the low end as the fastest-growing segment of the industry. Therefore, in 1993, 13 of the Gap Outlets and about 40 poorly performing Gap stores were converted into the Gap Warehouse division, which stocked merchandise specifically manufactured for the division.

Old Navy Clothing Co.

Then in early 1994 the Gap, headquartered in San Francisco, began the latest metamorphosis of the mass-merchandising division when it opened its first three Old Navy Clothing Co. units in the Bay Area and one near Los Angeles. With expectations for a rollout of up to 45 strip-mall stores in 1994 and early 1995, Gap would not comment on volume projections, but industry sources estimated that the division could reach annualized sales of $240 million, based on a potential core of about 80 stores.[21] The annual clothing mass market generally was estimated to total over $200 billion. Perhaps Old Navy was the inspiration of Gap executives who came face to face with an economic reality in the early 1990s: that scores of consumers were jobless or working two jobs to make ends meet and couldn't afford the pricey goods in regional malls where most Gap stores operated. Wall Street analysts said Old Navy stores, by offering a timely mix of lower prices and decent-quality clothes, albeit a few notches below the Gap merchandise, would make Old Navy successful.[22] Old Navy merchandise generally was priced about 30 percent lower than Gap clothing and also had specially designed products. "We're really going to school on this business," said Millard Drexler, Gap president. "It's too early to make predictions, but we will be aggressive about expanding the business."[23] Products made for Old Navy are no different from what was made for Gap Warehouses, but by using lighter-weight and less expensive fabrics than those used for regular Gap merchandise, Old Navy was able to meet its low price structure. For example, Old Navy Jeans were priced at $22 as compared with Gap's $34.

Initial Locations

The Old Navy locations in the Bay Area included one converted Gap Warehouse and two new properties, while the City of Commerce (near Los Angeles) location also was a converted Gap Warehouse. Old Navy stores were expected to average about 15,000 square feet and have nondescript exteriors and a friendly industrialized interior environment that featured appetizing fashion basics. The layout placed men's wear on the left, women's on the right, and children's in the rear. Baby clothes and large sizes also were carried later. Salespersons in black logo T-shirts paired with jeans or khaki pants greet shoppers by offering oversized black mesh Old Navy shopping bags (initially priced at $3) in shopping carts, many with baby seats. Store aisles were wide and boldly labeled, and the checkout counters were surrounded by impulse items such as socks and baseball caps. Another example of cost cutting was Old Navy's serviceable concrete floors, compared with Gap's hardwood floors and lush extras, such as inviting seating areas and abundant displays of fresh flowers, which were reserved for Banana Republic's locations. One industry observer commented that the Old Navy interior reminded one of a visit to the supermarket.

Creating an Image

Startup advertising for Old Navy was limited to full-page or double-page ads in regional newspapers and local billboards. The word *Gap* was used only on exterior store signs shown in the ads and was expected to be a short-term strategy to use the corporate name. Mr. Drexler said: "We wanted to help launch the business by trading on the equity of the Gap."[24] The ads listed a toll-free telephone number for potential customers to call to get further information, and when called, a recording gave product news, detailed the 30-day return policy, and pro-

vided directions to the nearest Old Navy. The recording also asked callers to leave a message on how they heard about the store. The name *Old Navy* was purported to be more about mental imaging than fashion reality—a denim work shirt is the closest thing to a nautical theme. Old Navy does not sell Navy-style or nautical-themed clothing. It was reported that Gap executives saw the name originally on an old building in Europe and liked it. When asked what is the store for, Richard Christman, vice-president of communications for Gap Inc., first pointed out that Old Navy was not an outlet shopping center store used to sell over-stocked Gap leftovers. "It's for the consumer without as much disposable income," said Christman. "You'll find great clothes at great prices. There's a great need for casual clothing at these price points," he said. "We've been getting a tremendous response."[25]

Competitors had taken what was known as the Gap "look" and underpriced it to reach the mass market. By opening Old Navy, Gap Inc. began to sell its own version of less expensive look-alikes. But Old Navy looked different than its Gap siblings. In between a cement floor and exposed-pipe ceilings, clothing was hung on and stacked in metal shelves. And customers purchased their bargains through check-out counters. But the clothing styles were pure Gap. Old Navy was awash in denim blue, khaki tan, navy, black, and white, and roughly 20 percent of its merchandise cost less than $22. But looking at the way the clothing was displayed and at the fixtures in Old Navy was to be reminded of the elan and quality of a retailer with pricier goods, whether it be Gap Inc.'s own Gap and Banana Republic stores or others like A/X Armani Exchange or a Ralph Lauren/Polo or a Tommy Hilfiger section in a department store. Unlike much of the apparel in this price range, Old Navy's clothes were distinctive, made from higher-quality fabrics like linen-and-cotton blends and with an attention to detail like embroidery. The store's layout included high-school lockers, stripped to bare metal and bereft of some doors, that serve as chic display cases. The overhead storage space so characteristic of budget retailers was concealed with canvas flaps that lend a vaguely nautical quality. Checkout counters were crafted from polished pressed board and galvanized metal—no Formica. The light to indicate that a cashier is free was a clever adaptation of the signal light one might find on a factory floor—not the generic bulb behind a plain plastic box.[26] One observer noted that Old Navy was the type of store you wished you could have shopped in when you were in college.[27] But in reality Old Navy was a one-stop location for families, since it had both men's and women's sections and also had baby and kids' clothing in the $10 to $20 range, thereby allowing an individual to spend a virtual lifetime attired in T-shirts, khaki, and denim.

GROWTH POTENTIAL AT GAP INC.

During an October 1994 consumer conference held by Roberson Stephens & Co. in New York, Warren Hashagen, senior vice-president for the Gap Inc., noted that Old Navy (then operating 28 units) could become Gap's largest division by the end of the decade by adding between 50 and 100 stores. Mr. Hashagen said: "It's a major growth vehicle for us, and we're very excited about the potential." To avoid cannibalization of the flagship Gap stores, Hashagen said that Old Navy stores would be located in different markets. "We've gone after a different customer and real estate base," he said. While the Gap division opts for regional malls and urban areas, Old Navy units generally were located in strip centers or power centers and targeted a more moderate customer than the Gap, noted Hashagen. He observed that there had been no "significant" negative effects on the Gap stores if the two concepts were located nearby but that the company tried not to "go head to head" with the two divisions.[28]

Growth of Old Navy coincides with a time of struggling with sluggish sales at the 866-unit Gap division. Mr. Hashagen noted that the Gap division is far from dead but has the challenge to "adapt and redefine the business" and is working hard to offer "a balance between fashion and basics" while seeking merchandise to tempt customers into making "incremental" purchases, including offering new product categories such as shoes and personal products such as fragrances, shampoos, conditioners, soap, bath gels and salts, and some gift items. Mr. Hashagan said that product-line extensions also would be offered in GapKids stores, including such merchandise as toys and shoes. Although Mr. Hashagan stressed that the Gap stores will not cut prices and that its initial markups will remain the same,

they will begin emphasizing "value" and will tout price in both print ads and in-store signage.[29]

Mr. Hashagen made additional comments to the effect that Banana Republic had been "turning out positive comp-store sales" and "margin improvements" and that the division was expected to "hit double-digit operating profit this year." He further noted that another growth vehicle for the Gap Inc. was its international division. He noted the Gap had stores in Canada, the United Kingdom, and France, with plans calling for opening Gap stores in Japan and Germany and Banana Republic stores in Canada in 1995. Mr. Hashagen said that the "only constraint" to international growth was high occupancy costs in Europe, particularly in the United Kingdom. Therefore, the Gap had taken to opening stores in basements or second floors rather than limiting locations to only ground level. "That has made a difference," he said. "But we won't take bad sites just to grow the business."[30]

Some Additional Outsider Viewpoints

While younger shoppers may avoid the Gap when they want the latest styles, many are still shopping there even if it's only for khakis or jeans. "It used to be cool, and it still is," said 28-year-old Richard Nardi of Pacific Heights, California. "It's prolific. You can't help [but] go in there."[31] A more positive viewpoint was taken by Alan Millstein, chairman of Fashion Network, in early 1995 when he made the observation that visibility will keep the Gap a force in the youth market. "They have the best locations of all the mall-based retailers and all the big stores [in cities]," he said. "The youth market for 14- to 22-year-olds who shop in suburbia is addicted to the Gap."[32] Barry Bryant, of Ladenbur, Thalmann & Co. Inc. (industry analysts), noted a switch to a higher percentage of fashion-forward styles from basics and said: "I suspect that women's fashion is driving the Gap store business."[33] Mr. Bryant noted that he was impressed with Gap's earnings, given that the company cut its promotions significantly in 1994, and he added that he believed that the Gap had succeeded in differentiating itself from the higher-priced Banana Republic division.

Positive observations also were made by Mr. Millstein when he said this about Old Navy: "It offers great prices and interesting ambience, and the first pilot stores that have opened have been outstanding successes. It is probably the most successful innovative specialty idea of the 1990s."[34] Kelli Arena, CNN correspondent on "Business News," who had a rather more skeptical viewpoint, said:"But the new chain won't help the Gap meet all its new challenges. Analysts say there are already too many Gap stores, with prices that are too high and a selection that's too limited. Plus, the Gap is cutting back expansion plans for Old Navy. Perhaps the hardest crowd to please are investors, who saw Gap stock fall 23 percent last year [1994], despite solid earnings growth. Word is they're waiting on the sidelines to see if the specialty retailer is really special after all."[35]

Outside Consultant

Mr. Drexler in mid-1995 decided that it would be wise to involve an outside consultant in analyzing Gap Inc.'s current situation with regard to both Old Navy and Gap stores. He was concerned about the viewpoint expressed by Kelli Arena and others (noted earlier) that there were too many Gap stores, that Gap prices were too high, and that Gap's merchandise selection was too limited. At the same time he was in a quandary about what rate of expansion to use in developing Old Navy stores. Expansion had not occurred as quickly as originally expected for Old Navy, and although no formal announcement of a slowdown had been made by Gap Inc., he was aware that many industry observers had the opinion that expansion of Old Navy had been purposely slowed by Gap executives. Mr. Drexler wondered about the effect Old Navy would have on sales from existing Gap stores. Would future growth be in the low end of the apparel market served by Old Navy? Or would future growth be best achieved by concentrating on revitalizing the Gap stores?

Questions

In order to answer these questions, the case analyst is expected to adopt the viewpoint of an outside consultant, as noted earlier.

1. Are there too many Gap stores?

2. Are Gap prices too high and merchandise selection too limited?

3. How effective have the Gap's recent advertising efforts been?

4. Which of the following alternatives offers the most likely opportunity for future growth and why?

   a. The Gap stores in the United States after revitalization

   b. The Gap stores through expansion of international locations

   c. The Old Navy division stores

5. Given your answer to Question 4, what would be your recommendation for how quickly Gap Inc. should expand the Old Navy division? What would be the optimal size (in number of stores) for this division?

Endnotes

1. Tom Vasich, "Mass-Market Clothing: With Old Navy Clothing Co., the Gap Imitates Itself with Lower Prices for a Vast Retail Audience Searching for Low Prices," *Orange County Metropolitan,* Business Dateline, August 1, 1994, Sec. 1, p. 46.
2. Pamela Street, "Three Tiers for the Gap: Company Profile," *Women's Wear Daily,* March 23, 1994, p. 5.
3. Andy Beckett, "FASHION/How We Fell into the Gap; Does the Gap Look Ordinary Now? Was It Just the Stars Who Made It Look Great? In America the Boom Is Over, But Is It Here?" *The Independent,* November 28, 1993.
4. *Ibid.*
5. *Ibid.*
6. *Ibid.*
7. *Ibid.*
8. *Ibid.*
9. *Ibid.*
10. Christina Duff, " 'Bobby Short Wore Khakis'—Who's He, and Who Cares?" *Wall Street Journal,* February 26, 1995.
11. *Ibid.*
12. *Ibid.*
13. *Ibid.*
14. *Ibid.*
15. Max Hicks and Wendy Tanaka, "The Gap Losing Its Cool Edge with Younger Set? Hip Gives Way to Mainstream Fashion," *San Francisco Examiner,* Business Section, February 17, 1995, p. 1.
16. *Ibid.*
17. Duff, *op cit.*
18. *Ibid.*
19. Beckett, *op cit.*
20. *Ibid.*
21. Street, *op cit.*
22. Cathleen Ferraro, "Gap's Low-Priced Store View for Last Cherry Creek Spot," *Rocky Mountain News,* July 12, 1994, p. 31A.
23. Steet, *op cit.*
24. *Ibid.*
25. Vasich, *op cit.*

26. Stephanie Strom, "How Gap Inc. Spells Revenge," *New York Times,* April 24, 1994, Late Edition, Final, Sec. 3, p. 1.
27. Vasich, *op cit.*
28. Jean E. Palmieri, "Gap Sees Old Navy Evolving into Its Biggest Division; Company Exec Details Growth Plans for Unit at Monday Conference; Gap Inc. Senior VP-Finance Warren Hashagen," *Daily News Record,* October 4, 1994, p. 3.
29. *Ibid.*
30. *Ibid.*
31. Matt Hicks and Wendy Tanaka, "The Gap Losing Its Cool Edge with Younger Set? Hip Gives Way to Mainstream Fashion," *San Francisco Examiner,* February 17, 1995, p. B-1.
32. *Ibid.*
33. Jennifer L. Brady, "Gap's Net Jumps 55% in Quarter," *Women's Wear Daily,* August 12, 1995, p. 2.
34. Kelli Arena, CNN "Business News," February 9, 1995.
35. *Ibid.*

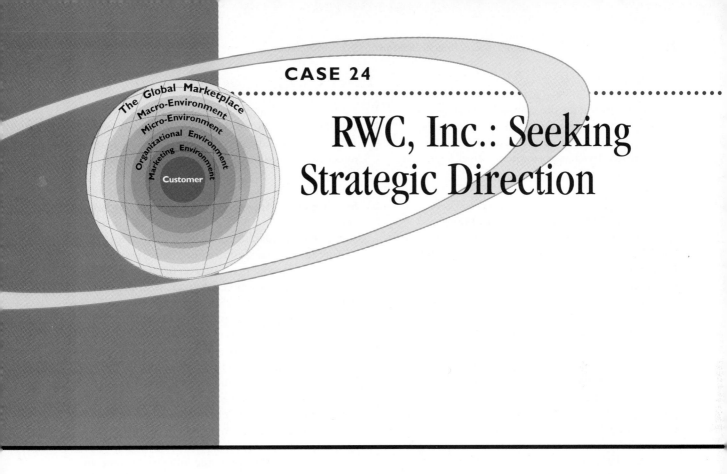

RWC, Inc.: Seeking Strategic Direction

This case was prepared by James W. Camerius, Professor of Marketing, and Brian G. Gnauck, Professor of Marketing, Northern Michigan University.

Richard Glenn, president and chief executive officer of RWC, Inc., was concerned about the future direction of the company when he called his senior management staff together at a Monday morning meeting in early January of 1995. He felt that the meeting would provide answers to a lot of critical questions. He was concerned about corporate goals and objectives that would need to be developed as management looked ahead to determine a corporate strategy. He knew that there should be an assessment of market opportunities and resources of the firm. He was aware that there would

have to be some revision of the current strategies of the firm and a plan developed for implementation and control of a revised plan. He was confident that the resulting executive summary would include a new growth strategy for the organization.

RWC, a firm with annual revenue of approximately $25 million, was headquartered in Bay City, Michigan. Its major business was the design of automated assembly lines (systems) for the appliance and automotive industries. The company was known for design leadership, engineering expertise, superior service, and high-performance equipment. Corporate management had developed important relationships with growing multinational firms that spanned nearly 50 years.

In 1988, however, RWC experienced a severe financial reversal based on several negative conditions in the marketplace. A plan to return the company to profitability included a number of significant organizational and operational changes, including the appointment of Richard Glenn as president. The following years were considered years of transition for the company. Management had responded successfully to a changing marketplace by taking advantage of a number of opportunities created by changes in the political, legal, and technological environment of the firm.

THE COMPANY AND ITS HISTORY

RWC, Inc., was founded by entrepreneur Leonard E. Nichols and several other individuals in Bay City. On January 18, 1945, the firm was incorporated as Resistance Welder Corporation. The company manufactured individual resistance welding machines designed to perform within a mass-production environment. The process of resistance welding combined pressure and high-energy heat to weld metals. During the 1950s, the firm completed its first automated assembly lines, which consisted of multiple station welding machines with automatic material transfer between stations.

The company's growth of its manufacturing base after 1957 went beyond Bay City. In 1979, RWC funded the startup of RWC Machinery (Canada), Ltd., and took a 60 percent interest in the venture. The managers of the venture held the balance of the stock. The company's mission was to parallel RWC's U.S. capabilities in the Canadian market on a downscaled basis. The company was consistently profitable and operated independently from RWC, Inc. In November, 1988, RWC, Inc.'s 60 percent share was sold to the minority shareholders.

In 1981, Midwest Laser Systems, Inc., was founded by RWC, Inc., and a group of its key people. RWC, Inc., held a 63 percent interest, and the balance of the stock was held by certain managers and individuals instrumental in launching the new company. The company had established a reputation in laser application thermoforming and smaller automatic assembly and manufacturing systems. MLS was basically independent of RWC, Inc., but developed a close working relationship with it in the sales, marketing, and manufacturing areas.

RWC, Inc., in 1983, also formed the first of its wholly owned subsidiaries, RWC Spare Parts, Inc., to develop a spare parts aftermarket sales as well as to supply the needs of RWC's affiliates (Canada and MLS). The company was wholly dependent on RWC for financial and general management support.

Huntington Automation, Inc., a wholly owned subsidiary in Huntington, Indiana, was founded in 1985. The objective of the company was to produce smaller automatic systems, to occasionally absorb excess business from RWC, Inc., and to be the low-cost production site (due to its low labor rates) for price-competitive projects. The company was very closely tied to RWC, Inc. In 1988, HAI opened a contract manufacturing division to produce metal closure devices used in the fiber barrel market. As a result of increasing pressures on financial and other corporate resources, management discontinued the subsidiary in 1988.

Over time, the firm added metal bending and forming machinery, as well as more sophisticated automated assembly lines utilizing computerized assembly equipment, to its product line. In 1979, the firm changed its name to RWC, Inc., to reflect expansion of its business beyond resistance welding machines into the field of automated fabrication. The firm historically supplied assembly systems to the automotive parts industry, and since the early 1990s, the appliance industry became an important customer. Entry into the appliance field led to the design and construction of the firm's first automatic refrigerator cabinet assembly line.

Subsequent growth in product diversification and market share led to numerous expansion programs in physical facilities. In 1995, the firm occupied a self-sufficient facility totaling 123,160 ft^2 in Bay City. It was located on a 12½-acre plant site adjacent to an interstate highway with easy access to air transport. The company had its own power substation, giving it ample power to completely test the largest assembly and welding equipment. When completed, the facilities of the company were believed to be adequate to supply the needs of the firm for 3 to 5 years.

Prior to fiscal year 1988, RWC had consistent break-even to slightly profitable years. During 1988, however, a reduction in volume, complicated by the culmination of an unsuccessful 4-year effort to produce an assembly system for a new television tube design for Zenith, created a $4.8 million loss, equating to $18.37 per share. The loss forced RWC's board to seek out a new president with turnaround experience. New management proceeded to reorganize the firm, establish a new system of financial control, and cut fixed costs to a level that reduced the break-even point to a $16.0 million revenue level annually.

In an effort to establish a strategic alliance with a strong partner that could provide needed financial backing, RWC sold a minority interest in the firm in November 1989 to Met-Coil Systems Corporation, an international producer of sheet metal products. At this time, Met-Coil was a profitable company producing annual revenues of $70 million. In January 1992, Met-Coil settled out of court a long-running patent infringement suit that damaged its financial condition. This event, combined with other problems, led Met-Coil to seek cash and sell its interest in RWC. The buyers were two investors, Charles Brenner, president of J. L. Schiffman & Co., and Jeffrey Herr, senior vice president of the Chicago Corporation. Brenner and Herr were active investors in small, established companies and had been RWC stockholders for 10 years. Subsequent stock acquisition brought their combined ownership to 55 percent.

CORPORATE MANAGEMENT

Richard W. Glenn became the chief executive officer (CEO) and president of RWC. Previously, he was president and CEO of a special machinery company owned by Vikers PLC of London, England. His employment experience also included 8 years in the manufacturing operations of the IBM corporation and 8 years as a research engineer in manufacturing processes for Western Electric Company.

Glenn reported to the board of directors. The board consisted of the president, executive vice president, and five outside directors, which included Brenner and Herr as majority stockholders and three others as representatives of minority interests. Reporting to the CEO were the subsidiary presidents as well as department heads from RWC subsidiary Midwest Laser Systems.

Sanford L. Lee, executive vice president and chief operating officer, joined RWC in 1973. He assumed his executive responsibilities as vice president of sales in 1978. His previous employment included 5 years with Teledyne Precision, Inc., in sales and marketing, 4 years as a manufacturing representative for Douglas Engineering Corporation, and 7 years as a foreman and engineer with General Motors Corporation.

William G. Perlberg was vice president, secretary, treasurer, and financial officer. Mr. Perlberg's prior experience included work as a controller of a stamping company that had revenues of approximately $30 million, 7 years on the staff of a public accounting firm, and 2 years as a staff accountant at a CPA firm.

Vice President of Manufacturing Kenneth C. Supanich joined RWC in 1972 as production manager, moving to the vice president position in 1988. Prior experience included 2 years as general manager of the Wilson Machine Company, 8 years as vice president and general manager of the Link Welder Corporation, 11 years as an applications engineer and manufacturing manager for Delta Associates, Inc., and 3 years as an engineering detailer.

Ronald G. Lain was appointed to the position of manager of applications engineering in 1988. He came to RWC in 1974 and served in a number of capacities, including vice president of engineering. Prior experience included service as a general manager at PSI, Inc., 7 years in various sales and estimating management responsibilities for welding and machinery companies, and 4 years as an engineering design leader for engineering and design organizations.

The management team also included Walter F. Malec, vice president for program management, who joined RWC in 1972 with far-reaching engineering experience; Brian P. Tobin, director of engineering, who joined in 1987 with extensive engineering experience; and Glenn R. Hergert, vice president marketing and sales, who assumed that position in 1988 with several years' experience in various sales and marketing positions. The RWC organization chart is shown in Exhibit A.

In 1995, RWC employed approximately 200 people, most of whom worked at the Bay City headquarters. The professional staff of approximately 80 people included those who performed engineering functions such as controlling, drafting, detailing, designing, checking, applications, project management, and supervision. Others performed administrative and operational functions including selling, program management, manufacturing, purchasing and finance. The manufacturing workforce of slightly more than half the company's employees was represented by a local of the U.S. Workers of America. The union represented workforce-performed manufacturing functions, which in-

EXHIBIT A
· · · · · · · · · · · · · · ·
RWC, Inc.: Organization Chart

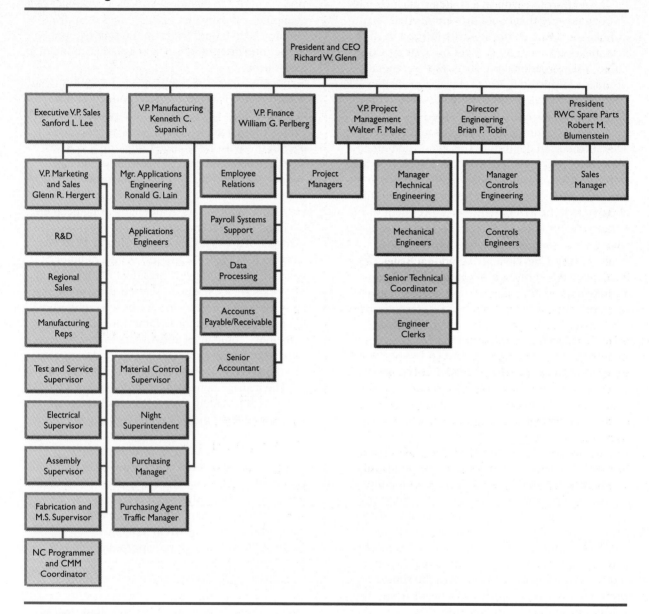

Source: Stifel, Nicolaus & Company, Inc., Consultant Report.

cluded machining, fabrication and assembly, electrical, technical, and maintenance work.

MARKET POSITIONING
· ·
The company's heritage was based on a commitment to technical expertise that was documented within the firm's design library and list of patents. Richard Glenn attributed customer loyalty, as evidenced by relationships with leading manufacturing companies that spanned nearly 50 years, to RWC's design and engineering abilities. In an RWC management report, the firm was positioned as "the technical and quality leader" and therefore felt it could justify selling at a premium price level in the market.

The RWC management report also described the firm as

> ...a design-and-build manufacturer of automated assembly machines and other special purpose manufacturing machinery. The company provides a turn-key installation tailored to meet the customer's specific, unique production needs including production output, labor content, floor space utilization, and precision tolerances. The company accomplishes its tasks through a combination of innovative concepts, engineering design, and incorporation of "standard building blocks."

CORPORATE BELIEFS

Glenn and other members of senior management concluded that the critical operational issues facing RWC were maintaining the firm's technical competitive edge and maintaining the lean cost structure obtained during the turnaround. The company felt it would accomplish this by senior management instilling policies or beliefs throughout the organization that would keep people focused on important issues. As part of a plan, management would implement a set of strategies that specifically addressed the competitive edge and cost structure. A listing of RWC corporate beliefs is shown in Exhibit B.

Management felt that these beliefs should not be compromised at any level in the organization. The beliefs defined the work ethic of the firm. The direction of the business was determined by a set of operations and sales strategies, as noted in the following sections.

OPERATIONS STRATEGIES

RWC's technical skills were considered by Rich Glenn to be an important competitive advantage. Customers had indicated the importance of these skills when selecting RWC. The skills there became the basis for developing operations strategies.

To remain competitive, RWC would

1. Invest in engineering and manufacturing skills.
2. Improve employee skills.
3. Identify and protect proprietary technology.

To retain cost control, RWC would

1. Improve control of the jobs.
2. Create quality.
3. Keep shop loaded to selected minimum capacity.
4. Tighten control of purchased parts.
5. Enhance financial controls.
6. Improve employee trust.
7. Manage fixed costs.

The preceding strategies would be implemented through a specific set of actions as deter-

EXHIBIT B
RWC Corporate Beliefs

Treat all individuals with respect.
Uncompromising standard of integrity.
Have pride in our work product and our company.
Provide excellent value and service to the customer.
Take the initiative to get a task done, take the time to do it right, and watch the details.
Value the skills of our people because they are our most important product.
Produce a positive cash flow.
Be highly knowledgeable of our customer needs.
Dedicated to meeting or exceeding budget and doing it on time.

Source: Stifel, Nicolaus & Company, Inc., Consultant Report.

mined by management. The development of a series of reporting systems ensured management that the company would meet its objectives and remain on track.

NATURE OF THE PRODUCT

RWC was primarily an engineering-driven designer of high-speed, precision-automated assembly systems and metal-joining equipment and provided related aftermarket support services. The company's products were supplied primarily to the appliance and automotive industries. RWC operated in the industrial automation business segment of the machine tool industry.

The company designed and built automated assembly systems to meet customers' specific requirements for precision, production output, labor content, and use of floor space. While each system was designed and manufactured to customer specifications, the company drew on a wide variety of proven techniques and standard components. These standard techniques and components, in addition to patented equipment designed by RWC, were engineered to create specialized systems.

Each RWC assembly was unique. They were categorized as nonsynchronous pallet systems, precision link carrousels, lift and carry synchronous systems, indexing dials, and synchronous pallet systems. RWC also designed and built, or purchased, standard components in addition to patented equipment designed by the company in order to provide automated systems. The components included feeder and placement units, handling devices, transfer units, weld stations, quality control units, diagnostic units, and others as needed.

The production cycle, which could take 6 to 18 months for existing designs and up to 2 years for new designs, involved the primary steps of sales/application engineering, R&D, mechanical and controls engineering, manufacturing, testing, and installation. The first contact between the customer and RWC was made by the sales and applications engineers. These engineers were responsible for guiding the project through the inquiry, concept, proposal, and purchase-order stages. Design engineers often were used at the early stage of the project lifecycle to ensure that the correct equipment capability and automation compatibility were built into the project and to develop customer confidence regarding RWC's ability to conceptualize and deliver the final product.

The next step in product development was using the engineering R&D lab to match the customer's product design with the correct manufacturing process. This process was the second step in ensuring that the most efficient design would be met by checking the manufacturing process against the customer product requirements for compatibility prior to release of a final machine design.

The third step was mechanical and controls engineering, where the actual equipment was laid out by RWC's full-service engineering department. Again, throughout the design phase, RWC worked closely with the customer to ensure that a cost-effective and efficient system was engineered.

Actual engineering and manufacturing were performed at the Bay City facility. Prior to shipment, to ensure performance and faster startup on delivery to the customer's plant, each machine and assembly line was tested within the production facility with simulated short-term actual production runs. The machines were large (hundreds of feet long) and complex items that took up huge amounts of space in the plant.

Finally, the automated assembly equipment was delivered to the customer's plant for setup and incorporation into actual production. RWC personnel remained with the equipment until it was fully functional at the customer's plant. Rich Glenn felt that financial ramifications would be significant if something did not meet specifications or buyer needs.

The physical life span of an automated assembly could exceed 25 years; however, obsolescence of the product manufactured could determine the working life of the line. As a percentage of RWC's total consolidated revenues, 96 percent was in automated equipment, and 4 percent was in standard equipment. Automated machine tool equipment ranged in price from less than $100,000 to more than $1 million; single assembly lines ranged in price from $2 million to more than $20 million, with the average of $6 million to $8 million.

THE COMPETITIVE ENVIRONMENT

RWC operated in the metal-forming machine tool and automatic assembly-line industries or, more generally, the automation equipment industry. The automation equipment industry was made up of a number of competitors, none of which, with the exception of Giddings and Lewis, Inc., had a dominant market share despite the considerable consolidation that appeared over the last decade. The market served by RWC was estimated at about $500 million as of 1993. The market share held by RWC was estimated to be about 5.5 percent. The breakdown of RWC revenue for 1993 by industry segment was 78 percent appliance, 16 percent airbag, and 6 percent other automotive.

The machine tool and automated assembly market was highly competitive. Direct competition was primarily from manufacturers of machine types similar to those produced by RWC. However, manufacturers of different machine types that were capable of performing comparable operations also were considered competitors. Additional competitors included builders of assembly lines who integrated machine tools built by others into an assembly line. Finally, a second tier of suppliers existed that produced the computer controls, robots, and machine components. RWC maintained the skilled engineering capability allowing it to compete primarily on design-build projects.

The average annual sales volume of RWC's principal competitors in the market was $10 to $30 million, with some exceeding $100 million. Principal competitive factors for automated machine tools and assembly lines included product performance, engineering, delivery, price, reputation, and service. The machine tool industry historically had been a cyclic business with relatively long lead times between order and shipments. Machine tool sales were affected by capital spending levels, interest rates, tax and depreciation policies, international competition, and currency exchange rates. The size of the entire automated assembly market was very large and was divided among hundreds of specialized suppliers. RWC's primary competitors included Taylor Winfield, Warren, Ohio; Gilman Corporation, Janesville, Wisconsin; and Newcor Corporation, Bay City, Michigan. Other competitors included Arco Automated Systems, Inc., Manor Welding, Inc., Detroit Tool, Inc., Giddings and Lewis Automation, Inc., Weldun International, Inc., and Wright Industries, Inc. The primary competitors are reviewed in Exhibit C.

MARKETING AND SALES

RWC's organization to perform the marketing and sales functions consisted of an executive vice president, a vice president of marketing and sales, and three regional sales managers and three manufacturer's representatives. The company's Applications Engineering and Research and Development Departments had direct-line responsibility to the vice president of marketing and sales with a strong working relationship with the executive vice president. They were important components of RWC's overall sales approach. Salespeople possessed engineering and manufacturing backgrounds and were technically trained. The company's sales territories are shown in Exhibit D.

The regional sales managers were staff positions and were compensated with salary, vehicles, expenses, and sales commission. Manufacturer's representatives were exclusive to RWC for machine tool and automated assembly sales and were compensated solely through commission arrangements based on a percentage of sales.

RWC's sales approach was to use a consultative relationship with the customer's engineers and purchasing departments. The salesforce visited major customers approximately every 2 weeks to discuss the company's product manufacturing process and attempted to uncover sales opportunities. Projects generally were awarded in closed, negotiated bids, but the low bidder was not necessarily given the contract. RWC was increasing its use of a partnering approach known as *simultaneous engineering*. The company worked with the customer's product design engineers to jointly design the product and assembly system to ensure product manufacturability, speed the time to production, and enhance the company's relationship with the customer.

Rich Glenn believed RWC's long-term relationships with major U.S.-based companies gave it a significant advantage in acquiring new projects. RWC had been selected as a manufacturing partner by Whirlpool for refrigerators, washing machines, and dishwasher cabinets; General Electric for the

EXHIBIT C
. . . .
Machine Tool and Automated Assembly Competitors

Acro Automation Systems, Inc.
Milwaukee, WI
Estimated sales: $13 million
Estimated employees: 118
Automatic assembly equipment, welding equipment

Banner Welder, Inc.
Germantown, WI
Estimated sales: $15 million
Estimated employees: 140
Welding equipment

Detroit Tool (a division of DT Industries)
Lebanon, MO
Estimated sales: $61 million
Estimated employees: 500
Metal cutting machines and special tool & die making

Giddings & Lewis Automation (a business segment of Giddings & Lewis, Inc., sales primarily by Gilman)
Janesville, WI
Estimated sales: $200 million
Estimated employees: 400
Assembly system machines and factory automation

Newcor–Bay City (a division of Newcor, Inc.)
Bay City, MI
Estimated sales: $27 million
Estimated employees: 200

Taylor Winfield (a division of Denton and Anderson)
Warren, OH
Estimated sales: $30 million
Estimated employees: 200
Welding and assembly equipment

Weldun International, Inc. (a division of Robert Bosch Corp.)
Bridgmen, MI
Estimated sales: $70 million
Estimated employees: 400
Factory automation and systems integration for computer aided manufacturing

Wright Industries, Inc.
Nashville, TN
Estimated sales: $61 million
Estimated employees: 400
Specialized assembly equipment

Source: Consulting Firm Report.

EXHIBIT D
················
RWC Sales Territories

Region	Sales Position
Southern Michigan	Regional manager
Illinois, Wisconsin, Iowa	Regional manager
Kentucky, Tennessee	Regional manager
Western Ohio	Manufacturer's representative
Mexico	Manufacturer's representative
Airbags (worldwide)	Manufacturer's representative

Source: Stifel, Nicolaus & Company, Inc., Consultant Report.

side-by-side refrigerator cabinet; Maytag for refrigerator cabinets; and the world's leading supplier of airbag initiators for airbag components. Exhibit E lists RWC's most significant customers in order of average sales.

The company's salesforce strived to develop personal relationships with customers' engineers. It attempted to maintain the relationship should the engineer accept a job with a new company. The company's salesforce had noted a tendency for customer engineers to change companies and worked

EXHIBIT E
················
RWC Primary Customers

Whirlpool
General Electric
OEA, Inc.
MABE (GE Mexican joint venture)
Raytheon (Amana, Speed Queen)
Maytag (Maytag, Admiral, Magic Chef)
Morton International, Inc.
Ford Motor Company
AC Delco (Division of GM)
Electrolux (White Consolidated/Frigidaire)

Source: Stifel, Nicolaus & Company, Inc., Consultant Report.

to establish sales opportunities at new companies through existing relationships.

RWC salespeople were responsible for uncovering sales opportunities, reviewing job specifications, and uncovering production needs and requirements not explicitly stated in job specifications. Once invited to bid, sales and applications engineering personnel coordinated the project through the firm's detailed estimated and risk-management process. All projects under bid were monitored closely by the salesforce, and customers were visited often by key executives, a regional manager, and an applications engineer prior to award of the project to ensure the quality of the RWC bid.

The company offered as standard a 90-day warranty on its equipment, although a 1-year warranty was generally provided to major customers.

BARRIERS TO ENTRY
●●●●●●●●●●●●●●●●●●●●●●●●●●●●●●●●●●●●

Although there were competing companies with access to greater financial resources than RWC, Rich Glenn believed that there were significant barriers to entry in highly engineered, high-speed automated systems marketed to large companies. To successfully enter or expand in this segment of the market, a competitor would need a skilled and experienced engineering department capable of conceptualizing and designing complex assembly systems, an extensive engineering CAD library from which to draw past plans to reduce engineering time and expense, and a skilled and experienced manufacturing force capable of building, troubleshooting, and testing the equipment. Rich Glenn felt that a potential competitor with prior experience would need to invest nearly a decade of personnel-hours to achieve the engineering and manufacturing experience and bid library required to compete profitably.

Another difficulty in building a business to compete with RWC in the refrigerator or certain automotive assembly markets was RWC's proprietary technology, which had been patented and was further protected by steep engineering and manufacturing learning curves.

Finally, the sale of an automated assembly system was a time-consuming, consultative process that generally was finalized in a negotiated bid among carefully selected vendors. Rich Glenn believed that the successful bidder often was not the low bidder. Customer relationships, reputation within the industry, and technical ability were primary sales success factors. Salespeople had to be technically trained and had to possess effective management skills to coordinate the sales process. Glenn felt that a competitor attempting to sell to the large companies that RWC had served for nearly 50 years would need to establish a trained and experienced salesforce and work to build long-term customer relationships. Glenn noted that to surmount these barriers, competition would require significant investment of time and money.

THE MACHINE TOOL INDUSTRY

Overview and Trends

RWC primarily served the appliance and automotive parts supply industries. Demand for the firm's products was influenced by cyclic demand for appliances and automotive parts, necessitating increased production capacity or equipment replacement, government-mandated product design changes, creation of new products that re-

quired new manufacturing lines, and international expansion of the firm's principal customers.

Machine tool sales rebounded strongly during 1993, to an inflation-adjusted level of $4.2 billion, from $3.4 billion for the comparable period in 1992, according to the U.S. Department of Commerce. The industry's recovery in 1993 was attributed to an 11 percent rise in capital spending, versus a 2.9 percent rise in 1992; an estimated average capacity utilization rate of 81.0 percent, versus 78.8 percent in 1992; and rising expenditures by the U.S. auto companies for machine tools, versus usually low purchases in 1992.

Continued growth in the U.S. GDP, capital spending, producers' durable equipment orders, and capacity utilization were expected to lead to higher machine tool orders in 1994. Standard & Poor's estimated 1994 GDP growth of 3 percent, a 10.3 percent rise in capital spending, an 11.8 percent increase in producers' durable goods orders, and capacity utilization of 83.1 percent. From his experience, Rich Glenn had concluded that capacity utilization rates in excess of 80 percent generally triggered new machine orders. Exhibit F illustrates new machine tool orders against the domestic capacity utilization rate. The U.S. Depart-

EXHIBIT F

Capacity Utilization Rate versus New Orders for Machine Tools

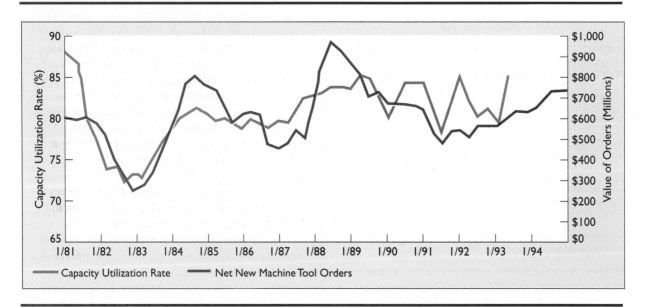

ment of Commerce estimated machine tool shipments to increase at a 10 percent inflation-adjusted rate in 1994 and at a 7 percent rate through the remainder of the decade.

Rich Glenn felt that the long-term outlook for the machine tool industry was favorable due to several issues: Modernization of U.S. industry was far from complete, the airbag industry was anticipated to grow at an annual rate of 21 percent over the next 5 years, Europe was on the verge of a major industrial restructuring effort, and increasing labor costs worldwide favored capital investment.

According to the U.S. Department of Commerce and Bureau of the Census, the average age of machine tools employed in the United States stood at a 53-year high. Glenn felt that the desire to replace aging equipment with efficient, modern equipment would create machine tool demand for several years. He also felt that machine tool sales would benefit from the cyclic upturn the automobile industry was experiencing. Automobile sales were anticipated to remain favorable for the next several years.

Glenn maintained that Europe faced a structural operating disadvantage relative to the United States and Asia and was on the verge of a major and long-term restructuring of industrial operations in order to reduce operating costs and become competitive globally. European manufacturers were anticipated to make sizable investments in new assembly systems and other highly engineered machine tools in order to reduce labor assembly hours and break-even levels.

Rich Glenn felt that the most important advantage for the machine tool industry was the worldwide trend toward capital investment to increase competitiveness, improve operations, and reduce costs, as opposed to investments in labor. Domestically, the Clinton administration's proposals for an increased minimum wage, worker retraining, and health care reform could raise labor costs and accelerate capital investment. The same trend was occurring in Europe, since large-scale workforce reductions were scheduled to occur over the next several years.

The Appliance Industry

RWC expanded into the appliance assembly business in response to the business potential created by two events: the National Appliance Energy Conservation Act of 1987 and the industry voluntary cooperation to redesign refrigerators to reduce the release of chlorofluorocarbons (CFCs).

The National Appliance Act of 1987 allowed the Department of Energy to set standards with the intent of reducing energy use by 25 percent every 5 years. The first 25 percent reduction required the redesign of major appliances and, consequently, the redesign of the machines that make these appliances. During this period, RWC built 18 of the 19 newly constructed refrigerator lines in the industry to satisfy energy-use requirements of the act. The important issue for the future was the fact that the act was ongoing. The next 25 percent reduction was set for 1998. RWC management believed that based on its experience in the early 1990s, significant work would be coming its way to meet this standard.

Chlorofluorocarbons (CFCs) have been identified as an environmental toxin that is released during the application of the foam insulator used in refrigerators. The foam insulator in these refrigerators was used not only for the insulation purpose, but it also gave rigidity and structure to the unit, since the gauge of the metal used in refrigerators had been reduced and in itself would not provide a rigid enough machine to be operational. The reduction of CFCs was a worldwide effort directed at all phases of the refrigeration industry. Thus the refrigerator business, in essence, was a small part of the total effort to reduce these CFCs.

The appliance industry, and specifically the appliance industry as it related to refrigerators, had encountered difficulty with efforts to improve the safety of the insulation material, meet the phaseout of the CFCs, meet the energy-reduction requirements of the National Appliance Act of 1987, and provide the consumer with a product that met desired size and design characteristics. As a short-run solution to this problem, the industry adopted the use of hydrochlorofluorocarbons (HCFCs) as an insulation material. HCFCs have lowered the ozone-depleting characteristic of CFCs, but they are scheduled for elimination in the future. The results of these changes were simply that the company believed that there will be design changes in refrigerators because of the elimination of HCFCs combined with the National Appliance Energy Act requirements.

RWC management noted that the Democratic party in the United States had aggressively proposed the phaseout of CFCs and HCFCs. Since the election of 1994, both houses of the Congress of the United States were controlled by the Republican party, which in some instances had moved to dampen the potential phaseout of these products.

The appliance industry had prepared for this changing environment with a fairly significant plan for capital expenditures. Whirlpool Corporation was planning to spend $884 million, Maytag $500 million, and General Electric $265 million. RWC management concluded that not all these expenditures would be related to the refrigerator business but felt that they would influence demand for automated assembly machines for the refrigerator business.

Management also felt that there was significant growth potential in world markets. Both Europe and Latin America represented great potential for domestic manufacturers. In addition, various companies had approached expansion on a worldwide basis either by buying production capacity in those areas or by entering into joint-venture relationships. Whirlpool had acquired Phillips NV's appliance division in 1991. Maytag acquired Hoover in 1988, and Maytag also was involved in a joint venture with Bosh-Seimans GMBH. RWC management believed that as European unification moved forward, the market would become similar to the United States with a concentration of manufacturers occurring and products becoming more homogeneous. It estimated that the European appliance market exceeded that of the United States by 25 percent, yet appliance saturation levels were only at about half of those of the United States.

The mature nature of the U.S. appliance market in some respects was perceived by many industry analysts as a negative regarding future demand for automated machines that made these appliances. Management felt, however, that as is true in any type of mature market, product innovations can continue to enhance the replacement demand for these products. Customer-driven design, such as user-friendly electronic controls, white-on-white coloring, rounded corners, and flush-to-cabinet design continued to gain popularity with consumers. Manufacturers had stated the desire to get such design changes to the market at a faster pace. All these issues could potentially, as RWC management noted, have a ripple effect regarding the demand for automated assembly machines for the refrigerator market.

Automotive Parts Supply Industry

Automotive parts companies generally fell into three main categories: original equipment, replacement parts, and nonautomotive parts. While replacement-parts sales were stable and were not directly affected by new car sales, original-equipment sales were highly cyclic and sensitive to the number, size, and complexity of cars and trucks produced. The industry was fragmented and composed of more than 2500 companies whose principal products were auto parts and many thousands of other companies whose output included auto parts. Parts makers tended to specialize in a few items requiring a high degree of skill and efficiency in an effort to spread R&D and engineering costs over a greater scale of production. Historically, original-equipment contracts were multisourced and covered one model year. Recent trends in the industry suggested that the norm had moved to single-source, multiyear contracts that covered the life of a vehicle model and included specific productivity-improvement and price-reduction targets. Automakers also announced a desire to work with fewer suppliers over a longer period of time and integrate them into an extended supplier network.

The automotive parts industry showed improvement beginning in 1992, pulling itself out of a 3-year decline. Original-equipment manufacturers (OEMs) benefited from the continued increase in car and truck production in North America, which reached a 21 percent increase in assemblies for the fourth quarter of 1993. Production was scheduled for a 13.3 million unit annual rate for the first quarter of 1994. The progress of OEMs was mitigated somewhat by the increased presence of the Japanese in the United States. Japanese automakers made use of fewer U.S.-supplied parts than did domestic producers such as General Motors, Ford, and Chrysler (Big Three). While some OEMs did benefit from increased sales to Japanese firms making automobiles in the United States, most firms were still waiting for the Japanese to live up to a 1992 promise of doubling purchases from U.S. parts suppliers. The U.S. Commerce Department, the Federal Trade Commission, and several U.S. legislators were investigating purchases of Japanese automakers and their long-term ties to Japanese suppliers.

Several hundred foreign parts companies had set up production within the United States to provide parts to Japanese manufacturers operating in the United States. The capacity of their factories exceeded the needs of Japanese automakers, and thus these suppliers were actively competing for Big Three contracts. While improved quality and efficiency of the U.S. suppliers had allowed foreign suppliers only limited success in winning Big Three contracts, industry analysts felt that the excess capacity in the industry could permanently depress industry prices.

RWC had supplied a variety of automated assembly systems to the automotive industry, including systems for the manufacture of body panel assemblies, shock absorbers, carburetor subassemblies, catalytic converters, brake shoes, spark plugs, oxygen sensors, and other automotive components, as well as components for mass transportation equipment. RWC continued to focus on traditional systems for the automotive market, while the firm's automotive growth strategy was to use niche sectors where unique RWC technology commanded an advantage. An example was patented technology developed for the manufacture of hybrid airbag initiator components.

RWC developed and patented the ball feed welder, an automatically controlled system for charging and sealing the canister component of an airbag inflator while under high pressure. The company also was a supplier of manufacturing equipment for the production of airbag ignitors (or squibs), which attach to and deploy the contents of the canister. The ball feed welder was based on technology developed and patented for automotive shock absorber production. The RWC shock absorber system remained the only method for charging and sealing a shock absorber that did not violate the component's rubber seal. RWC maintained an exclusive arrangement for the supply of certain equipment to Monroe, for whom the system was originally developed. RWC had supplied airbag gas-charging equipment to Morton, TRW, and Allied Bendix and had been selected as a preferred supplier by one of the world's leading suppliers of airbag initiators. RWC management targeted the airbag market for future growth because of legal mandates, new focus on side-impact protection, consumer and competitor pressures, expansion of the European market, and the preferred supplier status of RWC.

NHTSA's Passive Restraint Mandate

Beginning September 1, 1993, the National Highway Traffic Safety Administration (NHTSA) requirements mandated passive restraints for both the driver and passenger side on all cars sold in the United States. This legislation was later expanded to include light trucks, vans, and multipurpose vehicles. *Passive restraint* referred either to airbags, or passive seatbelts. The U.S. Congress enacted legislation in 1991 that promoted airbags as the preferred passive-restraint device, mandating airbags for both sides of the front compartment for all new cars manufactured for sales in the United States by the 1998 model year and light truck, vans, and multipurpose vehicles by 1999.

Occupant Side-Impact Protection

Having won hard-fought success with the mandate of driver and passenger side airbags, NHTSA indicated a shift in focus to upgrading occupant protection in side impacts. It was widely believed the side-impact issue would be addressed through the use of additional airbags mounted in the side of the vehicle. This translated into an increase, over time, in the number of airbags per vehicle from two to four or six. Volvo had announced the 1995 model year would include two side-impact airbags as standard equipment on the 850 Turbo model and a $500 option on other 850 models.

Consumer Preferences for Safety

Government regulation set in motion the demand for airbags. However, consumers had accelerated their proliferation by demonstrating a willingness to pay for safety. Airbags were ahead of schedule in meeting the government mandate for 100 percent installation by 1998, since most cars sold in the United States offered both driver and passenger airbags. Side-impact airbag protection was not expected to appear on luxury models until the late 1990s. However, with Volvo's announced inclusion of side-impact airbags on 1995 models, proliferation of side-impact airbags would likely occur more rapidly as competitors followed Volvo's lead. What was originally a government-mandated device was now a consumer-demanded feature, actively marketed by automakers as standard equipment.

Europe Represents a Very Large Potential Airbag Market

Europeans had shown a strong desire for safety; nearly 90 percent of Europeans wore seatbelts regularly. While airbags were not mandated in Europe, Mercedes-Benz, BMW, Volvo, and other manufacturers offered passenger and driver-side airbags to differentiate their automobiles, and other manufacturers announced plans to follow. The European market was widely expected to follow the United States, with consumer demand ultimately causing airbag installations in all vehicles. Market development was anticipated to lag the United States by 3 to 5 years. The European market was 50 percent larger than the U.S. market, making it the largest potential airbag market in the world.

RWC Partnered with Important Airbag Manufacturers

RWC was an important supplier of hybrid airbag initiator and inflator automated assembly equipment. The firm was aligned with the world's leading supplier of airbag initiators and with a global supplier of airbag modules. In addition, RWC had produced airbag equipment for other manufacturers of airbag modules.

The two major U.S.-based manufacturers of airbag modules expected significant growth to occur worldwide. Exhibit G illustrates international growth potential in millions of units.

Morton International had 20 airbag production lines at a cost of $10 million per line and was anticipating a $600 million investment in production lines and chemical processing by 1995. TRW, Inc., another major manufacturer of airbags, had plans

for expenditures totaling $130 million in 1993 and $130 million in 1994 for propellant, inflators, and modules for airbags. Airbag suppliers closely guarded the secrecy of their products and selected very few low-tier suppliers. RWC had built automated assembly equipment for Morton, TRW, and OEA (another significant supplier of airbag modules). Industry consultants noted that given the popularity of airbags and NHTSA's announced focus on side impacts, the number of airbag systems required to meet future new vehicle production could exceed 40 million annually. Suppliers, the consultants suggested, would need to increase production capability to meet the demand for initiator systems, meaning increased demand for RWC assembly systems.

THE SEARCH FOR A CORPORATE STRATEGY

Richard Glenn planned to call his senior management team together next week in another executive session. The meeting was to be an informal, free-for-all brainstorming session where important decisions concerning the company's future would be made. As Glenn sat over coffee with Sanford Lee, executive vice president, and chief operating officer, he shared his concerns about the company and its future.

> "If we did certain things, we could probably drive ourselves into a larger company," Glenn noted. "If we didn't do those things, we could remain small with different kinds of opportunities. We can either become a large corporation through a series of acquisitions and grow rev-

EXHIBIT G

Morton International Airbag Forecast (Millions of Units)

	1990	1991	1992	1993	1994	1995	1996	1997	1998
	3.2	4.9	6.5	12.0	20.0	31.0	34.0	39.0	43.0
% growth		53%	33%	85%	67%	55%	10%	15%	10%

Source: Morton International Report.

enues, or we can shrink down from a public company to a privately owned business. We're at the point now where there are a lot of different ways we can go."

Sanford Lee agreed: "I just got back from a conference, and the numbers, which came from a Whirlpool vice president, indicated that by the year 2005, the major appliance market in China will be four times the size of the U.S. If you are talking units, it's a tremendous market and opportunity," he noted.

"If we shift our attention from appliances to the airbag business, for example," suggested Glenn, "it's an entirely different story."

"You're right, it's different," Lee agreed.

"That's a safety item that goes in a car and nobody sees it. Well, it seems to me that there's an infinite demand for health and safety. When it comes to safety, people, just like medical, want the best 'medicine' possible, and they don't care about the cost as long as they are not paying for it directly. There's a lot of opportunity here as this market expands."

"I'm really looking forward to receiving input from the management team at the next executive meeting," Rich Glenn noted. "We need to decide on future corporate and marketing strategies which will bring stability to the organization and allow this firm to survive and grow in the future."

Nike, Inc. (1999)

This case was prepared by Robert J. Mockler of St. John's University, Dorothy G. Dologite of the City University of New York–Baruch College, and Paul Poppler of St. John's University. Edited by Julian W. Vincze.

Beaverton, Oregon–based Nike, Inc., has grown dramatically during the last decade. Nike, which designs, develops, and markets high-quality footwear, apparel, and accessory products worldwide, had consolidated revenues in 1988 of $1.2 billion but reached $9.5 billion by 1998 and has expectations for near-term growth to $15 billion. Their "swoosh" logo has become as familiar as McDonald's "golden arches," and much of the growth has been international. Nike's quality products are designed in-house after extensive research and development that uses high-tech innovations, but they also respond to fashion trends. They have stringently searched for sources of cheap but disciplined labor and are noted for sophisticated outsourcing of production to firms in developing nations.

However, the present economic crisis in Asia, when combined with changing customer taste in

footwear, indicated that industry growth would be minimal over the next few years. These factors as well as Nike's 1998 financial results had management concerned.

NIKE'S HISTORY

Phil Knight, cofounder and CEO, while an undergraduate runner at the University of Oregon, was coached by William J. Bowerman (also a cofounder of Nike), who redesigned a made-in-Japan running shoe and hired a band of students to hawk the shoes at track meets.[1] In 1962, Knight wrote a term paper about a business opportunity to create a better track shoe. Adidas shoes, made in West Germany, were then the best, but they were expensive and hard to come by in the United States. Knight reasoned that with cheap Japanese labor but American distribution and marketing, he could sell track shoes that rivaled Adidas in quality and undercut them in price and take over the market. After graduation in 1962, Knight and Bowerman each invested $500 so that Knight could travel to Japan and (using the name Blue Ribbon Sports) represent himself as a shoe importer to Onitsuka, the manufacturer of Tiger brand shoes. They were granted exclusive rights to distribute Tiger shoes in the western United States in 1964. By 1968, they had begun designing their own shoes and searching for Asian manufacturing sources.[2]

Nike's performance-oriented product innovations and outsourcing of production resulted in shoes that athletes wanted to wear and could afford. Knight and Bowerman's track connections got their shoes onto the feet of real runners just as jogging emerged as a new national pastime. In 1968, Blue Ribbon Sports became Nike, and the "swoosh" logo was born. Jon Anderson won the Boston Marathon wearing Nike shoes, Jimmy Conners won Wimbledon and the U.S. Open wearing Nike shoes, Henry Rono set four track and field records in Nike shoes, and members of the Boston Celtics and Los Angeles Lakers basketball teams were wearing Nike products. Sales and profits were doubling every year during the 1970s.

In the mid-1980s, after more than a decade of fast growth, Nike hit $1 billion in revenue. However, Nike misjudged the aerobics market, outgrew its own capacity to manage, and made a disastrous move into casual shoes. How? By making an aerobics shoe functionally superior to Reebok's but missing on styling. This also happened to Nike's casual shoes—viewed as funny looking. Nike confused consumers who viewed it as a running shoe company. Casual shoes sent a different message. Nike began to lose its magic. Retailers were unenthusiastic, athletes were looking at the alternatives, and sales slowed.

For three years ending in 1989, Nike wallowed in second place behind Reebok, whose sneakers became synonymous with aerobics. Nike lost its footing, and the company was forced to make a subtle but important shift. Instead of emphasizing just design and manufacture of their products, Nike focused more on the consumer and the brand. In a short time, it learned to be marketing oriented. Since then, Nike has resumed its leadership of the athletic footwear industry.[3]

Image

Nike built its brand through advertising slogans— "Bo Knows," "Just Do It," "There Is No Finish Line"—many became popular expressions.[4] The Nike brand became well known around the world. Through an exclusive agreement with The Athletics Congress, Nike became the sole provider of competitive uniforms for the U.S. track and field team until the twenty-first century. As a global brand franchise, Nike focused on distinct, culturally relevant messages that reflected the minds of sports and fitness enthusiasts everywhere. This focus allowed Nike to develop a consistent worldwide brand image, using the "swoosh" logo to enhance the perception of sneakers as upbeat, fun products, signifying the energy stored within, evoking images of technology, and being a visual shorthand for what was hip and meaningful. Nike's marketing themes—health, fitness, and self-empowerment—remained consistent.[5]

The Company

Nike designs, develops, and markets worldwide high-quality footwear, apparel, and accessory products. Distribution is through approximately 14,000 retailers in the United States and through a mix of independent distributors, licensees, and subsidiaries in approximately 82 countries. Manufacturing of most products (except Cole Haan) is outsourced to independent contractors—most located outside the United States. Apparel, however, is produced both domestically and abroad. The company's financial performance for the 3-year period ending in 1997 was remarkable, with revenues moving from $3.8 billion to $9.2 billion. Until 1998, the company believed it had great management, tremendous opportunities internationally, superb marketing ability, and brand-name appeal that was unparalleled in the industry.[6]

Product Offerings[7]

By the mid-1990s, consumers had gravitated to quality, one of Nike's strengths, but by 1998, they had become more value-oriented. Nike's revenue figures are reported by these categories: U.S. footwear, U.S. apparel, non-U.S. footwear, non-U.S. apparel, and other brands.

U.S. footwear products emphasized quality construction and innovative design, but U.S. footwear revenues in 1998 decreased 7 percent, or $255 million. The five largest footwear categories were training, basketball, running, kids, and Brand Jordan (which was reintroduced in 1998), together totaling approximately 80 percent of revenue. During 1998, Brand Jordan revenues increased 57 percent, but the others experienced decreases between 4 and 17 percent. However, the company also marketed shoes designed for aerobics, tennis, golf, soccer, baseball, football, bicycling, volleyball, wrestling, cheerleading, aquatic activities, and general outdoor activities. Golf and soccer showed increases of 71 and 74 percent in 1998.

U.S. apparel included active sports apparel as well as athletic bags and accessory items designed to complement Nike's footwear products, featuring the same trademarks and sold through the same marketing and distribution channels. Frequent use of "collections" of similar design or for specific purposes resulted in a revenue increase of 11 percent in 1998, with nearly all categories reporting growth: training up 10 percent, accessories up 6 percent, kids up 41 percent, tee-shirts up 5 percent, and golf up 57 percent. Team sports apparel was the only decrease, at 8 percent.

For non-U.S. footwear, despite the Asian economic crisis in 1998, revenues increased by 12 percent.

Non-U.S. apparel revenues increased by 21 percent in 1998 and represented 41 percent of Nike's total revenues. Europe increased 6 percent in footwear and 35 percent in apparel, Asia-Pacific had footwear down 8 percent but apparel up 34 percent, and the Americas reported footwear up 20 percent and apparel up 78 percent. Overall, the biggest country markets were Japan, United Kingdom, Canada, France, Italy, and Spain. The biggest declines were in Korea (minus 29 percent) and Germany (minus 6 percent).

Several lines of merchandise were sold under other brand names. Nike had a line of dress and casual footwear and accessories for men, women, and children under the brand name Cole Haan using a wholly owned subsidiary, Cole Haan Holdings, Inc. In January 1993, Nike had acquired Sports Specialties, Inc., which marketed a line of headwear with licensed team logos under the brand name Sports Specialties. The company also sold small amounts of various plastic products to other manufacturers through its wholly owned subsidiary, Tetra Plastics, Inc.

Product R&D

Nike's research and development (R&D) was a cornerstone of past successes. Technical innovations in footwear and apparel design received continued emphasis—striving for products that reduced injuries, aided athletic performance, and maximized comfort. In addition to its own staff specialists in the areas of biomechanics, exercise physiology, engineering, industrial design, and related fields, Nike also used research committees and advisory boards made up of athletes, coaches, trainers, equipment managers, orthopedists, podiatrists, and other experts who consulted with the company and reviewed designs, materials, and concepts for product improvement.

Logistics and Distribution

Nike had concentrated on the domestic (U.S.) market until 1981, when international strategies were formulated to service a growing foreign market. Nike initially reached more than 40 countries and, by 1993, had became the world's largest athletic footwear manufacturer, marketing in 82 countries.[8] Domestic sales through approximately 14,000 retailers accounted for approximately 59 percent of total revenues in 1998. Domestic retailers included a mix of department stores, footwear stores, sporting goods stores, tennis and golf shops, and other retail accounts. During the high growth years of 1995 to 1997, Nike made substantial use of its innovative "Futures" ordering program. Retailers could order 5 to 6 months in advance of delivery with the guarantee that 90 percent of their orders would be delivered within a set time period at a fixed price. However, in 1998, it became evident that during economic declines, this program resulted in overinventory positions for many retailers both domestically and especially in Asia. It necessitated large-scale sell-offs.

Nike had 17 company sales offices in the United States to market shoes and apparel, as well as 28 independent sales representatives for the sale of specialty products, such as golf, cycling, water sports, and outdoor wear. In addition, it operated 60 wholly owned retail outlets: 31 carried primarily closeout merchandise, 18 were Cole Haan stores, and 4 were Nike Town stores designed to showcase the company's products. High-profile Nike Town locations, called "concept shops," showcased the complete Nike line. The stores occupied 20,000 to 30,000 square feet and were designed as half art gallery and half walk-in advertisement. The concept was successful. Nike reported attracting on average 5000 people a week, with average spending of $50 from each customer.[9] The company's domestic distribution centers for footwear were located in Beaverton, Oregon, Wilsonville, Oregon, Memphis, Tennessee, Greenland, New Hampshire, and Yarmouth, Maine. Apparel products were shipped from the Memphis distribution center and from Greenville, North Carolina. Sports Specialties headwear was shipped from Irvine, California.

The largest volume category in retailers was discount stores, with 32 percent of the market. Shoe stores had 10 percent, department stores had 9 percent, athletic shoe stores had 9 percent, and sporting goods stores had 8 percent in the early 1990s. Discount stores carried many low-priced shoes but not the high-end, high-cost athletic footwear. Department stores, athletic footwear stores, and shoe stores, on the other hand, would carry more fashionable shoes with more varieties of choices. And for high-technology, high-performance and high-end athletic shoes, sporting goods stores and athletic shoe stores would have more to offer. All the stores were widely scattered, and they were the consumer's most preferred stores when they thought of buying a pair of athletic shoes.

In 1992, Nike opened its first 2000-square-foot concept shop at Macy's (San Francisco) and reported "pretty strong" sales gains. As a result, it quickly opened more of the Nike Town concept stores. Nike believed opportunities for increased sales depended on how its product met different retailers' needs. Nike placed more emphasis on in-store displays and offered less expensive shoes in discount stores and more fashionable, functional, and high-end shoes in department stores, sporting goods stores, and specialty athletic stores. Nike also adopted competitive distribution to retailers by selling through a direct ownership method designed not only to influence retail pricing but also to improve retailer relations.[10]

International Activities

Nike marketed internationally through independent distributors, licensees, subsidiaries, and branch offices. It operated 24 distribution centers in Europe, Asia, Canada, Latin America, and Australia and also distributed through independent distributors and licensees. International branch offices and subsidiaries of Nike were located in Australia, Austria, Belgium, Brazil, Canada, Chile, Costa Rica, Denmark, Finland, France, Germany, Hong Kong, Indonesia, Italy, Korea, Malaysia, Mexico, New Zealand, Norway, People's Republic of China, Spain, Sweden, Singapore, Switzerland, Taiwan, Thailand, The Netherlands, and the United Kingdom.

International operations in the footwear industry also were subject to risks such as possible revaluation of currencies, export tariffs, quotas, restrictions on the transfer of funds, and political instability. NAFTA provided an incentive for more investments in Mexico, and U.S. footwear companies were interested in Latin American markets.

FOOTWEAR INDUSTRY

In the 1970s, jogging, health and fitness, and sports had become national pastimes, particularly among the youth, leading to the dramatic growth of the industry. In the 1980s, the increasing popularity of aerobics brought a great number of women into the market.[11] Industry sales peaked in 1990 at $12.1 billion and had decreased to $11.6 billion in 1992 because of the worldwide recession and the changing habits of consumers, such as buying more all-purpose outdoor footwear and less expensive athletic shoes.

During the high growth 1980s, the leading companies were Nike, Reebok, L.A. Gear, Converse, Keds, Adidas, and Puma. The biggest two, Nike and Reebok, used aggressive advertising, cost reduction, and quality control as successful strategies. However, the athletic footwear industry reached a difficult point in the early 1990s.[12] A saturated male-oriented market, a weak economy, an upswing in nonathletic casual shoes, and a growing popularity of hikers, deck shoes, and other casual shoes contributed to the slowdown. Customers were buying less traditional athletic footwear.[13] Some industry experts expected that a market that consisted of casual, nonfunctional athletic footwear for outdoor activities would exist in the middle to late 1990s. The sales of hiking shoes, for example, had more than doubled, while the sales of athletic footwear had been declining in 1991. However, this prediction was not totally accurate in that Nike was able to achieve revenue growth of 24 percent in 1995, 32 percent in 1996, and an amazing 43 percent in 1997 just prior to the 1998 decrease.[14]

CUSTOMERS AND MARKETS

Customers, either domestic or international, could be classified into men, women, children, teenagers, and the elderly. To position their products effectively required companies to fully understand customers' needs as well as market trends.[15]

Domestic Market

Men   Surveys showed that only 14 percent of purchases were used for sports, 43 percent for everyday street wear, 26 percent for work or school, 3 percent for lounging or relaxing, and over 2 percent for visiting or entertaining. In the early 1990s, some people felt that the declining growth rate in the men's market and the high cost of promotion made the market much more competitive. However, since most men's sneakers were purchased for everyday street wear, manufacturers might respond by producing more high-quality athletic shoes in different colors and more casual styles.

Women   Only 8 percent of women's athletic shoes were used for sports, 40 percent for everyday street wear, 25 percent for work or school, and 4 percent for lounging or relaxing. Women usually spent more money and bought more pairs of athletic shoes than men, but this had begun to change. For the first time since the early 1980s, when women's buying habits were first tracked, women bought fewer athletic shoes and spent less in 1992[16] than in the previous year, and this trend continued. However, Nike designed a new footbed for women's shoes and in the fall of 1998 introduced it using women's concept shops within Nike's retail partners such as Dick's and The Finish Line.[17]

Children   Sixty percent were used for sports (80 percent of boys). Children's athletic shoes were the majority of the total number of pairs of children's footwear sold. Children in the 1990s influenced purchasing decisions of the family, ranging from what type of cars were purchased, to where families vacationed, to which restaurants they patronized. Although mothers still controlled buying, they were influenced by their children, who, in turn, were influenced by television commercials, other forms of advertisement, and peers. Often children preferred to dress in sweats and activewear, and so mothers would buy shoes that provided comfort and aided development of children's feet.[18]

Teenagers   Sixteen-year-old males were the primary consumers of the latest, and often the most expensive, products. Teens often could not buy without parental permission, but in an era of immediate gratification—"what you want is what you get"—teenagers paid high prices and were more influenced by styles and trends than comfort and fit. They owned from three to seven pairs. They purchased almost every 3 months. About one-third of teenagers said they wore only one athletic label.[19] Companies that provided current, fashionable, and stylish products and used intensive advertisement were targeting teenagers.

Elderly   Customers aged 65 and over were interested in soft and comfortable shoes with more functions and less fashion. Most athletic footwear sold to elderly was walking shoes.

International Market

International market expansion was expected to offer the greatest long-term growth potential, while the domestic athletic footwear market could be considered mature. Valued at $12 billion, this market was untapped in the early 1980s.[20] International operations had fueled overall growth of the U.S. footwear industry in the early 1990s, and although Nike's domestic sales had decreased in 1998, its international revenues grew by 12 percent. That fueled Nike's overall revenue growth of 4 percent in 1998. Customers in Europe, the Asia-Pacific region, Latin America, and Canada were interested in Nike's athletic footwear and apparel.

TECHNOLOGY AND FASHION

Technology, which was critical to product diversity and integrity, was one of the key ingredients driving the industry. Athletic footwear had become a supersleek construction of multiengineered materials using space-age technologies that cushioned the foot and had arch supports and waffled soles to allow the foot to exert its natural torque. First came Nike's Air shoe in 1979, and then came Reebok's Pump (replaced in 1998 by DMX cushioning technology) and Puma's Disc system sneaker.[21] Well-designed shoes addressed a major consumer concern—performance and preventing injury—for example, footwear developed for running would aid performance while preventing injury. Although technology was critical, however, fashion also became an important factor. The athletic look became socially acceptable, indeed fashionable, for a wide range of activities.

APPAREL AND ACCESSORIES

In the late 1960s, Adidas was the first footwear company to exploit its brand name by introducing sports clothing. By 1982, most companies with a strong brand image took the plunge into apparel. However, apparel was clearly different from shoes because it was driven primarily by fashion, not technical performance. Products became popular quickly but died quickly also, and there were many competitors waiting to duplicate popular designs.

Several footwear companies sold both performance leisure-wear and accessories. At the performance end of the spectrum, they competed with numerous small specialty outfits that focused on high-performance clothing for athletes. Performance-wear included tennis shirts and shorts, bicycle racing shorts and tops, snow-skiing apparel, and running shorts and pants. At the leisure end of the spectrum, they competed with hundreds of small sportswear firms that aggressively developed leisure-wear lines. Leisure-wear included t-shirts, light jackets, sweatsuits, shorts, socks, and long-sleeve shirts.

MANUFACTURING

The principal materials used were natural and synthetic rubber, vinyl and plastic compounds, nylon, leather, and canvas. To lower manufacturing cost, almost all sneakers were manufactured overseas, mainly in Asia,[22] often by independent contractors using designs from the United States, Japan, or Germany. U.S. companies and their contractors and suppliers bought raw materials in bulk because of ready availability in manufacturing countries.[23]

Labor costs and customs duties were constant concerns of companies that used overseas manufacturing operations. They were unable to predict whether additional customs duties, quotas, or other restrictions might be imposed on the importation of their products. The enactment of any such duties, quotas, or restrictions could result in increases in the cost of their products and adversely affect sales and profitability of a company and the industry. For example, in October 1997, the EU Commission imposed definitive antidumping duties on certain textile upper footwear imported from China and Indonesia. And then, in February of 1998, the EU Commission imposed definitive antidumping duties on certain synthetic and leather upper footwear originating in China, Indonesia, and Thailand. Such antidumping duties could have had considerable impact except that the textile footwear duties did not cover sports footwear, and in the case of synthetic and leather upper footwear duties, the so-called special technology footwear, which was for use in sporting activities, was expressly excluded.

Mainland China was expected by some industry observers to become the biggest footwear exporter due to its abundant supplies of cheap, easily trained workers. Until 1997, the economies of most East Asian countries were booming. However, Latin America and Eastern Europe also might become major manufacturing regions because they were nearer the U.S. and European markets and had lower transportation costs. Also, the labor costs in these regions were considered as low as those in Asia.

MARKETING

Although in many ways Nike's marketing had been driven by developing technologically advanced products, this alone did not account for its past success and envious growth. Effective logistics and distribution combined with effective integrated marketing communications (including advertising and the "swoosh") had enabled Nike to develop strong image and brand equity. Past marketing efforts had enabled Nike to achieve sales objectives while maintaining image and brand recognition. Like its competitors, Nike spent millions on brand advertising. The company used television, print advertisement, trade shows, sponsorships, and point-of-purchase (POP) displays. TV ads often featured top athletes or famous movie and singing artists. For many consumers, it was not the shoe's performance but the image as presented by popular sports celebrities in TV commercials that counted. Point of purchase (POP) was almost essential, because a powerful in-store presentation and display could help customers identify which technology belonged to which brand and persuade customers to purchase a certain product.

By 1998, Nike had begun reviewing all sponsorship contracts for professional and amateur athletes. The company preferred to have fewer spokespeople who would do more frequent ads. This would help to control advertising costs and create a more exclusive image for the company's products. Nike also contracted with coaches who made promotional appearances and who also could offer suggestions on product improvement. In addition, they often distributed sneakers to their student-athletes.[24]

But Nike did not restrict itself only to the use of "pull" marketing techniques. Widespread availability in a variety of retail outlets was a requirement for volume sales to occur. Nike's salesforce was noted for enthusiasm and effectiveness in setting up in-store displays, training retail sales clerks, and explaining any Nike-funded contests or special awards designed to motivate retailers.

COMPETITION

Much of the athletic footwear sales in the United States were controlled by Nike and Reebok. However, there were several other companies, including L.A. Gear, Asics Tiger Corp., Keds, Converse, Inc., Fila Footwear USA, Inc., and Adidas USA, Inc., all seeking to increase demand for their brands.

Reebok

Reebok International, Ltd., located in Stoughton, Massachusetts, experienced an 11.5 percent sales decline to $3.2 billion in 1998 from $3.6 billion in 1997. (For complete details, the reader should access Reebok's 1998 annual report at their Web location: *www.reebok.com.*)

Reebok and its subsidiaries designed and marketed active lifestyle and performance products, including footwear and apparel. The company's principal operating units included the Reebok Division, the Rockport Company, Inc., Greg Norman Collection, and RLS Polo Sport, the company having sold the AVIA Group International, Inc. division

in 1998. They concentrated on the Reebok division and recently hired Mr. Carl Yankowski as president and CEO to rebuild Reebok. In early 1999, he created six global strategic business units: Classic Footwear, Performance and Fitness Footwear, Global Apparel, Kids Products, Retail Operations, and Licensing/New Business.

Dominating operation, the Rockport division was positioned as a leader in quality, comfort, and performance in its walking, outdoors, boating, casual, and dress shoes but also markets a broad range of other products.[25] Sales in 1998 increased to $460 million, with U.K. sales continuing to improve as a result of an advertising campaign named "Uncompromise" that featured contemporary personalities such as famous drag queen RuPaul dressed as a man ("I am comfortable being a man"). The Greg Norman Collection division, which started out as an assortment of golf attire in 1991, currently included a variety of men's lifestyle clothing and accessories—from fashionable blazers, outerwear, socks, and belts to beach and volleyball gear. Sales reached $90 million in 1998.

The RLS Polo Sport division (previously called Polo Ralph Lauren) was based on Reebok International being the exclusive licensee for Ralph Lauren Footwear in North America. The portfolio of brands includes Polo Ralph Lauren, Ralph Lauren Collection, Lauren by Ralph Lauren, Polo Sport Ralph Lauren, and RLS/Polo Sport Ralph Lauren. 1998 sales totaled $73 million, and in February of 1999 the division introduced the RLX/Polo Sport brand, which was designed and manufactured to enhance performance and will be marketed for world-class athletes.

L.A. Gear

L.A. Gear, Inc., based in Los Angeles, California, until 1998 had designed, developed, and marketed a broad range of high-quality athletic and athletic-style and casual/lifestyle footwear for men, women, and children, primarily under the L.A. Gear brand name. However, after suffering a series of years of negative earnings,[26] L.A. Gear had reorganized as a privately owned company focusing solely on licensing its trademarks and brand names worldwide. It had signed a licensing agreement with ACI International to produce women's, children's, and men's footwear in the United States and Canada. ACI International's collection of L.A. Gear branded shoes was introduced at the WSA convention in Las Vegas in February of 1999. (For details, the reader should access the company's Web site at *www.lagear.com.*)

Asics Tiger Corp.

Asics had been successful in the early 1990s, becoming the number five U.S. branded athletic shoe company by 1992. Its sales had increased at an average annual rate of 38 percent since 1990. However, like L.A. Gear, the mid-1990s brought declining sales and losses instead of profits so that by 1999 Asics was being sold through only one major retailing organization and was struggling to survive. (For details, please access the company's Web site at *www.asicstiger.com.*)

Converse

Converse, Inc., of North Reading, Massachusetts, in 1998 reported that revenues decreased 31.5 percent to $308 million compared with $450 million in 1997. This resulted in a net loss for 1998 of $14 million, and the company noted that the reduction in revenues was primarily attributable to an industrywide oversupply of inventory and the related promotional activities necessary to move these excess quantities. Glenn Rupp, chairman and CEO, commented in the annual report, "Although dissatisfied with the financial performance, we are pleased with our substantial cost cutting efforts which, coupled with our substantially reduced inventory levels, place us in a favorable position upon a resurgence in the athletic footwear industry. We are also very encouraged by our recently announced development of an innovative new footwear technology containing helium." (For complete details, the reader is requested to access the company's Web site at *www.converse.com.*)

Keds

Keds is a part of the Stride Rite Corp., headquartered in Lexington, Massachusetts, which markets Keds, Stride Rite, Sperry Top-Sider, Tommy Hilfiger Footwear, and Nine West Kids brands of footwear in U.S. shoe stores, department stores, sporting goods stores, and marine supply stores. In Canada and internationally it markets through independent distributors and licensees. Stride Rite reported

1998 revenues of $539 million and noted that Keds posted its first sales increase since 1992. (For more details, the reader should access either of the following: *www.keds.com* or *www.striderite.com.*)

Fila

In his 1998 letter to shareholders (a part of the annual report), CEO Michele Scannovini noted that it was a difficult year for Fila—revenue fell for the first time after years of steady growth. Fila Holding S.P.A., the Italian company of which Fila USA is a part, reported that revenues declined approximately 23 percent from 1997 levels. Scannovini noted that for the first time in the past two decades, the U.S. athletic footwear market suffered a contraction as wholesale sales were reduced by over $500 million (equivalent to over 6 percent). (Complete details from Web site: *www.fila.com.*)

Adidas

Headquartered in Herzogenaurach, Germany, Adidas-Salomon AG in 1998 reported that it was the second-largest company in the sporting goods industry with an estimated 12 percent market share as measured in terms of worldwide sales. The company reported the second best results in its history, with global sales up 48 percent to total 9.9 billion Deutsche marks (approximately U.S. $5.7 billion). Marketing globally through almost 100 subsidiaries in all major markets, it had the following brand names: *Adidas*—footwear, apparel and accessories; *Erima*—teamsport apparel, swimwear, and accessories; *Salomon*—skis, snowboards, snowblades, ski boots and bindings, summer sports product, hiking boots, and trekking equipment; *Taylor Made*—golf equipment; *Mavic*—cycle components; and *Bonfire*—winter sports apparel. In predicting the 1999 global market environment, Adidas forecasted no growth—with the U.S. market in poor condition due to "too fast" expansion and thus expecting consolidation. (The reader interested in complete details should access Web site *www.adidas.com.*)

SOCIAL AND PUBLIC ISSUES

Due to the lavish endorsement deals between large footwear companies and top athletes, as well as promotional deals with coaches, public concern about the industry's influence and/or control of professional sports developed.[27] In 1990, Operation PUSH, an activist group, called for a public boycott of all Nike products because of some violent incidents in which inner-city youths appeared to have killed a youth just to steal Air Jordan or similar expensive shoes and apparel.[28] The activist group also presented the viewpoint that because the black community was Nike's primary U.S. market, the company did not employ enough black businesses as suppliers or hire enough black workers.[29] Nike reacted to these situations by holding lengthy negotiation sessions with leaders of inner-city minorities and pledged significant monetary resources to fund activities aimed at inner-city youths and also to increase the number of minority-owned suppliers it used and to increase the numbers of minorities it employed.

Nike and Reebok (in fact, almost all athletic footwear companies) imported their athletic footwear products from off-shore manufacturers. Many of these imported goods were purported to be manufactured in sweatshop environments or by prison labor. Importing prison products was illegal, and Congress seemed poised to impose crippling penalties on importers of forced-labor goods.[30] However, the largest public reaction was generated by TV journalists who reported that Nike and some well-known retailers were supporting the use of child labor. By interviewing on TV women workers and underage children employed by firms doing contracted manufacturing for Nike and other firms, it was suggested that Nike was thereby supporting both the exploitation of women, who were required to work in sweat-shop conditions that were unsafe, and also condoning the use of child labor. These social issues were difficult to refute and almost seemed to take on lives of their own. One public figure caught in this situation (due to her TV endorsements of the line of branded merchandise) was Kathy Lee Gifford.

FINANCIALS

Nike's financial results for the past 10 years are shown in Exhibit A. Even a quick glance at this table will indicate that Nike's financial results until fiscal year 1997 had placed it in an enviable position. However, fiscal year 1998 indicated a significant reversal. But Nike, although hurting, is not in financial difficulties of any kind, although return on assets is at a 10-year low. (For complete details, the reader should access Nike's complete annual report available to the public at *www.nike.com.*)

THE FUTURE

Philip H. Knight, chairman of the board and CEO, in his annual letter to stockholders noted that 1998 produced considerable pain, by far the worst of which was the laying off of 1600 friends and coworkers. (For complete details, the reader should access *www.nike.com.*) Knight cited the Asian economic meltdown, the popularity of brown shoes (i.e., nonathletic shoes), the labor practices social issue (mentioned above), past boring advertising aired by Nike, resignations of experienced employees (who often had become millionaires by owning Nike stock), and the layoffs as the factors that caused the 1998 results.

He also added that he had been criticized for expansion of headquarters. However, he answered this last criticism by saying, "Most of our troubles are really symptoms of a larger, more difficult problem: We are a very well-managed $5 billion company. Right now, though, we are a $10 billion company trying to get to $15 billion." Over the past 3 years Nike had grown from 9500 employees to 21,800, and Knight thought perhaps that this unchecked growth had likely obscured the ability to look objectively at what was happening to Nike. Now, he believed, it was time to stop adding employees and concentrate on training and assimilation.

Knight observed that Nike also needed to think about redundancies and inefficiencies in its structure. To facilitate international market expansion, Nike had built strong international regional headquarters designed to support the fledgling country businesses. Many of these countries grew into substantial businesses. Knight decided to reduce the size of the international regional headquarters and to bolster in-country organizations and thereby align costs more directly to in-country revenues. This also would permit a better focus on customer differences and peculiarities within country markets. At the same time, Knight moved to consolidate the warehouses servicing international markets. All these activities, including the exiting of certain manufacturing operations, resulted in a re-

EXHIBIT A
....
Nike's Financial History, Year Ended May 31 (In Millions, Except Per-Share Data and Financial Ratios)

	1998	1997	1996	1995	1994	1993	1992	1991	1990	1989
Revenues	$9,553.1	$9,186.5	$6,470.6	$4,760.8	$3,789.7	$931.0	$3,405.2	$3,003.6	$2,235.2	$1,710.8
Gross margin	3,487.6	3,683.5	2,563.9	1,895.6	1,488.2	1,544.0	1,316.1	1,153.1	851.1	636.0
Gross margin %	36.5%	40.1%	39.6%	39.8%	39.3%	39.3%	38.7%	38.4%	38.1%	37.2%
Restructuring charge	129.9	—	—	—	—	—	—	—	—	—
Net income	399.6	795.8	553.2	399.7	298.8	365	329.2	287.0	243.0	167.0
Basic earnings per common share	1.38	2.76	1.93	1.38	1.00	1.20	1.09	0.96	0.81	0.56
Diluted earnings per common share	1.35	2.68	1.88	1.36	0.99	1.18	1.07	0.94	0.80	0.56
Average common shares outstanding	288.7	288.4	286.6	289.6	298.6	302.9	301.7	300.4	299.1	297.7
Diluted average common shares outstanding	295	297	293.6	294	301.8	308.3	306.4	304.3	302.7	300.6
Cash dividends declared per common share	0.46	0.38	0.29	0.24	0.20	0.19	0.15	0.13	0.10	0.07
Cash flow from operations	517.5	323.1	339.7	254.9	576.5	265.3	435.8	11.1	127.1	169.4
Price range of common stock										
High	64.125	76.375	52.063	20.156	18.688	22.563	19.344	13.625	10.375	4.969
Low	37.750	47.875	19.531	14.063	10.781	13.750	8.781	6.500	4.750	2.891

EXHIBIT A *(continued)*

Nike's Financial History, Year Ended May 31 (In Millions, Except Per-Share Data and Financial Ratios)

	1998	1997	1996	1995	1994	1993	1992	1991	1990	1989
At May 31:										
Cash and equivalents	$108.6	$445.4	$262.1	$216.1	$518.8	$291.3	$260.1	$119.8	$90.4	$85.7
Inventories	1,396.6	1,338.6	931.2	629.7	470.0	593	471.2	586.6	309.5	222.9
Working capital	1,828.8	1,964.0	1,259.9	938.4	1,208.4	1,165.2	964.3	662.6	561.6	419.6
Total assets	5,397.4	5,361.2	3,951.6	3,142.7	2,373.8	2,186.3	1,871.7	1,707.2	1,093.4	824.2
Long-term debt	379.4	296.0	9.6	10.6	12.4	15	69.5	30	25.9	34.1
Redeemable preferred stock	0.3	0.3	0.3	0.3	0.3	0.3	0.3	0.3	0.3	0.3
Common shareholders' equity	3,261.6	3,155.9	2,431.9	1,964.7	1,740.9	1,642.8	1,328.5	1,029.6	781.0	558.6
Year-end stock price	46.000	57.500	50.188	19.719	14.750	18.125	14.500	9.938	9.813	4.750
Market capitalization	13,201.1	16,633.0	14,416.8	5,635.2	4,318.8	5,499.3	4,379.6	2,993.0	2,942.7	1,417.4
Financial Ratios										
Return on equity	12.5%	28.5%	25.2%	21.6%	17.7%	24.5%	27.9%	31.7%	36.3%	34.5%
Return on assets	7.4%	17.1%	15.6%	14.5%	13.1%	18.0%	18.4%	20.5%	25.3%	21.8%
Inventory turns	4.4	4.8	5	5.2	4.3	4.5	3.9	4.1	5.2	5.1
Current ratio at May 31	2.1	2.1	1.9	1.8	3.2	3.6	3.3	2.1	3.1	2.9
Current ratio at May 31 (diluted)	34.1	21.5	16.6	14.5	14.9	15.3	13.5	10.5	12.2	8.6
Geographic Revenues										
United States	$5,452.5	$5,529.1	$3,964.7	$2,997.9	$2,432.7	$2,528.8	$2,270.9	$2,141.5	$1,755.5	$1,362.2
Europe	2,143.7	1,833.7	1,334.3	980.4	927.3	1,085.7	919.8	664.7	334.3	241.4
Asia/Pacific	1,255.7	1,245.2	735.1	515.6	283.4	178.2	75.7	56.2	29.3	32
Canada, Latin America, and other	701.2	578.5	436.5	266.9	146.3	138.3	138.8	141.2	116.1	75.2
Total revenues	$9,553.1	$9,186.5	$6,470.6	$4,760.8	$3,789.7	$3,931.0	$3,405.2	$3,003.6	$2,235.2	$1,710.8

structuring charge of $129.9 million in the fourth quarter of 1998.

However, Knight also pointed out what he believed were the bright spots of 1998 by noting that he believed Nike's had the best production process in the industry, and that it had taken decades to develop. And he suggested that in the last 6 months of 1998 it had gotten even better. But he also noted that "Inventory is where you can get really killed in this industry. And, we got our bell rung pretty good in the fiscal '98. But we responded very quickly in our sales problems so that, as we go to press, our inventories are 'in line,' several months ahead of our original estimates." In the spring of 1998, Nike introduced the first line of Tiger Woods footwear and apparel, which helped the golf segment of Nike's business post a healthy global increase of 81 percent, while in October of 1998, Nike presented the first products in its Sports Timing category—the Triax running watch. Knight also noted that Nike continued to make strides in growing its women's business. But, he said, the clear winner in fiscal year 1998 had been European apparel, which was up 35 percent.

Nike clearly faced a situation that it had not foreseen nor expected and now faced the challenge of choosing an effective strategy for continued growth.

Endnotes

1. Susan Hauser, "To the Top," *People Weekly,* May 4, 1992, p. 142.
2. Stresser, J. B., and Laurie Becklund, "Swoosh, The Unauthorized Story of Nike and the Men Who Played There," *Harper Business,* 1993, p. 17.
3. Geraldine E. Willigan, "High-Performance Marketing: An Interview with Nike's Phil Knight," *Harvard Business Review,* July-August 1992, pp. 91-101.
4. *Ibid.*
5. Steve E. Holt, "Limousines for the Feet," *Graphic,* March 1993, pp. 89-98.
6. 1998 Annual Report—President's Letter to Stockholders, *www.nike.com.*
7. Please note that all sales revenue and percentages noted in

this section of the case were taken directly from Nike's 1998 Annual Report, available at *www.nike.com.*
8. Kevin Goldman, "Reebok Signs Up the Newest Star in Basketball in $15 Million Pact," *Wall Street Journal,* January 6, 1993, p. B8.
9. Elizabeth Comte, "Art for Shoes' Sake," *Forbes,* September 28, 1992, pp. 128–130.
10. Nike's 1998 Annual Report.
11. Staff writer, "Farewell . . . ," *Sports Illustrated,* February 19, 1990, pp. 77–82.
12. Rich Wilner, "The Battle for #3," *Footwear News,* February 1, 1993, pp. 12, 13, 47.
13. Rich Wilner, "Change, Though Inevitable, Never Comes Easily," *Footwear News,* July 26, 1993, pp. 28–29.
14. Nike's 1998 Annual Report.
15. Many of the figures in this section of the case were taken from Dick Silverman, "The Numbers Game," *Footwear News,* February 1, 1993, p. 54.
16. Staff writer, "Women's Total Athletic Shoe Sales Slip in '92," *Footwear News,* April 19, 1993, p. 19.
17. Nike 1998 Annual Report.
18. Michael Kormos, "Back to School Report, Doing the 'Rithmatic'," *Footwear News,* March 15, 1993, p. 14.
19. Laurie Sohng, "The Athletic Consumer, Age 14," *Footwear News,* February 1, 1993, pp. 44-45.
20. Staff writer, "Shoes," *Standard and Poor's Industry Reports,* October 1993, p. 77.
21. Joseph Perrira, "From Air to Pump to Puma's Disc System, Sneaker Gimmicks Bound to New Heights," *Wall Street Journal,* 1991, p. B5.
22. Staff writer, "Farewell . . . ," *Sports Illustrated,* February 19, 1990, pp. 77–82.
23. Mark Clifford, "Spring in Their Step," *Far Eastern Economic Review,* November 5, 1992, pp. 56–57.
24. Bill Brubaker, "In Shoe Companies' Competition, the Coaches Are the Key Players," *Washington Post,* March 11, 1991, p. A1.
25. Kevin Goldman, "Reebok Signs Up the Newest Star in Basketball in $15 Million Pact," *Wall Street Journal,* January 6, 1993, p. 88.
26. Staff writer, "L.A. Gear Posts Wider than Expected Loss for Fiscal 4th Period," *Wall Street Journal,* February 22, 1993, p. B6.
27. David Thigpen, "Is Nike Getting Too Big for Its Shoes," *Time,* April 26, 1993, p. 55.
28. Laurie Freeman, "Flat-Footed Ad Campaigns Try to Spark Sales as Sports Shoes Hit Plateau," *Stores,* August 1991, pp. 67, 82.
29. *Ibid.*
30. Amy Borrus, "Staunching the Flow of China's Gulag Exports," *Business Week,* April 13, 1992, pp. 51–52.

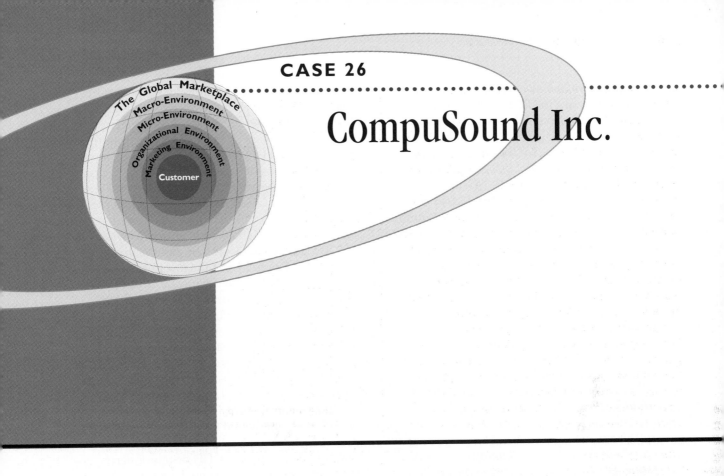

CompuSound Inc.

This case was prepared by James L. Bowey and Kimberley I. McKell, Bishop's University (Lennoxville, Québec).

On a Sunday evening in late February 1995, Bob Norman reviewed his notes from his latest meeting with CompuSound Inc.'s board of directors. He had mixed emotions. He recognized that the discipline being imposed by the board would ultimately result in a stronger CompuSound, the Kanata, Ontario, company he had founded in May 1992. At the meeting, the board had mandated hiring a vice president of marketing for CompuSound. The board's choice was a friend of the chairman.

Bob was confident and somewhat relieved that the new vice president of marketing would be starting on Monday morning. Hopefully, the

This case is intended for use as the basis for class discussion rather than to illustrate the effective or ineffective handling of a managerial situation. All events and individuals in this case are real and essential relationships are maintained, but people and company names have been disguised. Reprinted by permission of James L. Bowey.

pressure to gain shelf space and international distribution for CompuSound's critically acclaimed "CompuSound Pro" sound board would not be entirely on Bob's shoulders. Bob was generally in agreement with the addition of this new marketing executive. However, it would take a lot more sound board sales to cover the $50,000 Cdn annual salary. This figure did not include $30,000 in traveling expenses, including a $5000 trip to the March CeBIT 1995 trade show in Germany. The new vice president needed this immediate exposure to the sound board industry because his experience was unrelated to the computer industry.

Bob reflected on the progress and changes that his young company had undergone in its short history. CompuSound had launched the CompuSound Pro, its main product, at the March CeBIT 1994 trade show. During the remainder of 1994, CompuSound Pro had received very favorable reviews from many in the computer trade press, which prompted a deluge of interest from potential consumers, the PC industry, competitors, and even suppliers who wanted to license CompuSound technology.

Bob was convinced that the addition of the new vice president would help to settle many issues, including possible product repositioning. He recognized that any changes in the market position of CompuSound's sound board would entail rethinking the distribution and pricing strategies. Bob also was very concerned with how quickly the competition might replicate the CompuSound Pro sound board. Unless Bob escalated product development efforts, the CompuSound Pro would remain the company's only product. The amount of additional R&D required would be a function of the efficiency of the R&D team.

Additional R&D and marketing efforts might be difficult to fund, however. The company had nearly exhausted its initial shareholder capital. Fortunately, there did not seem to be a shortage of interested investors, including a local venture capital group. However, the potential investors all had different conditions for making additional investments. There were potential government financing sources. However, Bob wondered if the time and effort required to attract financing from the government would be worth it.

Bob was convinced that CompuSound's profit potential was enormous. He stated: "CompuSound has all the ingredients for success, but the investors take constant convincing and the number of meetings I've been attending to restructure our finances are affecting our daily operations, especially marketing." He believed that the board of directors, now major shareholders, would be patient, provided he could present a new approach. Bob planned to discuss these and other issues with his new vice president of marketing on Monday morning.

PC SOUND BOARD INDUSTRY DEVELOPMENT

When personal computers were first introduced, sound was available only through their internal speakers. The resulting sound was crude and unpleasant to the ear. It did little to enhance software applications. This situation changed in 1988, when a company named Ad Lib introduced the first frequency modulation (FM) synthesis sound board, using the Yamaha OPL2 chip. For the first time, sound was played through an external speaker; this breakthrough enhanced PC sound considerably. Soon after, Creative Labs of California introduced its first Sound Blaster board that incorporated 8-bit FM synthesis. Creative Labs then replaced its 8-bit board with a 16-bit board. Sound quality improved quickly, and the sound board industry grew rapidly.

The latest technological breakthrough in the sound board industry was the incorporation of a process called *wavetable synthesis.* In this process, the computer used recordings of actual instruments to reproduce sound rather than trying to replicate instrumental sound using FM synthesis. A trumpet sound was an actual trumpet with wavetable synthesis, not a poor FM synthesis imitation. Wavetable synthesis allowed personal computers to generate nearly CD quality sound.

The CompuSound Pro combined both wavetable synthesis and FM synthesis and also used the new-generation Yamaha OPL4 chip. The CompuSound Pro incorporated its own proprietary chip that integrated the technologies on a single board. This combination allowed consumers to generate all-round superior sound. This capability had positioned the CompuSound Pro board at the forefront of PC sound technology and was a source of pride for everyone at the company.

Company Background

Compu-Sound, Inc., was founded as a sole proprietorship in May 1992, by Bob Norman. Bob spent the first 15 years of his business career as a chartered accountant. He spent the next 10 years running his own niche market computer software business with several colleagues. Over the years, Bob accumulated numerous contacts in the personal computer industry, particularly in the engineering and manufacturing of printed circuit boards. The start-up capital for CompuSound, a young basement operation, came from Bob's May 1991 sale of his position in the computer software business to a public company. A year later, in May 1992, Bob turned his attention and capital to the development of a sound board that would outperform the less-than-adequate products that were available on the market. Bob had always had an ear for music and sound. His favorite hobby was tinkering with computers, and he wanted to apply his knowledge to meet other enthusiasts' needs.

Additionally, Bob Norman had an intense love for music technology that was not being satisfied by the market leader, Sound Blaster. Although Sound Blaster held a virtual monopoly in the PC sound market, its sound quality was not up to Bob's standards. Beyond Sound Blaster, there seemed to be high-quality sound boards on the market, but their prices were prohibitively expensive.

One of the reasons that Bob felt there was a major market in this area was the speed at which the demand for multimedia capabilities (simultaneous video, audio, and text functions) seemed to be converging with the demand for personal computers. All PC market trends looked to be pointing toward sound and CD-ROM drive peripherals or optional add-on accessories. The extraordinary demand for sound technology was being driven by the explosion of computer video games. The sophisticated software of these games and the marketing skills of companies such as Nintendo and Sega Genesis initiated the rapid development of PC sound capability.

Bob was convinced that he could deliver a better product at a lower price, particularly because one of the original industry leaders, Ad Lib, had gone bankrupt in 1991. According to Bob, "Ad Lib developed a terrific sound board, but its inability to meet delivery schedules and inadequate financing were largely responsible for the company's failure." Bob immediately hired AudioTech, the electronics and software engineering firm that had designed Ad Lib's technology. The AudioTech engineers had set an industry standard in PC sound technology and had over 7 years of experience with sound board technology. CompuSound developed its relationship with AudioTech, which was located only 2 hours away, into an exclusive alliance. AudioTech headed the research, design, and development effort for CompuSound under the close direction of Bob Norman.

CompuSound's products were manufactured by a local circuit board assembly company, FLEX Assemblers. CompuSound had managed to merge the brilliant sound technology of AudioTech with the manufacturing skills of FLEX Assemblers to create a state-of-the-art sound board. CompuSound protected itself by securing exclusive ownership of AudioTech's sound technology. Although Compu-Sound was responsible for any raw materials and

other inventories that FLEX Assemblers had acquired on its behalf, it was free to have its products manufactured elsewhere.

As of February 1995, CompuSound, Inc., employed seven people, of whom three were dedicated to the technical side of the business. The staff included a product specialist, a technical support specialist, a product tester, a managerial accountant, a secretary, a receptionist, and a part-time shipping clerk. Except for the accountant, most of the staff were employed in their first serious jobs at CompuSound. In terms of industry knowledge, the skills of the 22 year-old product specialist were exceptional. Bob had become increasingly dependent on the product specialist for insight into the quickly changing sound board industry. The product specialist also ran his own "Internet provider" business in his spare time, although the Internet activities sometimes conflicted with his responsibilities for taking sales calls and generating publicity for the CompuSound Pro.

Generally, Bob was very proud of his young, committed group of computer enthusiasts. He had personally trained his technical assistants, although he had to admit that their love and understanding of computers, especially the game applications, had proved invaluable to product improvements. Since the company's inception, Bob had handled the sales and marketing function.

CompuSound's sales had not been encouraging to date. The company only sold 1500 units over the prior 10-month period. However, Bob knew the CompuSound Pro sound board was unquestionably the best all-around product on the market. According to several industry experts, there was no other sound board with all the features of the Compu-Sound Pro. This seemed to be verified by a slight increase in European orders, as well as interest in licensing CompuSound's proprietary technology. By Feburary 1995, European orders surpassed domestic business. CompuSound had visited Europe initially with an appearance at the March CeBIT 1994 trade show in Germany. This trade show resulted in orders from a German distributor in the music channel. In contrast to North American sales, European export orders had been met with little price resistance. CompuSound also met with Philips Electronics of the Netherlands representatives at the show. Philips also was very interested in licensing CompuSound's technology. As of February 1995, the majority of CompuSound sales had come from distributors Bob had met at trade shows. Bob reiterated his claim at the February 1995 shareholder's meeting: "After almost 3 years of dedication and over $1.0 million of developmental investment, CompuSound, Inc., is about to capitalize on the multimedia superhighway frenzy."

PC Peripheral Market

Multimedia was the growing trend for PCs in the 1990s. A multimedia computer incorporated a CD-ROM drive, a sound board, and speakers. Consumers could obtain multimedia capabilities by purchasing computers that came "multimedia ready" from the manufacturer, upgrading their older personal computers with a multimedia upgrade kit, or buying a CD-ROM drive and sound board separately. The best prices were usually, but not always, obtained by purchasing either a multimedia-ready computer or an upgrade kit. Consumers also had the option of purchasing an optional upgrade at the original equipment manufacturer (OEM) level. The optional upgrade option was a small portion of the sound board market and was offered primarily by mail-order OEMs such as Gateway 2000.

The technology of the PC peripheral market had simply exploded over recent years. Computer environments that integrated audio, graphics, video, and other media had become the norm. In the mid-1990s, consumers expected multimedia capabilities from their personal computers, although they had difficulty keeping up with the latest technological trends. Consumers often were unsure of the quality, value, and technical differences of the peripherals needed for multimedia capability.

The PC market was broken down into informed buyers and uninformed buyers. The informed buyers were in the minority. Informed multimedia buyers were characterized by their higher income level, higher expenditure on hardware and software technology, a tendency to look beyond traditional retail channels for their multimedia purchases, and/or a tendency to purchase at computer specialty retail stores or through direct mail (Link Resources 1993, Home Media Consumer Survey).

As a rule of thumb, consumers who purchased multimedia-ready computers simply wanted multimedia capabilities. They were not concerned with having the best CD-ROM drive or the best sound board but were instead in search of the best cost deal. Consumers who upgraded through a multime-

dia kit also were looking for a good price. Usually, when a kit was sold, either the sound board or the CD-ROM drive was the featured product. As a result, there were virtually no high-quality multimedia upgrade kits that offered a top-notch CD-ROM drive and a superior sound board. Upgrading through buying all the components separately was the most expensive option. Computer owners were doing so because they wanted superior product quality. Either they had specific needs (e.g., musicians) or they simply wanted to have the best-quality product.

The average prices of sophisticated PC systems equipped with multimedia capabilities were tumbling (see Exhibit A). Multimedia add-on equipment and kit prices were subject to similar price pressures. With these price decreases, worldwide multimedia unit sales were expected to experience significant growth. In 1993, the United States dominated the demand for multimedia kit shipments and PCs shipped with sound capabilities, with 70 percent of worldwide market share. Europe followed, with 15 percent market share, and this percentage was expected to increase to 20 percent by 1996. Japanese end users accounted for 10 percent of the remaining market share (Dataquest: February 1994 World Estimates).

SOUND BOARD MARKET

Until February 1995, the sound board industry had grown quite rapidly, making it an attractive industry that had lured several new competitors. These competitors had introduced a wave of new sound board products in the fall of 1994. Some industry experts believed that the prospects for continued market growth were good; however, the market forecasts were mixed. One projection anticipated a 1995 increase and decline thereafter (see Exhibit B). Bob was slightly concerned about the Dataquest figures. He stated: "The CompuSound Pro does not compete in the low-end sound board market. Low-end sound boards will possibly be replaced by sound chips, and I think that this might cause an overall decline in sound board sales in a couple of years."

Some experts agreed that the major argument for this potential decline was that the original equipment manufacturers (OEMs) were increasingly manufacturing PCs with sound capabilities. Additionally, OEMs might soon be replacing sound

EXHIBIT A
················
Average Business Multimedia System Price (US$/unit)

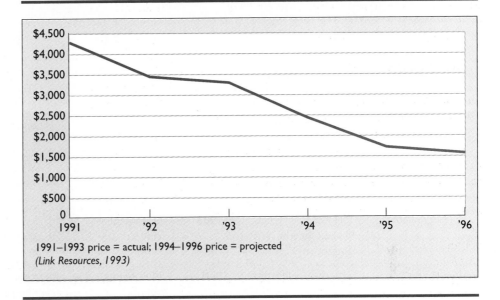

1991–1993 price = actual; 1994–1996 price = projected
(Link Resources, 1993)

board technology with a chip on the motherboard, eliminating the need for a separate sound board altogether. Sound board manufacturers would then be faced with a new marketing challenge—how to get consumers to upgrade the sound capabilities that were already present in their personal computers. Once the motherboard chip incorporated sound, the majority of the residual sound board market would be for high-end sound boards that catered to consumers who desired unusual capabilities adapted to their specific needs.

EXHIBIT B
················
Worldwide Sound Board Sales

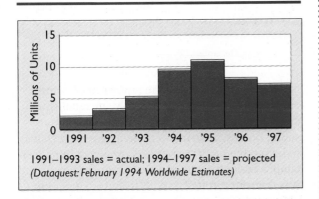

1991–1993 sales = actual; 1994–1997 sales = projected
(Dataquest: February 1994 Worldwide Estimates)

By February 1995, Bob believed that the markets remaining for the CompuSound Pro seemed to be (1) OEM based on delivery of a low-priced, high-performing sound board (or licensing of technology), (2) as an enhanced hardware add-on, or (3) as a product for very high-end music enthusiasts. Bob was convinced that his company would have at least 2 years before a sound chip on the motherboard could compete with the CompuSound Pro in terms of sound quality.

The increased competition of the fall of 1994 also had forced a decline in the price of sound boards. Bob had noticed many new competitors at the November COMDEX 1994 trade show in the United States (see Exhibit C). By February 1995, there was a significant gap between the manufacturer's suggested retail price and the street price at which a sound board was actually sold. Margins had been squeezed, particularly in the low-end market.

The sound board market was separated into three different price segments: low, medium, and high end. High-end boards, like the CompuSound Pro, all incorporated wavetable synthesis technology. One problem with incorporating wavetable synthesis was that the public did not fully understand and appreciate this technology. Most consumers, even those very knowledgeable about computers, often did not understand the difference

EXHIBIT C

Selected Information on Competitors

Company	Location	Year Formed	Product Expertise	Strategy	Sound Board
CompuSound Inc.	Kanata, Ontario	1992	Sound cards	Value/niche	CompuSound Pro
Creative Labs	Milpitas, California (head office in Singapore)	1981	Sound and video	Market domination	AWE32
Creative Labs	Milpitas, California (head office in Singapore)	1981	Sound and video	Market domination	Sound Blaster 16 ASP
Media Vision	San Jose, California	N/A	Multimedia, sound, and video	Mass market leadership	Pro 3D
Aztech Systems	Fremont, California (head office in Singapore)	1986	Multimedia, sound, video, CD-ROM	Price leadership	Wave Rider
Advanced Gravis	Burnaby, British Columbia	1985	Joy sticks, game pads, sound boards	Price/volume	Ultrasound Max
Ensoniq	Malvern, Pennsylvania	1982	Multimedia, musical instruments	Niche/volume	Soundscape
Turtle Beach Systems	York, Pennsylvania	1985	Sound cards	Total market segment coverage	Monterey
Roland	Los Angeles (Head office in Japan)	1972	Musical instruments, sound boards	Niche/ leadership	Rap-10

Source: CompuSound Inc., Internal Report based on press releases from various companies, December 1994.

between one sound board and another. Consumers, due to their lack of product knowledge, bought either multimedia-ready computers or whatever salespeople recommended to them. As a result, reviews in trade magazines carried much weight in the consumer purchase decision. Consumers had struggled to keep up with technology changes and had been forced to trust the reports of computer experts to keep them informed. Many retail store employees were surprisingly uneducated about sound boards, referring to trade magazine reviews to help them make "expert" recommendations. Certainly a major hurdle for any sound board company was consumer, retailer, and distributor education.

Price Cdn. $	Introduction Date of Latest Sound Board	Technical Rating by Compu-Sound (1 = Poor, 10 = Excellent)	Market Position	End-User Profile	How Sold
$395	March 1994	7	High end	Informed	Distributors, PC stores
$369	March 1994	6	High end	Informed Gamer and PC stores	Distributors
$249	1993	4	Middle end	Non-informed gamer	Distributors and PC stores
$299	1994	5-6	Middle-high end	Non-informed gamer	PC Distributors
$279	1994	5	Middle-high end	Non-informed gamer	OEM, distributors, PC stores
$269	1994	5	Middle	Informed	Distributors, PC stores, mail order
$269	1994	5	Middle-high	Informed	Music stores
$199	1994	4-5	Middle	Non-informed	Distributors, major chain stores
$549	1994	7	High	Pro user musician	Music distributors

MARKETING

Due to the lack of consumer education about sound board quality, product marketing played a larger role than product performance in the industry. Aggressive marketing and sales promotion expenditures were key to gaining distribution access and successful product sell through. Quite often consumers simply bought whatever was on display in retail stores. Bob was sometimes quite frustrated when he went to check out the CompuSound's retail competition. "How," he asked, "can people buy this garbage? The competition's quality and features are not even close to the CompuSound Pro."

Retailers typically carried one to three different sound boards in their stores. The sound boards often were bundled into multimedia kits. California's Creative Labs dominated the furious war for product shelf space with its line of sound boards called Sound Blaster. Sound Blaster had an enormous advantage because of its early positioning in the industry, as well as its excellent sales promotion and advertising skills. Sound Blaster compatibility had become a standard within the sound board industry, leading to further brand-name exposure. Consumers had become very familiar with the Sound Blaster brand and asked for it by name. Sound Blaster's extraordinary brand awareness had almost reached generic status.

Sound Blaster also offered a complete line of sound boards ranging from low to high end. Its high-end wavetable board called AWE32 was the direct competitor of the CompuSound Pro. Sound Blaster employed a very effective strategy of bundling its sound boards with well-targeted and attractive software packages. Many retailers could carry Sound Blaster as their only product line and satisfy all the perceived needs of the consumers. Retailers had deemed the best sound boards to be the ones that were the easiest to move off their shelves.

The three main sound board selling points had become sound quality, compatibility, and expandability. Sound quality was classified into two distinct categories, FM synthesis and wavetable synthesis boards, with wavetable synthesis providing clearly superior sound quality. Within these categories, however, consumers had to hear the sound boards for themselves to distinguish their sound quality. The compatibility feature of sound boards was important because the more systems that a sound board was compatible with, the less constrained the consumer's choice was when choosing future software applications. Upgrade features also were valued because they allowed consumers to add on features to their boards as they became available. This provided consumers with some assurance that their boards would not become obsolete.

MARKET SEGMENTS

There was little publicly available data on the sound board industry. During the last 12 months, press releases from various companies included the following:

- March 1994: Creative Labs introduced the Creative AWE32 sound board.

- June 1994: The CompuSound Pro received the "Candy Man" seal.

- January 1995: Turtle Beach Systems introduced the Tropez sound card.

Independent data revealed that more than 80 percent of sound boards were shipped to the home market in 1994 (Dataquest: February 1994 Worldwide Estimates). The home market was comprised of people using PCs in their homes instead of at work. The CompuSound team estimated that the sound board industry was broken down into three main market segments: the home and games market (70 percent), the business and multimedia market (25 percent), and the musician market (5 percent). These markets had the following distinct sound board purchase priorities (see table below):

(1 = most important, 5 = least important)

Market	Price	Sound Quality	Bundled Software	Bundled Hardware	Compatibility
Business/multimedia	4	3	1	2	5
Home/games	1	5	3	4	2
Musician	3	1	2	4	5

Source: CompuSound Inc., Internal Report Based on Bob Norman's Observations, September 1994.

The business market required custom-tailored hardware to meet distinct needs, along with full turnkey multimedia software presentation packages. Manufacturers generally had to service the business market through traditional distributors. These distributors in turn serviced value-added retailers (VARs) and multimedia houses. The business market also bought basic computer equipment, sound capabilities, and PC peripherals from large retail chains. These chains were supplied by these same distributors and sometimes directly with the manufacturers themselves. Several industry experts felt that sound quality was becoming more important to the business market, due to the growth in voice recognition and video conferencing software applications.

Home users required sound technology that was easily installed, problem-free, and met their perceived needs. Gamers, an integral part of the home market, wanted sound capabilities that exploited their game audio capabilities to the fullest, at a low price. Retailers usually were pressured by the home market for very competitive prices, and both the large retail chains and distributors were forced to work on low margins. As a result, distributors and retailers were not very interested in educating the home consumer about the feature comparability between sound board brands, preferring that manufacturers pull their brands through the channel.

The music market was distinct because musicians tended to ignore any sound technology made for the masses. Musicians also required specific audio features to meet their composing requirements. They mainly purchased their sound boards in specialist music shops that were supplied by music distributors. Retailers in the music segment spent time with their customers comparing various features, because sound quality and specific software were critical to purchase decisions.

Distributors in both the PC and music channels were quite powerful and had a tendency to send goods back to the manufacturers that did not sell through to the retailers. As the margins became increasingly squeezed throughout the distribution channels, manufacturers had to shoulder more of the responsibility of communicating their product features to retailers and consumers. This function was traditionally that of the distributors.

COMPETITION

The sound board industry was dominated by three companies who accounted for 95 percent of the entire market (see Exhibit D). Creative Labs (Sound Blaster), which sourced from Singapore, completely dominated the low end of the sound board industry. Overall, Sound Blaster accounted for about 60 percent of sound board sales. The other major competitors, Aztech Labs and Media Vision, controlled 17 and 18 percent of the market, respectively. Media Vision had expanded to take on other ventures in the computer peripherals' industry. This strategy met with disastrous results and nearly forced Media Vision into bankruptcy in 1994. Additionally, there were several other competitors that competed within the high-end sound board field, notably Turtle Beach, Roland, Advanced Gravis, and Ensoniq (see Exhibit C).

In the high-end sound board segment, sound quality was the primary issue rather than price. Technological advances had forced competitors at the high end to constantly improve their products. One industry expert suggested that the product lifecycle for a high-end product was about 2 years. Niche strategies often were successful in the high-end sound board market. Roland had successfully catered to the needs of aspiring musicians by offering a package that enabled the PC to transform into an actual recording studio. By February 1995, no other company had tried to compete in this niche market, and Roland had been left alone to enjoy its high margins and profits. Bob Norman was con-

EXHIBIT D

Estimated 1994 Sound Board Market Share

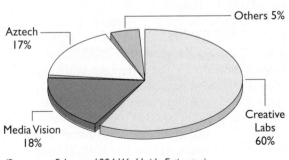

(Dataquest: February 1994 Worldwide Estimates)

vinced that the CompuSound Pro's sound quality was close to that of Roland while delivering features needed by gamers and business multimedia consumers.

COMPUSOUND'S PRODUCT LINE

CompuSound's product line was totally focused on sound boards for PCs. This strategy was somewhat unusual compared with other competitors, many of whom sold other peripheral products (see Exhibit C). Initially, some of these competitors also had been totally devoted to one segment of the sound board market and had later diversified their product lines.

At first, CompuSound had planned to introduce three sound boards into the marketplace, the CompuSound Basic, the CompuSound Amateur, and the CompuSound Pro. These products covered the low, medium, and high ends of the market, respectively. CompuSound had started shipping the CompuSound Pro in volume after the March CeBIT 1994 trade show, at a retail price of $395 Cdn. By February 1995, it was still the only sound board sold by the company. The company also offered several service-type products such as MIDI cables (for connecting PCs to electronic keyboards and guitars), add-on expansion boards, and extra software. These products were included as part of the product line in order to project the image of a company that was a full-service supplier of sound boards, as well as to ensure that the CompuSound Pro had maximum flexibility.

In terms of product features, Bob Norman was sure that no other board could touch the CompuSound Pro. The CompuSound Pro was considered state-of-the-art because it incorporated all the sound board standards and compatibility features. The CompuSound Pro had an extraordinary proprietary chip, the OPL4 chip by Yamaha, and a uniquely integrated circuit that could become the envy of the industry. The CompuSound Pro had unrivaled expansion capability because it could be fitted with any of four current optional add-on daughterboards and also left room for future growth. These daughterboards met the evolving needs of customers, such as providing 3D surround sound capability. The CompuSound Pro included many of the standard software programs expected

of a high-priced sound board, as well as several additional programs.

In terms of sound quality, Bob Norman was most inspired by the CompuSound Pro's being named the winner of the coveted "Candy Man" seal of approval in June 1994. Announced in a press release by CompuSound, the "Candy Man" had deemed that the CompuSound Pro was "Candy" tested, "Candy" certified, and "Candy" compatible. As of the November COMDEX 1994 trade show, the CompuSound Pro was the only sound board to have earned this honor. The "Candy Man" was a recognized producer of video game music who would most certainly add to the brand awareness of the CompuSound Pro.

The CompuSound Pro received numerous positive reviews in computer magazines in the United States: *PC Magazine* and *Computer Game Review* (October 1994) and *Computer Gaming World* (November 1994). In November 1994, CompuSound Pro also was reviewed well in Europe: *CD-ROM Now* (U.K.) and *WIN Magazine* and *Computer Persönlich* (Germany). The latest January 1995 reviews were found in *Computer Shopper* and *Computer Player* (United States) and in *PC Pro* (U.K.). Experienced PC users also raved about the CompuSound Pro on e-mail and Internet systems. In October 1994, the industry reviewer from *Computer Game Review* expressed his enthusiasm as follows:

> Gushing about sound boards is not something I generally do, but the CompuSound Pro is rather exceptional. Not only do you get quality sound …this card is so well-documented that Forrest Gump could install it.… This card performed flawlessly.… This card is nearly perfect.

These types of reviews from the trade journals and magazines were very encouraging to Bob Norman. However, the January 1995 *Computer Shopper* review brought into question the CompuSound Pro's ability to compete with the Roland sound board in terms of sound quality. Certainly the company had made every attempt to deliver the musician a product that had all the needed software as well as excellent sound at a cheaper price than Roland. Unfortunately, one influential critic negatively reviewed the CompuSound Pro for use by professional musicians, although he thought it was more than adequate for amateurs. Bob was slightly discouraged about this criticism. He insisted that the CompuSound Pro delivered similar sound quality to the Roland product.

By the fall of 1994, there were indications that the CompuSound Pro was on the verge of setting some of its own industry standards. At this time, Bob used his contacts at Yamaha USA, which supplied chips to CompuSound, to meet with Yamaha Japan representatives at the November COMDEX 1994 show. Armed with his product reviews for the CompuSound Pro, Bob enjoyed a very successful meeting with Yamaha Japan. The Yamaha people had asked if there was any possibility of licensing the entire CompuSound technology, which incorporated Yamaha's OPL4 chip. This type of endorsement by Yamaha (with its worldwide reputation in the music industry) was encouraging to Bob. Furthermore, Philips of the Netherlands was keen to send its engineers to Kanata to discuss a possible licensing agreement. The Philips interest had started initially through a personal meeting at the March CeBIT 1994 show in Germany. Bob was keen to visit Philips at the March CeBIT 1995 show to continue discussion of a possible relationship.

COMPUSOUND'S MANUFACTURING AND SOURCING

Bob Norman had recognized very early in the development of the sound board that there would be no advantage in manufacturing the sound board within the company. Bob Norman estimated the financial resources required to manufacture computer peripherals as far beyond his capital resources. Moreover, like most hardware segments of the PC industry, the economies of scale required would be prohibitive. Even the major players in the original equipment market were beginning to move toward outsourcing their production requirements.

Fortunately for CompuSound, Inc., the local region had managed to develop a respectable technological skill base. This base included a major supplier of circuit board assembly production for several multinational firms such as Northern Telecom and IBM. FLEX Assemblers, which was located within minutes of the CompuSound offices, became instrumental in the early development of the

CompuSound Pro. It had provided some of the seed capital and technology to CompuSound, with the thought of becoming one of its major suppliers. Bob Norman concluded that the proximity to such a major assembler was an important advantage for his company, particularly when it came to product development. However, the prices that FLEX Assemblers had quoted were not nearly as low as Bob had expected.

There was another important factor that forced CompuSound to avoid any investment into manufacturing assets. The Far East had already become a major supplier of low-end sound boards, and this region's role in the industry would undoubtedly grow. Although the quality was not yet up to North American standards, it seemed inevitable that Taiwan, Korea, and eventually China would be forces to be reckoned within the next couple of years. Since 1990, Singapore had become the most advanced in the production of low-end sound boards, primarily due to Sound Blaster's production base here.

COMPUSOUND'S DISTRIBUTION

CompuSound sold the CompuSound Pro through both PC and music distributors, primarily in parts of Europe and Canada. The European market was especially pleased with the high quality of the CompuSound Pro and was less susceptible to the marketing hype promoted by Sound Blaster. The CompuSound Pro was found in over 250 stores in Canada, including Future Shop and Adventure Electronics locations. Found mainly in larger cities across Canada, Future Shop was a computer superstore concept, whereas Adventure Electronics was a large national retail chain for electronic goods. Bob Norman wanted to increase CompuSound's share of the American market. By December 1994, the United States accounted for less than 10 percent of its total sales, most of which had come through direct sales (see Exhibit E). After reading the outstanding magazine reviews, American consumers were prompted to call CompuSound directly to purchase the CompuSound Pro.

In November 1994, CompuSound exhibited the CompuSound Pro at the Fall COMDEX 1994 trade show. The trade show had over 200,000 participants from the worldwide PC industry. The show

EXHIBIT E

Geographic Sales Breakdown of CompuSound, Inc., as of February 1995

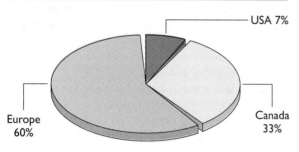

USA 7%

Canada 33%

Europe 60%

(CompuSound Inc., Internal Sales Report, December 1994)

was deemed a success by Bob Norman in that it resulted in several hundred inquiries. However, CompuSound did not have the salesforce to deal with these requests on a timely basis. The distribution infrastructure was so limited that it was difficult for CompuSound to handle the inquiries made by many international retailers and distributors. It was not unusual for a 3-month time period to pass for an initial inquiry to develop into a small test order by a retailer or distributor. Furthermore, these new customers expected generous payment terms, in-store promotional support and training, as well as the usual advertising commitments. CompuSound had planned to visit several trade shows in 1995, including March CeBIT 1995 in Germany. Although the show cost CompuSound approximately $40,000 Cdn, including the cost of a booth within the Canadian government pavilion and travel expenses, Bob hoped that the costs would pay off in terms of sound board sales.

CompuSound, Inc., was experiencing a distribution challenge. Bob had just started to understand that "because Sound Blaster is so dominant in the retail stores, it would take an enormous chunk of CompuSound's resources to get onto retail shelves." CompuSound was targeting three distinct channels (music, home, and business) in three different geographic regions (Europe, Canada, and the United States). The distinct customer target markets were very similar in all geographic areas. The dilemma that CompuSound was facing was how to reach each of these segments. By February 1995, CompuSound employed one sales agent for Canada and hoped to develop similar sales agents in each

of its target countries in Europe and selected regions in the United States. These representatives would be responsible for technical sales support, logistics, and servicing sales.

In Canada and Europe, CompuSound had recruited traditional distributors in both the home and music channels. These distributors purchased directly from CompuSound. The distributors were theoretically responsible for selling and providing product support, including educating dealers, retailers, resellers, and system consultants on the benefits of CompuSound Pro. Unfortunately, in practice, the distributors had been unsuccessful in selling the CompuSound Pro, and had been negligent in their duties to provide product support and education. These responsibilities had fallen back on CompuSound, Inc. Of further concern to CompuSound were that sound board distributor markups ranged from 7 to 15 percent, and retailer markups ranged from 20 to 30 percent. Bob Norman was starting to feel that these intermediaries were not earning their margins and were adding little value to the CompuSound Pro.

CompuSound sold some of its product directly to consumers at nearly full retail prices, although this was a negligible part of its sales to date. The higher margins from these direct sales were attractive, and the consumer who bought direct was usually a very informed end user who had little difficulty in installing the CompuSound Pro. Bob could not help wondering if direct-selling methods might not be a more profitable approach to reaching informed buyers. The costs of Internet marketing and other direct-selling methods seemed relatively low compared with using traditional distribution channels.

Another market opportunity that CompuSound was looking into was large contracts with original equipment manufacturers or manufacturers of other peripheral devices for computers. In addition to offering complete sound boards to OEMs, CompuSound could be in a position to offer them a portion of the proprietary components of the sound board and its technology. During November COMDEX 1994 show, CompuSound had started targeting manufacturers, such as IBM and Hewlett Packard, primarily in an upgrade option capacity. However, the preliminary feedback from the OEMs and primary research that CompuSound had undertaken indicated that upgrade options were a very limited market.

EXHIBIT F
. . . .
CompuSound, Inc.: Balance Sheet (Cdn. $), as of December 31, 1994

Current assets			Current liabilities		
Bank account	$	9,021	Bank loan	$	880,000
Accounts receivable, trade		31,883	Accounts payable		935,713
Accounts receivable, others		120,623	Accrued expenses		800
Inventory		1,122,859	Deductions at source		4,191
Deferred charges		1,043	Sales taxes		196
Income taxes		84,396			
Total current assets		1,369,825	**Total current liabilities**		1,820,900
Property and equipment		73,834	**Long-term liabilities**		
Other assets			Deferred credits		98,900
Development costs		961,970	Deferred tax credits		184,396
Start-up costs		81,263	Notes payable		17,798
Trademarks		5,249			
			Total liabilities		2,121,994
			Equity		
			Common stock		899,000
			Retained earnings		(528,853)
			Total liabilities and		
Total Assets		2,492,141	**Shareholder's equity**		2,492,141

Key financial data	
Average selling price to distributor/unit	$250 Cdn
Average retail selling price/unit	$395 Cdn
Actual sales to date	$375,000 Cdn
Gross margin[a]	10%–15%
Average monthly expenses during 1994[b]	$65–75,000 Cdn

[a]Depending on special discounts.
[b]Including salaries, marketing, distributor maintenance, and advertising costs.

COMPUSOUND'S FINANCIAL SITUATION

CompuSound's original financing of CompuSound, Inc., came from Bob Norman's previous business. It became apparent in early 1994, during the development of the first sound board prototype, that additional sources of capital would be required. When the company moved beyond its incubation stage, Bob was forced to invite other investors to participate as the company took on the financial burdens of growth and in the process gave up his controlling shareholder position. Bob expected he would have to find even more sources of capital in order to fund the continual development required to maintain a technological advantage. The provincial government had expressed an interest in becoming involved through either grants or loans. This government involvement was dependent on whether the company was able to meet certain export criteria.

There also was an opportunity to get a venture

capital group that focused on local entrepreneurial start-ups involved, once the company had achieved a critical mass of sales of $1.0 million Cdn per annum. In the meantime, the company's bank was not willing to extend the company any more credit because it had already exceeded its limits and had broken a few minor loan covenants. Bob thought, "If only these bankers understood the high quality of the CompuSound Pro, then they would get off my back."

Although CompuSound's current shareholders seemed to be interested in providing funding for continuing its operations and development, the present sales projections had to be revised before any capital would be forthcoming. The original budget was now 6 months old, and the projected sales had not materialized. It was now fairly clear that the 1994 forecast would become the 1995 forecast. The company seemed to be an entire year behind schedule. The board of directors, all shareholders, was acutely aware that the strategic positioning of the CompuSound Pro would significantly affect the sales volume and the gross margin contribution. Bob felt that one of the first priorities of the vice president of marketing would be a new marketing plan, including a detailed sales forecast.

Through February 1995, the company had sold 1500 units of CompuSound Pro at an average price to distributors of $250 Cdn (see Exhibit F for company balance sheet and other selected financial information). In 1993, CompuSound had projected sales for 1994 of 19,000 sound board units. All the potential sources of financing were adamant about the need for a detailed business plan. The board of directors was pushing management to complete the revised business plan as soon as possible. Several of the board members could be willing to provide either temporary or even longer-term capital, once a solid strategy was in place.

Bob decided that he should review the company's problems and accomplishments in light of the various market opportunities. He was very eager to get the new vice president of marketing focused on the right priorities. However, as he began to review his notes, it became clear that the next few months would be critical. One option would be to send CompuSound's new vice president to Europe for some further market investigation, although the Canadian and American distributors also needed immediate attention and nurturing. The market seemed to be changing very quickly, and Bob really could not wait to get working on the new product features for the CompuSound Pro. Bob decided to discuss these problems with his new executive first thing Monday morning. Bob then thought, "I can't wait to try out my new software for the CompuSound Pro."

North Country Bank & Trust

This case was prepared by Brian G. Gnauck, Dean and Professor of Marketing, and Samuel P. Graci, Professor of Accounting, Northern Michigan University.

On the evening before the deer season opened, Mr. John Crocker was indeed excited. John was at his camp in Michigan's Upper Peninsula with six lifelong, deer-hunting buddies. After dinner, John brought out his old rifle case and displayed his brand new 340 Weatherby magnum. "Wow!" said Pete, his hunting buddy of 15 years. Tim Compton chimed in, "That set you back a buck or two." Ed, John's best friend, said, "That is quite a weapon; let me see it." John, responding to Tim's comment, said, "It didn't cost me a dime." Tim immediately responded, "How's that? Come on, you gotta be kidding?"

How John obtained the weapon and its real value were all explained in a unique marketing program of North Country Bank & Trust of Manistique, Michigan, which was just one example of their unique approach to banking.

BACKGROUND

North Country Bank & Trust, formerly First Manistique Corporation, is a branch holding company with $327.5 million in assets as of June 1996. North Country Bank operates two commercial bank subsidiaries, First Northern Bank & Trust, headquartered in Manistique, Michigan, and South Range State Bank, located in South Range, Michigan. These banks operate 23 facilities (branches) in 20 communities in Michigan's Upper Peninsula. North Country Bank also owns and operates three other businesses: First Manistique Agency, which sells annuities as well as life, accident, and health insurance, First Rural Relending Company, a nonprofit relending company, and First Northern Services Company, a real estate appraisal company.

The company has experienced significant growth in assets as a result of acquisitions, having acquired two banks, one branch, and substantially all the banking assets and liabilities of a third bank since 1994. Effective January 31, 1996, the company acquired all the outstanding stock of the South Range State Bank, with assets of approximately $40 million. This acquisition may have an adverse effect on earnings because past results cannot be ensured in the future. The company is continuing to seek acquisitions in its existing or adjoining market areas to the extent suitable candidates and acceptable terms can be found. The company is a very aggressive bidder in the event a bank within its geographic region is for sale or agreeable to a merger. The company views the acquisition opportunities as limited and takes a very aggressive acquisition stance.

North Country Bank has experienced significant growth (see Exhibit A). This growth in assets has been a combination of internal growth as well as through merger and asset-acquisition activity.

Much of the internal asset growth was attributable to North Country Bank & Trust's innovative approach to marketing. Under the leadership of Ron Ford, the bank had deviated significantly from traditional bank practices and marketing methods. Among these nontraditional methods are deposit programs featuring Weatherby rifles, Big Bertha golf clubs, diamonds, grandfather clocks, and art prints, all innovative and effective approaches to demand deposit acquisition.

The company is in the process of selling 400,000 shares of common stock, which is expected to yield $10.668 million. The proceeds will be used to retire $2.9 million in bank debt, of which $1.9 million was incurred to acquire the South Range Bank. Another $4.3 million of the proceeds will fund expected future acquisitions. The balance will be used for working capital needs and to generally strengthen the financial position of the company.

THE WEATHERBY CERTIFICATE OF DEPOSIT PROGRAM

The Weatherby certificate of deposit program was typical of all these programs. This program basi-

cally provided the customer with a Weatherby rifle or shotgun in lieu of interest on a certificate of deposit (CD) with the bank. CDs with 3-, 9-, 12- or 20-year maturities were available to secure a rifle. For example, if a customer desired an Accumark 340 Weatherby magnum, a minimum deposit of $5673 for a 3-year period was required. If the customer deposited the money for as long as 20 years, it would require only $1189 (see Exhibit B). At the end of the deposit period, principal only is returned on the CD. For example, if customers purchased a 3-year, $5673 CD, they would receive their weapon at deposit time. At the end of the 3-year period, when the CD matures, $5673, the principal amount, is returned without any interest.

The purchase process works as follows: First, the buyer would select the firearm and fill out the appropriate information on the deposit agreement. Since a federal firearm license is required, a copy of that would be included with the purchase. In certain instances, required sales tax would be paid in addition to the deposit. North Country Bank & Trust provides free shipping as an incentive for the program, with delivery in about 4 to 6 weeks. The certificate of deposit could not be withdrawn prior to maturity. All the Weatherby products handled by the bank were new and included a Weatherby warranty as if they were purchased in a typical retail store. Since customers got the gun, they were required to pay income tax on North Country Bank & Trust's cost and were issued a 1099 for that tax year, analogous to paying tax on the CD's interest earnings.

Other certificate of deposit programs using Big Bertha golf clubs, diamonds, grandfather clocks, and prints worked in a similar fashion. Ron Ford was particularly proud of the Weatherby program. North Country Bank & Trust purchased rifles in lots of $250,000 and were consequently able to negotiate a lucrative purchase price. Typical margin on these types of weapons was 30 to 40 percent of *retail price*. The company advertised nationwide through sports magazines and operated an 800 phone number to handle inquiries and take orders. The program has been a great success and represents one of the highest-volume dealers for Weatherby rifles.

Weatherby rifles are viewed by the hunting community as a premium product. They are priced at the upper end of the mass-production weapons market. However, the typical retail consumer would seldom pay suggested retail price. Discounts of 10

EXHIBIT A

....

North Country Bank & Trust,
Manistique, Michigan, Selected Consolidated Financial Data

	1995 ProForma*	1994†	1993	1992	1991
Interest income	$ 24,990	$ 13,798	$ 7,942	$ 8,035	$ 8,085
Interest expense	11,001	6,053	3,543	3,788	4,551
Net interest income	13,989	7,745	4,399	4,247	3,534
Security gains (losses)	(19)	75	175	191	323
Provision for loan losses	811	330	125	239	232
Other income	1,587	1,037	795	577	407
Other expenses	11,076	6,101	3,715	3,277	2,714
Income before taxes	3,670	2,426	1,529	1,499	1,318
Cumulative effect of change in accounting for income taxes	0	0	13	0	0
Income taxes	1,047	458	260	331	321
Net income	$ 2,623	$ 1,968	$ 1,282	$ 1,168	$ 997
Per share					
Earnings	$ 1.25	$ 1.14	$ 1.05	$ 0.95	$ 0.82
Dividends	0.41	0.20	0.49	0.31	0.29
Book value	11.87	10.72	8.12	7.57	6.92
Ratios based on net income					
Return on average equity	11.44%	14.25%	13.33%	13.25%	12.24%
Return on average assets	.87%	1.01%	1.13%	1.15%	1.11%
Dividend payout ratio	32.80%	17.54%	46.67%	32.63%	35.37%
Shareholders' equity as a percent of average assets	7.58%	7.11%	8.45%	8.67%	9.46%
Financial condition					
Assets	$320,646	$253,098	$117,279	$106,798	$ 94,237
Loans	248,527	183,168	87,145	73,108	61,958
Securities	30,882	35,795	17,183	21,107	25,005
Deposits	277,014	223,436	103,717	94,257	82,786
Long-term borrowing	15,351	3,553	2,250	2,000	1,000
Shareholders' equity	25,006	22,483	9,943	9,260	8,467

*Gives effect to the company's recent acquisition of the South Range State Bank as if such acquisition had occurred on January 1, 1995.
†Per share data reflect 3 for 1 stock split, 23 April 1996.
Source: Prospectus.

EXHIBIT B
....
North Country Bank and Trust:
Weatherby Certificate of Deposit Program

Code	Package Description	Minimum Deposit Amount and Term Required to Earn Bonus				
		3-year	6-year	9-year	12-year	20-year
1	**ACCUMARK** *"New for 1996"* .257, .270, 7 mm, .300, .340 Weatherby Magnum, 7 mm Remington Magnum, .300 Winchester Magnum, 26" bbl.	$5673	$2838	$2037	$1636	$1189
	MARK V DELUXE					
2	.270, 7 mm, Weatherby Magnum .30-06 Springfield, 24" bbl.	$6318	$3160	$2268	$1832	$1324
3	.240, .257, .270, 7 mm .300, .340 Weatherby Magnum, 26" bbl.	$6619	$3311	$2376	$1919	$1386
	LAZERMARK					
4	.257, .270, 7 mm, .300, .340 Weatherby Magnum, 26" bbl.	$7090	$3546	$2544	$2055	$1485
5	.460 Weatherby Magnum, 26" with Accubrake	$9638	$4818	$3456	$2791	$2015
	MARK V SPORTER					
6	7 mm Remington Magnum, .300 Winchester Magnum, 24" bbl.	$4064	$2034	$1461	$1181	$ 854
7	.257, .270, 7 mm, .300, .340 Weatherby Magnum, 26" bbl.	$4247	$2126	$1526	$1234	$ 892
8	.30-06 Springfield, 22" bbl.	$4064	$2034	$1461	$1181	$ 854
	MARK V SYNTHETIC					
9	7 mm Remington Magnum, .300, .338 Winchester, 24" bbl. .257, .270, 7 mm, .300, .340 Weatherby Magnum, 26" bbl.	$3542	$1774	$1274	$1030	$ 745
	MARK V STAINLESS					
10	.257, .270, 7 mm, .300, .340 Weatherby Magnum, 26" bbl. 7 mm Remington Magnum, .300, .338 Winchester, 24" bbl.	$4688	$2346	$1684	$1361	$ 984

Source: North Country Bank & Trust's marketing literature.

EXHIBIT C

List Price and Probable Retail Selling Price of Weatherby Rifles

	List Price	Probable Retail Selling Price
Accumark	$ 1,199	$ 959.85
Mark V Deluxe	1,399	1,149.95
Lazermark	1,499	1,197.00
Mark V Sporter	899	714.95
Mark V Synthetic	749	599.95
Mark V Stainless	999	789.95

Source: Lindquist Sporting Goods.

to 20 percent off suggested retail occur in many markets (see Exhibit C).

Ron Ford sought out the best brands for his premium CD programs. He had tried but thus far has not been successful in securing Tiffany diamonds and Ping golf clubs. His ability to secure highly branded products like Weatherby and Big Bertha was one reason this premium program was so successful.

LAISSEZ-FAIRE BANKING

North Country Bank & Trust differentiated itself from other Upper Peninsula banks and banks in general by promoting an "easy going" informal style. Casual clothes are worn instead of the traditional blue or black suits. This is true of tellers as well as the CEO.

In addition, the bank presents itself in a friendly, almost homelike atmosphere. Popcorn is always available in the lobby, as well as coffee and pop. The bank provides pharmacy delivery and free legal advice. All these were significant deviations from traditional bank practices. They were, however, consistent with Mr. Ford's philosophy of meeting customer needs and style. He observed often that customers did not dress formally in the market served by North Country Bank & Trust. The bank, therefore, complemented the lifestyle of its customers.

WELCOME TO THE TYCOON CLUB

In an effort to instill savings in children, explain how banking works, and develop lifelong banking customers, North Country Bank & Trust created the Tycoon Club and the comic character Mr. Tycoon. As of 1996, there were about 3000 members of the Tycoon Club. The club sponsored Little League teams, promoted the club with guest appearances of Mr. Tycoon at fairs, outings, and picnics, and sold an array of Tycoon clothing. Special savings programs existed for Tycoon Club members. In addition, a loan program existed for young entrepreneurs. If, for example, a teenager wanted to buy a lawn mower to start a lawn mowing business, North Country Bank & Trust would loan the youngster the money.

The character Mr. Tycoon had achieved significant popularity in the local community around Manistique, Michigan, the headquarters of North Country Bank & Trust. Children related to Mr. Tycoon in a local sense as youth relate to Mickey Mouse or Donald Duck on the national scene.

The Tycoon Club emphasized savings at an early age and encouraged parents to save for very young children (1, 2, 3, and 4 years of age). These and other promotional efforts stressed the importance of saving early and developing lifelong saving habits. All evidence indicated that this program created customer loyalty at a very early age and secured customers for the bank for many years to come.

CHARACTERISTICS OF THE MARKETS SERVED BY NORTH COUNTRY BANK & TRUST

The rural Upper Peninsula of Michigan covers 14,000 square miles with a population of 320,000 people. It is approximately 300 miles east to west and 70 to 90 miles north to south. Its major cities are as follows:

- Marquette, population 25,000
- Sault Ste. Marie, population 14,448
- Escanaba, population 14,355
- Iron Mountain, population 8,314
- Houghton, population 7,512
- Ironwood, population 7,741

EXHIBIT D
················
**Rate of Return on Assets,
North Country Bank & Trust, First of America,
and Michigan Financial Corporation,
1993–1996**

Bank Holding Company	Return on Assets, %			
	1993	1994	1995	1996
North Country Bank and Trust	1.18	1.01	0.87	0.97
First of America	1.20	0.97	0.99	1.02
Michigan Financial Corporation	0.98	1.10	1.13	1.23

Source: Sheshunoff Banking Organization Quarterly.

Major industries of the Upper Peninsula include tourism, mining (iron ore), health care, gambling, and forest products. A long history of immigration from Finland, Italy, and Wales is partially responsible for a sense of rugged individualism that pervades the region.

The opening of deer season is equivalent to a "national holiday" in the Upper Peninsula. Many high schools and businesses close on November 15. Snowmobiling, cross-country and down-hill skiing, and showshoeing are major winter sports. The Upper Peninsula in its northern tier receives 150 inches of snow a year. The summertime brings lots of opportunities to sailboat or fish on Lake Michigan, Lake Huron, or the massive 31,000 square mile Lake Superior.

From a banking perspective, the Upper Peninsula of Michigan represents a $3 billion market. This market is served primarily by three bank holding companies: MFC First National, with assets of $783 million, North Country Bank & Trust, with $327 million in assets, and First of America, a $22 billion bank, headquartered in Kalamazoo, Michigan. This bank has business operations in Michigan, Ohio, Indiana, and Illinois. These three bank holding companies vary in their relative profitability. Exhibit D shows the relative rate of return on assets for these three companies for 1993 through the first 9 months of 1996.

Questions

1. Does the laissez-faire approach to banking used by North Country Bank & Trust make sense, or should it consider a more traditional approach?

2. Does the Weatherby, Big Bertha, diamond, grandfather clock, and picture premium program to secure demand deposits make economic sense from the bank's perspective as well as the customers' perspective? Are there nonfinancial implications of this program that benefit the bank? Do you believe this program should be continued?

3. Are the North Country Bank's profitability measures comparable with those of their competitors? How are these measures affected by the current rapid-expansion mode? As a potential investor, do the rapid-expansion and profitability measures add to the appeal of the forthcoming stock offering?

4. What are the marketing implications of the Mr. Tycoon program?

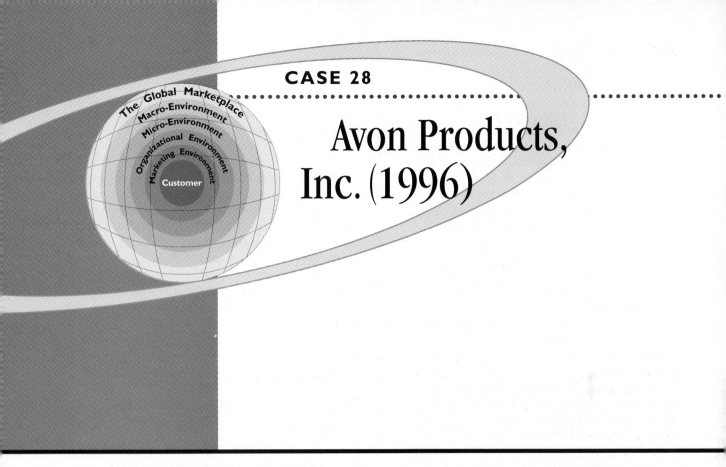

CASE 28

Avon Products, Inc. (1996)

This case was prepared by James Camerius, Professor of Management, Northern Michigan University, and James Clinton, Professor of Marketing, University of Northern Colorado.

James E. Preston is chairman and chief executive officer of Avon Products, Inc. (212-546-6015). Headquartered in New York City, Avon is one of the world's leading manufacturers and marketers of beauty products, including cosmetics, fragrances, toiletries, gifts, decorative apparel, and fashion jewelry. Avon was founded in 1886 and incorporated in 1916. Avon's business is exclusively direct selling by Avon representatives, with worldwide operations. During 1994, Avon sold Giorgio Beverly Hills, its remaining retail business. Avon products offered internationally vary by market, but most are substantially the same as those marketed domestically. Avon's 18-word vision statement is as follows: "To be the company that best understands and satisfies

the product, service and self-fulfillment needs of women, globally." As Preston notes:

> We are, uniquely among major corporations, a woman's company. We sell our products to, for and through women. We understand their needs and preferences better than most. This understanding guides our basic business and influences our choice of new business opportunities. We need to become, and are becoming, more customer-oriented and more market-driven.
>
> I can't think of a better definition of a women's company. And that has a lot of implications for us. If we are really going to be a preeminent company for women around the world, it requires that we have on a market to market basis, a very good understanding of where women are; what their needs, wants, and aspirations are; what the issues are; and what the trends are regarding women.

HISTORY

In the late 1800s, David McConnell, a door-to-door book salesman, had an idea that he believed would encourage women to buy his books. Following a common trade practice of the period, he gave prospective customers a gift of perfume to arouse their interest. Before long, he discovered that the perfume was more popular than the books. He formed a new firm, called the California Perfume Company. "I started in a space scarcely larger than an ordinary kitchen pantry," David McConnell noted in 1900. "My ambition was to manufacture a line of goods superior to any other and take those goods through canvassing agents directly from the laboratory to the consumer." McConnell based his business on (1) consumable products sold directly to the consumer, (2) an image of the company that captured the beauty and excitement of the state of California, and (3) a national network of sales agents organized during his years as a bookseller. A series of corporate principles, developed by Mc-Connell, provide direction and continue to influence decision making for Avon. These principles are shown in Exhibit A.

In 1920, Avon introduced a line of products called Avon that consisted of a toothbrush, cleanser, and vanity set. The Avon name was inspired by the area around the company's laboratory at Suffern, New York, which McConnell thought resembled the countryside of William Shakespeare's home, Stratford-on-Avon, England. The name of the line became so popular that in 1929 the company officially became Avon. By 1929, the company was selling low-cost home care and beauty products door to door and through catalogs in all 48 states.

In the early 1950s, the sales representatives' territories were reduced in size, a strategy that led to quadrupling the salesforce and increasing sales six-fold over the next 12 years. Avon advertisements appeared on television for the first time during this period. The famous slogan, "Ding Dong, Avon Calling," was first televised in 1954.

In 1960, total sales were $15 million, an 18 percent increase over the previous year; international sales were $8.2 million; and the company consisted of 6800 employees and 125,000 sales representatives. Sales continued to grow dramatically throughout the 1960s. By 1969, total sales had grown to $558.6 million, international sales were $193.1 million, and the firm had 20,800 employees and more than 400,000 sales representatives. Manufacturing plants, distribution centers, and sales branches were opened throughout the world as part of an expansion program.

The 1970s and 1980s presented Avon management with some of its greatest challenges. The strength of the U.S. dollar reduced the company's international profits; recession and inflation hurt sales. In 1975, about 25,000 Avon sales representatives quit due to decreased earning opportunities. Avon products were being outpaced by retail cosmetic firms offering jazzier products to women whose new attitudes favored more exciting product lines. The traditional direct sales approach was nearly toppled during this period by social changes management had not anticipated, such as the

EXHIBIT A

The Principles that Guide Avon

1.	To provide individuals an opportunity to earn in support of their well-being and happiness
2.	To serve families throughout the world with products of the highest quality backed by a guarantee of satisfaction
3.	To render a service to customers that is outstanding in its helpfulness and courtesy
4.	To give full recognition to employees and representatives, on whose contributions Avon depends
5.	To share with others the rewards of growth and success
6.	To meet fully the obligations of corporate citizenship by contributing to the well-being of society and the environment in which it functions
7.	To maintain and cherish the friendly spirit of Avon

Source: Avon Representative Success Book.

EXHIBIT B

Avon Products, Inc., Consolidated Statement of Income (In Millions, Except per Share Data)

Years Ended December 31	1995	1994	1993
Net Sales	$4,492.1	$4,266.5	$3,844.1
Costs, expenses, and other			
Cost of sales	1,769.0	1,672.1	1,497.0
Marketing distribution, and administrative expenses	2,215.6	2,098.8	1,913.9
Interest expense	41.3	50.8	45.2
Interest income	(19.4)	(22.1)	(25.3)
Other expense, net	20.6	33.1	18.7
Total costs, expenses, and other	4,027.1	3,832.7	3,449.5
Income from continuing operations before taxes, minority interest, and cumulative effect of accounting changes	465.0	433.8	394.6
Income taxes	176.4	163.5	150.8
Income from continuing operations before minority interest and cumulative effort of accounting changes	288.6	270.3	243.8
Minority interest	(2.5)	(5.5)	(6.9)
Income from continuing operations before cumulative effect of accounting changes	286.1	264.8	236.9
Discontinued operations			
Income, net of taxes	—	1.2	12.7
Loss of disposals, net of taxes	(29.6)	(25.0)	(10.0)
Cumulative effect of accounting changes, net of taxes	—	(45.2)	(107.5)
Net income	$ 256.5	$ 195.8	$ 132.1
Income (loss) per share			
Continuing operations	$ 4.19	$ 3.75	$ 3.28
Discontinued operations	(.43)	(.34)	.04
Cumulative effect of accounting changes	—	(.64)	(1.49)
Net income	$ 3.76	$ 2.77	$ 1.83
Average shares outstanding	68.24	70.59	72.06

growth in the number of working women. Direct sales firms were hurt in two major ways: Fewer women were at home for door-to-door salespeople to call on, and fewer women wanted to make money in their spare time by selling cosmetics to their neighbors. These trends continue throughout the 1980s. Avon lost $404 million in 1988. Avon's financial statements are shown in Exhibits B and C.

In the 1990s Avon's sales have increased every year primarily due to excellent sales internationally.

U.S. sales only amounted to 36 percent of total sales in 1994. Net income has been positive since 1988, growing to $195 million in 1994.

TOP MANAGEMENT

James Preston, age 55, became chairman of the board of Avon in 1989. He succeeded Chairman Hicks Waldron, who had been the force behind

EXHIBIT C
. . . .
Avon Products, Inc., Consolidated Balance Sheet (In Millions, Except per Share Data)

Years Ended December 31	1995	1994
Assets		
Current assets		
Cash, including cash equivalents of $60.5 and $132.5	$ 151.4	$ 214.8
Accounts receivable (less allowance for doubtful accounts of $32.6 and $27.3)	402.0	373.7
Inventories	466.3	412.8
Prepaid expenses and other	195.3	149.0
Total current assets	1,215.0	1,150.3
Property, plant, and equipment, at cost		
Land	53.5	54.3
Buildings and improvements	546.1	531.5
Equipment	569.9	560.9
	1,169.5	1,146.7
Less accumulated depreciation	631.7	618.3
	537.8	528.4
Other assets	300.0	299.6
Total assets	$2,052.8	$1,978.3
Liabilities and shareholders' equity		
Current liabilities		
Debt maturing within 1 year	$47.3	$61.2
Accounts payable	419.7	408.0
Accrued compensation	109.3	100.0
Other accrued liabilities	277.3	222.3
Sales and other taxes	101.8	95.7
Income taxes	289.9	253.8
Total current liabilities	1,245.3	1,141.0
Long-term debt	114.2	116.5
Employee benefit plans	390.8	366.6
Deferred income taxes	33.6	32.2
Other liabilities (including minority interest of $46.5 and $48.9)	76.2	136.4
Commitments and contingencies		
Shareholders' equity		
Common stock, par value $.50—authorized: $200,000,000		
Shares; issued 86,749,056 and 86,663,874 shares	43.4	43.3
Additional paid-in Capital	672.9	660.5
Retained earnings	325.8	212.4
Translation adjustments	(202.1)	(187.1)
Treasury stock, at cost—19,131,822 and 17,589,639 shares	(647.3)	(543.5)
Total shareholders' equity	192.7	185.6
Total liabilities and shareholders' equity	$2,052.8	$1,978.3

Avon's diversification into health care and other areas in the late 1970s. Preston joined the firm in 1964 as a trainee, rising to president of direct sales operations of the company in 1981 and president and CEO of the entire firm in 1988. During his tenure as head of direct selling, he was credited with turning the division around when many analysts thought such selling methods were outmoded. "Jim believes in the power of direct selling, and he has great capacity to communicate that vision," said Phyllis Davis, an Avon vice president who ran the sales organization in 1985.

Edward Robinson was elected executive vice president and chief financial officer of Avon in 1989 and president and chief operating office in 1993. Prior to joining Avon, he served as executive vice president, finance, and chief financial officer of RJR Nabisco. He started his career with an accounting degree, receiving a CPA license to practice in New York in 1968. Robinson was recruited specifically to reduce Avon's debt. Avon's corporate structure is shown in Exhibit D.

COMPETITORS

The direct selling industry consists of a few large, well-established firms and many small organizations that sell about every product imaginable including toys, animal food, collectibles, plant care products, clothing, computer software, and financial services. In addition to Avon, the dominant companies include Mary Kay (cosmetics), Amway (home maintenance products), Shaklee Corporation (vitamins and health foods), Encyclopedia Britannica (reference books and learning systems), Tupperware (plastic dishes and food containers), Electrolux (vacuum cleaners), and Fuller (brushes and household products). Avon is substantially larger in terms of sales representatives, sales volume, and resources than Mary Kay Cosmetics, Inc., its nearest direct competitor.

Other firms, such as Procter & Gamble Company, Unilever NV, and Revlon, Inc., sell cosmetics and personal-care products through retail stores. They too are important competitors facing Avon.

PRODUCTS

Avon is the world's largest direct selling organization and merchandiser of beauty products. Avon markets product lines to women in 120 countries through 1.9 million independent sales representatives who sell primarily on a door-to-door basis. Total sales in 1994 were $4.3 billion. The company's workforce consists of 30,400 employees. These numbers compare favorably to Avon's major competitor, Mary Kay Cosmetics (214-630-8787), whose 1994 sales were $1.2 billion.

Avon's product line includes skin-care items, makeup, perfume fragrances for men and women, and toiletries for bath, hair care, personal care, hand and body care, and sun care (see Exhibit E). Recognizable brand names include Skin-So-Soft, an item in the bath product area that benefits from wide publicity concerning alternative uses; Moisture Therapy; and Imari fragrance. Newer products include Avon Color, an entirely new line of more than 350 shades of lip, eye, face, and nail colors. The product line assures customers that Avon has just the right shade for them and that their total look can be coordinated. A New Perfecting Complex for Face, another new product, is the most successful skin care product in Avon history. There are approximately 600 items in the product line. Internationally, Avon's product line is marketed by emphasizing department store quality at discount store prices. The major categories and subcategories of products are shown in Exhibit F.

Avon is also the world's largest manufacturer and distributor of fashion jewelry, and it markets an extensive line of gifts and collectibles. A fashion apparel catalog, *Avon Style,* was added in 1994.

DOING BUSINESS GLOBALLY

In 1954, Avon opened sales offices in Venezuela and Puerto Rico to cultivate the Latin American market. Avon expanded into the European market in 1957 through its United Kingdom subsidiary, Avon Cosmetics, Ltd., and entered the Asian market in 1969 by way of Japan. In 1990, Avon became the first major cosmetics company to manufacture and sell products in China and the first American cosmetics company to enter East Germany. Sales of Avon International in 1994 were $2.73 billion, compared with Avon U.S. sales of $1.54 billion. More than three-fifths of the firm's direct selling sales and earnings come from outside the United States and the proportion is growing (see Exhibit G).

Satisfying the subtleties and intricacies of customer demand around the world requires that

EXHIBIT D

Avon's Organizational Structure (1995)

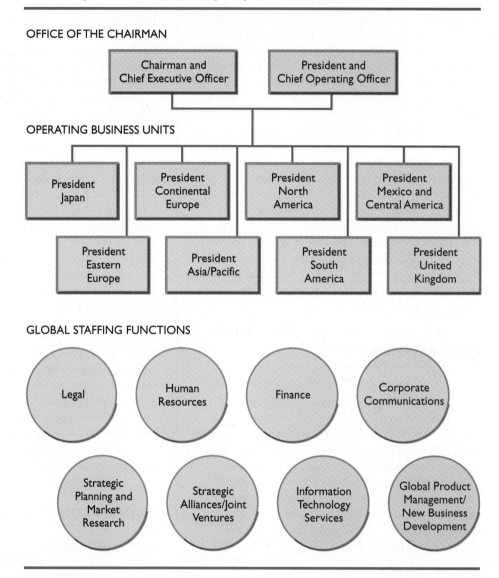

Source: *1994 Avon Annual Report.*

Avon's business varies from country to country and market to market. In the United States, for example, Avon offers Avon Select, a direct marketing program, whereby customers may buy Avon products via any one of four methods: (1) through their Avon representative, (2) by mail through special *Select* catalogs, (3) by the 1-800-FOR-AVON telephone number, or (4) by fax. Similar opportunities are offered worldwide.

In Taiwan, Avon products are sold by representatives in some 2000 storefront shops, where orders can be placed via fax for next-day delivery. In all cases, new programs are designed to complement the existing network of sales representatives. Avon spends 2 percent to 3 percent of annual sales on image-enhancing advertising and promotion programs worldwide to make customers aware of Avon products and purchase options available.

EXHIBIT E
....
Avon's Sales by Type of Product ($ in Millions)

Years Ended December 31	1994	1993	1992
Cosmetics, fragrances, and toiletries	$2,604.2	$2,375.2	$2,243.1
Gift and decorative	769.2	663.6	683.3
Apparel	480.3	350.0	296.9
Fashion jewelry and accessories	412.8	455.3	437.2
	$4,266.5	$3,844.1	$3,660.5

EXHIBIT F
....
Avon Product Line

Skin-care products
  Daily Revival Line: Everyday skin-care necessities
  Avon Visible Improvement Program: Problem-solving formulas
  Advanced Beauty Treatments: Items for aging skin
  Clearskin: For oily; blemish-prone skin
Makeup
  Advanced Foundation: Perfectors, enhancers, and finishers
  Color for Cheeks: Skin blush
  Color for Eyes: Eye shadow
  Mascara: Alternative formula
  Eye Makeup Removers: Lotion and gel
  Color for Lips: Lipsticks, pencils, and liners
  Color for Nails: Nail enamel in various colors
  Nail Solutions: For alternative nail needs
Women's fragrances
Fragrances for men
Toiletries
  Bath: Bubble bath, Avon bath line, shower gel, Skin-So-Soft
  Hair Care: Brushes, stylers, shampoos, and conditioners
  Personal Care: Deodorant, foot care, products, and hand soaps
  Hand and Body Care: Alternative skin care lines
  Sun Care: Sun protection and tanning systems
Jewelry
  Fashion Jewelry: Popular and designer collections
  Classic Jewelry: Traditional designs with timeless appeal
  Seasonal Jewelry: Gift specialties and personalized items
Gift Line
  Fine Collectibles: Steins, dolls, figurines, plates
  Gifts for the Home: Decorator items
  Seasonal Ornaments: Traditional to high-tech
  Children's Gifts: Toys, jewelry, and hair accessories
  Sawyers Unique Gifts for Men: Unique and innovative items
  Family Connections: Entertaining and educational videos, audiocassettes, compact discs, crafts, books,
    and games

EXHIBIT G
....
Avon's Sales by Geographic Area ($ in Millions)

	1994		1993		1992	
	Net Sales	**Pretax Income**	**Net Sales**	**Pretax Income**	**Net Sales**	**Pretax Income**
United States	$1,535.1	$201.2	$1,395.6	$152.8	$1,408.1	$140.8
International						
Americas	1,415.3	273.9	1,175.2	196.4	980.6	168.4
Pacific	664.3	89.7	625.6	90.9	542.8	84.0
Europe	651.8	15.3	647.7	53.5	729.0	31.5
Total international	2,731.4	378.9	2,448.5	340.8	2,252.4	283.9
Total from operations	$4,266.5	580.1	$3,844.1	493.6	$3,660.5	424.7
Corporate expenses		(84.9)		(69.0)		(73.1)
Interest expense		(50.8)		(45.2)		(43.7)
Other income (expense)		(10.6)		15.2		(17.9)
Total		$433.8		$394.6		$290.0

Note: Pretax income for geographic area data in 1992 includes the charge for restructuring costs of $96.0. The effect of this charge was to reduce the pretax income of United States, Europe, and the Americas by $54.4, $28.6, and $3.5, respectively, and to increase corporate expenses by $9.5.

Even retail stores are not ruled out by management as a viable alternative for the distribution of Avon products.

Enormous growth opportunities exist in countries with huge populations such as China, Indonesia, and India. In Eastern Europe, management is excited about the potential in Poland, Czechoslovakia, and Hungary. In the Pacific Rim area, countries such as Vietnam, Cambodia, and Laos are targeted as market opportunities.

In the emerging and developing markets of Latin America and the Pacific Rim, the retail infrastructure is undeveloped, especially in the interiors of those countries. Avon representatives provide consumers with an opportunity to buy a wide range of quality products at acceptable prices. In some developing markets, where access to quality goods is particularly difficult, Avon's direct selling method has opened up unprecedented prospects for women. In China, for example, women are so eager for Avon products that a projected 6-month inventory of lotion sold out in only 2 weeks. Keen demand for Avon products presents an extraordinary earnings opportunity for Avon representatives. Similarly, in Poland, Avon offers customers

access to cosmetics and personal-care items never before available to them. In one corporate study, Avon products were found satisfying such a pent-up demand that Polish women were willing to spend a considerable portion of their discretionary income on Avon products.

The move to become a global organization affected Avon in a number of different ways. The product line was strengthened and developed by identifying certain global brands that were important and sold on a worldwide basis.

AVON'S STRUCTURE
• •

Avon's three international regional headquarters were recently phased out and replaced by eight business units, each of whom is in charge of a major market or geographic region of the world, as illustrated in Exhibit H.

Responsibility for developing business plans and strategies for Avon around the world now rests with the Global Business Council (GBC). The GBC is comprised of the Office of the Chairman and

EXHIBIT H
....
1998 Earnings Opportunity ($ in Millions, Except per Share Data)

	1994	Margin	1998E	Margin
United States	$201	14.5%	$280	15.0%
Americas	274	19.4%	419	18.0%
Pacific	90	13.5%	138	15.0%
Europe	15	2.3%	78	10.0%
Total segment profits	$580	13.6%	$915	15.5%
Corporate expense	85		135	
Interest expense	51		55	
Other expense	11		20	
Pretax profits	$434		$705	
Taxes	164		268	
Minority interest	6		8	
Net income	$265		$429	
Shares outstanding	70.6		62.0	
EPS	$ 3.75		$ 6.90	

Source: Avon Products and CS First Boston estimates.
Note: E, estimated.

leaders of the eight operating business units (OBUs). OBU leaders represent six different nationalities and have an average of 25 years experience with Avon.

Some OBUs represent one country, an individual market whose size and profit contribution requires separate management attention. Other units include clusters of countries in areas where there are significant synergies and efficiencies in operating the countries as an integrated business organization. The leaders of all of the units report directly to the office of the chairman.

Also reporting to the office of chairman are eight global staff departments: Legal, Human Resources, Finance, Corporate Communications, Strategic Planning and Market Research, Strategic Alliances/Joint Ventures, Information Technology Services, and a new department—Global Product Management/New Business Development. Each department assumes worldwide responsibility for its function.

The new multinational Global Product Management Group is an essential factor in the new struc-ture. The group supports the entire company with Centers of Excellence to increase Avon's competitive advantage in the marketplace. With a global scope and multinational staffs, the centers are located around the world, wherever the appropriate expertise exists. The Global Product Management group is responsible for product management, global brands, global sourcing (raw materials) and logistics, worldwide manufacturing, product research and development, and certain global aspects of sales and customer service support.

Responsibilities of the Global Planning and Development group include new business development. This group manages Avon's emerging market ventures in China, Eastern Europe, Russia, and other parts of the former Soviet Union, as well as other new market ventures.

In reference to the organizational realignment when it was completed, Chairman Preston notes:

The new slimmed-down global organization makes us more responsive to local markets while providing economies in such areas as global manufacturing, purchasing and research and development. We also are able to better exchange best practices, growth initiatives and competitive information more rapidly from market to market. We want to become the embodiment of the phrase, "Think global, act local."

The new market-oriented structure is expected to speed decision making; eliminate unnecessary levels of management; allow sharing of successful business practices by previously autonomous divisions; and reduce overhead by centralizing such functions as purchasing, manufacturing, and research and development. Preston says, "the structure will put responsibility and accountability where they belong—in the hands of seasoned direct selling executives who best understand the needs of customers in their markets."

AVON TODAY

For any direct selling organization, new sales representatives bring in new customers, which are a vital component of growth. Avon's U.S. salesforce began to grow in 1994s third quarter, following several years of consistent declines. Recruitment of new sales representatives has increased and turnover is down. Avon added 1 million new customers in 1994.

Avon has instituted a revised training program for new representatives. The program focuses on helping salespersons get new customers and on teaching them how to determine what products to sell and how to sell more effectively. A greater effort is being made to ensure that district managers work with representatives on an ongoing basis to keep developing them.

In mid-1994, Avon changed its compensation program for district sales managers who now are on a salary plus bonus plan. The bonus had been based on volume, but now it is calculated on the increase in volume. The emphasis is much more clearly on growth. The upside potential is greater under the new plan and the motivation factor has proved highly successful. Representative morale is very high. Salespersons feel that Avon is once again committed to direct selling.

An important factor behind the increased motivation of Avon's salespeople is revitalization of the company's product line. New product activity has been heightened with more innovative products, such as Perfect Wear transfer-resistant lipstick and three-in-one (insect repellent, sunscreen, and moisturizer) Skin-So-Soft. The new lipstick sold 16 million units despite a price of $4 compared with other Avon lipsticks at $3. The new Skin-So-Soft generated $25 million of sales in seven months. Avon's recent fragrance launches—Far Away for Christmas 1994 and Natori for Mother's Day 1995—also were unusually successful.

Avon is working on modernizing its image. For the first time Avon is making use of promotion and merchandising techniques that have long been used at retail. These include gift or purchase with purchase, gift with premiums, and sampling—and they are being well received.

Expansion into apparel in the United States is also proving highly successful. In April 1994 Avon launched branded intimate apparel from Warnaco, believing that it offers compelling, unique advantages within a hotly competitive field. Avon's direct selling distribution system offers the advantages of free delivery and return compared with mail order competition. Moreover, Avon's studies found that most women do not like buying lingerie in stores because of poor service; in response, the company began a fit training program for its salespersons.

To further exploit its competitive advantages, Avon is presently testing a line of swimwear under the well-known Catalina brand. Avon offers both regular and larger sizes, which represents over 30 percent of the company's business. The test is going well, and a more full-scale introduction is likely next year. In the fourth quarter of 1995, Avon will launch a sportswear line designed by Diane von Furstenberg. The line will be proprietary to Avon, with prices ranging from $19 to $50 retail.

Avon has always been an excellent cash-flow generator, and the company has paid down most of its debt over the past few years while accumulating cash. This cash, along with the company's free cash flow, is earmarked to repurchase stock. The company so far has completed more than half of a seven million share repurchase program.

Following completion of heavy investments in 1995 in entering new geographic areas and building global internal information systems, management expects to generate $100 million to $150 million annually in free cash flow.

Manufacturing

Avon manufactures and packages almost all its cosmetic, fragrance, and toiletry products. Raw materials, consisting chiefly of essential oils, chemicals, containers, and packaging components, are purchased from various suppliers. Packages, consisting of containers and packaging components, are designed by its staff of artists and designers.

The design and development of new products are affected by the cost and availability of materials such as glass, plastics, and chemicals. Avon believes it can continue to obtain sufficient raw materials and supplies to manufacture and supply its own products.

Avon has 18 manufacturing laboratories around the world, three of which are principally devoted to the manufacture of fashion jewelry. In the United States, Avon's cosmetic, fragrance, and toiletry products are produced throughout the country. Most products sold in foreign countries are manufactured in Avon's facilities abroad.

The fashion jewelry line is developed by Avon's staff and produced in its two manufacturing laboratories in Puerto Rico and its manufacturing laboratory in Ireland, or by several independent manufacturers.

Distribution

Avon's products are sold worldwide by approximately 1.9 million sales representatives, approximately 440,000 of whom are in the United States. Almost all representatives are women who sell on a part-time basis. Representatives are independent contractors or independent dealers, not agents or employees of Avon. Representatives purchase products directly from Avon and sell them directly to their customers.

Avon's products are sold to customers through a combination of direct selling and marketing utilizing independent representatives, the mail, phone, or fax. Representatives go where customers are, either in the home or at the workplace. Representatives may sell in a territory, which typically averages 100 homes in the United States and from 100 to 150 homes in other countries. Representatives in the United States have the opportunity to take responsibility for sales in larger areas. Representatives also sell in offices, factories, schools, and hospitals.

In the United States, the representative contacts customers, selling primarily through the use of brochures that highlight new products and specially priced items for each 2-week sales campaign. Product samples, demonstration products, makeup color charts, and catalogs are also used. Generally, the representative forwards an order every two weeks to a designated distribution center. This order is processed and the products are assembled at the distribution center and delivered to the representative's home, usually by a local delivery service. The representative then delivers the merchandise and collects payment from the customer. Payment by the representative to Avon is customarily made when the next order is forwarded to the distribution center. The cost of merchandise to the representative varies according to the total order size for each 2-week sales campaign and averages approximately 60 percent of the recommended selling price.

In order to increase support of the representatives in the United States and allow them to run their business more efficiently—as well as to improve order processing accuracy—Avon has implemented electronic order systems technology. One of these systems permits Avon representatives to submit add-on orders with a touch-tone telephone, enabling them to augment orders already submitted by placing a phone call. Another system, Avon's Personal Order Entry Terminal, permits approximately 20,000 top-producing representatives in the United States to transmit orders electronically by phone line, 24 hours a day, 7 days a week.

Outside the United States each sales campaign generally lasts 3 or 4 weeks. Although terms of payment and cost of merchandise to the representative vary from country to country, the basic method of direct selling and marketing by representatives is essentially the same as that used in the United States, and substantially the same merchandising and promotional techniques are utilized.

Recruiting and training of representatives are the primary responsibility of district managers. In the United States each district manager has responsibility for a market area covered by 225 to 300 representatives. District managers are employees of Avon and are paid a salary and a commission based on purchases of Avon products by representatives in their district. Personal contacts, including recommendations from current representatives and local advertising, constitute the primary means of obtaining new representatives. Because of high turnover among representatives—a characteristic of the direct selling method—recruiting and training new representatives is continually necessary.

From time to time a question as to the legal status of representatives has arisen, usually in regard to possible coverage under social benefit laws that would require Avon (and in most instances, the representatives) to make regular contributions to social benefit funds. Although Avon has generally been able to address these questions in a satisfactory manner, the matter has not been fully resolved in all countries. If there should be a final determination adverse to Avon in a country, the cost for future—and possibly past—contributions could be so substantial in the context of the volume of business of Avon in that country that it would have to consider discontinuing operations in that country.

Promotion and Marketing

Sales promotion and sales development activities are directed toward giving selling assistance to representatives by making available sales aids such as brochures, samples, and demonstration products. In order to support the efforts of representatives to reach new customers, especially working women and other individuals who frequently are not at home, specially designed sales aids, promotional pieces, customer flyers, and product- and image-enhancing media advertising are used. In addition, Avon seeks to motivate representatives through the use of special incentive programs that reward superior sales performance. Periodic sales meetings with representatives are conducted by the district manager. The meetings are designed to keep representatives abreast of product line changes, explain sales techniques, and provide recognition for sales performance.

A number of merchandising techniques—including the introduction of new products, the use of combination offers, the use of trial sizes and the promotion of products packaged as gift items—are used. In general, for each sales campaign a distinctive brochure is published in which new products are introduced and selected items are offered at special prices or are given particular prominence. Cosmetic, fragrance, and toiletry products are available each sales campaign at a constant low price, and introductory specials and periodic sales on selected items are maintained for limited time periods.

Avon's sales and earnings have a marked seasonal pattern characteristic of many companies selling cosmetics, fragrances, and toiletries; gift and decorative products; and fashion jewelry. Christmas sales cause a sales peak in the fourth quarter of the year. Fourth-quarter net sales were 32 and 31 percent of full-year net sales in 1994 and 1993, respectively, and fourth quarter pretax income from continuing operations was 42 percent in 1994 and 1993.

Competitive Conditions

Avon's principal competitors are the large, well-known cosmetics and fragrances companies that manufacture and sell broad product lines through various types of retail establishments. Competitors in the gift and decorative products industry in the United States include retail establishments, principally department stores, gift shops, and direct mail companies.

Competition in the fashion jewelry industry also consists of companies that manufacture and sell fashion jewelry for women through retail establishments.

Intensity of competition that Avon faces in its foreign cosmetics, fragrances, toiletries, and fashion jewelry markets vary widely from country to country.

Avon believes that the personalized customer service offered by representatives; the high quality, attractive designs, and reasonable prices of its products; new product introductions; and the guarantee of satisfaction are significant factors in establishing and maintaining its competitive position.

Research Activities

Avon's research and development department is a leader in the industry, based on the number of new product launches of affordable, effective beauty treatments relevant to women's needs. Relationships with well-known dermatologists and other specialists supplement Avon's own research to deliver new formulas and ingredients. Each year Avon researchers test and develop more than 600 products in the cosmetic, fragrance, toiletry, and jewelry categories as well as analyze, evaluate, and develop gift and decorative products.

Avon has pioneered many innovative products, including Skin-So-Soft, its best-selling bath oil; BioAdvance, the first skin-care product with stabilized retinol, the purest form of vitamin A; and Collagen Booster, the premier product to capitalize on vitamin C technology. Avon also introduced the benefits of aromatherapy to millions of American women, encapsulated color for the Color-Release line, and introduced alpha-hydroxy acid for the Anew Perfecting Complex products.

Avon's R&D expenditures were $27.9 million in 1994, $28.5 million in 1993, and $27.9 million in 1992. This research included the activities of product research and development and package design and development.

Employees

At December 31, 1994, Avon employed approximately 30,400 persons, including 7900 in the United States and 22,500 in other countries. The number of employees tends to rise from a low point in January to a high point in November and decreases somewhat in December when Christmas shipments are completed.

Finance

Net income in 1994 was $195.8 million, or $2.77 per share, compared with $132.1 million, or $1.83 per share, in 1993.

United States   U.S. sales increased 10 percent to $1.54 billion and pretax income increased 32 percent to $201.2 million in 1994. The increase in sales reflects a 6 percent increase in average order size and a 4 percent increase in the number of representative orders. Units sold increased 5 percent over 1993. The sales improvement was driven by introduction of the new apparel line in 1994, a strong increase in sales of color cosmetics, and increases in most other major product categories. The increase in pretax income was primarily due to the sales increase and an improved operating expense ratio.

International   International sales increased 12 percent to $2.73 billion, and pretax income increased 11 percent to $378.9 million from $340.8 million in 1993. The sales increase reflects strong unit growth in the Americas region—most significantly Brazil—and in the Pacific Rim and the favorable impact of the weaker U.S. dollar in Japan and most European countries. These improvements were partially offset by unit declines in Europe, especially the United Kingdom and Germany, Venezuela, and Japan.

In the Americas region, sales increased 20 percent to $1.42 billion, and pretax income increased 39 percent to $273.9 million from $196.4 million in 1994. The sales increase was due to growth in all markets, except Venezuela—primarily in Brazil, Argentina, and Mexico. The significant increase in Brazil was due to the solid growth in the higher-priced categories of fashions and home products and higher-priced items such as Renew, a skin-care product, and the benefits of the new economic stabilization package implemented in July, which lowered inflation and improved consumer purchasing confidence. In addition, the number of representatives in Brazil at the end of 1994 increased 38 percent from the end of 1993, which enabled Avon to take advantage of the improved economic environment. Argentina's strong sales growth was driven by its image enhancement strategies and product line expansion, especially products like Renew and fashion lines.

Mexico's improvement reflects strong unit growth following successful market penetration and image building strategies. The large devaluation of the Peso in late December did not have a material impact on Mexico's results for the year. The sales decline in Venezuela reflects the significant currency devaluation and unsettled economic climate, which depressed consumer demand and negatively affected sales in all product categories.

In the Pacific region, sales increased 6 percent to $664.3 million, and pretax income decreased 1 percent to $89.7 million from $90.9 million in 1993. The increase in sales was due to unit growth in all Pacific Rim markets and the favorable impact of the weaker U.S. dollar in Japan. These improvements were partially offset by lower units sold in Japan. The decrease in pretax income was primarily due to higher operating expenses for expansion in China as part of a long-term growth strategy, partially offset by the sales growth in the Pacific Rim.

In the Europe region, sales increased 1 percent to $651.8 million, and pretax income declined 71 percent to $15.3 million from $53.5 million in 1993. The sales increase was due to the favorable impact of the weaker U.S. dollar against most European currencies, mainly in the fourth quarter, and unit growth in the developing Eastern European markets, Spain, and Italy. These improvements were partially offset by unit declines in the United Kingdom and Germany, reflecting weak economies in the retail and consumer nondurable segments and sales of lower-priced products in France. The decline in pretax income was primarily due to operational sales declines in Germany, the United Kingdom, and France, a high fixed-expense base in the region, and higher operating expenses related to expansion of Eastern European markets.

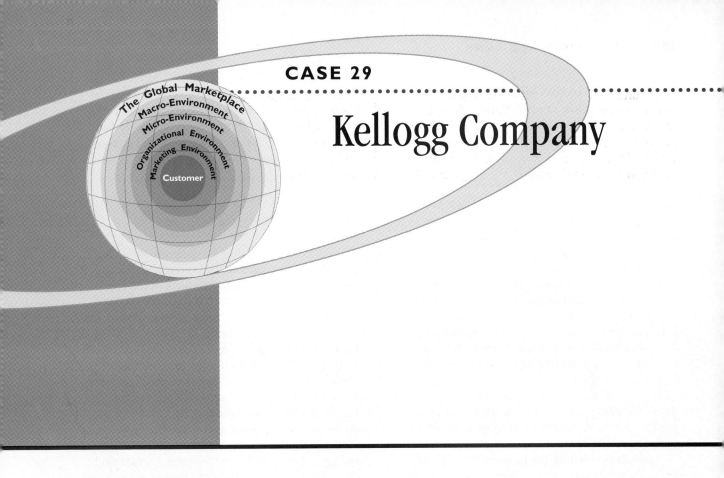

CASE 29

Kellogg Company

This case was prepared by Craig A. Hollingshead, W. Blaker Bolling, Richard L. Jones, and Ashli White of Marshall University.

From a news item in the *New York Times:*

> Battle Creek, January 25, 1995—Since the Kellogg Company posted fourth-quarter earnings on Friday, investors and analysts have become concerned that the company might be forced to adopt discounting measures to defend market share, weakening its profit margins. Last spring, Kellogg significantly cut back on discounting measures such as "buy one—get one free" offers on some of its best-selling cereals to lower costs and raise profits. The strategy succeeded at first, but then sales in Kellogg's core domestic cereal business fell, continuing a decline in market share that has seen Kellogg's brands go from over 40 percent of the $8 billion market in the late 1980s to 35 percent today.[1] Kellogg has assured investors that it will not reintroduce promotions. However, in re-

sponse to Kellogg chairman and chief executive officer Arnold Langbo's remark that Kellogg is "extremely sensitive toward further volume decline," Kellogg shares dropped by $2.75 on Friday to close at $54.25 on the New York Stock Exchange.

In Battle Creek, Michigan, headquarters of Kellogg Company, Chief Executive Officer and Chairman of the Board Arnold G. Langbo reflected back on the company's performance in 1994. Although Kellogg's sales increased for the fiftieth consecutive year and earnings increased for the forty-first time in 42 years, the company did not meet its growth objectives for the year. Kellogg remained the world's leading producer of ready-to-eat cereal products and controlled 43 percent of the global market. Even though Kellogg continued to lead the industry in 1994, it faced many challenges. Langbo was concerned with how the company would reach its marketing objectives and continue leading the industry, how it could maintain profit margin, and how it might increase its stock price, which was near a 3-year low in early 1995.

THE CEREAL INDUSTRY

Cereal grains milled into breakfast cereal is an $8 billion business worldwide. The worldwide demand for ready-to-eat cereal is in a long-term upward trend. Annual per capita cereal consumption in North America is 10.3 pounds, while the world's leading consumer of cereal, Ireland, topped at 17 pounds. However, cereal for breakfast is not part of the cultural tradition in many parts of the world. For example, in Africa and Asia, per capita cereal consumption runs well below 1 pound per year, offering a great opportunity for market development. In North America and Europe, an increasing consciousness of healthy diet and nutrition needs drives increased demand among adults. U.S. annual growth is estimated at 2 to 3 percent, with worldwide growth in the 5 to 7 percent range.

Competition within the industry centers around several companies. Kellogg Company is the worldwide leader with a 35 percent U.S. market share, 43 percent worldwide. Of the 10 most popular breakfast cereals in the world, six wear a Kellogg label. The number two player, and Kellogg's primary competitor, is General Mills, with a 25 percent U.S. market share. General Mills was a messy conglomerate in the early 1980s. Since 1985, however, it has sought to focus more on cereal products. Worldwide, General Mills formed joint ventures with Nestlé (Cereal Partners Worldwide) and PepsiCo (Snack Ventures Europe). Both are relatively new, and neither of these enterprises has scored significant success. General Mills' recent performance has been marred by disappointing returns from its Big G cereal business and violations of Food and Drug Administration (FDA) regulations. Unregistered pesticide traces were found in the company's raw oat supply. Although not a particular health hazard, this disrupted General Mills' production and marketing plans. Traditionally more broadly diversified than Kellogg, General Mills had recently sold off its three restaurant chains: Red Lobster, Olive Garden, and China Coast. The company retained Betty Crocker, Gold Medal, and Yoplait Products Divisions.

Other companies seeking market share were Quaker Oats, Ralston Purina, Kraft, General Foods, and Nabisco. With a growing worldwide demand, these companies had a chance to build markets and increase profits.

KELLOGG COMPANY

Kellogg Company and its subsidiaries are involved primarily in the manufacture and marketing of convenience foods. The main products of the company are ready-to-eat cereals, including Frosted Flakes, Corn Flakes, Apple Jacks, Frosted Mini-Wheats, Rice Krispies, Raisin Bran, Cracklin' Oat Bran, and Nut & Honey Crunch. These products are manufactured in 18 countries and distributed in more than 150. These cereals are sold primarily to grocery stores for resale to consumers and are marketed globally. In addition to ready-to-eat cereals, Kellogg produces or processes and distributes frozen dessert pies, toaster pastries, waffles, snacks, and other convenience foods in the United States, Canada, and other limited areas outside the United States. Some of these products include Pop-Tarts, Eggo waffles, Nutri-Grain Bars, Croutettes, and Corn Flake Crumbs.

The corporate culture at Kellogg is focused on the long-term well-being of the business. Management's primary objective is to increase shareholders' value over time. In order to reach this objective, the Kellogg Strategy was formed:

> Continued aggressive investment in new cereal markets, increased returns on existing investments, maximizing cash flows, and minimizing the cost of capital through appropriate financial policies.

At Kellogg, it was believed that the 16,000 employees were the company's most important competitive advantage.

Kellogg Company History

Kellogg Company's worldwide leadership came from the accidental invention of flaked cereal at the Battle Creek Sanitarium in 1894. The sanitarium was a famous Seventh Day Adventist hospital and health spa where exercise, fresh air, and a strict diet were offered. Sanitarium Superintendent Dr. John Harvey Kellogg and Will Keith Kellogg, his younger brother and business manager, invented many grain-based foods served at the facility.

The sanitarium served hard and tasteless bread. The Kellogg brothers conducted experiments to develop a better-tasting alternative. Wheat was cooked, forced through granola rollers, and then rolled into long sheets of dough. One day the brothers experienced a fortunate accident. A batch of wheat was cooked but then set aside, neglected. Later, the brothers decided to process the stale dough. Instead of producing long sheets of dough, the rollers flattened the wheat mixture into small, thin flakes. Toasted, these flakes tasted light and crispy.

The patients at the sanitarium liked these new flakes so well that they wanted to eat them at home. To satisfy that demand, the Kellogg brothers started the Sanitas Nut Food Company, selling the toasted wheat flakes by mail order. In 1898, Will Keith Kellogg extended the process to flaking corn. Seeing his brother's lack of interest in expanding the food company, W. K. Kellogg went into business for himself.

On April 1, 1906, the Battle Creek Toasted Corn Flake Company started production. W. K. Kellogg used his manufacturing and marketing ideas to promote his product. He added malt flavoring to the corn flakes to make them unique. He advertised to healthy people the benefits of a product with flavor, freshness, value, and convenience. Kellogg used most of his working capital to buy a full-page ad in *The Ladies Home Journal* in 1906. Results were amazing. Sales quickly went from 33 cases to 2900 cases per day. With continued advertising, the company's annual sales surged to more than a million cases by 1909. W. K. Kellogg became known for his innovative sales promotions, which included free samples and premiums. The company was renamed Kellogg Company in 1922.

Effective marketing led to the company's success. In addition, Kellogg constantly sought ways to improve the product. He was committed to providing consumers with information about diet and nutrition. Kellogg was the first company to print nutrition messages, recipes, and product information on cereal packages in the 1930s. By that time, products such as All-Bran and Rice Krispies had been introduced. Kellogg became an international

business when it built facilities in Canada, Australia, and England. In 1930, the W. K. Kellogg Foundation was established. Today, it is one of the largest philanthropic institutions in the world, funding projects in health, education, agriculture, leadership, and youth.

During the 1950s, products such as Corn Pops, Frosted Flakes, and Honey Smacks were introduced. Television also became an important part of advertising in the 1950s. As the mid-1960s approached, Pop Tarts and Product 19 were added.

Consumers began showing more interest in health and nutrition in the 1960s. So Kellogg Company provided information programs for schools, health organizations, and consumers. During the 1970s, Kellogg provided more detailed package labels, including amounts of sodium and dietary fiber. By the mid-1980s, packages included cholesterol, potassium, and nutrient information. New product introductions included Nutri-Grain, Crispix, Just Right, and Mueslix.

In Kellogg's continued commitment to health, the company led an All-Bran/National Cancer Institute campaign that produced more than 80,000 contacts to the National Cancer Institute (NCI) for information about the role of diet in reducing the risk of some kinds of cancers. Recently, Kellogg took pride in providing information to consumers about healthy lifestyles, cholesterol, and heart disease.

Production

Kellogg Company traditionally sought market leadership through production efficiency and product quality control, product innovation, and marketing effectiveness. The company spent considerable capital to maintain high-tech, high-capacity production capability. The result was low production costs but considerable excess capacity. To take advantage of possible economies of scale in production, there was constant pressure to build and maintain markets. New product innovations were an important part of this strategy. Kellogg moved Nutri-Grain from the health food store to the supermarket in 1981 and modified the production process to gain extended shelf life for the product.

Kellogg practiced Japanese-style total quality management (TQM) principles. The company strictly monitored product quality control. It made sure that new automated manufacturing machinery was thoroughly tested before it went on-line to serve a market. Worker teams monitored quality, controlled costs, and suggested improvements. Kellogg sought to improve inbound logistics by developing stronger relations with a limited number of suppliers.

Marketing

One of the roots of Kellogg's success was a strong marketing program. This was logical considering that the company marketed a low-priced, convenience good and that high volumes of repeat sales were necessary to maintain market share. The foundation of Kellogg's marketing strategy had been to offer a good product backed with high-performance promotion. The company used a mix of price and sales promotion to build and maintain market share. It believed that money spent to introduce good products would build market share. This was a successful strategy until the early 1990s. Success, for Kellogg, traditionally had been measured by market share.

The primary consumers of breakfast cereal products in the United States were children. Kellogg sought to serve this target market with its mainstay brands: Corn Flakes, Rice Krispies, Corn Pops, Honey Smacks, Froot Loops, Apple Jacks, and Raisin Bran had heavy consumption by kids. These products were in the maturity stage of their product lifecycle, but the market constantly renewed itself as younger children moved into the school-age years. Kellogg sought to maintain brand loyalty with a good-tasting product, vigorously promoted through advertising and coupon offers. In the past, Kellogg was known for new product innovation, rolling out four or five brand extensions a year. This rate of introduction was reduced recently to one, maybe two, per year.

One high-potential market niche was health-conscious adults. In the late 1980s, oat-bran products offered the promise of minimizing blood

cholesterol and reducing the chances of heart attack. Oat bran was "by far the most dramatic thing that has ever happened to the cereal industry," said one high-level industry executive. Oat bran and oat products doubled their market share to 18 percent in 1989, while the ready-to-eat cereal market grew only 1 to 2 percent. Kellogg, with only about 20 percent of its product line based on oats, was late to market with an acceptable brand. The company never really caught up. When it did offer a product, it cannibalized share from its existing offerings. Then the balloon burst. The health benefits of oat bran were placed in doubt. Consumers rebelled. Sales plummeted. Oat bran tasted like cattle feed—if it wasn't *really* good for you, people wouldn't eat it. Kellogg's Common Sense Oat Bran dropped from a 2 percent share to 0.7 percent. Cracklin' Oat Bran fell from 1.4 percent in 1990 to 0.4 percent in 1991.

Market share for Kellogg's domestic products had been slipping for a decade (see Table below). Kellogg's declining market share was the result of two factors: (1) product price increases accompanied by a heavy reliance on price-promotion spending and (2) increased competition. Kellogg raised prices six times, accompanied by heavy couponing in the 3 years preceding 1994. In 1994, the company cut back on coupons, maintained restraint on pricing, and spent money on increased advertising. Kellogg was concerned about the effect on its strategy when General Mills decreased prices. Low-priced private-label cereals, mostly from Ralston Purina, also were a concern. Kellogg's choice: Keep prices high and risk a further loss of market share or lower prices at the expense of profits—with no assurance that market share would increase. For the meantime, the focus was on profitability. Arnold Langbo calculated that price maintenance and selective couponing would increase profits more than simply cutting prices across the board. He thought that Kellogg's brand

Kellogg Company Domestic Market Share

Year	1986	1987	1988	1989	1990	1991	1992	1993	1994
%	42	41	42	40	37	39	37	37	35

equity and consumer loyalty were great enough that the public would tolerate price increases with no added value to the product. Langbo told a meeting of Wall Street analysts: "There are 140 brands of cereal being bought by very loyal consumers. Some of the fastest-growing brands are the most expensive, so it's not all about price."

In the early 1990s, Kellogg and its major U.S. competitors sought to maintain higher pricing and profitability by steadily increasing their use of price-promotion spending, including lots of buy-one-get-one-free offers, known as "bogos." However, this strategy failed to stop Kellogg's continued slide in U.S. market share. In 1994, Kellogg CEO Arnold Langbo said: "In the long run, bogos don't work. They borrow share. They don't earn share."

Kellogg also was hurt by its lack of appealing new cereal products that were needed to pull up U.S. volume. Kellogg's Healthy Choice cereals, introduced in early 1994, have performed well, but the overall new-product performance by Kellogg and its competitors since the early 1980s has been, at best, unspectacular.

Kellogg's Global Markets

Unlike some companies that sought product diversification to build profits, Kellogg concentrated on marketing cereal and other food products. Eighty percent of its worldwide sales came from cereal. The company's market development took the form of expanding to foreign markets. The company entered Canada in 1914 and by 1991 had 17 cereal plants located in 15 foreign countries. Since then, the company has added Argentina, Latvia, India, and China. In 1994, Kellogg controlled 43 percent of worldwide cereal sales.

Kellogg North America led its market with a 37 percent share in 1993. It enjoyed both good product quality control and high labor productivity. It also led the market in advertising expenditures. In addition to ready-to-eat cereals, Kellogg North America offered other grain-based convenience foods: frozen dessert pies, toaster pastries, waffles, granola bars, and snacks. In 1993, new product rollouts included Low Fat Granola Bars, Nutri-Grain Bars, new Eggo versions, Mini Eggos, and new flavors of Pop Tarts.

The best of the overseas beachheads seemed to be in the old British Empire (Britain, Ireland, Australia), where eating breakfast cereal was culturally

accepted. Kellogg Europe controlled 50 percent of the market, six times the share of its nearest competitor. During 1993, the company was selected first in customer service among all British manufacturers for the fourth year in a row. Ireland was the world's top cereal consumer, but market growth potential was still great. Kellogg gained 5 percent in sales volume in Ireland during 1993. A promising new market in this division was the Republic of Latvia. In a joint venture with Adazi Food Products, Kellogg opened a new cereal plant in 1993. This was the first Western cereal enterprise in the former Soviet Union. Cereal for breakfast was not a tradition in this region, so market potential could be great. Initially, demand would be low, but competition would be zero. Kellogg was substantially increasing advertising expenditures throughout Europe, trying to interest younger people in testing the convenience of cereal for breakfast or a snack instead of a croissant or *schwartzbrot*. This strategy was successful, resulting in a strong growth in the cereal business in continental Europe in the late 1980s and early 1990s.

So far as market potential was concerned, some countries had a very low market penetration rate. Worldwide cereal consumption averaged around 2 pounds per year, compared with North America's 10 pounds. Cereal for breakfast was not yet culturally accepted in certain areas. Kellogg marketing people thought it was merely a matter of education to get these consumers turned on to eating breakfast cereal. In some countries, there also was the matter of obtaining dairy products for topping. Some countries didn't drink a lot of milk and/or have an established dairy industry or an established channel of distribution that offered refrigeration. People did not have facilities to keep milk to pour over their Corn Flakes. Kellogg had a few cultural and infrastructure problems to solve before its market potential estimates could be realized.

Kellogg Asia Pacific controlled a 47 percent market share. New plants in India and China would serve millions of potential customers, more than one-third of the world's population. Here again, market development would require effecting significant changes in the traditional tastes and preferences of local consumers. Kellogg developed specific cereal products for niche foreign markets. A high-mineral multigrain cereal was developed for the health-conscious Australians, while in Japan, where fish and rice made a traditional breakfast,

Kellogg was offering Genmai Flakes, made from whole-grain rice.

Operations in the Latin America Division covered Mexico, Central America, and South America, and Kellogg dominated this market with 78 percent market share. This market share placed Kellogg in control of the developing markets as well. A new plant was under construction near Buenos Aires, Argentina, and capacity increases occurred at the plants in Bogota, Colombia; Maracay, Venezuela; and São Paulo, Brazil. Performance for the year in Latin America was favorable for the most part. However, disappointing results in Mexico had a negative impact on the overall performance of the division.

Opportunities for future growth were quite favorable with the increased interest in health and nutrition in Latin America. Kellogg had performed many different activities in order to make consumers more aware of the importance of nutrition. Some of the activities included school nutrition education programs, which covered 300,000 children in Mexico alone, fiber symposia, and nutritional newsletters to health professionals.

In an attempt to provide consumers with additional value in its products, Kellogg added extra vitamins to the cereals in Latin Americans' diets and added zinc to products in other selected countries. This adaptation of products to the culture was one of Kellogg's ways to boost cereal consumption.

THE COMPANY TODAY

Even with intense competition and many challenges faced by Kellogg during 1993, worldwide revenues increased by 2 percent. This was the forty-ninth consecutive year for increases. In the United States alone, sales rose by 6 percent. There were 24 new product introductions worldwide. Kellogg received 40 percent of its revenues from outside the United States.

In Europe, sales decreased 8 percent due to unfavorable foreign currency exchange rates. If this problem had not occurred, sales would have been up by 4 percent. Dividends increased for the thirty-seventh consecutive year, with 10 percent growth in 1993. Price-earnings multiple remained at one of the highest levels in the food industry. However, the performance of stock was disappointing.

In 1993, Kellogg decided to divest units that did not fit with long-term strategic plans. So the British carton container and Argentinian snack food businesses were sold for a total pretax gain of $65.9 million. (Other results of operations may be found in the financial statements provided at the end of the case.)

In 1994, Kellogg followed a price-maintenance policy to provide value to consumers. The company also cut back on coupons. Since then, the company's market share has been steady.

THE FUTURE

The future for Kellogg and the ready-to-eat cereal industry looked quite favorable at the end of 1995. Demand continued in a long-term upward trend, with growth estimated at 2 to 3 percent in the United States and 5 to 7 percent overseas. This continued growth would come with the increasing recognition by consumers of the nutritional value of cereal. Domestic growth also would come with the increasing ages of Baby-Boomers from young adulthood to middle age, where cereal consumption had grown steadily.

It also appeared that the trend among competitors in the industry was to cut promotional spending. These competitors could have unbounded opportunities to establish a position in the new markets that were being entered, such as India and China.

CEO Langbo has come to the conclusion: "If this business was ever easy, it isn't anymore."

EXHIBIT A
················
Kellogg Company and Subsidiaries: Consolidated Balance Sheet (At December 31, in millions)

	1993	1992
Current assets		
Cash and temporary investments	$ 98.1	$ 126.3
Accounts receivable, less allowances of $6.0 and $6.2	536.8	519.1
Inventories:		
Raw materials and supplies	148.5	167.7
Finished goods and materials in process	254.6	248.7
Deferred income taxes	85.5	66.2
Prepaid expenses	121.6	108.6
Total current assets	1,245.1	1,236.6
Property		
Land	40.6	40.5
Buildings	1,065.7	1,021.2
Machinery and equipment	2,857.6	2,629.4
Construction in progress	308.6	302.6
Accumulated depreciation	(1,504.1)	(1,331.0)
Property, net	2,768.4	2,662.7
Intangible assets	59.1	53.3
Other assets	164.5	62.4
Total assets	$4,237.1	$4,015.0
Current liabilities		
Current maturities of long-term debt	$ 1.5	$ 1.9
Notes payable	386.7	210.0
Accounts payable	308.8	313.8
Accrued liabilities:		
Income taxes	65.9	104.1
Salaries and wages	76.5	78.0
Advertising and promotion	233.8	228.0
Other	141.4	135.2
Total current liabilities	1,214.6	1,071.0
Long-term debt	521.6	314.9
Nonpension postretirement benefits	450.9	407.6
Deferred income taxes	188.9	184.6
Other liabilities	147.7	91.7
Shareholders' equity		
Common stock, $.25 par value		
Authorized: 330,000,000 shares		
Issued: 310,292,753 shares in 1993 and 310,193,228 in 1992	77.6	77.5
Capital in excess of par value	72.0	69.2
Retained earnings	3,409.4	3,033.9
Treasury stock, at cost: 82,372,409 and 72,874,738 shares	(1,653.1)	(1,105.0)
Minimum pension liability adjustment	(25.3)	
Currency translation adjustment	(167.2)	(130.4)
Total shareholders' equity	1,713.4	1,945.2
Total liabilities and shareholders' equity	$4,237.1	$4,015.0

EXHIBIT B
················
Kellogg Company and Subsidiaries: Consolidated Earnings and Retained Earnings
(Year ended December 31, in millions, except per share amounts)

	1993	*1992*	*1991*
Net Sales	$6,295.4	$6,190.6	$5,786.6
Other revenue (deductions), net	(1.5)	36.8	14.6
	6,293.9	6,227.4	5,801.2
Cost of goods sold	2,989.0	2,987.7	2,828.7
Selling and administrative expense	2,237.5	2,140.1	1,930.0
Interest expense	33.3	29.2	58.3
	5,259.8	5,157.0	4,817.0
Earnings before income taxes and cumulative effect of accounting change	1,034.1	1,070.4	984.2
Income taxes	353.4	387.6	378.2
Earnings before cumulative effect of accounting change	680.7	682.8	606.0
Cumulative effect of change in method of accounting for postretirement benefits other than pensions—$1.05 a share (net of income tax benefit of $144.6)		(251.6)	
Net earnings—$2.94, $1.81, $2.51 a share	680.7	431.2	606.0
Retained earnings, beginning of year	3,033.9	2,889.1	2,542.4
Dividends paid—$1.32, $1.20, $1.075 a share	(305.2)	(286.4)	(259.3)
Retained earnings, end of year	$3,409.4	$3,033.9	$2,889.1

Bibliography

Cohen, Waren, "A Crunch for Cereal Makers," *U.S. News & World Report,* March 28, 1994.

Elliott, Stuart, "Consumers Take Center Stage in a Campaign to Promote the Value of a Kellogg Breakfast," *New York Times,* July 20, 1994.

Erickson, Julie Liesse, "Schroeder: Kellogg Is Popping," *Advertising Age,* August 14, 1989, p. 3.

Erickson, Julie Liesse, "Why Schroeder Is Leaving Kellogg," *Advertising Age,* September 25, 1989, p. 6.

General Mills 1994 Annual Report.

Gibson, Richard, "Head of Kellogg's U.S. Cereal Business Resigns as Part of Management Shuffle," *Wall Street Journal,* July 5, 1994, p. B7.

Gibson, Richard, "Kellogg Tries to Keep Cereal Sales Crisp as Rivals Nibble Away at Market Share," *Wall Street Journal,* November 9, 1993, p. A5B.

Gibson, Richard, "Kellogg Earnings Increased 3.5% in Third Quarter," *Wall Street Journal,* October 24, 1994, p. A9A.

Kahn, Mir Maqbool Alam, "Kellogg Reports Brisk Cereal Sales in India," *Advertising Age,* November 14, 1994, p. 60.

"Kellogg Says It Plans to Further Cut Use of Discount Programs," *Wall Street Journal,* November 14, 1994, p. B5A.

Kellogg Company 1993 Annual Report.

Kellogg Company, Value Line, Edition 10, August 1994, pp. 1468, 1476, 1485.

Liesse, Julie, "Kellogg, Alpo Top Hot New Product List," *Advertising Age,* January 4, 1993, p. 66.

Liesse, Julia, and Judann Degnoll, "Kellogg's Golden Era Flakes Away," *Advertising Age,* August 31, 1990, p. 4.

Liesse, Julia, "Gen. Mills 1, Kellogg 0," *Advertising Age,* September 20, 1993, p. 2.

Liesse, Julie, "Kellogg's Prices Go Up, Up, Up," *Advertising Age,* August 9, 1993, p. 1.

Mitchell, Russell, "Big G Is Growing Fat on Oat Cuisine," *Business Week,* September 18, 1989, p. 29.

Mitchell, Russell, "The Health Craze Has Kellogg Feeling G-R-R-Reat," *Business Week,* March 30, 1987, pp. 52–53.

Moody's Industrial Manual, Vol. 2 (New York: Moody's Investors Service, Inc., 1993), pp. 4001–4004.

"The History of Kellogg Company," Kellogg Company pamphlet, 1992.

"¿Tiene usted los Corn Flakes?" *Forbes,* January 4, 1991, p. 168.

Sellers, Patricia, "How King Kellogg Beat the Blahs," *Fortune,* August 29, 1988, pp. 55–64.

Serwer, Andrew E., "What Price Brand Loyalty," *Fortune,* January 10, 1994, pp. 103–104.

Treece, James B., and Greg Burns, "The Nervous Faces Around Kellogg's Breakfast Table," *Business Week,* July 18, 1994, p. 33.

Woodruff, David, "Winning the War of Battle Creek," *Business Week,* May 31, 1991, p. 80.

Endnote

1. A conversation with Richard E. Lovell, manager, corporate communications, Kellogg's Company Corporate Headquarters, indicated a factual error in the news item. Kellogg's strategy of reducing price-promotion spending resulted in a 1 percent market share drop at first. This leveled off at 35 percent and has remained constant since then. The authors appreciate the great assistance provided by Mr. Lovell in the preparation of this case.

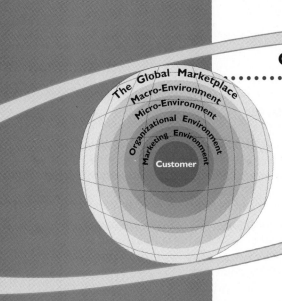

Cedar Falls Utilities and the Information Superhighway(D): TCI's Response

This case was prepared by Lynda L. Goulet and Peter G. Goulet of the University of Northern Iowa, Cedar Falls, Iowa.

Apparently TCI company doesn't care about its customers. First it increased rates last year 13 percent, then it started the fiber optics in Cedar Falls and not in Waterloo (Cedar Falls pays about 48 cents per channel and Waterloo pays about $1 per channel). Then it threatened to remove WGN, and, while everyone is concentrating on this, TCI decides to remove MTV and VH1 and the Comedy Channel, but only in Waterloo; Cedar Falls still has those channels, plus many more.

I am getting tired of its attitude toward their customers. . . . Now TCI is raising its rates another 7 percent this year. . . . Now the people of Waterloo can thank TCI for going back on its word to install fiber optics by 1999. [Editor noted that as of two weeks before this letter was written, TCI had not yet decided on this action.]

TCI lost many customers last year; now let's see how many it can lose this year. You can bet that Cedar Falls probably won't get the increase with Cedar Falls Utilities being there in competition. . . . TCI doesn't care if it upsets us. . . .[1]

On October 11, 1994, voters of the City of Cedar Falls, Iowa, authorized the city to establish a municipal broadband communications system to be operated as a municipal communications utility and issue $3 million of general obligation bonds to finance the project.[2]

As a result of this referendum, the city-owned, independently-managed Cedar Falls Utilities (CFU) implemented its fiberoptic broadband communications system and signed up its first customers in early 1996. The communications utility approved by voters was operated as a separate subsidiary of the existing utility operation and was intended to provide, among other things, cable entertainment services and fiberoptic communications services to the community. While the original project proposal called for $6 million of capital financing, the final investment, including working capital, came to roughly $7.5 million, with $3 million financed by the city and the rest coming from utility reserves.

Prior to the approval of the CFU project, TCI of Northern Iowa, a subsidiary of Tele-Communications, Inc. (TCI), the nation's largest provider of cable television services, renewed its franchise agreement with the City of Cedar Falls for 15 years. Part of TCI's new franchise agreement with the city was that it would upgrade service through the installation of the fiberoptic cable during 1995. This cable upgrade also was to provide 77-channel capacity.

TCI completed its promised system upgrade in Cedar Falls in mid-1996, signing up its first customers shortly after CFU. In spite of the fact that TCI had an established customer base and had enjoyed a nearly 20-year-long monopoly in Cedar Falls, and even though its new system was competitive with CFU's new utility, the cable giant did not encounter an easy road. The new system raised TCI's costs, and subsequent actions eroded public support, resulting in significant loss of subscribers. TCI's Cedar Falls service shared facilities with TCI's existing operation in Waterloo, Iowa, an adjacent community. While TCI's service in Waterloo was established first, it was not comparable with that provided in Cedar Falls, having only 40-channel capacity and utilizing standard coaxial cable. TCI's Waterloo/CF franchisees were part of a statewide business unit, owned in turn by its parent corporation, Tele-Communications, Inc. TCI's actions in the Cedar Falls market contributed to an erosion of support for the firm in Waterloo. Faced with these and other difficulties, the management of TCI of Northern Iowa had to decide how to proceed to return its performance to prior levels of success.

BACKGROUND ENVIRONMENT

The Local Market

Cedar Falls, Iowa, had an estimated population of about 34,300 in 1994, comprising approximately 11,000 households. In addition, the University of Northern Iowa (UNI) was home to about 13,000 students, 5000 of whom lived on campus in roughly 2400 dormitory units, while the remaining 8000 resided either in Cedar Falls or nearby communities. The city's population was growing by approximately 1000 people per year. Cedar Falls could be described as primarily a "white collar" community, with a median family income of $37,600 in 1990, slightly above both the state and national averages. Cedar Falls was located adjacent to Waterloo, a major industrial center with a population of roughly 75,000. At the end of 1996, the combination of both households and dorm rooms in Cedar Falls provided 12,000 to 13,000 "passings" (possible cable connections—equal to the available market).

Cedar Falls provided all traditional city services and owned and operated a municipal hospital (sold in early 1997), as well as a municipal utility (CFU) that provided electric, gas, and water services. In 1978, TCI (through a predecessor) began supplying cable television services to the city. In late 1994, TCI's franchise agreement with Cedar Falls was renewed for 15 years with a promise to upgrade service in 1995 at an estimated cost of $3.5 million. This improved technology would provide increased channel capacity and could be upgraded further to serve as the basis for interactive cable and other services. At the time of the new agreement, TCI supplied service to 68 percent of the available customers in the community. By contrast, cable companies in Iowa served just over 64 percent of the passings in the state, and nationally, the average rate of penetration was 61 percent. Further, TCI had just signed a 10-year exclusive agreement to serve the 2400 dormitory rooms at UNI.

Cedar Falls received local telephone service through U.S. West Communications and McLeod-USA (a regional phone company), both of which also provided access to all the major long-distance services. Cellular phone service was provided by 360° Communications and Cellular One. Finally, Cedar Falls was connected to Iowa's statewide fiberoptic cable network (ICN). The ICN was unique in the United States and was designed to connect all counties, governmental units, schools, universities, community colleges, libraries, hospitals, and other agencies throughout the state. At the end of 1994, the main "backbone" network of the ICN was completed, although most of the individual connections had not been made. One motivation for the establishment of the new CFU communications utility was to provide so-called broadband (high-capacity) fiberoptic connections to the ICN for voice and data transmission.

During the 1990s, Cedar Falls enjoyed a significant expansion in industrial development. By mid-1996, it was becoming clear that the new utility would attract businesses because it could give firms enhanced communications capability. At that time a major Internet service provider moved from Waterloo to Cedar Falls, setting off concerns in Waterloo that it might become less competitive economically if it did not enhance its own communications capability.

The National Environment

For several decades, the cable television industry has struggled to achieve growth and profitability. From its beginnings in the early 1950s, the industry grew to over 11,000 individual system franchises in the United States serving an estimated 65 million customers by 1997. While cable initially began as a way to enhance reception and provide coverage to communities that had limited ability to receive broadcast signals, by the 1970s the concept had expanded to include a dramatic increase in programmatic offerings. The establishment of satellite transmission and new cable-only networks such as ESPN, USA, A&E, and others changed the face of this medium.

While cable provided numerous advantages over broadcast television, by the mid-1990s the industry faced several significant issues: rising costs, rising prices to consumers, a declining image, consolidation of the industry, a rise in the number of substitute products and technologies, and regulatory threats.

Rising Costs/Prices A major disadvantage of cable, compared to its broadcast rivals, was that it

was a paid service. Subscriber fees, in turn, were a function of several issues. First, cable television was capital-intensive. Each cable system required a "headend" facility that received signals from the satellites that transmitted the various channel signals. Once the signal was reprocessed and decoded, it was retransmitted to subscribers. In addition, the system required hundreds of miles of cable. CFU had to lay a total of 334 miles of wire at roughly $20,000 per mile to construct its system in Cedar Falls in 1995. The cost of such capital investments had to be recovered through fees charged to subscribers.

The other major cost of cable was programming. Channels that were in demand from customers charged cable companies to carry them. Since established channels attracted subscribers, the cable firms had to carry these channels and charge their customers accordingly. However, as new channels were created, the demand for new programming rose, but the ratings (a count of households watching) for each channel fell on average. Only eleven of the largest cable-only channels such as TNT, USA, and ESPN received ratings over 1.0 in 1996, while broadcast channels (ABC, NBC) regularly received ratings as high as 15 to 20 for some shows.[3] In early 1996, cable television as a whole held a rating of 21.0, while ratings for the four major networks totaled 40.9. Ratings for public television, the minor networks, and independent stations totaled 17.1.[4] Because programs were paid for by advertising and advertising charges were dependent on ratings (higher ratings command higher prices), lower-rated channels had a difficult time buying new shows and had to try to recover costs through higher fees to the cable companies that wanted to transmit their signals.

Finally, to keep growing, cable companies have had to enter smaller markets, raising the average cost of their plant capacity per subscriber. This factor, and rising programming costs, forced the costs of cable companies to rise significantly. In an attempt to pass on these costs, cable companies raised prices. From 1983 to 1994, cable prices roughly doubled, while consumer prices as a whole increased only 50 percent. Early in 1997, two of the nation's largest providers, TCI (1) and Time Warner (2), both raised prices by as much as 7 percent. Basic programming costs (30 percent of the operating revenues) were expected to total $3.5 billion in 1997, up 14 percent from 1996. The cost of many key channels was rising as much as 20 percent per year. All this was occurring while competition also was increasing, making it more difficult for cable operators to pass these new costs on to consumers.[5]

Image   While cable became a more popular entertainment medium in the 1980s and 1990s, its image became increasingly tarnished by stories of poor service, billing problems, and bad attitudes on the part of its personnel. For a long time, this problem was ignored because cable had a monopoly, of sorts, on in-home entertainment. However, the rise of the direct-broadcast satellite system and other forms of competition, coupled with dissatisfaction over rising prices, forced the industry to try to take action to restore its image in early 1995. In March of that year, the National Cable Television Association (NCTA) launched a new national guarantee campaign comparing itself to such firms as UPS and others known for quality service.[6] Whether this campaign will be successful has yet to be determined. By early 1997, however, it was clear that some local operators had not improved their images, and sales of competitive services were still rising, while cable growth continued to slow down. It was estimated that annual subscriber growth would be less than 2.5 percent by the year 2000.

Consolidation   As with any industry entering a more mature phase of its lifecycle, the cable television industry has experienced significant consolidation. At the end of 1996, the industry was dominated by two giants, TCI and Time Warner. TCI led with roughly 14 million subscribers, or about 21 percent of the market. Time Warner followed closely with just under 12 million, or just over 18 percent of the market. The next four firms—Continental Cablevision, Comcast, Cox Communications, and Cablevision Systems—were roughly similar in size and served a total of 14.3 million subscribers, or about 22 percent of the market.[7] In Iowa, TCI was the dominant player, serving 530,000 of the 602,000 homes that received cable, for a market share of 88 percent.[8]

The impact of consolidation was not limited to the issue of company size. Expansion, and the corresponding replacement of copper wires with fiberoptics, required cable companies to incur huge amounts of debt, created major cash flow problems, and reduced the ability of these firms to take advantage of new technologies. Thus many of the major cable firms began to sell increasingly large pieces of their firms to partners in other segments of the communications industry. U.S. West Media, a "Baby Bell" spinoff, owned 25 percent of Time Warner's cable operation, for example. TCI tried to sell the whole firm to Bell Atlantic in 1993, but the deal fell through.[9]

Competition/Substitutes   For most of its existence as an industry, cable television lacked viable competitive substitutes. If a person wanted to watch 30 or 40 channels of entertainment, cable was the only source. In the 1980s, satellite systems were introduced to tap into the same satellites that the cable companies used to receive their programming so that individuals in rural areas especially could receive cable-type signals. These early satellite systems were expensive for the consumer to purchase. They did not really pose a major threat to the cable industry because they could receive only one signal at a time and could not accommodate multiple television sets.

In 1992, the Hughes Division of General Motors changed the cable landscape when it introduced a new satellite system, called DBS (direct broadcast satellite). It provided a digital signal that combined an array of the same channels that cable provided through a small, less costly satellite receiver. This digital signal provided cable programs without the cable. Several firms, including DirecTV and Dish, utilized this new system to provide not only standard cable fare but also programming not available on cable. The leading program provider, DirecTV, made arrangements with various networks to provide exclusive packaged pay services such as college and professional football, basketball, and movies that cable did not offer. Further, utilizing digital signals allowed the DBS system to provide better picture and sound quality than cable and enhanced its capability to take advantage of new digital television technology. It was estimated that by the end of 1997 more than 4 million rural and urban homes would be subscribers to this new satellite service. Further, the price of these small DBS receiving systems had fallen to only $150 by early 1997. However, DBS users paid $20 to $30 per month for a 40- to 50-channel lineup similar to standard cable, and the pay sports packages cost roughly $35 to $40 per month. Pay movie package costs were comparable with cable.

As the DBS threat increased, a consortium of cable companies led by TCI responded by increasing the marketing of their own satellite system called Primestar. While this system predated DBS, it was not as technically advanced and did not offer the complex pay TV packages offered by DBS providers. However, Primestar subscribers did not have to purchase any equipment. Both DBS and Primestar shared a weakness in comparison with cable. They could not offer local broadcast or weather channels on their systems. Thus subscribers to these systems needed a separate antenna to receive the four major networks and public television, but without the picture quality of typical cable systems.

In the mid-1990s, a new major player emerged in the television communications business that threatened to further disrupt the environment. Rupert Murdoch, CEO of News Corporation, Ltd., began to invest the fortune he made in his European tabloid newspaper and broadcasting empire in the United States. His ownership of newspapers, television stations, cable networks such as FX, and the new Fox television network made him a formidable force. In 1996, Murdoch launched a new firm called America Sky Broadcasting (Sky) based on partnerships with a firm called EchoStar and one of the DBS providers and announced plans to greatly expand the satellite cable business in the United States.[10]

Satellite television was viewed by many as a highly desirable medium because it did not require wires, thus saving the immense cost of a generally inflexible infrastructure. However, the required satellites are very costly. Motorola's Iridium project was originally estimated to cost in excess of $5 billion. Other firms, such as Hughes, Loral, GE, and McCaw (cellular phones) were expected to spend billions to put up as many as 1700 new satellites, 10 times the current number, to provide an array of communication services such as digital cellular phones, wireless Internet access, data transmission, expanded television services, and others. Some experts felt that, for a start, these services would provide more than $29 billion in annual revenue by the year 2000.[11] Note that while cable's emphasis is on wires, it, too, incurs satellite costs, though fewer than those of wireless firms.

While satellite and other forms of wireless television threatened the cable television industry, cable still had some advantages. Its infrastructure could provide a conduit for data and telephone transmission, as well as interactive or on-demand television. While this prospect existed even as the satellite systems were being launched, the cost of these applications and technological hurdles has slowed development of these applications. An interactive television experiment conducted by Time Warner in Tampa during the 1990s was abandoned in early 1997 because of lack of interest and high expenses for costly set-top boxes required to operate the system.

Perhaps the biggest potential application of the existing cable infrastructure is telephone transmission. However, current regulations and technology costs have thus far thwarted this application. The Cedar Falls Communication utility did make a limited entry into local phone business by using its fiberoptic cable to supply phone service to governmental agencies, thus saving the cost of a private carrier.

Regulation   In February 1996, Congress passed the telecommunications deregulation bill, which allowed local telephone companies, cable companies, and long-distance firms to freely enter each other's markets. Although these companies had already created many partnerships and joint ventures, the threat to the cable companies of these well-heeled competitors could prove to be worrisome. Further, both local phone companies and long-distance carriers had a better consumer image than cable companies (Exhibit A). When asked, 55 percent of consumers said they would buy cable-based telephone services if supplied by local or long-distance phone companies. Only 4 percent said they would buy these services if supplied by a cable firm.[12]

One critical regulation that affected the competition between cable and its competitors had to do with the local channels that cable systems carry on basic service. In 1996, all cable systems were required to carry all local broadcast affiliates available in their area as basic (low-cost) service. Because more than 60 percent of the viewers who received local stations received them through cable, loss of this access could have proved devastating for the local broadcasters. In October 1996, the Supreme Court heard a case trying to overturn these rules. That case was decided in the spring of 1997 in favor of the government to maintain the existing "must carry" rules. On the other hand, the DBS satellite carriers could not broadcast these local stations unless a subscriber otherwise had no access to local stations, such as in a rural area. This

EXHIBIT A
·················
Consumer Satisfaction

Percent of customers surveyed giving *excellent* or *good* ratings in each category to their cable television, local phone, and long-distance phone companies.

Service Attribute	Cable	Local Phone	Long Distance
Professional and courteous personnel	32.2%	54.6%	61.0%
Accurate, easy-to-read bills	39.8	55.9	61.7
Timely resolution of problems	29.8	50.2	54.0
Quick access to customer service reps	29.5	47.5	53.4
Value for money	16.1	35.3	50.3
High-quality transmission	32.0	57.7	61.7
Trustworthiness	25.7	50.0	56.5
Deserving of customer loyalty	23.3	48.4	54.6

Source: G. C. Hill, "It's War." *Wall Street Journal Reports, Telecommunications,* September 16, 1996, p. R4.

left DBS systems at a competitive disadvantage. However, in rural areas, many DBS suppliers were picking up distant broadcast stations, from New York City, for example, and rebroadcasting them to their customers. This was deemed a violation of copyright rules and barred. However, in early 1997, industry representatives from DBS and the National Association of Broadcasters came to an agreement that many felt might eventually lead to inclusion of broadcast networks on DBS.[13]

One way a major cable firm such as TCI might stifle competition was to buy or establish its own channels or contract with providers to have exclusive rights to certain channels, thereby shutting out the competition. Under existing regulations, this tactic was not allowed. All competitors, including CFU's system, had to be given access to all available channels at competitive prices. Thus a firm like TCI could not gain a channel advantage over an in-town rival such as CFU.

CFU COMMUNICATIONS UTILITY
··

As the Cedar Falls Communications Utility (CFU) began its marketing campaign in anticipation of initial customer connections in early 1996, it announced an initial lineup of 66 channels, compared with TCI's initial announcement offering 78 chan-

nels. Nineteen of CFU's channels were on basic cable at an initial cost of $7 per month, compared with 16 basic channels for $7.25 for TCI. CFU's expanded basic lineup was planned at 33 channels for $14 per month, while TCI planned 47 expanded service channels at $13.89. CFU was planning three HBO channels for $11, two Cinemax channels for $10, two Showtimes for $10, and an Encore/Starz package for $5. By contrast, TCI offered similar channels at slightly higher prices. Finally, CFU provided the Disney Channel as part of its expanded basic package, while TCI charged an additional $9.95 per month for that channel.[14] These prices and offerings reflected changes from those [that] appeared in the original feasibility study performed for CFU by Electrotek Concepts in 1994 (Exhibit B).

Exhibit B shows that 90 percent of TCI's customers purchased both basic and expanded cable in Cedar Falls in mid-1994. Further, counting each pay service (HBO, Showtime, etc.) taken as one subscriber, TCI served a total of 60.9 percent of its subscribers with one pay service. Nationally, however, TCI reported that it served the equivalent of 106 percent of its subscribers with at least one pay service, although only 15 percent of revenue came from its pay services.[15]

Initially, CFU developed two estimates for the number of subscribers it might sign up for its new

EXHIBIT B
....

Suggested Programming Structure for the Cedar Falls Cable Television System and Comparison to TCI's Cable Programming Price Structure

Programming	Suggested Price per Month	Estimated Cost per Month	Price per Month	Percent of Subscribers
	Cedar Falls System		TCI System	
Basic + expand. serv. (low)	$21.50	$3.25	$19.98	90%
Basic + expand. serv. (avg.)	$18.00	$3.25		
Premium channels (5)			$29.80 (all 5)*	
Home Box Office	$11.95	$6.24	$12.95	18.5%
Showtime	$10.95	$4.41	$11.95	7.6%
ENCORE	$ 1.75	$1.10	$ 1.75	19.7%
Disney	$ 8.95	$3.43	$ 9.95	5.4%
Movie Channel	$10.95	$4.60	$11.95†	9.7%

Note: The data reflect that the price for basic plus expanded service projected for CFU was expected to vary with the expected market penetration level (low or average). The price listed for TCI is the comparable price for basic plus expanded service which applies to the 90 percent of TCI's customers who take both.
*TCI offers numerous packaging options for premium pay channels.
†TCI offers Cinemax instead of The Movie Channel.
Source: Electrotek Concepts, Inc., and Public Financial Management, Inc.

cable service. The conservative estimate assumed that 3000 subscribers would subscribe in the first year of the project, with the total growing gradually to 3800 by the end of the fourth year. At this level CFU expected to be financially successful. In actual fact, by the end of its first year, CFU had gained just over 4800 subscribers, a number it never expected to obtain in the first 15 years of the project under its conservative estimate. According to statistics released by the Cedar Falls Cable Television Commission, in the 11 months ending in December 1996, TCI saw its subscriber numbers fall from 8600 to roughly 5650.[16]

As 1996 progressed, both TCI and CFU began to jockey lineups and prices. CFU increased its expanded basic offerings to 39 channels through the addition of 6 new channels, although prices remained as released in late 1995. As a result of the originally published lineup for CFU, TCI reacted by moving Disney into expanded basic at no charge, thus forgoing $10 per month per subscriber. It also added the Golf Channel, a key difference between the two firms. Initially, Golf was to be included only in a package requiring a converter box and an extra $5 charge. Under pressure from subscribers, this was later changed in September so that Golf and four other channels became part of expanded basic at no extra charge. In March, TCI noted 13 differences between the two services. By the summer of 1996, CFU had eliminated roughly half of those differences, including the Golf Channel, added in July, although TCI was still the only supplier of FX, Playboy, and later Ovation and Nick at Nite's TV Land. In mid-year, TCI also raised the price for expanded basic to $14.74, although it offered a promotion that would allow the customer to cut the cost of basic service by $2 per month if he or she subscribed to Sprint long-distance telephone service.

As the TCI/CFU competition progressed, many customers in the Waterloo market were wondering when they too would be included in the new higher-capacity, higher-quality cable world. When asked about this, Darrel Wenzel, general manager of TCI, said, "It's under negotiation." When asked about how well TCI could compete, Wenzel said, "[TCI would succeed with] more choices for the money, the best service, and the most experience." He also noted, "Customer service is where we have the advantage in manpower and training." Ken Alberts, general manager at CFU, responded when asked about CFU's service reputation, "It's all of those little things that you can't really put a price on, but that creates the kind of loyalty we've come to enjoy."[17]

When CFU initially sought permission to establish its new utility, it emphasized that two key reasons for the service would be the ability of the community to connect to the Internet through Iowa's ICN network and the added ability of the utility to lower its electric service costs through improved control over capacity utilization. When asked about CFU's proposed Internet access and various utility management options such as remote meter reading and electrical load management, TCI's Wenzel said, "Most of that is hype at this point. We really don't want to offer products that aren't deliverable." In early 1997, CFU began offering customers high-speed cable modem access to the Internet. CFU's cable modem service provided Internet access at 80 to 300 times the speed of conventional phone modems for a fixed price of $25 to $35 per month with no phone charges. This service was available to both individuals and business firms.

By mid-1996, the Waterloo officials, fearing that Cedar Falls might gain a competitive advantage in attracting and retaining business firms because of its new utility, and seeing that TCI had not yet announced any plans to upgrade its system in their city, made the decision to build a 60-mile-long fiberoptic "backbone" structure in their community to connect business and governmental offices to the ICN. While noting that this did not mean Waterloo would go into the cable television business, an official from McLeodUSA, Inc., the contractor installing the cable, noted, "We don't have any plan for providing cable TV, although the fiberoptic technology can certainly provide that kind of service."[18]

RECENT ACTIONS OF TCI

In the time between the initial establishment of TCI's fiberoptic "rebuild" in Cedar Falls and mid-1997, a number of significant events occurred. While many of these most strongly affected Waterloo subscribers, the publicity surrounding these events undoubtedly affected subscribers in both markets.

Corporate Actions

While TCI was the industry leader in cable television, all did not go well for the company in the mid-1990s. As noted earlier, an attempt to sell the company was aborted in 1993. Then Time Warner purchased Turner Broadcasting and its many popular networks: TNT, the ratings leader in cable; CNN; CNN Headline News; CNN Sports; TBS, the "superstation"; and the Cartoon Network. While TCI also was integrated, owning several networks through its Liberty Media subsidiary, Warner's production capabilities and its formidable libraries of MGM and Warner Brothers movies gave Time Warner a significant presence in programming software. Further, Disney, perhaps the most powerful entertainment giant, purchased the ABC network and with it gained ownership of ESPN, ESPN 2, and ESPN News. These major consolidations placed some of the most important programming on cable in the hands of TCI's competitors, reducing the firm's leverage in the industry. The death of TCI's former board chairman, Robert Magness, also created uncertainty as his shares of the company became available to current chairman, John Malone, if he could afford to buy them from the estate. If he could not or did not choose to buy them, they could go into the hands of a major purchaser who might make a deal with the estate.[19] In early 1997, rumors abounded that the company might again be "for sale." Malone had just given up his post as president and installed a new manager to be in charge of operations. Debt had climbed to over $14 billion, and the company had suffered significant losses in both 1995 and 1996. Prudential Securities' analysis of the company forecasted these losses to continue through 1998, although cash flow was expected to be positive.[20]

As TCI's losses mounted, its stock price declined, and pressure mounted for improvements. In response, TCI raised prices and cut costs. The cost-cutting moves largely took the form of layoffs, elimination of expensive popular channels, and substitution of new, less expensive ones such as the Animal Planet. It also planned to spin off its interest in the Primestar satellite venture. TCI announced its initial channel cuts late in 1996. The most visible cuts were the removal of WGN and MTV. In some markets TCI also dropped Comedy Central, VH1, Lifetime, BET, E!, the Travel Channel, A&E, Ovation, Bravo, TNN (Nashville), and the Weather Channel. Nationally, TCI subscribers did not react well to these changes, and by January 1997, many of the changes were rescinded in markets where the objections were the strongest. In many cases it was likely that these channels were reinstated at a lower cost to TCI than before the cuts because of TCI's bargaining power. As noted, advertising revenues depended on ratings. When TCI cut a channel, it reduced the total subscribers to that channel by 14 million. This would cause the channel to lose both advertising revenues and its license fee to TCI. With the threat of such a loss, it is likely that TCI gained considerable leverage. In the Waterloo–Cedar Falls market, things were a bit more strained.

Local Market Events

Channel Cuts   In the Waterloo–Cedar Falls market, the channel cuts that proved to be most difficult for TCI were WGN, which carried both Chicago Cubs and White Sox baseball, and MTV. After a good deal of backlash, WGN was restored to both markets. However, MTV presented a different story. Because of the higher channel capacity in Cedar Falls, MTV was restored to the lineup. However, in Waterloo, where capacity was only 40 channels, the firm did not restore MTV and VH1 service. This particular move created two types of protests, a petition to keep MTV off in Waterloo, led by area churches, and a series of subscriber protests to keep it on. According to the TCI manager, those against MTV outnumbered those in favor by a ratio of 2:1.[21] Initially, TCI's channel cuts were engineered at the corporate level. In contrast to TCI's practices, the channel lineup for the CFU cable system was determined by a committee of local citizens.

Price Increases   In conjunction with a corporate price increase, TCI raised prices for its new fiberoptic service in Cedar Falls, effective June 1, 1997. The price of basic service, initially $7.25, was scheduled to rise to $7.83, and expanded service was to rise from $13.97 to $14.81, for a total

package price of $22.64. At that point, CFU cable service was still priced at $21 for the total package.[22]

Subscriber Data   As noted earlier, in early 1997, TCI reported year-end subscriber data to the city of Cedar Falls, showing a loss of nearly 3000 subscribers. At that time there was some question as to the way these statistics were gathered and reported. In addition, the firm did not submit these statistics until just before a hearing where it was to show cause why it had not complied with the requirements of its franchise agreement to report these data. This was of some concern to the city because of the payment of franchise fees required by the contract with TCI. CFU paid these same fees, although it did not pay taxes.

Waterloo Franchise Agreement   TCI's fiberoptic rebuild in Cedar Falls created considerable interest among community leaders who wished to have Waterloo receive the same service. In February 1996, the Waterloo Cable Commission and TCI agreed to a renewal of their franchise agreement, extending it to 2018. The agreement was nonexclusive, allowing the possibility of a competitor in the market. The agreement also called for 77-channel capability and ostensibly was based on a new fiberoptic system. At least 40 percent of the new system was to be completed by December 31, 1997, and the rest was to be completed by the end of 1999. However, one year later TCI told the city of Waterloo that it would not be rebuilding the system with fiberoptic cable. It pointed out that its agreement with the city required only ". . . fiberoptic technology [or] something substantially similar and equally effective." Instead of fiber, the company said it would use so-called digital compression technology, which increased the capacity of traditional coaxial cable to a level similar to fiberoptic cable. Although the firm claimed it might build a fiber skeleton for computer access in the long-term future, it could not afford the $8 to $10 million it would cost to provide such a system for cable television. From the consumers' perspective, the digital compression system would require the use of set-top converter boxes to connect video equipment to the cable.[24]

Waterloo's reaction to this announcement was not positive. City officials felt the change away from fiberoptics might represent a breach of their contract with TCI. Cable Commissioner Chuck Angel said, "Our main concern is that we're going to be shortchanged with something that's at least equal to what we intended." The Waterloo city attorney said that if TCI did go to digital compression, the city would make the determination of whether this approach was comparable.[25]

THE FUTURE

Billions will be lost and billions will be made. In that order.

This view of the future of telecommunications from Don Valentine, a venture capitalist, captured his opinion about how successful industry competitors will be at entering one another's markets.[26] The advent of satellite television most certainly helped slow the growth of cable subscribers in the mid-1990s. While deregulation and technological advancements might offer opportunities for many firms in telecommunications to try to combine services such as Internet access, telephones, and cable television, wireless services may increasingly replace wires as the primary medium for transmission of information. Although wire-based cable and telephone infrastructures have placed major debt burdens on their owners, and while they are less flexible than new technologies, the new wireless infrastructure also will be extremely expensive, and building it may create great financial burdens for a number of firms.

TCI

As TCI looks to the future, both nationally and locally, it must determine how to stem the tide of subscriber defections and find the capital to keep its system competitive. Nationally, TCI passed more than 23 million homes, only 5 percent of which were supplied by fiberoptics.[27] In Cedar Falls, Iowa, the firm spent nearly $350 per passing to upgrade its system. Could it afford to do that across the country? The firm also must determine how to reverse the situation in Cedar Falls. Considerable revenue was lost in that market in 1996, and although some might be recovered in Waterloo, the firm must find some way to continue to service the costs of upgrade in this midsized market if it is to remain profitable. In Cedar Falls, fast cable modem

connections were available from CFU, but not from TCI. Service, too, may become an issue in this market. CFU built a looped cable system that was insulated from line breaks and blackouts. The new TCI system did not employ that architecture. Computer users require reliable service, especially for business applications. As the subscriber base shrinks, can TCI afford to maintain a full staff, or will it have to cut people to control costs? Finally, the company must determine to what degree the Cedar Falls–Waterloo market area is representative of its national market. If it is, what kind of strategy will be needed to cope?

CFU

CFU also faced issues in its future. In mid-1997, the utility's cable lineup had several open channel slots. CFU wondered if it should fill these slots quickly or wait until new channels became available and then make choices. CFU management knew that if it filled all its slots too soon and then was forced to make cuts in the future it could risk angering subscribers who liked the existing lineup. Further, if channels were added, price might become an issue. CFU was expected to contribute heavily to the revenues of the city of Cedar Falls but, on the other hand, had an obligation to pay off its bonds. These monetary concerns became more critical after the city sold its hospital. Should the utility raise subscriber fees? Should it be more aggressive in attempting to lure subscribers away from TCI? How should it approach marketing its new Internet service? If too many people requested service and CFU was forced to put them off because of a shortage of capacity and installation personnel its reputation could suffer. While these questions were not as pressing as those faced by TCI, they were still critical to CFU.

Endnotes

1. R. Mussman, Letter, *Waterloo Courier,* March 28, 1997, p. A6.
2. Refer to prior cases, "Cedar Falls Utilities and the Information Superhighway (A), (B), and (C)" in *Annual Advances in Business Cases 1996* for further information on the events described here.
3. J. Graham and A. Bash, "TNT Pops to Top of Cable Ratings," *USA Today,* December 16, 1996, p. 3D.
4. A. Bash, "Cable Infiltrating Network Territory," *USA Today,* March 11, 1996, p. 3D.

5. D. Lieberman, "Industry Factions Feud, Viewers Hit in Pocketbook," *USA Today,* March 14, 1997, pp. B1–B2.

6. D. Lieberman, "Ad Blitz Aims to Narrow Credibility Gap," *USA Today,* March 1, 1995, p. B1.

7. E. Lesley et al., "Cable TV: A Crisis Looms," *Business Week,* October 14, 1996, pp. 101–106.

8. M. Couch, "TCI Viewers Up In Arms," *Des Moines Register,* December 15, 1996, p. 6A.

9. Lesley et al., *op. cit.,* p. 106.

10. R. Grover et al., "Murdoch vs. Everyone," *Business Week,* December 9, 1996, p. 75ff.

11. E. Schine et al., "The Satellite Biz Blasts Off," *Business Week,* January 27, 1997, pp. 62–70.

12. Lesley et al., *op. cit.,* p. 105.

13. B. Gruley and M. Robinchaux, "TV Stations, Satellite Firms Reach Pact," *Wall Street Journal,* March 11, 1997, p. A2.

14. J. Jacobs, "CFU, TCI, Cable Competitors," *Waterloo Courier,* November 16, 1995, p. A4.

15. J. Friedman, Tele-Communications, Inc. Research Report, Prudential Securities, April 1997, p. 7.

16. "TCI Reluctantly Hands over C. F. Subscriber Data," *Waterloo Courier,* March 11, 1997, p. A1.

17. Jacobs, *op. cit.*

18. K. Potter, "Private Fiber-Optic Link Hooked up in Waterloo," *Waterloo Courier,* June 17, 1996, p. C1.

19. L. Sandler, "Heard on the Street," *Wall Street Journal,* April 16, 1997, p. C2.

20. Friedman, *op. cit.*

21. C. Willmsen, "TCI Plan Leaves MTV Unplugged," *Waterloo Courier,* January 26, 1997, p. A1.

22. P. Kinney, "TCI Will Increase Rates in Waterloo, Cedar Falls." *Waterloo Courier,* March 14, 1997, p. A1.

23. J. Jacobs, "TCI Reluctantly Hands over C. F. Subscriber Data," *Waterloo Courier,* March 11, 1997, p. A1.

24. T. Jamison, "TCI Cuts Fiber Out of Area's Diet," *Waterloo Courier,* February 2, 1997, p. A1.

25. K. O'Donoghue, "Officials Warn TCI Failure to Upgrade Could Breach Pact," *Waterloo Courier,* March 7, 1997, p. A1.

26. "Interview with Don Valentine," *Wall Street Journal Reports, Telecommunications,* September 16, 1996, p. R23.

27. Friedman, *op. cit.,* p. 7.

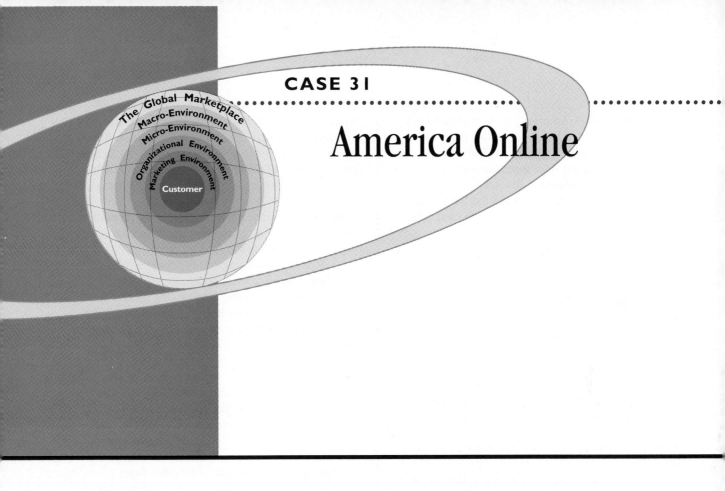

America Online

This case was prepared by Natalya V. Delcoure, Lawrence R. Jauch, and John L. Scott of Northeast Louisiana University.

America Online, Inc. (NYSE: AOL), was founded in 1985. This media company, with headquarters in Dulles, Virginia, has more than 10 million members and currently operates in the United States, Canada, the United Kingdom, France, and Germany. AOL provides on-line services including electronic mail, on-line conferencing, Internet access, news, magazines, sports, weather, stock quotes, mutual fund transactions, software files, games, computing support, and on-line classes.

According to the company, its mission is "to lead the development of a new interactive medium that eliminates traditional boundaries between people and places to create a new kind of interactive global community that holds the potential to change the way people obtain information, com-

This case was written based on published documents. It is intended to be used as a basis for class discussion rather than to illustrate either effective or ineffective handling of an administrative situation. Copyright © Lawrence R. Jauch and John L. Scott, 1997.

municate with one another, buy products and services, and learn."

To accomplish this mission, the company's strategy is to continue investment in the growth of its subscriber base, pursue related business opportunities often through joint ventures and acquisitions, provide a full range of interactive services, and maintain technological flexibility.

AOL's rapid growth and community orientation have made it the most popular, easiest, and well-known way for consumers to get on-line. In December 1996, AOL had 8.5 million member sessions a day, 7 million e-mails sent to 12 million recipients a day, and it accounted for approximately $750,000 per day in merchandise transactions.

However, AOL has not been trouble-free. On August 7, 1996, AOL threw 6 million subscribers off line for 19 hours due to software problems. America Online revealed that the glitch resulted from an error made by its working subsidiary, ANS Co., in reconfiguring software and from a bug in router software. The error cost AOL $3 million in rebates. On January 8, 1997, America Online suffered a partial outage that forced it to shut down half its system for 4 hours to find a problem. The problem was with an interface in a router device, which manages the flow of data in the network. The outage drew front-page headlines around the world, as millions of users were unable to access electronic mail, the Internet, and a variety of services and publications on-line for nearly a day.

AMERICA ONLINE COMPANY PROFILE

America Online emerged from a firm founded in the early 1980s as Control Video Corp., aimed to create an on-line service that specialized in games. It failed to meet strong competition from the Apple II and Commodore 64. Control Video was reorganized as Quantum Computer Services and became a custom developer of on-line services for other companies. Over time, Quantum managed to persuade Tandy Corp. and Apple Computers to offer a new service called Applelink Personal Edition. At the last minute, Apple withdrew from the deal and left Quantum holding a lot of software it had developed expressly for Applelink. In 1989, Quantum was only scraping by, and it did not have much money for splashy ad campaigns to attract computer users to its new service—America Online. So it came on the market with a unique approach, which was to blanket the countryside with diskettes containing America Online software. As the years went by, the company changed the way it accounted for the costs of acquiring subscribers and its pricing plans, but America Online, Inc., had never actually made any money in its entire history. At the same time, America Online had positioned itself apart from traditional print and television companies as the first "digital media company." Similar to television, the company produces digital content and distributes it digitally and allows a customer to interact digitally.

AOL Organization

AOL Corporation now oversees the operations of several subsidiaries and three divisions: AOL Networks, ANS Access, and AOL Studios. The corporation comprises the core business functions of finance, human resources, legal affairs, corporate communications, corporate development, and technology. AOL Technologies is responsible for delivering research, development, network/data-center operations, and member support to the other America Online divisions, technology licensees, and joint-venture partners. The group is also responsible for support functions—including technical support, billing, and sales.

AOL Networks is responsible for extending the AOL brand into the market, developing new revenue streams, advertising, and on-line transactions. AOL Networks is led by Robert Pittman, president, formerly managing partner and CEO of Century 21 and cofounder of MTV Network.

ANS Access is responsible for the telecommunications network. The network consists of more than 160,000 modems connecting 472 cities in the United States and 152 cities internationally. Nearly 85 percent of the American population can dial into AOLNet on a local number. For America Online's members who travel, GlobalNet offers access in approximately 230 additional cities in 83 countries. The ANS technical team is responsible for architecture, design, development, installation, management, and maintenance of hardware and software for the nationwide corporate data networks and Internet backbone by which communications take place.

AOL Studios, formerly AOL Productions, runs AOL's innovative chat (iChatco), games (INN), local (Digital City), and independent (Greenhouse) programming properties. AOL Studios is the newest division in AOL. It is working on development of leading-edge technology for broadband and midband distribution, interactive brands that can be extended into other media properties such as TV and radio, and managing joint ventures with companies including Time-Warner and CapCities/ABC. World-Play, built from ImagiNation Network entertainment, is the provider of computer on-line games for AOL. ImagiNation Network was founded in 1991 and became an independent subsidiary of AOL in 1996.

Digital City provides local programming, news, services, chat rooms, and commerce to AOL members as well as to the Internet at large. To date, Digital City has been launched nationally in Washington, D.C., Boston, Philadelphia, Atlanta, San Francisco, and Los Angeles. Digital City planned to expand to over 40 cities in 1997. Digital City, Inc., is owned by Digital City LP. AOL owns a majority interest in that entity, and the Tribune Company owns the remaining interest.

Advanced CO+RE Systems, Inc., a wholly owned subsidiary of America Online, provides network services for AOLnet, together with Sprint Corporation and BBN Corporation. Through this subsidiary, America Online designs, develops, and operates high-performance wide-area networks for business, research, education, and government organizations.

In February 1996, AOL merged with the Johnson-Grace Company, a leading developer of compression technology and multimedia development and delivery tools. Using the Johnson-Grace technology, America Online is able to deliver the data-intensive graphics and audio and video capabilities using narrow-band technologies, even over the slower-speed modems currently used by most AOL members.

2Market, Inc., is a joint venture of America Online, Apple Computer, and Medior. It provides retail catalog shopping CD-ROMs that include on-line ordering capabilities. In 1997, America Online, along with Netscape Communications and Disney's ABC unit, announced plans to launch ABCNEWS.com, a 24-hour news service.

Since the beginning of 1995, the company also acquired Advanced Network and Services, Inc. (ANS), Ubique, Ltd., Navisoft, Inc., Global Network Navigator, Inc. (GNN), BookLink Technologies, Inc., and Redgate Communications Corporation. ANS was used to build the AOLNet telephone network and has now been traded to WorldCom in return for CompuServe. (This transaction is discussed more fully later.) Ubique, Ltd., was an Israeli company that developed unique and personable ways to interact over the Internet, notably Virtual Places. Navisoft, Inc., made software such as that which allowed AOL's users to author Web pages. GNN was AOL's flat-rate full Web service provider. However, AOL's flat-rate pricing scheme rendered GNN redundant. BookLink Technologies, Inc., produced software to browse the Web. Redgate Communications Corporation was a multimedia services corporation with a specialization in using multimedia in marketing.

AOL is also planning to go in to the bookselling business in a joint venture with Barnes & Noble, but the timing is still uncertain.

AOL Marketing

The goals of the firm's consumer marketing programs are to increase the general visibility of America Online and to make it easy for customers to experiment with and subscribe to its services. AOL attracts new subscribers through independent marketing programs such as direct mail, disk inserts and inserts in publications, advertising, and a variety of comarketing efforts. The company has entered into comarketing agreements with numerous personal computer hardware, software, and peripheral production companies, as well as with certain of its media partners. These companies bundle America Online software with their products and cater to the needs of a specific audience.

America Online also has been expanding into business-to-business markets, using AOL's network to provide customized network solutions to both individual businesses and professional communities and industries. These private AOLs (the PAOLs) offer the ease of use America Online is known for, as well as customized features and functionality accessible only by preauthorized users, access to the fleet of AOL distribution platforms, secure communications, and information. The company offers these products using a direct salesforce and direct marketing and through resellers and system integrators.

America Online uses specialized retention programs designed to increase customer loyalty and satisfaction and to maximize customer subscription life. These retention programs include regularly scheduled on-line events and conferences; the regular addition of new content, services, and software programs; and on-line promotions of upcoming on-line events and new features. The firm also provides a variety of support mechanisms such as on-line technical support and telephone support services.

In May 1995, America Online introduced its Web browser, which provides integrated World Wide Web access within the AOL services. The integrated approach allows the user to seamlessly use the full suite of America Online features, including chat room, e-mail gateways and mailing lists, File Transfer Protocol, USENET newsgroups, WAIS, and Gopher.

In the summer of 1997, America Online planned to offer its 8 million members a three-dimensional gaming world, CyberPark. The company will try to compete with such heavyweights as Microsoft, the Internet Gaming Zone site, and MCI, which will launch a service in 1997 that allows computer users to play their favorite CD-ROM games. The projected earnings are expected to reach $127 million in 1997, but there are still some technical problems to overcome and the uncertainty of how much to charge future users.

America Online has included international market expansion in its strategy to gain competitive advantage. In April 1995, AOL entered into a joint venture with Bertelsmann, one of the world's largest media companies, to offer interactive services in Europe: Germany (November 1995), the United Kingdom (January 1996), and France (March 1996). Bertelsmann agreed to contribute up to $100 million to fund the launch of the European services, provided access to its book and music club membership base of over 30 million, and offered its publishing content to the joint venture on a most favored customer basis. In addition, Bertelsmann acquired approximately a 5 percent interest in America Online and designated a member of the company's board of directors. AOL contributed interactive technology and management expertise, proprietary software licenses and development services, and staff training and technical support in order to develop, test, and launch the interactive services in Europe. Subscribers to the European services enjoy access to America Online's services in the United States, and U.S. subscribers enjoy access to the European services.

AOL Canada, launched in January 1996, features local content and services. In Ocober 1996, AOL Canada offered Canadian members software, thirteen local channels, billing in Canadian dollars, e-mail, message boards, and easy access to the Internet through a Web browser. AOL Canada's key partners include Citytv, an internationally renowned broadcaster and program producer; MuchMusic, Canada's first national music television channel; *Shift Magazine,* Canada's hottest publication in media; Intuit Canada, makers of the world's leading personal finance software, Quicken; and Southam New Media, a wholly owned subsidiary of Southam, Inc., Canada's largest news organization.

In May 1996, America Online announced a partnership with Mitsui & Co., one of the world's largest international trading companies, and Nikkei, one of Japan's leading media companies with respected business and computer publications. The joint venture consists of Mitsui & Co. owning 40 percent, Nikkei 10 percent, and AOL 50 percent. Japanese partners contributed more than 120 years of experience and credibility in the Japanese market, a strong management team, and $56 million to fund the launch of the Japanese service. America Online brings to the venture its ability to develop, manage, and execute interactive on-line services in the United States, Europe, and Canada.

America Online's wildly successful marketing ploy of flat-rate pricing in the United States turned out to contribute to AOL's latest problem. About 75 percent of AOL's customers took the flat-rate offer. As a result, total daily AOL customer use soared from 1.6 million hours on-line in October 1996 to more than 4 million hours in January 1997. (These problems are described more fully later in this case.)

Meeting Customer Needs

The company provides tools to its members so that they can control their child's or teen's experience on-line without cramping the adults who enjoy using AOL's services to talk to other adults. Parental controls can block or limit the use of chat, instant messages, e-mail, binary files, newsgroups, or the Web. Different on-line areas support different values. For instance:

- *ACLU Forum:* This encourages lively yet responsible debate. Illegal activities (harassment, distribution of illegal materials) are not permitted in this area.

- *Womens' Network:* This is a women-friendly and safe space for chatting, learning, teaching, and networking, but men are still welcome to join the communication.

- *Christian Chat Room:* This allows fellowship among Christian members. In this space, proselytizing is forbidden.

- *Kids Only:* This gives children their own space on-line for searching help with homework, sending e-mail, and hanging out in chat rooms. Parental control can be set up in this area.

The average adult spends about an hour on-line, but the average kid spends three. Currently, there are 4.1 million kids surfing the Net. By 2000, it is expected that there will be 19.2 million. Kids, who spent $307 million in 1996 on on-line services, will spend $1.8 billion by 2002, and this is why media and Web giants are scrambling to offer new kid-friendly sites. Fox TV features cartoons and kid shows. Disney gave AOL first crack at hosting Daily Blast, which offers kids games, comics, and stories for $4.95 per month or $39.95 per year. "But," says Rob Jennings, vice president for programming for AOL networks, "We felt we had a good mix already." Yahooligans! offers kids-friendly Web sites for free. AOL still has partnerships with other media giants such as Disney rival Viacom, Inc.'s Nickelodeon unit for other offerings.

Since 1994, AOL has offered a Kids Only area featuring homework help, games, and on-line magazines, as well as the usual fare of software, games, and chat rooms. The area gets about 1 million 8- to 12-year-old visitors monthly.

In April 1996, America Online began to see the effect of seasonality in both member acquisitions and in the amount of time spent by customers using its services. The company expects that member acquisition is to be highest in the second and third fiscal quarters, when sales of new computers and computer software are highest due to holiday seasons (AOL's fiscal year ends June 30.) Customer usage is expected to be lower in the summer months, due largely to extended daylight hours and competing outdoor leisure activities.

AOL Employees

As of June 30, 1996, America Online had 5828 employees, including 1058 in software and content development, 3271 in customer support, 199 in marketing, 1099 in operations, and 291 in corporate operations. None of AOL's employees is represented by a labor union, and America Online has never experienced a work stoppage.

AOL employs numerous part-time workers around the world known as "remote staff." These are volunteer staff who develop content and provide both marketing and operations functions. Remote staff write informational articles, produce graphics, host chat rooms, provide technical assistance, and fulfill various support functions. Remote staff duties vary. Some may work as little as 10 hours per week or more than 40 hours per week. AOL's remote staff is compensated for these services with "community leader accounts"—a membership for which the staff members are not charged. Relatively few remote staff members are paid as independent contractors.

AOL's flat-rate pricing plan had a serious impact on its remote staff. Prior to the flat rate, members paid about $3 per hour of on-line access. Hence a "free" account would have a monthly value of approximately $300 for a staff member who spent 3 hours per day on-line.

After the flat-rate pricing plan, this account's value fell to $20. This enormous decrease in incentives led many remote staff members to resign their positions. The positions hardest hit were those for which the job pressures were highest, including AOL's guides and Techlive. Guides served to police AOL's chat rooms and to assist users with whom they came in contact. Techlive assisted users with computer problems, computer use, and navigation of AOL. Techlive is now buried beneath menu options that do not hint that real-time on-line help is available.

AOL Finance

Exhibits A and B present the financial statements for fiscal years 1995 and 1996. About 90 percent of the firm's revenues are generated from on-line subscription fees. AOL's other revenues are generated from sales of merchandise, data network services, on-line transactions and advertising, marketing and production services, and development and licensing fees. The increase of over $600 million in service revenues from 1995 to 1996 was attributed primarily to a 93 percent increase in AOL subscribers.

This is expected to undergo radical change, due to the flat rate pricing, with much less revenue coming from subscriber fees, which AOL hopes to make up by increases in the other revenue streams.

Cost of revenue, which includes network-related costs, consists of data and voice communication costs and costs associated with operating the data centers and providing customer support. These increased almost $400 million from 1995 to 1996. This increase was related to a growth of data communication costs, customer support costs, and royalties paid to information and service providers.

For fiscal year 1996, marketing expenses in-

EXHIBIT A

Income Statement (Year Ended June 30; Amounts in Thousands, Except per Share Data)

	1997	1996	1995
Revenues			
On-line service revenues	$1,429,445	$991,656	$344,309
Other revenues	255,783	102,198	49,981
Total revenues	1,685,228	1,093,854	394,290
Costs and expenses			
Cost of revenues	1,040,762	638,025	232,318
Marketing	409,260	212,710	77,064
Write-off of deferred subscriber acquisition costs	385,221	—	—
Product development	58,208	43,164	11,669
General and administrative	193,537	110,653	42,700
Acquired research and development	—	16,981	50,335
Amortization of goodwill	6,549	7,078	1,653
Restructuring charge	48,627	—	—
Contract termination charge	24,506	—	—
Settlement charge	24,204	—	—
Total costs and expenses	2,190,874	1,028,611	415,739
Income (loss) from operations	(505,646)	65,243	(21,449)
Other income (expense), net	6,299	(2,056)	3,074
Merger expenses	—	(848)	(2,207)
Income (loss) before provision for income taxes	(499,347)	62,339	(20,582)
Provision for income taxes	—	(32,523)	(15,169)
Net income (loss)	$ (499,347)	$ 29,816	$ (35,751)
Earnings (loss) per share			
Net income (loss)	$(5.22)	$0.28	$(0.51)
Weighted average shares outstanding	95,607	108,097	69,550

creased 176 percent over fiscal year 1995. This was attributed primarily to an increase in the size and number of marketing programs designed to expand the subscriber base.

Product development costs include research and development, other product development, and the amortization of software. For fiscal year 1996, these costs increased 277 percent over fiscal year 1995 and increased as a percentage of total revenues from 3.6 to 4.9 percent. The increases in product development costs were attributable primarily to an increase in the number of technical employees. Product development costs, before capitalization and amortization, increased by 242 percent.

For fiscal year 1996, general and administrative costs increased 159 percent over fiscal year 1995

and decreased as a percentage of total revenues from 10.8 to 10.1 percent. The increase in general and administrative costs was related to higher personnel, office, and travel expenses related to an increase in the number of employees. The decrease in general and administrative costs as a percentage of total revenues was a result of the substantial growth in revenues, which more than offset the additional general and administrative costs, combined with the semivariable nature of many of the general and administrative costs.

Acquired research and development costs relate to in-process research and development purchased with the acquisition of Ubique, Ltd., in September 1995. Acquired research and development costs relate to in-process research and devel-

EXHIBIT B

Consolidated Balance Sheet (June 30; Amounts in Thousands; Except per Share Data)

	1997	1996	1995
Assets			
Current assets			
Cash and cash equivalents	$124,340	$118,421	$ 45,877
Short-term investments	268	10,712	18,672
Trade accounts receivable	65,306	49,342	32,176
Other receivables	26,093	23,271	11,381
Prepaid expenses and other current assets	107,466	65,290	25,527
Total current assets	323,473	267,036	133,633
Property and equipment at cost, net	233,129	111,090	70,919
Other assets			
Restricted cash	50,000	—	—
Product development costs, net	72,498	44,330	18,949
Deferred subscriber acquisition costs, net	—	314,181	77,229
License rights, net	16,777	4,947	5,579
Other assets	84,618	29,607	9,121
Deferred income taxes	24,410	135,872	35,627
Goodwill, net	41,783	51,691	54,356
Total assets	$846,688	$958,754	$405,413
Liabilities and stockholders' equity			
Current liabilities			
Trade accounts payable	$ 69,703	$105,904	$ 84,640
Other accrued expenses and liabilities	297,298	127,876	23,509
Deferred revenue	166,007	37,950	20,021
Accrued personnel costs	20,008	15,719	2,863
Current portion of long-term debt	1,454	2,435	2,329
Total current liabilities	554,470	289,884	133,362
Long-term liabilities			
Notes payable	50,000	19,306	17,369
Deferred income taxes	24,410	135,872	35,627
Deferred revenue	86,040	—	—
Minority interests	2,674	22	—
Other liabilities	1,060	1,168	2,243
Total liabilities	$718,654	$446,252	$188,601
Stockholders' equity			
Preferred stock, $.01 par value; 5,000,000 shares authorized, 1,000 shares issued and outstanding at June 30, 1997 and 1996	1	1	—
Common stock, $.01 par value; 300,000,000 and 100,000,000 shares authorized, 100,188,971 and 92,626,000 shares issued and outstanding at June 30, 1997 and 1996, respectively	1,002	926	767
Unrealized gain on available-for-sale securities	16,924	—	—
Additional paid-in capital	617,221	519,342	252,668
Accumulated deficit	(507,114)	(7,767)	(36,623)
Total stockholders' equity	128,034	512,502	216,812
Total liabilities and equity	$846,688	$958,754	$405,413

opment purchased as part of the acquisitions of BookLink Technologies, Inc. (Booklink), and Navisoft, Inc. (Navisoft).

The amortization of goodwill increase relates primarily to America Online's fiscal 1995 acquisitions of Advanced Network & Services, Inc., and Global Network Navigator, Inc., which resulted in approximately $56 million of goodwill. The goodwill related to these acquisitions is being amortized on a straight-line basis over periods ranging from 5 to 10 years. The increase in amortization of goodwill results from a full year of goodwill recognized in fiscal year 1996 compared with only a partial year of goodwill recognized in fiscal year 1995.

Other income (expenses) consists of interest expense and nonoperating charges net of investment income and nonoperating gains. The change in other income (expenses) was attributed to the $8 million settlement of a class action lawsuit partially offset by an increase in investment income.

Nonrecurring merger expenses totaling $848,000 were recognized in fiscal year 1996 in connection with the merger of America Online with Johnson-Grace Company. Nonrecurring merger expenses totaling $2,207,000 were recognized in fiscal year 1995 in connection with the mergers of AOL with Redgate Communications Corporation, Wide Area Information Servers, Inc., and Medior, Inc.

In December 1993, the company completed a public stock offering of 8 million shares of common stock, which generated net cash proceeds of approximately $62.7 million. In April 1995, the joint venture with Bertelsmann AG to offer interactive on-line services in Europe, netted approximately $54 million through the sale of approximately 5 percent of its common stock to Bertelsmann. In October 1995, AOL completed a public offering of 4,963,266 shares of common stock, which generated net cash proceeds of approximately $139.5 million. In May 1996, America Online received approximately $28 million through the sale of convertible preferred stock to Mitsui in its joint venture with Mitsui & Co., Ltd., and Nohon Keizai Shimbun, Inc., to offer interactive on-line services in Japan. The preferred stock has an aggregate liquidation preference of approximately $28 million and accrues dividends at a rate of 4 percent per annum. Accrued dividends can be paid in the form of additional shares of preferred stock. Exhibit C

EXHIBIT C

Market Price of Common Stock

For the Quarter Ended	High	Low
September 30, 1994	$10.28	$ 6.88
December 31, 1994	14.63	7.47
March 31, 1995	23.69	12.31
June 30, 1995	24.06	16.75
September 30, 1995	37.25	21.38
December 31, 1995	46.25	28.25
March 31, 1996	60.00	32.75
June 30, 1996	71.00	36.63
September 30, 1996	37.75	34.65
December 31, 1996	33.38	32.25

shows the history of share prices of AOL's common stock.

America Online has financed its operations through cash generated from operations and the sale of its capital stock. AOL has financed its investments in facilities and telecommunications equipment principally through leasing. American Online leases the majority of its facilities and equipment under noncancelable operating leases. The communications network requires a substantial investment in telecommunications equipment, which America Online plans to finance principally through leasing. The company has never declared, nor has it paid, any cash dividends on its common stock. AOL currently intends to retain its earnings to finance future growth.

The company uses its working capital to finance ongoing operations and to fund marketing and content programs and the development of its products and services. American Online plans to continue to invest in computing and support infrastructure. Additionally, AOL expects to use a portion of its cash for the acquisition and subsequent funding of technologies, products, or businesses complementary to the company's current business.

For example, America Online is investing in the development of alternative technologies to deliver its services. AOL has entered into agreements with several manufacturers of personal digital assistants

(PDAs are low-powered, hand-held computers), including Sony, Motorola, Tandy, and Casio, to bundle a palmtop edition of America Online's client software with their PDAs. AOL is participating in early cable trials using cable as the conduit into PCs and has announced future support of ISDN, which allows digital transmission, as opposed to the analog transmission of telephones, and wireless, similar to cell phone and satellite transmission. By the time that cable modems are poised for market penetration, a new generation of competitive telephone modems may be available. In the paging market, AOL has entered into agreements with AT&T Wireless Services and MobileMedia to provide their paging customers who subscribe to AOL with mobile access to certain America Online services.

AOL'S ENVIRONMENT

AOL is subject to federal and state regulations applicable to business in general. However, America Online must keep up with changes in the regulatory environment relating to telecommunications and the media. Additional legislative proposals from international, federal, and state government bodies in the areas of content regulations, intellectual property, privacy rights, and state tax issues could impose additional regulations and obligations on all on-line service providers. For a long time, such companies as AT&T, Western Union, and RCA dominated the telecommunications industry. The courts deregulated the telephone industry in the 1980s. Although technology and market development made passage of new telecommunications legislation inevitable, it took about 10 years to frame it. Even though the Telecommunications Reform Act of 1996 meant to remove many of the regulatory barriers and make it easier for telecom companies to invest in the information superhighway, so far it has made little difference.

The Department of Commerce and the U.S. Trade Representative have pushed the World Trade Organization to open up the telecom sector to more service and equipment competition. As a result of trade negotiations in Singapore, tariffs on many telecommunications products and services will be reduced, with great potential benefit to U.S. firms. Additional talks were under way in Switzerland in 1997 that may permit U.S. telecommunica-

tions companies to compete on equal footing with providers in Europe and elsewhere.

Telephone companies are collecting high revenues as computer and on-line services expand. One study found that local carriers collected revenues totaling $1.4 billion in 1995 from second phone lines used mainly for Net links while spending only $245 million to upgrade their networks for the additional usage. Phone companies experienced 8 to 9 percent profit growth in 1996 since second phone line installations at homes grew 25 percent. Both local carriers and on-line service providers agree that there is a necessity to build higher-capacity networks to satisfy the increasing demand for public phone networks to meet the growing trend in cybersurfing.

The future of technology is difficult to predict but can affect AOL's future strategy. Some speculate that interactive TV is going to be replaced by network computers (such as those from Sun). Some argue that Internet connections should be available to people who want to use them and that public monies should be provided to ensure access for all. There is a growing place for satellite and fiber in the new communication system. Technology trends are sometimes born of social change. Here are some of the most important trends to watch for the next 5 years:

- The world phone could be a satellite wireless phone that uses digital technology. A combination of Global System for Mobilization (GSM) and satellite technologies could be the model for the world phone. Pioneers such as Wildfire Communications, Lucent Technologies, Dialogic, and VDOnet are among hundreds of alternative carriers that try to unite PCs, phone, e-mail, fax, and video into a seamless fabric. They are designing software that sends phone calls around the world on the Internet very cheaply. The line dividing computers and telephones, voice and data is blurring. Building on the union of data networks and computers, the Internet has become the new global communications infrastructure for businesses.

- Personal communication systems (PCSs) could broadside local telecom carriers. Projections are that local exchange carriers must brace for a loss of 35 percent of high-margin business customers and 25 percent or more of their residential shares to PCS providers. Mobile subscribers could represent 17 percent of traditional wire-line carrier business by 2010. VocalTec, Ltd., leading maker of Internet telephony products, recently broadened the appeal by introducing gateways that connect the Internet to standard phone systems—allowing PC users to call non-PC users on their phones, and vice versa. Vocal-Tec claims it saves $10,000 a month on phone bills between the company's New Jersey and Israeli offices.

- Wireless convergence. Commercial mobile wireless will include mobile satellite, and satellite communication will overlap coverage and mobility with cellular/PCS. Cordless telephony will play major roles. Several years ago, Microsoft Corp. and Novell, Inc., tried to apply computer-telephony integration technology to any desktop by creating competing standards for connecting phone systems to PC networks. But the products, TAPI and TSAPI, which allowed desktop computer users to receive and manage phone calls through their PCs, went nowhere. Now, a wave of products built on TAPI and TSAPI that work with standard telecom equipment is hitting the market. Users can select a handful of names from a database and command the phone switch to set up a conference call with all of them. Pacific Bell is testing a sophisticated messaging service on 300 wireless-phone customers in San Diego. It answers incoming phone calls, screens them, and automatically routes them to wherever you are—a conference room, your home office, or a shopping mall. For a richer media experience, many companies are concentrating on desktop video-conferencing products from Intel, C-Phone, and VDOnet, among others. These products are very cost-efficient and price-compatible.

- Asynchronous transfer mode. ATM carrier services are still expensive. Originally developed by Bell Laboratories for high-speed voice networks, ATM has now been adapted for data applications. They are able to move data at 155 mb/s, whereas advanced modems top out at 56 kb/s. The Defense Department uses a fiberoptic ATM network between the United States and Germany. The Mayo Clinic in Rochester, Minnesota, uses ATM for "telemedicine"—doctors can videoconference with patients. ATM switches account for an estimated savings of $200,000 per month for the American Petroleum Institution, which uses this tool to transmit drilling-site data over satellite. This technology is moving quickly into the public phone network, which increases the speed of the global communications network.

- Residential gateways will let customers plug in telecom carriers and cable companies' networks and give users more control.

Increased competition makes it hard to make money by selling unlimited on-line access. Service providers have to upgrade their equipment to handle higher modem speeds and install separate equipment and phone lines for rival technologies. Sales of new modems are expected to be huge, driven by the Internet boom. AOL signed a deal with U.S. Robotics, which was scheduled to start turning on telephone access numbers on February 27, 1997, to give subscribers log-on access at a faster speed. Currently, the only high-speed (56 kb/s) modems that America Online customers can use are made by U.S. Robotics, which now controls a quarter of the market. Modems from the Open 56K Forum Group—available in March 1997—cannot talk to those of U.S. Robotics. Most of the Open 56K Group will have modems out in March 1997. U.S. Robotics has dominated the market; thus it appears that AOL chose well. The number 2 modem maker, Hayes Microcomputer Products, Inc., registered more than 40,000 people for a deal it offered on the company's Web page: Customers can get their high-speed modems for $99 by sending in any brand modem. U.S. Robotics sells its superfast modems for $199 for a version that is installed into the computer or $239 for an external model.

Use of the Net has increased dramatically the demand for techies. An estimated 760,000 people are working for Net-related companies alone. The Internet is full of companies' ads wanting programmers. A new study by the Information Technology Association of America estimates that 190,000 "infotech" jobs stand vacant in U.S. companies—half in the information industry. The situation can get worse, because the number of college students in computer science has fallen 43 percent in the past decade. Net-related companies are spending millions of dollars recruiting employees. In 1996, pay for infotech workers rose by 12 percent to 20 percent, while average annual pay for software architects rose to $85,600.

The on-line services market is highly competitive. Major direct competitors include Prodigy Services Company, a joint venture of International Business Machines Corp. and Sears, Roebuck and Co.; e-World, a service of Apple Computer, Inc.; GEnie, a division of General Electric Information Services; Delphi Internet Services Corporation, a division of News Corp.; Interchange, a service of AT&T Corp.; and Microsoft Corp., which launched its on-line service under the name Microsoft Network. Microsoft has been devoting considerable resources and energy to focus the firm and its products squarely on the Internet. The Internet directory services are another source of competition, including NETCOM On-Line Communication Services, Inc., Bolt, Beranek & Newman, Inc., Performance System International, UUNET Technologies with Internet MCI, Yahoo, Inc., Excite, Inc., Infoseek Corporation, and Lycos, Inc. Finally, software providers such as Intuit, Inc., and Netscape Communication Corporation are another category of competitors.

America Online is by far the largest on-line service, with 10 million American members as of 1997. CompuServe was the second largest service prior to AOL acquiring it. The Microsoft Network is the second largest on-line service, with 2.3 million subscribers. But a great deal of the competition comes from the small local Internet providers, who were the catalyst that drove AOL to the flat-rate pricing plan.

The imperatives for global communications look very promising. Telecom and data networks should become a lifeline for nations, businesses, and individuals. The Internet is pushing world financial markets and the flow of goods and services. The Net has the potential to revolutionize business and human lives, but it also has the danger that the network can be a vehicle of isolation. Communication by fax, modem, wireless handset, videoconferencing, or telecommuting can create personal isolation. A high-tech world may need to be counterbalanced by community, family, and person-to-person contacts.

The Internet and more advanced computing, plus training for people to understand and partici-

pate in the network, have obvious educational potential.

THE FLAT-RATE DEBACLE

Through December 31, 1994, America Online's standard monthly membership fee for its service, which included 5 hours of services, was $9.95, with a $3.50 hourly fee for usage in excess of 5 hours per month. Effective January 1, 1995, the hourly fee for usage in excess of 5 hours per month decreased from $3.50 to $2.95, while the monthly membership fee remained the same.

In October 1995, AOL launched its Internet Service, Global Network Navigator (GNN), which was aimed at consumers who wanted a full-featured Internet-based service but without the full-service quality of AOL. The monthly fee for GNN was $14.95. This fee included 20 hours of service per month with a $1.95 hourly fee for usage in excess of 20 hours per month. In May 1996, AOL announced an additional pricing plan, which was oriented to its heavier users and called Value Plan. It became effective July 1, 1966, and included 20 hours of services for $19.95 per month with a $2.95 hourly fee for usage in excess of 20 hours per month.

AOL usage increased dramatically when the company announced its plans to offer flat-rate unlimited pricing in October 1996. AOL switched its more than 7 million members to unlimited access for $19.95 a month. Its network was deluged by subscribers, many of whom could not log onto the system during peak evening hours or on weekends. Exhibit D shows comparative data before and after this new pricing policy.

Following the second shutdown of its system in January 1997, the company's chairman and CEO, Steve Case, emphasized that AOL took full responsibility for the "busy signals":

> When we decided . . . to introduce unlimited use pricing, we were well aware that usage would increase substantially. We did some consumer testing and operations modeling to generate usage forecasts, and we began building extra capacity in advance of the December launch of unlimited pricing. We thought that there would be some problems with busy signals during our

EXHIBIT D
················
AOL System Use Before and After Flat-Rate Pricing

Average AOL	January 1997	September 1996
Member daily usage	32 minutes	14 minutes
Daily sessions	10 million	6 million
Total hours daily	4.2 million	1.5 million
Total hours per month	125 million (est.), (Dec.: 102 million)	45 million
Peak simultaneous usage	260,000	140,000
Average minutes per session	26 minutes	16 minutes

peak periods in some cities. . . . But we expected those problems to be modest, and not too long in duration.

AOL has tried to decrease the "busy signal" by increasing the size and pace of the system capacity expansion by bringing in new hardware, installing circuits, adding 150,000 new modems, increasing the number of customer service representatives to 4000, offering a toll-free line, and reducing marketing efforts. Mr. Case even asked the customers for help by moderating their own use of AOL during peak hours.

Even so, AOL became fodder for comics and lawsuits. In one comic strip, the customer is shown on the telephone conversing with "customer service":

Caller: "I am not getting my money's worth with your on-line service."
Service: "Good news, sir! We have just cut our rates."
Caller: "Your lines are always busy. . . . I can't get on-line!"
Service: "Don't forget you get unlimited time on-line for no extra charge."

A number of AOL customers filed lawsuits against the company in more than 37 states, charging the firm with civil fraud, breach of contract, negligence, and violation of state consumer-protection statutes. The negative publicity from the "busy signals" allowed other on-line providers the opportunity to expand their number of subscribers and increase their revenues from advertising and merchandising fees.

America Online began a refund offer to its members, and the attorneys general in several states agreed to support its proposed plan to members. The plan involved the following refund policy: Customers had a choice of a free month on-line or up to $39.90—the cost of 2 months of its unlimited service. In addition, AOL increased customer service staffing to handle member cancellations so that calls were answered within 2 minutes. Also, AOL gave customers the opportunity to cancel their membership through mail, fax, or toll-free number.

In the meantime America Online was facing another legal problem, this time from its shareholders. On February 24, 1997, shareholders sued in U.S. District Court in Virginia alleging that AOL directors and outside accountants violated securities laws in the way the company did its accounting. The online giant took a $385 million charge in October 1996, for marketing expenses it had capitalized.

The various problems facing America Online raised serious doubts among analysts about its ability to meet its goal to earn $60 million in fiscal year 1998 (ending in June) without more revenues from sources outside of operations. An analyst with Smith, Barney & Company believed that the $1.7 billion company had a cash flow problem that could force AOL to raise cash through bank loans or another stock offering—which would be the company's fourth. "The worst time to go to the market is when you need to," notes Abe Mastbaum, money manager of American Securities.

Prior to 1997, AOL was able to maintain its positive cash flow through the addition of new members. Due to overload of the system, brought on by flat-rate pricing, new members cannot be added as aggressively as needed. The company will have to develop new sources of revenue, such as on-line advertising and fees on electronic transfers, or charge additional fees for premium channels. AOL launched its first premium channel in July of 1997. Its premium games channel allows people from around the world to play both traditional games, such as hearts, and new games against each other. It charges $2 per hour for the premium games channel.

Since AOL did not have the infrastructure in place to handle the increased usage that came with the revised pricing structure, America Online planned to hold its membership at 8 million and spend $350 million to expand system capacity and customer support. Then a large acquisition substantially changed system capacity.

In April 1997, rumors were heard about AOL acquiring CompuServe from WorldCom. America Online declined to comment. CompuServe said the company is in "external discussions" regarding a deal. Buying CompuServe would add much-needed network capacity to AOL's strained system. These speculations gave a boost to both companies' stock: CompuServe's shares jumped 12 percent to $11; AOL's stock was up 7.6 percent to $45.75. A month before, CompuServe Corp. had quietly cut 500 jobs, or 14 percent of its workforce, which was the latest evidence of the on-line company's troubles as it lost members in an intense competition with America Online and other rivals. The cuts left CompuServe's home office in Columbus, Ohio, with about 3200 employees who were primarily on-line content and service specialists. At the same time, CompuServe posted a $14 million quarterly loss, and 3 days later the company's president and chief executive, Robert J. Massey, resigned. In September 1997, AOL bought CompuServe.

CompuServe was acquired in exchange for AOL's ANS Communications Subsidiary. AOL also received $175 million in cash. This added 100,000 modems to AOL's system for the short term. AOL also received long-term network commitments from WorldCom. AOL expected that the exchange would allow it to focus on its core assets— AOL Networks and AOL Studios. CompuServe would be retained as a brand name with continued marketing to small business and professional markets but with AOL's expanded content and ease of use. The companies plan to collaborate on the future development of a broadband communications network, as opposed to the current narrow-band network that consists mainly of telephone lines.

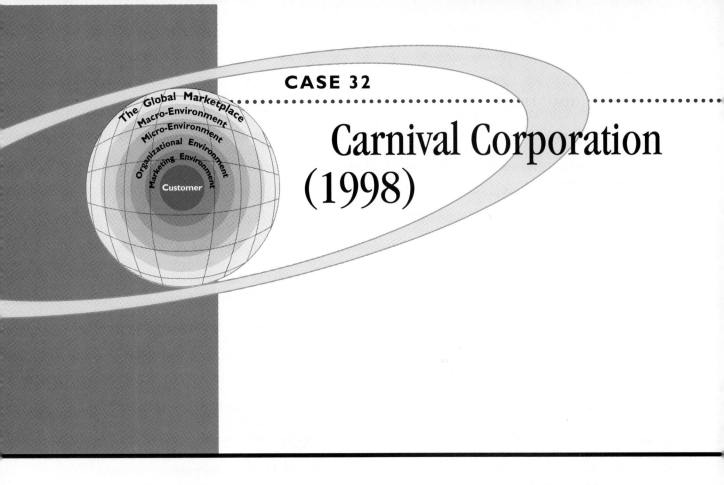

Carnival Corporation (1998)

This case was prepared by Professors Michael J. Keeffe, John K. Ross III, and Bill J. Middlebrook of Southwest Texas State University.

Carnival Corporation, in terms of passengers carried, revenues generated, and available capacity is the largest cruise line in the world and is considered the leader and innovator in the cruise travel industry. Given its inauspicious beginnings, Carnival has grown from two converted ocean liners to an organization with two cruise divisions (and a joint venture to operate a third cruise line) and a chain of Alaskan hotels and tour coaches. Corporate revenues for fiscal year 1997 reached $2.4 billion, with net income from operations of $666 million. And the growth continues, with May 1998 revenues up $100 million over the same quarter in 1997 to $1.219 billion. Carnival has several "firsts" in the cruise industry, with over 1 million passen-

gers carried in a single year and the first cruise line to carry 5 million total passengers by fiscal year 1994. Currently, its market share of the cruise travel industry stands at approximately 26 percent overall.

Carnival Corporation CEO and Chairman, Mr. Micky Arison, and Carnival Cruise Lines President, Mr. Bob Dickinson, are prepared to maintain the company's reputation as the leader and innovator in the industry. The company has assembled one of the newest fleets catering to cruisers, with the introduction of several "superliners" built specifically for the Caribbean and Alaskan cruise markets, and expects to invest over $3.0 billion in new ships by the year 2002. Additionally, the company has expanded its Holland American Lines fleet to cater to more established cruisers and plans to add three of the new ships to its fleet in the premium cruise segment. Strategically, Carnival Corporation seems to have made the right moves at the right time, sometimes in direct contradiction to industry analysts and cruise trends.

The case was prepared for classroom purposes only and is not designed to show effective or ineffective handling of administrative situations. Reprinted by permission of Dr. John K. Ross III.

THE CRUISE INDUSTRY
• •

Cruise Lines International Association (CLIA), an industry trade group, has tracked the growth of the cruise industry for over 25 years. In 1970, approximately 500,000 passengers took cruises for three consecutive nights or more, reaching a peak of 5 million passengers in 1997, an average annual compound growth rate of approximately 8.9 percent (this growth rate has declined to approximately 2 percent per year over the period from 1991 to 1995). At the end of 1997, the industry had 136 ships in service with an aggregate berth capacity of 119,000. CLIA estimates that the number of passengers carried in North America increased from 4.6 million in 1996 to 5 million in 1997, or approximately 8.7 percent. CLIA expects the number of cruise passengers to increase to 5.3 million in 1998, and with new ships to be delivered, the North American market will have roughly 144 vessels with an aggregate capacity of 132,000 berths.

Carnival has exceeded the recent industry trends, and the growth rate in the number of passengers carried was 11.2 percent per year over the 1992 to 1996 period. The company's passenger capacity in 1991 was 17,973 berths and had increased to 31,078 at the end of fiscal year 1997. Additional capacity will be added with the delivery of several new cruise ships already on order, such as the *Elation,* which went into service in early 1998, adding 2040 to the passenger capacity.

Even with the growth in the cruise industry, the company believes that cruises represent only 2 percent of the applicable North American vacation market, defined as persons who travel for leisure purposes on trips of 3 nights or longer, involving at least one night's stay in a hotel. The Boston Consulting Group, in a 1989 study, estimated that only 5 percent of persons in the North American target market have taken a cruise for leisure purposes and estimated the market potential to be in excess of $50 billion. Carnival Corporation (1996) believes that only 7 percent of the North American population has ever cruised. Various cruise operators, including Carnival Corporation, have based their expansion and capital spending programs on the possibility of capturing part of the 93 to 95 percent of the North American population who have yet to take a cruise vacation.

The Evolution of Cruising
• • • • • • • • • • • • • • • • • • • •

With the replacement of ocean liners by aircraft in the 1960s as the primary means of transoceanic travel, the opportunity for developing the modern cruise industry was created. Ships no longer required to ferry passengers from destination to destination became available to investors with visions of a new vacation alternative to complement the increasing affluence of Americans. Cruising, once the purview of the rich and leisure class, was targeted to the middle class, with services and amenities similar to the grand days of first-class ocean travel.

According to Robert Meyers, editor and publisher of *Cruise Travel* magazine, the increasing popularity of taking a cruise as a vacation can be traced to two serendipitously timed events. First, television's "Love Boat" series dispelled many myths associated with cruising and depicted people of all ages and backgrounds enjoying the cruise experience. This show was among the top 10 shows on television for many years according to Nielsen ratings and provided extensive publicity for cruise operators. Second, the increasing affluence of Americans and the increased participation of women in the workforce gave couples and families more disposable income for discretionary purposes, especially vacations. As the myths were dispelled and disposable income grew, younger couples and families "turned on" to the benefits of cruising as a vacation alternative, creating a large new target market for the cruise product that accelerated the growth in the number of Americans taking cruises as a vacation.

CARNIVAL HISTORY
• •

In 1972, Ted Arison, backed by American Travel Services, Inc. (AITS), purchased an aging ocean liner from Canadian Pacific Empress Lines for $6.5 million. The new AITS subsidiary, Carnival Cruise Line, refurbished the vessel from bow to stern and renamed it the *Mardi Gras* to capture the party spirit. (Also included in the deal was another ship later renamed the *Carnivale.*) The company's start was not promising, however, because on the first voyage the *Mardi Gras,* with over 300 invited travel agents aboard, ran aground in Miami Harbor.

The ship was slow and guzzled expensive fuel, limiting the number of ports of call and lengthening the minimum stay of passengers on the ship to break even. Mr. Arison then bought another old ocean vessel from Union Castle Lines to complement the *Mardi Gras* and the *Carnivale* and named it the *Festivale*. To attract customers, Mr. Arison began adding diversions on-board, such as planned activities, a casino, nightclubs, discos, and other forms of entertainment designed to enhance the shipboard experience.

Carnival lost money for the next 3 years, and in late 1974, Ted Arison bought out the Carnival Cruise subsidiary of AITS, Inc., for $1 cash and the assumption of $5 million in debt. One month later, the *Mardi Gras* began showing a profit and through the remainder of 1975 operated at more than 100 percent capacity. (Normal ship capacity is determined by the number of fixed berths available. Ships, like hotels, can operate beyond this fixed capacity by using rollaway beds, pullmans, and upper bunks.) Ted Arison (then chairman), along with Bob Dickinson (who was then vice president of sales and marketing) and his son Micky Arison (then president of Carnival), began to alter the current approach to cruise vacations. Carnival went after first-time and younger cruisers with a moderately priced vacation package that included air fare to the port of embarkation and home after the cruise. Per diem rates were very competitive with other vacation packages, and Carnival offered passage to multiple exotic Caribbean ports, several meals served daily with premier restaurant service, and included all forms of entertainment and activities in the base fare. The only things not included in the fare were items of a personal nature, liquor purchases, gambling, and tips for the cabin steward, table waiter, and busboy. Carnival continued to add to the shipboard experience with a greater variety of activities, nightclubs, and other forms of entertainment and varied ports of call to increase its attractiveness to potential customers. Carnival was the first modern cruise operator to use multimedia advertising promotions and established the theme of "Fun Ship" cruises, primarily promoting the ship as the destination and ports of call as secondary. Carnival told the public that it was throwing a shipboard party and everyone was invited. Today, the "Fun Ship" theme still permeates all Carnival cruise ships.

Throughout the 1980s, Carnival was able to maintain a growth rate of approximately 30 percent, about three times that of the industry as a whole, and between 1982 and 1988, its ships sailed with an average of 104 percent capacity (currently they operate at 104 to 105 percent capacity, depending on the season). Targeting younger, first-time passengers by promoting the ship as a destination proved to be extremely successful. Carnival's 1987 customer profile showed that 30 percent of the passengers were between the ages of 25 and 39 with household incomes of $25,000 to $50,000.

In 1987, Ted Arison sold 20 percent of his shares in Carnival Cruise Lines and immediately generated over $400 million for further expansion. In 1988, Carnival acquired the Holland America Line, which had four cruise ships with 4500 berths. Holland America was positioned to the higher-income travelers, with cruise prices averaging 25 to 35 percent more than similar Carnival cruises. The deal also included two Holland America subsidiaries, Windstar Sail Cruises and Holland America Westours. This success, and the foresight of management, allowed Carnival to begin an aggressive "superliner" building campaign for its core subsidiary. By 1989, the cruise segments of Carnival Corporation carried over 750,000 passengers in 1 year, a "first" in the cruise industry.

Ted Arison relinquished the role of chairman to his son Micky in 1990, a time when the explosive growth of the 1980s began to subside. Higher fuel prices and increased airline costs began to affect the industry as a whole, and the Persian Gulf War caused many cruise operators to divert ships from European and Indian ports to the Caribbean area of operations, increasing the number of ships competing directly with Carnival. Carnival's stock price fell from $25 in June of 1990 to $13 late in the year. The company also incurred a $25.5 million loss during fiscal 1990 for the operation of the Crystal Palace Resort and Casino. In 1991, Carnival reached a settlement with the Bahamian government (effective March 1, 1992) to surrender the 672-room Riveria Towers to the Hotel Corporation of the Bahamas in exchange for the cancellation of some debt incurred in constructing and developing the resort. The corporation took a $135 million write-down on the Crystal Palace for that year.

The early 1990s, even with industrywide demand slowing, were still a very exciting time. Carnival took delivery of its first two superliners, the *Fantasy* (1990) and the *Ecstasy* (1991), which were to further penetrate the 3- and 4-day cruise market and supplement the 7-day market. In early 1991, Carnival took delivery of the third superliner, *Sensation* (inaugural sailing November 1, 1993), and later in the year contracted the fourth superliner, to be named the *Fascination* (inaugural sailing 1994).

In 1991, Carnival attempted to acquire Premier Cruise Lines, which was then the official cruise line for Walt Disney World in Orlando, Florida, for approximately $372 million. The deal was never consummated because the involved parties could not agree on price. In 1992, Carnival acquired 50 percent of Seabourn, gaining the cruise operations of K/S Seabourn Cruise Lines, and formed a partnership with Atle Byrnestad. Seabourn serves the ultra-luxury market with destinations in South America, the Mediterranean, Southeast Asia, and the Baltics.

The 1993 to 1995 period saw the addition of the superliner *Imagination* for Carnival Cruise Lines and the *Ryndam* for Holland America Lines. In 1994, the company discontinued operations of Fiestamarina Lines, which attempted to serve Spanish-speaking clientele. Fiestamarina was beset with marketing and operational problems and never reached continuous operations. Many industry analysts and observers were surprised at the failure of Carnival to successfully develop this market. In 1995, Carnival sold a 49 percent interest in the Epirotiki line, a Greek cruise operation, for $25 million and purchased $101 million (face amount) of senior secured notes of Kloster Cruise Limited, the parent of competitor Norwegian Cruise Lines, for $81 million. Kloster was having financial difficulties, and Carnival could not obtain common stock of the company in a negotiated agreement. If Kloster were to fail, Carnival Corporation would be in a good position to acquire some of the assets of Kloster.

Carnival Corporation is expanding through internally generated growth, as evidenced by the number of new ships on order (see Exhibit A). Additionally, Carnival seems to be willing to continue with its external expansion through acquisitions if the right opportunity arises.

In June, 1997, Royal Caribbean made a bid to buy Celebrity Cruise Lines for $500 million and assumption of $800 million in debt. Within a week, Carnival had responded by submitting a counter-offer to Celebrity for $510 million and the assumption of debt and then 2 days later raising the bid to $525 million. However, Royal Caribbean seems to have had the inside track and announced on June 30, 1997, the final merger agreements with Celebrity. The resulting company will have 17 ships with approximately 30,000 berths.

However, not to be thwarted in its attempts at continued expansion, Carnival announced in June 1997 the purchase of Costa, an Italian cruise company and the largest European cruise line, for $141 million. External expansion continued when on May 28, 1998, Carnival announced the acquisition of Cunard Line for $500 million from Kvaerner ASA. Cunard was then merged with Seabourn Cruise Line (50 percent owned by Carnival), with Carnival owning 68 percent of the resulting Cunard Line Limited.

THE CRUISE PRODUCT

Ted and Micky Arison envisioned a product where the classic cruise elegance along with modern convenience could be had at a price comparable with land-based vacation packages sold by travel agents. Carnival's all-inclusive package, when compared with resorts or a theme park such as Walt Disney World, often is priced below these destinations, especially when the array of activities, entertainment, and meals is considered.

A typical vacation on a Carnival cruise ship starts when the bags are tagged for the ship at the airport. Upon arriving at the port of embarkation, passengers are ferried by air-conditioned buses to the ship for boarding, and luggage is delivered by the cruise ship staff to the passengers' cabins. Waiters dot the ship offering tropical drinks to the backdrop of a Caribbean rhythm, while the cruise staff orients passengers to the various decks, cabins, and public rooms. In a few hours (most ships sail in the early evening), dinner is served in the main dining rooms, where wine selection rivals the finest restaurants and the variety of main dishes is designed to suit every palate. Diners can always order double portions if they decide not to save room for the variety of desserts and after-dinner specialties.

After dinner, cruisers can choose between many forms of entertainment, including live music, dancing, nightclubs, and a selection of movies, or they can sleep through the midnight buffet until

EXHIBIT A
. . . .
Carnival and Holland America Ships Under Construction

Vessel	Expected Delivery	Shipyard	Passenger Capacity*	Cost (millions)
Carnival Cruise Lines				
Elation	03/98	Masa-Yards	2,040	$300
Paradise	12/98	Masa-Yards	2,040	300
Carnival Triumph	07/99	Fincantieri	2,640	400
Carnival Victory	08/00	Fincantieri	2,640	430
CCL Newbuild	12/00	Masa-Yards	2,100	375
CCL Newbuild	2001	Masa-Yards	2,100	375
CCL Newbuild	2002	Masa-Yards	2,100	375
Total Carnival Cruise Lines			15,912	$2,437
Holland America Line				
Volendam	6/99	Fincantieri	1,440	274
Zaandam	12/99	Fincantieri	1,440	286
HAL Newbuild	9/00	Fincantieri	1,440	300
Total Holland America Line			4,260	$860
Windstar Cruises				
Wind Surf	5/98	Purchase	312	40
Total all Vessels			20,484	$3,337

*In accordance with industry practice, all capacities indicated are calculated based on two passengers per cabin, even though some cabins can accommodate three or four passengers.

breakfast. (Most ships have five or more distinct nightclubs.) During the night, a daily program of activities arrives at the passengers' cabins. The biggest decisions to be made for the duration of the vacation will be what to do (or not to do), what to eat and when (usually eight separate serving times not including the 24-hour room service), and when to sleep. Service in all areas from dining to housekeeping is upscale and immediate. The service is so good that a common shipboard joke says that if you leave your bed during the night to visit the head (sea talk for bathroom), your cabin steward will have made the bed and placed chocolates on the pillow by the time you return.

After the cruise, passengers are transported back to the airport in air-conditioned buses for the flight home. Representatives of the cruise line are on hand at the airport to help cruisers in meeting their scheduled flights. When all amenities are considered, most vacation packages would be hard-pressed to match Carnival's per diem prices that range from $125 to $250 per person per day de-

pending on accommodations. (Holland America and Seabourn are higher, averaging $300 per person per day.) Occasional specials allow for even lower prices, and special suite accommodations can be had for an additional payment.

CARNIVAL OPERATIONS
. . . .

Carnival Corporation, headquartered in Miami, is composed of Carnival Cruise Lines; Holland America Lines, which includes Windstar Sail Cruises as a subsidiary, Holland America Westours, Westmark Hotels, and Airtours; and the newly created Cunard Line Limited. Carnival Cruise Lines, Inc., is a Panamanian corporation, and its subsidiaries are incorporated in Panama, the Netherlands Antilles, the British Virgin Islands, Liberia, and the Bahamas. The ships are subject to inspection by the U.S. Coast Guard for compliance with the Convention for the Safety of Life at Sea (SOLAS), which requires specific structural requirements for safety of passengers at sea, and by the U.S. Public Health Service for sanitary standards. The company is also regulated in some aspects by the Federal Maritime Commission.

At its helm, Carnival Corporation is led by CEO and Chairman of the Board Micky Arison and Carnival Cruise Lines President and COO Bob Dickinson. Mr. A. Kirk Lanterman is the President and CEO of the Holland American cruise division, which includes Holland America Westours and Windstar Sail Cruises. (A listing of corporate officers is presented in Exhibit B.)

The company's product positioning stems from its belief that the cruise market is actually comprised of three primary segments with different passenger demographics, passenger characteristics, and growth requirements. The three segments are the contemporary, premium, and luxury segments. The contemporary segment is served by Carnival ships for cruises that are 7 days or shorter in length

EXHIBIT B
. . . .
Corporate Officers of Carnival Corporation

Micky Arison
    Chairman of the board and chief executive officer, Carnival Corporation
Gerald R. Cahill
    Senior vice president finance and CFO, Carnival Corporation
Lowell Zemnick
    Vice president and treasurer, Carnival Corporation
Robert H. Dickinson
    President and COO, Carnival Cruise Lines
A. Kirk Lanterman
    Chairman of the board and CEO, Holland America Lines
Howard S. Frank
    Vice chairman and chief operating officer, Carnival Corporation
Roderick K. McLeod
    Senior vice president marketing, Carnival Corporation
Meshulam Zonis
    Senior vice president operations, Carnival Cruise Lines
Peter T. McHugh
    President and COO, Holland America Lines

Source: Carnival Corporation, 1998.

and feature a casual ambiance. The premium segment, served by Holland America, serves the 7-day and longer market and appeals to more affluent consumers. The luxury segment, while considerably smaller than the other segments, caters to experienced cruisers for 7-day and longer sailings and is served by Seabourn. Specialty sailing cruises are provided by Windstar Sail Cruises, a subsidiary of Holland America.

Corporate structure is built around the "profit center" concept and is updated periodically when needed for control and coordination purposes. The cruise subsidiaries of Carnival give the corporation a presence in most of the major cruise segments and provide for worldwide operations.

Carnival has always placed a high priority on marketing in an attempt to promote cruises as an alternative to land-based vacations. It wants customers to know that the ship in itself is the destination and the ports of call are important, but secondary, to the cruise experience. Education and the creation of awareness are critical to corporate marketing efforts. Carnival was the first cruise line to successfully break away from traditional print media and use television to reach a broader market. Even though other lines have followed Carnival's lead in selecting promotional media and are near in total advertising expenditures, the organization still leads all cruise competitors in advertising and marketing expenditures.

Carnival wants to remain the leader and innovator in the cruise industry and intends to do this with sophisticated promotional efforts, by gaining loyalty from former cruisers, and by refurbishing ships, varying activities and ports of call, and being innovative in all aspects of ship operations. Management intends to build on the theme of the ship as a destination given their historical success with this promotional effort. The company capitalizes and amortizes direct-response advertising and expenses other advertising costs as incurred. Advertising expense totaled $112 million in 1997, $109 million in 1996, $98 million in 1995, and $85 million in 1994.

FINANCIAL PERFORMANCE
. . . .

Carnival retains Price Waterhouse as independent accountants, the Barnett Bank Trust Company of North America as the registrar and stock transfer agent, and its class A common stock trades on the

New York Stock Exchange under the symbol CCL. In December 1996, Carnival amended the terms of its revolving credit facility primarily to combine two facilities into a single $1 billion unsecured revolving credit facility due 2001. The borrowing rate on the $1 billion revolver is a maximum of LIBOR* plus 14 basis points, and the facility fee is 6 basis points.

Carnival initiated a commercial paper program in October 1996, which is supported by the $1 billion revolver. As of November 30, 1996, the company had $307 million outstanding under its commercial paper program and $693 million available for borrowing under the $1 billion revolver.

The consolidated financial statements for Carnival Cruise Lines, Inc., are shown in Exhibits C and D, and selected financial data are presented in Exhibit E.

Customer cruise deposits, which represent unearned revenue, are included in the balance sheet when received and recognized as cruise revenues

*LIBOR rate means, for an interest period for each LIBOR (London Interbank Offer Rate) rate advance comprising part of the same borrowing, the rate determined by the agent to be the rate of interest per annum (i) rounded upward to the nearest whole multiple of 1/100 of 1 percent per annum, appearing on Telerate screen 3750 at 11:00 A.M. (London time) two business days before the first day of such interest period for a term equal to such interest period and in an amount substantially equal to such portion of the loan, or if the agent cannot so determine the LIBOR rate by reference to Telerate screen 3750, then (ii) equal to the average (rounded upward to the nearest whole multiple of 1/100 of 1 percent per annum, if such average is not such a multiple) of the rate per annum at which deposits in U.S. dollars are offered by the principal office of each of the reference lenders in London, England, to prime banks in the London interbank market at 11:00 A.M. (London time) two business days before the first day of such interest period for a term equal to such interest period and in an amount substantially equal to such portion of the loan. In the latter case, the LIBOR rate for an interest period shall be determined by the agent on the basis of applicable rates furnished to and received by the agent from the reference lenders two business days before the first day of such interest period, subject, however, to the provisions of Section 2.05. If at any time the agent shall determine that by reason of circumstances affecting the London interbank market (i) adequate and reasonable means do not exist for ascertaining the LIBOR rate for the succeeding interest period or (ii) the making or continuance of any loan at the LIBOR rate has become impracticable as a result of a contingency occurring after the date of this agreement which materially and adversely affects the London interbank market, the agent shall so notify the lenders and the borrower. Failing the availability of the LIBOR rate, the LIBOR rate shall mean the base rate thereafter in effect from time to time until such time as a LIBOR rate may be determined by reference to the London interbank market.

on completion of the voyage. Customers also are required to pay the full cruise fare (minus deposit) 60 days in advance, with the fares being recognized as cruise revenue on completion of the voyage.

Property and equipment on the financial statements are stated at cost. Depreciation and amortization are calculated using the straight-line method over the following estimated useful lives: vessels, 25 to 30 years; buildings, 20 to 40 years; equipment, 2 to 20 years; and leasehold improvements at the shorter of the term of lease or related asset life. Goodwill of $275 million resulting from the acquisition of HAL Antillen, N.V. (Holland America Lines), is being amortized using the straight-line method over 40 years.

During 1995, Carnival received $40 million from the settlement of litigation with Metra Oy, the former parent company of Wartsila Marine Industries, related to losses suffered in connection with the construction of three cruise ships. (Wartsila declared bankruptcy in late 1994.) Of this amount, $14.4 million was recorded as other income, with the remainder used to pay legal fees and reduce the cost basis of the three ships.

On June 25, 1996, Carnival reached an agreement with the trustees of Wartsila and creditors for the bankruptcy that resulted in a cash payment of approximately $80 million. Of the $80 million received, $5 million was used to pay certain costs, $32 million was recorded as other income, and $43 million was used to reduce the cost basis of certain ships that had been affected by the bankruptcy.

By May 31, 1998, Carnival had outstanding long-term debt of $1.55 billion, with the current portion being $58.45 million. This debt is composed primarily of $306.8 million in commercial paper and a number of unsecured debentures and notes of less than $200 million each at rates ranging from 5.65 to 7.7 percent.

According to the Internal Revenue Code of 1986, Carnival is considered a controlled foreign corporation (CFC), since 50 percent of its stock is held by individuals who are residents of foreign countries and its countries of incorporation exempt shipping operations of U.S. persons from income tax. Because of CFC status, Carnival expects that all its income (with the exception of U.S. source income from the transportation, hotel, and tour businesses of Holland America) will be exempt from U.S. federal income taxes at the corporate level.

EXHIBIT C
....
Carnival Corporation: Consolidated Statements of Operations (in Thousands)

Years Ended November 30	Six-Month Comparison								
	May 31, 1998	May 31, 1997	1997	1996	1995	1994	1993	1992	1991
Revenues	$1,219,196	$1,117,696	$2,447,468	$2,212,572	$1,998,150	$1,806,016	$1,556,919	$1,473,614	$1,404,704
Costs and expenses									
Operating expense	669,951	634,622	1,322,669	1,241,269	1,131,113	1,028,475	907,925	865,587	810,317
Selling and administrative	163,784	156,219	296,533	274,855	248,566	223,272	207,995	194,298	193,316
Depreciation and amortization	89,266	82,658	167,287	144,987	128,433	110,595	93,333	88,833	85,166
	923,001	493,564	1,786,489	1,661,111	1,508,112	1,362,342	1,209,253	1,148,718	1,088,799
Operating income before affiliated	296,195	244,197	660,979	551,461					
Income from affiliated	(13,034)	11,694	53,091	45,967					
Operating income	283,161	232,503	714,070	597,428	490,038	443,674	347,666	324,896	315,905
Other income (expense)									
Interest income	5,885	3,382	8,675	18,597	14,403	8,668	11,527	16,946	10,596
Interest expense, net of capitalized interest	(24,735)	(31,536)	(55,898)	(64,092)	(63,080)	(51,378)	(34,325)	(53,792)	(65,428)
Other income (expense)	(662)	2,105	5,436	23,414	19,104	(9,146)	(1,201)	2,731	1,746
Income tax expense	6,861	6,353	(6,233)	(9,045)	(9,374)	(10,053)	(5,497)	(9,008)	(8,995)
	(12,651)	(19,696)	(48,020)	(31,126)	(38,947)	(61,909)	(29,496)	(43,123)	(62,081)
Income before extraordinary item	270,510	212,807	666,050	566,302	451,091	381,765	318,170	281,773	253,824
Extraordinary item									
Loss on early extinguishment of debt								(5,189)	
Discontinued operations									
Hotel casino operating loss									(33,173)
Loss on disposal of hotel casino									(135,463)
Net income	$270,510	$212,807	$666,050	$566,302	$451,091	$381,765	$318,170	$276,584	$84,998

Source: 1997 and 1998 10K's and 10Q's.

Carnival Corporation: Consolidated Balance Sheets (in Thousands)

Years Ended November 30	May 31, 1998	1997	1996	1995	1994	1993	1992
Assets							
Current assets							
Cash and cash equivalents	$120,600	$139,989	$111,629	$53,365	$54,105	$60,243	$115,014
Short-term investments	9,414	9,738	12,486	50,395	70,115	88,677	111,048
Accounts receivable	66,503	57,090	38,109	33,080	20,789	19,310	21,624
Consumable inventories (average cost)	76,226	54,970	53,281	48,820	45,122	37,245	31,618
Prepaid expenses and other	102,754	74,238	75,428	70,718	50,318	48,323	32,120
Total current assets	375,497	336,025	290,933	256,378	240,449	253,798	311,424
Property and equipment (at cost)							
Less accumulated depreciation and amortization	5,469,814	4,327,413	4,099,038	3,414,823	3,071,431	2,588,009	1,961,402
Other assets							
Goodwill (less accumulated amortization)	403,077	212,607	219,589	226,571	233,553	237,327	244,789
Long-term notes receivable				78,907	76,876	29,136	
Investment in affiliates and other assets	425,715	479,329	430,330	128,808	47,514	21,097	38,439
Net assets of discontinued operations	37,733	71,401	61,998			89,553	89,553
	6,711,836	5,426,775	5,101,888	4,105,487	3,669,823	3,218,920	2,645,607
	$6,711,836	$5,426,775	$5,101,888	$4,105,487	$3,669,823	$3,218,920	$2,645,607
Liabilities and shareholders' equity							
Current liabilities							
Current portion of long-term debt	58,457	59,620	66,369	72,752	84,644	91,621	$97,931
Accounts payable	187,897	106,783	84,748	90,237	86,750	81,374	71,473
Accrued liabilities	169,048	154,253	126,511	113,483	114,868	94,830	69,919
Customer deposits	755,890	420,908	352,698	292,606	257,505	228,153	178,945
Dividends payable	44,619	44,578	32,416	25,632	21,190	19,763	19,750
Reserve for discontinued operations						34,253	36,763
Total current liabilities	1,215,911	786,142	662,742	594,710	564,957	549,994	474,781
Long-term debt	1,557,016	1,015,294	1,277,529	1,035,031	1,046,904	916,221	776,600
Convertible notes			39,103	115,000	115,000	115,000	
Other long-term liabilities	23,907	20,241	91,630	15,873	14,028	10,499	9,381
Shareholders' equity							
Class A common stock (1 vote/share)	5,949	2,972	2,397	2,298	2,276	2,274	1,136
Class B common stock (5 votes/share)		550	550	550	550	550	275
Paid in capital	871,676	866,097	819,610	594,811	544,947	541,194	539,622
Retained earnings	2,912,499	2,731,213	2,207,781	1,752,140	1,390,589	1,089,323	850,193
Other	1,799	4,816	546	(4,926)	(9,428)	(6,135)	(6,381)
Total shareholders' equity	3,791,923	3,605,098	3,030,884	2,344,873	1,928,934	1,627,206	1,384,845
	$6,711,836	$5,426,775	$5,101,888	$4,105,487	$3,669,823	$3,218,920	$2,645,607

Source: 1997 and 1998 10K's and 10Q's.

EXHIBIT E
....
Carnival Corporation: Selected Financial Data by Segment (in Thousands)

Years Ended November 30	1997	1996	1995	1994	1993	1992
Revenues						
Cruise	$2,257,567	$2,003,458	$1,800,775	$1,623,069	$1,381,473	$1,292,587
Tour	242,646	263,356	241,909	227,613	214,382	215,194
Intersegment revenues	(52,745)	(54,242)	(44,534)	(44,666)	(38,936)	(34,167)
	2,447,468	2,212,572	1,998,150	1,806,016	1,556,919	1,473,614
Gross operating profit						
Cruise	1,072,758	913,880	810,736	726,808	598,642	552,669
Tour	52,041	57,423	56,301	50,733	50,352	55,358
	1,124,799	971,303	867,037	777,541	648,994	608,027
Depreciation and amortization						
Cruise	157,454	135,694	120,304	101,146	84,228	79,743
Tour	8,862	8,317	8,129	9,449	9,105	9,090
Corporate	971	976				
	167,287	144,987	128,433	110,595	93,333	88,833
Operating income						
Cruise	656,009	535,814	465,870	425,590	333,392	310,845
Tour	13,262	21,252	24,168	18,084	14,274	23,051
Corporate	44,799	40,362				
	714,070	597,428	490,038	443,674	347,666	333,896
Identifiable assets						
Cruise	4,744,140	4,514,675	3,967,174	3,531,727	2,995,221	2,415,547
Tour	163,941	150,851	138,313	138,096	134,146	140,507
Discontinued resort and casino	518,694				89,553	89,553
Corporate		436,362				
	5,426,775	5,101,888	4,105,487	3,669,823	3,218,920	2,645,607
Capital expenditures						
Cruise	414,963	841,871	456,920	587,249	705,196	111,766
Tour	42,507	14,964	8,747	9,963	10,281	11,400
Corporate	40,187	1,810				
	$497,657	$858,645	$465,667	$597,212	$715,477	$123,166

Source: 1997 and 1998 10K's and 10Q's.

The primary financial consideration of importance to Carnival management involves the control of costs, both fixed and variable, for the maintenance of a healthy profit margin. Carnival has the lowest break-even point of any organization in the cruise industry (ships break even at approximately 60 percent of capacity) due to operational experience and economies of scale. Unfortunately, fixed costs, including depreciation, fuel, insurance, port charges, and crew costs, which represent more than 33 percent of the company's operating expenses, cannot be reduced significantly in relation to decreases in passenger loads and aggregate passenger ticket revenue. [Major expense items are air fares (25 to 30 percent), travel agent fees (10 percent), and labor (13 to 15 percent). Increases in these costs could negatively affect the profitability of the organization.]

PRINCIPAL SUBSIDIARIES
• •

Carnival Cruise Line
• • • • • • • • • • • •

At the end of fiscal year 1996, Carnival operated 11 ships with a total berth capacity of 20,332. Carnival operates principally in the Caribbean and has an assortment of ships and ports of call serving the 3-, 4-, and 7-day cruise markets (see Exhibit F).

Each ship is a floating resort including a full maritime staff, shopkeepers and casino operators, entertainers, and complete hotel staff. Approximately 14 percent of corporate revenue is generated from shipboard activities such as casino operations, liquor sales, and gift shop items. At various ports of call, passengers also can take advantage of tours, shore excursions, and duty-free shopping at their own expense.

Shipboard operations are designed to provide maximum entertainment, activities, and service. The size of the company and the similarity in design of the new cruise ships has allowed Carnival to achieve various economies of scale, and management is very cost-conscious.

Although the Carnival Cruise Lines division is increasing its presence in the shorter cruise markets, its general marketing strategy is to use 3-, 4-, or 7-day moderately priced cruises to fit the time and budget constraints of the middle class. Shorter cruises can cost less than $500 per person (depending on accommodations) up to roughly $3000 per person in a luxury suite on a 7-day cruise, including port charges. (Per diem rates for shorter cruises are slightly higher, on average, than per diem rates for 7-day cruises.) Average rates per day are approximately $180, excluding gambling, liquor and soft drinks, and items of a personal nature. Guests are expected to tip their cabin steward and waiter at a suggested rate of $3 per person per day and the bus boy at $1.50 per person per day.

Some 99 percent of all Carnival cruises are sold through travel agents, who received a standard commission of 10 percent (15 percent in Florida). Carnival works extensively with travel agents to help promote cruises as an alternative to a Disney or European vacation. In addition to training travel agents from nonaffiliated travel/vacation firms to sell cruises, a special group of employees regularly visits travel agents posing as prospective clients. If the agent recommends a cruise before another vacation option, he or she receives $100. If the travel agent specifies a Carnival cruise before other options, he or she receives $1000 on the spot. During fiscal year 1995, Carnival took reservations from about 29,000 of the approximately 45,000 travel agencies in the United States and Canada, and no one travel agency accounted for more than 2 percent of Carnival revenues.

On-board service is labor-intensive, employing help from some 51 nations—mostly third-world countries—with reasonable returns to employees. For example, waiters on the *Jubilee* can earn approximately $18,000 to $27,000 per year (base salary and tips), significantly greater than could be earned in their home country for similar employment. Waiters typically work 10 hours per day, with approximately 1 day off per week for a specified contract period (usually 3 to 9 months). Carnival records show that employees remain with the company for approximately 8 years and that applicants exceed demand for all cruise positions. Nonetheless, the American Maritime Union has cited Carnival (and other cruise operators) several times for exploitation of its crew.

Holland America Lines
• • • • • • • • • • • • • • • •

On January 17, 1989, Carnival acquired all the outstanding stock of HAL Antillen N.V. from Holland America Lines N.V. for $625 million in cash. Carnival financed the purchase through $250 million in retained earnings (cash account) and borrowed the other $375 million from banks at 0.25 percent over the prime rate. Carnival received the assets and operations of the Holland America Lines, Westours, Westmark Hotels, and Windstar Sail Cruises. Holland America currently has seven cruise ships with a capacity of 8795 berths, with new ships to be delivered in the future.

Founded in 1873, Holland America Lines is an upscale (it charges an average of 25 percent more than similar Carnival cruises) line with principal destinations in Alaska during the summer months and the Caribbean during the fall and winter, with some worldwide cruises of up to 98 days. Holland America targets an older, more sophisticated cruiser with fewer youth-oriented activities. On Holland America ships, passengers can dance to the sounds of the Big Band era and avoid the discos of Carnival ships. Passengers on Holland America

EXHIBIT F
• • • • • • • • • • • • • •
The Ships of Carnival Corporation

Name	Registry	Built	First in Company	Service Cap*	Gross Tons	Length/ Width	Areas of Operation
Carnival Cruise Lines							
Carnival Destiny	Panama	1996	1997	2,642	101,000	893/116	Caribbean
Inspiration	Panama	1996	1996	2,040	70,367	855/104	Caribbean
Imagination	Panama	1995	1995	2,040	70,367	855/104	Caribbean
Fascination	Panama	1994	1994	2,040	70,367	855/104	Caribbean
Sensation	Panama	1993	1993	2,040	70,367	855/104	Caribbean
Ecstasy	Liberia	1991	1991	2,040	70,367	855/104	Caribbean
Fantasy	Liberia	1990	1990	2,044	70,367	855/104	Bahamas
Celebration	Liberia	1987	1987	1,486	47,262	738/92	Caribbean
Jubilee	Panama	1986	1986	1,486	47,262	738/92	Mexican Riviera
Holiday	Panama	1985	1985	1,452	46,052	727/92	Mexican Riviera
Tropicale	Liberia	1982	1982	1,022	36,674	660/85	Alaska, Caribbean
Total Carnival ships capacity:	20,332						
Holland America Line							
Veendam	Bahamas	1996	1996	1,266	55,451	720/101	Alaska, Caribbean
Ryndam	Netherlands	1994	1994	1,266	55,451	720/101	Alaska, Caribbean
Maasdam	Netherlands	1993	1993	1,266	55,451	720/101	Europe, Caribbean
Statendam	Netherlands	1993	1993	1,266	55,451	720/101	Alaska, Caribbean
Westerdam	Netherlands	1986	1988	1,494	53,872	798/95	Canada, Caribbean
Noordam	Netherlands	1984	1984	1,214	33,930	704/89	Alaska, Caribbean
Nieuw Amsterdam	Netherlands	1983	1983	1,214	33,930	704/89	Alaska, Caribbean
Rotterdam IV	Netherlands	1997	1997	1,316	62,000	780/106	Alaska, Worldwide
Total HAL ships capacity:	10,302						
Windstar Cruises							
Wind Spirit	Bahamas	1988	1988	148	5,736	440/52	Caribbean, Mediterranean
Wind Song	Bahamas	1987	1987	148	5,703	440/52	Costa Rica, Tahiti
Wind Star	Bahamas	1986	1986	148	5,703	440/52	Caribbean, Mediterranean
Total Windstar ships capacity:	444						
Total capacity:	31,078						

*In accordance with industry practice, passenger capacity is calculated based on two passengers per cabin even though some cabins can accommodate three or four passengers.

ships enjoy more service (a higher staff-to-passenger ratio than Carnival) and have more cabin and public space per person and a "no tipping" shipboard policy. Holland America has not enjoyed the spectacular growth of Carnival cruise ships but has sustained constant growth over the decade of the 1980s and early 1990s with high occupancy. The operation of these ships and the structure of the crew are similar to the Carnival cruise ship model, and the acquisition of the line gave the Carnival Corporation a presence in the Alaskan market where it had none before.

Holland America Westours is the largest tour operator in Alaska and the Canadian Rockies and provides vacation synergy with Holland America cruises. The transportation division of Westours inludes over 290 motorcoaches comprised of the Gray Line of Alaska, the Gray Line of Seattle, Westours motorcoaches, the McKinley Explorer railroad coaches, and three day boats for tours to glaciers and other points of interest. Carnival management believes that Alaskan cruises and tours should increase in the future due to a number of factors. These include the aging population wanting relaxing vacations with scenic beauty coupled with the fact that Alaska is a U.S. destination.

Westmark Hotels consist of 16 hotels in Alaska and the Yukon territories and also provides synergy with cruise operations and Westours. Westmark is the largest group of hotels in the region providing moderately priced rooms for the vacationer.

Windstar Sail Cruises was acquired by Holland America Lines in 1988 and consists of three computer-controlled sailing vessels with a berth capacity of 444. Windstar is very upscale and offers an alternative to traditional cruise liners with a more intimate, activity-oriented cruise. The ships operate primarily in the Mediterranean and the South Pacific, visiting ports not accessible to large cruise ships. Although catering to a small segment of the cruise vacation industry, Windstar helps with Carnival's commitment to participate in all segments of the cruise industry.

Seabourn Cruise Lines

In April 1992, the company acquired 25 percent of the capital stock of Seabourn. As part of the transaction, the company also made a subordinated secured 10-year loan of $15 million to Seabourn and

a $10 million convertible loan to Seabourn. In December 1995, the $10 million convertible loan was converted by the company into an additional 25 percent equity interest in Seabourn.

Seabourn targets the luxury market with three vessels providing 200 passengers per ship with all-suite accommodations. Seabourn is considered the "Rolls Royce" of the cruise industry and in 1992 was named the World's Best Cruise Line by the prestigious Condé Naste Traveler's Fifth Annual Readers Choice Poll. Seabourn cruises the Americas, Europe, Scandinavia, the Mediterranean, and the Far East.

Airtours

In April 1996, the company acquired a 29.5 percent interest in Airtours for approximately $307 million. Airtours and its subsidiaries constituted the largest air-inclusive tour operator in the world and is publicly traded on the London Stock Exchange. Airtours provides air-inclusive packaged holidays to the British, Scandinavian, and North American markets. Airtours provides holidays to approximately 5 million people per year and owns or operates 32 hotels, 2 cruise ships, and 31 aircraft.

Airtours operates 18 aircraft (one additional aircraft is scheduled to enter service in the spring of 1997) exclusively for its U.K. tour operators, providing a large proportion of their flying requirements. In addition, Airtours' subsidiary Premiair operates a fleet of 13 aircraft (one additional aircraft is also scheduled to enter service with Premiair in the spring of 1997), which provides most of the flying requirements for Airtours' Scandinavian tour operators.

Airtours owns or operates 32 hotels (6500 rooms) that provide rooms to Airtours' tour operators principally in the Mediterranean and the Canary Islands. In addition, Airtours has a 50 percent interest in Tenerife Sol, a joint venture with Sol Hotels Group of Spain, which owns and operates three additional hotels in the Canary Islands providing 1300 rooms.

Through its subsidiary Sun Cruises, Airtours owns and operates two cruise ships. Both the 800-berth *MS Seawing* and the 1062-berth *MS Carousel* commenced operations in 1995. Recently, Airtours acquired a third ship, the *MS Sundream*, which is the sister ship of the *MS Carousel*. The *MS*

Sundream is expected to commence operations in May 1997. The ships operate in the Mediterranean, the Caribbean, and around the Canary Islands and are booked exclusively by Airtours' tour operators.

Costa Crociere S.p.A.

In June 1997, Carnival and Airtours purchased the equity securities of Costa from the Costa family at a cost of approximately $141 million. Costa is head-quartered in Italy and is considered Europe's largest cruise line with seven ships and 7710-passenger capacity. Costa operates primarily in the Mediterranean, northern Europe, the Caribbean, and South America. The major market for Costa is southern Europe, mainly Italy, Spain, and France. In January 1998, Costa signed an agreement to construct an eighth ship with a capacity of approximately 2100 passengers.

Cunard Line

Carnival's most recent acquisition has been the Cu-nard Line, announced on May 28, 1998. Comprised of five ships, the Cunard Line is considered a luxury line with strong brand name recognition. Carnival purchased 50 percent of Cunard for an estimated $255 million, with the other 50 percent being owned by Atle Brynestad. Cunard was immediately merged with Seabourn and, the resulting Cunard Cruise Line Limited (68 percent owned by Carnival), with its now eight ships, will be headed by the former president of Seabourn, Larry Pimentel.

Joint Venture with Hyundai Merchant Marine Co., Ltd.

In September 1996, Carnival and Hyundai Merchant Marine Co., Ltd., signed an agreement to form a 50-50 joint venture to develop the Asian cruise vacation market. Each has contributed $4.8 million as the initial capital of the joint venture. In addition, in November 1996, Carnival sold the cruise ship *Tropicale* to the joint venture for approximately $95.5 million cash. Carnival then chartered the vessel from the joint venture until the joint venture is ready to begin cruise operations in the Asian market, targeting a start date in or around the spring of 1998. The joint venture borrowed the $95.5 million purchase price from a financial insti-

tution, and Carnival and HMM each guaranteed 50 percent of the borrowed funds.

This arrangement, however, was short-lived, since in September 1997, the joint venture was dissolved, and the company repurchased the *Tropicale* for $93 million.

FUTURE CONSIDERATIONS

Carnival's management will have to continue to monitor several strategic factors and issues for the next few years. The industry itself should see further consolidation through mergers and buyouts, and the expansion of the industry could negatively affect the profitability of various cruise operators. Another factor of concern to management is how to reach the large North American market, of which only 5 to 7 percent has ever taken a cruise.

With the industry maturing, cruise competitors have become more sophisticated in their marketing efforts, and price competition is the norm in most cruise segments. (For a partial listing of major industry competitors, see Exhibit G.) Royal Caribbean Cruise Lines also has instituted a major shipbuilding program and is successfully challenging Carnival Cruise Lines in the contemporary segment. The announcement of the Walt Disney Company entering the cruise market with two 80,000-ton cruise liners by 1998 should significantly impact the family cruise vacation segment.

With competition intensifying, industry observers believe the wave of failures, mergers, buyouts, and strategic alliances will increase. Regency Cruises ceased operations on October 29, 1995, and has filed for Chapter 11 bankruptcy. American Family Cruises, a spin-off from Costa Cruise Lines, failed to reach the family market, and Carnival's Fiestamarina failed to reach the Spanish-speaking market. EffJohn International sold its Commodore Cruise subsidiary to a group of Miami-based investors that then chartered one of its two ships to World Explorer Cruises/Semester at Sea. Sun Cruise Lines merged with Epirotiki Cruise Line under the name of Royal Olympic Cruises, and Cunard bought the Royal Viking Line and its name from Kloster Cruise, Ltd., with one ship of its fleet being transferred to Kloster's Royal Cruise Line. All these failures, mergers, and buyouts occurred in 1995, which was not an unusual year for changes in the cruise line industry.

EXHIBIT G
················
Major Industry Competitors

Celebrity Cruises, 5200 Blue Lagoon Drive, Miami, FL 33126

Celebrity Cruises operates four modern cruise ships on 4-, 7-, and 10-day cruises to Bermuda, the Caribbean, the Panama Canal, and Alaska. Celebrity attracts first-time cruisers as well as seasoned cruisers. Purchased by Royal Caribbean on July 30, 1997.

Norwegian Cruise Lines, 95 Merrick Way, Coral Gables, FL 33134

Norwegian Cruise Lines (NCL), formally Norwegian Caribbean Lines, was the first to base a modern fleet of cruise ships in the Port of Miami. It operates 10 modern cruise liners on 3-, 4-, and 7-day eastern and western Caribbean cruises and cruises to Bermuda. A wide variety of activities and entertainment attracts a diverse array of customers. NCL has just completed reconstruction of two ships and is building the *Norwegian Sky,* a 2000-passenger ship to be delivered in the summer of 1999.

Disney Cruise Line, 500 South Buena Vista Street, Burbank, CA 91521

Disney has just recently entered the cruise market with the introduction of the *Disney Magic* and *Disney Wonder.* Both ships will cater to both children and adults and will feature 875 staterooms each. Each cruise will include a visit to Disney's private island, Castaway Cay. Although Disney currently has only two ships and the cruise portion of Disney is small, its potential for future growth is substantial with over $22 billion in revenues and $1.9 billion net profits in 1997.

Princess Cruises, 10100 Santa Monica Boulevard, Los Angeles, CA 90067

Princess Cruises, with its fleet of nine "Love Boats," offers 7-day and extended cruises to the Caribbean, Alaska, Canada, Africa, the Far East, South America, and Europe. Princess's primary market is the upscale 50-plus experienced traveler, according to Mike Hannan, senior vice president for marketing services. Princess ships have an ambiance best described as casual elegance and are famous for their Italian-style dining rooms and onboard entertainment.

Royal Caribbean Cruise Lines, 1050 Caribbean Way, Miami, FL 33132

RCCL's nine ships have consistently been given high marks by passengers and travel agents over the past 21 years. RCCL's ships are built for the contemporary market, are large and modern, and offer 3-, 4-, and 7-day as well as extended cruises. RCCL prides itself on service and exceptional cuisine. With the purchase of Celebrity, RCCL has become the largest cruise line in the world with 17 ships and a passenger capacity of over 31,100. Plans include the introduction of six additional ships by the year 2002. In 1997, RCCL had net income of $175 million on revenues of $1.93 billion.

Other Industry Competitors (Partial List)	
American Hawaii Cruises	(2 ships, Hawaiian Islands)
Club Med	(2 ships, Europe, Caribbean)
Commodore Cruise Line	(1 ship, Caribbean)
Cunard Line	(8 ships, Caribbean, worldwide)
Dolphin Cruise Line	(3 ships, Caribbean, Bermuda)
Radisson Seven Seas Cruises	(3 ships, worldwide)
Royal Olympic Cruises	(6 ships, Caribbean, worldwide)
Royal Cruise Line	(4 ships, Caribbean, Alaska, WW)

Source: Cruise Line International Association, 1996, and company 10K's and annual reports.

EXHIBIT H
....
Liners Completed and Placed in Service during the Past 3 Years

Carrier and Vessel Name	Passengers	Year
Carnival Cruise Lines, *Elation*	2040	1998
Carnival Cruise Lines, *Destiny*	2642	1997
Carnival Cruise Lines, *Inspiration*	2040	1996
Celebrity Cruises, *Mercury*	1870	1997
Celebrity Cruises, *Galaxy*	1870	1996
Costa Cruises, *Costa Victoria*	1950	1996
Holland America Line, *Veendam*	1266	1996
Holland America Line, *Rotterdam VI*	1316	1997
Princess Cruises, *Dawn Princess*	1950	1997
Princess Cruises, *Grand Princess*	2600	1998
Radisson Seven Seas Cruises, *Paul Gaugin*	320	1997
Royal Caribbean Cruises, *Rhapsody of the Seas*	2000	1997
Royal Caribbean Cruises, *Enchantment of the Seas*	1950	1997
Royal Caribbean Cruises, *Splendour of the Seas*	1800	1996
Royal Caribbean Cruises, *Grandeur of the Seas*	1850	1996
Royal Caribbean Cruises, *Visions of the Seas*	2000	1998

Future Liners Now under Construction		
Carrier and Vessel Name	**Passengers**	**Expected Launch**
Disney Cruise Line, *Disney Magic*	1740	Summer, 1998
Carnival Cruise Lines, *Paradise*	2040	Winter, 1998-99
Disney Cruise Line, *Disney Wonder*	1740	Winter, 1998-99
Carnival Cruise Lines, *Triumph*	2758	1999
Holland America Line, *Volendam*	1440	1999
Holland America Line, *Zaandam*	1440	1999
Norwegian Cruise Line, *Norwegian Sky*	2000	1999
Princess Cruises, *Sea Princess*	1950	1999
Princess Cruises, *Ocean Princess*	2022	1999
Radisson Seven Seas, unnamed	490	1999
Renaissance Cruises, *R3*	684	1999
Renaissance Cruises, *R4*	684	1999
Royal Caribbean Cruises, *Voyager of the Seas*	3114	1999
Carnival Cruise Lines, *Victory*	2642	2000
Carnival Cruise Lines, unnamed	2100	2000
Costa Cruises, unnamed	1950	2000
Celebrity Cruises, unnamed	1950	2000
Delta Queen Steamboat Co., unnamed	225	2000
Holland America Line, unnamed	1380	2000
P & O Cruises, unnamed	1840	2000
Royal Caribbean Cruises, *Project Eagle*	3114	2000
Silversea Cruises, unnamed	396	2000
Celebrity Cruises, unnamed	1950	2001
Princess Cruises, unnamed	2600	2001
Princess Cruises, unnamed	2600	2001
Royal Caribbean Cruises, unnamed	2000	2001
Silversea Cruises, unnamed	396	2000
Royal Caribbean Cruises, unnamed	3114	2002
American Hawaii Cruises, 2 unnamed		Undetermined

Source: Cruise News @ *http://www.cruise-news.com/.*

The increasing industry capacity is also a source of concern to cruise operators. The slow growth in industry demand is occurring during a period when industry berth capacity continues to grow. The entry of Disney and the ships already on order by current operators will increase industry berth capacity by over 10,000 per year for the next 3 years, a significant increase. (See Exhibit H for new ships under construction.) The danger lies in cruise operators using the "price" weapon in their marketing campaigns to fill cabins. If cruise operators cannot make a reasonable return on investment, operating costs will have to be reduced (affecting quality of services) to remain profitable.

This will increase the likelihood of further industry acquisitions, mergers, and consolidations. A "worst case" scenario would be the financial failure of weaker lines.

Still, Carnival's management believes that demand should increase during the remainder of the 1990s. Considering that only 5 to 7 percent of the North American market has taken a cruise vacation, reaching more of the North American target market would improve industry profitability. Industry analysts state the problem is that an "assessment of market potential" is only an educated guess, and what if the current demand figures are reflective of the future?

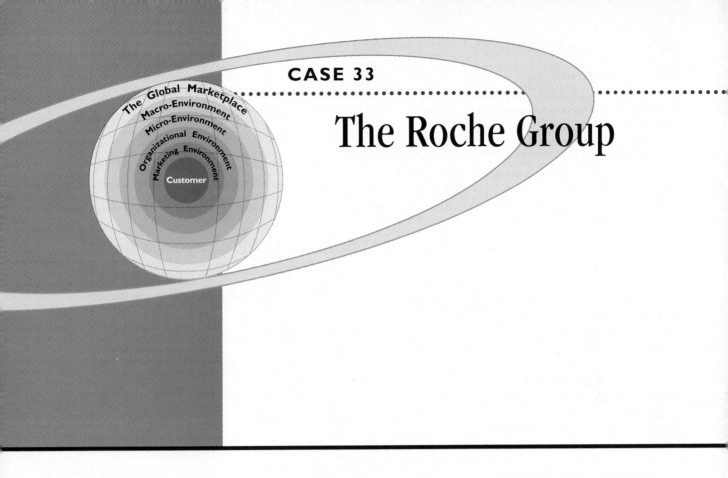

The Roche Group

This case was prepared by James W. Clinton of The University of Northern Colorado and James W. Camerius of Northern Michigan University.

The Roche Group, which is headquartered in Basel, Switzerland, has made a series of strategic moves since 1986, which were expected to prepare the company for the twenty-first century: Companies have been sold, companies have been bought, and internal alignments have been made to strengthen the company's core businesses.

The Roche Group was a leading multinational pharmaceutical company that manufactured, processed, distributed, and marketed its products and services worldwide. Revenues for 1994, derived from the company's four core businesses (pharmaceuticals, vitamins and fine chemicals, flavors and fragrances, and diagnostics) were 14.7 billion Swiss francs, a company record. Although 26.6 percent of the company's property, plant, and equipment were located in Switzerland, only 2 per-

cent of its sales were in Switzerland. Roche was engaged in businesses characterized by extreme competition in a very complex environment. Significant consolidation that had already occurred within the pharmaceutical industry was continuing, and industry competitors were being forced to question their product lines, their organization, their mission, and their strategies. Not all major participants in the industry agreed on which course of action was essential for survival and growth (see Appendix).

HISTORY

Roche was founded in 1896 by Dr. Fritz Hoffmann. The family name of the woman he married was La Roche. At that time, it was the custom to add the wife's name to one's business title—thus Hoffmann-La Roche.

Dr. Hoffman founded the company because of his faith in a sirolin syrup that he had developed to treat coughs and sneezing. The product was well received, and Hoffmann subsequently established subsidiaries in Paris (1903), New York (1905), Vienna (1907), London (1909), St. Petersburg (1910), and Yokohama (1911).

Roche became a public company in 1919. In 1934, Roche began industrial-scale production of synthetic vitamins. Flavors and fragrances were added in the 1960s, and the Diagnostics Division was formed in 1968.

Valium, a tranquilizer drug product used to treat anxiety and nervousness, and introduced in 1963, was the company's first major pharmaceutical success. Another Roche success was Rocephin, an antibacterial, which was introduced in 1982. Rocephin not only has become Roche's top-selling pharmaceutical product but also was the number one hospital injectable product in the world for preventing infection and treating infectious disorders. On a positive note for the company, Rocephin's patent protection was not scheduled to expire until the end of the decade.

A STRATEGIC TRANSITION

Between 1986 and 1994, Roche divested most of the acquisitions purchased years earlier and which had been designed to diversify the company's product mix. Selected for divestment were (1) weak performers (i.e., companies that failed to return what the company considered a satisfactory return on investment), (2) those companies which lacked critical mass, or (3) those companies in which Roche could not build critical mass through acquisitions at reasonable purchase prices. Divestitures were as follows:

1. (1988) Kontron, manufacturer of instruments and electronics
2. (1989) Maag, plant protection
3. (1989) Medi-Physics, diagnostics
4. (1992) Microbiology, diagnostics
5. (1993) Animal Health, vitamins and chemicals

Concurrent with these divestitures, Roche made significant acquisitions and additional investments designed to strengthen its core businesses. Most of Roche's businesses, except for fragrances, were considered, to a large extent, recession-resistant. Acquisitions and investments made by Roche were as follows:

1. (1990) Genentech, biotechnology
2. (1991) Fritzche, Dodge, flavors and fragrances
3. (1991) Cetus/Chiron, PCR technology, diagnostics
4. (1991) Nicholas, OTC medical products
5. (1992) Compuchem, clinical labs, drug testing
6. (1993) Fisons, OTC medical products
7. (1994) Syntex, transplant medicine, analgesics, and rheumatology
8. (1994) Agri-Bio, poultry disease treatments

As a result of these divestments and acquisitions, Roche's degree of diversification narrowed. Changes in the company's product mix, as they have evolved between 1986 and 1994, appear in Exhibit A. In the 1980s, Roche also entered into two major strategic alliances (several other similar agreements undertaken with Genentech were overtaken by Roche's purchase of Genentech): Roche-Glaxo and Roche-Amgen.

Roche's geographic distribution of sales and related assets, capital expenditures, and employees are shown in Exhibit B.

1. *Roche-Glaxo.* The largest alliance in the global pharmaceutical industry was initiated 10 years ago when Roche agreed to market pharmaceutical manufacturer Glaxo's drug Zantac, a treatment for ulcers, in the United States.

2. *Roche-Amgen.* Roche and the pharmaceutical manufacturer Amgen formed the second-largest strategic alliance in the pharmaceutical industry to market Amgen's Neupogen, which was used to reduce the negative effects that may be associated with medical products used to fight cancer. Roche marketed Neupogen in Europe. Zantac and Neupogen thus were able to capitalize on Roche's strength in marketing.

Roche's subsidiary, Syntex, formed a 50-50 joint venture with Procter & Gamble in 1994 to market the over-the-counter analgesic product naprosyn under the trade name Aleve. The company also formed a joint venture with the U.S. conglomerate company Cargill to develop a new production process for vitamin E.

EXHIBIT A

Roche Group, Sales by Business Segment, as a Percent of Sales, 1986, 1990, 1992, and 1994

	Percentage of Total Sales			
Business Segment	*1986*	*1990*	*1992*	*1994*
Pharmaceuticals	41.0%	49.7%	53.2%	56.6%
Vitamins/fine chemicals	26.0	24.8	23.7	21.7
Diagnostics	11.0	13.6	12.1	10.8
Fragrances and flavors	11.0	11.0	10.4	10.3
Other	11.0	0.9	0.6	0.6
Totals	100.0	100.0	100.0	100.0

Source: Roche Group, Annual Report, 1994; Roche Presentation to Financial Analysts, May 1995.

RESEARCH AND DEVELOPMENT

A global presence was crucial to Roche because of the astronomical cost of pharmaceutical research and the need to spread research expenses across many markets. To develop a new drug typically required 10 years of research and an investment of approximately $300 million. Pharmaceutical companies needed to introduce at least one good product every year to remain profitable and competitive.

Areas in which Roche conducted research included the central nervous system, infectious diseases, oncology and virology, inflammatory and autoimmune diseases, metabolic disorders, cardiovascular diseases, bronchopulmonary diseases, and dermatology. Criteria used by Roche to select research projects were scientific merit, medical need, market potential, and expected time to market. These criteria, as well as pressures to reduce drug prices and the high cost of R&D, have forced the company to focus on innovative drugs that repre-

EXHIBIT B

Roche Group, Sales, Operating Assets Employed, Capital Expenditures (millions of Swiss francs), and Number of Employees, by Geographic Area, 1994

	Sales	*Operating Assets Employed*	*Capital Expenditures*	*No. of Employees*
Switzerland	301	3,366	308	10,512
European Union	4,041	3,569	285	13,628
Rest of Europe	714	259	27	1,177
Total Europe	5,056	7,194	620	25,317
North America	5,839	9,023	565	24,581
Latin America	1,342	1,087	34	5,452
Asia	1,986	1,407	125	4,643
Africa, Australia, Oceania	525	288	11	1,388
Combined total	14,748	18,988	1,355	61,381

Source: Roche Group, Annual Report, 1994.

sented therapeutic breakthroughs. Consequently, after Roche and Syntex resources were combined, research efforts were rationalized and concentrated on those which showed the most promise.

Roche had five research centers: (1) Nutley, New Jersey, (2) Palo Alto, California, (3) Welwyn, Great Britain, (4) Basel, Switzerland, and (5) Kamakura, Japan. Although Roche held ownership of over two-thirds of Genentech's stock, Genentech of San Francisco operated as an autonomous company, independent of Roche, and Genentech's stock continued to be traded on the New York Stock Exchange. The 1994 Annual Report noted that Roche and Genentech were engaged in joint research into cancer and the central nervous system.

Each of the centers was assigned a particular area of research responsibility. Furthermore, research was decentralized to capitalize on where the scientific talent was located and thus improve performance. Roche also entered into cooperative research agreements with selected leading universities and biotechnology companies.

Roche spent 16 percent of total sales on R&D and 24 percent (the highest in the industry) of its pharmaceutical sales on R&D. It was considered to be a key factor in the company's success. Roche's objectives were to (1) develop innovative products with long-term patent protection that would lower health care costs and (2) take those new pharmaceutical products to market as quickly as possible. Patents were country-specific; that is, the company was required to apply for a patent in each country in which patent protection, typically 15 to 20 years, was sought. Roche (according to *The Pocket Roche*, p. 93) had over 10,000 patents and patent applications in over 100 countries.

Roche planned to submit for approval six new pharmaceutical products between 1995 and 1997. An additional seven are in late stages of development. New applications were being investigated for existing drugs, while research into new drugs continued.

Roche would, as well, develop an "orphan drug" (so-called because the target consumer population was small), Vesanoid, for use in the treatment of acute leukemia. R&D costs were not expected to be recovered. Roche was committed to the development of lifesaving drugs, as well as those drugs which may show less impressive returns but produce medical breakthroughs.

A Roche manager estimated that there were no effective treatment drugs for two-thirds of known illnesses. Roche's president has been quoted as saying that pharmaceuticals represent the least-saturated market in the world. In other words, there were a vast number of drug products yet to be discovered, which represented significant potential for investigation, research, and development.

MARKETING AND OPERATIONS

The company managed an annual compound growth rate in sales of 8 percent between 1986 and 1994, which was primarily internally generated, since sales of acquired businesses only slightly exceeded sales of divested businesses. Construction projects underway or completed in 1994 included sites in Florence, South Carolina, Basel, Nutley, New Jersey, East Hanover, New Jersey, Singapore, and Fukuroi, Japan. Roche has taken measures to reduce pollution at the source through either new or improved process technology or through energy conversion to cleaner fuels. Safety and environmental production audits were conducted throughout the organization at production, premix, and distribution centers.

Roche estimated that by 1995 it ranked eighth in the world in sales of pharmaceuticals, number one in the sale of pharmaceuticals to hospitals, and number three in sales of OTC products in Europe. Roche was estimated to be the global leader in vitamin sales, with a 50 percent market share, the global leader in the sale of carotenoids (pigments appearing in vegetable oils and some animal fats), number two in fragrances and flavors, with a market share of 11 percent, and number one (or coequal) in laboratory services revenues in the United States.

Pharmaceuticals

Worldwide 1994 sales for pharmaceuticals were 8.3 billion Swiss francs, up 7 percent from 1993 sales of 7.8 billion. This segment's respective subdivisions, that is, prescription drugs, OTC products, and Genentech, were up 7 percent, unchanged, and up 18 percent, respectively. Prescription drugs represented 77 percent of sales; OTC, 13 percent; and Genentech, 10 percent. Acquisition of Genentech and Syntex expanded Roche's global market share in pharmaceuticals.

The purchase of a majority stake in Genentech (of South San Francisco, California) coincided with a major drop in the value of the U.S. dollar with respect to the Swiss franc. Roche owned approximately 67 percent of Genentech common stock, up from an initial purchase of 60 percent of the company's stock. Roche deliberately chose not to acquire all the shares of Genentech so that Genentech's scientists and managers would have the opportunity to benefit and profit from increased value in the shares of stock through the purchase of stock options. To preserve Genentech's very unique research approach, Roche took the further step of placing only three of its executives on the thirteen-member Genentech board of directors.

Genentech's 1994 sales rose 27 percent from the preceding-year figures, while income, including licensing royalties, rose 25 percent to $795.4 million. Genentech was expected to have a "blockbuster" in Pulmozyme, a medical product used in the treatment of cystic fibrosis, an inherited disease that attacked the lungs.

Purchase of Syntex of Palo Alto, California, for approximately $5.3 billion, announced in May 1994, was closed at the end of October 1994. The strength of the Swiss franc, coupled with Roche's healthy balance sheet, enabled the company to purchase Syntex with internally generated funds except for a short-term bridge loan. Approximately $3.0 billion of the purchase price represented goodwill, which Roche charged off directly against retained earnings, contributing to a decline of about 700 million Swiss francs in shareholders' equity. Intangible assets (patents, technology, know-how, trademarks, licenses, etc.) associated with the purchase had an estimated value of 3 billion Swiss francs, which was to be amortized over 15 years. The consolidation of Syntex's staff with that of existing Roche facilities was expected to result in a reduction of 5000 positions. Roche offered transfers, severance packages, early retirement, and outplacement assistance to those employees affected by the acquisition.

A Syntex pharmaceutical product, CellCept, was used in conjunction with organ transplants to assist the body to accept the transplanted organ, kidneys in particular, when the body rejected the organ. CellCept was approved by the Food and Drug Administration (FDA) in May of 1995.

Roche had not entered the OTC market in the United States (except through the joint venture with Procter & Gamble previously mentioned) and Japan. Roche, long term, however, wanted to develop a global presence in this area.

Vitamins and Fine Chemicals

Sales for this segment in 1994 totaled 3.2 billion Swiss francs, down 2.0 percent from 1993 sales. Sales, however, in terms of local currencies, actually rose 5 percent. Sales by product category were vitamins, 60 percent; fine chemicals (for use in food, pharmaceuticals, and cosmetics), 23 percent; and carotenoids, 17 percent. Geographic sales were concentrated in Europe (42 percent) and North America (31 percent).

A beta-carotene plant was built in Freeport, Texas. Several new vitamin forms were introduced. Market growth experienced its best success in the Far East and Latin America. Improvements in processes for the production of vitamin B_2 and carotenoids were developed. In addition, the company was building a new technical center in Sisseln, Switzerland, to develop new and improved production technologies. The company also planned to be a major player in the China market by participating in joint ventures and providing technological consultation to keep product costs low.

To improve economies of scale in logistics, the division centralized product distribution at four distribution centers. In response to industrial customers forming partnerships to consolidate purchases and increase their buying clout, Roche integrated its Europe, Africa, and Middle East marketing organizations. To address intense competition from low-wage countries in Asia, Roche increased productivity through both concentration and expansion of production, improvement of production processes, and development of new markets.

Roche, in a move reflective of its corporate culture, distributed tablets free to 2 million children worldwide to help combat the problem of vitamin A deficiency.

Diagnostics

Sales revenues for the Diagnostics Division declined 7.1 percent from 1.7 billion Swiss francs in 1993 to 1.6 billion Swiss francs in 1994. Diagnostics' 1994 sales were derived from two businesses: Roche Biomedical Laboratories (63 percent of sales) and Roche Diagnostic Systems (37 percent).

The sales decline was attributed primarily to intense competition for market share and government cost controls that forced lower fees for laboratory services. Fees also came under pressure because of the increased buying power of managed care organizations that had been achieved through market consolidation, that is, the merger of service providers.

The 1994 merger of Roche Biomedical Laboratories (RBL) of Burlington, South Carolina (which represented 63 percent of this industry segment's sales), with National Health Laboratories of La Jolla, California, was expected to improve this division's competitive position. The merger created a new company, Laboratory Corporation of America (LabCorp), which was estimated to have a 13 percent market share of independent laboratory revenues, equaling that of coleader in the field, MetPath, and moving ahead of SmithKline's 10 percent. The merger joined RBL, whose revenues were derived primarily from the eastern United States, with NHL, whose sales were geographically dispersed throughout the United States. In addition to the assets of RBL, Roche contributed $186.7 million. In return, Roche received a 49.9 percent share of LabCorp and 8.3 million warrants convertible to LabCorp shares in the year 2000.

Roche Diagnostic Systems generated revenues through sales in clinical chemistry and drug monitoring (58 percent), polymerase chain reaction (PCR), in which genetic materials can be copied millions of times over to assist in detecting infectious diseases, cancer, or hereditary disorders (14 percent), immunochemistry (16 percent), hematology (10 percent), and other areas (2 percent). The company was number one in the industry in PCR technology. The company recently developed an automated system for laboratory testing of a broad range of diseases that was fast, secure, and efficient. Like other sectors of the health care industry, Diag-

nostic Systems responded to price pressures from health care regulators by consolidating operations.

Fragrances and Flavors

Sales revenues for this industry segment were 1.5 billion Swiss francs in 1994, up 6.2 percent over 1993. Fragrances (used in perfumes, toiletries, cosmetics, soaps and detergents, and household and industrial products) represented 39 percent of sales; flavors (compounds for use in foods, beverages, pharmaceuticals, oral hygiene products, and animal foods), 36 percent; and specialties (which included cosmetic and synthetic fragrance ingredients, natural essences, and sunscreen agents), 25 percent. Sales by region were as follows: Europe, 42 percent; North America, 34 percent; Asia/Pacific, 16 percent; and South America, 8 percent. Research was presently focused on the biology of the skin, natural flavors, and the sense of smell with regard to natural scents.

Roche was number two in the industry, behind number one International Fragrances and Flavors. Fragrances and flavors companies Roure and Givaudan, respectively, formerly separate Roche units, were merged into one division in 1991.

As was the case in the other divisions, production was concentrated at fewer facilities to improve productivity. The division also paid special attention to key accounts and, by improving responsiveness to their needs, increased sales to these high-volume customers.

MANAGEMENT AND ORGANIZATION

A key Roche objective was to be a leader in the industries in which it competed, not necessarily number one but perhaps number two or three. The thrust of the company was to focus on research and innovation, above-average profitability in its core businesses, and improved efficiency. The company strongly believed that new drug discoveries would do more to improve health care and contain medical costs than any other alternative, since drugs not only were cheaper than other health care methods but also could shorten hospital stays.

Roche Holding, Ltd., formed in 1989, directly controlled 127 subsidiary units in 55 countries. The eight largest subsidiaries, as reported in the company's 1994 Annual Report, were (1) F. Hoffmann-

La Roche, Ltd., Basel, Switzerland; (2) Hoffmann-La Roche Inc., Nutley, New Jersey; (3) Roche S.p.A., Milan, Italy; (4) Hoffmann-La Roche Aktiengesellschaft, Grenzach, Germany; (5) Produits Roche S.A., Neuilly-sur-Seine, France; (6) Societe Chimique Roche S.A., Village-Neuf, France; (7) Roche Products Limited, Welwyn, Great Britain; and (8) Nippon Roche K.K., Tokyo, Japan.

The Roche Group had four major divisions, as described earlier. Subsidiaries within each division reported to their respective division heads. Changes in organizational alignments were made to decentralize and flatten the organizational structure to speed communications and decision making and encourage management initiative. In keeping with these objectives, in 1990, costs formerly charged off to the corporate headquarters were assigned to the four major businesses, decentralizing responsibility and decision making.

At the corporate level, a functional organization included the following elements: (1) audit, (2) finance and accounting, (3) human resources, (4) investor relations, (5) public policy, (6) research and development, and (7) safety and environmental protection. Members of Roche's board of directors and executive committee are shown below:

Roche Group, Board of Directors:
Mr. Fritz Gerber, Chairman
Dr. Lukas Hoffmann, Vice-Chairman
Dr. Andres F. Leuenberger, Vice-Chairman,
    Delegate to General Management
Professor Kurt Jenny
Dr. Armin M. Kessler
Dr. Henri B. Meier
Dr. Jakob Oeri
Dr. h.c. Paul Sacher
Professor Werner Stauffacher
Professor Charles Weissmann

Roche Group, Executive Committee:
Mr. Fritz Gerber, Chairman and CEO
Dr. Andres F. Leuenberger, Vice-Chairman
Dr. Henri B. Meier, Finance, Accounting
Dr. Markus Altwegg, Pharma Stammhaus Basel,
    Group Informatics
Mr. Jean-Luc Belingard, Diagnostics Division
Dr. Roland Bronnimann, Vitamins, Fine
    Chemicals Division
Professor Jurgen Drews, Research and
    Development
Dr. Franz B. Humer, Pharmaceuticals Division

FINANCE

Roche stock was traded on the Zurich, Geneva, and Basel, Switzerland, stock exchanges. American investors could invest in Roche through the U.S. ADR program (American Depository Rights), which was nonvoting stock issued through the Bank of New York (BONY). The ADR program was launched in 1992 with the express purpose of giving U.S. investors easier access to investment in the company. In 1990, to attract international investors, Roche adopted international accounting standards (IASs) in the filing of the company's financial reports.

After consolidated net income for the Roche Group rose from 2.5 billion Swiss francs (CHF) in 1993 to 2.9 billion CHF in 1994, the market value of Roche's common stock continued to appreciate. (See Exhibit C.) In the summer of 1995, Roche's publicly traded stock was valued at slightly more than the combined market value of Swiss competitors Ciba-Geigy and Sandoz, despite the fact that Ciba-Geigy's sales were almost twice those of Roche, reflecting investors' optimistic appraisal of Roche's growth and profit potential. Estimates of the common stock market capitalization of the top pharmaceutical companies in the world, as of July 31, 1995, had Roche on top at $66.9 billion, Merck second at $63.8 billion, Sandoz at $26.4 billion, and Ciba-Geigy at $21 billion (*Wall Street Journal,* October 2, 1995, p. R32). In 1986, reflecting the shift in industry leadership, comparable stock capitalization figures for Roche, Merck, Sandoz, and Ciba were 9 billion, 19 billion, 7 billion, and 13 billion CHF, respectively.

Between 1991 and 1995, Roche issued six innovative financial instruments (for a total of about $6 billion). These funds were obtained at an average of 3 percent interest and were then deployed to obtain a yield of 9 percent on investments in marketable securities. The six financial instruments employed by Roche and the colorful labels assigned to these issues were as follows:

1. The *bull spread.* Roche issued $1 billion in bonds at a coupon rate of $3\frac{1}{2}$ percent in 1991. Detachable warrants, which were exercised in 1994, enabled each holder of 100 warrants to receive 10,000 Swiss francs in cash.

2. The *knockout.* Roche Holdings, Inc., issued bonds with a nominal value of $1.42 billion in 1993, paying an interest rate of $2\frac{3}{4}$ percent. De-

EXHIBIT C
················
Roche Holding, Ltd.: Selected Financial Data, 1985–1994 (in millions of Swiss francs)

	1985	*1986*	*1987*	*1988*
Sales	8,940	7,822	7,705	8,690
Depreciation/amortization	498	497	492	538
Research and development	1,196	1,123	1,210	1,419
Net income	452	416	482	642
Cash from operations	—	—	—	—
Long-term assets	5,524	5,509	5,361	5,396
Current assets	7,058	7,344	8,315	9,880
Total assets	12,582	12,853	13,676	15,276
Shareholders' equity	7,954	8,321	8,703	10,075
Minority interests	7	5	5	5
Long-term liabilities	2,649	2,690	2,777	2,768
Current liabilities	1,972	1,837	2,191	2,429
Capital expenditures	542	529	520	652
No. of employees, end of year	45,477	46,513	47,498	49,671
Net income as a % of sales	5.1	5.3	6.3	7.4
Net income as a % of sh. equity	5.7	5.0	5.5	6.4
R&D as a % of sales	13.4	14.4	13.8	13.9
Current ratio (as a percent)	357.8	399.8	379.6	406.8
Equity as a % of total assets	63.2	64.7	63.6	66.0
Sales per employee (000 CHF)	197	168	162	175
Number shares outstanding (000)	16	16	16	16
Number nonvoting equity securities (000)	61.4	61.4	61.4	61.4
Total shares and nonvoting equity securities (000)	77.4	77.4	77.4	77.4
Net income per share and nonvoting equity security (CHF)	56	52	60	80
Dividend per share and nonvoting equity security (CHF)	12	12	13	14
Total dividends (millions CHF)	100	100	102	161

Source: Roche Group, Annual Report, 1994.

tachable warrants, exercisable in 1996, entitled the holder of 60 warrants to receive either 6000 Swiss francs in cash or one nonvoting equity security.

3. *Lyon I* and *Lyon II* (liquid yield option notes). In 1993, Roche Holdings, Inc., issued $1.42 billion of zero coupon bonds (sold at a discount) that were redeemable in 1988 and 2003 either for cash or American Depository Shares of Roche Holding, Ltd., at a specified conversion rate for each $1000 of principal.

4. The *samurai*. In 1994, Roche Financial Management issued bonds, with detachable warrants, valued at 100 billion yen ($1.4 billion) at a coupon rate of 1 percent. The warrants, exercisable in 1998, entitled the holder of 100 warrants to receive one of the following: (a) one nonvoting equity security, (b) cash equal to the

1989	1990	1991	1992	1993	1994
9,814	9,670	11,451	12,953	14,315	14,748
597	521	822	880	930	979
1,419	1,444	1,727	1,998	2,269	2,332
852	948	1,482	1,916	2,478	2,860
—	1,718	1,980	2,673	2,976	3,120
5,080	6,937	8,478	9,293	9,522	13,549
12,200	15,880	16,567	18,290	21,404	22,684
17,280	22,817	25,045	27,583	30,926	36,233
11,624	13,243	14,429	16,046	17,914	16,422
5	446	511	581	625	861
3,280	5,799	7,029	6,809	7,921	10,034
2,371	3,329	3,076	4,147	4,466	8,916
908	907	1,139	1,293	1,407	1,355
50,203	52,685	55,134	56,335	56,082	61,381
8.7	9.8	12.9	14.8	17.3	19.4
7.3	7.2	10.3	11.9	13.8	17.4
14.5	14.9	15.1	15.4	15.9	15.8
514.6	477.0	538.6	441.0	479.3	254.4
67.3	60.0	59.7	60.3	59.9	47.7
195	184	208	230	255	240
800	800	1,600	1,600	1,600	1,600
3,330	3,330	7,026	7,026	7,026	7,026
4,130	4,130	8,626	8,626	8,626	8,626
103	115	172	222	287	332
19	21	28	37	48	55
157	173	236	312	404	474

nonvoting equity security prices, or (c) 7100 Swiss francs in cash.

5 and 6. The *gold option* and the *Helveticus* were two other major bond issues, and each returned over $1 billion to Roche under favorable terms.

Financial investments made by Roche were significant. At the end of 1994, Roche actively managed marketable securities totaling 13.1 billion Swiss francs—almost the equivalent of the firm's entire investment in long-term assets and over 62 percent more than the value of the firm's plant and equipment. Liquid funds gave the company the flexibility to invest in operations as opportunities arose and also enhanced its ability to negotiate a satisfactory price for such investments.

Since 98 percent of Roche's sales were outside Switzerland, the company used various strategies to reduce its vulnerability to currency and interest-rate risks. These included the purchase of derivative financial instruments, forward exchange contracts, options, and currency swaps.

In 1994, Roche's dividend payout ratio remained at around 16 percent. Most of the company's profits were reinvested in the company in the form of R&D and acquisitions. The low payout ratio also limited investors' tax liability and the potential for payment of double taxation. Ceiba-Geigy and Sandoz, Basel's other two major pharmaceutical companies, also had a low payout ratio, but not as low as Roche.

Unlike publicly traded companies in the United States, Roche was not required under Swiss law to maintain records of shareholders. Shares of stock, including nonvoting equities, were issued to bearer, and for this reason, the company did not keep a register of shareholders. Roche was obligated, however, to state in its annual report that the Roche family owned more than 50 percent of the company's common stock.

A COMPLEX GLOBAL ENVIRONMENT

Roche and other pharmaceutical companies faced a challenging global environment. Major issues the company had to consider in developing future strategies included the following:

1. Choice of one or more strategic organizational configurations that would include

    a. Growth through either internal or external means, or both, that would include both acquisitions and divestments.

    b. Concentration on a limited number of products and services versus diversification intended to deal with an uncertain future.

    c. Diversification into different industries or within the health care industry at another level in the channels of distribution, similar to Merck's 1993 purchase of Medco.

    d. Site selection worldwide that optimized functional operations, such as production, marketing, and research and development.

    e. Number and size of commitments to strategic alliances, as well as choice of alliance partners.

2. The need to maintain the goodwill of governments so that prescription medicines could be priced at levels that struck a balance between health benefits to patients and economic benefits to Roche that made further drug research feasible. Although the Japanese government, for example, mandated price cuts in prescription drugs, it was believed to be fair in its approval of prices for innovative products that enabled pharmaceutical companies to receive a fair return. "Me too" products that failed to differentiate themselves from previously introduced pharmaceuticals, however, did not obtain very good prices or margins.

3. The need to adapt to and compensate for government restrictions placed on pharmaceutical manufacturers and health care providers. In Germany, for example, in 1993, the government froze drug prices and placed tight controls on prices for diagnostic services. In Japan, in addition to biennial government-imposed price cuts on pharmaceuticals, hospitals and doctors were under pressure to curtail discretionary drug use. The French government imposed cost controls on prescription drug prices. The Italian government also mandated major reductions in prescription drug prices and the amounts reimbursed to consumers. These moves by the Italian government led to a decline of 7 percent in the overall Italian market for pharmaceuticals (although Roche still was able to increase its Italian sales by 3 percent during 1994).

4. The unresolved health care reform debate in the United States concerning the fate of universal health care proposals and how ensuing federal and state legislation would impact the pricing of health care products and services. Related to this was the pressure on the U.S. Congress to reduce spending by making cuts in large government health care programs such as Medicare and Medicaid.

5. Economic uncertainty in Latin and South America due to inflation and unemployment and political instability in the Middle East and Africa made it difficult either to negotiate contracts with governments or to successfully market more expensive prescription drug products.

6. Increased pressure by medical insurance programs to reduce costs (drug costs were estimated to represent 7.5 percent of total health care costs). Health maintenance organizations (HMOs) have grown in size and number and have applied relentless pressure on prices charged for drugs and diagnostic services. In Germany, hospitals formed cooperative buying units to negotiate lower pharmaceutical prices based on increased value of purchases.

7. The increased presence, promotion, and acceptance of generic medicines has applied pressure on drug manufacturers to market initially patented medications under newly named generic labels to combat low-priced competition.

8. Increased sales of over-the-counter (OTC) medicines due to increasing numbers of consumers choosing to self-medicate and the shift of some previously prescribed medications to OTC status placed increased pressure on pharmaceutical manufacturers to clearly differentiate their products and demonstrate their superior efficacy.

9. The need to educate relevant industry stakeholders, particularly consumers, providers, and regulators, concerning actual and potential savings and economies contributed by prescription medicines to the total health care system, i.e., the extent to which timely use of medications avoided or moderated the use of more expensive in-patient care that included hospitalization, the use of technology, and perhaps more expensive treatment modalities.

10. The challenge of developing effective medicines for major diseases associated with the increasingly large over-65 population, which, as a group, lived longer but also increased the likelihood of its exposure to a broader range of gerontologic ailments.

11. Major fluctuations in international currencies that in some cases have turned profitable operations into losses and have increased the criticality of decisions made with respect to the location, acquisition, and disposition of resources and facilities.

APPENDIX: The Pharmaceutical Industry

The pharmaceutical industry was centuries old and the treatment of diseases had come a long way since the use of herbs and "magical" incantations. Medicine men and magical potions from the Dark Ages have been displaced by researchers, scientists, clinicians, and the economies of scale possible through global marketing and manufacture of health care products and services. The pharmaceutical industry was a multi-billion dollar industry that was dominated by a dozen major multinational companies. The industry also was unique in that the Swiss companies Ciba-Geigy, Sandoz, and Roche, three of the world's largest pharmaceutical companies, were each headquartered in Basel, less than a mile away from one another, and each was founded approximately a century earlier to produce and market different but related products.

Many of the industry's competitors, including both Sandoz and Ciba-Geigy, were more diversified than Roche, relying on horizontal diversification to enter manufacturing areas other than pharmaceuticals.

A brief overview of a few of Roche's major competitors (Ciba-Geigy, Ltd., Sandoz International, Ltd., Merck & Co., Inc., the Hoechst Group, and the Glaxo Group, Ltd.) appears below. Both these companies and Roche pursued similar strategies in a variety of fields. Each company, for example,

1. Spent heavily on research, which was vital to company growth and profitability.

2. Not only conducted its own research but joined with others to conduct research.

3. Contracted research projects out to specialized companies and leading universities.

4. Established research centers dedicated to specialized areas of inquiry.

5. Formed strategic alliances to manufacture and distribute drug products.

6. Was increasingly aware of the importance of generic (i.e., products whose original patents had expired and now were manufactured by others without payment of royalties to the developer of the patented drug) and over-the-counter (OTC) drug products.

7. Was sensitive to currency exchange-rate fluctuations.

8. Cut staff and facilities in selected areas to increase competitiveness and productivity but also expanded other facilities to achieve economies of scale.

9. Sought new markets in eastern Europe and the Far East, particularly China.

10. Considered and evaluated acquisition and merger partners while divesting businesses that seemed incompatible with its core businesses.

11. Found its sales and profits coming under increased governmental surveillance and control throughout the world.

12. Increased its degree of decentralization of operations.

13. Took an active role in minimizing the impact of its facilities on the environment.

Despite these similarities, however, there also were differences. A few of these differences are noted in the discussion that follows.

Ciba-Geigy sales for 1994 totaled 22.1 billion CHF, down slightly from 1993 sales of 22.6 billion, whereas net profit rose in 1994 to 1.9 billion from 1.8 billion CHF. Shareholders' equity declined to 15.5 billion CHF in 1994 from 17.1 billion CHF, due primarily to a charge of 2.5 billion in goodwill related to acquisitions against retained earnings and secondarily to currency translation adjustments. During 1994, Ciba-Geigy acquired a 49.9 percent share of the health care company Chiron and the OTC product line of Rhone-Poulenc Rorer in both the United States and Canada. Ciba was engaged in three major businesses: health care, agriculture, and industry (dyes, chemicals, pigments, etc.), whose share of total sales totaled 39.7, 21.7, and 38.6 percent, respectively.

Sandoz acquired the Gerber Products Company, the leading U.S. baby food manufacturer, in 1994 for $3.8 billion. Sandoz's chairman believed that this purchase was the most important in the company's history, which was designed to establish nutrition as the company's second core business and assist the company to reduce its risks in the pharmaceutical industry that were associated with increased government controls and price pressures. Like Roche, Sandoz financed most ($2 billion) of its purchase price of Gerber internally and the remainder with a bridge loan of $1.8 billion.

Goodwill associated with the Gerber purchase was written off in 1994 against the stockholders' equity. Sandoz's 1994 sales of 15.9 billion CHF (up 5.1 percent from 1994) were distributed among its divisions as follows: pharmaceuticals, 45 percent; nutrition, 18 percent; chemicals, 14 percent; Agro (crop protection agents), 9 percent; construction and environment, 8 percent; and seeds, 6 percent. The company's pharmaceutical division accounted for 77 percent of total research and development (R&D), which was equal to 17.4 percent of pharmaceutical sales. In January 1994, Sandoz divested one of its chemical division companies, Alphen, whose product line did not fit in with the company's other chemical products.

Merck, whose headquarters was at Whitehouse Station, New Jersey, recorded sales of $15 billion in 1994, an increase of 43 percent over 1993 sales, which took into account the company's purchase of Medco Containment Services (for about $6.6 billion) in November 1993. Without consideration of Medco, sales for Merck rose 7 percent in 1994 above 1993.

In 1994, Merck's net income rose 38 percent to $3.0 billion, including Medco, and 12 percent when Medco was excluded. Unlike the Swiss companies, which immediately wrote off goodwill resulting from acquisitions, Merck chose to amortize goodwill over a 40-year period, thus preserving growth in its net income. Medco was a pharmacy benefit management company whose mail-service pharmacies and retail pharmacy networks dispensed 130 million prescriptions in 1994. One in every seven Americans, 40 million, was covered by a Medco drug benefit. Merck sales in 1994 were distributed in approximately the following percentages: pharmaceuticals, 62.9 percent; Medco, 27.4 percent; animal health and crop protection, 6.9 percent; and specialty chemicals, 2.8 percent. Early in 1995, Merck sold off its specialty chemical businesses to focus on the other core businesses.

The Hoechst Group of Frankfurt, Germany, was more diversified than most participants in the pharmaceutical industry. Sales were distributed as follows: chemicals, 27 percent; health, 24 percent; fibers, 15 percent; polymers, 14 percent; engineering and technology, 12 percent; and agriculture, 8 percent. The company's 1994 sales totaled 49.6 billion German marks (average 1994 exchange rate was about 1.4 marks per dollar), an increase of 7.8 percent over the prior year. Sales of the health division rose 2.6 percent over the previous year. Germany was the company's largest market for pharmaceutical products. Of total sales, about 60 percent were in Europe and 30 percent in North America. At the beginning of 1994, Hoechst controlled no more than 1 percent of the U.S. market for pharmaceutical products. However, later in 1994, Hoechst purchased the U.S. pharmaceutical company Marion Merrell Dow for over $7 billion and Copley, a U.S. generics drug manufacturer. Hoechst also purchased the U.S. diagnostic firm, Syva, in 1995.

Glaxo, whose headquarters was in London, England, increased 1994 sales by 15 percent to 5.7 billion British pounds (1995 average rate of exchange was 1.0 British pound equivalent to $1.55) over the previous year of 4.9 billion British pounds. Sales in the United States, Europe, and the rest of the world accounted for 43, 35, and 22 percent of sales, respectively. The company's product line consisted entirely of medicines, including ethical (prescribed by a physician) drugs and OTC drugs. Glaxo had subsidiary companies in 70 countries that operated under a decentralized system of management.

Manufacturers of OTC drug products, i.e., those which did not require a doctor's prescription and which were frequently used to treat minor illnesses, such as colds and sleeplessness (which also were treated with prescription drugs), also competed for consumers' health care dollars. Some OTC manufacturers applied for and received approval from the Food and Drug Administration (FDA) to sell drugs over the counter that previously were sold only by prescription. SmithKline Beecham's Tagamet, a drug used to treat heartburn and acid indigestion, and approved for OTC sale by the FDA in 1995, was an example of such a product.

Company owned

greater controe over operations than franchises

Kentucky Fried Chicken and the Global Fast-Food Industry

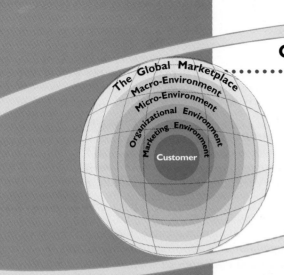

This case was prepared by Jeffrey A. Krug of the Department of Business Administration, University of Illinois at Urbana-Champaign.

Kentucky Fried Chicken Corporation (KFC) was the world's largest chicken restaurant chain and third largest fast-food chain. KFC held over 55 percent of the U.S. market in terms of sales and operated over 10,200 restaurants worldwide in 1998. It opened 376 new restaurants in 1997 (more than one restaurant a day) and operated in 79 countries. One of the first fast-food chains to go international during the late 1960s, KFC has developed one of the world's most recognizable brands.

Japan, Australia, and the United Kingdom accounted for the greatest share of KFC's international expansion during the 1970s and 1980s. During the 1990s, KFC turned its attention to other international markets that offered significant opportunities for growth. China, with a population of over one billion, and Europe, with a population roughly equal to the United States, offered such opportunities. Latin America also offered a unique

Reprinted by permission of the author, Jeffrey A. Krug, University of Illinois at Urbana-Champaign.

opportunity because of the size of its markets, its common language and culture, and its geographic proximity to the United States. Mexico was of particular interest because of the North American Free Trade Agreement (NAFTA), a free-trade zone between Canada, the United States, and Mexico that went into effect in 1994.

Prior to 1990, KFC expanded into Latin America primarily through company-owned restaurants in Mexico and Puerto Rico. Company-owned restaurants gave KFC greater control over its operations than franchised or licensed restaurants. By 1995, KFC also had established company-owned restaurants in Venezuela and Brazil. In addition, it had established franchised units in numerous Caribbean countries. During the early 1990s, KFC shifted to a two-tiered strategy in Latin America. First, it established 29 franchised restaurants in Mexico following enactment of Mexico's new franchise law in 1990. This allowed KFC to expand outside its company restaurant base in Mexico City, Guadalajara, and Monterrey. KFC was one of many

U.S. fast-food, retail, and hotel chains to begin franchising in Mexico following the new franchise law. Second, KFC began an aggressive franchise building program in South America. By 1998, it was operating franchised restaurants in 32 Latin American countries. Much of this growth was in Brazil, Chile, Colombia, Ecuador, and Peru.

COMPANY HISTORY

Fast-food franchising was still in its infancy in 1952 when Harland Sanders began his travels across the United States to speak with prospective franchisees about his "Colonel Sanders Recipe Kentucky Fried Chicken." By 1960, "Colonel" Sanders had granted KFC franchises to over 200 take-home retail outlets and restaurants across the United States. He had also succeeded in establishing a number of franchises in Canada. By 1963, the number of KFC franchises had risen to over 300, and revenues had reached $500 million.

By 1964, at the age of 74, the Colonel had tired of running the day-to-day operations of his business and was eager to concentrate on public relations issues. Therefore, he sought out potential buyers, eventually deciding to sell the business to two Louisville businessmen—Jack Massey and John Young Brown, Jr.—for $2 million. The Colonel stayed on as a public relations man and goodwill ambassador for the company.

During the next 5 years, Massey and Brown concentrated on growing KFC's franchise system across the United States. In 1966, they took KFC public, and the company was listed on the New York Stock Exchange. By the late 1960s, a strong foothold had been established in the United States, and Massey and Brown turned their attention to international markets. In 1969, a joint venture was signed with Mitsuoishi Shoji Kaisha, Ltd., in Japan, and the rights to operate 14 existing KFC franchises in England were acquired. Subsidiaries also were established in Hong Kong, South Africa, Australia, New Zealand, and Mexico. By 1971, KFC had 2450 franchises and 600 company-owned restaurants worldwide and was operating in 48 countries.

Heublein, Inc.

In 1971, KFC entered negotiations with Heublein, Inc., to discuss a possible merger. The decision to seek a merger candidate was partially driven by Brown's desire to pursue other interests, including a political career (Brown was elected governor of Kentucky in 1977). Several months later, Heublein acquired KFC. Heublein was in the business of producing vodka, mixed cocktails, dry gin, cordials, beer, and other alcoholic beverages. However, Heublein had little experience in the restaurant business. Conflicts quickly erupted between Colonel Sanders, who continued to act in a public relations capacity, and Heublein management. Colonel Sanders became increasingly distraught over quality control issues and restaurant cleanliness. By 1977, new restaurant openings had slowed to about 20 per year. Few restaurants were being remodeled, and service quality had declined.

In 1977, Heublein sent in a new management team to redirect KFC's strategy. A "back-to-the-basics" strategy was immediately implemented. New unit construction was discontinued until existing restaurants could be upgraded and operating problems eliminated. Restaurants were refurbished, an emphasis was placed on cleanliness and service, marginal products were eliminated, and product consistency was reestablished. By 1982, KFC had succeeded in establishing a successful strategic focus and was again aggressively building new units.

R. J. Reynolds Industries, Inc.

In 1982, R. J. Reynolds Industries, Inc. (RJR), merged Heublein into a wholly owned subsidiary. The merger with Heublein represented part of RJR's overall corporate strategy of diversifying into unrelated businesses, including energy, transportation, food, and restaurants. RJR's objective was to reduce its dependence on the tobacco industry, which had driven RJR sales since its founding in North Carolina in 1875. Sales of cigarettes and tobacco products, while profitable, were declining because of reduced consumption in the United States. This was mainly the result of an increased awareness among Americans about the negative health consequences of smoking.

RJR had no more experience in the restaurant business than did Heublein. However, it decided to take a hands-off approach to managing KFC. Whereas Heublein had installed its own top management at KFC headquarters, RJR left KFC management largely intact, believing that existing KFC managers were better qualified to operate KFC's businesses than were its own managers. In doing so, RJR avoided many of the operating problems that plagued Heublein. This strategy paid off for RJR as KFC continued to expand aggressively and profitably under RJR ownership. In 1985, RJR acquired Nabisco Corporation for $4.9 billion. Nabisco sold a variety of well-known cookies, crackers, cereals, confectioneries, snacks, and other grocery products. The merger with Nabisco represented a decision by RJR to concentrate its diversification efforts on the consumer foods industry. It subsequently divested many of its nonconsumer food businesses. RJR sold KFC to PepsiCo, Inc., one year later.

PEPSICO, INC.

Corporate Strategy

PepsiCo, Inc., was formed in 1965 with the merger of the Pepsi-Cola Co. and Frito-Lay, Inc. The merger of these companies created one of the largest consumer products companies in the United States. Pepsi-Cola's traditional business was the sale of soft drink concentrates to licensed independent and company-owned bottlers that manufactured, sold, and distributed Pepsi-Cola soft drinks. Pepsi-Cola's best known trademarks were Pepsi-Cola, Diet Pepsi, Mountain Dew, and Slice. Frito-Lay manufactured and sold a variety of snack foods, including Fritos Corn Chips, Lay's Potato Chips, Ruffles Potato Chips, Doritos, Tostitos Tortilla Chips, and Chee-tos Cheese Flavored Snacks. PepsiCo quickly embarked on an aggressive acquisition program similar to that pursued by RJR during the 1980s, buying a number of companies in areas unrelated to its major businesses. Acquisitions included North American Van Lines, Wilson Sporting Goods, and Lee Way Motor Freight. However, success in operating these businesses failed to live up to expectations, mainly because the management skills required to operate these businesses lay outside of PepsiCo's area of expertise.

Poor performance in these businesses led then-chairman and chief executive officer Don Kendall to restructure PepsiCo's operations in 1984. First, businesses that did not support Pepsi-Co's consumer product orientation, such as North American Van Lines, Wilson Sporting Goods, and Lee Way Motor Freight, were divested. Second, PepsiCo's foreign bottling operations were sold to local businesspeople who better understood the culture and business environment in their respective countries. Third, Kendall reorganized PepsiCo along three lines: soft drinks, snack foods, and restaurants.

Restaurant Business and Acquisition of KFC

PepsiCo first entered the restaurant business in 1977 when it acquired Pizza Hut's 3200-unit restaurant system. Taco Bell was merged into a division of PepsiCo in 1978. The restaurant business completed PepsiCo's consumer product orientation. The marketing of fast food followed many of the same patterns as the marketing of soft drinks and snack foods. Therefore, PepsiCo believed that its management skills could be easily transferred among its three business segments. This was compatible with PepsiCo's practice of frequently moving managers among its business units as a way of developing future top executives. PepsiCo's restaurant chains also provided an additional outlet for the sale of Pepsi soft drinks. Pepsi-Cola soft drinks and fast-food products also could be marketed together in the same television and radio segments, thereby providing higher returns for each advertising dollar. To complete its diversification into the restaurant segment, PepsiCo acquired Kentucky Fried Chicken Corporation from RJR-Nabisco for $841 million in 1986. The acquisition of KFC gave PepsiCo the leading market share in chicken (KFC), pizza (Pizza Hut), and Mexican food (Taco Bell), three of the four largest and fastest-growing segments within the U.S. fast-food industry.

Management

Following the acquisition by PepsiCo, KFC's relationship with its parent company underwent dramatic changes. RJR had operated KFC as a semiautonomous unit, satisfied that KFC management understood the fast-food business better than they. In contrast, PepsiCo acquired KFC in order to complement its already strong presence in the fast-food market. Rather than allowing KFC to operate autonomously, PepsiCo undertook sweeping changes. These changes included negotiating a new franchise contract to give PepsiCo more control over its franchisees, reducing staff in order to cut costs, and replacing KFC managers with its own. In 1987, a rumor spread through KFC's headquarters in

Louisville that the new personnel manager, who had just relocated from PepsiCo's headquarters in New York, was overheard saying that "there will be no more home grown tomatoes in this organization."

Such statements by PepsiCo personnel, uncertainties created by several restructurings that led to layoffs throughout the KFC organization, the replacement of KFC personnel with PepsiCo managers, and conflicts between KFC and PepsiCo's corporate cultures created a morale problem within KFC. KFC's culture was built largely on Colonel Sanders' laid-back approach to management. Employees enjoyed relatively good employment stability and security. Over the years, a strong loyalty had been created among KFC employees and franchisees, mainly because of the efforts of Colonel Sanders to provide for his employees' benefits, pension, and other nonincome needs. In addition, the southern environment of Louisville resulted in a friendly, relaxed atmosphere at KFC's corporate offices. This corporate culture was left essentially unchanged during the Heublein and RJR years.

In stark contrast to KFC, Pepsi-Co's culture was characterized by a strong emphasis on performance. Top performers expected to move up through the ranks quickly. PepsiCo used its KFC, Pizza Hut, Taco Bell, Frito Lay, and Pepsi-Cola divisions as training grounds for its top managers, rotating its best managers through its five divisions on average every 2 years. This practice created immense pressure on managers to continuously demonstrate their managerial prowess within short periods, in order to maximize their potential for promotion. This practice also left many KFC managers with the feeling that they had few career opportunities with the new company. One PepsiCo manager commented, "You may have performed well last year, but if you don't perform well this year, you're gone, and there are 100 ambitious guys with Ivy League MBAs at PepsiCo who would love to take your position." An unwanted effect of this performance-driven culture was that employee loyalty often was lost, and turnover tended to be higher than in other companies.

Kyle Craig, president of KFC's U.S. operations, was asked about KFC's relationship with its corporate parent. He commented:

The KFC culture is an interesting one because I think it was dominated by a lot of KFC folks, many of whom have been around since the days of the Colonel. Many of those people were very

intimidated by the PepsiCo culture, which is a very high performance, high accountability, highly driven culture. People were concerned about whether they would succeed in the new culture. Like many companies, we have had a couple of downsizings which further made people nervous. Today, there are fewer old KFC people around and I think to some degree people have seen that the PepsiCo culture can drive some pretty positive results. I also think the PepsiCo people who have worked with KFC have modified their cultural values somewhat and they can see that there were a lot of benefits in the old KFC culture.

PepsiCo pushes its companies to perform strongly, but whenever there is a slip in performance, it increases the culture gap between PepsiCo and KFC. I have been involved in two downsizings over which I have been the chief architect. They have been probably the two most gut-wrenching experiences of my career. Because you know you're dealing with peoples' lives and their families, these changes can be emotional if you care about the people in your organization. However, I do fundamentally believe that your first obligation is to the entire organization.

A second problem for PepsiCo was its poor relationship with KFC franchisees. A month after becoming president and chief executive officer in 1989, John Cranor addressed KFC's franchisees in Louisville in order to explain the details of the new franchise contract. This was the first contract change in 13 years. It gave PepsiCo greater power to take over weak franchises, relocate restaurants, and make changes in existing restaurants. In addition, restaurants would no longer be protected from competition from new KFC units, and it gave PepsiCo the right to raise royalty fees on existing restaurants as contracts came up for renewal. After Cranor finished his address, there was an uproar among the attending franchisees, who jumped to their feet to protest the changes. The franchisees had long been accustomed to relatively little interference from management in their day-to-day operations (a tradition begun by Colonel Sanders). This type of interference, of course, was a strong part of PepsiCo's philosophy of demanding change. KFC's franchise association later sued PepsiCo over the new contract. The contract remained unresolved until 1996, when the most objectionable parts of the contract were removed by KFC's new president and CEO, David Novak. A new contract was ratified by KFC's franchisees in 1997.

PepsiCo's Divestiture of KFC, Pizza Hut, and Taco Bell

PepsiCo's strategy of diversifying into three distinct but related markets—soft drinks, snack foods, and fast-food restaurants—created one of the world's largest consumer products companies and a portfolio of some of the world's most recognizable brands. Between 1990 and 1996, PepsiCo grew at an annual rate of over 10 percent, surpassing $31 billion in sales in 1996. However, PepsiCo's sales growth masked troubles in its fast-food businesses. Operating margins (profit as a percent of sales) at Pepsi-Cola and Frito Lay averaged 12 and 17 percent between 1990 and 1996, respectively. During the same period, margins at KFC, Pizza Hut, and Taco Bell fell from an average of over 8 percent in 1990 to a little more than 4 percent in 1996. Declining margins in the fast-food chains reflected increasing maturity in the U.S. fast-food industry, more intense competition among U.S. fast-food competitors, and the aging of KFC and Pizza Hut's restaurant base. As a result, PepsiCo's restaurant chains absorbed nearly one-half of PepsiCo's annual capital spending during the 1990s. However,

they generated less than one-third of PepsiCo's cash flows. Therefore, cash was diverted from PepsiCo's soft drink and snack food businesses to its restaurant businesses. This reduced PepsiCo's return on assets, made it more difficult to compete effectively with Coca-Cola, and hurt its stock price. In 1997, PepsiCo spun off its restaurant businesses into a new company called Tricon Global Restaurants, Inc. (see Exhibit A). The new company was based in KFC's headquarters in Louisville, Kentucky. PepsiCo's objective was to reposition itself as a packaged goods company, to strengthen its balance sheet, and to create more consistent earning growth. PepsiCo received a one-time distribution from Tricon of $4.7 billion, $3.7 billion of which was used to pay off short-term debt. The balance was earmarked for stock repurchases.

FAST-FOOD INDUSTRY

According to the National Restaurant Association (NRA), food-service sales topped $320 billion for the approximately 500,000 restaurants and other food outlets making up the U.S. restaurant industry in 1997. The NRA estimated that sales in the fast-food segment of the food service industry grew 5.2 percent to $104 billion, up from $98 billion in

EXHIBIT A

Tricon Global Restaurants, Inc.—Organizational Chart (1998)

Tricon Global Restaurants, Inc.
Corporate Offices
(Louisville, Kentucky)
Andrall Pearson, Chairman and CEO
David Novak, Vice Chairman and President

Kentucky Fried Chicken Corporation
(Louisville, Kentucky)
Jeffrey Moody, Chief Concept Officer
Charles Rawley, Chief Operating Officer

Pizza Hut, U.S.A.
(Dallas, Texas)
Michael Rawlings, President & CCO
Aylwin Lewis, Chief Operating Officer

Taco Bell Corp.
(Irvine, California)
Peter Waller, President & CCO
Thomas Davin, Chief Operating Officer

Tricon Restaurants International
(Dallas, Texas)
Peter Bassi, President

1996. This marked the fourth consecutive year that fast-food sales either matched or exceeded sales in full-service restaurants, which grew 4.1 percent to $104 billion in 1997. The growth in fast-food sales reflected the long, gradual change in the restaurant industry from an industry once dominated by independently operated sit-down restaurants to an industry fast becoming dominated by fast-food restaurant chains. The U.S. restaurant industry as a whole grew by approximately 4.2 percent in 1997.

Major Fast-Food Segments

Six major business segments made up the fast-food segment of the food service industry. Sales data for the leading restaurant chains in each segment are shown in Exhibit B. Most striking is the dominance of McDonald's, which had sales of over $16 billion in 1996. This represented 16.6 percent of U.S. fast-food sales, or nearly 22 percent of sales among the nation's top 30 fast-food chains. Sales at McDonald's restaurants average $1.3 million per year, compared with about $820,000 for the average U.S. fast-food restaurant. Tricon Global Restaurants (KFC, Pizza Hut, and Taco Bell) had U.S. sales of $13.4 billion in 1996. This represented 13.6 percent of U.S. fast-food sales and 17.9 percent of the top 30 fast-food chains.

Sandwich chains made up the largest segment of the fast-food market. McDonald's controlled 35 percent of the sandwich segment, while Burger King ran a distant second with a 15.6 percent market share. Competition had become particularly intense within the sandwich segment as the U.S. fast-food market became more saturated. In order to increase sales, chains turned to new products to win customers away from other sandwich chains, introduced products traditionally offered by non-sandwich chains (such as pizzas, fried chicken, and tacos), streamlined their menus, and upgraded product quality. Burger King recently introduced its Big King, a direct clone of the Big Mac. McDonald's quickly retaliated by introducing its Big 'n Tasty, a direct clone of the Whopper. Wendy's introduced chicken pita sandwiches, and Taco Bell introduced sandwiches called "wraps," breads stuffed with various fillings. Hardee's successfully introduced fried chicken in most of its restaurants. In addition to new products, chains lowered pricing, improved customer service, cobranded with other fast-food chains, and established restaurants in nontraditional

locations (e.g., McDonald's installed restaurants in Wal-Mart stores across the country) to beef up sales.

The second largest fast-food segment was dinner houses, dominated by Red Lobster, Applebee's, Olive Garden, and Chili's. Between 1988 and 1996, dinner houses increased their share of the fast-food market from 8 to over 13 percent. This increase came mainly at the expense of grilled buffet chains, such as Ponderosa, Sizzler, and Western Sizzlin'. The market share of steak houses fell from 6 percent in 1988 to under 4 percent in 1996. The rise of dinner houses during the 1990s was partially the result of an aging and wealthier population that increasingly demanded higher-quality food in more upscale settings. However, rapid construction of new restaurants, especially among relative newcomers, such as Romano's Macaroni Grill, Lone Star Steakhouse, and Outback Steakhouse, resulted in overcapacity within the dinner house segment. This reduced per-restaurant sales and further intensified competition. Eight of the sixteen largest dinner houses posted growth rates in excess of 10 percent in 1996. Romano's Macaroni Grill, Lone Star Steakhouse, Chili's, Outback Steakhouse, Applebee's, Red Robin, Fuddruckers, and Ruby Tuesday grew at rates of 82, 41, 32, 27, 23, 14, 11, and 10 percent, respectively.

The third largest fast-food segment was pizza, long dominated by Pizza Hut. While Pizza Hut controlled over 46 percent of the pizza segment in 1996, its market share has slowly eroded because of intense competition and its aging restaurant base. Domino's Pizza and Papa John's Pizza have been particularly successful. Little Caesars is the only pizza chain to remain predominantly a take-out chain, although it recently began home delivery. However, its policy of charging customers $1 per delivery damaged its perception among consumers as a high-value pizza chain. Home delivery, successfully introduced by Domino's and Pizza Hut, was a driving force for success among the market leaders during the 1970s and 1980s. However, the success of home delivery drove competitors to look for new methods of increasing their customer bases. Pizza chains diversified into nonpizza items (e.g., chicken wings at Domino's, Italian cheese bread at Little Caesars, and stuffed crust pizza at Pizza Hut), developed nontraditional items (e.g., airport kiosks and college campuses), offered special promotions, and offered new pizza variations with

EXHIBIT B
....
Leading U.S. Fast-Food Chains (Ranked by 1996 Sales, $000s)

Sandwich Chains	Sales	Share	Family Restaurants	Sales	Share
McDonald's	16,370	35.0%	Denny's	1,850	21.2%
Burger King	7,300	15.6%	Shoney's	1,220	14.0%
Taco Bell	4,575	9.8%	Big Boy	945	10.8%
Wendy's	4,360	9.3%	Int'l House of Pancakes	797	9.1%
Hardee's	3,055	6.5%	Cracker Barrel	734	8.4%
Subway	2,700	5.8%	Perkins	678	7.8%
Arby's	1,867	4.0%	Friendly's	597	6.8%
Dairy Queen	1,225	2.6%	Bob Evans	575	6.6%
Jack-in-the-Box	1,207	2.6%	Waffle House	525	6.0%
Sonic Drive-In	985	2.1%	Coco's	278	3.2%
Carl's Jr.	648	1.4%	Steak 'n Shake	275	3.2%
Other chains	2,454	5.2%	Village Inn	246	2.8%
Total	46,745	100.0%	Total	8,719	100.0%

Dinner Houses	Sales	Share	Pizza Chains	Sales	Share
Red Lobster	1,810	15.7%	Pizza Hut	4,927	46.4%
Applebee's	1,523	13.2%	Domino's Pizza	2,300	21.7%
Olive Garden	1,280	11.1%	Little Caesars	1,425	13.4%
Chili's	1,242	10.7%	Papa John's	619	5.8%
Outback Steakhouse	1,017	8.8%	Sbarros	400	3.8%
T.G.I. Friday's	935	8.1%	Round Table Pizza	385	3.6%
Ruby Tuesday	545	4.7%	Chuck E. Cheese's	293	2.8%
Lone Star Steakhouse	460	4.0%	Godfather's Pizza	266	2.5%
Bennigan's	458	4.0%	Total	10,614	100.0%
Romano's Macaroni Grill	344	3.0%			
Other dinner houses	1,942	16.8%			
Total	11,557	100.0%			

Grilled Buffet Chains	Sales	Share	Chicken Chains	Sales	Share
Golden Corral	711	22.8%	KFC	3,900	57.1%
Ponderosa	680	21.8%	Boston Market	1,167	17.1%
Ryan's	604	19.4%	Popeye's Chicken	666	9.7%
Sizzler	540	17.3%	Chick-fil-A	570	8.3%
Western Sizzlin'	332	10.3%	Church's Chicken	529	7.7%
Quincy's	259	8.3%	Total	6,832	100.0%
Total	3,116	100.0%			

Source: Nation's Restaurant News.

an emphasis on high-quality ingredients (e.g., Roma Herb and Garlic Crunch pizza at Domino's and Buffalo Chicken Pizza at Round Table Pizza).

Chicken Segment

KFC continued to dominate the chicken segment, with 1997 sales of $4 billion (see Exhibit C). Its nearest competitor, Boston Market, was second with sales of $1.2 billion. KFC operated 5120 restaurants in the United States in 1998, eight fewer restaurants than in 1993. Rather than building new restaurants in the already saturated U.S. market, KFC focused on building restaurants abroad. In the United States, KFC focused on closing unprofitable restaurants, upgrading existing restaurants with new exterior signage, and improving product quality. The strategy paid off. While overall U.S. sales during the last 10 years remained flat, annual sales per unit increased steadily in 8 of the last 9 years.

Despite KFC's continued dominance within the chicken segment, it has lost market share to Boston Market, a new restaurant chain emphasizing roasted rather than fried chicken. Boston Market has successfully created the image of an upscale deli offering healthy, "home style" alternatives to fried chicken and other "fast foods." It has broadened its menu beyond rotisserie chicken to include ham, turkey, meat loaf, chicken pot pie, and deli sandwiches. In order to minimize its image as a fast-food restaurant, it has refused to put drive-thrus in its restaurants and has established most of its

EXHIBIT C

Top U.S. Chicken Chains

Sales ($ M)	1992	1993	1994	1995	1996	1997	Growth Rate (%)
KFC	3,400	3,400	3,500	3,700	3,900	4,000	3.3
Boston Market	43	147	371	754	1,100	1,197	94.5
Popeye's	545	569	614	660	677	727	5.9
Chick-fil-A	356	396	451	502	570	671	11.9
Church's	414	440	465	501	526	574	6.8
Total	4,758	4,952	5,401	6,118	6,772	7,170	8.5
U.S. restaurants							
KFC	5,089	5,128	5,149	5,142	5,108	5,120	0.1
Boston Market	83	217	534	829	1,087	1,166	69.6
Popeye's	769	769	853	889	894	949	4.3
Chick-fil-A	487	545	534	825	717	762	9.0
Church's	944	932	937	953	989	1,070	2.5
Total	7,372	7,591	8,007	8,638	8,795	9,067	4.2
Sales per unit ($000s)							
KFC	668	663	680	720	764	781	3.2
Boston Market	518	677	695	910	1,012	1,027	14.7
Popeye's	709	740	720	743	757	767	1.6
Chick-fil-A	731	727	845	608	795	881	3.8
Church's	439	472	496	526	531	537	4.1
Total	645	782	782	782	782	782	3.9

Source: Tricon Global Restaurants, Inc., *1997 Annual Report;* Boston Chicken, Inc., *1997 Annual Report;* Chick-fil-A, corporate headquarters, Atlanta; AFC Enterprises, Inc., *1997 Annual Report.*

units in outside shopping malls rather than in free-standing units at intersections so characteristic of other fast-food restaurants.

In 1993, KFC introduced its own rotisserie chicken, called Rotisserie Gold, to combat Boston Market. However, it quickly learned that its customer base was considerably different from that of Boston Market's. KFC's customers liked KFC chicken despite the fact that it was fried. In addition, customers did not respond well to the concept of buying whole chickens for take-out. They preferred instead to buy chicken by the piece. KFC withdrew its rotisserie chicken in 1996 and introduced a new line of roasted chicken called Tender Roast, which could be sold by the piece and mixed with its Original Recipe and Extra Crispy Chicken.

Other major competitors within the chicken segment included Popeye's Famous Fried Chicken and Church's Chicken (both subsidiaries of AFC Enterprises in Atlanta), Chick-fil-A, Bojangle's, El Pollo Loco, Grandy's, Kenny Rogers Roasters, Mrs. Winner's, and Pudgie's. Both Church's and Popeye's had similar strategies—to compete head on with other "fried chicken" chains. Unlike KFC, neither chain offered rotisserie chicken, and nonfried chicken products were limited. Chick-fil-A focused exclusively on pressure-cooked and char-grilled skinless chicken breast sandwiches, which it served to customers in sit-down restaurants located predominantly in shopping malls. As many malls added food courts, often consisting of up to 15 fast-food units competing side by side, shopping malls became less enthusiastic about allocating separate store space to food chains. Therefore, in order to complement its existing restaurant base in shopping malls. Chick-fil-A began to open smaller units in shopping mall food courts, hospitals, and colleges. It also opened free-standing units in selected locations.

Demographic Trends

A number of demographic and societal trends contributed to increased demand for food prepared away from home. Because of the high divorce rate in the United States and the fact that people married later in life, single-person households represented about 25 percent of all U.S. households, up from 17 percent in 1970. This increased the number of individuals choosing to eat out rather than eat at home. The number of married women working outside the home also has increased dramatically during the last 25 years. About 59 percent of all married women have careers. According to the Conference Board, 64 percent of all married households will be double-income families by 2000. About 80 percent of households headed by individuals between the ages of 25 and 44 (both married and unmarried) will be double-income. Greater numbers of working women increased family incomes. According to *Restaurants & Institutions* magazine, more than one-third of all households had incomes of at least $50,000 in 1996. About 8 percent of all households had annual incomes over $100,000. The combination of higher numbers of dual-career families and rising incomes meant that fewer families had time to prepare food at home. According to Standard & Poor's *Industry Surveys,* Americans spent 55 percent of their food dollars at restaurants in 1995, up from 34 percent in 1970.

Fast-food restaurant chains met these demographic and societal changes by expanding their restaurant bases. However, by the early 1990s, the growth of traditional free-standing restaurants slowed as the U.S. market became saturated. The major exception was dinner houses, which continued to proliferate in response to Americans' increased passion for beef. Since 1990, the U.S. population has grown at an average annual rate of about 1 percent and reached 270 million people in 1997. Rising immigration since 1990 dramatically altered the ethnic makeup of the U.S. population. According to the Bureau of the Census, Americans born outside the United States made up 10 percent of the population in 1997. About 40 percent were Hispanic, while 24 percent were Asian. Nearly 30 percent of Americans born outside the United States arrived since 1990. As a result of these trends, restaurant chains expanded their menus to appeal to the different ethnic tastes of consumers, expanded into nontraditional locations such as department stores and airports, and made food more available through home delivery and take-out service.

Industry Consolidation and Mergers and Acquisitions

Lower growth in the U.S. fast-food market intensified competition for market share among restaurant chains and led to consolidation, primarily through mergers and acquisitions, during the mid-1990s. Many restaurant chains found that market share could be increased more quickly and cheaply by acquiring an existing company rather than building new units. In addition, fixed costs could be spread across a larger number of restaurants. This raised operating margins and gave companies an opportunity to build market share by lowering prices. An expanded restaurant base also gave companies greater purchasing power over supplies. In 1990, Grand Metropolitan, a British company, purchased Pillsbury Co. for $5.7 billion. Included in the purchase was Pillsbury's Burger King chain. Grand Met strengthened the franchise by upgrading existing restaurants and eliminated several levels of management in order to cut costs. This gave Burger King a long-needed boost in improving its position against McDonald's, its largest competitor. In 1988, Grand Met had purchased Wienerwald, a West German chicken chain, and the Spaghetti Factory, a Swiss chain.

Perhaps most important to KFC was Hardee's acquisition of 600 Roy Rogers restaurants from Marriott Corporation in 1990. Hardee's converted a large number of these restaurants to Hardee's units and introduced "Roy Rogers" fried chicken to its menu. By 1993, Hardee's had introduced fried chicken into most of its U.S. restaurants. Hardee's was unlikely to destroy the customer loyalty that KFC long enjoyed. However, it did cut into KFC's sales, because it was able to offer consumers a widened menu selection that appealed to a variety of family eating preferences. In 1997, Hardee's parent company, Imasco, Ltd., sold Hardee's to CKE Restaurants, Inc. CKE owned Carl's Jr., Rally's Hamburgers, and Checker's Drive-In. Boston Chicken, Inc., acquired Harry's Farmers Market, an Atlanta grocer that sold fresh quality prepared meals. The acquisition was designed to help Boston Chicken develop distribution beyond its Boston Market restaurants. AFC Enterprises, which operated Popeye's and Church's, acquired Chesapeake Bagel Bakery of McLean, Virginia, in order to diversify away from fried chicken and to strengthen its balance sheet.

The effect of these and other recent mergers and acquisitions on the industry was powerful. The top 10 restaurant companies controlled almost 60 percent of fast-food sales in the United States. The consolidation of a number of fast-food chains within larger, financially more powerful parent companies gave restaurant chains strong financial and managerial resources that could be used to compete against small chains in the industry.

International Quick-Service Market

Because of the aggressive pace of new restaurant construction in the United States during the 1970s and 1980s, opportunities to expand domestically through new restaurant construction in the 1990s were limited. Restaurant chains that did build new restaurants found that the higher cost of purchasing prime locations resulted in immense pressure to increase annual per-restaurant sales in order to cover higher initial investment costs. Many restaurants began to expand into international markets as an alternative to continued domestic expansion. In contrast to the U.S. market, international markets offered large customer bases with comparatively little competition. However, only a few U.S. restaurant chains had defined aggressive strategies for penetrating international markets by 1998.

Three restaurant chains that had established aggressive international strategies were McDonald's, KFC, and Pizza Hut. McDonald's operated the largest number of restaurants. In 1998, it operated 23,132 restaurants in 109 countries (10,409 restaurants were located outside the United States). In comparison, KFC, Pizza Hut, and Taco Bell together operated 29,712 restaurants in 79, 88, and 17 countries, respectively (9126 restaurants were located outside the United States). Of these four chains, KFC operated the greatest percentage of its restaurants (50 percent) outside the United States. McDonald's, Pizza Hut, and Taco Bell operated 45, 31, and 2 percent of their units outside the United States. KFC opened its first restaurant outside the United States in the late 1950s. By the time PepsiCo acquired KFC in 1986, KFC was already operating restaurants in 55 countries. KFC's early expansion abroad, its strong brand name, and its managerial experience in international markets gave it a strong competitive advantage vis-à-vis other fast-food chains that were investing abroad for the first time.

Exhibit D shows *Hotels'* 1994 list of the world's 30 largest fast-food restaurant chains (*Hotels* discontinued reporting these data after 1994). Seventeen of the 30 largest restaurant chains (ranked by number of units) were headquartered in the United States. There were a number of possible explana-

EXHIBIT D
....
The World's 30 Largest Fast-Food Chains (Year-End 1993, Ranked by Number of Countries)

	Franchise	Location	Units	Countries
1	Pizza Hut	Dallas, Texas	10,433	80
2	McDonald's	Oakbrook, Illinois	23,132	70
3	KFC	Louisville, Kentucky	9,033	68
4	Burger King	Miami, Florida	7,121	50
5	Baskin Robbins	Glendale, California	3,557	49
6	Wendy's	Dublin, Ohio	4,168	38
7	Domino's Pizza	Ann Arbor, Michigan	5,238	36
8	TCBY	Little Rock, Arkansas	7,474	22
9	Dairy Queen	Minneapolis, Minnesota	5,471	21
10	Dunkin' Donuts	Randolph, Massachusetts	3,691	21
11	Taco Bell	Irvine, California	4,921	20
12	Arby's	Fort Lauderdale, Florida	2,670	18
13	Subway Sandwiches	Milford, Connecticut	8,477	15
14	Sizzler International	Los Angeles, California	681	14
15	Hardee's	Rocky Mount, North Carolina	4,060	12
16	Little Caesar's	Detroit, Michigan	4,600	12
17	Popeye's Chicken	Atlanta, Georgia	813	12
18	Denny's	Spartanburg, South Carolina	1,515	10
19	A&W Restaurants	Livonia, Michigan	707	9
20	T.G.I. Friday's	Minneapolis, Minnesota	273	8
21	Orange Julius	Minneapolis, Minnesota	480	7
22	Church's Fried Chicken	Atlanta, Georgia	1,079	6
23	Long John Silver's	Lexington, Kentucky	1,464	5
24	Carl's Jr.	Anaheim, California	649	4
25	Loterria	Tokyo, Japan	795	4
26	Mos Burger	Tokyo, Japan	1,263	4
27	Skylark	Tokyo, Japan	1,000	4
28	Jack in the Box	San Diego, California	1,172	3
29	Quick Restaurants	Berchem, Belgium	876	3
30	Taco Time	Eugene, Oregon	300	3

Source: Hotels, May 1994; 1994 PepsiCo, Inc., Annual Report.

tions for the relative scarcity of fast-food restaurant chains outside the United States. First, the United States represented the largest consumer market in the world, accounting for over one-fifth of the world's gross domestic product (GDP). Therefore, the United States was the strategic focus of the largest restaurant chains. Second, Americans were more quick to accept the fast-food concept. Many other cultures had strong culinary traditions that were difficult to break down. Europeans, for example, had histories of frequenting more midscale

restaurants, where they spent hours in a formal setting enjoying native dishes and beverages. While KFC was again building restaurants in Germany by the late 1980s, it previously failed to penetrate the German market, because Germans were not accustomed to take-out food or to ordering food over the counter. McDonald's had greater success penetrating the German market because it made a number of changes in its menu and operating procedures in order to better appeal to German culture. For example, German beer was served in all of McDonald's German restaurants. KFC had more success in Asia and Latin America, where chicken was a traditional dish.

Aside from cultural factors, international business carried risks not present in the U.S. market. Long distances between headquarters and foreign franchises often made it difficult to control the quality of individual restaurants. Large distances also caused servicing and support problems. Transportation and other resource costs were higher than in the domestic market. In addition, time, cultural, and language differences increased communication and operational problems. Therefore, it was reasonable to expect U.S. restaurant chains to expand domestically as long as they achieved corporate profit and growth objectives. As the U.S. market became saturated and companies gained expertise in international markets, more companies could be expected to turn to profitable international markets as a means of expanding restaurant bases and increasing sales, profits, and market share.

KENTUCKY FRIED CHICKEN CORPORATION

KFC's worldwide sales, which included sales of both company-owned and franchised restaurants,

grew to $8.0 billion in 1997. U.S. sales grew 2.6 percent over 1996 and accounted for about one-half of KFC's sales worldwide. KFC's U.S. share of the chicken segment fell 1.8 points to 55.8 percent (see Exhibit E). This marked the sixth consecutive year that KFC sustained a decline in market share. KFC's market share has fallen by 16.3 points since 1988, when it held a 72.1 percent market share. Boston Market, which established its first restaurant in 1992, increased its market share from 0 to 16.7 percent over the same period. On the surface, it appeared as though Boston Market's market-share gain was achieved by taking customers away from KFC. However, KFC's sales growth has remained fairly stable and constant over the last 10 years. Boston Market's success was largely a function of its appeal to consumers who did not regularly patronize KFC or other chicken chains that sold fried chicken. By appealing to a market niche that was previously unsatisfied, Boston Market was able to expand the existing consumer base within the chicken segment of the fast-food industry.

Refranchising Strategy

The relatively low growth rate in sales in KFC's domestic restaurants during the 1992–1997 period was largely the result of KFC's decision in 1993 to

EXHIBIT E

Top U.S. Chicken Chains—Market Share (%)

	KFC	Boston Market	Popeye's	Chick-fil-A	Church's	Total
1988	72.1	0.0	12.0	5.8	10.1	100.0
1989	70.8	0.0	12.0	6.2	11.0	100.0
1990	71.3	0.0	12.3	6.6	9.8	100.0
1991	72.7	0.0	11.4	7.0	8.9	100.0
1992	71.5	0.9	11.4	7.5	8.7	100.0
1993	68.7	3.0	11.4	8.0	8.9	100.0
1994	64.8	6.9	11.3	8.4	8.6	100.0
1995	60.5	12.3	10.8	8.2	8.2	100.0
1996	57.6	16.2	10.0	8.4	7.8	100.0
1997	55.8	16.7	10.1	9.4	8.0	100.0
Change	−16.3	16.7	−1.9	3.6	−2.1	0.0

Source: Nation's Restaurant News.

begin selling company-owned restaurants to franchisees. When Colonel Sanders began to expand the Kentucky Fried Chicken system in the late 1950s, he established KFC as a system of independent franchisees. This was done in order to minimize his involvement in the operations of individual restaurants and to concentrate on the things he enjoyed the most—cooking, product development, and public relations. This resulted in a fiercely loyal and independent group of franchises. PepsiCo's strategy when it acquired KFC in 1986 was to integrate KFC's operations in the PepsiCo system, in order to take advantage of operational, financial, and marketing synergies. However, such a strategy demanded that PepsiCo become more involved in decisions over franchise operations, menu offerings, restaurant management, finance, and marketing. This was met by resistance with KFC franchises, who fiercely opposed increased control by the corporate parent. One method for PepsiCo to deal with this conflict was to expand through company-owned restaurants rather than through franchising. PepsiCo also used its strong cash flows to buy back unprofitable franchised

restaurants, which could then be converted into company-owned restaurants. In 1986, company-owned restaurants made up 26 percent of KFC's U.S. restaurant base. By 1993, they made up about 40 percent (see Exhibit F).

While company-owned restaurants were relatively easier to control compared with franchises, they also required higher levels of investment. This meant that high levels of cash were diverted from PepsiCo's soft drink and snack food businesses into its restaurant businesses. However, the fast-food industry delivered lower returns than the soft drink and snack foods industries. Consequently, increased investment in KFC, Pizza Hut, and Taco Bell had a negative effect on PepsiCo's consolidated return on assets. By 1993, investors became concerned that PepsiCo's return on assets did not match returns delivered by Coca-Cola. In order to shore up its return on assets, PepsiCo decided to reduce the number of company-owned restaurants by selling them back to franchisees. This strategy lowered overall company sales but also lowered the amount of cash tied up in fixed assets, provided PepsiCo with one-time cash flow benefits from initial fees

EXHIBIT F

KFC Restaurant Count (U.S.)

	Company-Owned	% Total	Franchised/Licensed	% Total	Total
1986	1,246	26.4	3,474	73.6	4,720
1987	1,250	26.0	3,564	74.0	4,814
1988	1,262	25.8	3,637	74.2	4,899
1989	1,364	27.5	3,597	72.5	4,961
1990	1,389	27.7	3,617	72.3	5,006
1991	1,836	36.6	3,186	63.4	5,022
1992	1,960	38.8	3,095	61.2	5,055
1993	2,014	39.5	3,080	60.5	5,094
1994	2,005	39.2	3,110	60.8	5,115
1995	2,026	39.4	3,111	60.6	5,137
1996	1,932	37.8	3,176	62.2	5,108
1997	1,850	36.1	3,270	63.9	5,120
1986–1993 Compounded annual growth rate					
	7.1%		−1.7%		1.1%
1993–1997 Compounded annual growth rate					
	−2.1%		1.5%		0.1%

Source: Tricon Global Restaurants, Inc., 1997 Annual Report; PepsiCo, Inc., Annual Reports, 1994, 1995, 1996, 1997.

charged to franchisees, and generated an annual stream of franchise royalties. Tricon Global continued this strategy after the spin off in 1997.

Marketing Strategy

During the 1980s, consumers began to demand healthier foods, greater variety, and better service in a variety of nontraditional locations such as grocery stores, restaurants, airports, and outdoor events. This forced fast-food chains to expand menu offerings and to investigate nontraditional distribution channels and restaurant designs. Families also demanded greater value in the food they bought away from home. This increased pressure on fast-food chains to reduce prices and to lower operating costs in order to maintain profit margins.

Many of KFC's problems during the late 1980s surrounded its limited menu and inability to quickly bring new products to market. The popularity of its Original Recipe Chicken allowed KFC to expand without significant competition from other chicken competitors through the 1980s. As a result, new product introductions were never an important element of KFC's overall strategy. One of the most serious setbacks suffered by KFC came in 1989 as KFC prepared to add a chicken sandwich to its menu. While KFC was still experimenting with its chicken sandwich, McDonald's test marketed its McChicken sandwich in the Louisville market. Shortly thereafter, it rolled out the McChicken sandwich nationally. By beating KFC to the market, McDonald's was able to develop strong consumer awareness for its sandwich. This significantly increased KFC's cost of developing awareness of its own sandwich, which KFC introduced several months later. KFC eventually withdrew its sandwich because of low sales.

In 1991, KFC changed its logo in the United States from Kentucky Fried Chicken to KFC in order to reduce its image as a fried chicken chain. It continued to use the Kentucky Fried Chicken name internationally. It then responded to consumer demands for greater variety by introducing several products that would serve as alternatives to its Original Recipe Chicken. These included Oriental Wings, Popcorn Chicken, and Honey BBQ Chicken. It also introduced a dessert menu that included a variety of pies and cookies. In 1993, it rolled out Rotisserie Chicken and began to promote its lunch and dinner buffet. The buffet, which

included 30 items, was introduced into almost 1600 KFC restaurants in 27 states by year-end. In 1998, KFC sold three types of chicken—Original Recipe and Extra Crispy (fried chicken) and Tender Roast (roasted chicken).

One of KFC's most aggressive strategies was the introduction of its Neighborhood Program. By mid-1993, almost 500 company-owned restaurants in New York, Chicago, Philadelphia, Washington, D.C., St. Louis, Los Angeles, Houston, and Dallas had been outfitted with special menu offerings to appeal exclusively to the black community. Menus were beefed up with side dishes such as greens, macaroni and cheese, peach cobbler, sweet-potato pie, and red beans and rice. In addition, restaurant employees wore African-inspired uniforms. The introduction of the Neighborhood Program increased sales by 5 to 30 percent in restaurants appealing directly to the black community. KFC followed by testing Hispanic-oriented restaurants in the Miami area, offering side dishes such as fried plantains, flan, and tres leches.

One of KFC's most significant problems in the U.S. market was that overcapacity made expansion of free-standing restaurants difficult. Fewer sites were available for new construction, and those sites, because of their increased cost, were driving profit margins down. Therefore, KFC initiated a new three-pronged distribution strategy. First, it focused on building smaller restaurants in nontraditional outlets such as airports, shopping malls, universities, and hospitals. Second, it experimented with home delivery. Home delivery was introduced in the Nashville and Albuquerque markets in 1994. By 1998, home delivery was offered in 365 U.S. restaurants. Other nontraditional distribution outlets being tested included units offering drive-thru and carry-out service only, snack shops in cafeterias, scaled-down outlets for supermarkets, and mobile units that could be transported to outdoor concerts and fairs.

A third focus of KFC's distribution strategy was restaurant cobranding, primarily with its sister chain, Taco Bell. By 1997, 349 KFC restaurants had added Taco Bell to their menus and displayed both the KFC and Taco Bell logos outside their restaurants. Cobranding gave KFC the opportunity to expand its business dayparts. While about two-thirds of KFC's business was dinner, Taco Bell's primary business occurred at lunch. By combining the two concepts in the same unit, sales at individual restaurants could be increased significantly. KFC believed that there were opportunities to sell the Taco Bell concept in over 3900 of its U.S. restaurants.

Operating Efficiencies

As pressure continued to build on fast-food chains to limit price increases, restaurant chains searched for ways to reduce overhead and other operating costs in order to improve profit margins. In 1989, KFC reorganized its U.S. operations to eliminate overhead costs and increase efficiency. Included in this reorganization was a revision of KFC's crew training programs and operating standards. A renewed emphasis was placed on improving customer service, cleaner restaurants, faster and friendlier service, and continued high-quality products. In 1992, KFC reorganized its middle-management ranks, eliminating 250 of the 1500 management positions at KFC's corporate headquarters. More responsibility was assigned to restaurant franchisees and marketing managers and pay was more closely aligned with customer service and restaurant performance. In 1997, Tricon Global signed a 5-year agreement with PepsiCo Food Systems (which was later sold by PepsiCo to AmeriServe Food Distributors) to distribute food and supplies to Tricon's 29,712 KFC, Pizza Hut, and Taco Bell units. This provided KFC with significant opportunities to benefit from economies of scale in distribution.

INTERNATIONAL OPERATIONS

Much of the early success of the top 10 fast-food chains was the result of aggressive building strategies. Chains were able to discourage competition by building in low-population areas that could only support a single fast-food chain. McDonald's was particularly successful because it was able to quickly expand into small towns across the United States, thereby preempting other fast-food chains. It was equally important to beat a competitor into more largely populated areas where location was of prime importance. KFC's early entry into international markets placed it in a strong position to benefit from international expansion as the U.S. market became saturated. In 1997, 50 percent of KFC's restaurants were located outside the United

States. While 364 new restaurants were opened outside the United States in 1997, only 12 new restaurants were added to the U.S. system. Most of KFC's international expansion was through franchises, although some restaurants were licensed to operators or jointly operated with a local partner. Expansion through franchising was an important strategy for penetrating international markets because franchises were owned and operated by local entrepreneurs with a deeper understanding of local language, culture, and customs, as well as local law, financial markets, and marketing characteristics. Franchising was particularly important for expansion into smaller countries such as the Dominican Republic, Grenada, Bermuda, and Suriname, which could only support a single restaurant. Costs were prohibitively high for KFC to operate company-owned restaurants in these smaller markets. Of the 5117 KFC restaurants located outside the United States in 1997, 68 percent were franchised, while 22 percent were company-owned, and 10 percent were licensed restaurants or joint ventures.

In larger markets such as Japan, China, and Mexico, there was a stronger emphasis on building company-owned restaurants. By coordinating purchasing, recruiting and training, financing, and advertising, fixed costs could be spread over a large number of restaurants, and lower prices on products and services could be negotiated. KFC also was better able to control product and service quality. In order to take advantage of economies of scale, Tricon Global Restaurants managed all the international units of its KFC, Pizza Hut, and Taco Bell chains through its Tricon International Division located in Dallas, Texas. This enabled Tricon Global Restaurants to leverage its strong advertising expertise, international experience, and restaurant management experience across all its KFC, Pizza Hut, and Taco Bell restaurants.

Latin-American Strategy

KFC's primary market presence in Latin America during the 1980s was in Mexico, Puerto Rico, and the Caribbean. KFC established subsidiaries in Mexico and Puerto Rico, from which it coordinated the construction and operation of company-owned restaurants. A third subsidiary in Venezuela was closed because of the high fixed costs associated with running the small subsidiary. Franchises were used to penetrate other countries in the Caribbean whose market size prevented KFC from profitably operating company restaurants. KFC relied exclusively on the operation of company-owned restaurants in Mexico through 1989. While franchising was popular in the United States, it was virtually unknown in Mexico until 1990, mainly because of the absence of a law protecting patents, information, and technology transferred to the Mexican franchise. In addition, royalties were limited. As a result, most fast-food chains opted to invest in Mexico using company-owned units.

In 1990, Mexico enacted a new law that provided for the protection of technology transferred into Mexico. Under the new legislation, the franchisor and franchisee were free to set their own terms. Royalties also were allowed under the new law. Royalties were taxed at a 15 percent rate on technology assistance and knowhow and 35 percent for other royalty categories. The advent of the new franchise law resulted in an explosion of franchises in fast-food, services, hotels, and retail outlets. In 1992, franchises had an estimated $750 million in sales in over 1200 outlets throughout Mexico. Prior to passage of Mexico's franchise law, KFC limited its Mexican operations primarily to Mexico City, Guadalajara, and Monterrey. This enabled KFC to better coordinate operations and minimize costs of distribution to individual restaurants. The new franchise law gave KFC and other fast-food chains the opportunity to expand their restaurant bases more quickly into more rural regions of Mexico, where responsibility for management could be handled by local franchisees.

After 1990, KFC altered its Latin American strategy in a number of ways. First, it opened 29 franchises in Mexico to complement its company-owned restaurant base. It then expanded its company-owned restaurants into the Virgin Islands and reestablished a subsidiary in Venezuela. Third, it expanded its franchise operations into South America. In 1990, a franchise was opened in Chile, and in 1993, a franchise was opened in Brazil. Franchises were subsequently established in Colombia, Ecuador, Panama, and Peru, among other South American countries. A fourth subsidiary was established in Brazil, in order to develop company-owned restaurants. Brazil was Latin America's largest economy and McDonald's primary Latin American investment location. By June 1998, KFC operated 438 restaurants in 32 Latin American countries. By comparison, McDonald's operated 1091 restaurants in 28 countries in Latin America.

Exhibit G shows the Latin American operations of KFC and McDonald's. KFC's early entry into Latin America during the 1970s gave it a leadership position in Mexico and the Caribbean. It also had gained an edge in Ecuador and Peru, countries where McDonald's had not yet developed a strong presence. McDonald's focused its Latin American investment in Brazil, Argentina, and Uruguay, countries were KFC had little or no presence. McDonald's also was strong in Venezuela. Both KFC and McDonald's were strong in Chile, Colombia, Panama, and Puerto Rico.

Economic Environment and the Mexican Market

Mexico was KFC's strongest market in Latin America. While McDonald's had aggressively established restaurants in Mexico since 1990, KFC retained the leading market share. Because of its close proximity to the United States, Mexico was an attractive location for U.S. trade and investment. Mexico's population of 98 million people was approximately one-third as large as the United States and represented a large market for U.S. companies. In comparison, Canada's population of 30.3 million people was only one-third as large as Mexico's. Mexico's close proximity to the United States meant that transportation costs between the United States and Mexico were significantly lower than to Europe or Asia. This increased the competitiveness of U.S. goods in comparison with European and Asian goods, which had to be transported to Mexico across the Atlantic or Pacific Ocean at substantial cost. The United States was, in fact, Mexico's largest trading partner. Over 75 percent of Mexico's imports came from the United States, while 84 percent of its exports were to the United States (see Exhibit H). Many U.S. firms invested in Mexico in order to take advantage of lower wage rates. By producing goods in Mexico, U.S. goods could be shipped back into the United States for sale or shipped to third markets at lower cost.

While the U.S. market was critically important to Mexico, Mexico still represented a small percentage of overall U.S. trade and investment. Since the early 1900s, the portion of U.S. exports to Latin America had declined. Instead, U.S. exports to Canada and Asia, where economic growth out-

EXHIBIT G
....
Latin American Restaurant Count: KFC and McDonald's (as of December 31, 1997)

	KFC Company Restaurants	KFC Franchised Restaurants	KFC Total Restaurants	McDonald's
Argentina	—	—	—	131
Bahamas	—	10	10	3
Barbados	—	7	7	—
Brazil	6	2	8	480
Chile	—	29	29	27
Columbia	—	19	19	18
Costa Rica	—	5	5	19
Ecuador	—	18	18	2
Jamaica	—	17	17	7
Mexico	128	29	157	131
Panama	—	21	21	20
Peru	—	17	17	5
Puerto Rico & Virgin Islands	67	—	67	115
Trinidad & Tobago	—	27	27	3
Uruguay	—	—	—	18
Venezuela	6	—	6	53
Other	—	30	30	59
Total	207	231	438	1,091

Source: Tricon Global Restaurants, Inc.; McDonald's, 1997 Annual Report.

EXHIBIT H
....
Mexico's Major Trading Partners—% Total Exports and Imports

	1992		1994		1996	
	Exports	Imports	Exports	Imports	Exports	Imports
U.S.	81.1	71.3	85.3	71.8	84.0	75.6
Japan	1.7	4.9	1.6	4.8	1.4	4.4
Germany	1.1	4.0	0.6	3.9	0.7	3.5
Canada	2.2	1.7	2.4	2.0	1.2	1.9
Italy	0.3	1.6	0.1	1.3	1.2	1.1
Brazil	0.9	1.8	0.6	1.5	0.9	0.8
Spain	2.7	1.4	1.4	1.7	1.0	0.7
Other	10.0	13.3	8.0	13.0	9.6	12.0
% Total	100.0	100.0	100.0	100.0	100.0	100.0
Value ($M)	46,196	62,129	60,882	79,346	95,991	89,464

Source: International Monetary Fund, *Direction of Trade Statistics Yearbook,* 1997.

paced growth in Mexico, increased more quickly. Canada was the largest importer of U.S. goods. Japan was the largest exporter of goods to the United States, with Canada a close second. U.S. investment in Mexico also was small, mainly because of past government restrictions on foreign investment. Most U.S. foreign investment was in Europe, Canada, and Asia.

The lack of U.S. investment in and trade with Mexico during this century was mainly the result of Mexico's long history of restricting trade and foreign direct investment. The Institutional Revolutionary Party (PRI), which came to power in Mexico during the 1930s, had historically pursued protectionist economic policies in order to shield Mexico's economy from foreign competition. Many industries were government-owned or controlled, and many Mexican companies focused on producing goods for the domestic market without much attention to building export markets. High tariffs and other trade barriers restricted imports into Mexico, and foreign ownership of assets in Mexico was largely prohibited or heavily restricted.

Additionally, a dictatorial and entrenched government bureaucracy, corrupt labor unions, and a long tradition of anti-Americanism among many government officials and intellectuals reduced the motivation of U.S. firms for investing in Mexico. The nationalization of Mexico's banks in 1982 led to higher real interest rates and lower investor confidence. Afterward, the Mexican government battled high inflation, high interest rates, labor unrest, and lost consumer purchasing power. Investor confidence in Mexico, however, improved after 1988, when Carlos Salinas de Gortari was elected president. Following his election, Salinas embarked on an ambitious restructuring of the Mexican economy. He initiated policies to strengthen the free-market components of the economy, lowered top marginal tax rates to 36 percent (down from 60 percent in 1986), and eliminated many restrictions on foreign investment. Foreign firms can now buy up to 100 percent of the equity in many Mexican firms. Foreign ownership of Mexican firms was previously limited to 49 percent.

Privatization

The privatization of government-owned companies came to symbolize the restructuring of Mexico's economy. In 1990, legislation was passed to privatize all government-run banks. By the end of 1992, over 800 of some 1200 government-owned companies had been sold, including Mexicana and AeroMexico, the two largest airline companies in Mexico, and Mexico's 18 major banks. However, more than 350 companies remained under government ownership. These represented a significant portion of the assets owned by the state at the start of 1988. Therefore, the sale of government-owned companies, in terms of asset value, was moderate. A large percentage of the remaining government-owned assets were controlled by government-run companies in certain strategic industries such as steel, electricity, and petroleum. These industries had long been protected by government ownership. As a result, additional privatization of government-owned enterprises until 1993 was limited. However, in 1993, President Salinas opened up the electricity sector to independent power producers, and Petroleos Mexicanos (Pemex), the state-run petrochemical monopoly, initiated a program to sell off many of its nonstrategic assets to private and foreign buyers.

North American Free Trade Agreement (NAFTA)

Prior to 1989, Mexico levied high tariffs on most imported goods. In addition, many other goods were subjected to quotas, licensing requirements, and other nontariff trade barriers. In 1986, Mexico joined the General Agreement on Tariffs and Trade (GATT), a world trade organization designed to eliminate barriers to trade among member nations. As a member of GATT, Mexico was obligated to apply its system of tariffs to all member nations equally. As a result of its membership in GATT, Mexico dropped tariff rates on a variety of imported goods. In addition, import license requirements were dropped for all but 300 imported items. During President Salinas' administration, tariffs were reduced from an average of 100 percent on most items to an average of 11 percent.

On January 1, 1994, the North American Free Trade Agreement (NAFTA) went into effect. The passage of NAFTA, which included Canada, the United States, and Mexico, created a trading bloc with a larger population and gross domestic product than the European Union. All tariffs on goods traded among the three countries were scheduled to be phased out. NAFTA was expected to be particularly beneficial for Mexican exporters because reduced tariffs made their goods more competitive in the United States compared with goods exported to the United States from other countries. In 1995, one year after NAFTA went into effect, Mexico posted its first balance of trade surplus in 6 years. Part of this surplus was attributed to reduced tariffs resulting from the NAFTA agreement. However, the peso crisis of 1995, which lowered the value of the peso against the dollar, increased the price of goods imported into Mexico and lowered the price of Mexican products exported to the United States. Therefore, it was still too early to assess the full effects of the NAFTA agreement. (See Exhibit I for further details.)

Foreign Exchange and the Mexican Peso Crisis of 1995

Between 1982 and 1991, a two-tiered exchange-rate system was in force in Mexico. The system consisted of a controlled rate and a free-market rate. A controlled rate was used for imports, foreign debt payments, and conversion of export proceeds. An estimated 70 percent of all foreign transactions were covered by the controlled rate. A free-market rate was used for other transactions. In 1989, President Salinas instituted a policy of allowing the peso to depreciate against the dollar by one peso per day. The result was a grossly overvalued peso. This lowered the price of imports and led to an increase in imports of over 23 percent in 1989. At the same time, Mexican exports became less competitive on world markets.

In 1991, the controlled rate was abolished and replaced with an official free rate. In order to limit the range of fluctuations in the value of the peso, the government fixed the rate at which it would buy or sell pesos. A floor (the maximum price at which pesos could be purchased) was established at Ps 3056.20 and remained fixed. A ceiling (the maximum price at which the peso could be sold) was established at Ps 3056.40 and allowed to move upward by Ps 0.20 per day. This was later revised to Ps 0.40 per day. In 1993, a new currency, called the *new peso,* was issued with three fewer zeros. The new currency was designed to simplify transactions and to reduce the cost of printing currency.

When Ernesto Zedillo became Mexico's president in December 1994, one of his objectives was to continue the stability of prices, wages, and exchange rates achieved by ex-President Carlos

EXHIBIT I
Selected Economic Data for Canada, the United States, and Mexico

Annual Change (%)	1993	1994	1995	1996	1997
GDP growth					
Canada	3.3	4.8	5.5	4.1	—
United States	4.9	5.8	4.8	5.1	5.9
Mexico	21.4	13.3	29.4	38.2	—
Real GDP growth					
Canada	2.2	4.1	2.3	1.2	—
United States	2.2	3.5	2.0	2.8	3.8
Mexico	2.0	4.5	−6.2	5.1	—
Inflation					
Canada	1.9	0.2	2.2	1.5	1.6
United States	3.0	2.5	2.8	2.9	2.4
Mexico	9.7	6.9	35.0	34.4	20.6
Depreciation against $U.S.					
Canada (C$)	4.2	6.0	−2.7	0.3	4.3
Mexico (NP)	−0.3	71.4	43.5	2.7	3.6

Source: International Monetary Fund, *International Financial Statistics,* 1998.

Salinas de Gortari during his 5-year tenure as president. However, Salinas had achieved stability largely on the basis of price, wage, and foreign-exchange controls. While giving the appearance of stability, an overvalued peso continued to encourage imports, which exacerbated Mexico's balance of trade deficit. Mexico's government continued to use foreign reserves to finance its balance of trade deficits. According to the Banco de Mexico, foreign currency reserves fell from $24 billion in January 1994 to $5.5 billion in January 1995. Anticipating a devaluation of the peso, investors began to move capital into U.S. dollar investments. In order to relieve pressure on the peso, Zedillo announced on December 19, 1994 that the peso would be allowed to depreciate by an additional 15 percent per year against the dollar compared with the maximum allowable depreciation of 4 percent per year established during the Salinas administration. Within 2 days, continued pressure on the peso forced Zedillo to allow the peso to float freely against the dollar. By mid-January 1995, the peso had lost 35 percent of its value against the dollar, and the Mexican stock market plunged 20 percent. By November 1995, the peso had depreciated from 3.1 pesos per dollar to 7.3 pesos per dollar.

The continued devaluation of the peso resulted in higher import prices, higher inflation, destabilization within the stock market, and higher interest rates. Mexico struggled to pay its dollar-based debts. In order to thwart a possible default by Mexico, the U.S. government, International Monetary Fund, and World Bank pledged $24.9 billion in emergency loans. Zedillo then announced an emergency economic package called the *pacto* that included reduced government spending, increased sales of government-run businesses, and a freeze on wage increases.

Labor Problems

One of KFC's primary concerns in Mexico was the stability of labor markets. Labor was relatively plentiful, and wages were low. However, much of the workforce was relatively unskilled. KFC benefited from lower labor costs, but labor unrest, low job retention, high absenteeism, and poor punctuality were significant problems. Absenteeism and punctuality were partially cultural. However, problems with worker retention and labor unrest also were the result of workers' frustration over the loss of

their purchasing power due to inflation and government controls on wage increases. Absenteeism remained high at approximately 8 to 14 percent of the labor force, though it was declining because of job security fears. Turnover continued to be a problem and ran at between 5 and 12 percent per month. Therefore, employee screening and internal training were important issues for firms investing in Mexico.

Higher inflation and the government's freeze on wage increases led to a dramatic decline in disposable income after 1994. Further, a slowdown in business activity, brought about by higher interest rates and lower government spending, led many businesses to lay off workers. By the end of 1995, an estimated 1 million jobs had been lost as a result of the economic crisis sparked by the peso devaluation. As a result, industry groups within Mexico called for new labor laws giving them more freedom to hire and fire employees and increased flexibility to hire part-time rather than full-time workers.

RISKS AND OPPORTUNITIES

The peso crisis of 1995 and resulting recession in Mexico left KFC managers with a great deal of uncertainty regarding Mexico's economic and political future. KFC had benefited from economic stability between 1988 and 1994. Inflation was brought down, the peso was relatively stable, labor unrest was relatively calm, and Mexico's new franchise law had enabled KFC to expand into rural areas using franchises rather than company-owned restaurants. By the end of 1995, KFC had built 29 franchises in Mexico. The foreign-exchange crisis of 1995 had severe implications for U.S. firms operating in Mexico. The devaluation of the peso resulted in higher inflation and capital flight out of Mexico. Capital flight reduced the supply of capital and led to higher interest rates. In order to reduce inflation, Mexico's government instituted an austerity program that resulted in lower disposable income, higher unemployment, and lower demand for products and services.

Another problem was Mexico's failure to reduce restrictions on U.S. and Canadian investment in a timely fashion. Many U.S. firms experienced problems getting required approvals for new ventures from the Mexican government. A good example was United Parcel Service (UPS), which sought government approval to use large trucks for deliveries in Mexico. Approvals were delayed, forcing UPS to use smaller trucks. This put UPS at a competitive disadvantage vis-à-vis Mexican companies. In many cases, UPS was forced to subcontract delivery work to Mexican companies that were allowed to use larger, more cost-efficient trucks. Other U.S. companies such as Bell Atlantic and TRW faced similar problems. TRW, which signed a joint-venture agreement with a Mexican partner, had to wait 15 months longer than anticipated before the Mexican government released rules on how it could receive credit data from banks. TRW claimed that the Mexican government slowed the approval process in order to placate several large Mexican banks.

A final area of concern for KFC was increased political turmoil in Mexico during the last several years. On January 1, 1994, the day NAFTA went into effect, rebels (descendants of the Mayans) rioted in the southern Mexican province of Chiapas on the Guatemalan border. After 4 days of fighting, Mexican troops had driven the rebels out of several towns earlier seized by the rebels. Around 150—mostly rebels—were killed. The uprising symbolized many of the fears of the poor in Mexico. While ex-President Salinas' economic programs had increased economic growth and wealth in Mexico, many of Mexico's poorest felt that they had not benefited. Many of Mexico's farmers, faced with lower tariffs on imported agricultural goods from the United States, felt that they might be driven out of business because of lower-priced imports. Therefore, social unrest among Mexico's Indians, farmers, and the poor could potentially unravel much of the economic success achieved in Mexico during the last 5 years.

Further, ex-President Salinas' hand-picked successor for president was assassinated in early 1994 while campaigning in Tijuana. The assassin was a 23-year-old mechanic and migrant worker believed to be affiliated with a dissident group upset with the PRI's economic reforms. The possible existence of a dissident group raised fears of political violence in the future. The PRI quickly named Ernesto Zedillo, a 42-year-old economist with little political experience, as their new presidential candidate. Zedillo was elected president in December 1994. Political unrest was not limited to Mexican officials and companies. In October 1994, between 30 and 40 masked men attacked a McDonald's restaurant in the tourist section of Mexico City to show their opposition to California's Proposition 187, which would have curtailed benefits to illegal aliens (primarily from Mexico). The men threw cash registers to the floor, cracked them open, smashed windows, overturned tables, and spray-painted slogans on the walls such as "No to Fascism" and "Yankee Go Home."

KFC faced a variety of issues in Mexico and Latin America in 1998. Prior to 1995, few restaurants had been opened in South America. However, KFC was now aggressively building new restaurants in the region. KFC halted openings of franchised restaurants in Mexico, and all restaurants opened since 1995 were company-owned. KFC was more aggressively building restaurants in South America, which remained largely unpenetrated by KFC through 1995. Of greatest importance was Brazil, where McDonald's had already established a strong market-share position. Brazil was Latin America's largest economy and a largely untapped market for KFC. The danger in ignoring Mexico was that a conservative investment strategy could jeopardize its market-share lead over McDonald's in a large market where KFC long enjoyed enormous popularity.

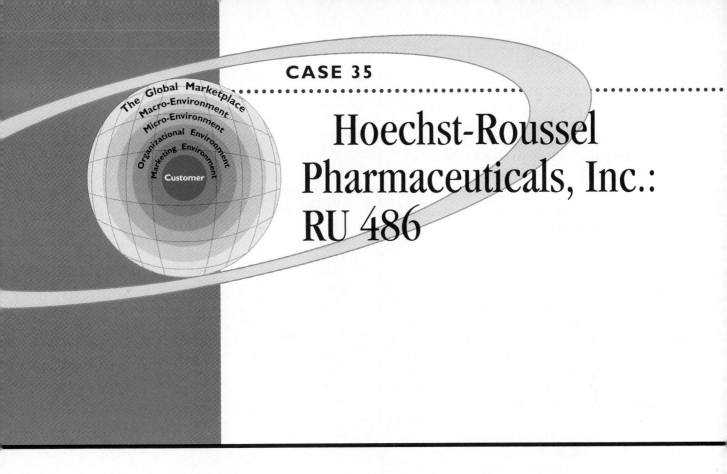

CASE 35

Hoechst-Roussel Pharmaceuticals, Inc.: RU 486

This case was prepared by Jan Willem Bol and David W. Rosenthal of Miami University.

In July 1991, the management of Hoechst-Roussel Pharmaceuticals had as yet made no public announcement as to their plans for marketing RU 486 in the United States. The product had been available for testing in very limited quantities, but the steps necessary to bring the new drug to market had not yet been taken.

This case was originally written by Laura Case, Gail Geisler, Chris Peacock, Sherri Thieman, and Elisabeth Wolf. Originally presented at a meeting of the North American Case Research Association, November 1991. This case was written from public sources, without the cooperation of management, solely for the purpose of stimulating student discussion. All incidents and individuals are real, although some names have been changed at the request of the individuals. All other rights reserved jointly to the author and the North American Case Research Association (NACRA). Copyright © 1993 by the *Case Research Journal* and Jan Willem Bol.

RU 486 was a chemical compound that was commonly referred to as "the morning after pill" in the press. The compound had the effect of preventing a fertilized egg from attaching to the uterine wall or ensuring that a previously attached egg would detach. The pill had been thoroughly tested in several European countries with significant success.

RU 486 had become the focus for a great amount of publicity, press coverage, and industry speculation. The compound also was the center of a series of U.S. Senate hearings. Activists, both in support of and in opposition to RU 486, had sought to influence the company's course of action since the product's inception.

Pharmaceutical industry observers suggested that the company was not marketing the product aggressively in order to "maintain a low profile." It was clear that the Hoechst-Roussel management had an ongoing and very complex issue to resolve as to the disposition of RU 486.

THE DRUG INDUSTRY

The drug industry consisted of three primary components: biologic products, medicinals and botanicals, and pharmaceutical preparations. Pharmaceuticals were generally classified into one of two broad groups:

- Ethical pharmaceuticals—drugs available only through a physician's prescription

- Over-the-counter (OTC) drugs, both generic and proprietary (drugs sold without prescription)

The pharmaceutical industry had grown steadily since 1970 as a result of rising health care costs throughout the world and continuing product innovations from manufacturers. From 1970 to 1980, worldwide sales grew at an average of 10 to 12 percent in real dollars. In the 1980s, growth was slightly lower, about 7 percent, and real growth rates were expected to decrease slightly during the early 1990s, the projected rate being from 6 to 8 percent. The growth rates varied considerably among countries and product categories. An estimated breakdown of 1987 worldwide sales of ethical pharmaceuticals by country or region, with projected growth rates, is shown in Exhibit A.

Size and Composition

In the late 1980s, the industry was not particularly concentrated; the top four firms comprised slightly less than 10 percent of the market. Within specific product categories, however, there were much higher concentration levels, the top four competitors often sharing 40 to 70 percent of total sales. Exhibit B lists 1987 pharmaceutical sales of the leading global pharmaceutical companies.

Research and Development

The overall health of the pharmaceutical industry was measured by the number of products it developed, the value of its exports, and the high level of its profits. These factors were, in turn, directly affected by the amount of dollars spent on research and development.

The U.S. drug industry spent some $6 billion on R&D in 1988, up from $5.4 billion in 1987 and $4.7 billion in 1986. As a percentage of sales, the drug

EXHIBIT A

Leading Pharmaceutical Markets

Country	1987 Sales U.S. Millions	1990–1995 Growth Potential
United States	23,979	Moderate
Japan	15,690	Moderate
Germany	6,527	Moderate
France	5,992	Moderate
China	4,890	Low
Italy	4,690	High
United Kingdom	3,370	Low
Canada	1,710	Moderate
South Korea	1,500	High
Spain	1,480	Moderate
India	1,400	High
Mexico	1,300	Declining
Brazil	1,180	Declining
Argentina	856	Declining
Australia	685	Moderate
Indonesia	590	Moderate
Others	33,200	High

Source: Thompson from Arthur D. Little Inc.

industry spent more on R&D than any other major industry group. In 1988, research accounted for more than 15 percent of revenues. Exhibit C lists research and development expenditures for some of the leading pharmaceutical companies.

The Outlook in 1991

There were a number of positive factors affecting the industry at the beginning of the 1990s. The demographic growth trend in the over-65 segment of the population presented both a larger and more demanding market. The nature of the pharmaceutical business tended to make sales and revenues recession-resistant. High and increasing profit margins tended to attract capital in order to support the ambitious R&D needs of the industry.

Not all conditions were positive. Pharmaceutical firms had been increasingly criticized for their drug pricing policies. Critics argued that relatively

EXHIBIT B
....
Twenty Leading Global Pharmaceutical Companies

Company	Country	1987 Sales, $US000
Merck & Co., Inc.	U.S.	$5,060,000
American Home Products Corp.	U.S.	5,020,000
Pfizer Inc.	U.S.	4,910,000
Hoechst Corp.	Germany	4,610,000
Abbott Laboratories	U.S.	4,380,000
Smithkline Beckman Corp.	U.S.	4,320,000
American Cyanamid Co.	U.S.	4,160,000
Eli Lilly & Co.	U.S.	3,640,000
Warner-Lambert Co.	U.S.	3,480,000
Schering Plough Co.	U.S.	2,690,000
Upjohn Co.	U.S.	2,520,000
Sterling Drug Inc.	U.S.	2,300,000
Squibb Corp.	U.S.	2,150,000
Schering Corp.	U.S.	1,900,000
E. R. Squibb & Sons Inc.	U.S.	1,800,000
Hoffman-LaRoche Inc.	Switzerland	1,500,000
Miles Inc.	U.S.	1,450,000
Glaxo Inc.	U.S.	937,000
Rorer Group Inc.	U.S.	928,000
A. H. Robins	U.S.	855,000

Source: Estimates based on various industry sources. The figures should be regarded as approximations due to differences in fiscal years of companies, and variations in data due to different definitions of pharmaceutical sales.

low manufacturing costs should be reflected in the pricing of drugs and that high profit levels proved their point. Generic (unbranded) drugs continued their trend of high growth, supplanting the higher-profit, proprietary segment of the market. Liability costs and the costs associated with compliance with increasingly complex and restrictive regulations continued to soar.

Drug companies in the United States were essentially free to price their products as they wished. This was contrary to the policies in many countries outside the United States, where pharmaceutical prices were strictly regulated by governmental agencies. However, as a result of the rapid increase of health care costs during the 1970s and 1980s, there was a movement toward a more restrictive pricing environment both at the state and federal levels. In order to make their operations more efficient and acquire economies of scale,

many companies had chosen to form alliances with other firms. A trend toward consolidation through merger and acquisition resulted.

The growth of the generic drug segment posed a significant problem to the industry because generic products were priced much lower than proprietary products. The price of a generic drug was often as much as 50 percent lower than the price of the corresponding proprietary drug. All 50 states had laws that permitted substitution of generic drugs for proprietary drugs. As a result, the generic drug market doubled in sales from 1983 to 1987.

Pharmaceutical companies faced extensive product liability risks associated with their products. This was especially true for "high risk" products such as vaccines and contraceptives. The cost of liability insurance to cover these adverse effects had forced many companies to coinsure or curtail

EXHIBIT C

....

Research and Development Expenditures (Sales in Millions of Dollars)

	1986		1987		1988	
Company	Sales	%	Sales	%	Sales	%
Abbot	$295	8	$361	8	$455	8
Bristol-Myers	311	8	342	8	394	7
Johnson & Johnson	521	7	617	8	674	7
Hoechst Group	395	10	540	10	608	10
Eli Lilly	420	13	466	13	541	13
Merck	480	12	566	11	669	11
Pfizer	336	7	401	8	473	9
Rorer Group	70	8	82	9	103	10
Schering-Plough	212	9	251	9	298	11
SmithKline	377	10	424	10	495	10
Squibb	163	9	221	10	294	11
Syntex	143	15	175	16	218	17
Upjohn	314	14	356	14	380	14
Warner-Lambert	202	7	232	7	259	7

Source: Annual Reports.

their research efforts in these areas. In 1991, liability insurance coverage for the manufacture and sale of contraceptives was in most cases impossible to obtain. As a result of this "insurance crunch," the industry had become polarized. Only small companies with few assets and large corporations with the ability to self-insure tended to market contraceptives.

The pharmaceutical industry's high profit levels and "heavy" expenditure on marketing make it a frequent target for attack by political figures and consumer advocates. Critics suggested that the pharmaceutical companies priced drugs so high that only wealthy patients could afford treatment. Marketing expenditures were blamed for "overprescribing," or the tendency for physicians to rely too heavily on drugs for treatment. Marketing also was blamed for hiding from physicians information regarding side effects and contraindications in order to boost sales.

Outpatient Drug Coverage

....

Regulation of health care played an important role in the pharmaceutical industry. Increasingly complex regulations both at the state and federal levels resulted in corresponding increases in costs of compliance. Further, the political nature of the regulatory system often resulted in uncertainty for the industry. For example, the outpatient drug coverage provision of the Medicare catastrophic health insurance bill was expected to have both a positive and negative impact on the U.S. market, with the overall impact uncertain. Scheduled to begin a 3-year phase-in period in 1991, the plan was to cover 50 percent of Medicare beneficiaries' approved drug expenditures, after an annual deductible of $600 was met. Although the new coverage was expected to expand the overall market, it also made the industry more dependent on the federal government, whose reimbursements were increasingly affected by cost constraints. Further, policies regarding other social issues, such as race or sex discrimination, abortion, and even environmental protection came into play for those health care facilities which dealt with Medicare recipients. The documentation necessary to show compliance with the relevant regulation was sure to result in increased costs for facilities. Pharmaceutical company managers were uncertain what effect such regulation would have on specific products.

HOECHST CELANESE

Hoechst Celanese was a wholly owned subsidiary of Hoechst AG of Frankfurt, Germany. Hoechst AG and its affiliates constituted the Hoechst Group, one of the world's largest multinational corporations, encompassing 250 companies in 120 nations. The Hoechst companies manufactured and conducted research on chemicals, fibers, plastics, dyes, pigments, and pharmaceuticals. The United States was the largest and fastest-growing segment for the Hoechst product lines and was often the key to establishing worldwide marketing capability.

Within its Life Sciences Group, Hoechst Celanese, in affiliation with Roussel-Uclaf (a French pharmaceutical company), provided leading products to the prescription drug markets in the United States. The division was referred to as Hoechst-Roussel Pharmaceuticals Incorporated (HRPI). Exhibit D lists the primary prescription drugs provided by HRPI to the United States health care market.

The company also marketed stool softeners and laxatives, including Doxidan and Surfak, directly to consumers, and was developing potential drugs for many conditions, including Alzheimer's disease, cardiovascular disease, some kinds of tumors, and dia-

betes. HRPI had not previously invested in research into contraceptives or abortion drugs.

ROUSSEL-UCLAF

Roussel-Uclaf, founded in Paris, France, was engaged in the manufacturing and marketing of chemical products for therapeutic and industrial use, perfumes, eyeglasses, and nutritional products. In addition, Roussel was one of the world's leading diversified pharmaceutical groups. Within its pharmaceutical group, Roussel poured its research dollars into a wide range of product categories, including antibiotics, diuretics, steroids, and laxatives.

Roussel employed 14,759 people, and its 72 subsidiaries yielded a total net income of over $84 million in 1988. Ownership was held by two groups: the German company Hoechst AG, with 54.5 percent of common stock, and the French government, with 36 percent.

In 1979, George Teutsch and Alain Belanger, chemists at Roussel-Uclaf, synthesized chemical variations on the basic steroid molecule. Some of the new chemicals blocked receptors for steroids, causing inhibition of the effects of the steroids, including the hormones involved in sexual reproduction. Because of the controversy surrounding birth control, Roussel had maintained a company policy not to develop drugs for the purpose of contracep-

EXHIBIT D

Hoechst-Roussel's Prescription Drugs

Drug Name	Description
Lasix (furosemide)	A widely prescribed diuretic.
Clarofan (cefotaxime)	One of the largest selling third-generation cephalosporin antibiotics used to treat infections.
Topicort (desoximetasone)	A steroid applied to the skin.
Streptasea (streptokinase)	A product used to dissolve clots in blood vessels, e.g., in the treatment of heart attack.
Trental (pentoxifylline)	Improves arterial blood flow, and is used to treat intermittent claudication (leg pain associated with arteriosclerosis).
Diabeta (glyburide)	An oral antidiabetic agent used in the treatment of non-insulin-dependent diabetes.

Source: Hoechst AG 1988 Annual Report.

tion or abortion and did not want to pursue research into the type of compounds that had been synthesized by Teutsch and Belanger. However, Dr. Etienne-Emile Baulieu, one of Roussel's research consultants, argued persuasively that such compounds represented a revolutionary breakthrough and might have many important uses other than those involved with reproduction, and Roussel continued its research. The research led directly to the discovery, by Dr. Baulieu, of RU 486, and Roussel began manufacturing the drug in the early 1980s.

HISTORY

The trade name for RU 486, a synthesized steroid compound, was Mifepristone. The company referred to the product as a "contragestive," something between a contraceptive and an abortifacient, and marketed it as an alternative to surgical abortion. Like birth control, it could prevent a fertilized egg from implanting on the uterine wall and developing. It could also ensure that an implanted egg "sloughed off" or detached, making the product more like a chemical abortion. Its use was primarily intended for first trimester pregnancies, because if taken up to 49 days after conception, it was 95 percent successful. In the office of the doctor or woman's health center, a woman would take a 600-mg dose of RU 486. She would return 2 days later for a prostaglandin injection or pill, which would result in a vaginal blood flow 2 to 5 days later that was comparable to that of a menstrual period and which lasted approximately 1 week. A follow-up visit to her doctor would then determine whether the abortion was complete and make sure the bleeding had been controlled. If the fertilized egg was not completely expelled, a surgical abortion could then be performed. Researchers believed that the success rate would approach 100 percent when dosage levels were more defined. A few patients did feel slight nausea and cramps. Complications were rare, but it was recommended that the drug be taken under a physician's care because of the potential for heavy bleeding or the failure to abort.

The drug was first offered to the French market in September of 1988. During the time it was on the market, 4000 women used the drug, reporting a 95.5 percent success rate. However, during this period strong protests and proposed worldwide boycotts of Hoechst products (Roussel's German parent company) brought about the removal of RU 486 from the market and all distribution channels. Dr. Baulieu said the company's decision was "morally scandalous." At this point the French government, which owned 36 percent of Roussel-Uclaf, intervened. Two days after the pill's removal, Health Minister Claude Evin ordered RU 486 back into production and distribution in France, saying, "The drug is not just the property of Roussel-Uclaf, but of all women. I could not permit the abortion debate to deprive women of a product that represents medical progress." Since then, the product had been sold only to authorized clinics. Over 100 French women took the drug each day. Thus approximately 15 percent of all French abortions were conducted through the use of RU 486.

Because RU 486 triggered such strong emotion for and against its use, Roussel management was hesitant to make it available to the world. A Roussel researcher, Dr. Eduoard Sakiz, commented: "We just developed a compound, that's all, nothing else. To help the woman. . . . We are not in the middle of the abortion debate." Roussel held the patent to the compound, but willingly supplied it for investigations around the world.

The only U.S. research on RU 486 was a joint effort of the Population Council, a nonprofit research organization in New York City, and the University of Southern California. Early results showed a 73 percent efficacy rate. Shortly after the drug became legal in France, China was able to officially license the use of the drug and by 1991 was close to manufacturing the drug itself. In 1990, Roussel management decided to market RU 486 to Great Britain, Sweden, and Holland as well.

It was generally believed that groups opposed to abortion under any circumstances had been largely responsible for keeping the drug out of the United States. Similarly, interest in research on the drug in the United States had apparently been curtailed by the intimidating tactics of the antiabortion groups. No U.S. drug maker had sought a license from Roussel. However, other compounds, similar to RU 486, were in the process of development by pharmaceutical companies both in the United States and worldwide.

No long-term risks or effects had been found to result from continuous use of the drug, nor were any problems expected from its occasional use.

There was no information about how the drug might affect a fetus if the woman decided to continue her pregnancy after RU 486 failed, because the limited number of reported failures had all been followed by surgical abortions. Some studies reported that the drug seemed to suppress ovulation for 3 to 7 months after use. One medical journal did report that use of the drug created birth defects in rabbits, but the results could not be duplicated in rats or monkeys.

RU 486's primary function was obviously that of an abortifacient. It was thought that the drug was particularly beneficial for three segments of the population. First, it would be important in the developing nations, where many women lacked access to medical facilities and the anesthetics needed for surgical abortion. Second, it would be useful among teenagers, whose use of contraceptives was erratic at best. Third, it would be useful for women who for various reasons were unable to use other methods successfully.

Secondary markets were potentially available as well because RU 486 functioned by inhibiting progesterone. The drug could, therefore, be beneficial in the treatment of Cushing's disease, in which an overactive adrenal gland releases too much of a steroid similar to progesterone. The drug also could be used to treat types of cancer that depend on progesterone for growth, such as tumors of the breast and other cancers of the reproductive system and endometriosis (abnormal growth of uterine lining). In addition, RU 486 had potential for treatment of the nearly 80,000 women yearly who have ectopic pregnancies, a dangerous condition in which the egg develops outside the uterus.

In France, the availability of RU 486 was limited, and the product was used only under medical supervision. Because of these conditions the price was high, about $80 (U.S. dollars). Industry analysts believed that with larger markets and an increased production scale, the cost of the drug could be reduced in the United States. U.S. industry consultants believed that when drug companies identified the large profit potential associated with RU 486, U.S. interest in the drug would grow.

POLITICAL AND LEGAL ENVIRONMENT

The management of Hoechst-Roussel faced considerable problems with the introduction of RU 486 into the United States. The process of obtaining Food and Drug Administration (FDA) approval was not likely to begin without the vocal support of American women who saw the drug as an important means to achieve more personal and political control over their fertility. The process of satisfying FDA requirements was likely to require considerable time and expense. Despite criticisms, the FDA had shown little inclination to reduce the time required for licensing new drugs, and the politically sensitive aspects of RU 486 were unlikely to speed the process.

Although the approval process for RU 486 could have in theory been significantly shortened because of the test data already generated by foreign researchers, no American company had yet petitioned the FDA to even begin the process. The standards required before the FDA would approve a new drug were (1) safety for the recommended use and (2) substantial evidence of efficacy. The clinical trials and testing occurred in three phases. Statistically, of 20 drugs which entered clinical testing under the FDA, only 1 would ultimately be approved for the market. It frequently cost a pharmaceutical company up to $125 million and 15 years to move a contraceptive from the lab to approval for the market.

With RU 486, the FDA had apparently resolved to be even more restrictive than normal. Special policies and exceptions to their normal FDA rules had been enacted. Under normal circumstances the FDA allowed patients to ship certain unapproved drugs into the country if the drugs were to be used to treat life-threatening conditions. The agency refused to apply these rules to RU 486. FDA Commissioner Frank Young had written to a Congressional representative that the FDA would not permit RU 486 to be imported into the United States for personal use—for *any* reason.

The FDA did not, however, change an established rule that might permit RU 486 to be imported for the purpose of a "secondary use" such as the treatment of breast cancer. The FDA did not have jurisdiction to regulate the administration of a drug by a physician, so a doctor could theoretically prescribe the RU 486, which had been presumably imported for treatment of breast cancer, for the purpose of inducing abortions. However, the potential liability for a physician who chose to prescribe RU 486 in this manner was probably sufficient to render this possibility remote.

RU 486 was not without its advocates. The National Academy of Sciences recommended that RU 486 be marketed in the United States but also reported that for that to be possible, the FDA would have to streamline its stringent rules for the approval of new contraceptives. It also recommended that pharmaceutical companies be given federal protection from liability suits so they would be encouraged to reenter the contraceptive business.

If the federal government approved the pill, an individual state could not limit a doctor's decision to prescribe it. The fundamental tenet of the United States Supreme Court decision *Roe* v. *Wade* was that abortion in the first trimester should remain free from intrusive regulation by the state. Thus *Roe* v. *Wade* would permit U.S. use of RU 486 as an abortifacient to be administered under close medical supervision. The remote possibility of use of RU 486 as a monthly antifertility drug would also be well within abortion law, and perhaps would allow RU 486 to be treated under law as a contraceptive.

Paradoxically, some observers argued that the United States was most likely to witness the appearance of RU 486 if the *Roe* v. *Wade* decision were overturned and abortion again became illegal. It was suggested that a black market for the pill would evolve to meet the need for illegal abortions. Dr. Sheldon Siegel of the Rockefeller Foundation stated, "If there is a serious attempt to constrain further progress and further knowledge about RU 486, then it is likely that a black market manufacturer and supply system would develop."[1] The black-market scenario posed very serious health risks for women. Many could suffer side effects, especially in the absence of medical supervision. Still more frightening was the idea that women using the pill illegally would not have access to the backup of safe surgical abortion.

THE CONTRACEPTIVE INDUSTRY

As of 1991 there were nearly 6 million unwanted pregnancies each year in the United States, and as a result, there were 1.5 to 2 million abortions. Yearly, there were 500,000 pregnancy-related deaths and 200,000 of those were from improperly performed abortions.[2] Up to half of these unwanted pregnancies and deaths could have been prevented if women had more birth control options. In 1991, American contraceptive research had come to a virtual halt, causing the United States to fall far behind other countries in developing new techniques. In the early 1980s, eleven companies in the United States did research in the contraceptive field, but by 1991 only two were engaged in such studies. Political opposition and the possibility of large liability suits appeared to be the most important reasons for the decline in focus on these drugs.

In 1991 several "morning after" abortifacients had been approved by the FDA for use in the United States. These drugs, based on prostaglandins, which are powerful hormones that can cause serious side effects, were distributed only to hospitals approved by the manufacturer, the Upjohn Company. The drugs were only available by prescription and under the most controlled conditions. The FDA allowed the drugs to be used only for second trimester pregnancies. The drugs were neither advertised to the public nor promoted to physicians by company sales representatives. Likewise, samples of the drugs were not provided to the medical profession. Jessyl Bradford, spokeswoman for Upjohn, stated, "We believe that our commitment to provide a safe and effective alternative to saline and surgical procedures is a responsible one. However, we do not promote abortion. It is an individual decision, made in consultation with a physician. We make no effort to influence such decisions."[3]

The contraceptive market was relatively small, its value being about $1 billion yearly worldwide. Within this market, $700 million was accounted for by the use of oral contraceptives. There were, however, nearly 3 million women in the United States who used nonoral methods.[4] The profit margin on contraceptives was very high. To illustrate, the U.S. government, buying in bulk for shipment overseas, was able to buy a monthly supply of birth control pills for about 18 cents, whereas the average consumer paid about $12 a month. The leader in the contraceptive field was a company named Ortho, which sold contraceptive pills, diaphragms, spermicides, and other products for family planning (e.g., home pregnancy kits). Ortho was continuing to develop improved oral contraceptives that would provide better cycle control and have fewer side effects; however, as mentioned previously, the estimated cost of development of a contraceptive from the laboratory to the market was estimated at $125 million.

Although pro-life forces attributed the decline in contraceptive development in the United States to their efforts, companies and outside experts argued that the reduction was the result of three main factors: high research costs, relatively low potential profit, and the enormous risk that liability suits presented. Robert McDonough, spokesman for Upjohn Company, said, "[Upjohn] terminated its fertility research program in 1985 for two reasons. There was an adverse regulatory climate in the U.S.; it was increasingly difficult to get fertility drugs approved. And there was a litigious climate. . . . Litigation is terribly expensive, even if you win."[5]

In 1988, an $8.75 million judgment was passed against GD Searle in favor of a woman injured by the company's Copper-7 intrauterine device. Similarly, Dalkon Shield cases forced the AH Robbins Company into bankruptcy. In the late 1980s, AH Robbins was forced to establish a $615 million trust fund to compensate victims of IUD-caused pelvic infections and deaths. Such settlements made liability insurance for contraceptive manufacturers nearly impossible to obtain.

One of the few organizations in the United States that continued research on contraceptives was the Population Council, a nonprofit organization backed by the Rockefeller and Mellon foundations. The Population Council had been conducting U.S. studies on RU 486 on a license from the French developer. Additional support for contraceptive development was evident in proposed litigation that would provide $10 million for the "development, evaluation, and bringing to the marketplace of new improved contraceptive devices, drugs, and methods." If passed, the legislation would put the federal government into the contraceptive marketing business for the fist time.

TECHNICAL ISSUES

RU 486 acts as an antiprogesterone steroid. Progesterone is a hormone which allows a fertilized embryo to be implanted on the inner wall of the uterus. Progesterone also reduces the uterus's responsiveness to certain contractile agents that may aid in the expulsion of the embryo. Additionally,

progesterone helps the cervix to become firm and aids in the formation of a mucous plug which maintains the placental contents. All these steps are necessary for an embryo to properly develop into a fetus. Without progesterone, which initiates the chain of events, an embryo cannot mature.

RU 486 masks the effects of progesterone by binding to the normal receptors of the hormone and prohibiting a proper reaction. The embryo cannot adhere to the uterine lining, so the subsequent changes do not occur and the normal process of menstruation (shedding of the uterine wall) begins.

The Population Council sponsored two studies (1987 and 1988) at the University of Southern California that examined the efficacy of RU 486. The tests were all conducted on women within 49 days of their last menstrual cycle. In the 1987 study, 100 mg per day for 7 days was 73 percent effective and 50 mg per day was 50 percent effective. In the 1988 study, one 600-mg tablet was 90 percent effective.

The studies were conducted without prostaglandin, a compound which dramatically increases the effectiveness of RU 486. With prostaglandin, RU 486 was tested at 95.5 percent efficacy.

The general conclusions drawn from the Population Council research were that RU 486 was more effective at higher doses and that the earlier it was administered in the gestational period, the greater its efficacy.

OPPOSITION AND SUPPORT

The National Right to Life Committee of the United States played an important role in keeping RU 486 from being introduced in the United States. The group referred to RU 486 as the "death pill," claiming that a human life begins at conception and that RU 486 intervenes after conception. A former vice president of Students United for Life said in 1990:

> RU 486 is a poison just like cyanide or other poisons. Poisons are chemicals that kill human beings. . . . RU 486 is such a poison which kills the growing unborn human being.[6]

Antiabortionists also resisted the marketing of RU 486 because in clinical testing, women were required to agree to surgical abortions if the drug was unsuccessful. Pro-lifers also suggested that by simply taking a pill to end a pregnancy, a woman was evading the moral significance of the act. One antiabortion legislator, Republican Congressman from California Robert Dornan, wrote a letter to his colleagues in 1986 to gain support to curtail federal funding for the testing of the pill. He stated his concerns as follows:

> The proponents of abortion want to replace the guilt suffered by women who undergo abortion with the moral uncertainty of self-deception. Imagine with the Death Pill, the taking of a pre-born life will be as easy and as trivial as taking aspirin.

Pro-life groups reacted strongly and even violently to prevent the drug's introduction into the U.S. market. The U.S. Right to Life group began its campaign by pressuring the French company which originated the pill, Roussel-Uclaf. At one point, as a result of the efforts and the influence of this group, which included bomb threats on Roussel executives, the company temporarily discontinued its production of RU 486. Subsequently, the strategy of the group was focused on preventing the drug's introduction in the United States. The transfer of pressure to the U.S. domestic market occurred as a result of RU 486's expansion into the British and Chinese markets and the resultant fear that the United States was the next logical market for introduction.

Pro-life groups continued their letter-writing campaign to Roussel and extended the campaign to Roussel's parent company, Hoechst AG. Further, they threatened to boycott Hoechst's American subsidiary, Hoechst Celanese. The right-to-life campaign succeeded in getting Hoechst to place a "quarantine" on the drug, limiting its distribution to current markets.

Another strategy used by antiabortionists included putting pressure on the U.S. Congress to limit federal funding for research on the drug. Such limitations would strongly impede the FDA approval process. At the same time, pro-life members of Congress continued to lobby for legislation to prohibit further testing. The position of the President, and the increasingly conservative character of the Supreme Court, suggested that the introduction of RU 486 would meet stiff resistance.

In addition to the antiabortion concerns, pro-life groups and some feminist groups were concerned over the short- and long-term physical dangers associated with the use of the drug. Advocates for the pill stressed that a main advantage of the drug was that it was a "safe" method of abortion as compared to the probabilities of injury associated with surgical abortion. The safety claim was largely unsubstantiated, however, due to the lack of available objective test results. According to the *Yale Journal of Law and Feminism*, "The level of ignorance about the long-term effects of RU 486 makes it premature to apply the adjective 'safe.' "[7] Although Dr. Baulieu stated that studies had been performed using rabbits and immature human eggs, no direct objective evidence from these tests had been provided to substantiate his claims of safety.

There were additional concerns that the drug could harm subsequent offspring or cause malformation in unsuccessful abortions. Baulieu admitted that there had been cases where the drug was unsuccessful in causing the abortion and the women had foregone surgical abortion. He indicated that there had been no evidence of maldevelopment. RU 486 was said to be "quickly flushed from a woman's system, making long-term effects less likely." This claim had not yet been proved through empirical evidence.

Although the efficacy of RU 486 was increased significantly when used in conjunction with a prostaglandin, the possibility of incomplete abortion remained. Such a condition was dangerous because of the potential for the tissue remaining in the uterus to cause infection. The threat to the health and life of the woman was, therefore, a reasonable concern.

The final concern that pro-lifers had about the dangers of RU 486 was that it had been proved to be ineffective on ectopic pregnancies, pregnancies which occur in the fallopian tubes or the ovary rather than in the uterus. The concern was that the number of ectopic pregnancies in the United States was on the rise and that women with ectopic pregnancies who used RU 486 and thus believed themselves no longer pregnant were in danger of dying if their fallopian tubes burst.

Gynecologists and obstetricians were mixed in their views toward the introduction of RU 486 into the United States. Pressure from doctors belonging to the World Congress of Obstetrics and Gynecology had forced the French government to require Roussel-Uclaf to resume distribution of the drug after its 1988 withdrawal. However, some doctors considered the product to be unnecessary. One prominent gynecologist and obstetrician believed that there were other chemical alternatives available and stated:

> The drug will be a fiasco for whoever decides to market it due to the stink from Right to Life groups.... We already have similar forms of chemical abortifacients that are legal and are used in the U.S. For example, Ovral is used as a "morning after" pill. In residency ... when a rape victim came into the emergency room, she was given one dose of Ovral and then another one in the morning. This makes the uterus incapable of conception which is similar to the effects of RU 486. This method is 95.5 percent effective whereas RU 486 alone [without prostaglandins] is only up to 90 percent effective. Not many people are aware that this goes on so there is not much publicity.[8]

RU 486 was not without supporters. The controversy surrounding the drug elicited the attention of many consumer and political groups. Family planning establishments such as Planned Parenthood Federation of America, World Health Organization, and the Population Council, and feminist groups such as the Committee to Defend Reproductive Rights, Boston Women's Health Book Collective, and the National Women's Health Network, all supported the drug. During the period that Roussel had stopped production and sales of RU 486, the World Congress of Gynecology and Obstetrics had planned to ask physicians to boycott Roussel products if the company did not reverse its decision. Kelli Conlin, president of National Organization for Women in New York, called for a campaign urging U.S. pharmaceutical companies to test abortion drugs such as RU 486. She said, "Companies cannot let these (anti-abortion) groups push them around. And that group is really a minority."[9]

Right-to-life groups considered RU 486 to be a particular threat because one of their main avenues of action had been picketing abortion clinics and making the process more difficult for those [women] who chose to terminate their pregnancies. RU 486 could be used in a doctor's office, thus making pickets and public demonstrations less effective. Further, the drug was to be used within the first 7 weeks of pregnancy, and the emotional appeal of showing developed fetuses in danger of abortion would be limited since all that is observed is bleeding similar to menstruation. One fear of pro-life groups was that if RU 486 became common, the very term "abortion" could become obsolete. Dr. Baulieu told the "MacNeil-Lehrer News Hour" in September, 1986, that "Abortion, in my opinion, should more or less disappear as a concept, as a fact, as a word in the future...."

If RU 486 was authorized for use, it would be possible for a woman to take the pill safely and privately very soon after missing her period without ever knowing whether she was actually pregnant or not. In fact, if used monthly, there was some question whether it should actually be labelled an "abortion drug." Depending on when it was taken, RU 486 worked virtually the same way as the "pill" or an IUD. Normally, the pill prevented pregnancy by suppressing ovulation, but certain forms (containing lower doses of hormones to reduce the side effects) occasionally failed to suppress ovulation and instead prevented the fertilized ovum from implanting in the uterus. The IUD, too, worked by irritating the uterus and preventing implantation. If RU 486 was used within 8 days of fertilization, it brought about the same effect.

One of the reasons given most often in support of RU 486 was safety. The United States had one of the highest percentages of accidental pregnancies in the industrialized world. According to the World Health Organization, "Surgical abortions [in the world] kill 200,000 women each year. Companies are retreating from research in abortion for fear of controversy, special interest pressure, and product liability questions—creating a major health care crisis."[10]

Likewise, there were increased safety problems when the abortion was postponed until later stages of pregnancy. Women facing an unwanted pregnancy often attempted to avoid the physically and emotionally painful abortion decision by ignoring it. If the abortion options were less harsh, it was thought that many women would face up to their situations more immediately and, therefore, more safely. Polls indicated that "Americans tend to oppose early abortions much less fervently and in fewer numbers than late abortions."[11]

Pro-life groups argued that conception is equivalent to fertilization, thus making RU 486 a form of chemical abortion. However, the federal courts and the American College of Obstetrics and Gynecology defined "conception" as implantation. In 1986, the Federal Appeals Court overturned an Illinois law that had used the pro-life definition in its legislation pertaining to abortion. The implantation definition was based on the fact that 40 to 60 percent of all fertilized ova fail to implant. Some pro-choice advocates suggested that if the pro-life argument were carried to its logical (but absurd) conclusion, women should be required to take progesterone to encourage implantation and prevent accidental death of the fertilized ova.

One of the most significant reasons for support for the introduction of RU 486 was the improvement it provided over other abortion options. With RU 486, there would be "no waiting, no walking past picket lines, no feet up in stirrups for surgery." In many cases, abortion clinics would be unnecessary. The clinics, instead, could be replaced by a few 24-hour emergency clinics that could treat any potential complications. It would make the abortion decision much more a personal matter. In some cases it would remove the psychological agony of deciding on an abortion at all. Women who took the pill just a few days after missing their period would never even know if they had been pregnant. Considering the extreme emotional trauma an abortion often causes, this was considered by supporters to be a great benefit. Finally, the cost of RU 486 would make it much more attractive than other methods. According to a *Newsweek* article, "If RU 486 is approved, Planned Parenthood plans to make it available free or 'at cost' at its family planning centers."[12]

A number of industry observers suggested that the availability of RU 486 in the U.S. market was inevitable. They argued that there were enough people who supported RU 486 for a black market to develop. Such a market was even more likely because the drug was already legal and easily available in other countries. Some radical groups even called for their members to support the illegal use of RU 486. Norma Swenson of the Boston Women's Health Book collective argued that RU 486 would save so many women from death by "botched abortions" that it would be worth it for women's groups to encourage its underground use. According to Swenson, "Using RU 486 . . . would be a type of civil disobedience."

CONCLUSION

The management of Hoechst-Roussel held the legal and moral responsibility for the decision regarding introduction of RU 486 to the United States. It was clear that, regardless of its direction, the decision would have far-reaching implications for vast numbers of people—not only Hoechst-Roussel's stockholders and customers, but also U.S. society as a whole. It also was evident that the pressures being brought to bear would continue to build.

Endnotes

1. "60 Minutes," April 9, 1989.
2. *Time*, February 26, 1990, p. 44.
3. "Letter to Columbia from Upjohn," 1987.
4. *Business Week*, April 1, 1985, p. 88.
5. "Letter to Columbia from Upjohn," 1987.
6. Personal telephone conversation, April 1990.
7. *Yale Journal of Law and Feminism*, 1(75) (1989), p. 96.
8. Personal telephone conversation, April 1990.
9. *New York Times*, October 27, 1988, pp. A1, B18.
10. *Business Week*, November 14, 1988.
11. D. R. Mishel, *American Journal of Obstetrics and Gynecology*, June 1988, pp. 1307–1312.
12. *Newsweek*, December 29, 1988, p. 47.

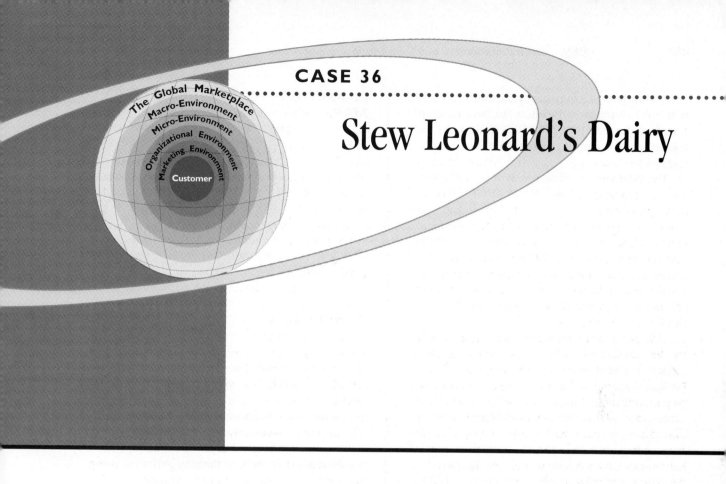

CASE 36

Stew Leonard's Dairy

This case was prepared by Charles B. Shrader, Steven A. Rallis, and Joan L. Twenter of Iowa State University.

Stewart (Stew) J. Leonard's father, Leo Leonard, owned and operated a small dairy route with four milk trucks. As a young boy, Stew often helped his father with deliveries. By the time Stew was in high school he was operating his own milk route (Leonard, 1993). Stew pursued a college education in hopes that it would prepare him to one day run the dairy. After Stew's graduation from college, his father passed away and Stew took over the dairy.

In the late 1960s, the state of Connecticut decided to build a highway through the land used for the dairy. Furthermore, the proliferation of supermarkets and refrigerators had made the cost of running a milk delivery route prohibitive. So Stew decided to move and start a new store. In 1968 the

This case is intended to be used as a basis for classroom discussion rather than to illustrate either effective or ineffective management practices. Partial support for writing the case was provided by the Murray G. Bacon Center for Ethics in Business. Copyright © 1998 by the *Business Case Journal* and Charles B. Shrader, Steven A. Rallis, and Joan L. Twenter.

Small Business Administration loaned Stew $500,000, the largest loan granted to that date, to start a dairy store in Norwalk, Connecticut. Leonard and his wife, Marianne, knew they were risking their net worth of $100,000, but on the basis of his experience selling dairy products since he was a child, he was convinced his ideas would work. He expected to be competitive with other area stores by stocking mostly his own products in a specialized dairy store (Fishman, 1985).

Stew Leonard and his wife formed a partnership. He refused to form a corporation because he wanted to be liable for any losses (Fishman, 1985). Before opening, he visited many food stores across the country gathering information on what worked and what did not (Slater, 1991). During one visit he met a farmer who was bottling and selling milk on the premises (Fishman, 1985). Leonard decided his store would do the same. Calculating the cost of the SBA loan and other credit, Leonard estimated he needed to sell $20,000 a week to survive. Through long hours and attention to detail, Leonard realized $21,850 in his first week in business. By midweek he was so optimistic about reaching the $20,000 mark that he took his wife on a trip to Grenada in the Caribbean.

The following week, an incident occurred that was to become the foundation of the Stew Leonard management philosophy. The incident began when a customer complained that the eggnog she recently purchased was sour. Stew tasted the eggnog and concluded that the customer was wrong. He told her so and added, "We sold over 300 half-gallons of eggnog this week, and you're the only one who's complained." The customer angrily left the store and stated she would never come back (Leonard, 1987). Later that evening Leonard could not get the scene out of his mind. Upon reflection, he acknowledged that not only had he failed to empathize with the customer, but he had ignored the potential repercussions of the complaint. His wife, Marianne, said that her husband had just lost a valuable customer over a $.99 carton of eggnog. This was a customer who may have later spent thousands of dollars on groceries, money that Stew Leonard's dairy store would now never see. This mistake led Stew Leonard to a mission statement for his business:

> Rule 1: The customer is always right!
> Rule 2: If the customer is ever wrong, reread rule 1!

These rules, which were engraved on a 6000-pound boulder and placed at the entrance of the store, became the credo upon which Stew Leonard built his business (Leonard, 1987). By the end of the 1980s, the store had grown from two cash registers, 6000 square feet, and $20,000 a week in sales to a retail grocery with more than 2 dozen registers, 37,000 square feet, and annual sales in excess of $100 million (Penzer, 1991). By 1991 a second store had been opened on a 40-acre complex in Danbury, Connecticut. Although the mission statement formed the backbone of the strategy which enabled the organization to expand 27 times in roughly 20 years, Stew Leonard implemented additional strategies to achieve his business's remarkable growth—a growth so remarkable that Stew Leonard's did more business per square foot than any business of any kind in the world (Raphel, 1989).

MARKETING AND CUSTOMER RELATIONS

Initially, Stew Leonard stocked his dairy store with just under a dozen items. Eventually, the store topped out at 800 items (the typical supermarket stocked 15,000). Stew differentiated his store by eliminating the middleman and passing the savings on to his customers (Suters, 1991).

Stew also sold the idea of freshness. Customers knew they could count on the freshest produce, milk, cheese, meats, and baked goods. A glass-enclosed milk processing plant was located in the center of the store, where customers could see their milk being produced (Fishman, 1985). Beth Leonard, Stew's daughter, ran the bakery, which filled the store with the aroma of croissants, cookies, and muffins (Adams, 1991). Free samples and recipes were always made available to customers.

To further distinguish itself from other food stores, Stew Leonard's added entertainment to the marketing mix (Englander, 1989). A petting zoo with barnyard animals was placed in the parking lot, encouraging parents to bring children. Animated singing animals filled the store, and employees roamed the aisles in cow, chicken, and duck costumes (Leonard, 1993). All of this was part of Leonard's emphasis on making grocery shopping an enjoyable experience (Slater, 1991).

Building on the mission statement, *The Customer Is Always Right,* Stew Leonard's adopted other customer service systems. A liberal return policy provided internal checks and balances, which required employees to constantly monitor quality. Even if a Stew Leonard "team member" knew that a customer was returning an item the store did not sell, the customer got his or her money back (Adams, 1991). Stew once said:

> Out attitude is that everybody's honest. If we occasionally run into someone who isn't, we just take it on the chin. But the important point is that 999 out of 1,000 customers are honest. We simply refuse to let one dishonest customer determine how we are going to treat the other 999. (Stew Leonard, *Management Review,* October 1987).

Stew Leonard's exhibited a special commitment to following up on customers' comments. A suggestion box was filled to capacity each day (Englander, 1989). By 11:00 A.M. each morning, all the complaints and suggestions were typed and submitted to the appropriate department. Managers held weekly meetings to report what had been done with the customers' suggestions.

Customer feedback also was gathered through in-store focus groups. Each month ten specially selected customers were given $20 worth of store gift certificates in return for which they met with store managers and offered suggestions on what items should be stocked and how items should be displayed (Bennett, 1992).

There were other small acts of kindness as well. For example, free ice cream cones were given randomly to customers, customers' pictures with Stew Leonard's shopping bags were posted near the entrance, and elderly customers were given free rides to the dairy in a bus provided by the store (Englander, 1989; Feldman, 1989). By conducting business in this manner, Stew Leonard's earned tremendous customer trust and loyalty over the years (Hill, 1993).

EMPLOYEE RELATIONS

Employees, referred to as *team members,* were well-trained in customer relations. Many employees also were Leonard family members.

The large number of family members working for the company contributed to the company's culture. Of the company's 1200+ employees, 25 percent had worked at Stew Leonard's for at least 5 years and over half had family as coworkers (Leonard, 1993). Stew believed in nepotism (*Review of Business,* 1991). He was an ardent supporter of employing relatives as team members; he believed they worked much harder because the presence of a relative was like another boss watching over them (Fishman, 1985).

Team members understood that a job at Stew Leonard's required that they provide superior customer service (Weinstein, 1993). The company's two stores were open 364 days a year, and team members were required to work during various times of the day and on holidays. Also, team members were expected to be well groomed and display positive attitudes. As a result of Stew's hiring practices, the store had a 60 percent turnover rate—much better than the supermarket industry average of 82 percent (Weinstein, 1993).

Curiosity about Stew Leonard's training and customer relations methods ran strong among business firms. Inquiries from companies like Kraft, Citibank, and IBM led to the creation of Stew Leonard University by Stew's daughter, Jill (Adams, 1991). "Stew U" was a 4-hour seminar intended to give insight into Stew Leonard's operation. Throughout the seminar, attendees were taught methods of how to handle dissatisfied customers, appropriate behaviors of team members, and management tips for motivating team members (Adams, 1991).

Stew Leonard's offered its employees a variety of incentive programs to heighten the level of customer service, such as

1. A monthly "One Idea Club," where 10 team members and a department manager went to other supermarkets and on the basis of that experience made suggestions for improving store departments (Englander, 1989).

2. A "Superstar of the Month," nominated by co-workers and department managers, for achievement of safety, cleanliness, and attendance. Winners had their photographs posted in the store and were awarded $100 (Bolger, 1988; Englander, 1989).

3. "Ladders of Success" charts placed near checkout lanes demonstrating team members' career progression. Stew Leonard's company fully supported a promotion-from-within policy (Bolger, 1988; Englander, 1989).

4. Retail gift certificates valued up to $500 if team members' ideas were implemented (Bolger, 1988).

5. Fifty-dollar awards to team members who referred new hires (Bolger, 1988).

6. An ABCD (Above and Beyond the Call of Duty) award—a polo shirt embroidered with "ABCD Award"—to employees who performed beyond the duties of their jobs (Bolger, 1988).

7. A "Hall of Fame," which consisted of workers who performed admirably during their careers (Bolger, 1988).

8. An Outstanding Performance Award given to three high achievers at the annual Christmas party (Englander, 1989).

9. A recreation program, supplemented by employee vending machine funds, providing outings and trips to workers at discount rates (Englander, 1989).

10. A "Stew's News" company newsletter—called the ultimate company newsletter by *Inc.* magazine—filled with information about bonus plans, contests, and customer comments. Births, parties, anniversaries, illnesses, and organization successes were included (Adams, 1991).

11. A "Name Game" reward for cashiers who thanked customers by name. Customers dropped cashiers' names in a box, and at the end of each week, the three cashiers who thanked the most customers by name received $30 (Penzer, 1991).

These activities were used by Stew Leonard Dairy to focus team members on the mission statement. Leonard knew everybody was motivated by different things. Occasionally, Stew would place extra dollars in pay envelopes along with thank-you notes (which he wrote hundreds of every year) for employees who performed exceptionally well (Penzer, 1991). Impromptu inducements were often granted to team members. It was not uncommon for Stew Leonard or the other managers to hand out lunch or dinner certificates for special performance such as coming in on a day off (Penzer, 1991).

THE ORGANIZATION

Stew Leonard's overall company goal—customer satisfaction—determined the design of the organization. It was a simple, relatively informal structure. Because the business was a partnership, there was no board of directors or shareholders. There also were no required annual reports or meetings. The partners gained and lost in proportion to the success of the business and were personally liable for financial obligations. The partnership paid no taxes as an entity; rather, Stew and Marianne were taxed directly for their portion of the business' income.

All four of Stew Leonard's children were actively involved in the business and held corporate titles. Stew Jr., the oldest, was president. He originally planned on working for an accounting firm after earning his M.B.A. at UCLA but became involved in every detail of the company. Tom managed the Danbury store, which opened in the fall of 1991. Beth, after obtaining her masters degree in French and working for a croissant distributor, originated and managed the high-volume in-store bakery (Fishman, 1985). Jill Leonard was the vice president of human resources (Weinstein, 1993). And, of course, Marianne, Stew Sr.'s wife, continued to provide support as she had from the beginning.

Marianne's brothers, Frank H. Guthman and Stephen F. Guthman, served as executive vice president and vice president of finance, respectively (Pastore, 1993). Most company decisions were made by the family. However, lower-level employees were allowed a great deal of discretion, especially in the area of customer service.

The company preferred "in-house" control practices. Customers were asked to pay cash for gift certificates and were encouraged to use cash for other purchases (Levy, 1993). Stew did not make much use of outside consultants in his business. He preferred using the in-house customer focus groups for business advice. Being privately held, the company did not publicly reveal its profits (Bolger, 1988). Profits, however, were significant enough to fund the store's numerous expansions as well as a large second home for Stew and his children. The second home, located in St. Maarten in the Caribbean, was named "Carpe Diem" (Latin for "seize the day") (Steinberg, 1993).

As the business grew from a small dairy to superretailer to world's largest dairy store, the Stew Leonard's story was one of customer satisfaction, employee development, and tremendous growth. Over the years the store received numerous awards and accolades. For example:

- An award for entrepreneurial excellence from President Ronald Reagan

- The Connecticut Small Business Advocate of the Year Award

- A citation from the *Guiness Book of World Records* for doing more business per square foot than any store of any kind in the world

In addition, a certified in-house Dale Carnegie training school, attended by Fortune 500 firms, was operated in conjunction with Stew Leonard University. In 1991, Stew Leonard's Dairy was nominated for the Malcolm Baldrige National Quality Award in the service category, and might have become the first retail organization ever to win the award had not the company decided to withdraw from the competition.

In addition to all the other awards, a 1993 issue of *Chief Information Officer* (*CIO*), a publication for data processing and computer programming professionals, named Stew Leonard's as one of the 21 recipients of their customer service award (Pastore, 1993). Criteria for winning this award included a company's successful integration of management information systems and customer service. The store was commended for its ability in tracking sales and using point-of-sale data. The sophisticated system also helped managers anticipate heavy traffic periods so that cash registers could be staffed adequately and product shortages avoided.

TROUBLE LOOMS

On August 25, 1991, Stew Leonard Sr. was questioned by a Norwalk, Connecticut, reporter about a visit from the Criminal Investigation Division of the Internal Revenue Service. On August 9, 1991, the IRS raided the homes of several company officers, seizing boxes of records and cash (Kanner, 1993). Stew Leonard said that the raid "came out of the blue" and that he was "as surprised as anyone else" (Heller, 1991). But U.S. customs agents had stopped him back in June of 1991, when, with $80,000 in cash, he boarded a flight to St. Maarten in the Caribbean (Kanner, 1993). Leonard had not filled out the forms required for taking large sums of money out of the country, and this eventually led to the IRS confiscation of store records (Levy, 1993). Nevertheless, Leonard maintained that he did not know what prompted the IRS agents to enter the store with a search warrant on August 9 (IRS probing records, 1991).

Leonard and his son, Tom, manager of the Danbury store, told the news reporters and the public that the IRS was simply conducting a routine audit. However, the Criminal Investigation Division of the IRS did not conduct "audits," which involved possible civil violations; it investigated possible criminal violations of internal revenue laws (Heller, 1991).

Most people in the community reacted with disbelief to news of the investigation. Many of Stew Leonard's customers found it impossible to believe that any wrongdoing had taken place, regarding the Leonard family as a pillar of honesty in the community. Ironically, it was Stew Leonard's sophisticated computer system that gave the IRS the primary evidence it needed to charge Leonard and other executives with tax evasion.

THE GUILTY PLEA

On July 22, 1993, the U.S. Department of Justice announced that Stewart J. Leonard Sr., Frank H. Guthman, Stephen F. Guthman, and company general manager Tiberio (Barry) Belardinelli had pleaded guilty in federal court to federal tax conspiracy charges. The four defendants admitted that between 1981 and August 9, 1991, they had defrauded the IRS by skimming more than $17 million from Stew Leonard's Dairy in Norwalk, Connecticut. It had taken the IRS almost 2 years to determine the full extent of the tax evasion scheme. Along with paper records and large sums of cash, the IRS found other items indicating the executives' aversion to paying taxes (Steinberg, 1993).

According to the IRS, Stew Leonard had avoided $6.7 million in taxes between 1981 and 1991 by not reporting $17 million in sales during that period (Wamae, 1993). They also reported that it was the largest computer-driven criminal tax evasion case in U.S. history, calling the fraud a crime of the twenty-first century (Levy, 1993).

Stew Leonard Jr., president of the Norwalk store, was cited as having knowledge of the tax conspiracy (Kanner, 1993). A *New York Times* article reported that part of the plea bargain arrangement was that no charges would be brought against Stew Jr. (Steinberg, 1993). Observers speculated that the IRS may have given Stew Jr. immunity in order to persuade his father to plead guilty. According to the IRS, Stew Sr. was initially turned in by an employee who had recently been fired (Berman, 1996).

THE "EQUITY PROGRAM"—SKIMMING

In Frank Guthman's basement, in a hollowed-out edition of the 1982 *New England Business Directory,* the Criminal Investigation Division of the IRS discovered a computer program that the executives had named "Equity" (Ingram, 1993). Apparently, the program had been developed in the latter part of 1981 by Jeffrey Pirhalla, Stew Leonard's computer programmer. Frank Guthman had instructed the programmer to create the program in order to reduce sales data stored on Stew Leonard's computer. Frank Guthman also had directed Pirhalla to write the program so that it would reduce Stew Leonard's financial and bank deposit data.

Witnesses in the court proceedings testified that Stew Leonard Sr. and the other executives were informed of the use of this tax evasion tool. In general, the program enabled the defendants to enter a dollar figure that matched a cash receipt withdrawal for the day. Typical cash diversions were $10,000 to $15,000 per day. Furthermore, the program allowed the company to keep dual books that generated accounting spreadsheets disclosing "actual" and "reported" sales. To appease previous IRS auditors, Stew Leonard's had provided "reported" sales data, while the actual sales data were utilized only for store operations.

As part of the scheme, Belardinelli and the Guthmans set up a system that transferred universal product code (UPC) scanner information from the cash registers to two different computer record systems. One set of records systematically understated sales by a predetermined amount. Belardinelli destroyed the tapes with the "real" sales data generated daily from the cash registers. Then he secretly removed cash from bank deposit bags in his office, and the skimmed cash was hidden in "vaults" and "fireplaces" constructed specifically for the execution of this crime. Correspondingly, investigators identified personal and partnership tax forms that were falsely submitted to the IRS.

SHORTWEIGHTING

To make matters worse, on July 23, 1993, a day after the tax evasion announcement, the Connecticut State Consumer Products Department charged Stew Leonard's with violating state labeling laws

(Barron, 1993). A series of inspections involving a check of 2658 products in the Norwalk store revealed that 730 of the products checked weighed less than what the label stated —they were *short-weighted*—and 500 items carried no labels or were improperly labeled (Tosh, 1993). The Consumer Products Commissioner reported that this rejection rate, 46.3 percent, was much greater than the statewide average of 5 percent (Ingram, 1993).

Some industry experts believed the short-weighting charges were not fair and were merely the bureaucratic attempt of a vengeful state to embarrass the family (O'Neill, 1996). They maintained that store scales were accurate and that the variance noted by investigators was not atypical of other stores. Stew Jr. argued that because the company sold so many handpacked and precooked items, product weight could not always be perfectly accurate (Kanner, 1993; Zemke, 1993).

Each of the 1230 violations was subject to a $500 maximum fine (Barron, 1993). Stew Leonard's had already been assessed fines of $10,500 for similar violations at the Danbury store. The company planned to appeal the Danbury store fines as well as the potentially costly fines on the alleged 1230 violations (Barron, 1993; Zwiebach, 1993).

THE AFTERMATH

News of the crime drew harsh criticism from industry professionals and the media but caused only a minor decline in sales (Zwiebach, 1993). Some customers condemned the elder Leonard and the store for being hypocritical (Ingram, 1993). The majority of Stew Leonard's clientele was angrier about the shortweighting than the tax evasion. Indeed, many people believed that the tax fraud was a private rather than a business issue (Ingram, 1993). Several shoppers even expressed sympathy for Leonard and his family and pledged they would continue to support the company (Crispens, 1993). As had happened early in the investigation, in 1991, some community members thought the IRS was overreacting, even harassing the company. One customer stated that it was okay for the store to cheat the government because everybody else does it (Crispens, 1993). *The Danbury News Times* polled 5323 of its readers, and 4556 said they would continue to shop at Stew Leonard's (Kanner, 1993). Employees of Stew Leonard's, including

Leonard Jr., stated that business was good and that they were 100 percent behind the fallen founder (Ingram, 1993).

Stew Leonard was sentenced to 52 months in prison and ordered to pay $15 million in back taxes, penalties, and interest (IRS interview, 1995). He was also fined $850,000 for court and probation costs, but this fine was later reduced to $650,000 by a federal appeals court judge (Silvers, 1994). The resulting $650,000 was still much larger than the usual $100,000 fine for tax fraud, because Leonard had profited so greatly from the scheme (Silvers, 1994). Leonard's brothers-in-law, Frank H. Guthman and Stephen F. Guthman, were sentenced to 41- and 18-month prison terms, respectively (Wamae, 1993). Frank Guthman's plea agreement provided that he pay $335,000 in tax, penalties, and interest. Stephen Guthman was not fined. Belardinelli received no prison sentence but was fined $15,000 and put on probation for 2 years (Wamae, 1993).

Leonard gave no reason for the crime he committed, although he did apologize to customers and employees. At one point, the Leonards insinuated that the tax scheme had been suggested by their lawyer (now deceased) as a way to raise capital for expansion (Kanner, 1993). Later, in 1994, after reflecting on the crisis while in prison, Leonard commented that "Somehow, I just lost sight of my core values" (Silvers, 1994). After the incident, the company continued to grow and was even planning to open a third store. Stew Leonard was scheduled to be released from a Schuylkill, Pennsylvania, prison in December 1997 (Suters, 1995; Berman, 1996).

DAMAGE CONTROL

Once Stew Sr. was in prison, Stew Jr. had to step up and fill the leadership void. Stew Jr. began running the Norwalk store, which was still in his mother's name. Stew Jr., Tom, and their sisters, Jill and Beth, owned and operated the new Danbury store (Berman, 1996). They were now faced with monumental decisions regarding damage control. How would they be able to maintain the business? How could they regain goodwill and customer confidence? How could they overcome the stigma associated with skimming and shortweighting? Would they be able to get along without Stew Sr.? What steps could they take to ensure that wrongdoing

like this wouldn't happen again? How could they restore the company's reputation?

There were other worries as well. Stew Sr.'s health was in question. Prior to entering prison, he had to have a heart valve and hip replaced (Farrelly, 1993).

To make matters worse, in early 1996, it was reported that Tom was under a grand jury investigation for skimming cash from store vending machines (Berman, 1996). According to investigators, Tom had been skimming cash from pop machines, hot dog vendors, and other vending locations in the store. Stew Jr. would almost certainly be called to testify before the grand jury.

Stew Jr. had been responsible for withdrawing from the Baldrige Award competition in 1991, a move he had made only because of the criminal investigations (O'Neill, 1996). Now he wondered if he could put the store back into contention for the prestigious award.

Young Stew Jr. knew he must direct his attention immediately to the challenges facing him. He knew his father would want to return to store management and that it was his mission to pave the way. He pondered how he would be able to regain customers' faith and redeem the Leonard family name.

References

Adams, M. "The Udder Delights of Stew U." *Successful Meetings,* 403 (March 1991), pp. 59–61.

Barron, J. "Stew Leonard's Is Cited for Shorting Customers." *New York Times,* July 24, 1993, p. L24.

Bennett, S. "What Shoppers Want." *Progressive Grocer,* 71(10), October 1992, pp. 73–78.

Berman, P. "Like Father, Like Son." *Forbes,* May 20, 1996, pp. 44–45.

Bolger, B. "Stew Leonard: Unconventional Wisdom." *Incentive,* 162(11), November 1988, pp. 36–40.

Crispens, J. "The Reaction from Shoppers: Luke-Warm to Mildly Stewed." *Supermarket News,* Aug. 2, 1993, p. 42.

Englander, T. "Stew Leonard's: In-Store Disneyland." *Incentive,* 163(1), January 1989, pp. 26–30.

Farrelly, P. T., Jr. "Leonard to Begin Sentence Today at Medical Facility." *The Hour,* Nov. 29, 1993, pp. 1–2.

Feldman, D. "Companies Aim to Please." *Management Review,* 78(5), May 1989, pp. 8–9.

Fishman, Davis K. *Stew Leonard's—The Disney World of Supermarkets* (New York: Curtis Brown Publishers, Mar. 11, 1985).

Heller, J. "At Stew Leonard's Business as Usual Despite IRS Audit." *The Fairpress* (Norwalk, weekly edition), sec. CG, Aug. 15, 1991, p. 54.

Hill, J. M. "Supermarkets Can Beat Warehouse Clubs, But Not on Price Alone." *Brandweek,* 34(1), January 1993, p. 25.

Ingram, B. "Stew, We Hardly Knew Ye." *Supermarket Business,* September 1993, pp. 157–158.

"IRS Crime Unit Probing Records." *The Advocate* (Stamford, CT), Aug. 22, 1991.

IRS. Telephone interview with Larry Marini, state investigator, Criminal Investigation Division, Connecticut, March 1995.

Kanner, B. "Spilled Milk." *New York,* 26(42), Oct. 25, 1993, pp. 68–74.

Leonard, S. "Love That Customer!" *Management Review,* 76(10), October 1987, pp. 36–39.

Leonard, S., Jr. "The Customer Is Always Right." *Executive Excellence,* 10(8), 1993, pp. 16–17.

Levy, C. J. "Store Founder Pleads Guilty in Fraud." *New York Times,* July 23, 1993, pp. B1, B4.

O'Neill, H. Telephone interview with consultant who worked with Stew Leonard's in making the Baldrige Award application, August 1996.

Pastore, R. "A Virtual Shopping Spree." *CIO,* 6, August 1993, pp. 70–74.

Penzer, E. "Secrets from the Supermarket." *Incentive,* 165(8), August 1991, pp. 67–69.

Raphel, M. "Confidence Is Number One." *Direct Marketing,* 52(5), September 1989, pp. 30, 32.

Silvers, S. "Judge Reduces Stew's Fine." *Connecticut Post,* October 27, 1994, pp. A1, A13.

Slater, Les. Interview, in *Review of Business,* 13, Summer-Fall 1991, pp. 10–12.

Steinberg, J. "Papers Show Greed Calculation and Betrayal in Stew Leonard Case." *New York Times,* Oct. 22, 1993.

Stew Leonard's Fact Sheet, 100 Westport Avenue, Norwalk, CT.

Suters, E. T. "Stew Leonard: Soul of a Leader." *Executive Excellence,* 8(6), June 1991, pp. 13–14.

Suters, E. T. Telephone interview, April 1995. Author, *The Unnatural Act of Management.*

Tosh, M. "Mislabeling Charge May Be More Taxing." *Supermarket News,* Aug. 2, 1993, p. 43.

Wamae, C. H. "Leonard Checks in at Federal Hospital." *Connecticut Post,* Nov. 30, 1993, p. A7.

Weinstein, S. "How to Hire the Best." *Progressive Grocer,* 72(7), July 1993, pp. 119–122.

Zemke, R. "Piling On." *Training,* 30(10), October 1993, p. 10.

Zwiebach, E. "Stew Leonard's Reports Sales Dip." *Supermarket News,* Aug. 2, 1993, pp. 42–43.